Jean-Luc
GODARD

a guide to
references and resources

A
Reference
Publication
in
Film

Ronald Gottesman
Editor

Jean-Luc GODARD

a guide to references and resources

JULIA LESAGE

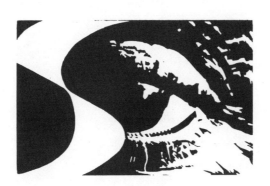

G.K.HALL&CO.

70 LINCOLN STREET, BOSTON, MASS.

Distributed in the United Kingdom and Europe by
George Prior Associated Publishers Ltd.,
37-41 Bedford Row, London
WC1R 4JH, England

Library of Congress Cataloging in Publication Data
Lesage, Julia.
  Jean-Luc Godard, a guide to references and resources.

  (A Reference publication in film)
  Includes indexes.
  1. Godard, Jean Luc, 1930-   I. Title.
II. Series.
PN1998.A3G6237   016.79143'0233'0924   79-15674
ISBN 0-8161-7925-5

This publication is printed on permanent/durable acid-free paper
MANUFACTURED IN THE UNITED STATES OF AMERICA

In memory of Charles Eckert

Contents

Preface

In this bibliographic study I have tried to annotate as completely as possible the critical writings of Jean-Luc Godard, his published interviews, and the criticism written about his work. My assumption was that the study should be as inclusive as possible. When I have included entries with incomplete bibliographic data, they usually cite articles which I was not able to read but which were referred to by other sources, or articles from film archives' clipping files where the page numbers were not indicated. Several previous bibliographies on Godard (see Entries 1833, 1505, 1088, 1684, 1111, 1657, 1425, 1399, 1268) and the clipping files at the Museum of Modern Art and the Lincoln Center Library for the Performing Arts in New York provided the starting point for and the "heart" of this study.

In the annotated guide to the critical writings about Godard, Part IV, and in the distribution guide, Part VII, I have used the French and English titles for Godard's films interchangeably, as has been done with their distribution in England, Canada, and the United States; generally the annotation reflects the titles used by the critics and distributors themselves. In the index, the entries are listed under the French-language title to which the English-title entry will then refer.

Part III, the synopses of the films, presented a whole series of critical challenges. In writing a synopsis of a film by a director whose work is characterized by disjuncture, what does one summarize? Surely not just the "plot." Even in the brief space of a "synopsis," I tried to demonstrate the interplay of themes and cinematic structures, both visual and audio, in the films. And for the later films, where the visual tracks are much more abstract and are constructed on the basis of visual symbolism, I have summarized the political concepts expressed on the sound track and indicated the kind of visual symbolism used to present each concept. In a sense, the synopses are the "proof" of the generalizations offered in Part II, the critical survey of Godard's work.

In preparing the annotations in Part IV on the critical writings about Godard, I relied primarily on the resources of the major university libraries in Chicago — the University of Illinois Circle Campus Library, Regenstein Library at the University of Chicago, and the Northwestern University

Library. The staff of the University of Illinois Interlibrary Loan Department tirelessly sent for reprints of hundreds of articles not available in Chicago. Their assistance was the most invaluable aid I received on this project, and I wish to express my gratitude to them for their thoroughness and patience.

Because every project such as this has to have a cut-off point where the researcher stops gathering and starts summarizing, I would like to indicate where I stopped searching for articles and where a future film bibliographer might begin. For example, Godard's films constantly premiered at film festivals in the 1960s. Yet I did not systematically read all the "festival" articles in the American and European press, although many such articles are, in fact, annotated in this study. Since most major newspapers and film periodicals, as well as general cultural reviews, publish film festival round-ups and since I have indicated here in the credits (Part III) the major festivals in which Godard's films appeared, one could presumably pursue 1960s festival roundups to get a more precise, international overview of critics' initial reactions to Godard's films.

Also listed in the credits in Part III are the dates when Godard's films opened in several major cities. A systematic search of all the major newspapers in any of these cities — principally New York, Paris, London, and Montreal — the week the film opened would undoubtedly yield more reviews. However, since I started this project by working from several major bibliographies whose authors had already undertaken such a search, I did not try to duplicate their efforts except to verify and annotate the entries they listed. A critical task which no film scholar has yet attempted is to ascertain when a major director's films have opened in every major city in his/her country of origin — or in the major cities of the United States, or in every capital city of the world — and then to trace systematically what the critical reception has been to that director's films in the newspapers and magazines in each city. In this light, I myself have found sporadic information about Godard's critical reception in Chicago, San Francisco, and even Buenos Aires, but no information at all about his films' reception in Rome, Hamburg, Oslo, Toronto, Mexico City, Lima, Havana, Cairo, or Hong Kong. Because the *New York Times* and the London *Times* each publishes a complete index, Godard's reception can be traced more thoroughly in those two cities. If film scholars were to go beyond established indices to trace a director's critical reception internationally, we would get information not only about that director but also a more accurate picture of distribution patterns, shifts in taste, and cross-cultural influences on the reception of certain types of films.

The listing of distributors, Part VII, is as current as possible, but distribution information is subject to rapid change. This list was primarily drawn from the sources used by the Film Center of the Art Institute of Chicago in preparing a retrospective of Godard's work in May-June 1977. It is possible to contact distributors and either view films on their premises or get films released for close study. If one wishes to do this, it is wise to have a letter in hand from a publisher and an outline of one's forthcoming book. New Yorker Films and Grove Press were exceptionally accommodating to me in the course of this research, and I want to thank them for their assistance. In general in the United States, film research is hampered by a lack of access to original texts. The synopses of Godard's films in Part III derive in many cases from my single viewings at film festivals or multiple viewings in a commercial theater, with my memory now refreshed from notes then scribbled in the dark. If I was lucky, I could taperecord the sound track, or have later reference to a published script (although these are rarely sufficient in terms of cinematic descriptions). Surely, it would not cut into a film's rentals but only enhance a director's reputation and the demand for her/his films if distributors systematically made available to major film study centers videotaped copies of films to be used for research purposes only.

In addition to the assistance mentioned above, I wish to thank the following people for their direct help on this project: Ron Gottesman, Linda Turner, Patricia Erens, Virginia Wexman, Bill Van Wert, Royal Brown, and James Monaco. Chuck Kleinhans has offered his constant support, companionship, and encouragement. Charles Eckert, who supervised my dissertation on Godard and to whose memory this book is dedicated, was too briefly in my life as a friend, but the vitality of his writing still remains to bring the memory of him as a person keenly to mind.

January 1979   JL

ON USING THIS BOOK

In the annotations, I have presented key notions raised by the reviewer, or I have tried to indicate what unique information about Godard's life, milieu, or work this review could provide the reader. Some materials on the events of May 1968 and on French film production are included in the bibliography which may not mention Godard by name but which have a direct bearing on his work. Interviews with multiple interviewers are listed under the first name given in the article followed by the notation *et al.*, the names of the rest of the interviewers are then listed in the body of the annotation and in the index.

Frequently page numbers were unavailable and are not given here. For works listed here which I could not personally consult, the source where that review was originally cited is indicated here in one of three ways: either the complete source is given or there is a cross-reference to another entry or the source is referred to by an abbreviation; the abbreviations are explained immediately below:

API	*Alternative Press Index.*
Bowles	Stephen E. Bowles. *Index to Critical Film Reviews, Vol. 1: Critical Film Reviews A-M.* New York: Burt Franklin, 1974.
BFI Bibliography	British Film Institute Book Library Bibliography No. 19, "Jean-Luc Godard." A seventeen-page selection of French- and English-language material on Godard. *See* Entry No. 2419.
Dietrich's IBZ	Dietrich's *Internationale Bibliographie der Zeitschriftenliteratur aus allen Gebeiten des Wissens*
FLI	*Film Literature Index* (from 1973 to present).
Guide to P.A.	*Guide to the Performing Arts* (1957 to present, appearance irregular).
Index analytique.	See annotation for *Périodex.*
IIFP	*International Index to Film Periodicals* (from 1972 to present).
MMRI	*Multi-Media Reviews Index,* later titled *Media Review Digest.*
Périodex	An annotated guide to French-language periodicals, before 1973 entitled *Index analytique* (1966–1972). Montreal: La Centrale des Bibliothèques and the Quebec Minister of Education.
Schuster	Mel Schuster. *Motion Picture Directors: A Bibliography of Magazine and Periodical Articles, 1900–1970.* Metuchen, N.J.: Scarecrow Press, 1971.

I
Biographical Background

Installed in the Sonimage Studios with the coworker and coproducer of his films, Anne-Marie Miéville, Jean-Luc Godard has returned to Switzerland after a long detour through Paris. Permeating Godard's entire oeuvre is the sense of his being an outsider, an onlooker, a provincial observer of the mores of large, urban, capitalist centers. This can be seen in *A Bout de souffle*, where Godard used Seberg, with her strongly accented French, to comment wittily on the reception of U.S. women in France. It continues in his political films such as *Loin du Viêt-Nam, Pravda,* and *Ici et ailleurs,* where Godard tries to understand what a European (and, by extension, U.S.) intellectual's involvement in anti-imperialist struggles means when history and that person's own national and class position has placed her/him at a certain distance from those struggles.

Godard not only moved away from Switzerland at the young age of nineteen, he also broke emotionally from his family, something which he considers intellectually and politically beneficial. His parents, who divorced while he was a teenager, enacted the conflicts of many middle class families; as a consequence Godard's films constantly have dealt with the sexual politics of the couple relationship, and more recently with *Numéro deux,* with the politics of the family. In the late 1960s Godard said that he escaped from the bourgeois family merely to enter a bigger "family," the self-affirming world of film production and critical fame, and it was only in the mid-1960s that he began to question that dubious security as well.

Godard was born in 1930, the second of four children, to a Swiss physician and the daughter of a rich Parisian banking family, the Monods. His father had his own clinic in Nyon, in the canton of Vaud, where Godard lived through his primary school years. A French citizen by birth, Godard was naturalized as a Swiss citizen during World War II and kept his Swiss passport throughout his sojourn in Paris. He was particularly attached to his mother, Odile, and it was her premature death in a motorcycle accident on the streets of Lausanne that caused him to make the final break with his family.

Godard's secondary school years were spent in Switzerland and at the Lycée Buffon in Paris, from where, at the age of nineteen in 1949, he enrolled

1

in the Sorbonne to pursue a degree in ethnology. Or perhaps he just wanted to continue to get money from his father and live in Paris. In the years 1949–59, before he made *A bout de souffle*, Godard lived the life of a bohemian cinephile in Paris, with periods spent in Switzerland or traveling. Perhaps he became immersed in the world of constant film viewing through a friend of the family, Jacques Doniol-Valcroze, to whom his mother had introduced him. He does not seem to have attended class regularly at the Sorbonne. In postwar Paris, where the educational apparatus had hardly recovered from the Occupation, a sensitive adolescent like Godard who wanted a broad cultural education was more likely to pursue it through viewing paintings, reading existentialist philosophy, going to the theater, and viewing films than through going to class. Especially in the cinéclubs and the Cinémathèque, one could see that whole rash of late thirties and early forties U.S. films that were part of U.S. aid to postwar European recovery. Godard says that before the age of eighteen or nineteen he was not a film buff but had an "encyclopedic inclination," wanting to grasp everything through painting or literature. Godard's voraciousness for literature, which he fed by skimming and by reading the beginnings and ends of books, has been commented on by many of his friends, and his voraciousness for film viewing was for many years just as great. According to Jacques Rivette, by 1949, he, Godard, Astruc, Rohmer, and Truffaut were running into each other constantly in the Cinémathèque at the Rue Messine or the Cinéclub in the Quartier Latin. Rivette said they were seeing about four films a day, 1,000 films a year, not counting re-viewings.

During this period, Godard and his fellow film addicts reinforced in each other the notion that they would be film directors, sure that their films would be very different from the established "Cinema of Quality" that was popular in France at the time. They admired U.S. cinema, especially *film noir*, for its fast pace, emotional directness, and distinctive visual style. In 1950, Godard paid for and acted in an experimental forty-minute film by Rivette, which depicted a group of people sitting speechlessly around a table. Along with his friends, Godard founded the short-lived *Gazette du cinéma*, but, according to Rivette, Godard — who signed his articles Hans Lucas — attached little importance to his writing. They all thought of writing criticism, says Rivette, only as a tool to *see* films better. Godard also began to write for *Cahiers du cinéma* and to act in other films by his friends.

Godard's income was finally cut off by his family, and he moved back and forth from Paris to Switzerland, trying to make a living. He stole openly; his thefts reputedly included money from the cash box of *Cahiers du cinéma*, his grandfather's first editions of Valéry (this Parisian gentleman had been secretary to Valéry as an avocation), 500 F. from friend Paul Gégauff's jacket, money from the open safe of a radio company (he spent days in a Swiss jail for that), and from his father's clinic (he arranged for thugs to break in). In Switzerland he was a delivery boy for a bookstore, cameraman and assistant editor for Zurich TV, and construction worker on the Grande-Dixence Dam. He deliberately took his last job so as to make a profit-making film which would let him live for a year or two in Paris while preparing a feature film. Before that job, his father had sent him on a five-month trip to visit relatives in South America, perhaps to get the youth out of legal troubles. After working on the dam, Godard got a job writing the gossip column for the daily *Les Temps de Paris*. In this job, he took quotations from books and attributed them to whichever movie star he was writing about.

In 1954 his mother was killed, and in 1955 and 1956 he immersed himself totally in a world of cinema. In 1955, shooting *Une Femme coquette* in Geneva, Godard did the camerawork, directing and editing as well as act in the film. In 1956 he returned to writing reviews after a lapse of four years, now in *Cahiers du cinéma* and *Arts*.

In 1956 he collaborated on and acted in his friends' films and in 1956–57 he worked as a professional film editor. In 1957 Chabrol got him a better job in the publicity department of Twentieth Century Fox through which position he met producer and lifelong friend Georges de Beauregard. Godard made three shorts, produced by Pierre Braunberger: *Histoire d'eau*, from footage abandoned by Truffaut; *Tous les garçons s'appellent Patrick*, from a script by Rohmer; and *Carlotte et son Jules*, shot in his own apartment. The latter two films were refused by the Selection Committee at Tours for being too amateurish.

In 1959 Godard was working for Beauregard after leaving his job at Fox. Beauregard sent him to work on a film called *The Fisherman of the Island*, for which Godard directed one comic love sequence set in a school of fish. Then he left and came back to Paris. When Godard proposed four scripts of his own to Beauregard (possibly *Une Femme est une femme* was among them), the first New Wave features had already triumphed at the international festivals, and Beauregard chose the script for *A bout de souffle*, thinking that Truffaut's scenario and Chabrol as "technical advisor" might safeguard his investment. The worst that Beauregard thought could happen, as he said later, was that Godard might "fill the film full of citations."

To film *A bout de souffle*, Godard asked his cameraman, Raoul Coutard, what film stock would give the most realistic effect; they actually spliced together an extrasensitive 35mm film stock ordinarily used for still news photography to make up reels of cinema film. Coutard says of Godard's technique that Godard would ask where one should set up the camera and then deliberately seek out the opposite effect. Sometimes Godard would describe setups in terms of shots from other films. To follow his actors around the streets in filming *A bout de souffle*, Godard pushed Coutard around in a wheelchair, a child's wagon, and a postal cart with holes drilled in the side so as to hide the camera. After the rushes were in, Godard was surprised, saying he thought he had filmed *Scarface* but finding that what he had was *Alice in Wonderland*. In the four months that elapsed between the first screenings of that film and its general release, *A bout de souffle* earned a certain notoriety. It won the Jean Vigo Prize, a record of the score was put out by Columbia, a novel vaguely inspired by the film was published, and a critical polemic was pursued by critics in the daily press.

A bout de souffle brought Godard fame, but he was thought by his friends to be retiring and shy. He had lived with Danish actress Anna Karina, a woman ten years younger than himself, for over a year and had introduced her to everyone as his wife, so it came as a surprise when he married her in March 1960. In April and May, 1960, Godard filmed *Le Petit Soldat* in Geneva, but that film was banned in September and not shown for three years, damning its lead actor, the newcomer Michel Subor, to obscurity. Godard made this film and a number of subsequent ones as a paen to Karina. With her he made the studio production of *Une Femme est une femme* (he would prefer location shooting after that). He began one of many altercations with producers when he was to make *Eva* for the Hakim Brothers but did not want to work with Jeanne Moreau. Truffaut said that even before his marriage Godard had always been in love with child-women, graceful, nonchalant, and decorative, and Jean Clay explained Godard's abandoning the production of *Eva* as his fear of working with "adult women."

In 1961 and 1962 Godard was active in both filmmaking and acting in others' films, but his abandoned projects in those years also reveal both his personality and his aesthetic and political concerns. He prepared a scenario of *France la douce* about a leftist man and a right wing woman, and he had actually started to film *Pour Lucrèce*, a study of theatricality, language, and the relation of rehearsal and script to finished product. He never finished this latter project. Indeed he abandoned it on the first day of shooting because he wanted to join Karina in Madrid, where she was acting in the film *Schérézade*, and he used his profits on *Vivre sa vie* to pay off his actors and crew.

In December 1963 Godard shot *Les Carabiniers* under arduous conditions, actually filming, for example, thirty-one shots in one day. In 1964, that film was a colossal critical and box office failure. *Le Petit Soldat*, finally shown, evoked strong mixed reactions in the press. By now critics were beginning to take strong pro- or anti-Godard stands, using the types of epithets or praise that follow him even to this day.

Le Mépris was a big-budget project, filmed while Godard was fighting with both his producers and his wife. Coutard said he had expected Godard to abandon that film as well to join Karina in Paris, and that the whole film was one "expensive letter made by Godard to explain something to his wife." Internal to *Le Mépris* are other indications that the film can be read in autobiographical terms. The character Prokosch probably represents Joseph E. Levine, as Godard portrays in Prokosch the crassness and corruption of contemporary film production. Godard's arguments with the film's producers continued even into distribution, when Carlo Ponti changed the Italian-release version so much that Godard found it necessary to have his name removed from the film.

The years 1964 and 1965 were ones of great fame for Godard. He founded Anouchka films with Karina, and that production company would co-produce most of the rest of his films. He filmed *Bande à part* and *La Femme mariée* in a continuing, nonexclusive arrangement with Columbia. He visited the United States and thought of doing a television program there, but abandoned his plans. Nevertheless, he began to state a desire then which he would frequently mention in interviews and which eventually came to fruition in the seventies: to do essay-like or journalistic pieces for television. He also wanted to do *Pour Lucrèce* or *Bérénice*, and his proposed *France la douce* was now to be about Communists, a provincial election, and a student from the UEC — the Communist Party student organization. The cineclub at Annecy had a complete Godard retrospective, and for that Godard talked on a series of panels, November 6–8, 1964. These were partially televised in the series *Cinéastes de nôtre temps*; and another television program, *Pour le Plaisir*, filmed by Jacques Doniol-Valcroze, was based on extracts from Godard's films.

In 1965 Godard made *Alphaville* and *Pierrot le fou*, and he also stormily divorced Karina. He made friends with a group of young people in Paris, which inspired him to make what he now considers his first effort to make a specifically political film. This was *Masculin-Féminin*, filmed in Paris in November and December, 1965, between two rounds of Gaullist elections. From 1966 on, Godard's statements to the press took on an increasingly politicized tone, as did his films. He chafed at the ideological and financial strictures of the film industry, the French governmental system of film finance and censorship, and the Ministry of Culture itself. In 1966 he published a letter in *Le Nouvel Observateur* protesting André Malraux's censorship of Rivette's *La Religieuse*. Godard shot *Made in U.S.A.* and *Deux ou trois choses que je sais d'elle* in the summer of 1966, and these as well as his two films completed in 1967 contain trenchant critiques, still from within a bourgeois intellectual framework, of capitalist social and economic structures and the personal relations which they engender. Because of his own intellectual and political development, Godard, of all the New Wave filmmakers, would be the most receptive to and the most affected by the civil rebellion in France in 1968.

In 1967 Godard made contact with the far-left publication, *Cahiers marxistes-léninistes*. Future collaborator Jean-Pierre Gorin was on the editorial board. *La Chinoise* was preceded by this inquiry into and contact with groups of far-left students, especially at the University of Nanterre. Because the 1968 student "take-overs" were to start in Nanterre, the film was later seen as prophetic. Acting in this film was Anne Wiazemsky (she previously had appeared in a film Godard greatly admired, Bresson's *Au hazard Balthazar*), and she married Godard in July 1967. Gorin said that although he did not start making films with Godard until 1969, he began at this point a friendship with Godard, consisting mostly of long political conversations, that was to last over the next few years. Godard also worked collectively with the group of filmmakers making *Loin du Viêt-Nam* in an act of political protest against the Vietnam War. In the fall of that year he shot *Weekend*, which was to be his last big-budget, wide-screen film until *Tout va bien*. He expressed his total dissatisfaction with the U.S., French, Italian, Japanese, and Russian film industries and the types of films they produced. His critique of "bourgeois film form" would be a constant theme in interviews for years to come.

In December 1967 and January 1968, he shot part of *Le Gai Savoir*, commissioned by ORTF but never shown on TV or commercially in theaters in France. In February and March, 1968, Godard commenced his career as a political activist by leading the protests against the firing of Henri Langlois, revered director of the French Cinémathèque; Godard was even hit by police as he led street demonstrations for Langlois in the Trocadero. During the May 1968 rebellion, Godard filmed in the streets but did not take an active role in the collective efforts by French media workers to reorgainze commerical and governmental structures of mass communication. However, along with François Truffaut, Claude Lelouch, and Claude Berri, he effected a total shutdown of the Cannes Festival. In June, he went to England to film *One Plus One* and then returned to France without completing or perhaps intending to complete the shooting. He shot the color-sequence parts of *Une Film comme les autres* in July and then returned to England in August to complete *One Plus One*. He edited *Le Gai Savoir*, which was censored, and traveled to Cuba with Anne Wiazemsky and possibly planned to make a film there. (Strangely, in his films as a whole, he does not make explicit reference either to Cuban films or Cuban cinema. While he scores both Russian film and Russian "revisionist" politics, he only uses posters of Cuban leaders or Cuban revolutionary songs in his films to indicate symbolically a "good" kind of communism.) Other projects undertaken that year include filming in the United States, where Godard planned to make a film about the student and Black Power movements, and a trip to Canada where he planned to film but did not. Gorin has said that they discussed making a film,

Communications, that might last two days and would be about all aspects of communications, but if that project ever came to fruition it was only in a truncated way with the television series Godard made in 1976 with Anne-Marie Miéville, *Sur et sous la communication*.

After the events of May 1968, Godard seemed to be searching both for the best way to make a political film and the best way to integrate his metier, filmmaking, with militant Marxist-Leninist political activity. What the actual political groups are that he associated with is unclear (see 1972, Leblanc, Entry No. 1698 and Entry No. 1699 for the most complete explanation of political references in *Vent d'est* and *Luttes en Italie*). In 1968 and 1969, Godard associated with members of two "Maoist" groups, each of whom had principled differences with the other. (One "line" — Jean-Henri Roger's — influenced *Pravda* and *British Sounds*; the other — Gorin's — is most clearly in evidence in *Vent d'est* and *Luttes en Italie*.

It is in Godard's films of those years and in interviews that his social political ideas and his concepts about political filmmaking most clearly emerge. In this book, the plot summaries of the films will indicate some of the aesthetic-political ideas developed by Godard at this time, and I have analyzed the political content of his films at greater length elsewhere (See 1976, Lesage, Entry No. 1982). Because Godard was influenced anesthetically by the work of both Bertolt Brecht and U.S. avant-garde filmmakers, particularly Andy Warhol, the political concepts in his films cannot be grasped directly but only reflected upon as they are presented to us in an artistically manipulated way.

In 1969 Godard attempted to work collectively with various political militants. In February he shot *British Sounds* in England for London Weekend Television (never shown) with Jean-Henri Roger. In March he went to Czechoslovakia with Roger and Paul Burron, where they filmed images off Czech television and clandestinely in and around Prague. In May or June, leaders from the past May's events, such as Daniel Cohn-Bendit, and also leftist actors and filmmakers gathered in Italy to make a political "Italian western" with Godard. This project was to be a collective effort. According to Jean-Pierre Gorin, the group could not reach an aesthetic or political accord on what to do, and the participants just played around in the sun and/or argued. Gorin came from Paris to join them, and he and Godard "took charge of" and finished the film.

From that time on, Roger no longer worked with Godard, and Gorin became Godard's close associate until 1973, when they separated. Gorin said that he edited *Vent d'est* while Godard simultaneously edited *Pravda*; when it was obvious that both films were so similar the two men realized the collective production was not only an ideal but that Godard had, in fact, reached a certain anonymity. To further the end of demystifying Godard's fame, they "reclaimed" all of Godard's 1969 work and labeled his work up until 1972 as that of the Dziga Vertov Group. Indeed, a number of militants regularly contributed ideas to Godard's work. However, the actual production decisions were made and most work was done by only Godard and Gorin. We do not know what contribution their regular coworkers made in those years, especially their cameraman, Armand Marco.

In December 1969 Godard and Gorin filmed *Luttes en Italie* for Italian television, which never showed it. The same fate befell *British Sounds*, made for British television, and *Pravda*, made for German television. The Palestinian group, Al Fatah, asked Godard and Gorin to make a film about their struggles, and they began filming in Lebanon and Jordan in February. This project, then entitled *Till Victory*, was to be a militant tool for the Palestinians, but in that form it was never completed, partly because Godard and the groups he was working with could not come to an adequate political-aesthetic analysis which both sides could agree upon to shape the film and also because the Jordanians killed most of the film's participants in Amman in September 1970. The "distance" of Europeans from that struggle became the basis upon which Godard and Miéville would reedit these rushes in 1976 as *Ici et ailleurs*.

In April 1970 Godard and Gorin consented to do a tour of U.S. universities arranged by Grove Press, with whom they had just signed a contract to do *Vladimir and Rosa* and one or two other films. They toured with the film *See You at Mao (British Sounds)* in order to raise money for the Palestine film, and Godard showed his storyboard for that film to campus audiences and to Mark Woodcook, who filmed *Godard in America: Two American Audiences*. During this tour, Godard and Gorin sparred verbally with politicized New Left university audiences, whom the filmmakers seemed not to take seriously; consequently the two were not well received, especially at Berkeley and Yale. In Paris, Godard also did commercial films to make money for the Palestine film. He and Gorin filmed *Vladimir and Rosa* in Paris, which was financed by Grove and also by German television. Just as he felt about *One Plus One*, also an effort to film others' struggles, Godard was later to reject *Vladimir and Rosa* as political "garbage." In Paris in 1970 and 1971, Godard worked on the short-lived Marxist far-left publication, *J'Accuse*, and was associated with the Secours Rouge Group, an association of left-wing intellectuals around the writer André Glucksmann; this group acted as a support to ongoing far-left militant activity.

In 1971 Godard and Gorin began plans for a film that was to speak to a popular audience, supposedly to the whole spectrum of the middle class, but Godard was injured in a motorcycle accident and recuperated from it slowly, subsequently requiring surgery. He and Gorin filmed the feature *Tout va bien* using two famous militant actors, Yves Montand and Jane Fonda (they had hoped to work closely with Godard politically on the film but did not). *Tout va bien* opened in May 1972 in Paris while everyone else was at Cannes. Its short-lived run greatly disappointed Godard and Gorin, who had fully anticipated making a commercially successful Marxist and Brechtian film.

Letter to Jane was made as an aesthetic and political statement to accompany *Tout va bien* at various film festivals, especially in the United States. However, it was seen as unfairly critical of a U.S. militant against the war. In 1973 Godard and Gorin had a brief U.S. speaking tour with *Tout va bien* while they were buying video equipment. At this point, their attitude toward audiences seems to have changed as they engaged mainly bourgeois intellectual audiences — including many politicized students — not ironically but openly, as equals.

In 1973 Godard and Gorin terminated their partnership. Gorin moved to California where he teaches and plans to make a documentary film about twins who created their own language. He no longer considers himself a "political" filmmaker. Godard, who had divorced Anne Wiazemsky, announced that he was going to do a film, *Moi, je*, with her in color video, but the project was never completed. In 1974 or 1975, Godard and his present coworker Anne-Marie Miéville established the Sonimage film and video production studio in Grenoble. There they have coproduced all of Godard's work to the present. In terms of themes and film form, there is a great continuity between Godard and Miéville's current work and Godard's past films, now integrating in ever new ways Godard's concerns about class, imperialism, ideological structures, left-wing "bourgeoisification," the mass media, and sexual and family politics.

II
Critical Survey of Oeuvre

At the end of Jean-Luc Godard's and Anne-Marie Miéville's film *Numéro deux*, made in 1977, Godard self-consciously and a bit sadly faces the camera. His posture seems to sum up a major conflict seen throughout his work: he must stand alone as a creative genius although he has constantly struggled to forge a collective, modernist, politicized art.

As we see Godard in that sequence, he switches on and off images of family life and of a woman on the video monitors in his studio. In voice off, the woman protagonist summarizes both her situation and that of individuals in general under capitalism with their fragmented personal lives, alienated labor, sexual and family politics, and false consciousness generated especially by the mass media. The woman states that although it is she who does the understanding, it is always "he" who commands, who tells what to do and when to do it. "What's worse," she says, perhaps echoing Miéville herself, "I say it for him. And him, him in my place, working, in my place. . . . His is special work, more so because it's paid. But to let other people speak for you is a crime, especially when you are unpaid. . . . I ought to be there and I'm not. Not yet."

That Godard and Miéville have a woman speak the key summary lines is important since Godard, the romantic creator of *A bout de souffle, Une Femme est une femme,* and *Pierrot le fou,* has often been accused of misogyny, especially in portraying women as unfeeling betrayers. However, throughout his career, in numerous other films, especially *Vivre sa vie, Une Femme mariée, Deux ou trois choses que je sais d'elle, Vladimir et Rosa,* and *Tout va bien,* Godard has portrayed and politically analyzed issues of women's oppression with a seriousness and thoroughness not matched by any other major male film director.

Miéville is acknowledged yet still not openly accepted as collective co-creator with Godard. Godard's name still brings in money for their films and achieves the critical recognition, or even the rejection. And Godard himself, although he has chosen to work collectively since his radicalization in 1968, is still politically an isolated artist, making the films he feels will be needed by a future communist society as well as by current radical movements for social change. *Numéro deux* ends with the image of the middle-aged artist

11

turning off the images of family life on his monitors, listening to a romantic crescendo of a Léo Ferré song about escaping into fantasy from the bitterness of daily life, and laying his head in his arms on the control deck — an image of death, despair, or sleep. From Michel Poiccard in *A bout de souffle* and Ferdinand-Pierrot in *Pierrot le fou* to this image of Godard, there is a direct line of continuity in the type of romantic outsider depicted, but that outsider is no longer presented in an obliquely autobiographical way. Godard the director, with the collaboration of his partner Miéville, has now made himself and that romantic image of himself into a cinematic icon.

CRITICAL APPROACHES TO GODARD

Critics favorable to Godard's films have usually preferred one term of the contradiction which Godard and Miéville here try to deal with to the other — the romantic or the political Godard. The "romantic" Godard has been praised for his tenderness; his capturing of the fugitive moment or the chaos of modern life; his autobiographical and subjective tendencies — especially his homages to and expressed bitterness about his first wife, Anna Karina; his personal, subjective monologues spoken in voice off; his love of spontaneity in filming and in his direction of actors; his painterly use of color; and his emotional, abruptly edited musical scores.

Critics who prefer the socially committed Godard fall into two more camps. Many militant leftists reject Godard's wit and modernism, as well as his romanticism. They find Godard's work private, anarchistic, obscurantist, elitist, insolent, and either too heavily theoretical and preachy or too topical. Another group of left cultural critics, and I would place myself among these, appreciate the way Godard contrapuntally brings both documentary elements and abstract ideas from the social and historical world to bear on a film's story. Such juxtaposition of elements not only breaks up dramatic tension but also opens up whole new intellectual contexts which amplify the social, cultural and political resonance of each Godard film.

In particular, Godard uses editing with a social and intellectual wit. He manipulates different modes of visual and verbal discourse, often humorously, so as to provoke thought about contemporary society and about film itself. To appreciate this side of Godard is to appreciate the "Brechtian" Godard — *that* Godard develops character in a nonpsychological way; delights in parenthetical material and obtrusive details; develops narratives with many ellipses, discontinuities, and ruptures in tone — both between shots and sequences and within a given take; ever more heavily depends on visual symbolism; and either pares down or crowds signifying elements into a given shot.

Internal to a shot that makes a social comment, multiple reflections on the way that shot functions are made available to the spectator all at once. For example, a shot of a book title stands out as a tight, static close-up, visually unrelated to what has just been seen, especially if juxtaposed against shots of dramatic action. At the same time, the book title has its own referential value — both in what the words say and in what we may or may not know about the author and the author's intellectual position in France. Godard may use the color of the book jacket ironically, especially if red, white, or blue. We notice whether it stands in contrast to or reinforce something else in the film. If it follows an interview or a monologue, or is accompanied by music shown in the previous scene to be coming from a jukebox, then its significance lies not only in the words presented in the title but also in Godard's juxtaposition of modes of discourse.

In the more political films, shots are often inserted which seem outside the narrative flow. These dislocating inserts act as Brecht said titles or back projections should, that is, as footnotes which introduce some extra bit of related information for the spectators' intelligent consideration. Such inserted material reminds us, the audience, that our world is outside the film's action, and at the same time it conveys a sense of the interrelation of artistic linguistic, iconic (visual representational), architectural, sexual, class, and economic structures both within the film and in the world. Every Godard film, even the less explicitly political ones, examines various levels of how people communicate within a given historical context. And each film makes cinematic technique a direct object of consideration.

The tone of Godard's films is as contradictory as his own artistic stance. He shifts constantly from "obviousness" and heaviness to playfulness and wit. His earlier work, such as *A bout de souffle, Une Femme est une femme, Bande à part,* and *Alphaville,* was often praised for its fugitive, fantasy quality. It was also scorned by many French critics for its low schoolboy humor. Godard delights in gags, parody, and word play — down to simplistic, bad puns. In those films with a direct social commentary, Godard (and his collaborators, first Gorin, then Miéville) constantly insert shots of book jackets, intertitles (often in red, white, and blue), and symbolic, flat images, posters and photos — frequently written over in Godard's own handwriting. These bring with them an intellectual and political humor. They are both exaggerated and suggestive, obtrusive yet slyly witty — and they usually leave it to the spectator to figure out the political point. Often Godard's humor is mainly cinematic — found in filmic parody, in non-naturalistic, saturated color, in spontaneity and a documentary capturing of on-the-street happenings, in manipulation of film stock and lighting, in an inventive use of the long take, and, above all, in the startling editing of both image and sound. Other times, Godard's humor is subjective and emotional, especially when he pokes tender fun at his romantic male protagonists and their pretensions.

Godard is a modernist director, but one unlike his fellow innovators in the narrative arts in France. His humor is never purely a game. He enjoys chance but does not rely on it. He never asserts that there are no specific truths, nor does he try to create a work like a Chinese puzzle box, as the "new novelists" do. He does use certain techniques reminiscent of the Absurdists, who rose to the height of their popularity in the French theater in the 1950s. He shares Ionesco's preoccupation with the problems of translation and the cultural devaluation of words, the banality of language, and the accumulation and intensification of symbolic visual details. Like Beckett, he uses metaphorical sets, often farcical dialogue, and fragmented characterization. Arthur Adamov's dramatic tactic of abrupt, brutal violence, usually social violence, which Adamov uses as a narrative structuring device, reminds one of all the automobile accidents, murders, and moments of violence artificially presented in Godard's films. The image of a character being run over by a car and being swept off the street into the garbage by street cleaners, found in Adamov's *The Parody*, could also have come from a film like *Weekend*.

However, many visual artists from Expressionism and Dada to Pop Art and concrete poetry have also used visual elements such as those used by Godard, particularly letters and numerals, precisely for their shock value and the incongruity of their incorporation within an otherwise representational scene. Beyond enjoying surprising audiences with an ever-new presentation of once-familiar types of visual material, Godard almost always uses non-narrative inserts to make us think about the social process behind what we see. Like the Pop artists and also the concrete poets, Godard delights in an art that takes as its matter all social communication: messages and their content and their mode of presentation. Yet unlike these other modern artists, Godard uses inserted photographic and symbolic material to expand on its social signification. His most political films are about ideas, and to express ideas he has simultaneously created new cinematic equivalents for them and has imported a whole range of intellectual, sociological, political, psychological, and artistic concepts which he has found expressed in images from his own milieu.

As with the audiences for most modernist works, people watching Godard's films cannot rely merely on identification, catharsis, and a story line. They are, especially with Godard's post-1968 films, led to create their own aesthetic experience. However, Godard's distancing effects, particularly the humorous ones, have increasingly been used by him to formulate a political aesthetic, which fact separates him from almost all other avant-garde film directors. His films are often directly polemical, even though the political line is often presented in a distanced, i.e., refracted and symbolic way.

Godard has had to teach audiences how to read his own films at the same time that he has striven to teach them how to "read" the media. As I mentioned, his wit and use of obtrusive elements more frequently than not lead audiences to make judgments about narrative and cinematic technique and the concepts these embody. Increasingly Brechtian, Godard's films refer to a specific class and sexual-political structure beyond art that Godard in a polemical way wants to use his art to change.

Only a combined filmic and political analysis of Godard's films can provide an accurate, efficient, and integrative method for approaching his work. If I assert that Godard is the most influential filmmaker of the sixties, that statement must be understood in both aesthetic and social terms. Many critics have a purely formalist appreciation of Godard's films or analyze only single films or pick out just one strand of his work to esteem. Some critics discuss these films in terms of "life" and fail to understand Godard's close relation to a specific intellectual and sociopolitical milieu. Very many critics have stopped liking or writing about Godard's "political" work from *Le Gai Savoir* on, and few have found the major strands or "voices" that would tie together Godard's career as a whole. Apolitical critics often do not know or care about the issues in left politics and Marxist aesthetics which have preoccupied Godard and his collaborators since 1968; at the same time, many leftist cultural critics automatically reject Godard as elitist along with their rejection of the rest of the cinematic avant-garde.

Godard's intellectual scope can be seen not merely in his accomplishments as an avant-garde director but also in the complexity of these films' social, psychological, and political themes. Throughout his work, Godard has dealt with problems of communication, interpersonal relations, and false consciousness. In film after film, he has analyzed language, translation, the media, education, and the difficulty of communication. Sometimes emotionally and sometimes analytically, he throws himself into a nexus of issues that deal with the quality of personal life — especially themes of sentimentality, adolescence, prostitution, and urban alienation. He also has more specifically political concerns which include critiques of both Communist party revisionism, economism, and cultural narrowness and of U.S. imperialism — specifically the U.S.-style consumerism which has "Americanized" French life, U.S. intervention in Vietnam, and imperialism in Czechoslovakia, Palestine, and Portugal. Godard and Miéville's more recent efforts to demonstrate the functioning of the mass media in the West embrace all these concerns — as they simultaneously consider interpersonal dynamics and family life at the same time that they deal with history, strategy on the left, and an anticapitalist critique.

GODARD'S CINEMATIC TECHNIQUE

Cinematically Godard has developed a specific set of filmic techniques that stamp all his films with his mark. Considering his cumulative work in purely formal terms, one could easily analyze Godard as an auteur. He is unique in the way he deals with images and sounds, and he has introduced into commercial feature films very specific kinds of modernist cinematic effects. In particular, it is on the level of the shot — both as filmed and as edited — that his intellectual shock tactics are most clearly defined. In terms of visual style, from *A bout de souffle* on, Godard's use of jump-cuts, hand-held camera, and elliptical editing has made us look at familiar outdoor settings in a new way. In the films before 1968, Godard especially enjoyed playing off contradictory elements against each other — the realistic along-side the implausible, written signs juxtaposed against other images, static interviews followed by rapid action, thingness versus living people — in a narrative he often merely used to reveal the incoherence of events. He constantly strips the familiar of its inconspicuousness.

In Godard's films, the clash of seemingly discontinuous shots throws each shot into relief; the characters are presented visually in contradictory ways; the camera swings back and forth, catching a detail at the edge, framing a character in an unexpected way. Sometimes the camera movements seem gratuitous, and sometimes Godard's use of extremely long takes and traveling shots makes the audience wonder what he could possibly show next before cutting to another shot. The editing, the composition of the frame, the angles of the shots, and the color control lead the spectator to consider previously taken-for-granted elements in a new way and to consider them intellectually. Godard sometimes uses these techniques ironically or satirically, as in his fondness for ketchup-colored blood, and sometimes to comment on conventional film and television practice and on the ideology of film form — as in his eye level close-ups of someone talking to the camera in interview style.

Increasingly, in his attack on unreflective photographic representation, Godard has used the human figure, costume, gesture, action, and locale not for their iconic, representational value, but in a totally stylized and symbolic way. In the post-1968 films he has drastically reduced the connotations carried by images: they must be read as symbols. Furthermore, he has always used the written word imaginatively, especially in the title frames which call attention to both the linguistic form and the social use of the words presented on the screen. Finally, Godard incorporates other filmic texts into his films, thus commenting on his own departure from and debt to the very texts cited. His films thus become self-reflexive texts, a kind of art criticizing art. Increasingly, from 1966 on, he has used stylization to make a political point about film form.

Godard's juxtaposition of and implicit commentary on entire modes of discourse — both cinematic and extracinematic — his insertion of seemingly undigested documentary material from his own milieu, and his use of single shots to represent whole political concepts are all of as much interest to the film viewer as is the story line or, in the later films, the exposition of a political idea. He keeps intact the referential aspect of much of his filmed material and expands on its conventional meaning, especially through his abrupt editing technique. Because of this, we notice the uniqueness of the isolated images, particularly the elements of Godard's urban milieu — its people, language, signs, color patterns, planes, architecture, and culture. In other words, Godard's collage technique generally reinforces a sense of artifice while still preserving the heterogeneity of the inserted elements, which are not then reduced merely to advancing the plot as, for example, a shot of a "wanted" poster does in a western.

NONPSYCHOLOGICAL DEVELOPMENT OF CHARACTER

Godard has created a variety of tactics in framing and composition which he typically uses to develop character or advance the narrative in an unexpected way. A major character may be filmed as a tiny figure against a vast urban backdrop, connoting both personal and social malaise. Two lovers or husband and wife are often seen constantly moving around in and out of frame as the camera either moves or stays fixed in a long take, the composition being a visual symbol of their coming together or moving apart. In his presentation of female characters, especially from 1964 on, rather than use photography conventionally to encourage the audience's romantic yearning, identification, and desire, Godard instead films women so as to comment on such conventions. In particular, he often uses expressionless close-up of faces, often with a voice off relating a character's story or analyzing the social group or situation that determines that character's predicament.

The actions of the characters are often not continued naturalistically from one shot to the next; a sequence of actions may be connected by jump cuts, gestures may be repeated, or a character may be shown giving a set speech separated from the dramatic action, such as in *Tout va bien*. Characters may perform actions in a single plane parallel to the camera. Such a filming technique creates a highly exaggerated visual flatness and is used especially in the films from *Le Gai Savior* on, although often found in the films before that. In *Made in U.S.A.* and *La Chinoise*, the characters are frequently filmed standing against a wall. In many films they are shown addressing the camera directly, lit from the front and not performing any action except talking — if that. In *Vent d'est* and *Luttes en Italie*, the human figures (one can no longer call them characters) are shown either in symbolic, static tableaux or performing very minimal symbolic gestures. In *Le Gai Savoir*, Godard exaggerates a technique of visual repetition, developed earlier in films such as *La Femme mariée*. He films Berto and Léaud in a minimalist way against a darkened background and manipulates their positions and glances in a way that leads the spectator to consider the various visual combinations possible within a given image. In *Tout va bien, Vladimir et Rosa*, and *Le Gai Savior*, Godard has a man and a woman repeat the same minimal gestures; in the latter two films, these occur while one is positioned behind the other. Such images symbolize sexual role playing, and the switching of positions symbolizes women's struggles to change power relations between the sexes. In the films from 1967 on, we do not and cannot make the lives and the feelings of the characters our own because they speak as if they are quoting a third-person text, turn to the camera to show the process of acting, and are developed in a nonpsychological way.

DOCUMENTARY

Over and over again, Godard uses his films to explore philosophically, stylistically, and politically the relation between documentary and artifice in cinema, and in particular he often tries to elucidate the ideology of newsreel style filming. Perhaps more than any other director, he works not only from a personal style of directing and editing, but he also uses that style to question what kind of filmmaking and media production in general is best suited to give us the Truth. He frequently imitates TV-newscast visual compositions, films on the street, or captures "spontaneous" gestures of his actors "candid-camera" style. He prefers professional actors to amateurs, yet he also directs those actors with an eye toward spontaneity, and sometimes he films them talking to real-life people "playing themselves." He is famous for his rapid shooting style and his ability or preference to use whatever he gets, thus working on low budgets and using most of what he shoots in the finished film. Yet he consistently uses both the visual and the sound track to question what the newsreel, the television interview, and the documentary filmmaking style can and do present to us — a blend of fiction and reality. In our own lives, he asks, what are fictions, what are roles, and what are dangerous lies? He uses spontaneity and documentary reflections in his film both for their own sake aesthetically and to challenge the modes, possibilities, distortions, and limits of communication in the dominant culture.

The use of documentary footage is particularly important in Godard's more explicitly political films. Like Brecht, Godard came to reject the ideology of naturalism. He found that the only authentic artistic realism lay in elucidating the social mechanism behind appearances, and that a correct view of reality had to be created and did not come from a presentation of surface appearances. To take one film as an example, *Deux ou trois choses*, Godard presents images — very often extreme close-ups — of what seem the least significant and most "natural" aspects of urban life, and he uncovers the social structure and the ideology behind these so-called trivial or banal things — such as a box of soap, a gas station, or the daily routine of a working class wife. The documentary footage — the shots of apartment buildings, construction, pedestrians, stores, and billboards in Paris — trace out at least implicitly the capitalist social relations that connect human life and necessities with the seemingly inhuman morass of images, construction, and material things found in a contemporary urban milieu. Both visually and verbally, Godard demonstrates the interrelation of words, images, objects, architecture, city traffic, and persons, and also their relation to the film's theme: prostitution, taken in the larger sense as a metaphor for advanced capitalist France.

SYMBOL AND EMBLEM

From 1967 on, Godard's films (and those coproduced with Gorin or Miéville) present social criticism in a complex, intellectualized way. Images, words, and sound are used not merely as pictorial or auditory representations but as symbols — that is, as arbitrary abstractions of social concepts. This is particularly true of the Dziga Vertov Group films of 1969. The organizing principle of *Luttes en Italie*, like *Pravda*, is that of repetition, in which images are reiterated with minimal variation, while the voice-off commentary reevaluates the images in successively more profound ways. Most often these images make sense only if interpreted as symbols.

Although most directors of feature films have used the image primarily in its connotative, representational function, one of the early theorists of the communicative possibilities of film, Sergei Eisenstein, advocated a type of cinema that would carry on a complex conceptual discourse. Eisenstein insisted that intellectual concepts could be conveyed by a "collision" of images that had been abstracted from their ordinary representational context. With a similar intent, Godard and his coproducers from *Le Gai Savoir* on have structured their films symbolically, waging an attack on unreflective photographic representation. More precisely, in these films the visual symbols are usually emblems.

In general terms, an emblem can be defined as a picture accompanied by a word or a motto, occasionally by more extensive verbal exposition, for a moral or didactic purpose. Since cinema incorporates action and movement, both within the frame and by the camera, Godard's emblems include gestures, such as a raised fist, and camera movement. Movement from left to right in *Pravda* and *Tout va bien* both within the frame and by the camera, for example, is emblematic of political shifts. In general in the post-1968 films, Godard tries to strip the image of its multivalence and make it stand as a one-to-one symbol for some social or historical process. And in both his earlier films and those after 1968, he often uses color emblematically. Red, white, and blue usually stand for a purified communism, not the traitorous French Communist Party version, and this pure communism is also frequently symbolized by the word *lutte* (struggle) handwritten over a photo or on a white frame in red.

In *Numéro deux* Godard and Miéville use a specific video technique emblematically. They overlay in silhouette the image of the person listening, thus emphasizing the mutuality of communication and the frequent miscomprehension, resentment, or "erasure" of the listener, especially if that person is a woman or child. In all the post-1969 films, repeated phrases, songs, and ideas on the sound track, tied to repeated images and the printed word or an emblematic use of color on the visual track, emphasize some historical or social process and often "explain" in a telegraphic way what we are seeing on the visual track. In this way, the opening of *Vladimir et Rosa* repeats the words *theoretically* and *practically* as we see repeated shots of a photo of Lenin, a young man studying, a movie camera, and a tape recorder. To expand on such a sketchy political indication about the necessary direction for militant filmmaking, at several points in the film, voices over comment on the filmmakers' need to learn how to create "correct" images and sounds in order to portray militant activity and to aid it.

This description makes Godard's use of emblems sound very mechanical, but actually in his films from *Le Gai Savoir* to *Vladimir et Rosa*, often considered his "driest" or most heavily theoretical films, he shared that delight in the graffiti, zany photos, and political posters — especially from Cuba and China — that accompanied the occupation of the Sorbonne in May 1968. In *Vladimir et Rosa*, for example, the political leaders Vladimir Lenin and Rosa Luxemburg are symbolized visually by the emblems of "Vladimir" and "Rosa" hippie tee-shirts. In the films of this period, the dialogue provides a commentary on the imagery, and the written words — usually positive political "signals" — often act as the motto or inscription which gives the didactic lesson of the traditional emblem.

THE WRITTEN WORD

Godard not only specifically used the written word as a motto for an emblem in the films from 1968 to 1970, but he has also consistently used the written word as the title for a sequence. Both filmed inserts with writing on them and intertitles function regularly as summary statements within the narrative. Furthermore, Godard is fascinated with the semantic and linguistic possibilities of isolated words and phrases. He combines and plays with many kinds of syntaxes all at once: kinetic, coloring, verbal cinematic and poetic syntax. As James Ronald Green noted (Entry No. 1684), Godard often uses written words in the way that concrete poets do, particularly in the titles flashed on the screen during the film or in his writing on the image. In *Numéro deux,* the titles appear on computer printouts which replace each other letter by letter and which thus create other "words" or suggestions of words that only appear temporarily on the screen. Often the intertitles that look like neon signs, especially in the films of 1966 and 1967, fascinate us as visual abstractions; other times the intertitles call attention to their ideological bias. In his use of the word as an image, Godard captures the tension between motion and stasis in the very material process of writing, and he shows the kinesis inherent in that process, a kinesis we usually only perceive as the movement from left to right in reading, and from the top to the bottom of the page or screen. He often renders points simultaneously — by flashing a text or various elements of it on the screen, often at different points in the rectangular composition of the frame; by repeating the same word, either in one image or successively; or by presenting a very short message rapidly for the audience to read in one glance.

THE LONG TAKE/COLOR

I must emphasize that Godard's cinematic innovations are often delightful for their sheer virtuosity and are not necessarily significant for any social commentary. This is true of his mastery of the long take and of the Technicolor spectrum. In his direction of actors, Godard has always absorbed chance into his work, but, especially in the earlier films, we sense his directorial presence behind the spontaneous gestures captured by the camera and behind the composition of the frame and the seemingly free camera movements. Godard makes us clearly aware of the virtuosity of the long takes, which he often uses to film "natural" settings, whether outdoors or indoors, in places such as apartments or Parisian cafes. He makes the technique as noticeable as the story. Furthermore, because of his editing technique, what was perhaps captured spontaneously is always presented in a highly intellectualized form, as a constant interrogation of how sense is transmitted and practiced in film.

Godard is extremely versatile in his use of the long take. Characteristic of his films from 1966 on, as Brian Henderson (Entry No. 1459) points out, is a lateral tracking shot that always films objects and people at a critical distance from the camera; the characters are arranged within a single plane perpendicular to the camera's line of sight. In such shots, Godard's compositions seem flat, and this flatness changes the way the viewer "reads" the image. It makes it easier to explore or elicit a new reading of the semiotic codes within that image, particularly in terms of Godard's intent in the film as a whole.

Not only does the long take heighten the presentation of the urban milieu so that we are more aware of the social codes in the mise en scène, but Godard uses both fluid and "flat" long takes to film conversations in an unconventional way. Over and over again he interferes with a conversation's "naturalness" — as seen, for example, in the conversations and arguments between couples in Le Petit Soldat, Une Femme est une femme, Le Mépris, and La Chinoise, and in the entire set of relations between the students living together in La Chinoise. He uses his cinematic technique to reflect both on the "rules" of a conversation as such interaction might occur in daily life and also on how these interactions traditionally have been filmed.

Godard often uses long takes to reject film as entertainment and to criticize society. Masculin-Féminin was shot with an almost completely fixed camera. In addition, Godard put important details at the very edge of the screen and/or on it only momentarily, again reinforcing the film's theme of the problems of communication. British Sounds opened with a long ten-minute tracking shot of workers on an actual assembly line in England while the commentary discussed the causes of alienation, defined in Marxist terms, and the boredom that workers suffer. Vent d'est's static form throughout the film is intended as an attack on entertainment films and on bourgeois concepts of representation.

Although Godard sometimes uses color romantically, he also uses it to comment on the narrative or interfere with narrative tension. He stripped the political act in La Chinoise of all drama by filming the "assassination" sequence in excessively cheerful color, and similarly Vladimir et Rosa and Tout va bien he filmed reenactments of student protests in bright color. On the other hand, he used a restrained black and white somberness to express the banality of violence in Le Petit Soldat, Les Carabiniers, and Alphaville. Masculin-Féminin, which Godard said was the first film in which he tried to analyze France politically, was shot in very dark grey tones. Les Carabiniers was processed three times to get a special grainy effect like old newsreel photography. Alphaville was also shot in grainy black and white film, the harsh contrasts of which were emphasized in Godard's use of single-source lighting, such as an uncovered bulb swinging from a wire. Le Gai Savoir was one of the first films in which Godard "stripped down" the image so as to examine language; the film was shot in color, but the action (conversations) took place mostly against the background of a blacked-out room. Godard is capable of a spectacular use of painterly color, as in Pierrot le fou and Weekend, but he will also vary or mismatch the color if that suits his political purpose or theme.

CINEMATIC REFLEXIVITY

In the type of imagery which he incorporates on the level of the shot and in the composition of the shot, Godard elicits a reflection on the visual medium itself. Perhaps the most obvious way in which Godard's films reflect on cinema itself is in their citation of other films. Within his films Godard uses movie posters, real-life film directors playing themselves, clips from others' films, and a wide range of loving imitation of the shots and styles of many directors. In his borrowings of film texts and references, Godard often makes the original sources obvious, either as a joke or as a serious reinforcement of the theme. Thus Michel encounters a *Cahiers du cinéma* hawker in *A bout de souffle*; Charlotte does not know what Auschwitz is as she watches Resnais' documentary about the concentration camps, *Nuit et tinieblas*, in *La Femme mariée*, and the characters are presented emblematically as from a western in *Vent d'est*.

To criticize the "truth" of newscasts and documentary films, in almost all of his films Godard utilizes sequences of film interviews, either with real, historically important personages or with the characters. Each time, he provokes reflection on the degree of communication achieved by any interview, the bias of the questioner, the pose of the respondent, and the kind of information that is or can be gained. In visual style, these sequences, often shot in a single take with an immobile camera, look like a parody of television interviews. Godard plays with this visual-verbal convention in order to interrogate the function of languages and communication in general.

His use of parody, of television styles, and of film-within-film is sometimes merely a tour de force but more often serves to comment on the dream world of film and television and its effect both on the lives of the characters in his films and by implication on our lives. In his pre-1968 films he undermines this dream world from within the cinema of spectacle. After 1968 his attack is more direct and he tries to create a totally different film form and function. In *Made in U.S.A.* and *Vent d'est*, the dream world of Hollywood cinema is seen to be a major ideological reinforcement of U.S. imperialism. The films from 1968 on, especially the ones made with Miéville, refute traditional cinema and television on many levels — formally, economically, politically, psychologically — and phrase a warning to the left not to let its politics and tactics be limited, disastrously, by the means of communication currently in use all over the world. In these political films Godard and his collaborators made their attack on traditional cinema and television in both the aesthetic and political commentary within the films themselves and in the ascetic, emblematic, and intellectualized form of their films, which was intended to shock audiences, even militants, out of their habituation to entertainment and spectacle.

THE SOUND TRACK

Finally, even though published scripts of a director's films are invaluable critical tools, especially when they indicate the shots, the published scripts of films by Godard (and his collaborators) do not do justice to the way he uses sound, both verbal and nonverbal, in a lyrical and/or analytical way. As with the visual elements , Godard uses sound as a plastic element which he manipulates in the editing stages of the film. In the dialogue itself, he mixes widely varying verbal modes, and he especially likes to overlay love scenes with various kinds of discourse such as jokes, slang, lessons, and comments on or citations from literature. Just as Godard mixes many different kinds of visual texts in his films, so too he thrusts at us many modes of verbal communication, often distanciated or only partly intelligible. Thus we hear interviews, lessons, recitations, monologues, declamations, characters' reading aloud from books or periodicals, citations read by a voice off, monologues, intellectual discussions on a given theme, Godard's, Gorin's, or Miéville's own voices, television announcing, shortwave radio messages, tape recordings, computer language, and popular songs blasting from jukeboxes or playing from a stereo headset.

In terms of content, the sound track is used, in part, to develop the narrative line. But it has other functions as well. It especially bears the weight of one of Godard's major concerns: to explore how language functions in contemporary society. He investigates this problem early in his films, but in the course of his career he states it in increasingly Brechtian, political terms. Susan Sontag (Entry No. 1214) proposed that Godard's work (through *Weekend*) was really about language. The increased importance of the sound track in his later films would seem to reinforce such an interpretation, for although Godard uses a variety of images to present different *kinds* of political situations and concepts in those films and also to show different *ways of presenting* political concepts, nevertheless the predominant stylistic feature of the films from *Le Gai Savoir* on is that the sound track shapes the film. It contains all the directly stated political messages and is denser and more complicated than the image track. Often the image is a mere emblematic illustration of a point made on the sound track. In the films of this later period, disparate visual material often seems to be rudely juxtaposed, or a static image is held which "tells" us little in and of itself. The sound track makes explicit comments on how these elements and images fit into the film as a whole and what relation they have to the world in which we and Godard live. Such combinations of sound and image usually result in new concepts — principally about language, education, sexual politics, ideology, Communist party revisionism, and film itself.

In most of these films, Godard and Gorin or Miéville go to great lengths to avoid having a third person narrator or an actor with whom we can identify just deliver the directors' notion of the truth, the correct line. Concepts are presented to be worked with. In this period, Godard spoke of creating a cinema that would function like a blackboard. The written words and spoken ones that are so often repeated, such as *lutte, savoir,* and *revolution,* are signal words which represent concepts to which we are expected to give our approval, but the context of which we must work out for ourselves. In these explicitly political films, in fact, the audience is never spoon-fed a revolutionary program. If Godard and his collaborators overlay "false images" with "correct sounds," as the tactic is explained in *Pravda*, that means that they are trying to get people to correct and adjust their interpretation of the image, particularly the film and television image, in the light of social process. The bluntness of political statement means that viewers must think about the film in an explicitly political way or they won't "receive" the film at all. They are not allowed to absorb the film as an emotional experience. They must actively bring their minds to consider the words and ideas presented, particularly because the image track is so flat. On the other hand, the sound tracks' political lessons are often simplistic or exaggerated. We may hear prescriptions, blunt statements of right and wrong, ritualistic repetitions, or jokes. These films deliberately use such effects in the verbal presentation of the political message so that there is no omniscient godlike voice in the film.

Verbal wit characterizes all Godard's films. *A bout de souffle* played with Jean Seberg's American accent and her bad French; her incomprehension of *dégeulasse* provided the punch line of the film. Godard said of that film that the reason he had used jump cuts was to eliminate any boring bits of conversation. In *Bande à part* he announced a plot summary for "latecomers" and gave some indications about the action and related subjects that added little to our understanding. Odile in that film, always looking for true love, sang, "Hugging a Dream that Can't Come True." In *Deux ou trois choses,* made in 1966, the husband, Robert, sat in his apartment at his ham radio, earphones on, and listened to a Jules Feiffer futuristic newscast about Lyndon Johnson's bombing Hanoi in 1966, Haiphong in 1968, Peking in 1969, and finally Moscow, the joke having the horror of propelling present reality unchanged or worsened into the future. In *La Chinoise* a group of adolescents held classes in an apartment over vacation. They gave lectures, discussed political theory, presented skits, and from behind a stack of *Quotations from Chairman Mao* they chanted their political slogans in unison. Much of this the audience saw as frivolous or witty, no matter how seriously the characters themselves took it. *Le Gai Savoir* introduced a type of wit that could continue to the present in Godard's films; the conversations here are full of disjunctures, puns, foolishness, free associations, metaphoric language, and political jokes.

In a 1972 interview, Jean-Pierre Gorin told me why he and Godard regularly used the words of others as texts for their films: "Why write it if it's already been written?" As the text of his films, either in the words given to the characters or in a voice-off commentary, Godard has always used frequent reference to and quotations from literature and magazines — starting with the discussion of Faulkner in *A bout de souffle*. In general, the citations from literature highlight the theatricality of the actions in the films. They usually have a direct purpose in establishing character or reinforcing the film's theme, but they also bring with them the resonance of a larger cultural frame of reference. In watching a Godard film, the spectators are not expected to catch all the words or know where citations come from. Viewers are to be teased by the quotations, to let literary references wash over them in a wave of words.

It is, however, tempting to go reference hunting through Godard's films to try to identify all the literary texts used, and all the references to and statements by political figures. Godard's films seem "literary" and idea-filled, yet he manages to offer his borrowings from others in a fresh, frequently self-reflective way. He uses verbal texts to interfere with a story line and also to comment on it both ideologically and emotionally.

In the pre-1968 films, Godard himself often intervenes on the sound track. This not only introduces a subjective element directly into the film, but more often enhances the work's Brechtian-style theatricity. Also in the pre-1968 films, Godard seems to state some of his own pet ideas by means of the characters' monologues, although we have to evaluate the ideas expressed in each case in terms of the characters' roles. Among the ideas delivered by characters that seem to echo ideas of Godard himself on freedom, language, politics, and art are the following: Bruno's statement on cinema and liberty in *Le Petit Soldat*, Nana and Brice Parain's conversations about language and responsibility in *Vivre sa vie*, Roger Leenhardt's monologue on memory (as well as the other monologues) in *La Femme mariée*, Richard Po's tape in *Made in U.S.A.*, Lemmy Caution's citation from Eluard in *Alphaville*, Ferdinand's reflections in *Pierrot le fou*, and Guillaume's ideas on political theater in *La Chinoise*.

It is not always just to convey a positive idea that Godard uses extensive verbal commentaires. I have already mentioned the effect of having the final long political monologue in *Numéro deux* be delivered by a woman's voice while we see the isolated figure of Godard the creator in his studio. Godard often seeks an emotional impact as well as a distancing effect when he uses the long monologue, interview, or voice off. In *La Femme mariée*, the fact that each of the characters at the dinner party in Charlotte and Pierre's apartment delivers a monologue reveals that they are emotionally widely distant with only certain points of congruity in their ideas, points of which we but not they are aware. In contrast, Brice Parain's exposition of a philosophy of language to Nana in *Vivre sa vie* conveys a sense of intimacy between him and Nana. Ferdinand's lines and the voice off in *Pierrot le fou*, crammed as they are with citations from literature, express nostalgia and a desire to escape. Even in a film with the coldness of suburban Paris architecture and that city's "noise pollution," *Deux ou trois choses*, Godard's voice-off commentary — delivered in a raspy whisper and confessing Godard's own anxieties about aptness of expression in art, as well as expressing his political convictions — conveys a vague desire for intimacy on the narrator's part.

Godard's use of music and noise serves the same function. At times it conveys a direct emotional impact — from lyricality to harshness. Other times it comments on the action, such as in the jukebox song of love in the swimming pool sequence of *La Femme mariée*, which comments not only on Charlotte's sex life but on that of a young couple and also that of two adolescent girls talking about sex and love. In *Vivre sa vie* Godard underscores our sympathy for Nana by introducing crescendos of music which represent her emotions. In that film, as in others, he also emphasizes that music is a material element of cinema and not some spiritual force, as he frequently breaks off the music abruptly, in the editing, to silence. He uses the same tactic of a "romantic" music track to comment on yearnings for escape, especially from the traps that both the nuclear family and alienated labor enmesh us in, *Numéro deux*. The same kind of orchestral music that is found in *Vivre sa vie* is used ironically in *Weekend*, where it rises in crescendo during an erotic monologue at the beginning of the film, making the audience strain to hear the words and thus leading them to realize just how emotionally engaged in the sexual tale they are, a comment on how audiences will identify with and become involved in the most outrageous of plots if that plot is about sex. And in a more positive way, on the sound track of *Le Gai Savoir*, there is a Cuban revolutionary song whic is supposed to elicit a positive response from the audience. It designates a political stance which is implied as a goal, but not programatically stated, by the entire film.

Noise from city streets, noise of guns, noise of water from the tap — all these have a thematic use in Godard's films, but like the music, they are often presented as overly loud and then broken off into abrupt silence, so that we are aware of the artifice of noise recorded for cinema. This editing tactic, characteristic of Godard's films, provides the audio equivalent of the jump cut. In 1968, after its use in *Weekend*, rock music also became an important element in a few of Godard's films, as he flirted with the counterculture in *Le Gai Savior*, *One Plus One*, and *One American Movie*, but he then seems to have rejected audio elements like rock music in favor of more overly political comment. His use of the Léo Ferré ballad in *Numéro deux* signals a return to an older style.

As sound came to dominate over the image in the films from *Le Gai Savior* on, Godard defended his break from his previously spectacular visual style. In the documentary *Godard in America*, filmed while he and Gorin toured U.S. college campuses in 1970, Godard explained, "There are too many images, so each one cancels the other. Hollywood makes a lot of images . . . but always uses the same sounds everywhere. We have to work on complexity from the sound point of view for a few years and on simplicity from the image of view, and then we will know where we are coming from."

FILM AND POLITICS

If the aim of all modernist works is to produce a new consciousness in the spectator (usually the modernist artist acts out of some awareness of the narrowness of bourgeois modes of thought), Godard's modernism aims to displace the spectator ideologically, to move her/him away from illusion into a closer relation to social reality. Specifically this means that Godard, alone and with his collaborators, has tried to convey an understanding of the social role of film and television form and a specific understanding of dialectics, class, sexual politics, the media, false consciousness and the need to act to control one's own life. Godard's films are modernist art works that provide more than the pleasures of irony or a puzzle; they seek to force audiences to create political solutions for themselves.

Like Brecht, Godard uses art to reveal and enhance social contradictions and specifically to unmask the mechanisms of bourgeois ideology at work in the dominant narrative arts. Godard's films question both reality and the forms by which we represent that reality. His post-1968 work stands as an affirmation that people can effect a more adequate relation between themselves and the world — we could, these films say, view the media differently, initiate political struggles that go beyond economic demands, and listen not only to the "voices" of white, bourgeois men, but to those previously unheard — in particular, children, workers, women, and peoples of the Third World.

For Godard, to be critical is a political act. His films lead spectators to take up a different, displaced ideological position, from which they can understand the narrowness of their previous stance — an understanding Godard feels especially leftists will need if they are to change people's currently "empty," alienated, and oppressive lives. One of the major theoretical considerations in current left thought is the role that the mass media play in the "bourgeoisification" of working class consciousness, in maintaining U.S. imperialism, in managing class conflict, and in masking social and sexual-political contradictions. Godard has never committed himself as filmmaker to a specific political party. Yet he has increasingly defined his filmmaking role first as anti-capitalist, and then as leftist and antipatriarchal. Although his cinematography is magnificently inventive, he has not just provided us with a protean variety of new forms of cinematic representation. A political filmmaker often desperately making films before the revolution is in sight, in an utopian way Godard continues to make films for the revolution to come.

III
The Films:
Credits, Notes and Synopsis

1 OPÉRATION BÉTON

Producer:	Jean-Luc Godard
Production Company:	Actua-film (Geneva)
Director:	Jean-Luc Godard
Screenplay:	Jean-Luc Godard
Director of Photography:	Adrien Porchet
Process:	35mm, black and white
Music:	Handel, Bach
Cast:	Jean-Luc Godard (Commentary).
Filmed:	On location at the Grande-Dixence Dam, Switzerland, 1954
Running Time:	20 minutes
Released:	Paris, July 2, 1958, along with *Tea and Sympathy*
Distribution:	France - Gaumont

Notes

Godard financed the film out of his own salary as a construction worker on the Grande-Dixence Dam.

Synopsis

In straightforward documentary fashion, this film shows the workers constructing the Grande-Dixence Dam in Switzerland. No commentators give any more details about the film.

2 UNE FEMME COQUETTE

Producer:	Jean-Luc Godard
Director:	Jean-Luc Godard
Screenplay:	Hans Lucas (pseud. Godard)
Based on:	Guy de Maupassant's novella *Le Signe (The Swan)*
Director of Photography:	Hans Lucas (pseud. Godard)
Process:	16mm, black and white

Editing:	Hans Lucas (pseud. Godard)
Music:	Bach
Cast:	Maria Lysandre (the woman), Roland Tolma (the man), Jean-Luc Godard (the client)
Filmed:	On location in Geneva, 1955
Running Time:	10 minutes

Notes

It is what happens after this story ends that is the subject of the "Swedish-porn" film-within-a-film in *Masculin-Féminin*.

Synopsis

"The plot is about a respectable young married woman who, fascinated by the come-on look with which a prostitute attracts her customers, is tempted to try it out. Just to see if it works. And it does. Pursued by a stranger to the very door of her apartment, she finally gives in to him because she is expecting her husband at any moment, and this seems the quickest way of getting the man out of the house. It is curious that although the short follows the story [*Le Signe* by de Maupassant] closely, it stops at the moment the importunate stranger forces his way into the apartment. . . .

"Stylistically, many of Godard's devices are already in evidence: 'Rapid' cutting, unmatched shots, and hand-held camera; pleonastic use of dialogue (we see the words of a letter, while the actress simultaneously reads them aloud); flash-shots; the big American car; false timing (as the narrator says she saw a man leave the prostitute's flat, we actually see him *entering* it); alternation of sunny takes with grey ones in what are supposed to be two immediately consecutive shots. For the first time, we see one of his actresses shaking her head, fluffing up her hair, swirling it around. Finally, Godard himself makes an appearance in the film as one of the prostitute's customers." Reprinted from Richard Roud, *Jean-Luc Godard*, Second Edition, Collection Cinema One (London: Secker and Warburg; Bloomington: Indiana University Press, 1970), pp. 154–55. Reprinted by permission of the author. Copyright 1970. *See* Entry No. 1505.

3 TOUS LES GARÇONS S'APPELLENT PATRICK

Alternate Title:	*Charlotte et Véronique*
Producer:	Pierre Braunberger
Production Company:	Films de la Pléïade
Director:	Jean-Luc Godard
Screenplay:	Éric Rohmer
Director of Photography:	Michel Latouche
Process:	16mm, black and white
Sound:	Jacques Maumont

Editing:	Cécile Decugis
Music:	Beethoven, Pierre Monsigny
Cast:	Jean-Claude Brialy (Patrick), Anne Colette (Charlotte), Nicole Berger (Véronique)
Filmed:	On location in Paris, 1957
English-Language	
Release Title:	*All the Boys Are Called Patrick*
Running Time:	21 minutes
Distribution:	
France:	Gaumont
England:	Connoisseur
USA	Pyramid Films

Notes

Cost: 10,000 F. Shown in Paris along with *Un Temoin dans le ville.*

Synopsis

Visually this short film uses a grainy, black and white low-contrast photography, shot mostly outdoors on an overcast grey day so that medium tones predominate. The women characters are not physically glamorous but wistful and simple, rather like Odile in *Bande à part*. Patrick, on the other hand, changes his appearance from a hip man wearing sunglasses while flirting with Charlotte to a more studious type wearing a tie while flirting with Véronique.

Charlotte is sitting outside the Luxembourg gardens reading Hegel, when Patrick tries to pick her up. He keeps following her around and she gets rid of him by setting the time and place for a date. He then meets Véronique in a cafe, with whom he also makes a date. Visual jokes in that sequence include a copy of *Cahiers du cinéma* lying on a table, and someone reading the newspaper *Arts*, the headline of which is, "The French Cinema Is Dying under the Weight of False Legends."

The two women are roommates and in their apartment they each talk about the new man they have met, finding it ironic that both are named Patrick. Typical Godard "citations" in this early film include a James Dean poster on the wall, and the two women alternately singing lines of a popular song: "It looks like love./It could be love./It should be love." They also sing, perhaps in homage to Hitchcock's *The Man Who Knew Too Much*, "Que será, será."

The next day the two women are out on the street looking at postcards. They see Patrick flirting with another young woman in the Rue Dufflot and discover that it is the same man they had both made dates with. He kisses his new friend and sends her off in a taxi. Charlotte and Véronique shrug their shoulders as if to say, "That's love," and go off together. Patrick, too, realizes that they saw him and does not care.

4 UNE HISTOIRE D'EAU

Producer:	Pierre Braunberger
Production Company:	Films de la Pléiade
Director:	Jean-Luc Godard and François Truffaut
Screenplay:	François Truffaut, Jean-Luc Godard (Narration)
Director of Photography:	Michel Latouche
Sound:	Jacques Maumont
Editing:	Jean-Luc Godard
Cast:	Jean-Claude Brialy (The man), Caroline Dim (The woman), Jean-Luc Godard (Narrator, the man's voice)
Filmed:	On location in a flooded region near Paris in late 1957 or early 1958 by Truffaut, who then abandoned the footage
Running Time:	20 minutes; 12 minutes in England
Released:	Paris, March 1961, along with *Lola*
Distribution:	
France:	Unidex
England:	Connoisseur
USA:	FACSEA

Notes

Godard called this an hommage to Mack Sennet. For an account by Truffaut of the film's genesis, *see* Roud, Entry No. 1505, pp. 156–57.

Synopsis

Visually, the film depends on a strong interest in the documentary presentation of the flooded Paris countryside and the actual farmers stranded in it. The visuals contrast with the voice off commentary, which is literary, whimsical, and full of digressions and nonsequiturs, and runs throughout the film giving the female protagonist's stream-of-consciousness impressions. There is very little dialogue, and often the woman's voice off speaks in the past tense, as if the incident had already happened.

The woman comes downstairs outside her house and discovers the flood. She sings a snatch of a folk song. Shots of the area are shown as the voice off talks poetically about the situation. The woman crosses a few planks, gets a boat, and lands on dry land in a car with whose driver she intends to hitchhike to Paris. As they drive, the voice off cites literary references constantly while visually the flooded landscape is seen through the window.

The car gets stuck. The woman's voice off tells of a lecture in which Aragon wanted to talk about "the art of the digression," and says how dull the man next to her is because he can talk only about his Ford Taunus (she labels him a "Fordiste"). Helicopter shots of the flooded Paris countryside are shown. When the car gets stuck again, the two cannot push it out, so they abandon it. They continue on foot, the man citing Baudelaire. He pursues her. In voice off she declares, "as usual I can't care less for the image; it's the text that's important. But this time I'm wrong, because everything here is lovely." She then goes on to sing about a girl being seduced by the wolf. She concludes, "He kisses me. He caresses me."

In the flooded countryside, a person on a farmhouse roof signals for help. The voice off says the driver told jokes in a wager to make her laugh, the penalty being made to love again, and she recounts several of his meaningless, stale jokes. She then says he seems to have won.

They find a boat to get them back to the Ford, and they start on their way again. Once again, the countryside and the flooded farms are seen from the window. The voice off commentary says that the man rebuked the woman for not being "serious," that she executed a series of word plays, and that he made an inane statement about his car again: "The more the Fordiste accelerated, the quicker my amorous feeling disappeared." On arriving in Paris, however, the voice off indicates that she'd probably stay the night with him because if water inundates France, that makes her happy.

5   CHARLOTTE ET SON JULES

Producer:	Pierre Braunberger
Production Company:	Films de la Pléïade
Director:	Jean-Luc Godard
Screenplay:	Jean-Luc Godard
Director of Photography:	Michel Latouche
Sound:	Jacques Maumont
Editing:	Jean-Luc Godard
Assistant Editor:	Cécile Decugis
Music:	Pierre Monsigny
Cast:	Anne Colette (Charlotte), Jean-Paul Belmondo (Jean, Charlotte's old lover), Gérard Blain (Charlotte's new friend), (Belmondo's voice dubbed by Godard in post-synchronization.)
Filmed:	In Godard's hotel room, Rue de Rennes, Paris, 1958
English-Language Release Title:	*Charlotte and Her Jules*
Running Time:	20 minutes; 14 minutes in England
Released:	Paris, March 1961, along with *Lola*
Distribution:	
France:	Unidex
USA:	

Notes

Godard made this film as an hommage to Jean Cocteau. Cost: 5,550 F. Godard dubbed in his own voice because Belmondo had to go into military service.

Synopsis

As the film opens, a convertible pulls up and a young woman gets out, leaving her date to wait. The woman, played by Anne Colette, enters Jean-Paul Belmondo's apartment. During the film, Belmondo sits on the bed, walks around the room, types, changes his shirt, tries on various ties, gets washed while still gesturing and talking, paces, tries to get the woman's attention, holds her, pushes her on the bed, and finally tries to kiss her. She then tells him she has come back only to pick up her toothbrush and walks out.

This single joke is enhanced by Belmondo's logorrhea. He talks constantly and the woman says almost nothing. He begins by declaring, "I knew you'd return," and proceeds to both harass and court her. For example, "What do you two do when you're together?" he asks and then interrupts her before she can get more than a few words out with his, "But let me finish my sentence." She shouldn't want to get into films, he says. "What is cinema? A huge head grimacing in a tiny room." Knowing someone waits for her below, he asks why she has come back, but does not wait for an answer. He insults her, puts words in her mouth, says they both love each other, and declares that he can't live without her. Finally he concludes, "I know. You, too, cannot live without me. Is that why you've come back?" She answers and leaves.

Anne Colette enters wearing a spotted dress and a summer hat with a ribbon around it. She is eating an ice cream cone. During Belmondo's monologues she plays games with her fingers, gestures behind his back, puts her hat on him, checks herself out in the full-length mirror, looks down at her lover in his car below, shakes her head yes and no in response to one question, dances a bit, airs herself all over with a small electric fan, sits with Belmondo on the bed, and when he tries to kiss her, grabs her toothbrush and runs out.

Except for a few cutaway shots to a high angle close-up of the lover waiting outside in his car, the film contains mostly long shot-sequences filmed with a fluid, moving camera in a very small space (in fact, Godard's own apartment). Many of the shifts in and emphases on various types of compositional possibilities within the mobile long-take foreshadow the visual wit of Godard's later work.

6 A BOUT DE SOUFFLE

Producer:	Georges de Beauregard
Production Companies:	Impéria Films, Société Nouvelle de Cinéma (S.N.C.)
Director:	Jean-Luc Godard
Screenplay:	Jean-Luc Godard
Based on:	An original treatment by François Truffaut

Directory of	
Photography:	Raoul Coutard
Process:	Black and white
Screen Ratio:	1 x 1,33
Camera Operator:	Claude Beausoleil
Sound:	Jacques Maumont
Artistic &	
Technical Advisor:	Claude Chabrol
Assistant Director:	Pierre Rissient
Editing:	Cécile Decugis
Assistant Editor:	Lila Herman
Music:	Martial Solal, Mozart's Clarinet Concerto, K.622
Cast:	Jean Seberg (Patricia Franchini), Jean-Paul Belmondo (Michel Poiccard, alias Laszlo Kovacs), Daniel Boulanger (Police Inspector Vital), Henri-Jacques Huet (Antonio Berrutti), Roger Hanin (Carl Zombach), Van Doude (Journalist Van Doude), Liliane Robin (Liliane), Michel Favre (Plainclothes inspector), Jean-Pierre Melville (Parvulesco), Claude Mansard (Used car dealer, Claudius), Jean Domarchi (Drunk), Jean-Luc Godard (Informer), André-S. Labarthe, Jean-Louis Richard, François Mareiul (Journalists at Orly), Richard Balducci (Tolmatchoff), Philippe de Broca, Michael Mourlet, Jean Douchet, Jacques Sicilier, Guido Orlando, Jacques Serguine, Louiguy, Virginie Ullman, Emile Villion, José Bénazéraf, Madame Paul, Raymond Ravanbaz
Filmed:	On location in Paris and Marseilles, August 17-September 15, 1959
English-Language	
Release Title:	*Breathless*
Cost:	400,000 N.F.
Running Time:	89 minutes
Released:	
Paris:	March 16, 1960 (Helder, Vivienne, Scala and Balzac theaters — 260,058 first-run tickets were sold)
England:	July 1961
USA-New York:	February 7, 1961 (Fine Arts Theater)
Prizes:	Berlin Film Festival, 1960 — Best Direction; Prix Jean Vigo, 1960; German Critics' Prize for Photography to Coutard
Distribution:	
France:	Impéria Films
Italy:	Euro
England:	B.L.C., British Lion
USA:	Contemporary/McGraw-Hill

Notes

A 45 rpm record was made by Columbia of the music from the film.

Truffaut wrote this scenario originally in 1955–56. It was to have been his project after *Les Mistons*. First he tried to do this film with Jean-Claude Brialy, then with Gérard Blain (seen in *Histoire d'eau*). Then he suggested that Eduardo Molinario use it as Molinario's film. Finally he gave it, in fifteen typed pages, to Godard three years later. 1963, Clay, Entry No. 264.

The censors cut one long shot from the film which shows Patricia and Michel on the Champs Elysées and Eisenhower's meeting with De Gaulle taking place in the background.

Synopsis

With the help of a young woman whom he does not take with him, Michel Poiccard steals a large Oldsmobile in Marseilles. While driving recklessly toward Paris, he finds a gun in the glove compartment. Two policemen pursue him for speeding. Michel drives off the highway, raises the hood, and preemptorily shoots the policeman who returns to find him. Michel flees on foot across a field, a tiny figure seen in long shot.

The next morning in Paris, Michel looks for money. First he seeks Patricia Franchini, who is not in; he steals her hotel key and uses her bathroom. He then visits another woman in another hotel. She is going to work and has no time for him; he steals money from her purse.

On the Champs Elysées he meets the American woman, Patricia, who is dressed in a New York *Herald Tribune* tee-shirt and is selling newspapers. He asks her to come to Rome with him, but she is not eager to go. They decide to meet that evening. We see the first of a number of close-ups of newspaper articles that appear as a leitmotif in the film and relate the police's progress in solving the murder of the highway patrolman.

On the Avenue Georges V in the Inter-Americana Travel Agency, Michel seeks an associate, Mr. Tolmatchoff, to be paid for some deal, but the check needs the signature of a Mr. Berrutti, whom Michel seeks throughout the film. Two policemen come in and look for Michel just as he is leaving. Michel imitates a Bogart-style gesture in front of a poster advertising Bogart in a Robert Aldrich film. Michel robs a man in a restaurant toilet to pay for dinner with Patricia, steals a car to take her home, and is furious when she will not spend the night with him because she has a date with a journalist, Van Doude. The latter asks her to interview a novellist, Parvulesco, at Orly, which she does the next day. Michel spies on her with Van Doude, buys a *France-Soir*, and is lying in Patricia's bed when she comes back to her room the next day. The couple banter and spend time there together. Michel steals another car to take Patricia to Orly for her interview, which is filmed in a style parodying interviews with celebrity artists. When Michel tries to sell the stolen car to a used car dealer, the man takes the car, brandishes a *France-Soir* in front of Michel's face, and refuses to pay. Michel beats him up, robs him, takes a taxi back to pick up Patricia, and then goes to Berrutti's, but the man is not in.

At the *Herald Tribune* office, the police ask Patricia about Michel. Evasively, she takes the inspector's phone number and escapes from being followed via a window in a movie theater bathroom. She meets Michel in another cinema showing a western. That night they steal two more cars. The newspaper headlines announce "Net closes around Michel Poiccard." Finally, at St. Germain-de-Près, they meet up with Berrutti, who promises to cover the check the next day and who provides them with an apartment to stay in. In the morning Patricia leaves the apartment and phones the police to turn Michel in, but goes back and tells Michel about it. He refuses to flee, meets Berruti in the street, gets the money, and is gunned down by the arriving police. Michel curses Patricia with his dying words, but she does not understand his French.

Many shots seem to be included to develop a unique view of Paris, rather than the story line (e.g., the street lights going on at dusk, all the kiosks where Michel buys papers). The conversations between Michel and Patricia contain many nonsequiturs; the characters' motivations, particularly Patricia's, are not explained. Plot ellipses and sometimes confusion arise from the extensive use of jump cuts and the introduction of secondary characters — such as Tolmatchoff, Berrutti, and Van Doude — whose background is not explained at all.

7 LE PETIT SOLDAT

Producer:	Georges de Beauregard
Production Company:	S.N.C., Impéria Films
Director:	Jean-Luc Godard
Screenplay:	Jean-Luc Godard
Director of Photography:	Raoul Coutard
Process:	Black and white
Camera Operator:	Michel Latouche
Sound:	Jacques Maumont
Assistant Director:	Francis Cognany
Script Continuity:	Suzanne Schiffman
Editing:	Agnès Guillemot
Assistant Editors:	Nadine Marquand, Lila Herman
Music:	Maurice Leroux
Cast:	Michel Subor (Bruno Forestier), Anna Karina (Véronica Dreyer), Henri-Jacques Huet (Jacques), Paul Beauvais (Paul), Laszlo Szabo (Laszlo), Georges de Beauregard (Activist leader), Jean-Luc Godard (Bystander at railroad station), Gilbert Edard
Filmed:	On location in Geneva, April-May 1960
English-Language Release Title:	*The Little Soldier*

Running Time:	88 minutes
Released:	
Paris:	January 25, 1963 (at Marbeuf, Eldorado, Lynx, Les Vedettes, Cinévog, Saint-Lazare, Danton Theaters — 74,126 tickets sold in first-run Paris theaters.
England:	June 1963
Montreal:	1963 Film Festival, along with *Les Carabiniers*
USA-New York:	New York Film Festival, September 1965
Censorship:	Banned by French Board of Censors and Minister of Information for over two years from fall 1960 to January 25, 1963, when it was passed with minor cuts; some shots were cut showing French agents torturing Véronica, and her lines to Bruno: "You'll lose this war because you have no ideal." (1963, Martin, Entry No. 299)
Distribution:	
France:	Impéria Films
Italy:	Panta
England:	Academy Cinema
USA:	Not currently in distribution

Synopsis

The protagonist, Bruno Forestier, often narrates his thoughts and events in voice off. Visually, we see him as a tacky tough guy, a cinema noir hero, enmeshed in a world of violence. He officially works as a reporter with the French News Agency in Geneva but is actually a deserter from the French army now working with French terrorists against Algerians.

Driving around Geneva in an open U.S. convertible, Bruno leaves off a roll of film at work and meets his friend Hugh, who tells him about a beautiful woman who wants to be photographed. They meet her at the Bergues Bridge, where an itinerant photographer takes their picture and shoves the ticket, No. 1,418, at Bruno. Bruno makes a pretext to leave, and in a complex series of maneuvers, he takes a train at 14 hr. 18 min., gets a signal to get off from a woman reading a story to a child, and is met by a taxi that takes him to a small farm by a river. He gets in one of a number of parked cars with French license plates.

In the car two men, Jacques and Paul, ask what has become of Bruno and the money they gave him. They listen to the radio and tell Bruno to kill the newscaster — antiwar Swiss radio journalist, Arthur Palivoda. For some vague personal reason Bruno refuses, even under the threat of expatriation or death. When they get to Geneva, he escapes but is not pursued.

Bruno meets Véronica for a date in her rather empty apartment. He constantly photographs her. They talk at length about their attitudes and backgrounds. At night, Bruno and Véronica go to his hotel. Two men steal Bruno's car and use it in a hit-and-run accident to frame Bruno to assassinate Palivoda.

Bruno is being driven in a car by the French agents, who pull up alongside Palivoda. Bruno cannot fire, and then is distracted by seeing Véronica on her bike who waves while Palivoda drives off. Bruno is now suspected of being a double agent. He gets away this time, but as he tries to leave Geneva he is caught by Algerian agents who torture him in a small apartment by means of drowning and electric shock. He jumps out of the apartment window, not knowing how high it is. It is ground level and he gets away.

He returns to Véronica's, where she confesses that she is a left-wing agent who has been ordered to follow him but declares that now she wants to flee the country with him. Bruno decides to kill the Swiss journalist to get passports for them to leave the country; but after he leaves the apartment for a meeting with Jacques, set up over the phone, French agents seize Véronica. Bruno is told that Véronica is a hostage. He shoots Palivoda on the busy streets of Geneva and then finds out Véronica had been hideously tortured and killed. His last lines, spoken as he goes from the news agency into the streets, reaffirm the individualistic, apolitical stance he has taken throughout the film: "There was only one thing left I could do: learn not to be bitter. But I was content, because I had a whole lot of time waiting ahead of me."

8   UNE FEMME EST UNE FEMME

Producers:	Georges de Beauregard, Carlo Ponti
Production Company:	Rome-Paris Films
Director:	Jean-Luc Godard
Screenplay:	Jean-Luc Godard
Based on:	An idea by Geneviève Cluny
Director of Photography:	Raoul Coutard
Process:	Techniscope or Franscope; Eastmancolor
Sound:	Guy Villette
Assistant Director:	Francis Cognany
Script Continuity:	Suzanne Schiffman
Production Manager:	Phillippe Dussart
Set and Art Direction:	Bernard Evian
Editing:	Agnès Guillemot
Assistant Editor:	Lila Herman
Music:	Michel Legrand
Song:	"Chanson de Angéla," by Legrand and Godard
Cast:	Anna Karina (Angéla), Jean-Claude Brialy (Émile Récamier), Jean-Paul Belmondo (Alfred Lubitsch), Marie Dubois (Suzanne), Marion Sarraut (Second prostitute), Nicole Paquin (First prostitute), Jeanne Moreau (Woman in bar), Catherine Demongeot
Filmed:	In the Studio Saint-Maurice and on location in Paris, November 1960-January 1961

English-Language	
Release Title:	*A Woman Is A Woman*
Running Time:	84 minutes
Released:	
Berlin:	Berlin Film Festival, July 1, 1961
Paris:	September 6, 1961 (La Rotonde, Avenue, Studio Publicis, Vendôme Theaters — 56,323 tickets sold in first-run Paris theaters)
England:	London Film Festival, October 1961; general release, March 1967
USA-New York:	New York Film Festival, September 1964; general release, November 3, 1964 (Murray Hill Theater)
Prizes:	Berlin Film Festival: Jury's Special Prize; Best Actress Award to Karina
Distribution:	
France:	Unidex
Italy:	Euro
England:	Amanda
USA:	Contemporary/McGraw-Hill

Notes

Godard took the idea for this film from the actress, Geneviève Cluny. He wrote the original scenario in 1958; then Philippe de Broca used the same idea for *The Love Game;* in 1960 Godard decided to use it, too. (1964, Anon., "Glorious Nut," Entry No. 339)

Synopsis

Angéla sees her lover Émile Récamier at a cafe and again at a bookstore where they look at books for children and for expectant mothers. Angéla works at a tacky cafe striptease joint on Rue Fbg. St. Denis. Backstage is a magic wall, behind which the women walk and reemerge either in their show costumes or their street clothes. The decor is red, the customers few and bored, and the music tape-recorded. When not at work, Angéla is usually seen wearing a plaid skirt, a baggy sweater, and red knee socks; she often looks pathetic and naive.

Alfred Lubitsch, a friend of Angéla's and Émile's, works putting parking tickets on cars. A bill collector tries to collect a 52,000 F. hotel bill from him; the two men exchange insults in the street in a sequence humorously filmed like a western shootout. Alfred meets Angéla on the street and flirts with her.

Angéla lives with Émile and wants to have his baby. In their apartment we see her dialing a complex formula on a plastic "fertility" gadget given to her by one of her coworkers: she could conceive today. That night she burns the roast. Émile refuses to have a baby because he does not want to marry yet. They quarrel. He rides his bike around the room. She proclaims she will ask the first man she·sees to be the father. Two detectives come into the apartment, looking for terrorists' bombs. Intertitles tell Angéla's and Émile's assumptions. Alfred comes and is asked to father her child. They disappear into the bathroom and giggle, which infuriates Émile. Later that night Angéla and Émile fight in their bedroom, communicating only by book titles.

The next morning Émile phones home and the quarrel continues. Angéla fries an egg, which she flips up into the air. The neighbor woman knocks and tells Angéla there is another call for her, and the neighbor sticks the phone out into the hallway between the two apartments. When Angéla goes back inside, she catches the suspended egg in the frypan. The call was from Alfred, whom she agreed to meet in a cafe.

We see the empty faces of the men at the striptease joint and a cinema verité view of the Parisian streets as Angéla and Suzanne discuss in voice off Suzanne's Communist Party affiliation, their stripping as a job, and Alfred — Suzanne's former lover. Angéla meets Alfred at a cafe. He tries to convince her of his love, tells her the story of a woman who loses two lovers (the plot of Godard's *Montparnasse-Levallois*), and shows her a snapshot of Émile with another woman. The camera studies their reactions as a jukebox plays a bitter, antiromantic song by Charles Aznavour.

Angéla and Émile make up but continue to fight about having a baby. Émile looks unsuccessfully for Angéla at the striptease joint and then goes to a prostitute. Angéla goes to Alfred's. Émile phones Alfred, who is given the message by a neighbor, an old man, who lives in the adjoining, tiny rooftop flat. The phone call impels Angéla to return home; there she tries to avoid Émile but seems pursued by him and the camera into a corner. She tells him she has slept with Alfred in order to have a baby. Once again they get books to argue with in their bedroom. They make up and Émile decides to make the baby potentially his own.

9 "LA PARESSE" in LES SEPT PÉCHÉS CAPITAUX

Producer:	Joseph Bercholz
Production Companies:	Films Gibé, Franco-London Films (Paris); Titanus (Rome)
Director:	Jean-Luc Godard. (Other sketches by Sylvain Dhomme, Philippe de Broca, Jacques Demy, Edouard Molinario, Roger Vadim, and Claude Chabrol)
Screenplay:	Jean-Luc Godard
Director of Photography:	Henri Decaë
Process:	Dyaliscope
Camera Operator:	Jean-Paul Schwartz
Sound:	Jean-Claude Marchetti, Jean Labussière
Assistant Director:	Marin Karmitz
Production Manager:	Jean Lavie
Editor:	Jacques Gaillard

Music:	Michel Legrand
Cast:	Eddie Constantine (Himself), Nicole Mirel (Herself, the starlet)
Filmed:	On location in Paris, September 1961
English-Language Release Title:	"Laziness" or "Sloth" in *The Seven Capital Sins*
Running Time:	113 minutes (whole film)
Released:	
Paris:	March 7, 1962
England:	London, June 1966 (National Film Theater)
USA-New York:	November 1962 or January 16, 1963 (Sutton Theater)
Distribution:	
France:	Consortium Pathé
Italy:	Titanus
USA:	Embassy Pictures (Joseph E. Levine)

Notes

Godard: "I wanted to use a famous actor who was well-known as a personality. I could do it with Constantine because he's a solid block, a block of intelligence and precision, but a block just the same." Roud said Godard had wanted to use the heaviest camera available, a Mitchell, but had to use a Debrie. (1972, Roud, Entry No. 1505, pp. 158-159)

Synopsis

At the film studios at Saint Cloud, starlet Nicole Mirel is seen lounging beside the Seine, reading. There is a large car parked across from her. She sees director Eddie Constantine get into the car. She asks for a lift to Paris. He obliges. The soundtrack is Hawaiian music. He doesn't talk except to say: "Tout me fatigue." (Everything makes me tired.)

"The sun and death are not to be looked in the face," he says. She wangles a part in his next film. They stop for gas. (The filling station is shot from many different angles.) She gets him a sandwich — something easy to chew — paté. He opens the door to look at his untied shoelace. He offers the station attendant an extra 10,000 francs, but the attendant refuses to tie it. He has to tie it himself.

As they are driving again, she asks, "What are you thinking about?" Yes, he says. As they go under the underpass, Hawaiian music playing in the car radio is cut abruptly to silence, but resumes again when they are in Mirel's Paris apartment. There is also an abrupt visual cut as the car comes out of the underpass to an ascending elevator, from which the protagonists presumably have just come. They are walking along an interior landing.

Eddie and Nicole are *chez elle*. He reads a book but doesn't cut the pages. She runs up and downstairs, very busy. He condescends to unzip her dress. She walks around in her underwear. Eddie takes a tour of the house. She tells the servants not to leave the kitchen for the next twenty minutes. Nude, she walks into the bedroom and calls to him. He replies that it bothers him to get dressed afterwards. She explains, "That's the end!"

The narrator states in voice off, "Who said laziness was the mother of all other vices? On the contrary, as we have just seen it prevents them!"

(Summary drawn from synopsis by James Monaco, dated March 1972, and description in 1970, Roud, Entry No. 1505.)

10 VIVRE SA VIE

Producer:	Pierre Braunberger
Production Company:	Films de la Pléïade
Director:	Jean-Luc Godard
Screenplay:	Jean-Luc Godard
Based on:	The book, *Où en est la prostitution?* by Judge Marcel Sacotte (Paris: Buchet-Castel); Edgar Allen Poe's "The Oval Portrait."
Director of Photography:	Raoul Coutard
Process:	Kodak xx, negative
Screen Ratio:	1 x 1, 33
Camera Operators:	Claude Beausoleil, Charles Bitsch
Sound:	Guy Villette
Grip:	Jean Philippe
Electrician:	Coquet Frères
Traveling:	Pierre Durin
Installations:	Bernard Largemain
Machinery:	Chrestien Frères
Special Effects:	Jean Fouchet
Assistant Directors:	Jean-Paul Savignac, Bernard Toutblanc-Michel
Script Continuity:	Suzanne Schiffman
Production Manager:	Roger Flextoux
Production Assistants:	Jean Fitdam, Ida Fassio, Claude Laporte, Georges Cravenne,M.-L. Parolini
Costumes:	Christiane Fageol
Hairdressing:	Simone Knapp, designs by DeAlexandre
Make-up:	Jackie Reynal
Editing:	Agnés Guillemot
Assistant Editor:	Lila Lakshmanan
Music:	Michel Legrand
Song:	"Ma Môme, elle joue pas les starlettes," by Jean Ferrat (music) and Pierre Frachet (lyrics)
Sound Mix:	Jacques Maumont
Cast:	Anna Karina (Nana Kleinfrankenheim), Sady Rebbot (Raoul), André-S. Labarthe (Paul), Guylaine Schlumberger (Yvette), Gérard Hoffman (Man to whom Nana is sold), Monique Messine (Élisabeth), Paul Pavel (Photographer), Dimitri Dinoff (Dimitri), Peter Klassowitz (Nana's lover-voice dubbed by Godard), Éric Schlumberger (Luigi), Brice Parain (Himself), Henri Atal (Ar-

	thur), Gilles Queant (Client), Odile Geoffrey (Barmaid), Laszlo Szabo (Wounded man), Gisèle Hauchecorne (Concierge), Marcel Charton (Policeman), Jacques Flourency (Film spectator), Jean Ferrat (Man at jukebox watching Nana), Jean-Paul Savignac (Soldier in bar), Mario Botti (The Italian)
Filmed:	On location in Paris, February-March 1962
English-Language Release Title:	*My Life to Live (It's My Life,* England)
Running Time:	85 minutes (3 minutes cut by British censor)
Released:	
Paris:	September 20, 1962 (Avenue, Bonaparte, Festival, and Plaza Theaters — 148,000 tickets in first-run Paris theaters)
England:	London Film Festival, October 1962; general release, December 1962
USA-New York:	September 1963
Prizes:	Venice Film Festival, August 28, 1962 — Jury's Special Prize, Italian Critics Prize; London Film Festival Awards; German Critics' Prize, Best Foreign Film 1962-63
Distribution:	
France:	Panthéon, Films de la Pléïade
Italy:	Dear U.A.
England:	Miracle
USA:	Contemporary/McGraw-Hill

Notes

Cost, approximately $40,000.

Synopsis

Vivre sa vie summarizes its sequences by Brechtian-style intertitles. More than in *A bout de souffle* or *Une femme est une femme,* Godard provides a rich and detailed characterization of the protagonist, Nana, by showing her economic status, environment, sense of self-determination, and inner character. He reveals character through milieu, often filmed documentary style, and by theatrical means. Godard develops Brechtian techniques such as pointed summary statements and representative tableaux to explain conceptually certain moments of Nana's life. He both involves us emotionally and makes us reflect on emotion, especially by using a highly romantic musical score, which is played only in phrases and is often cut abruptly to silence.

The film opens in a cafe where Nana and her husband Paul, whom she has left, are filmed entirely from behind their backs as they engage in a long conversation about themselves and their son. They play pinball; Paul tells her a story about a chicken that had no soul.

In the record shop where she works, Nana tries unsuccessfully to borrow 2,000 F. from the woman there. Her concierge keeps her out of her apartment. She meets Paul on the street, gets some photos of her son, refuses to have dinner with Paul, and goes to the cinema, where we see close-ups of the suffering Falconetti in Dreyer's *Jeanne d'Arc*. Nana avoids the advances of the man next to her, whom she had let pay her way. In a cafe, she meets a journalist whom she wants to take her picture so she can get into film. She tries to borrow 2,000 F. and agrees to spend the night with him.

At the police station, Nana answers questions, claiming she had only put her foot on a 1,000 F. bill which some woman had lost. She had no idea what to do now. On the streets, she is propositioned and accepts. She demands 4,000 F. and gets 5,000, but she refuses to let the client kiss her.

On the street, she meets an old friend, Yvette, also gone into prostitution. They go to a cafe. Yvette claims she could not help herself, whereas Nana claims full responsibility for her acts. Yvette's friend Raoul shows her his notebook crudely listing his profits as a pimp. A man bleeding from machine gun wounds enters the cafe and Nana runs out.

In another cafe, Nana is writing to a madame in a brothel soliciting employment; her letter is similar to one written by an aspirant *au pair* girl. Raoul enters and persuades Nana to work for him. In a cinema verité sequence, prostitutes on the street are seen from a traveling car while a voice off, supposedly Raoul's, explains the sociological aspects of prostitution in Paris. Following this is an elliptical series of images which show Nana with various clients, the context of each encounter unexplained.

In a cafe, Raoul meets one of his friends. Nana plays the jukebox and does a carefree dance to attract the attention of a young man playing billiards alone. In a hotel Nana provides a client with another woman and sits alone. In a bar she meets philosopher Brice Parain, with whom she has a long conversation about language's inadequacy.

She is shown in a room with the young man, whom we see reading Poe's "The Oval Portrait," which is about an artist whose art killed his wife; Godard's voice off narrates the story. Nana and the young man embrace; they are seen in shadow while subtitles indicate their words of love.

Raoul thrusts Nana into a car. He has sold her but does not receive the agreed upon sum. In a final sequence, filmed in long shot on a shabby side street in a style reminiscent of Rossellini, we see a shootout between the men. Nana is held by Raoul as a shield and is accidentally killed. She dies with exaggerated spasms and her body is left abandoned on the street.

11 "LE NOUVEAU MONDE" in ROGOPAG

Italian release title:	*Il nuovo mondo*
Producer:	Alfredo Bini
Production Companies:	Société Lyre Cinématographique (Paris), Arco Film (Rome), Cineriz (Rome)

Director:	Jean-Luc Godard (other episodes by Roberto Rossellini, Pier Paolo Pasolini, and Ugo Gregoretti)
Screenplay:	Jean-Luc Godard
Director of Photography:	Jean Rabier
Sound:	Hervé
Production Manager:	Yves Laplache
Editing:	Agnès Guillemot
Assistant Editor:	Lila Lakschmanan
Music:	Beethoven Quartets 7, 9, 10, 14, 15
Cast:	Alexandra Stewart (Alexandra), Jean-Marc Bory (Narrator), Jean-André Fieschi, Michel Delahaye, André-S. Labarthe (His voice), Jean-Luc Godard (A pill-popping pedestrian)
Filmed:	In Paris, November 1962
Running Time:	20 minutes
Released:	
Italy:	March 1963
England:	London Film Festival, October 1963
USA-New York:	New York Film Festival, September 1963
Distribution:	
Italy:	Cineriz
USA:	Macmillan/Audio Brandon

Notes

"*Rogopag* was banned [in Italy] shortly after its release and later released, with cuts in the Pasolini film, under the title of *Laviamoci il cervello (Let's Wash Our Brains)*." (1972, Brown, Entry No. 1656). It was also censored and not shown in France.

Synopsis

Like *Alphaville, Le Nouveau Monde* presents a science fiction story of a grim future ironically set in contemporary Paris. The narrator, a middle class man, tells in voice off the changes that occur in Parisians' psyche and behavior after a high altitude atomic explosion. The film opens with shots of Paris city streets: these shots are patterned formally in the editing and some shots were taken at night, some overexposed. Other visual interest is added by the fact that each time the narrator reads the newspaper, it is a different publication.

In a love-making sequence in the narrator's apartment between him and his lover, Alexandra, she declares, "I ex-love you," and is seen wearing a knife in her underpants. Later, in a sequence in a swimming pool, she is still wearing the knife, and we see her kissing another man.

Pedestrians all over Paris pop pills in their mouths, which leads the narrator to sense that the whole city has somehow changed. In his apartment, in a sequence filmed with a static camera and a planimetric composition, the narrator sits at the table reading a newspaper and the woman enters in and out of frame, offering to bring him a Coca-Cola for breakfast. Nervously his glance darts back and forth to follow her. She keeps taking pills and declares to a woman friend on the phone that she will come but does not know if she will come. She goes out, again telling the narrator, "I ex-love you."

Alone, he looks out the apartment window and ruminates on "the death of logic." He starts to keep a notebook in which we see the words: "last testimony to the world of liberty."

The plot is of such slight interest and the narrator, like the one in "Antici-pation," is so deliberately wooden, we can hardly care about either. The delight of the film lies in its two visual tricks and in its visual patterning. The two "tricks" are the use of the knife as a threatening prop which never figures in the action, and the characters' constant pill-popping, which reveals a public psychosis. Visually, the film is innovative in the following ways: use of overexposure; editing of shots in which the line of filmed action or the visual perspective is constantly coming at us from a different direc-tion; use of headlines and the printed word — often accompanied by "canned" sounds of bombardment; a fixed camera, often held at 90° in a planimetric composition; visual elements in odd places in the frame (in one love sequence a radiator is always visible); artificial movement of the charac-ters in and out of frame or to the right or left of frame. The sequences inside the man's apartment often look like the quarrel sequence in *Le Mépris*.

12 LES CARABINIERS

Producers:	Georges de Beauregard, Carlo Ponti
Production Companies:	Marceau Films, Cocinor Films, Rome-Paris Films, Laetitia (Rome)
Director:	Jean-Luc Godard
Screenplay:	Jean-Luc Godard, Jean Gruault, and Roberto Rossellini
Based on:	A play by Benjamin Joppolo, *I Carabinieri*, adapted to a version for the French stage by Jacques Audiberti
Director of Photography:	Raoul Coutard
Process:	Black and White, Kodak negative
Screen Ratio:	1 x 1:33
Camera Operator:	Claude Beausoleil
Sound:	Jacques Maumont, Hortion
Assistant Directors:	Charles Bitsch, Jean-Paul Savignac
Production Manager:	Roger Scipion
Art Direction:	Jacques Fabre
Editing:	Agnès Guillemot
Assistant Editor:	Lila Lakshmanan
Music:	Philippe Arthuys

Cast: Marino Mase (Ulysse), Albert Juross (Michel-Ange),
                                Genevieve Galéa (Vénus), Catherine Ribeiro (Cléopâtre),
                                Gérard Poirot (1st Carabinier), Jean Brassat (2nd
                                Carabinier), Alvaro Gheri (3rd Carabinier), Barbet
                                Schroder (Car Salesman), Odile Geoffroy (Young parti-
                                san woman), Roger Coggio and Pascale Audret (Couple
                                in car), Catherine Durant (Woman in film-within-the-
                                film), Jean Grault ("Bébé's" father), Jean-Louis Comolli
                                (Soldier), Wladimir Faters (Revolutionary), Jean Mon-
                                signy (Soldier), Gilbert Servien (Soldier).
Filmed: On locations in and near Paris, in three weeks from De-
                                cember 1962-January 1963
English-Language
  Release Title: *Les Carabiniers*
  England: *The Soldiers*
Running Time: 80 minutes
Released:
  Paris: May 31, 1963 (Lord-Byron, Studio, Saint-Germain Thea-
                                ters)
  England: London Film Festival, October 1963; general release, Oc-
                                tober 1964
  Montreal: 1963 Film Festival (See 1968, Sarris, Entry No. 1196, for
                                mention of Godard's "fame" at that festival)
  Venice: 1966 Film Festival, Cultural Session
  USA-New York: New York Film Festival, September 27, 1967; general
                                release, April 24, 1968 (Bleecker Street Cinema, New
                                Yorker Theater)
Distribution:
  France: Cocinor
  England: Academy, Connoisseur
  USA: FACSEA

Notes

The film was a colossal box-office failure in Paris, playing for three weeks,
and Godard, in an unprecedented way, responded to the critics one by one
in an article in *Cahiers du cinéma* (1963, Godard, Entry No. 2216). French
censors prohibited the film to those under 13 years of age.

Synopsis

Les Carabiniers uses Brechtian tactics in the plot, characterization, and
cinematography to comment on war. The opening shots are taken from a car
shown in jump cuts to be driving out of Paris. Two carabiniers (soldiers) in a
jeep zigzag across a field and arrive at a shack where four characters live —
Michel-Ange, a porcine fellow sitting in a wheelbarrow reading comics;
Vénus, a young woman preparing a bath in the barnyard; her mother
Cléopâtre; and Ulysse, a thin angular man with a cigar who fights with one
of the carabiniers.

Upon hearing that the soldiers have come from the king — his message is a standarized handbill marked ℝ for *roi* — all go inside the cabin where they hear about the "mobilization." Their "friend," the king, will make these bumpkins rich if the men go off to war. The carabiniers rattle off a list of what soldiers are entitled to; it includes nosegays, arches de triomphe, splendid sites, breaking eyeglasses, and not paying in restaurants.

The lumpen protagonists' long career at war is represented by a great variety of cinematic means, including shots of airplanes, documentary sounds and images of war, staged shots of men marching right and then left on a plain behind a jeep, picture postcards home plus the written messages on them, a sequence of Michel-Ange terrorizing a woman and riding her piggyback around her house, the execution of partisans, shots of the Pyramids, Michel-Ange and Ulysse saluting a scarred Statue of Liberty, their bombing out a house, and their entering a deserted city — Paris — on a motorbike and sidecar past lifeless surburban highrise apartment buildings. Throughout, the men act like savages, with no understanding of what they do.

Michel-Ange is shown at the cinema; he avoids an oncoming filmed train in a reenacted Lumière film and during another short film tries to seize a filmed "woman of the world" from her bathtub. Back out in the countryside, the soldiers cook up a pot of eels, capture more partisans, and execute a fair-haired young woman. She recites a poem by Mayakovsky and appeals to them as "brothers," as the sailors did in *Potemkin*. Her words temporarily paralyze her executors; then Michel-Ange keeps shooting at her corpse, shouting, "She's still moving." After further shots of the war and postcard messages home, Ulysse is shown trying to commandeer a Masarati from a Paris showroom. The salesman intimidates him into paying, so he robs two women on the street to get the necessary cash.

Back home, Cléo and a lover frolic and dance to Victrola music on the plain. Vénus announces Michel-Ange's and Ulysse's return; Cléo hurriedly puts away the record player and summarily dismisses her "friend," who has a car parked in the field.

The returning soldiers announce that they are rich. As proof, they lay out packets of trophies, picture postcards, on a table. The packets are arranged in categories: e.g., Antiquity (all tilt heads to look at the Leaning Tower), Middle Ages, the Renaissance, and Modern Times. The men lay out some cards one way, some upside down. In the section called Cars, there are golden coaches, Abyssinian chariots, and wheelbarrows. The women swap cards, saying such things as, "The Parthenon is ruined. I don't want it." In the section on Women, some photos are vulgar, others artistic reproductions ("*That* Cleopatra will have to change her name").

The carabiniers return in their jeep. The family demand the final reward, the "title deeds" from the king. The carabiniers pin medals on them and say the family cannot take possession until the war is over and the king has won.

The protagonists go to the city, where, as a radio program in voice-over indicates, a civil war between a right and a left faction is taking place, complete with chaos, looting, and executions. The original carabiniers probably have changed sides; now they wear as an insignia a black cross on a white field, whereas before they had worn a white cross on a black field. The carabiniers lead Michel-Ange and Ulysse inside a house and execute the two with machine guns.

13 "LE GRAND ESCROC" in LES PLUS BELLES ESCROQUERIES DU MONDE

Producer:	Pierre Roustang
Production Companies:	Ulysse Productions, Lux-C.C.F. (Paris); Primex Films (Marseilles); Vidès Cinematografica (Rome); Toho/Towa (Tokyo); Cesar Film Productie (Amsterdam)
Director:	Jean-Luc Godard (other sketches by Roman Polanski, Ugo Gregoretti, Claude Chabrol, Hiromichi Horakawa)
Screenplay:	Jean-Luc Godard
Director of Photography:	Raoul Coutard
Process:	Dyaliscope or Franscope, color (U.S. print in black and white)
Sound:	Hervé
Assistant Director:	Charles Bitsch
Production Manager:	Philippe Dussart
Editing:	Agnès Guillemot
Assistant Editor:	Lila Lakshmanan
Music:	Michel Legrand
Cast:	Jean Seberg (Patricia Leacock), Charles Denner (The swindler), Laszlo Szabo (Police inspector), Jean-Luc Godard (Narrator, voice off; also shown wearing a fez and filming Seberg while she, as Patricia, is taking pictures)
Filmed:	On location in Marrakesh, January 1963
English-Language Release Title:	*The Beautiful Swindlers*
Running Time:	90 minutes (whole film, without Godard sketch); 25 minutes (Godard sketch only)
Released:	
Paris:	As a short, August 14, 1964 with a revival of King Vidor's *Our Daily Bread* at several art houses
England:	London Film Festival, November 24, 1967, sketch shown.
Note:	Godard's sketch deleted for Paris premiere (August 1964) and not shown as part of English language version.
Distribution: (Film without Godard Sketch)	
France:	Lux
USA:	Originally with Jack Ellis Films, by arrangement with Walter Reade Organization (Continental Distributing)

Notes

Visually and in terms of the plot, this film seems closely derivative from or a hommage to Rossellini's sketch from *Rogopag,* the omnibus film Godard made *Le Nouveau Monde* for, his project immediately preceding this one.

Le Grand Escroc is the French title for Herman Melville's *The Confidence Man,* which Patricia is seen reading in the film.

Sketch was deleted because distributors thought it "too philosophical."

Synopsis

"Le Grand Escroc" is similar in plot to Rossellini's sketch from *Rogopag,* itself made in a style similar to Godard's films. Rossellini there had presented an Italian stewardess on an Asian route who makes home movies while abroad. In "Le Grand Escroc," Godard shows a U.S. television reporter, Patricia Leacock (probably a reference to U.S. cinema verité director, Richard Leacock), constantly filming while in Morocco. As in a *A Bout de souffle* Godard uses Jean Seberg with her heavily accented French to play Patricia, the stereotypically assertive, charming, self-centered, and insensitive American woman tourist — here, a reporter. Godard uses images of Patricia's filming and of what she films, as well as a plot about a philanthropist's giving away counterfeit money, to draw witty parallels between cross-cultural misunderstandings, con games, and the problematic nature of cinematic truth/fiction.

The film opens with Patricia reading Melville's *The Confidence Man* in her hotel room in Marrakesh. Speaking in English, she arranges a date with a lover over the phone. She seems disappointed that he is returning to the United States. During their conversation, we see three extreme close-ups of words from the pages of her book: "Charity does not think evil. /Charity endures all things /Charity believes everything." Patricia then sits on her bed loading her movie camera, planning to film in Medina.

There is a cut to an exterior location with palm trees, Patricia adjusting her lens, and Arab music playing in the background. Patricia looks toward us. Godard, wearing a fez and smoking a cigarette, moves to look through the viewfinder of the camera filming Seberg. Patricia/Seberg looks up away from her camera, surprised, and smiles. Cut to Godard who calls, "Camera." We then see Patricia filming, with the sound of her camera clearly audible. This camera sound and the audio motifs of the Arab music and cries return at various times to underscore the film's two interconnected themes: cinema's truth/fiction and cross-cultural (mis)understanding.

In Medina (first seen in extreme long shot), the *escroc* or the con man points his finger at us. A chauffer-driven car pulls up; the *escroc* gets out and gives away money to the crowd. Patricia, seen in the crowd in long shot, tries to film him. He drives off.

Patricia buys a striped burnoose from a vendor. Two Moroccan policemen seize the money she has paid with, and take her off in the police car. Patricia's interview with the police inspector consists more of flirtation than interrogation. They speak in English. She films him as he asks her to define "reporting." With the sound of her camera constantly heard in the background, she says that she films real things, places, and people: "truth motion pictures, cinema verité." He understands that to mean "documentary films, like Jean Rouch," and says he, too, searches for the truth in other ways but thinks no one ever finds it. Patricia explains she is filming the *Reader's Digest* series, "The Most Extraordinary Man I Ever Met." The detective offers to drive her to meet her date, and when the date does not show up, they arrange to drive together to Casablanca in the morning.

Again Patricia sees the *escroc* giving away money in the bazaar, and again she tries to film him. She takes a cab to follow him when he flees.

On the outskirts of the city, Patricia, dressed in a striped burnoose, is seen filming. A reverse shot reveals the con man carrying an old printing press into a shack. He comes out and talks to Patricia in paradoxical and idealistic language. He explains his scheme to create a worldwide philanthropic organization. She tells him that she will just film him, not tell the police. She only wants to seek out the truth. "To show to other people," he responds. "Well, you're stealing from me, and you, too, give it to others."

As Patricia drives with the inspector in his jeep across mountainous terrain, we find that she has told him about the incident so she can "have a clear conscience." "Are you sure that's all?" he asks disgustedly. As they stop by the side of the road, she says yes, that the *escroc* had turned his back on her and left her perplexed. She films the detective, who is sitting in the jeep, and then turns to film an Arab going down the road on a burrow. It is the *escroc* unrecognized. He recedes into the distance. Off screen we hear Patricia's and Godard's comments on fiction and reality. Godard cites, in French, Shakespeare's, "All the world's a stage . . . " The last shot is an extreme close-up of Patricia filming accompanied by the sound of the running camera.

14   LE MÉPRIS

Producers:	Georges Bearuegard, Carlo Ponti, Joseph E. Levine
Production Companies:	Rome-Paris Films, Films Concordia, Compagnia Cinematografica Champion
Director:	Jean-Luc Godard
Screenplay:	Jean-Luc Godard
Based on:	Alberto Moravia's novel, *Il disprezzo (A Ghost at Noon)*
Director of Photography:	Raoul Coutard
Process:	Technicolor
Screen Ratio:	Franscope

Sound:	William Sivel
Assistant Director:	Charles Bitsch
Production Managers:	Philippe Dusart, Carlo Lastricati
Script:	Suzanne Schiffman
Costumes:	Janine Autre
Editing:	Agnès Guillemot
Assistant Editor:	Lila Lakshmanan
Music:	Georges Delerue (Italian version, Piero Piccioni)
Cast:	Brigitte Bardot (Camille Javal), Michel Piccoli (Paul Javal), Jack Palance (Jeremy Prokosch), Fritz Lang (Himself), Giorgia Moll (Francesca Vanini), Jean-Luc Godard (Assistant director to Lang), Linda Veras (A siren)
Filmed:	On location in Rome and Capri (including in Curzio Malaparte's villa), April-June 1963
English-Language Release Title:	*Contempt*
Italian-Language Release Title:	*Il disprezzo*
Running Time:	100 minutes in France, 103 minutes in USA, 84 minutes in Italy
Released:	
Paris:	December 27, 1963 (withdrawn from 1963 Venice Film Festival by Joseph E. Levine) (212,107 tickets sold in first-run Paris theaters)
England:	London, November 3, 1967 (National Film Theater)
Montreal:	Opened Fifth Montreal Film Festival, 1964
USA-New York:	December 18, 1964 (Lincoln Art Theater)
Distribution:	
France:	Marceau-Cocinor
Italy:	Interfilm
England:	Avco-Embassy
USA:	Macmillan/Audio Brandon

Notes

"Godard had his name removed from the credits of the Italian version. Ponti cut footage from the Odyssey sequence, replaced Delerue's musical score with a jazz score by Piero Piccone, used the same color process throughout (Godard had a harsher color process for Rome, a more limpid one for Capri), and dubbed it all into Italian — making Moll's role senseless." (1972, Roud, Entry No. 1505; 1972, Brown, Entry No. 1656.)

Central French Catholic Film Censor Board advised adults not to see this film.

Synopsis

This 70mm color film is framed by cinematic references internally, with sequences of film production both introducing and concluding the film.

Paul and Camille Javal are in their bedroom. Camille (Bardot) is nude, filmed through colored filters. Camille asks Paul if he loves each part of her body. They affirm their love, Paul concluding, "I love you totally, tenderly, tragically."

Paul, Francesca Vanini — secretary and multilingual translator for U.S. producer Jeremy Prokosch, Prokosch, and Fritz Lang meet at Prokosch's Rome studios to see the rushes of Lang's version of *The Odyssey*. Throughout the film, Vanini translates each person's comments for Prokosch, and also his demands. Prokosch wants to hire Paul to write more scenes for the film, adding sex and drama and portraying Ulysses as a modern neurotic. He feels sure Paul needs more money to support "a beautiful wife." The rushes of Lang's *Odyssey* consists mostly of static close-ups of or tracking shots around statues of the gods, often painted, and a high angle long shot of a naked woman swimming in the Mediterranean. Citing Hölderlin, Lang says the film is about "the absence of the gods."

Outside, Paul introduces Camille to Prokosch, who invites them both to his villa for a drink. Prokosch asks Camille to ride there in his red sports car. She seems to expect Paul to stand up for her against Prokosch's attentions, but Paul tells her to go on, as there's room for only one passenger. The red car speeds off. Paul arrives at the villa by taxi a half-hour late. There Prokosch has been showing Camille the grounds, putting his arm around her waist, and she is clearly, albeit silently, angry at Paul for having left her with Prokosch alone. Going into the villa looking for a bathroom, Paul encounters Francesca Vanini in the living room changing her sweater. She is crying, and Paul converses with her and finally touches her hair, in a gesture of sympathy, at which point Camille enters and sees them.

On the way home Camille expresses her dislike for Prokosch, who has spouted pompous platitudes and displayed the power of his money all day. In a half-hour section, composed mostly of long takes and shot sequences, the camera follows Paul and Camille as they move about, come together, and move apart in a prolonged quarrel, moving from room to room in their newly purchased and partially decorated apartment. Because of the way the field and reverse shots are composed, in the first third of this section, we see things from Paul's point of view, the second third from Camille's, then from Paul's. They argue over whether or not to accept Prokosch's invitation to go to his villa in Capri, about Paul's working for Prokosch, and about their relationship.

They meet Lang, Prokosch, and Vanini at a small film theater where a woman is auditioning for the part of Naussica. Lang recites Brecht's poem about selling lies in Hollywood to earn a living. Paul asks Camille why she feels contempt for him. When she ascertains that Lang is also going to Capri, she seems to accept Prokosch's invitation as fate and is seen crying.

At the villa in Capri, Paul and Fritz Lang walk along the high cliffs with Paul telling Lang that Ulysses really did not want to return to Penelope, so he took ten years to get back to Ithaca. She had faithfully waited for him, and when he delayed killing the suitors, she felt contempt for him. Ulysses was then constrained to kill the suitors to regain her love.

Camille sunbathes on the villa roof and later sits upstairs in a window and kisses Prokosch. After seeing that, Paul tells Prokosch he will not write a script for the film and that he took the job for money but would rather write for the theater. When Paul meets Camille, sunbathing again, she has more disdain for him than ever. He asks her if they should stay or go, if he should give up the job, but she says it's too late, that he's "not a man." The next morning Paul finds a note from Camille; she's left for Rome with Prokosch and will get a hotel room by herself once she's there.

At a gas station, Camille tells Prokosch she plans to become a secretary in Rome. Close-ups of words from Camille's farewell note are intercut with shots of Prokosch's red Alfa Romeo in an accident and a close-up of the car crashed into a truck, with Camille and Prokosch immobile and covered with blood.

In the last sequence, Paul goes to say goodbye to Lang, filming at the villa. That director, accompanied by Godard playing the assistant director, continues filming *The Odyssey*, the last image being of the empty sea and the sky.

15 "MONTPARNASSE-LEVALLOIS" in PARIS VU PAR

Producer:	Barbet Schroeder
Associate Producer:	Patrick Bauchau
Production Companies:	Films du Losange, Barbet Schroeder
Director:	Jean-Luc Godard (other sketches directed by Claude Chabrol, Jean Douchet, Eric Rohmer, Jean-Rouch, Jean-Daniel Pollet)
Screenplay:	Jean-Luc Godard
Based on:	*Les Contes de lundi* by Jean Giraudoux, an anecdote told by Belmondo in *Une Femme est une femme*.
Director of Photography:	Albert Maysles
Process:	Shot in 16mm Ektachrome, printed in 35mm Eastmancolor
Sound:	René Levert
Editing:	Jacqueline Reynal
Cast:	Johanna Shimkus (Monika), Philippe Hiquilly (Ivan, the sculptor), Serge Davri (Roger, the garage mechanic)
Filmed:	In the sculptor Philippe Hiquilly's own atelier in Paris, December 1963-January 1964
English-Language Release Title:	"Montparnasse-Levallois" in *Six in Paris*
Running Time:	18 minutes, 96 minutes total film
Released:	
Paris:	Cannes Film Festival, May 19, 1965; Paris release, October 13, 1965

England: London Film Festival, November 1965; general release,
                         February 1966
USA-New York: NY Film Festival, September 1965; general release, March
                         2, 1969 (New Yorker Theater)
Distribution:
  France: Sodireg
  England: Amanda
  USA: New Yorker Films

Notes

Of all Godard's films, this least has his visual style. André Téchiné (1965, Entry No. 608) says this sketch was only "organized," not directed, by Godard, who left the cameraman at complete liberty.

Synopsis

One night a woman sends two letters to two men friends. She posts the letters and then decides she'd mixed the two envelopes and sent each letter to the wrong person. She first goes to the man she loves the most, a man making "action sculpture," huge abstract metal pieces, in a workshop that looks like a garage. He keeps on working with his blowtorch, making lots of noise, as she tries to talk to him. (Her accent is noticeably Canadian.) She takes off her sweater and tries to interest him physically. She tells about the letter to the other man, which she thinks the sculptor will receive: "I told him that I loved him, but I don't. I was going to tell him that tonight." The sculptor throws her out.

She goes from there to the other lover, a garage mechanic and metal worker. His garage looks just like the sculptor's atelier. She tells him about the letter, tries to assure him she loves only him, and is thrown out. The film ends with a shot of the Chevron sign at his garage.

The film is subtitled, "an action film." Not only does the sculptor make action sculpture, but the film is shot in long takes with little cutting and has more narrative continuity than most of Godard's films. In that sense, it is the least characteristic of Godard's work and looks more like Maysles' film than Godard's.

16   BANDE À PART

Production Companies: Anouchka Films, Orsay Films
Director: Jean-Luc Godard
Screenplay: Jean-Luc Godard
  Based on: Novel, *Fool's Gold (Pigeon Vole)* by Delores and B. Hitch-
                         ens
Director of
  Photography: Raoul Coutard
Camera Operator: Georges Liron
Sound: René Levert, Antoine Bonfanti

Assistant Director:	Jean-Paul Savignac
Production Manager:	Philippe Dussart
Editing:	Agnès Guillemot
Assistant Editor:	Françoise Collin
Music:	Michel Legrand
Cast:	Anna Karina (Odile), Claude Brasseur (Arthur), Sami Frey (Franz), Jean-Luc Godard (Voice-off narrator), Louisa Colpeyn (Madame Victoria), Danièle Girard (English teacher), Ernest Menzer (Arthur's uncle), Chantal Darget (Arthur's aunt), Michèle Seghers and Claude Makovski (Pupils in English class), Georges Staquet (Légionnaire), Michel Delahaye (Doorman at language school)
Filmed:	On location in Paris, February-March 1964
English-Language Release Title:	*Band of Outsiders* (in England, *The Outsiders*)
Running Time:	97 minutes
Released:	
Venice:	1966 Film Festival, Cultural Session
Germany:	Berlin Film Festival, July 5, 1964
Paris:	August 5, 1964; it ran for 5 weeks in first-run theaters in Paris to 42,200 people
England:	London Film Festival, November 1964; general release, November 1964
USA-New York:	New York Film Festival, September 1964; general release, March 1966 (Beekman Theater)
Distribution:	
France:	Columbia
England:	Gala, Columbia
USA:	Swank

Notes

Financed through Columbia Pictures for $120,000. (1966, Crowther, "Hollywood Woos Foreign Talent," Entry No. 675)

Synopsis

This film is loosely structured like a "heist" story, but its protagonists' adolescent concerns and its pace — a rambling tour of grey, wintery, suburban Paris — give the film a nonchalant, even melancholy tone, rather than one of adventure or tension. There are many long shots and long takes of the characters' driving back and forth from city to suburb, or around in circles in a factory yard near Odile's house, and also of their going on foot circuitously from the factory yard to the house across a small canal.

Two young men — Franz, a tall, thin young man wearing a fedora, and Arthur, a stocky youth wearing a stocking cap — drive past Odile's home, a large suburban house facing a canal. Franz says that Odile, a young woman in his English class, has told him about a pile of money in a cupboard there. It belongs to her guardian Aunt Victoria's friend, Mr. Stolz. The boys go to

Franz's Berlitz-style English class, held in a tacky building. There Arthur meets and flirts with Odile while the teacher gives an impossible dictation from *Romeo and Juliet*.

The two young men bully Odile into participating in the robbery. She seems to be Aunt Victoria's servant as well as ward. When Odile looks in Mr. Stolz's room to see how much money there is, she forgets to replace an overcoat that had been in the cupboard, thus arousing Victoria's suspicions.

While waiting for Odile, Franz and Arthur read newspapers on the river bank opposite the house and declaim to each other violent headlines from the news. Odile takes some meat from her refrigerator to feed to a tiger in a nearby menagerie. Arthur races his car around the factory yard, saying he wants to race in the Indianapolis 500. They drive to a cafe where Franz and Arthur compete for Odile's attention, and the three dance in a spontaneous chorus line formation, as Godard's voice off tells the feelings of each. Franz and Arthur flip a coin to see who can spend an evening with Odile; Arthur wins.

In the Metro, Arthur and Odile express tentative words of love. In a long sequence there, a voice-off monologue, possibly conveying Odile's feelings if not her conscious thoughts, tells of her identifying with a general human sadness. During this monologue, we see close-ups of Odile and people in the Metro and long shots of people in the city.

Arthur's family also seems to know about the money, and his uncle, a stocky, brawling "Legionnaire from Dienbienphu," himself plans to rob the house. Therefore, Arthur insists that they make the robbery the next day. Odile expresses her fear to Franz and they talk of escaping either to the Far North or to South America. The trio do the world's fastest tour of the Louvre and are seen racing down its corridors.

When they get to Odile's yard, the boys force Odile to give them black stockings to put over their face. They enter the house. Odile is terrified, so they tie her hands and gag her, but they release her when they find the door to Stolz's room locked. The three take a long ladder from the garage to try to get in from the outside, but the window is also locked. Arthur hits Odile out of frustration.

The next day they return and tie and gag Aunt Victoria, stuffing her into a downstairs closet. Little money is now to be found; just some currency in the refrigerator. Aunt Victoria seems dead. Arthur's uncle leaves from Paris and drives toward the house in his white car. As the three youths start to drive away, Arthur insists on going back alone to see how Aunt Victoria is and to look for the money. Franz keeps driving, but when he sees Arthur's uncle's white car, he turns back.

Arthur finds the cash in the dog house, but is shot by his uncle. Arthur is, in fact, shot many times but he does not fall. Finally he shoots once, kills the uncle, and then dies himself with great spasms. Another car comes in; it is Mr. Stolz, who is met by an alive Aunt Victoria. The onlooking Franz and Odile escape and drive away. With the money they did get, they go off to South America; in a clearly fantasy ending, the last shot is of them on shipboard, accompanied by a pet terrier.

17   LA (UNE) FEMME MARIÉE

Production Companies:	Anouchka Films, Orsay Films (Paris)
Director:	Jean-Luc Godard
Screenplay:	Jean-Luc Godard
Includes:	Rewritten scene from Racine's *Bérénice*; long monologue from Louis-Ferdinand Céline's novel, *Mort à crédit*
Director of Photography:	Raoul Coutard
Process:	Black and white
Camera Operators:	Roger Liron, Jean Garcenot
Sound:	Antoine Bonfanti, René Levert, Jacques Maumont
Electricians:	Fernand Coquet, Henri Schickel
Travelling:	Robert Cambaurakis
Machinery:	Bernard Largemain, Roger Schleich
Assistant Directors:	Claude Othnin-Girard, Jean-Pierre Léaud, and Hélène Kalouguine
Script Continuity:	Suzanne Schiffman and Catherine Savignac
Production Managers:	Philippe Dussart, Maurice Urbain
Production Assistants:	Jean-Claude Durand, Jane Marie Oliver, Christine Brierre, Patricia Finaly
Art Direction:	Henri Nogaret
Props:	Joseph Gerhard
Costumes:	Laurence Clairval
Editing:	Agnès Guillemot, Françoise Collin
Assistant Editors:	Andrée Choty, Gérard Pollicand
Music:	Extracts from Beethoven's Quartets Nos. 7, 9, 10, 14, 15; jazz by Claude Nougaro, "La Java"
Song:	"Quand le film est triste," by J. D. Loudermilk, G. Aber, L. Morisse; sung by Sylvie Vartan
Laboratory:	G.T.C. (Paris-Joinville)
Cast:	Macha Méril (Charlotte Giraud), Bernard Noël (Robert, the lover), Philippe Leroy (Pierre, the husband), Roger Leenhardt (Himself), Rita Maiden (Mme. Céline, the maid), Margaret Le-Van and Véronique Duval (Two young women at the pool), Chris Tophe (Nicholas, the little boy), Georges Liron (The physician)
Filmed:	In Paris, interiors mostly at 2 Elysée, and Orly Airport, June-July 1964
English-Language Release Title:	*The (A) Married Woman (The -- in USA; A -- in England)*
Running Time:	95 minutes, originally 98 minutes

Released:
  Italy: Venice Film Festival, September 8, 1964 (before censor-
                            ship) as *La Femme marièe*
  Paris: December 4, 1964 (at Studio Publicis, Vendôme and
                            Gaumont Rive Gauche), as *Une Femme mariée*; it ran for 4
                            weeks in these first-run theaters to 67,943 people.
  England: April 1965
  USA-New York: August 16, 1965 (Baronet Theater)
Distribution:
  France: Columbia
  England: Gala, Columbia
  USA: Swank

Notes

French censors forced a few cuts and a change of title, so as not to imply that guiltless infidelity was characteristic of most married women in France. Released to viewers over 18 years old.

Bowsley Crowther notes that Columbia Pictures financed the film for $100,000. (1966, "Hollywood Woos Foreign Talent," Entry No. 675)

French governmental censors also forced Godard to cut a sequence filmed by Jacques Rozier showing the topless bathing suit fad at the Côte d'Azure, and a long section of Mme. Céline's monologue, drawn from Ferdinand Céline's *Mort à crédit*, about love-making with her husband.

The Central French Catholic Board of censors recommended that adults avoid this film.

Synopsis

Charlotte Giraud and her lover Robert are at his apartment. We see a montage of their bodies and faces against the background of white sheets. As the two dress, Godard utilizes shots of book titles (*Souls, Age of Nylon*), radio announcements about traffic accidents (similar to those in *Weekend*), and Robert's possessions to comment on the characters' roles and middle-class status. (Actor Robert has a portrait of Molière. He sells Charlotte a "posture improving" belt like his.) They leave in Robert's car. A voice-off commentary speaks about emotional life in a way that Charlotte cannot utter for herself. The commentary enters throughout the film, especially over exterior shots showing Charlotte as a small figure swallowed up by her consumer-oriented milieu.

Charlotte slinks down in the car seat. She tells Robert to let her off at a major department store, Printemps Nation, to buy a bra, but she only rushes through the store to take two more taxis to pick up her small son, Nicholas, at school. Shots of perfume ads, billboards, and the taxi meter contain words that comment ironically on her affair and her fear of being followed — *My Sin, Pretext, Triumph, Free.*

She meets husband Pierre at a private airport; he has flown in a small plane along with a guest, real-life filmmaker and philosopher Roger Leenhardt. She escapes from Pierre's embrace. At home, the couple quarrels before dinner, at which point Charlotte reveals her resentment about Pierre's previously having had her followed by a detective. When guest Leenhardt arrives, they describe their home to him in the language of a real estate brochure. The three each give a monologue — filmed in television style close-up. Pierre speaks on memory, Charlotte on the present, and Leenhardt on the intellect. Nicholas comes in and gives a monologue on some process he has mastered.

Later Charlotte and Pierre quarrel over some records. She wants to play "*Erotica*," which is just the sound of a woman laughing. They chase each other from bedroom to living room via hallway and porch (visually similar to *A Night at the Opera*). Finally the two make love in a sequence which looks almost the mirror opposite of that which opened the film. Here the voice-off commentary expresses anxieties about love; Pierre says he wants a child; Charlotte feels happy.

The next day Charlotte and her maid, Mme Céline, discuss ads and techniques for improving one's bust. In the kitchen, Mme. Céline delivers a lusty monologue, drawn from Céline's novel, *Mort à crédit*, to tell Charlotte all her physical marital pleasures.

Charlotte, who works as a fashion editor, goes to a swimming pool where she directs the photographing of models in swimsuits (shown in negative). Afterwards, sitting in the poolside bar, she leafs through a magazine filled with all the ads that shape women's lives. As she tries to eavesdrop on two adolescent women talking about their first sexual experiences, her eye scans a headline, "Here's what every woman should know. She does. She doesn't." The young women's conversation is almost inaudible due to the sound of pinball machines; the film summarizes their words in subtitles. The jukebox plays Sylvie Vartan's "Sad Songs Always Make Me Cry."

At the doctor's, Charlotte tries to talk about physical pleasure, her uncertainty about the father of her child, and contraception, but the doctor will not speak to her real concerns and instead answers her questions in pseudo-scientific, coldly "objective" terms. Outside, Charlotte falls down while running across the street. The camera focuses on billboards to create intertitles, or else actual intertitles are used in this and the next section, including *Eve Dreams* (*Rêves*), *What Will Be, Take a Stand, Danger*.

Robert is leaving for Marseilles to act in *Bérénice*. Charlotte meets him at the Orly Cinema, which is playing a Hitchcock film and Alain Resnais' *Nuit et tinieblas*. Charlotte sees part of the latter (earlier she could not identify what Auschwitz was). Then she and Robert do an elaborate Hitchcock-style maneuver in the airport waiting room: Robert, wearing dark glasses, walks past her, dropping his key by her feet. She ascertains the room number and returns the key to him. They have only an hour to spend together in a barren airport hotel room. In voice off Charlotte interviews Robert, seen in close-up, about what it means to him to be an actor; in bed they recite parts from *Bérénice*, rewritten by Godard. Robert says that Charlotte has tears in her eyes. The last shot is of a man's and a woman's hands withdrawing out of frame against the background of a white sheet.

18   ALPHAVILLE: UNE ÉTRANGE ADVENTURE DE LEMMY CUATION

Producer:	André Michelin
Production Companies:	Chaumiane (Paris), Filmstudio (Rome)
Director:	Jean-Luc Godard
Screenplay:	Jean-Luc Godard
Director of Photography:	Raoul Coutard
Camera Operator:	Georges Liron
Sound:	René Levert
Assistant Directors:	Charles Bitsch, Jean-Paul Savignac, Hélène Kalouguine
Production Manager:	Philippe Dussart
Editing:	Agnès Guillemot
Music:	Paul Misraki
Cast:	Eddie Constantine (Lemmy Caution), Anna Karina (Natacha von Braun), Akim Tamiroff (Henri Dickson), Howard Vernon (Professor Léonard Nosferatu, alias von Braun), Laszlo Szabo (Chief engineer), Michael Delahaye (Von Braun's assistant), Jean-André Fieschi (Professor Heckell), Jean-Louis Comolli (Professor Jeckell), A man with a laryngectomy (Alpha 60's voice), Christa Lang, Jean-Pierre Léaud
Filmed:	On location in Paris, January-February 1965. "It was filmed in the most futuristic buildings in Paris — the new snail-shaped Maison de la Radio and the new wing-topped Palais des Expositions, at the Rond-Point de la Défense — as well as inside the office of Les Machines Bull, which make computers." (1965, Genêt, Entry No. 536)
English-Language Release Title:	*Alphaville*
Running Time:	98 minutes
Released:	
Berlin	"Festival Winner" (1965, Crowther, Entry No. 513)
Paris:	May 5, 1965; 160,000 people saw it in first-run theaters from May to August.
England:	London Film Festival, November 1965; general release, March 1966
USA-New York:	New York Film Festival, September 1965; general release, October 25, 1965 (Paris Theater)

Distribution:
France:	Athos
Italy:	Medusa
England:	Academy, Connoisseur
USA:	Swank

Notes

The film opened in New York at a gala benefit for the N.Y. Civil Liberties Union, with $12.50 for admission and $17.50 reception. (1965, Crowther, Entry No. 512)

Synopsis

Tough-looking Lemmy Caution drives into Paris or Alphaville at night and registers at a large hotel as Ivan Johnson, reporter for *Figaro-Pravda*. A weary-looking blonde woman leads him along endless corridors to his room and is rejected by him when she offers to bathe with him. As the camera faces Lemmy's bed, to the right we see the bathroom, brilliantly lit, and to the left a rather dark "jukebox" room, connected to both the bathroom and bedroom.

A figure from the left is seen smashing into Lemmy in the bathroom and a fight ensues, during which Lemmy shoots and kills "the inspector." Lemmy sits the woman in a chair, takes flash photos of her, and shoots holes through the breasts of a pinup which he has her hold over her head. After he pushes her out, Natasha von Braun comes up, wearing a dark dress that compliments her long dark hair. Her way of behaving confuses Lemmy. They agree to meet for the "Festival."

At a phone station Lemmy is accosted by a man whom he stabs and leaves in a phone booth. A photograph of Professor von Braun on the wall is the same as a photo Lemmy carries, and he is surprised that the telephone operator, as well as many people he asks on the street (all filmed in extreme long shot), all know that man. Lemmy goes to another hotel and waits for a Mr. Dickson. Dickson comes and cannot pay his rent. He takes the money which Lemmy gives him, pays up, gets a bottle of beer, and goes upstairs. On the stairs they talk in front of a bare, swinging light bulb. Dickson staggers and seems ill. He explains the despair engendered by the technocracy of Alpha 60, the giant computers running Alphaville. (Alpha 60 itself is seen often in the film. It is a flashing beacon against a black background, shown in extreme close-up). In his room, Dickson makes love with a prostitute as Lemmy stands half-hidden behind the closet door. Either the exertion or poison kills Dickson. Before dying, he gives Lemmy a book hidden under his pillow, Paul Eluard's *Capital de doleur*, and whispers, "Conscience, tenderness, make Alpha 60 destroy itself." Lemmy photographs the corpse and leaves.

Lemmy drives to where Natasha works, the Institute of General Semantics. There she and coworkers sit and copy Alpha 60's words, which are interspersed with bizarre surreal line drawings intended to illustrate its concepts. Lemmy is bored and leaves. He goes with Natasha to the "galareception," where dissidents are stood on a diving board over a swimming pool, make final speeches about love and faith and courage, and are stabbed by Esther Williams-type bathing beauties. There Lemmy tries to speak to Professor von Braun, a refugee from the Outerlands, but he is trapped by von Braun's henchmen in an elevator and is beaten up. Natasha looks on and cries.

Lemmy is taken to be interrogated by a computer unit. As he sits in a darkened room, facing a flashing light, several hanging microphones revolve around his head. His philosophical statements confuse the computer. He is taken to the chief engineer, who explains Alpha 60 to him and takes him on a tour of the computer center, where Alpha 60's "brains" look rather like the inside of the phone company. He hears that Alpha 60 has declared war against his homeland, the Outerlands. He escapes and returns to his hotel.

Natasha has been forbidden to see him, but comes anyway. He teaches her new emotions by having her read Eluard's poetry. She learns the words *consciousness* and *tenderness* and remembers her early life in the Outerlands. We see long takes of Lemmy and Natasha moving around the room, and a montage of close-ups as they embrace and dance against the light. Intercut are images of a police car racing through the city toward their hotel.

The police arrive and order Natasha to tell "Story No. 842," which she does mechanically. Lemmy laughs at the joke, sufficient reason for him to be arrested, roughed up, and interrogated by the computer again. He escapes by smashing through a locked door, but sees Natasha being dragged in the building as he leaves. He kills von Braun, and presumably decommissions Alpha 60 — either by a shot fired into it or by the questions he had asked it. He steals a car and is chased through snow-covered streets, finally driving down a flight of stone stars. Alpha 60's words become confused. Inhabitants of Alphaville stagger and fall dead, especially in the corridors of the computer center. Lemmy finds Natasha there and keeps her alive by forcing her to think about the word *love*. They stagger down long corridors and drive out the city streets at night. Natasha learns by herself to say the saving words, "I love you."

19   PIERROT LE FOU

Producers:	Georges de Beauregard, Dino de Laurentiis
Production Companies:	Rome-Paris Films, Dino de Laurentiis Cinematografica
Director:	Jean-Luc Godard

Screenplay:	Jean-Luc Godard
Based on:	The thriller novel, *Obsession*, by Lionel White; in France, *Le Demon de onze heurs* in the "Serie Noire" (Gallimard)
Director of Photography:	Raoul Coutard
Process:	Techniscope, Eastmancolor
Camera Operator:	Georges Liron, Jean Garçenot
Sound:	René Levert
Assistant Directors:	Philippe Fourastié, Jean-Pierre Léaud
Production Manager:	René Demoulin
Production Assistant:	Roger Scipion
Art Direction:	Pierre Guffroy
Editing:	Françoise Collin
Music:	Antoine Duhamel
Song:	"Ma Ligne de chance" and "Jamais je ne t'ai dit que je t'aimerai toujours" by Duhamel and Bassiak (45 rpm record released of Karina and Bassiak singing the two songs, and Duhamel playing theme from film)
Sound Mix:	Antoine Bonfanti
Cast:	Jean-Paul Belmondo (Ferdinand Griffon), Anna Karina (Marianne Renoir), Dirk Sanders (Marianne's brother or lover), Raymond Devos (Man on pier), Graziella Galvani (Mrs. Griffon), Roger Dutoit (Gangster), Hans Meyer (Gangster), Jimmy Karoubi (Dwarf, gangster), Christa Nell (Mme. Staquet), Pascal Aubier (Second brother), Pierre Hanin (Third brother), Princess Aïcha Abadie (Herself), Samuel Fuller (Himself), Alexis Poliakoff (Sailor), Laszlo Szabo (Political exile from Santo Domingo), Jean-Pierre Léaud (Young man in cinema)
Filmed:	On location in Paris and in Hyères in the south of France, June-July 1965
English-Language Release Title:	*Pierrot le fou (Crazy Pete)*
Running Time:	112 minutes
Released:	
Italy:	Venice Film Festival, August 29, 1965
Paris:	November 5, 1965 (128,019 tickets sold in first-run Paris theaters)
England:	London Film Festival, November 1965; general release, April 1966
USA-New York:	New York Film Festival, September 1966; general release, January 8, 1969 (72nd Street Playhouse)
Distribution:	
France:	S.N.C. Impéria
Italy:	De Laurentiis-Medusa
England:	Gala
USA:	Contemporary/McGraw-Hill

Notes

The film ran for more than a year at one theater in the Latin Quarter. (1968,

Mussman, "Introductory Notes," Entry No. 1167) It was censored for those under 18 because of its "intellectual anarchism." (1970, Simsolo, Entry No. 1518)

Synopsis

Throughout the film the dialogue is exaggerated, funny, filled with non sequiturs, and often lyrical, but never naturalistic.

Ferdinand Griffon sits in the bath reading Elie Faure's *L'Histoire d'art* to his daughter. In the bedroom, he argues with his wife about going to her mother's party. A couple arrives to go with them; the man, Frank, has brought his "niece" Marianne Renoir to babysit.

At the party we see groups of guests, filmed through red, yellow and blue filters, speaking advertising cliches or acting outrageously. Ferdinand meets U.S. director Samuel Fuller and finds out from the filmmaker what cinema is. Ferdinand borrows Frank's car keys to go home and while departing, throws a fistful of cake at the guests. He then drives the babysitter home; we see them in a fixed shot through the windshield, across which colorful lights rhythmically flash. They speak of having a past love affair and they listen to radio news about Vietnam. Against his wishes, Marianne calls Ferdinand "Pierrot."

Marianne is fixing breakfast for Ferdinand in her apartment. (She is identified with a Renoir painting, he with a Picasso — red vs. blue being the color symbolism of their love throughout the film.) A corpse stabbed in the neck with scissors, rifles, and guns stacked up in the corner of a room, Frank's entrance and his being knocked over the head by Marianne, and a pursuit and shootout in her apartment complex are presented confusedly and almost casually. A series of phrases uttered by the protagonists indicates some complicated shady business, possibly political, involving Marianne's brother Fred.

The couple escapes in a stolen red car. They beat up gas station attendants to get gasoline, drive south into central France, and destroy their car alongside a burning wreck in the countryside around which are strewn bloody bodies. In the car was a suitcase containing U.S. currency which the gangsters had thought was in Marianne's apartment; Ferdinand tried to get it out of the trunk, but Marianne had shot a bullet into the gas tank. The couple steals a Ford Galaxy from a service lift in a gas station; they get cash from the owner's jacket, left in the car, and dress in clothes from their new-found luggage. Arriving at the Riviera, Ferdinand drives that car into the sea, and the two pull the luggage out and trudge with it down the sand. As they make love on the beach, the camera remains fixed on the moon; Ferdinand tells a tale about what happened when the moon was colonized by U.S. and Russian astronauts.

They escape to an island where they try to live out an idyll of love. We see them with a brightly colored parrot and a tame fox. Ferdinand tells Marianne to buy books and he keeps a diary (entries shown in close-up). Marianne wants to buy records and a phonograph; she is totally bored. He wants to communicate in words, she in feelings. In boredom, she throws the last of their cash into the sea; to get money they perform anti-imperialist skits about Vietnam for some U.S. sailors who are tourists, and Marianne steals all the money from the officer's hand. The couple sing and dance through the woods.

Marianne and Ferdinand are fishing by a river and arguing. Suddenly she fearfully recognizes someone, a midget. She tells Ferdinand to wait five minutes for her in a restaurant but then phones from an apartment to summon him. In that apartment the midget threatens to torture her to tell where the suitcase full of dollars is, but she kills him with a scissors.

When Ferdinand enters he finds only Marianne's red dress and blood everywhere. Two men there in grey suits torture him to find out where the money and/or Marianne are. Ferdinand is seen walking along a railroad track and on the docks of Toulon in sequences intercut with close-ups of his diary; the sound track here gives, via the protagonists' voices off, some brief, confused statements about the plot development. In Toulon, Ferdinand goes to a cinema where he sees Vietnam newsreel footage that bores him and also Godard's *Le Grand escroc*. He works on the yacht of the elderly Princess Aïcha Abadie, who always speaks as if being interviewed.

Marianne finds him, says she'd met her "brother" Fred by accident in Toulon, and gets Ferdinand involved in some kind of gun-running episode with Fred; this episode is presented visually in short, unconnected images and is described on the sound track in terms of novels by Stevenson, Faulkner, London, and Chandler. The protagonists are involved in a bloody holdup, presumably stealing money from other gangsters. Ferdinand delivers a suitcase with $50,000 to Marianne, who is waiting for him in a bowling alley. She abandons him, escaping with Fred by boat. On the quay, desperately watching them drive off, Ferdinand meets Raymond Devos, a crazy old man obsessed by a melody once associated with his first love. Ferdinand takes a boat to an island and shoots Fred and then, probably accidentally, Marianne, as the fugitives run on a path toward a villa.

Ferdinand phones his Paris home, but the maid does not recognize his voice. Marianne dies. Ferdinand paints his face blue, wraps yellow and red strips of dynamite around his head, lights the fuse, and is blown up — seemingly as he is trying to put the fuse out.

20 MASCULIN-FÉMININ

Production Companies: Anouchka Films, Argos Films (Paris), Svensk Filmindustrie, Sandrews (Stockholm)

Director:	Jean-Luc Godard
Screenplay:	Jean-Luc Godard
Freely based on:	Two novels by Guy de Maupassant: *La Femme de Paul* and *Le Signe*; LeRoi Jones' *Dutchman*; Vauthier's *Prodiges*
Director of Photography:	Willy Kurant
Process:	Black and white
Sound:	René Levert
Assistant Directors:	Bernard Toublanc-Michel, Jacques Barratier
Production Manager:	Philippe Dussart
Production Assistants:	Pascal Aubier, Penni Jacques
Editing:	Agnès Guillemot, Marguerite Renoir
Music:	Francis Lai, J.J. Debout, Mozart's Clarinet Concerto, K. 622
Cast:	Jean-Pierre Léaud (Paul), Chantal Goya (Madeleine), Marlène Jobert (Élisabeth), Michel Debord (Robert), Catherine-Isabelle Duport (Catherine-Isabelle), Eva Britt Strandbert ("She" in the film-within-the-film), Birger Malmsten ("He" in the film-within-the-film), Elsa Leroy (Miss Nineteen Year Old, Elsa), Françoise Hardy (Companion to the U.S. officer in car), Brigitte Bardot and Antoine Bourseiller (Couple rehearsing in cafe), Chantal Darget (In extract from "Le Métro Fantôme")
Filmed:	In Paris, November-December 1965
English-Language Release Title:	*Masculine-Feminine*
Running Time:	103 minutes in USA; previously 110 minutes
Released:	
Berlin:	Summer, 1966, Film Festival
Paris:	April 22, 1966 (108,749 tickets sold in first-run Paris theaters)
England:	June 1967
USA-New York:	New York Film Festival, September 1966; general release, September 18, 1966 (Little Carnegie)
Distribution	
France:	Columbia
Italy:	Cormons
England:	Gala
USA:	Swank

Synopsis

Visually this somber-toned, black and white film is dominated by its many long shots of the protagonists traversing crowded Paris streets and many interior sequences in Parisian cafes or apartments. In the latter, the camera frequently stays fixed on the face of one adolescent character interrogating or being interrogated by another. The film opens in a cafe where 21-year-old Paul engages the young woman at the next table, Madeleine in conversation. At another table, a couple quarrels, the man leaves with his small son, and his wife fires a pistol at him as he exits. Paul meets his friend Robert at another cafe where they talk about left politics and their most recent dates.

Presumably Madeleine, who aspires to be a recording star, secures employment for Paul on a magazine where she works or has worked. They converse in the employees' bathroom and Paul persuades her to go out with him.

On the street, Madeleine introduces Paul to Élisabeth and Catherine, her roommates. Together Paul and Robert distract an army chauffeur so Paul can paint "Peace in Vietnam" on a S.H.A.F.E. limousine. In the Métro at night the two friends witness a scene extracted from LeRoi Jones' *Dutchman*, a violent dispute between two black men and a white woman.

In the bathroom in their apartment, Catherine and Élisabeth discuss sexuality and speculate whether or not Paul might be a good lover. Paul meets Madeleine in a cafe and asks her to marry him. She is evasive. They are distracted by a couple reading aloud and an old man and young woman conversing.

Paul, Élisabeth, and Madeleine meet at a dancing place and then have a drink at a soda bar across from a pinball arcade, a photomat, and a recording booth. The two women leave and a young blonde woman offers to let Paul take photos in the photomat with her barebreasted, which he does. He then records a love record to Madeleine. A man from the bowling alley comes after Paul with a knife but unpredictably stabs himself instead and collapses in Paul's arms.

At night Paul meets Robert in a laundromat. Robert reproaches Paul politically for his individualism, but Paul can only think of Madeleine whom he's asked to move in with because he's lost his room.

In their shared apartment, Paul is eating with Catherine, who talks about contraception. The other two women arrive. Paul listens to classical music in the living room with Catherine and then goes to sleep with Madeleine in a big double bed which Élisabeth also shares.

Paul now works for the French Public Opinion Institute and interviews Miss Nineteen Year Old, who naively talks at length about everything. While waiting for Madeleine at a restaurant, Paul and Élisabeth begin eating; Élisabeth takes the occasion to warn him against Madeleine and her friends. He repudiates her remarks and says that Madeleine is pregnant. The latter arrives. Elsewhere in the bar a prostitute, the woman who had shot her husband earlier, reproaches a German client for his nationality, and dramatist Antoine Bourseillier and Brigitte Bardot rehearse lines from Vauthier's *Prodiges*.

At the cinema, in the men's room, Paul sees two men making love. After the film starts, he leaves his seat and goes around the outside of the theater to the projection booth to protest that the film is being shown in the wrong ratio. The film itself parodies sadistic pornography.

At the apartment, first in the bathroom and then in the kitchen, Robert and Catherine engage in a long conversation, questioning each other about their lives, habits, and opinions. Paul and Catherine are then seen walking down the street when a man borrows matches from Paul. Paul runs to get his matches back, only to return to announce the man had immolated himself, crying "Peace in Vietnam." Paul and Catherine later meet Madeleine at her recording studio, where she is recording a song. As they exit, a radio reporter interviews her and she asks Paul as her "secretary" to get her car. He calls her bluff, getting a limousine by phoning the War Ministry as a "General Doniol."

In a long monologue accompanying shots of people in the streets and in front of stores — crowds often including himself — Paul describes the failure of his investigative reporting. His words reflect Godard's own concerns about the betrayal of language and the commercial manipulation of the means of communication.

At a police station, Catherine and Madeleine give depositions about Paul's death. He fell from the window of an apartment he was purchasing: it was possibly suicide, possibly an accident.

21   MADE IN U.S.A.

Producer:	Georges de Beauregard
Production Companies:	Rome-Paris Films, Anouchka Films, S.E.P.I.C. (Paris)
Director:	Jean-Luc Godard
Screenplay:	Jean-Luc Godard
Based on:	A novel, *The Juggler*, by Richard Stark; in French, *Rien dans le Coffre*, "Serie Noire" (Gallimard)
Director of Photography:	Raoul Coutard
Process:	Techniscope, Eastmancolor
Camera Operations:	Georges Liron, Jean Garcenot
Sound:	René Levert
Travelling:	Ortion
Assistant Directors:	Charles Bitsch, Claude Bakka, Jean-Pierre Léaud, Philippe Pouzenc
Script Continuity:	Suzanne Schiffman
Production Manager:	René Demoulin
Production Assistants:	Roger Ferret, Roger Scipion, Colette Roy
Photographer:	Marylou Parolini
Make-up:	Jackie Reynal
Editing:	Agnès Guillemot
Assistant Editor:	Geneviève Letellier
Music:	Robert Schumann, Symphony No. 3; Ludwig von Beethoven, Symphony No. 5, and Piano Trio
Song:	"As Tears Go By" by Mick Jagger and Keith Richard
Sound Mix:	Jacques Maumont
Cast:	Anna Karina (Paula Nelson), Laszlo Szabo (Richard Widmark), Yves Alfonso (David Goodis), Jean-Pierre

Léaud (Donald Siegal), Jean-Claude Bouillon (Inspector Aldrich), Kyoko Kosaka (Doris Mizoguchi), Ernest Menzer (Edgar Typhus), Elaine Giovagnoli (Dentist's assistant), Marianne Faithfull (Herself, woman in a cafe), Rémo Forlani (Worker in bar), Sylvain Godet (Robert MacNamara), Jean-Pierre Biesse (Richard Nixon), Jean-Luc Godard (Voice of Richard Politzer), Claude Bakka (Man with Marianne Faithful), Philippe Labro (Himself), Marc Dudicourt (Barman), Eliane Giovagnoli (Dentist's assistant), Alexis Poliakoff (Man with notebook and red phone), Roger Scipion (Dr. Korvo), Danièle Palmero (Chambermaid in hotel), Rita Maiden (Woman who gives Paula information), Isabelle Pons (Journalist), Philippe Pouzenc (Policeman), Fernand Coquet (Bill poster), Miguel (Dentist), Annie Guégan (Young woman in bandages), Marika Perioli (Young woman with dog), Jean-Philippe Nierman (Note-taking policeman), Charles Bitsch (Taxi driver), Daniel Bart (Policeman)

Filmed:	On locations in Paris, July-August 1966
English-Language Release Title:	*Made in U.S.A.*
Running Time:	90 minutes
Released:	
Italy:	1967 Pesaro Festival, outside competition.
Paris:	January 27, 1967 (Lord Byron, Astor, Cinévog, St. Lazare, Atlas, Bonaparte, Studio St. Germain Theaters — 59,329 tickets sold in first-run Paris theaters)
England:	London Film Festival, December 3, 1966
USA-New York:	New York Film Festival, September 27, 1967
Distribution:	
France:	Lux Films, C.C.F.
Italy:	Lux

Notes

Not distributed in the United States because of a lawsuit over original novel rights.

Godard finished shooting *Made in U.S.A.* on August 11, yet began *Deux ou trois choses*, August 8. Reputedly he went from one set in the morning to the other in the afternoon.

Godard was the constant reference point at the 3rd International Festival for a New Cinema at Pesaro, 1967. There *Made in U.S.A.* was "projected the last night . . . as the glorious prototype of the new cinema." (1967, Collet, Entry No. 857)

Synopsis

Made in U.S.A. suggests rather than develops a plot about conspiracies, assassinations, torture, and international connections between governmental figures, the press, and criminals. Furthermore, the vivid, primary-colored visual track surrealistically connotes aspects of political intrigue. The images that Godard finds most apt to portray contemporary political life on an international scale are ones that he borrows from Disney, comicstrips, *noir* detective novels and films, and his own past films (e.g., filming characters in a planimetric composition against a flat wall, witty or symbolic intertitles, striped dresses on the protagonist, and saturated glaring colors). Modes of discourse on the sound track vary widely. They include comic strip-like dialogue, poetry, a Mick Jagger-Keith Richard song, a tape-recorded Marxist analysis of Gaullist France — played so loud that it is hard to hear the words distinctly, a loud jet plane which always comes in to drown out the assassinated man's last name, machine gun fire, the protagonist's existential monologues, and a bartender's delivering a lesson in linguistics and meaning vs. nonmeaning.

Credits dedicate the film: TO NICK AND SAM / WHO RAISED ME / TO RESPECT / IMAGE AND SOUND. The protagonist Paula Nelson is first seen lying on a hotel bed with a crime novel, *Adieu la vie, adieu l'amour* and a copy of *Newsweek*. She talks about her lost love (Richard Politzer) and discusses with the maid the fact that the Communists lost the last local election there in Atlantic City. Outside are police inspector Aldrich and two political henchmen, Widmark and Donald Siegal.

We hear a knock on Paula's door and the gangster Typhus, a short man wearing a panama hat, enters. He tells Paula that the war in Morocco has made her mean. She asks him how Richard died. Typhus wants to work with her and split the profits from whatever she finds out about Richard. She hits him over the head with a shoe, knocks him out, and drags him back to his own hotel room. A voice off declares, "Already fiction carries away reality . . . I seem to be plunged into a film by Walt Disney, but played by Humphrey Bogart, therefore a political film." In Typhus' pocket she finds the address of Dr. Samuel Korvo and the word "autopsy." David Goodis, a poet and Typhus's nephew, enters. Doris Mizoguchi plays the guitar in the shower. David talks about his love for Doris and tries to complete a poem about her, which Paula completes for him.

A rapid montage of seventeen quick shots is accompanied by a Beethoven piano trio and two massive chords which punctuate the action. Paula is seen in various positions against a red wall. A woman puts on a white coat. Paula loads a gun and hides it in a hollowed out *Larousse gastronomique*. She trains the gun on the doctor's assistant, and then she uncovers a bloody bandaged head of a corpse in a dentist's chair to reveal a skull with marble eyes bulging out. She runs into a clinic with Typhus. Neon signs at night are seen as Marianne Faithfull sings in voice off in English the first line of a Jagger-Richard song, "As Tears Go By."

Paula, a bartender, and a patron at a bar play word games and discuss linguistics and the meaning of words and sentences. "The tables are on the glasses . . . The window is looking at the eyes of Mademoiselle . . . The dictionary has only three windows . . . I am what you are. He is not what we are . . . They have got what we haven't." Widmark and Donald come into the bar, Donald wearing a huge badge saying, "Kiss me, I'm Italian." Marianne Faithfull sits abandoned by her lover and sings the entire song, "As Tears Go By." As she sings, we see close-ups of Widmark, Donald, and Paula. Paula has tears in her eyes.

Paula walks past women exercising in a women's health club. She tries to find out from Doctor Ludwig, who signed Richard's death certificate and who has some connection with Widmark, what the cause of Richard's death really was. The doctor knows about Paula and answers evasively. Paula vows to avenge Richard's death. As she leaves Ludwig's, she is followed by Donald. The voice off says she knows she is risking her life, but she may be able to discover something which she could sell to the opposition press afterwards. She plans to pick up Richard's things and then meet an anonymous female caller in a garage. She is knocked out and awakens to find Widmark and Donald in the garage (pinball machine is prominent in the mise en scene). In a conversation with Widmark, interspersed with frames from comic strips, she gets some information about Richard's death. Widmark is "chief organizer for the fifth region" and wants to ascertain if Paula knows where "it" is. They play part of Politzer's tape.

The three go back to the hotel where they see the bloodied bodies of the murdered Doris Mizoguchi and Edgar Typhus. The police handcuff Paula, but Inspector Aldrich releases her in the custody of Widmark, to whom she says, "I'm sure it was you who killed Dick." David Goodis is seen in handcuffs, hysterically accusing Paula of killing his uncle. Aldrich says to Paula that if Richard Po ("Polizer" is always drowned out in the film) didn't die naturally, he must have committed suicide.

Paula says several times, "I can't tell you how much I hate the police." An insert here shows Dr. Ludwig's assistant phoning. In the next sequence we see a young woman answering questions which Paula asks in voice off. The woman says Richard had told her something before he died; "they" tortured her with a razor blade to find out, and subsequently she has tried to commit suicide.

The word LIBERTÉ, painted on a white plaster wall, is shot up with machine-gun fire. Paula goes to an advertising agency that seems to make huge stand-up cardboard figures used outside of movie houses. Prominent in the mise en scene, these figures connote the ideological consequences of certain "icons" in Western society. These include Disney characters, lovers, a Nazi, a bathing beauty, and a cowboy. A woman, Madame Céline, secretly comes over to tell Paula that she knew Richard when he was living in a villa outside Atlantic City on Rue Preminger. Outside the building Widmark is waiting for Paula and tells her David Goodis told the police his accusations had been a mistake. Two detectives and a man with a Tommy gun who had been following Paula get in the car with Paula and Widmark. They drive off.

Paula is in her hotel room packing her clothes on the blood-stained bed. Widmark looks on. Shots of Paula walking in the streets are intercut with words being typed. Beethoven chords are heard in the background. Paula is in David's hotel room as he first types with one finger and then puts a silencer on a gun. There is a visual and audio montage of neon signs; chamber music; a close-up of a tape playing; more of Richard Po's analysis; Paula stealing a gun from a store; a bloodied bandaged woman; Paula standing against a wall looking bewildered; and Paula listening to Richard's tape in a dark room. At this point Paula's reflections and Richard's analysis are heard at length. Paula and Donald are in the garage. The voice off tells that Donald has brought Paula's pictures of Richard's death and says he killed Typhus. She shoots Donald and searches his pockets. Marianne Faithfull sings in voice off.

In a park Paula and Inspector Aldrich talk. He says that she can leave Atlantic City if she wants to, for he has "received the order from Paris to close the whole affair provisionally." They discuss Paula's political involvements as a reporter for the weekly L'Express. Widmark is seen giving money to Dr. Ludwig's assistant, who says to him, "It's the last time." Paula meets two of Widmark's associates, Richard Nixon and Robert MacNamara, who say they enjoy all these assassinations. Intertitles show the word LIBERTÉ being shot up by machine-gun fire and the words LEFT, YEAR ZERO. Paula and Widmark stand in front of a green poster and simultaneously address monologues to the camera. So that each will have a "guarantee" against the other, each one writes a confession of murder, Paula saying that she killed Typhus and Widmark saying that he killed Politzer. Each reads the other's confession aloud. Now that she has "found out" about him, Widmark attempts to kill Paula, but David Goodis kills Widmark first with the silenced revolver. David proclaims that now, thanks to Paula, he can finish his novel. She fears that "fiction" will reveal the truth, which must not be known, so she kills David. Her voice, taped, is played from a dictaphone, as she questions her existence, her words, and her actions — "which escape from me, not only when I have finished, but before I have even started." We see Paula at night dictating into the dictaphone.

There is a cut to an exterior shot, showing a traffic light in the daytime. Standing by a toll booth, Paula recognizes journalist Philippe Labro, driving a car owned by a major French commercial radio station. He seems unsurprised when Paula says that she has killed two people, and he is glad to give her a ride. Over a shot of the paperback title — LEFT, YEAR ZERO, we hear Schumann's Fourth Symphony (a combination of image and sound which

Godard said connoted hope). Speaking as they are driving, Paula predicts many struggles in the years to come and fears being tired and giving up the struggle in advance. Philippe says that the right and the left comprise an "outdated equation" and will not change, because the left is "sentimental" and the right as "stupid as it is vicious." "How should it be?" asks Paula. Blue, red, and white letters present the word FIN.

22   DEUX OU TROIS CHOSES QUE JE SAIS D'ELLE

Production Companies:	Anouchka Films, Argos Films, Les Films du Carosse, Parc Film (Paris)
Co-Producer:	François Truffaut
Director:	Jean-Luc Godard
Screenplay:	Jean-Luc Godard
Based on	Articles, "La Prostitution dans les grands ensembles," by Catherine Vimenet, in *La Nouvel Observateur*, March 29 and May 10, 1966
Director of Photography:	Raoul Coutard
Process:	Techniscope, Eastmancolor
Camera Operators:	Jean Garcenot, Georges Liron
Sound:	René Levert
Traveling ("Perchman"?)	Robert Cambourakis
Assistant Directors:	Charles Bitsch, Isabel Pons, Robert Chevassu
Script Continuity:	Suzanne Schiffman
Production Managers:	Philippe Senné, Claude Miler
Production Assistant:	Marilou Parolini
Costumes:	Gitt Marrini, Dora Balabanow (clothes changes, etc.)
Hairdressing:	Renée Guidet
Makeup:	Jackie Reynal
Editing:	Françoise Collin, Chantal Delattre
Music:	Beethoven Quartet No. 16
Sound Mix:	Antoine Bonfanti
Cast:	Marina Vlady (Juliette Jeanson), Roger Monsoret (Robert Jeanson), Anny Dupery (Marianne), Jean Narboni (Roger, the friend), Raoul Lévy (John Bogus, the American), Jean-Luc Godard (Narrator, voice off), Christophe and Marie Bourseiller (Christophe and Solange Jeanson), Joseph Gehrard (Mr. Gérard), Helena Bielicic (Woman in bathtub), Robert Chevassu (Electricity meter reader), Yves Beneyton (Young man — longhaired client), Jean-Pierre Laverne (Author), Blandine Jeanson (Student), Claude Miller (Bouvard), Jean-Patrick Lebel (Pécuchet), Juliet Berto (Woman talking to Robert in cafe), Anna Manga (Woman in basement), Banjamin Rosette (Man in basement), Helene Scott: (Woman playing pinball)
Filmed:	In the Paris region, August 8-September 8, 1966
English-Language Release Title:	*Two or Three Things I Know about Her*
Running Time:	95 minutes

Released:
Paris:	March 17, 1967 (Political Science Night, Théâtre des Champs-Elysées); general release, March 18, 1967 (Marbeuf, La Marotte, Studio Medicis le Dragon — 88,845 tickets sold in first-run Paris theaters).
England:	London Film Festival, November 24, 1967
Italy:	Bergamo Festival, Fall 1968
USA-New York:	New York Film Festival, September 25, 1968
Prizes:	Marilyn Monroe Prize, 1967

Distribution:
France:	U.G.C., C.F.D.C. Films, Sirius (Argos-Foreign Sales)
Italy:	Cormons
USA:	New Yorker Films

Synopsis

Deux ou trois choses que je sais d'elle presents a series of episodes in one day in the life of Juliette Jeanson. She is a working class housewife who lives in one of the high rise apartment complexes in suburban Paris and who resorts to occasional prostitution to "get along," that is, to maintain a middle class life-style for her family. Her character is never developed psychologically, and the film shows as much of the urban milieu as it does of her, usually with bright objects in primary colors in the mise en scene. The sound track is filled with a deafening barrage of traffic and construction noises. Godard's whispered commentary enters in voice off; his discussions of epistemology and ontology are heavily influenced by poet Francis Ponge. Close-ups of all or part of book titles from the paperback series, "Ideés" serve as Brechtian "footnotes" to the action, providing a sociopolitical interpretation of what we see.

On the porch of a high rise apartment, Marina Vlady stands as Godard presents her to us as an actress. Inside, the character Juliette quotes from "Madame *Express*" to her husband Robert and his friend Roger, as they listen to shortwave broadcasts about Johnson's bombing Hanoi. Robert praises his wife's ability to buy things—this radio and also an Austin car. Later, as Juliette and Robert are in their red, white, and blue bedroom, their small son comes in to relate a dream about two twins, North and South Vietnam, who turned into one person.

Somewhere else, as a woman is bathing, the Electricity Board meter reader walks right into her bathroom. Outside, the camera passes over building sites and a sign, AZUR. Inside, an older man looks out a window. In his rather empty apartment decorated with travel posters, a young man and a prostitute are in one room making love. Juliette comes and leaves off her crying young daughter in the older man's living room, where he is also caring for several other children. A stack of cans on a table indicate that he is paid in produce rather than cash.

Juliette walks through downtown Paris, looks at clothes in a department store, meets a woman friend in a bar, and is solicited there by a pimp. In the cafe, she and another woman leaf through magazines. The camera lingers on several extreme close-ups of swirling espresso coffee as Godard in voice off whispers philosophically about speech and the reality it does or does not express.

Juliette enters a sleazy hotel room with travel posters on the wall. She is with a young man with freckles, a client. The word "beauty" is filmed from the reverse side of a window as she tells in voice off how she feels about being a prostitute.

A woman in her forties, seen outdoors against the background of construction and apartment buildings, talks to the camera about how hard it is to find a job at her age.

At the beauty parlor, Juliette talks to her friend Marianne, the manicurist. Another employee, Paulette, a French-Algerian immigrant, addresses the camera about her interests and how she spends her time. Juliette and Marianne go to the garage where Robert works to pick up the Austin. The red car is shown entering the garage several times as the voice off questions how best to film a scene.

A French-Algerian boy is questioned by the voice off about his family. Marianne and Juliette meet an eccentric client, U.S. war correspondent John Bogus, who has them walk around his hotel suite with TWA flight bags over their heads while he takes their picture. When Bogus and Marianne go off to another room, Juliette sits and thinks about thought.

Sitting in a cafe waiting for Juliette, Robert talks to a young woman about sex. Somewhere else, two young men named after Flaubert's characters Bouvard and Pécuchet copy sentences out of stacks of paperback books and send out for food. In the cafe, Nobel Prize author Ivanov talks to a woman companion with pseudo-intellectual condescension. A black woman prostitute is seen with a client in a basement boiler room.

Juliette and Robert drive home and find their son sitting on the stairs. He reads aloud his theme, "Friendship," which tells his attitude toward girls. Juliette expresses dissatisfaction to Robert about their monotonous life. He operates his radio set. Behind their bed hangs a painting of an outlined female figure with fingers squeezing her neck. They read in bed and briefly discuss their relationship. We see in close-up the glowing tip of Juliette's cigarette, the title IDEÉS, and a zoom back from an array of consumer products in boxes arranged on the apartment complex's lawn.

23 "ANTICIPATION, OU L'AMOUR EN L'AN 2,000" in LE PLUS VIEUX MÉTIER DU MONDE

Producer: Joseph Berholz
Production Companies: Les Films Gibé, Francoriz (Paris); Rialto Films (Berlin);
                                         Rizzoli Films (Rome)

Director:	Jean-Luc Godard (other sketches by Franco Indovina, Mauro Bologni, Philippe de Broca, Michel Pfleghar, Claude Autant-Lara
Screenplay:	Jean-Luc Godard
Director of Photography:	Pierre Lhomme and Service de Recherches du Laboratoire L.T.C.
Process:	Eastmancolor, both positive and negative
Assistant Director:	Charles Bitsch
Production Manager:	André Cultei
Production Assistant:	Tonio Suné
Editing:	Agnès Guillemot
Music:	Michel Legrand
Cast:	Jacques Charrier (Male space traveler, John Demetrios), Anna Karina (Miss Conversation, Eléonor Roméovitch, called Natacha), Marilù Tolo (Miss Physical Love, Marlène), Jean-Pierre Léaud (Bellboy), Daniel Bart, Jean-Patrick Lebel
Filmed:	On location in Paris and at Orly Airport, November 1966
English-Language Release Title:	"Anticipation," *The Oldest Profession*
Running Time:	Whole film-original, 115 minutes; English version, 97 minutes. Godard sketch, approximately 20 minutes
Released:	
Paris:	April 21, 1967, in a program in Paris art houses called "Star Short Films"
England:	October 20, 1967
New York:	November 8, 1968
Distribution:	
France:	Athos
Italy:	Cineriz
England:	Miracle
USA:	Macmillan/Audio Brandon

Notes

English version dubbed. Godard's film was originally tinted different colors in different sequences, with full color only at the end. Released film did not do this; sketch seen as planned at Hyères Festival, 1967, and at the Trieste Science Film Festival.

Synopsis

John Demetrios, an alien military man from another planet who speaks in a choppy, mechanical way, disembarks at Orly. Immigration control consists of his having the palms of his hands scrutinized. He is taken to the airport hotel by a military escort. A prostitute, Marlène, dressed in Paco Rabanne metallic clothes, is given to him, but she is programmed just to make physical love and not to talk and she does not excite him. Demetrios protests over the phone and is sent another woman, dressed in bouffant, white, ultrafeminine clothes. This woman, Eléonor Roméovitch, just knows the sentimental words of love, does not undress, and never stops talking. Together this couple invent the kiss. In this way they can unite words and physical love and can make "love, conversation, and progress at the same time." Here the visual image turns to full color.

Godard's original intent was that some of the sequences be tinted, others be in negative, others bleached out, others have excessive contrast — so that there would often be an erasing of exact lines. Furthermore, some sequences were to be printed entirely in red, some in yellow, some in blue; each time the color of the sequence changed, the narrator would announce, "Coleur europeén", "Coleur soviétique," or "Coleur chinoise" (perhaps so that the various modes of love-making portrayed could also be viewed as a witty comment on larger cultural traditions, or sexual mores under capitalism and socialism). The first two attempts at love-making were to be printed in negative and the figure of the protagonist often blurred. This was to be Godard's first attempt to destroy or deconstruct the image itself. However, the laboratory did not follow instructions, and the general release print is uniformly beige, with only one color sequence at the end. The original version has been seen only at a few festivals and art houses but is not the version released in the United States. *See* 1967, Comolli, Entry No. 858; and 1972, Roud, Entry No. 1505.

24 LA CHINOISE, OU PLUTÔT À LA CHINOISE

Production Companies:	Productions de la Guéville, Parc Films, Simar Films, Anouchka Films, Athos Films
Director:	Jean-Luc Godard
Screenplay:	Jean-Luc Godard
Based on (probably):	Paul Nizan's *La Conspiration* (Paris: Gallimard, 1939)
Director of Photography:	Raoul Coutard
Process:	Eastmancolor
Screen Ratio:	1x1,66
Camera Operator:	Georges Liron
Sound:	René Levert
English Subtitles:	Mark Woodcock
Assistant Director:	Charles Bitsch
Production Manager:	Philippe Dussart
Editing:	Agnès Guillemot
Assistant Editors:	Delphone Desfons, Marguerite Renoir
Music:	Karl-Heinz Stockhausen; Schubert, Piano Sonata, Opus 120; Vivaldi
Cast:	Anne Wiazemsky (Véronique), Jean-Pierre Léaud (Guillaume), Michel Semeniako (Henri), Lex de Bruijn (Kirilov), Juliet Berto (Yvonne), Omar Diop (Omar), Francis Jeanson (Himself), Blandine Jeanson (Blandine), Elaine Giovagnoli

Filmed:	On locations in Paris and Nanterre, March 1967; in Antoine Bourseillier's apartment
English-Language Release Title:	*La Chinoise*
Running Time:	90 minutes
Released:	
Paris:	Avignon Festival, July 1967; general release, August 30, 1967 — 92,815 tickets sold at first-run Paris theaters
Venice:	1968 Festival
England:	London Film Festival, November 24, 1967
USA-New York:	April 3, 1968 (Kips Bay Theater)
Prizes:	Special Prize of Jury, Venice Film Festival, 1967
Distribution:	
France:	Athos
Italy:	Cormons
USA:	Leacock-Pennebaker Films

Synopsis

Visually *La Chinoise* is marked by its use of glaring primary colors, particularly red — emblematic of Maoist, antirevisionist communism; political slogans written on the walls and blackboards; precisely executed camera movements and/or compositions which indicate political shifts or positions within the student group; character types to represent specific political stances; and Brechtian-style skits acted by students, especially Véronique and Guillaume.

The major part of the film consists of the self-education and debates of five young people who are staying in a suburban apartment loaned to Véronique for the summer. The reject the *embourgeoisement* of the French Communist party and wish to learn new approaches to political action from the example of the Chinese cultural revolution. Guillaume introduces himself to the camera as an actor seeking a new form for political theater. Yvonne tells of her life on the farm (accompanied by shots of a farm) and of her occasional prostitution, which she still engages in. A black philosophy student, Omar, who is not actually a member of the group, lectures on some of the tenets of Maoism. His talk is accompanied visually by photos of political leaders, especially Lenin. Véronique discusses the revolutionary potential of students, their distance from the working class, and the need to shut down the university as the first step toward reorganizing education — which the Red Guard did in China. Accompanying her monologue are shots of the slums and the high rise apartments in Nanterre. Guillaume lectures on Méliès and Lumière, finding Méliès the more "Brechtian" of the two. Véronique enacts a skit on Vietnam; she plays a Vietnamese calling on Kosygin for help, only to find the latter has made a pact with the Esso tiger for "peace" in Vietnam. Kirilov presents himself as the anemic, dark-haired, darkly dressed artist. He lectures on art and literature; he erases the names of many writers, starting with Sartre, from a blackboard, and leaves the name of only one on the board, Brecht. The other member of the cell is Henri, a young scientist and the lover of Yvonne.

Véronique and Guillaume discuss the problem of "struggling on two fronts" in terms of her ability to listen to music and study at the same time, which he challenges. She retorts by saying she doesn't love him in order to make him see that one *can* love and work at the same time. The group strongly criticizes Henri as revisionist for advocating peaceful coexistence and for defending established Communist parties in the capitalist West, where, he says, violent insurrections and street fighting are not politically viable. In contrast to his position, the group votes to constitute itself as a terrorist cell. They expel Henri. In sequences intercut with the group conference, we see Henri being interviewed at home, while eating breakfast, about his reactions to his expulsion.

In a lengthy shot-sequence, filmed in a moving train, Véronique discusses terrorism with her professor, Francis Jeanson. She is in the left of the frame, he in the right, and the French landscape flashes by in the background. During the Algerian war, in real life, Jeanson had defended the terrorists' bombing Parisian cafes. Now he describes his cultural political work doing theater in the provinces, and he tries to dissuade the fictional Véronique from terrorism.

Back at the apartment, Kirilov has a revolver and says he will commit suicide if he cannot use it politically. But the group draws lots and chooses Véronique. She is to assassinate the Soviet cultural minister who has come to inaugurate new buildings at the University of Nanterre. The nihilist Kirilov commits suicide. Véronique is shown being driven on a bright sunny day to a suburban hotel where the Soviet cultural minister is staying. After coming out, she decides she's read the room number incorrectly and killed the wrong man. She comes back again after doing the job correctly, and she and her male companion drive off.

In various symbolic sequences, we see Guillaume's efforts to create a political street theater. Véronique's friends, two women, come back to their apartment and clean up the walls. Véronique goes inside from the porch, closes the shutters, and declares in voice off, "I thought I'd made a great stride forward, but I've discovered that, in fact, I just made the first timid steps in a long march."

25 "CAMÉRA-OEIL" in LOIN DU VIÊT-NAM

Organizers:	Jacqueline Mappiel, Andréa Haran
Production Company:	Groupe S.L.O.N.
Directors:	Assembled by Chris Marker. Directors in whole film include Godard, Agnès Varda, Marker, William Klein, Alain Resnais, Claude Lelouch, and Joris Ivens. Varda's sketch is not in final version.

Screenplay:	Jean-Luc Godard — "Caméra-Oeil"
Photography:	Willy Kurant, Jean Boffety, Kieu Tham, Bernard Zitzerman, Théo Robiché, Denis Clairval, Alain Levant (Godard's sketch), Ghislan Cloquet
Process:	Eastmancolor
Sound:	Antoine Bonfanti, Harold Mauri
Reportage:	Michèle Ray, Roger Pic, Marceline Loridan, François Maspero, Chris Marker, Jacques Sternberg, Jean Lacoutre
Production Manager:	Andréa Haran
Production Assistants:	Pierre Grunstein, Alain Franchet, Didier Beaudet, Florence Malraux, Roger deMonestral, Marie-Louise Guinet
Still Photography:	Ethel Blum, Michèle Bouder
Animation:	Jean Larivière
Editing:	Jacques Meppiel
Assistant Editors:	Ragnard, Jean Ravel, Colette Leloup, Eric Pluet, Albert Jurgenson
Music:	Michel Fano, Michel Capdenat, Georges Aperghis
"Banc-titre":	Christian Quinson
Principal Collaborators:	(Listed in its entirety because of variations, especially in spelling, with other sources. From 1970, Roud, Entry No. 1505) Michèle Ray, Roger Pic, K.S. Karol, Marceline Loridan, François Maspero, Chris Marker, Jacques Sternberg, Jean Lacoutre, Willy Kurant, Jean Bosty, Kieu Tham, Denis Clairval, Ghislan Cloquet, Bernard Zitzerman, Alain Levant, Théo Robichet, Antoine Bonfanti, Harold Maury, Claire Grunstein, Alain Franchet, Didier Baudet, Florence Malraux, Marie-Louise Guinet, Roger de Menestrol, Ragnar, Jean Ravel. Colette Leloup, Eric Pluet, Albert Jurgenson, Ethel Blum, Michèle Bouder, Christian Quinson, Jean Larivière, Maurice Carrel, Bernard Fresson, Karen Blanquernon, Anne Bellec, Valerie Mayoux, Mrs. Ann (Norman) Morrison
Filmed:	In USA (demonstrations on Wall Street), Vietnam, Cuba, and France
English-Language Release Title:	*Far from Vietnam*
Running Time:	115 minutes (90 minutes in English version); Godard's sketch, 15 minutes
Released:	
Besançon:	Trade union showing, October 18, 1967
Paris:	December 13, 1967
Canada:	Montreal Film Festival, August 1967
England:	London Film Festival, November 29, 1967; general release, December 28, 1967
USA-New York:	Film Festival, October 1967; general release, June 6, 1968
Distribution:	
France:	Films 13
England:	Contemporary
Italy:	Audax
USA:	New Yorker Films

Notes

Film was finished a few days before it premiered at Montreal Film Festival. (1967, Ciment, Entry No. 849).

Film was disputed over and excluded from 1967 Venice Film Festival. (1967, Anon., *Times*, London, Entry No. 786)

Synopsis

Godard peers through the viewfinder of the camera and twiddles with the controls; the lights and the camera itself are aimed directly at the audience. Intercut are some of the masks from the political theater skits of *La Chinoise*, photos of Che's corpse, grainy newsreel images of military jets and bombings, scenes of striking French factory workers and demonstrations — these are images of the historical situation to which Godard will refer.

The sound track consists of Godard's monologue, some of which is paraphrased below:

"I'm a prisoner of the world power of Hollywood films and am struggling against the U.S. movie. To demonstrate war's bestiality, I thought of photographing a woman's nude body and then showing what the impact of bullets would do to it; but I had to abandon that project because it would have taken too much research. I'm full of ideas, but ideas aren't much.

"I don't know what one can do about Vietnam but I feel one ought to do something. That's why I bring a reference to Vietnam into every one of my films. Perhaps the best thing to do is to let Vietnam invade us, which also is, of course, difficult. I'm as isolated from Vietnam and the working class as the working class is isolated from Vietnam; both are in my films but never a part of filmic production.

"I am a filmmaker making a film. That's my job. At the same time, I'm also concerned about the war in Vietnam — that's also my job. I'm thinking out loud but talking to you, on screen, shooting a film but talking to you. I wanted to get these two things together — being concerned and making something out of that concern."

"I wanted to go to Vietnam to make a movie. I requested permission from the North Vietnamese government, and after a period of several months was told that the permission would not be granted because of my vague ideology. I agreed that such a film by me might be dangerous."

26 AMORE E RABBIA

Italian original version:	"L'Aller et retour des enfants prodigues: andate e ritorno dei figli prodighi" in *Vangelo 70*
French release: version:	"L'Amour" in *La Contestation*
Producer:	Carlo Lizzani
Production Companies:	Castoro Films (Rome); Anouchka Films (Paris)

Director:	Jean-Luc Godard (other episodes by Bernardo Bertolucci, Pier Paolo Pasolini, Carlo Lizzani, Marco Bellochio, Elda Tattoli
Screenplay:	Jean-Luc Godard
Director of	
Photography:	Alain Levant
Process:	Eastmancolor
Screen Ratio:	Techniscope
Sound:	Guy Villette
Assistant Director:	Charles Bitsch
Editing:	Agnès Guillemot
Music:	Giovani Fusco
Cast:	Christine Guého (She), Catherine Jourdon (Female witness), Nino Castelnuovo (He), Paolo Pozzesi (Male witness)
Filmed:	In 1967 on a roof garden in Paris
Running time:	26 minutes
Released:	
Berlin:	Festival, summer 1969, as *Amore e rabbia*
Paris:	June 1970, Le Marais Theater
England:	London Film Festival, November 24, 1967
Distribution:	
France:	Films Jacques Leitienne
Italy:	Italnoleggi

Notes

Valerio Zurline made a sketch released separately as the feature-length *Seduto alla sua destra*, which was replaced in *Vangelo 70* by Bellochio and Tattoli's sketch. Bellochio would not participate in a film with a title about the gospel, so the title was changed to *Amore e rabbia (Love and Rage)*.

Synopsis

On a flowery terrace of an old urban mansion, a couple discusses love and revolution. He is a revolutionary Arab; she, a bourgeois Jewess. Their two young chaperones discuss cinema, illusion and reality, and their friends' relationship. In this Franco-Italian production, the woman, Christine, or her blonde bridesmaid speak French; each of their phrases is responded to in Italian (occasionally with phrases duplicating each other) by the young man, Nino, or his brunette best man. The two witnesses do not let the lovers out of their sight and aid in breaking up the romance, so that the couple part, going back to their respective families.

"Godard describes the girl [sic] with very much the same chopped-up editing technique he used in *Une Femme mariée*. This affectionate little film strongly suggests the beauty and impossibility of love in a world where revolution is immanent." (1970, Marcorelles, Entry No. 1476)

See also 1967, C., L., No. 841; 1974, Collet, Entry No. 1833; 1970, Roud, Entry No. 1505.

27 LE WEEK-END

Production Companies:	Films Copernic, Comacico, Lira Films (France); Ascot-Cineraïd (Rome)
Director:	Jean-Luc Godard
Screenplay:	Jean-Luc Godard
Director of Photography:	Raoul Coutard
Process:	Eastmancolor
Sound:	René Levert
English Subtitles:	Sonja Mays Friedman
Assistant Director:	Claude Miler
Production Managers:	Ralph Baum, Philippe Senné
Editing:	Agnès Guillemot
Music:	Antoine Duhamel; Mozart, Piano Sonata, K. 576
Song:	"Allô, allô, tu m'entends?" by Guy Béart
Cast:	Mireille Darc (Corinne), Jean Yanne (Roland), Jean-Pierre Kalfon (F.L.S.O. Leader), Valérie Lagrange (His companion), Jean-Pierre Léaud (Saint-Just and man in phone booth), Yves Beneyton (F.L.S.O. Member), Paul Gégauff (Pianist), Daniel Pommereulle (Joseph Balsamo), Virginie Vignon (Marie-Madeleine), Yves Alfonso (Tom Thumb), Blandine Jeanson (EmilyBronte/young woman in farmyard), Ernest Menzer (Cook), Georges Staquet (Tractor driver), Juliet Berto (Woman in car crash/F.L.S.O. member), Anne Wiazemsky (Woman in farmyard/F.L.S.O. member), Jean Eustache (Hitchhiker), J.C. Guilbert (Tramp), Monsieur Jojot, Isabelle Pons, Michel Cournot (Man in farmyard), Laszlo Szabo (The Arab speaking for his black brother)
Filmed:	In the Paris area, September-October 1967
English-Language Release Title:	*Weekend*
Running Time:	95 minutes
Released:	
Venice:	28th Venice Film Festival, September, 1967
Paris:	December 29, 1967
England:	July 5, 1968
Berlin:	Summer 1969, Film Festival
USA-New York:	New York Film Festival, September 27, 1968; general release, September 30, 1968 (72nd Street Playhouse)
Distribution:	
France:	Athos
Italy:	Magna
England:	Connoisseur
USA:	Grove Press

Notes

Condemned by Legion of Decency in USA.

Synopsis

Intercut with the fable-like action are red, white, and blue intertitles which comment on the action in a self-reflective, political, or just humorous way. I shall indicate some of these in translation in brackets.

A bourgeois couple, Corinne and Roland, are entertaining a male friend in a Paris apartment. As Roland talks on the phone, Corinne and the friend wish Roland and her father would die in an auto accident. A high-angle shot shows a collision of a red and a blue car in the streets below; the owners fight viciously and the red car drives off. Roland tells *his* lover on the phone that he'd already tried to kill Corinne twice.

Corinne sits on a table in bra and pants, silhouetted against a window near which her lover or psychiatrist is sitting. She talks at length about a sexual experience. The music rises and periodically drowns out her words. [ANAL/YSIS]

While leaving their parking lot, Corrine and Roland fight with a small boy who was shooting arrows at their car. [SCENE FROM PARIS LIFE] They back into another car and then fight with the child's parents — weapons consist of red spray paint, tennis balls, and a shotgun.

A single, long, lateral tracking shot reveals the following: a colossal traffic jam on a country highway; a stalled traveling menagerie; our couple ignoring the carnage and passing all the cars; a multiple crackup with cars being towed away, blood on the road, and bodies strewn in the ditch.

In a small town, the couple and employees from an Esso gas station impassively witness a crash between a Triumph and a tractor and an ensuing argument, consisting primarily of class-based insults, between the farmer-driver and a bourgeios woman passenger from the Triumph. [SS/SS STRUGGLE/THE CLASS STRUGGLE] In her car the driver, a rich young man, lies dead, covered with ketchup-colored blood. The onlookers are shown in static poses, filmed in snapshot style. [FAUX/TOGRAPHE or FALSE/PHOTO]. The farmer and the woman embrace and walk away arm in arm.

During another traffic jam, hands come from behind and attack Corinne and Roland, who fight off their unseen attackers. The couple pick up two passengers, Marie-Madeleine and Joseph Balsamo, who force them at gunpoint to drive the opposite way. Joseph proclaims miraculous powers which he proves by having Corrine pull a rabbit from the dashboard, but he angers the couple by refusing to fulfill their crass dreams. Corinne grabs the gun from Marie-Madeleine; she insists Joseph prove his magic powers by changing wrecked cars in a field to sheep — which he does. [THE EXTERMINAT-ING ANGEL]

The couple's car is burnt in yet another multiple, bloody, body-strewn smashup. In a grassy field they encounter Saint-Just pacing and declaiming from a book; later they encounter the same person now in street clothes, in a roadside phone booth singing a message of love. As they try to steal his car, he fights them off. They walk past more wrecks and then meet two storybook characters — Emily Bronte and Tom Thumb. Emily discourses on a pebble, seen in huge close-up, and she is then burnt alive by our couple, who also talk about themselves being in a movie.

A Mozart piano concerto is played in a farmyard, the camera panning and tracking in several 380° circles from the vantage point of the piano to show us the peasant onlookers. The couple hitches a ride in the pianist's truck, and then Roland makes Corinne carry him piggyback. As they wait by the side of the road, he lets a tramp rape her. They miss several rides but finally get one in a garbage truck. The two garbagemen, an African and an Arab, eat sandwiches in front of the famished couple and deliver political speeches — each speaking for the other — about tribal primitivism, racism, and imperialism. [WORLD/3]

The couple arrive at their destination, Oinville. While Corinne bathes, they discuss their frustration at getting Corinne's mother to split the inheritance with them. [SCENE FROM LIFE IN THE PROVINCES] The mother returns from shopping, carrying a skinned rabbit. They kill her. We see a close-up of the rabbit on the ground sloshed with red paint (blood).

They burn up the mother's body in her car near a wrecked plane and then try to steal food from a family picnicking by the roadside. A group of young hippies with machine guns capture everyone and march them through a woods to their camp. There, by a lake, a rock combo beats out a drum rhythm, and dispersed members of the gang contact each other via shortwave radio, using code names such as *The Searchers, Battleship Potemkin, Gosta Berling,* and *Johnny Guitar.* The cannibal cooks prepare a captured woman for butchering by dropping raw eggs on her and putting a live fish between her thighs. [TOTEM AND TABOO]

Roland tries to escape and is shot. The butcher kills a goose and live pig, slitting its throat. The hippie leader declaims to drum music. In a shootout in a farmyard [ARIZONA JULES], a young hippie woman dies while reciting a poem. [DISCONTINUITY] Corinne is seen sitting next to the hippie leader munching on a bone that probably comes from Roland. [*END OF STORY/END OF CINEMA*]

28 LE GAI SAVOIR

Production Companies:	Originally O.R.T.F. (French Radio-Television), later Anouchka Films, Gambit, Bavaria Atelier (Munich)
Director:	Jean-Luc Godard
Screenplay:	Jean-Luc Godard
Based on:	Rousseau's *Emile* (loosely); title is the translation of Nietzsche's *Die Fröhliche Wissenschaft*

Director of	
Photography:	Jean Leclerc
Process:	Eastmancolor; shot in 35mm; released in U.S. in 35mm and 16mm
Editing:	Germaine Cohen
Music:	Revolutionary songs, especially Cuban
Cast:	Juliet Berto (Patricia Lumumba), Jean-Pierre Léaud (Emile Rousseau)
Filmed:	At the Joinville Studios, December 1967-January 1968; edited after June 1968
English-Language Release Title:	*Le Gai Savoir*
Running Time:	91 minutes
Released:	
Berlin:	Berlin Film Festival, June 28, 1969
Paris:	1969, Cinéma Nationale Populaire
USA-New York:	New York Film Festival, September 27, 1969; general release, June 5, 1970 (The New Yorker Theater)
England:	July 12, 1969
Distribution:	
Italy:	D.A.E.
England:	Kestrel Productions
USA:	Twyman

Notes

The O.R.T.F. commissioned this film but refused to show it and sold the rights back to Godard.

At the Berlin Film Festival, the critical reaction was "disastrous." (1969, Roud, Entry No. 1337).

French censors forbid the showing of the film in commercial cinemas or on TV.

Synopsis

A young man, Emile Rousseau, enters a dark area. A young woman, Patricia Lumumba, carrying a clear plastic umbrella, joins him. They carry on a metaphorical political discussion about politics and culture, especially in the context of French student life and Third World revolutions. They often describe each other in the third person. They seek to learn about language, television ("We're on TV, aren't we?"), a "reduced" society — in the Marcusian sense of one-dimensional, and the "disordered speech" that that society produces. Intercut with their discussion are shots of people on Paris streets; photos with handwritten words, often political ones, over them (red writing is used for revolutionary concepts); and inserts of book covers, photos of Vietnam atrocities, and portraits of political or historical figures. They must, the couple say, go back to the zero degree of cinema, to dissolve its sounds and images, to find its structure. After that, they will criticize themselves and find either rules of cinematic production or sure reference points.

Visually, these opening sequences base their interest on their formal patterning, with one character entering right or left and sitting in the foreground and the next time, the other person repeating the same gesture or, more likely, its mirror opposite with some slight variation. Juliet Berto, playing Patricia, characteristically twiddles her hair or puts her fingers near her mouth. After the couple leave their first session together, we see photos of Che, Mao, and the Vietnamese, and we hear Cuban revolutionary songs. And w as the couple returns, a whispered voice off presents, in highly poetic and metaphoric terms, the concept of cultural revolution coming from the "East." The two young people sitting in the darkened room discuss the relation between sexual and political repression, noting especially the ways this issue was raised in May 1968. Godard also attacks the traditional radical press, such as *L'Humanité*, for which Patricia poses for lingerie ads. The whispered voice off advises the two to learn about, "1. Theory, strategy, content, hence discourse; 2. Form, hence grammar."

Patricia and Emile, in voice off, give a small boy in a red shirt, filmed against a blue background, a word association test. The boy associates "heaven" with "God," "Mamma" with "character," "Lumière" with "cinema," and "magician" with "Communist." He gives no response to "solution," "sexual," "mathematics," "loneliness," or "pleasure," among other words. We then see an old man being interviewed in much the same way. He fears the tape recorder, does not respond much to questions about sexuality ("Freud" means "sex" to him), discusses his craft — saddlemaker, and associates "nice" with "country." He associates "colonialism" with the old French colonies and cannot respond to many terms, especially political ones. The two interviews illustrate what concepts are repressed or distorted through the mechanisms of bourgeois ideology.

The next session shows the protagonists watching television images and discussing the need to refuse the "self-evident truths" and "enslaved" sounds and images emanating from the bourgeois cultural apparatus. "What is a false image? A false sound? . . . It is DeGaulle talking to the students, Johnson talking to the North Vietnamese." Particularly blacks and Third World countries have had their images "censored, prostituted, misled, fragmented, and tortured."

Patricia sits on a stool and reads a children's dictionary, noting how the words which illustrate the letters of the alphabet reinforce the bourgeois order and also noting which words are missing — "the real words." $M =$ "mandolin," "more," "medal," but "merde" is not there. $A =$ "auto," not "art." $S =$ "Saturday" or "soap," not "sex" or "strike." P is not illustrated by "psychoanalysis" or "police." C is not equated with "culture" or "capitalism" or "class." F = "family" and "food," but not "fascism." And to illustrate "food," "DeGaulle's flunkies give this sentence, 'There's food on the table.' But what about the children in Biafra?" Better than words, images can be laid on top of each other to reveal and bring out contradictions. "Not representation; presentation. Not spectacle; struggle."

With their backs to us, the youths discuss what is *not* transmitted by film and television and how the educational and communications apparatus, technology, and sexuality have all been transformed into "instruments of repression." Each character then stands behind the other and lends the other his/her voice; in the first instance, the man is the "mask" for the woman; in the second, she assumes his militant role and surprises the police. Dressed in a fancy antebellum outfit, Patricia reads an unintelligible text that talks about women's "nature" almost in terms of a gothic romance. Finally, to complete a parallel between sexism and racism, in a sequence called IMPERIALIST FILM — BLACK FRANCE, the young man squeezes the young woman's neck as he tries to get her to hum his note while she insists on singing her scale.

A blacked-out sequence demonstrates the confused politics of the May events. We hear overlaid sounds of Godard's whispered commentary, "documentary" sounds — perhaps taped from the radio or TV — of speeches made by students and bureaucrats during May-June 1968, and other confused sounds. An image of a sleepy woman depicts the boredom rhetoric induces, even if it is presenting correct ideas. A cartoon with *le gai savoir* written over it shows children (= the students?) on a swing hung from a tree. They swing so high that they go all the way over the branch. The whispered voice off asserts that students must join workers.

Before the two youths leave the darkened studio, they discuss other film directors' potential ability to make political films. Both "method and sentiment" are needed to combine images and sounds correctly. Godard whispers, "This is not the film that should be made, but if a film is to be made, it must follow some of the paths shown here."

29 CINÉTRACTS

Producer:	Paid for by filmmaker
Director:	Jean-Luc Godard (Chris Marker and Alain Resnais also made some cinétracts)
Director of Photography:	Jean-Luc Godard
Process:	One 100-foot reel of black-and-white 16mm film
Editing:	Film edited in camera
Filmed:	Possibly in Nanterre in March during the uprisings there; possibly in Paris during the events of May-June 1968
Running time:	3 minutes each

Distribution:
France:	Circulated in student assemblies, factories on strike and political action committees in May 1968
England:	The Other Cinema

Notes

Each *cinétract* was to be shot in one day and cost/sell for 50 F. Films were unsigned but Godard's are recognizable because they often consisted of writing over an image, with some of the same frames being repeated in *Le Gai Savoir*.

Synopsis

In May 1968 *cinétracts* provided a kind of alternate "information service" and an alternate aesthetic, formed in reaction to the mass media and the commercial cinema. To make *cinétracts* the filmmakers would often film a written message or a photo or some graffiti that appeared on the walls of Paris in those months. Godard's messages in his *cinétracts* included comments on the relations between aesthetics and politics, between sexual/personal liberation and political liberation (these are not concerns of the French Communist Party). Freud, Marx, Brecht, Mao, Cuban revolutionary songs, and references to the Chinese cultural revolution all entered Godard's citations as conceptual and political "equals" in those years.

All the images from one *cinétract*, which seems to be Godard's because the handwriting over the image resembles his, appear in a series of photographs in *Art and Confrontation* (1968, Godard, Entry No. 2258). The film consists of ads and photos with words written across them, the sum of the words forming a political comment, perhaps taken from the graffiti that covered Paris at the time. Below I indicate which words are written over which images in the succession in which they appear.

Writing	*Photograph*
The kings (written three times)	Blank frame
The kings (written eight times)	Cartoon of man flirting with woman in a bar
of imperialism	Ad of man in scuba diving outfit with woman kneeling by him; caption — "a real man's life."
have transformed	Aggressive male figure from Marvel comics
technological progress	Written across woman's bra in lingerie ad
and sexuality	Cover of "Kwai" comics, "for adults," showing U.S. marine running, machine gun blazing
into an instrument	Two pin-ups of nude women
of repression	Ad for Schick razors with razor and blades in foreground, woman nuzzling barechested man in background; caption — "Success doesn't come just from shaving with a Schick injector, but it helps. . . .

Below are further descriptions of specific *cinétracts* by Godard, drawn from 1976, Segal, Entry No. 1976, which includes photographs of stills.

In one tract, a text by DeGaulle is reproduced in intertitles, which are intercut with photos of student encounters with the police, photos that expose DeGaulle's words as a lie. There are also visual parallels and contradictions between the photos and the placement of the words. The text, written in Godard's handwriting in lower case, would cumulatively read as follows (only a few words are in each intertitle):

"There is a solution. It is participation that changes people's condition in this milieu of modern civilization . . . The Republic and liberty will be assured (title: *will be aSSured*) and progress, independence, and peace won. The Republic must live, and France must live."

In another tract, numbered "10," intertitles present the words *reflect* or *idem*, plus an indication of the number of seconds the next shot will last (from eight to twelve seconds). Example: *reflect/12 seconds*. The shots alternating with the intertitles are of photos, often with writing over them, which present a complex ideological message — e.g., book covers juxtaposed and also written over. The last shot shows a cover of *L'Express* with a photo of a U.S. soldier wounded in Vietnam, eyes covered with bandages. Over the photo is written *reflect everything*, and this image lasts till the end of the reel.

30 UN FILM COMME LES AUTRES

Director:	Dziga-Vertov group
Process:	16mm Ektachrome; black and white
Cast:	Militant students from Nanterre and workers from Renault auto factory
Filmed:	In Flins, July 1968, in a grassy field "at the foot of the H.L.M. in Flins." (1970, Collet, Entry No. 1425) Footage by Godard from May 1968 demonstrations in Paris.
English-Language Release Title:	*A Film like Any Other*
Running Time:	110 minutes
Released: USA-New York:	Film Festival, December 29, 1968
Distribution: USA:	Leacock-Pennebaker

Notes:

English release version has two magnetic sound tapes (French and English) to be played along with the visual track. The English translation is in one voice so both the long conversation and the interruption of other cited texts cannot be distinguished on it.

Synopsis

The visual track of this film consists of color footage of a small group of young adults sitting in a grassy field and conversing on a sunny summer day. There is a single tall building in the background, and the camera directs our attention to the grass, people's hands and legs, and people listening — but we do not see the face of the person talking.

Intercut with this conversation is documentary black and white footage from the May demonstrations — cars burning, youths fighting with the police, massed thousands marching down the boulevards, Daniel Cohn-Bendit addressing crowds, students mimeographing leaflets, and striking workers. These images are rarely accompanied by "documentary" sounds from the events filmed.

The major aspect of the film's construction, "struggle" on the sound track, is lost in the univoice English translation (see credits), since the viewer is expected to listen to the flow of conversation among a small group of people whose faces are not seen talking but each of whom has a certain point of view and who should be recognizable by voice. The members of the group discuss their political goals, sometimes disagree, and strive to evaluate the revolutionary events of the month before. Topics they take up include the role of the Communist Party as active collaborator with the government in putting down revolution, new forms of rank and file labor organization, the revolutionary role of students, and the notion of the society of the spectacle. No single person's point of view is emphasized as "right" or most important, and the whole conversation flows spontaneously — at a heightened level of awareness, mutual support, and politicization.

Godard had intended the sound track to be the major locus of "struggle" in the film, but this is entirely lost in the univoice English version. According to Baconnier (1969, Entry No. 1263), another line of commentary in the film "recapitulates, explains, sometimes carries on a dialogue, sometimes preaches, or offers diverse citations — from Mao to Homer, Marx to Shakespeare. Sometimes the two sound bands run together, so that nothing is clearly audible. . . ."

The conflict between the two kinds of images (a pastoral scene accompanied by verbal analysis and frenetic documentary footage deprived of its accompanying "agitated" documentary sound) and the two sound bands was supposed to reflect the political conflict between the spontaneous action of the May events and political analysis. At this point in his careeer, Godard both prized spontaneous rebellion against established authority and wanted some way to grow from it. He used the two kinds of images and the sound tracks to portray the struggle between idealism and scientific theory, seeking that kind of revolutionary theory that could have turned the 1968 civil rebellion into a revolution.

31 ONE PLUS ONE

Producers:	Ian Quarrier, Michael Pierson
Executive Producer:	Eleni Collard
Production Company:	Cupid Production, Ltd.
Director:	Jean-Luc Godard
Screenplay:	Jean-Luc Godard
Director of Photography:	Anthony Richmond
Process:	Eastmancolor; released in 16mm and 35mm versions, shot in 35mm.
Camera Operator:	Colin Corby
Sound:	Arthur Bradburn and Derek Ball
Assistant Directors:	Tim Van Rellim and John Stoneman
Production Managers:	Clive Freedman, Paul de Burgh
Editing:	Ken Rowles, Agnès Guillemot
Music:	Mick Jagger and Keith Richard
Song:	"Sympathy for the Devil"
Cast:	Rolling Stones (Mick Jagger, Keith Richard, Brian Jones, Charlie Watts, Bill Wyman), Anne Wiazemsky (Eve Democracy), Ian Quarrier (Fascist porno book seller), Frankie Dymon, Jr. (Himself), Bernard Boston (Himself), Sean Lynch (Narrator), Danny Daniels, Clifton Jones (Black power militant), Ilario Pedro, Roy Stewart, Limbert Spencer, Tommy Ansar, Michael McKay, Rudi Patterson, Mark Matthew, Karl Lewis, Niké Arrighi, Françoise Pascal, Joanna David, Monica Walters, Glenna Forster-Jones, Elizabeth Long, Jeanette Wild, Harry Douglas, Colin Cunningham, Graham Peet, Matthew Knox, Barbara Coleridge
Filmed:	In London, Olympic Recording Studios, Barnes; Lombard Wharf near Fulham R.R. Bridge, Lombard Row, Battersea; and Cambert Sands, Sussex — in June and August 1968, with interruptions
English-language Release Title:	*One Plus One, Sympathy for the Devil*
Released:	
Berlin:	Film Festival
Paris:	May 7, 1969
London:	Film Festival, November 30, 1968
USA-New York:	April 26, 1970 (Murray Hill)
Distribution:	
England:	Connoisseur
France:	Images Distribution
USA:	New Line Cinema

Notes

Godard shot the Stones sequences for three days in June, producing two and a half hours of rushes. He seemed to have abandoned the film but came back to England the third week in July and did location shooting for the Black Power, book store, and Eve Democracy sequences.

Between *Weekend* and *Tout va bien*, *One Plus One* was the only Godard film to have regular commercial distribution in France.

Ian Quarrier added the completed song at the end of the film and changed the title. Godard punched him in the nose at the premier in London and disowned the *Sympathy for the Devil* version of the film. In its New York opening, both versions ran, on alternate nights.

The film was entered in but rejected from the Rio and Edinburgh Festivals. Brazil ruled out all "revolutionary" films, and Godard and the États Généraux unsuccessfully tried to get other directors to boycott the Rio Festival. See 1968, Anon., London *Times* article, Entry No. 1018; and 1969, Moskowitz, Entry No. 1330.

Synopsis

One Plus One, made in ten eight-minute shot-sequences, has five sequences showing the Rolling Stones in their recording studio. These alternate with other, symbolic sequences. Occasional visual inserts intrude, showing a woman painting political slogans outdoors, as well as audio inserts of a "novel" being read aloud. In the Stones sequences the camera sweeps in fluid, beautifully composed, 360° takes around the studio. Mick Jagger sits with his guitar and sings again and again each phrase of "Sympathy for the Devil." The rest of the musicians sit in separate recording booths with headsets, absorbed in their work as they listen to and feed into the 16-track sound system. We see onlookers, technicians, and workers, some standing unconcerned behind a plywood partition.

Two sequences filmed in an automobile junkyard in Battersea near the Fullham railway bridge over the Thames show Black Power militants reading from black authors and enacting symbolic situations with white women and with guns. In the first of these sequences, entitled "Outside," one man sits in a wheelbarrow reading LeRoi Jones' *Blues People*. The camera swings 90° to show two men on a car with a tape recorder, discussing how the genocide of native American Indians has parallels with the situation of blacks. The camera tracks to the other end of the yard, passing one militant reading from Eldridge Cleaver's *Soul on Ice* about interracial sexual relations. A red Mini-car enters the yard, and two young women and a girl dressed in long white shifts or nightgowns are forced out at gunpoint. The women are taken off to be executed by the bridge, where we see a crane marked Rapier and a power station putting out filthy smoke. The camera tracks back to the man with the tape recorder.

In a later sequence in the same location, entitled "Inside," a man addressing the camera talks about love, patience, brotherhood, and nonviolence.

The women's bloodied bodies are left strewn over the cars. Two black women reporters interview and tape the responses of one man who gives long militant answers to their questions. The camera swings in a 90° pan from that interview to men tossing rifles hand-to-hand from left to right while reciting slogans such as, "Up against the wall, mother fucker." The last man piles the guns on the bodies of two of the white women; when the women are covered, he removes the guns one by one and the men toss them back down the line right to left. Off screen we hear random rounds of firing.

In a contrasting sequence, entitled "alL abOut eVE," Anne Wiazemsky as Eve Democracy moves enigmatically about a leafy green forest. She wears a white shirtwaist dress with a full skirt and a flowered yoke. On a telephone, there in the forest, she tries to phone Lumumba, but gets no answer. A group parodying a TV interview team, especially one male reporter with a microphone, pursue her and ask her a series of long, leading questions, usually in cliché phrasing, about the relation of culture to revolution. The cameraman scrambles about, cables are juggled, and the interviewer-director flips the pages of his notebook. Questions asked include: "The U.S., in fighting Communism abroad, is creating Communism in our own society? America really wants the Vietnam war and its coverage by television? The only way to become a revolutionary intellectual is to cease being an intellectual?" The woman answers only, "Yes" or "No," sometimes with prompting.

In a central sequence, "Heart of the Occident," an owner of a pornographic bookstore, played by the film's producer, Ian Quarrier, stands at his shop reading extracts from *Mein Kampf* aloud, especially about the triumph of individualism. Displayed are many cheap novels, scandal sheets, a few film magazines, and scores of sex magazines, the covers of which represent images of sadism, perversion, war, crime, fascism, and violence. The camera passes in lateral pans across these. Below the magazines on display are boxes labeled with titles such as PICTURE ROMANCE, THRILLER, and WESTERN (= major film genres, too). The camera swings in pendulum fashion back and forth from Quarrier to two long-haired prisoners, possibly Jewish, whom all the customers slap, even a little girl, in lieu of paying Quarrier. As they enter, the customers also give Quarrier the raised hand of the Nazi salute. The young hippie prisoners' responses to each slap is to shout revolutionary slogans such as "Vive Che," "Victory to the NLF," and "Long live Mao." The camera moves in on them as they gaze at us, breaking the rhythm of the lateral pans.

At various points in the film we see briefly Eve Democracy painting protest slogans on the walls, cars, bridges, and billboards of London, as well as on the glass windows of the Hilton, where, in fact, Wiazemsky and Godard were staying. The slogans include: FREUDEMOCRACY, CINEMARXIST, FBI + CIA = TWA + PANAM, $\frac{MAO}{R}$, *soVietCong*, and

Sight anD Sound. Furthermore, intermittantly on the sound track we hear the text of a novel which is a cross between pornography and a fascist adventure story, with characters who are figures in bourgeois news, such as Pope Paul, Nixon, Brezhnev, John Birch, and Regis Debray. (Sample: "We have ways of taking care of nosey detectives," sneered General Westmoreland.) This "novel" is read in an expressionless, staccato voice by a Bolivian revolutionary hiding out in a London lavatory waiting for "Uncle Mao's yellow submarine" to collect him.

The last two intertitles are "Changes in a Society" (the word ONE is emphasized in the original French) and "Under the Stones, the Beach" (with the words USSR and ONE emphasized in the original). In this sequence, Eve Democracy is pursued by armed blacks and gunned down on the beach. The cast and production crew appear, Godard runs out to pour artificial blood on Wiazemsky's white gown, and her body is hoisted on a camera crane up over the beach. The blue sky is in the background; a red flag and a black flag on either side of her flap in the brisk wind blowing in from the sea. The camera on the crane swings free, first right, then left.

At the end of Godard's version of this film, the screen goes black, the song is never finished, the sound fumbles, and we hear Godard's voice saying that he is fed up and wants to go home. Quarrier's version freezes the last images and dubs in the completed version of "Sympathy for the Devil."

32 BRITISH SOUNDS

Producers:	Irving Teitelbaum, Kenith Trodd
Production Company:	Kestrel Productions for London Weekend Television
Director:	Jean-Luc Godard along with Jean-Henri Roger in the name of the Dziga Vertov Group
Screenplay:	Jean-Luc Godard
Researcher:	Mo Teitelbaum
Director of Photography:	Charles Stewart
Process:	Eastmancolor; filmed and released in 16mm only
Sound:	Fred Sharp
Editing:	Elizabeth Kozmian
Cast:	Production line of MG sports car, British Motor Co., Cowley, Oxford; students from Oxford; students from Essex; feminist from *Black Dwarf* paper (narration); a group of militant workers from the Dagenham area
Filmed:	February, 1969
English-Language Release Title:	*British Sounds* (U.S.: *See You at Mao*)
Running Time:	52 minutes
Distribution:	
England:	The Other Cinema
USA:	Grove Press

Notes

The film was commissioned in 1968 by London Weekend Television; it was never shown on TV, but a panel on the program *Aquarius*, early in 1970, "explained" and discredited the film. The Other Cinema premiered it after buying it from Kestrel Productions.

Godard earned $4,000 for this film.

Synopsis

Godard constructed this film about Britain in six sequences, all of which uses a simple image track — there are mostly long shot sequences with simple camera movement or a static camera. As the title indicates, the sound track carries the complex political thought and the images serve as symbols or emblems of that thought.

Sequence One: Image: A lateral ten-minute tracking shot gives a documentary view of workers on the assembly line making MGs at the "model" British Motor Corporation plant in Oxford. Ambient noise seems irritatingly loud; Godard actually used two noise tracks — one synchronous of the men's voices, hammering, and machines, and another harsher and louder track of machine noise. Two voices off intermittently give political messages. A man reads from the Communist *Manifesto* about the effects of wage labor under capitalism, and a little girl is tutored to repeat the important dates and events in the history of Britain's class struggle.

Sequence Two: A nude woman is shown in three shots — walking up and down stairs in her apartment, talking on a telephone, and standing. This last shot is held in extreme close-up for a seemingly long time, showing the woman's pubic area, thighs, and stomach. In voice off, a woman reads a feminist text analyzing women's history, sexuality, work, and relation to the class struggle. A man's voice occasionally interrupts to ask how to pose questions about women's exploitation.

Sequence Three: Image: A middle class man on a television monitor, in sepia tones, gives what seems to be a parody of a news broadcast. Intercut are occasional shots of isolated workers going about their tasks. Sound: The newscaster gives a speech in synchronized sound, scoring dishonest and lazy workers, foreigners, and "colored people" and praising U.S. involvement in Vietnam. The workers have no voice on the sound track, but at the end we do hear voice off whispers saying, "Unite," and "Strike," possibly from studio technicians.

Sequence Four: "Workers' Sounds." Godard considered this the central or most admirable group in the film: a group of Trotskyist workers gathered around a table at an apartment speak about their job conditions, especially the speed-ups. The camera pans about the room and does not reveal the face of the speaker at any given moment until it reaches the face of the young man who is discussing the need to form a revolutionary party to combat capitalism. The little girl in voice off is occasionally heard reciting her working class history. Intertitles read FORd USa; A GOOD COMRADE; and MORE — the latter two titles in red. The girl's voice declares, "To break with the Hollywood system induces a radical change of aesthetics."

Sequence Five: "Students' Sounds." A group of radical Essex University students make posters and rewrite Beatles' lyrics; e.g., "You say Nixon, I say Mao." They are heard in synchronized sound. The voice off analyzes how to create images and sounds that will oppose capitalist images and sounds: "Self-evident truths belong to bourgeois philosophy. Images do not speak for themselves. There is only a pattern of contradictions permeating society. Film needs a correct line to go through and beyond this."

Sequence Six: "Sound of the Revolution." A hand covered with blood (Godard's hand?) moves slowly across mud and snow covered ground to grasp a red flag lying there. Red covers the screen. Fists burst through paper Union Jacks. A hand waves a red flag, and then the flag is seen waving. The sound track contains the following modes of political discourse: revolutionary songs from many countries; united voices saying, "Solidarity"; the statement, "The bourgeoisie created a world in its image. Comrades, let us destroy that image"; and united voices chanting the line from *Marat-Sade*, "We want a revolution now." At this point the film flashes the final title across the screen, "There's no end to the class struggle."

33 PRAVDA

Producer:	Claude Nedjar
Production Company:	Centre Européen Cinéma-Radio-Télévision — for German TV. A documentary section of the Czech Cinematographic Institute paid for the shooting.
Directors:	Dziga Vertov Group — Jean-Luc Godard, Jean-Henri Roger, Paul Burron, Jean-Pierre Gorin
Screenplay:	Jean-Luc Godard
Based on	Brecht's *Me-ti*, writings of Mao Tse-tung
Process:	16mm, Agfa-Gevart color
Editing:	Jean-Luc Godard
Cast:	Godard's voice - Vladimir (Lenin), Woman's voice - Rosa (Luxemburg)
Filmed:	In Czechoslovakia clandestinely, off Czech television and in and around Prague, March 1969
English-Language Release Title:	*Pravda*
Running Time:	58 minutes
Distribution:	
England:	The Other Cinema
USA:	Grove Press

Note: There was a political shift in the Dziga Vertov group during the making of the film, with Roger dropping out and Gorin taking a greater role as Godard's coworker between the shooting and editing of the film.

Grove Press paid $6,000 for U.S. rights.

Released: Shown privately to militants. July 1972, *Cahiers du cinéma* workshop, Avignon. In April 1971, Godard visited European capitals and provincial French film societies to show the Dziga Vertov Group films, which had no distributors. (1971, Sery, Entry No. 1617)

Synopsis

In *Pravda* we see a series of images "seized" clandestinely in Czechoslovakia. In the first section of the film, these are presented as the "concrete situation" in Czechoslovakia, and are described by the voices off — Vladimir and Rosa. In the second section, the two voices paraphrase Mao to analyze the internal causes of the Communist "unreality" in Czechoslovakia and to expose the contradictions there, namely "Occidentalism and revisionism in practice." Third, as the voices off try to elaborate a "just" sound track to put over the "false" image track, they consider in depth the following topics: the role of the cadres in maintaining the revolution, the reeducation of intellectuals, the peasantry (a tale is cited in its entirety from Brecht's *Me-ti*), the army, the dictatorship of the proletariat. These are presented as the major Marxist-Leninist strategies for fighting revisionism. In concluding the film, the voices off summarize how to arrive at an adequate theory, again following Mao; theory must come through social practice, struggle for production, the class struggle, and scientific experimentation.

A limited number of symbolic images are edited together in different combinations, according to the topics analyzed on the sound track. The following list of images are grouped according to the political concept they are associated with and not according to their order of appearance.

Concept: capitalism in Czechoslovakia; U.S., Western European, and USSR economic imperialism. Images: Hertz, "Fly," and Honeywell billboards, neon signs; toy guns and model U.S. jet planes; slot machines (= USSR manipulation of Czech currency); tourist hotel; "Paris" movie theater; black limousine.

Concept: daily life, analyzed politically. Images: old people walking down the street, tiny apartment room, fruit vendor, children playing ball in a railroad yard, a beach near large apartment complexes.

Concept: sex and glamour peddled by U.S.-type consumerism; in general, consumerism is analyzed as a strategy for buying off worker discontent over not having control over production and political life. Images: women's clothes and jewelry ads, "Mr. Muscle" poster, *Angelika* film poster, woman newscaster said to be wearing cashmere sweater, worker carrying photo of naked woman, a wedding, still of a nude woman from *Loves of a Blonde*, a man in a motorcycle helmet looking in a display window at "today's program," which is advertised by photos of nude women.

Concept: production, the working class, or the means of production, organization of production (especially Taylorism). Images: factories, men in factories, men at lathes, steel being smelted, long-haired worker digging a ditch, women weavers, secretaries in an office.

Concept: the peasantry. Images: cherry trees not belonging to anyone, haying, farmer on a wagon, small country store, tractors, workers in fields.

Concept: student life. Images: students dancing, fenced-in schoolyards, student uprisings, Russian soldiers walking past students sitting on steps — possibly at the university.

Concept: the reeducation of the intellectuals, the proletariat's seeking to recapture control of culture and intellectual life. Image: adult students in a classroom.

Concept: the Russian presence in Czechoslovakia. Images: Russian tanks, missiles, plane in a field, soldiers on the street.

Concept: Brezshnev and Kosygin. Image: cartoon of two crows — "two crows who took themselves to be nightingales."

Concept: militant, authentic communism. Images: red rose held by a child, red tram going left, red car facing left, car with red flag, underexposed shots of a student meeting, historical film shown on television about WW II militants in Resistance, student uprisings, truck going left, red frames, posters of Che and Lenin and Vietnam, gun tinted red.

Concept: revisionism, communism that has fallen back into capitalist ways. Images: rose trampled in mud, tram car going left and then right, red car facing right, TV image of workers' council, photos and TV images of Czech political leaders.

Concept: film production. Images: neon Agfa sign, camera person with red flag over face, color test strip from laboratory.

34 VENT D'EST

Producer:	Georges de Beauregard, Gianni Barcelloni, and Ettore Rohoch
Production Companies:	CCC (Berlin), Polifilm (Rome), Anouchka, Film Kunst (Berlin)
Director:	Dziga-Vertov Group
Screenplay:	Jean-Luc Godard, Daniel Cohn-Bendit, Jean-Pierre Gorin, Gianni Barcelloni, Sergio Bazzini
Director of Photography:	Mario Vulpiani
Process:	16mm, Eastmancolor 7254; also 35mm blow-up
Sound:	Antonio Ventura, Carlo Diotalevi

Costumes:	Lina Nerli Tavani
Editing:	Jean-Pierre Gorin, Enzo Micarelli
Production Assistants:	Isabelle Pons, Gianni Amico
Cast:	Gian Maria Volonte (Cavalryman), Anne Wiazemsky (Woman in petticoat), Glauber Rocha (Himself), José Varela (Guide), George Gotz, Christiana Tullio Altan (Bourgeois woman), Fabio Garriba, Jean-Luc Godard and film crew (Themselves), Allen Midgette (Indian), Marco Ferreri, Paolo Pozzesi (Union representative), Vanessa Redgrave (Woman with movie camera), Daniel Cohn-Bendit (Himself)
Filmed:	On location in Italy, on the western town set at Elios Studios, and the sound stage at DePaoli's Studios, May or June 1969
English-Language Release Title:	*Wind from the East*
Running Time:	100 minutes
Distribution:	
France:	Cineriz (Angelo Rizzoli)
Italy:	D.A.E.
England:	The Other Cinema
USA:	New Line Cinema, Films Incorporated
Released:	
France:	Cannes, 1970. Shown in "Directors Fortnight," 1970, Roud, Entry No. 1505.
USA:	New York Film Festival, 1970

Notes

Gianni Barcelloni (Cineriz) originally offered $1 million in advance for an Italian western directed by Godard, written by Cohn-Bendit, and starring Volonte.

Lokin (1971, Entry No. 1595) says film caused an uproar at Cannes.

Shown privately in France to militants. July 1972, *Cahiers du cinéma* Seminar, Avignon.

Synopsis

Vent d'est uses symbolic characters taken from the western — a cavalryman (symbolically = the ruling class), a woman in a flounced petticoat and a young man (= bourgeois youth who ally themselves with the working class), an Indian (= Third World struggles), and an additional figure, a "union representative" (= sell-out unions and Communist parties). These figures execute very simple actions or stay in static poses. Godard uses them to symbolize some political concept or social role in an arbitrary, emblematic symbolism rather than a metonymic one.

Voices off, primarily women's voices, present a dense political discourse through various kinds of distanciated speech — such as past events told in the third person, fictional events related as history, and repeated phrases.

No single strategy offers the correct formula for action; the film presents political concepts and forces us to evaluate them if we are to "receive" the film at all.

Below are summarized the images and the corresponding concepts discussed on the sound track (Image — Concept). A long list of handwritten points, regularly repeated and added to in the intertitles, is here indicated in capital letters; and the summary below does not give the whole list but only the last point added.

A couple lies in a field, hands chained; woman wears white flounced petticoat — Woman tells about strike in her childhood and how union leader sold out.

Actors in woods put on makeup; Indian faces camera — How can we make revolutionary films in the light of Russian history? Dziga Vertov vs. Eisenstein.

1. THE STRIKE. In a procession through the woods, union representative and cavalry man abuse Indian, who escapes — The history of a strike is told, analyzing revisionism and the failure of unions.

Union representative reads from Waldek-Rochet — Union leaders talk and never do anything for workers.

WHAT IS TO BE DONE? Couple lying in the grass discuss what to do — Student politics reflect left-wing infantilism, as discussed by Lenin.

In idyllic country scene, union representative accompanies woman in pink dress with parasol — Stories are told of bourgeois women and Communist Party members aiding reactionary forces.

4. THE GENERAL ASSEMBLY. Members of the film company, participants of May 1968 in France, argue. Posters of Mao and Stalin. WANTED FOR MURDER. IT'S NOT A JUST IMAGE, IT'S JUST AN IMAGE. REPRE $$ ION, REPRE SS ION. A confused discussion of Stalinism and Socialist Realism leads to questioning how to create a "just image of repression."

6. THE ACTIVE STRIKE. Young man in profile — Letter written to friend about strike is read.

7. THE POLICE STATE. In a canyon, characters fight cavalryman on horseback with his saber drawn. The camera movement is intrusive. DEFEAT/PROVOCATION. Two men are shown hanged, upside down, in the woods — The proletariat's enemies and its forms of resistance are the same across national lines.

NEW DEFEAT/NEW PROVOCATION. Cavalryman chokes woman; blood is thrown onto her hair. ANOTHER FIGHT, ANOTHER DEFEAT, AND SO TO VICTORY. SUCH IS THE PEOPLE'S LOGIC — Woman describes strikes by miners, technicians, high school students. Second woman offers tactical advice to revolutionaries.

Black screen — In the second part of the film, try to correct your mistakes, an integral part of your moving toward Marxist education.

LIAISON WITH THE PEOPLE. Intercut with shots of farmers, industrial sites, trucks on the road, shanty towns, and blocks of apartment buildings are shots of young man and woman together — To escape from the dominant ideology (also prevalent in Russian filmmaking) and to "go to the people" effectively, left filmmakers must develop theory.

Cavalryman on horseback, shouting, "I am General Motor," leads Indian by rope around neck — Hollywood and Russian filmmaking (a drugged cinema, not a class cinema) tries to make us believe the dream is more real than reality itself.

At a crossroads, with arms outstretched, Glauber Rocha says go either to the "unknown" political cinema or right to the "divine, marvelous," Third World one. A young woman with a camera goes left.

Gian Maria Volonte sits near a waterfall and addresses us. In the foreground are the sound and camera persons; in the distance, below, swimmers — We hear how cinema seduces us and how filmmakers must struggle against bourgeois notions of representation.

EDUCATION. Union representative and Miss Althusser hand out books. The Indian bites his like a sandwich and walks past a table of guns — Communist Party intellectuals treat comrades "like the enemy," because the intellectuals do not act from "the people's point of view."

COMBAT. Student plays a flute. CRITICISM. He holds a rifle and a flute. COMBAT. He makes a mistake and stops. TRANSFORMATION — Only criticism and self-criticism and participation in the class struggle lead to learning and growth.

Union representative examines inert, bloodied young man at cavalryman's request. Young woman cleans man's face with a white cloth — Class-based medicine in France is compared to people's medicine in China.

Young woman reads book by Proust, then one by PCF Central Committee member. A hand holding a sickle swings at her neck and a hammer comes down over her head. Indian reads *Capital* — "Death to bourgeois and revisionist culture." Use Marx, Lenin, and Engels as guide to action and as model for methods of argumentation and problem solving.

COMBAT/CRITICISM. Young woman tries to read from a book. Indian and now-bloodied young man, carrying pick and shovel, yell, "strike," at her — The class nature of the university and tasks of political student organizations are discussed.

THE WORKER-DIRECTED FACTORY. Red frames alternate with scratched-up shots of assembled film company and tree tops — Confused voices from the film company alternate with woman's voice analyzing inadequacy of workers' collectives in Yugoslavia.

Young woman eats and looks at self in mirror — We need theory.

Woman in pink dress films scenery; man photographs actor carrying a gun and rushing through a stream — Photography's invention allowed the bourgeoisie to disguise reality and to identify class enemies.

Indian by stream examines guns, picks up camera and photographs his rifle — How can revolutionaries wrest cinema from the controlling ideology?

THE ARMED STRUGGLE. Hands fabricate weapons, leave fingerprints on paper. Paris scenes include a factory, street life, boule players, man passing out leaflets — Warnings and instructions for militants are given.

CIVIL VIOLENCE. Woman in pink dress and cavalryman eat from same plate — Woman utters "correct" formulae for behavior; man curses. Female voice off analyzes sexual politics in class terms.

Union representative walks in meadow, reading. He helps young man up riverbank by extending rifle butt. Young man turns rifle on representative and then aids young woman and Indian up — Union representative reads about peaceful coexistence. Female voice off explains our need now to struggle on two fronts: against "the eternal lies of the bourgeoisie," and "its ally, revisionism."

35   LOTTE IN ITALIA/LUTTES EN ITALIE

Production Company:	Cosmoseion (Rome) for the R.A.I. (Italian Radio and Television), Anouchka Films
Director:	Dziga Vertov Group (Jean-Luc Godard and Jean-Pierre Gorin)
Screenplay:	Probably Jean-Pierre Gorin, primarily
Based on:	Louis Althusser's concept of ideology, published in 1969 and later translated as "Ideology and Ideological State Apparatuses," in *Lenin and Philosophy*. Trans. Ben Brewster (New York: Monthly Review Press, 1971.
Process:	16mm, Eastmancolor 7254
Editing:	Jean-Pierre Gorin and Jean-Luc Godard
Cast:	Christiana Tullio Alan (Paola Taviani), Anne Wiazemsky (Store clerk), Jerome Hinstin (Young man), Paolo Pozzesi-Narrator (Italian)
Filmed:	In Godard's apartment in Paris, 1969; a few shots of factories in Italy
English-Language Release Title:	Not released with English soundtrack or subtitles (translation of title: *Struggles in Italy*)
Running Time:	76 minutes; Italian version runs 55 minutes
Distribution and release:	
Italy:	In competition at Bergamo Festival, September 2–10, 1970
France:	Privately by Godard to militants and at film festivals. At the Hyères Festival in 1969 and 1970 and at the Avignon Festival in 1969, there were special programs of parallel cinema, and Godard's post-1968 films were probably shown there. *Vent d'est, Pravda,* and *Luttes en Italie* were

	shown at a *Cahiers du cinéma* workshop in Avignon in 1972.
USA:	Double-system copy in Pacific Film Archives, French sound track

Synopsis

The major figure in *Luttes en Italie* is never developed enough to be justly called a "character." She is Paola, an Italian university student working for Lotta Continua, a Communist organization to the left of the left of the Italian Communist Party (hereafter PCI). This woman is shown in symbolic tableau, usually static, in poses that each represent a whole social and personal situation. These tableaux, with minor variations, are repeated in different combinations four times throughout the film as the young militant comes to a more profound understanding of her own ideological position. In the last section, black frames that had appeared throughout the film are replaced by shots of a factory; these symbolize "production relations," the knowledge of which capitalist ideology suppresses.

All the commentary is carried by voices off: we hear some dialogue, but mostly a young woman's voice analyzes her situation politically. She speaks in the first and second person about herself ("I" or "you"). In the French version, a translating voice speaks over the original Italian sound track; this translation is neither simultaneous nor exhaustive. In the summary below, most of the symbolic tableaux are described the first time they appear. Their repetition and the relation of commentary to image in the montage form an essential part of the film's political discourse, which cannot be replicated here. The spoken, political content, drawn from the theories of Louis Althusser, is also only indicated summarily below. The format is as follows: Image — major concept from sound track.

Woman, first raised — Dialectical concepts of the world; struggle against idealistic ones.

Woman's hands writing, leftist pamphlets and books on the table — We need theory to analyze Palestinian, anti-imperialist, struggles.

Woman on the telephone — The PCI does not wage class struggles, only economic and parliamentary ones.

Woman reading *L'Unità* and *Pekin-Information* — PCI paper predicts a "calm winter" without strikes; the Chinese say politics should command the economy.

Two heads seen from rear, seemingly of a young man and woman studying or talking — idealistic lectures at the university on the "essence" of things are all the same.

In an apartment, a standing woman teaches a seated male worker math — The university student cannot teach in the practical way that workers need.

Paola looks at a shirt in a store; woman sales clerk — Paola tries to talk to the clerk; manual labor is contrasted to intellectual labor.

Close-up of a woman's hands in front of a soup bowl; a tea tray surrounded by pills, pill boxes, and ampules; woman putting on makeup in the bathroom — Arguments with her family are presented and she analyzes the contradictions of her position there, as well as those expressed through women's anxieties and bodily concerns.

Woman's hand on handle, closing bedroom door — She expresses her need for a love affair yet dislikes the isolation of the "couple."

Woman selling *Lotta Continua* on the street; woman at university standing under sign pointing to lecture hall; woman buying train ticket — Police, university, and transport officials all want to check her "identity" papers.

Inverse composition, woman looking in mirror; woman facing camera; black frame — How can she reflect on and recompose all these compartments of her life, until now seen in idealistic terms and defined as the predominant ideology defines them?

Paola and sales clerk in elevator — She realizes how ideology functions to organize her everyday behavior in Italian capitalist society, how social life determines thought, and what her demand for "privacy" means.

Woman working in a garment factory; woman cutting out a paper pattern of a mannequin representing society — Just going to work in a factory won't give her the correct line; she will have to analyze concretely the specific situation in Italy.

Advertising photos of a bourgeois couple with an infant, families — How can they become a revolutionary couple? If they had a child, they'd be more accepted as a "family," but they would also carry their own political struggle to a new stage.

Woman and math student — Theoretical understanding will transform one's political practice and vice versa. All the intellectual fields the woman has studied are rethought in terms of the objective, real contradictions that they reflect.

Intertitle: MIRAFIORI, SETTEMBRE, 1969; photo of massed Fiat workers — Ideology is the necessarily imaginary rapport between myself and my conditions of existence.

Worker at machine — The black spaces will be replaced by this shot, which represents what bourgeois ideology represses, production relations, the factor that defines one's social conditions.

Woman buying sweater; exterior shot of factory, woman at university standing under sign to lecture hall — Ideology is always expressed by means of an institutional apparatus, which organizes material practice according to institutional rituals prescribed for that practice. Here the university is the voice of the state. Woman challenges her science professor not to speak of true and false ideas without telling where those ideas came from. The family and the police are also ideological apparatuses, organizing material comportment and shaping that society *as* a capitalist society.

Woman facing camera — As a militant, she has understood that the determinant area for struggle is the political and ideological sphere of state power. In the other regions of her life, she must rethink subjectivity in class terms. How can one be a militant actress on Italian TV? What should the progressive sector of the intelligensia do? This film indicates the areas of work and struggle that must be pursued.

36 ONE P.M.

Original Title:	*One American Movie (One A.M.)*
Production Company:	Leacock-Pennebaker, Inc.
Director:	Jean-Luc Godard, shooting; D.A. Pennebaker and Richard Leacock, release version
Screenplay:	Jean-Luc Godard / D.A. Pennebaker
Director of Photography:	Richard Leacock, D.A. Pennebaker
Process:	16mm Ektachrome
Editing:	D.A. Pennebaker
Music:	Jefferson Airplane
Cast:	Rip Torn, Tom Hayden, LeRoi Jones, Jefferson Airplane, class in Ocean Hill-Brownsville, Eldridge Cleaver and Black Panthers, Anne Wiazemsky, Jean-Luc Godard, Richard Leacock, Tom Luddy, Paula Madder, Mary Lampson, two girls from Harlem, woman executive from Wall Street.
Filmed:	In New York City (Harlem, Wall Street), Newark, N.J., and Berkeley, in November 1968
English-Language Release Title:	*One P.M.* (1971)
Running Time:	90 minutes
Released: USA-New York:	Whitney Museum, February 10, 1972
Distribution: USA:	Leacock-Pennebaker, New Yorker Films

Notes

Godard and Gorin came to New York in March 1970 to edit the footage and abandoned the project because they felt in conflict with Leacock-Pennebaker's cinema verite style. (*See* 1976, Walsh, Entry No. 2010)

Godard's footage was edited by Leacock and Pennebaker along with sequences they shot showing Godard at work and being interviewed.

The police's dispersal of the Jefferson Airplane playing on a rooftop is also shown.

Synopsis

(Film is composed of sequences shot by Richard Leacock and D.A. Pennebaker as well as by Godard; it was completed by Pennebaker.)

Two black girls pick up a tape recorder off a belaying post by the New York City waterfront. They skip along the harbor listening to it. Rip Torn, wearing an Indian headdress, walks and sits in the woods as he listens to and repeats a speech from a tape recorder. It seems to be a speech by Tom Hayden that is being filmed later in the movie.

Torn ascends 45 floors in an elevator on a construction site (the Random House Building, Third Avenue and Fiftieth Street). He is seen against the background of a darkening skyline at twilight. His action is to continue the same procedure of repeating after the tape recorder, on which a speech discusses social alienation, and strategy for rebellion, especially action in the streets. Torn gets out, walks across a plank to look around, and then descends in the elevator.

In a residential garden in Berkeley, Tom Hayden is talking about the relations between blacks and whites. Godard, wearing a red scarf and smoking, walks around Hayden and gives a few directions to the camera operators and sound people who are in plain view. A woman is eating a hamburger and another woman offers Hayden a cup of coffee. Long circular shot-sequences emphasize first Godard directing, then Hayden, then the sound woman, then the spectators, then Godard in close-up.

Accompanied by other Black Panthers, Eldridge Cleaver is interviewed. These men are in a plain-walled room and are filmed under a glaring light. Cleaver talks about prisoners but quickly gets into his main topic, that being filmed has been a bad experience for the Panthers, including being filmed by the radical American Documentary Films and Newsreel. All black artists, he says, have to deal with the Mafia, and Godard, as part of the film establishment, is also a part of the Mafia. In a sequence not originally planned, Godard, had Ameer Baraka and friends filmed playing in a Black-Afro band on a Newark street, offering a black power mass. Godard is in the background observing as Baraka is seen singing and chanting with a group of five others at dawn. Baraka is wearing an orange parka and a maroon and pale-blue turban and is playing a xylophone. The six sing: "We are your nightmare. Some are raped; some are burned; some are decapitated. I praise the black man. I praises the black man." It is a traditionally edited sequence.

Godard is seen listening to the end of Cleaver's talk. Godard and Torn rehearse with the tape recorder, as in the beginning. There is a cliché skyscraper shot of New York, panning down to a street scene. The camera follows a woman lawyer, with Godard interviewing her as she walks to work at her Wall Street office. Godard instructs the lawyer about the next scene. We see both the camera people shooting inside the building and shots of what they filmed. An officious type interrupts them to find out if they have permission to film there. Godard introduces himself. There is a tracking shot of the lawyer walking down long corridors and black and white footage of offices.

In an indoor sequence in Berkeley, Hayden criticizes Godard for the way the film is being made. It is hard to think, Hayden says, because there is too much movement. He says that it was a very unnatural way for him to speak. Godard replies that art is not natural but is completely abstract; in fact, the film is honest because it shows the camera, and it indicates that Hayden is speaking in an unnatural situation. There is a shot of Torn practicing with the tape recorder. A group of people sit in a dimly-lit living room (in Berkeley?) listening to a tape recording of Cleaver. Godard sits on a sofa, a cat on his lap playing with his tie. There is a cut to Cleaver, analyzing the Algerian experience.

Shot of New York city skyline, pan inside to lawyer at her desk. She speaks of business and social progress. She says that she is thirty, was in the Peace Corps in Guatemala where she did community action work among natives and raised chickens, and now wants to work on Wall Street because business is the most important tool to develop the underdeveloped sections of our and other countries. Today we're developing Brooklyn; and tomorrow, who knows?

Rip Torn enters a grade-school science class with mostly black children. He is wearing a Confederate officer's uniform and declares that he is going to take his "business techniques" and "develop" the classroom. Godard is sitting in the back row. The children articulately discuss their situation in Ocean Hill-Brownsville; they express a distrust for the head of the New York Teacher's Union, Albert Shanker, and for the newspapers, "which lie about our school." Torn hands out toy guns and reenters in an army uniform. The children shoot him down and generally have a good time. Torn is seen in a car, driving, and talking about the last scene. He talks about goals for education and says the children are still "penned up in the plantation" and are "sold out to the system."

The Jefferson Airplane give a concert on a midtown Manhattan rooftop. Long-shots show people gathered around the bottom of the building and others hanging out windows to hear. The top of the apartment building has ornate cornices, and the camera zooms in and out on the musicians. The police come to arrest them, and one policeman stops the film by putting his hand over the lens. There is a sequence showing a marching grade school band in the streets, as the police protect it.

We see a shot of a sign "The Wrecking Corporation of America," then a title, PRESENTS, and then, in time-lapse filming, a building being torn down. The last shot shows Godard standing by a window, filmed from the outside. He motions to the camera to quit, then pulls down the shade.

(Synopsis based on my notes and those of James Monaco)

37 VLADIMIR ET ROSA

Production Company:	Grove Press, German Television (Munich Tele-Pool)
Director:	Dziga Vertov Group (Jean-Luc Godard and Jean-Pierre Gorin)
Cast:	Jean-Luc Godard - Himself (Vladimir Lenin), Jean-Pierre Gorin-Karl Rosa (after Rosa Luxemburg), Anne Wia-zemsky (Ann, women's liberation militant), Juliet Berto (Juliet, Weatherwoman, hippie), Yves Alfonso (Yves, revolutionary student from Berkeley), Claude Nedjar. People playing these roles are unknown (Jacky, maladjusted worker; Dave Dellinger, a pacifist M.D.; Bobby X, a Black "already accused of killing a cop"; Judge Julius T. Hoffman; William Kunstler, lawyer; Jury; Police)
Filmed:	1970
English-language Release Title:	*Vladimir and Rosa*
Running Time:	106 minutes
Opened in New York:	April 16, 1971
Distribution:	
France:	Festival of Hyères, 1971
USA:	Grove Press

Notes

Godard and Gorin had a contract with Grove Press to make several films. Only this one was completed.

Grove Press also released a totally different version of the same film under the same title with shots from the Godard-Gorin film intercut with shots of participants in the Chicago 7 trial watching and reacting to the film.

Synopsis

This film uses predominantly symbolic sequences, as in the 1969 films, but it also has more acted sequences, particularly burlesques of the courtroom proceedings in the Chicago 7 trial. The format for describing the film is the same as for *Luttes en Italie:* Image — Major concepts expressed on the sound track.

Alternation primarily of the following images: Vladimir and Rosa tee-shirts draped over the engine of a red car; Lenin's face; a camera; Nagra tape recorder; words, *theory* and *practice*; photos and drawings of militants; black frames — This film will pay for the Palestine film. How can we make the best film about justice, both theoretically and practically?

Police chasing and beating students bloody — The United States oppresses students advocating nonviolent revolution.

Mug shots of actors playing the defendants, the Chicago 7; same characters in costumes and locales that indicate their social/political position — The riot in Chicago had been organized by the police; the student defendants (listed and described) were carefully picked.

Judge in red robes doodling and writing across photos of a nude woman; jury members seen together and singly, heads going one way and then another in unison — Background story of Chicago 7 is told, as are Kunstler's objections and Godard's and Gorin's analysis of legal process.

Godard and Gorin walking up and down on either side of the net in a tennis court, talking to each other and stuttering — We must film a process, showing all the contradictions in the repressive situation we are involved in.

Shots of workers in Paris, of Jackie, "the maladjusted worker" — Jackie is too much of an individualist, but he would beat up his boss.

Dave Dellinger in his study, writing in blood — Dellinger's pacifism and reliance on petition writing are critiqued.

Godard and Gorin on tennis court, pacing back and forth, game in progress; black frame — It's not so easy to make the "scientific breakthrough", and how can we show that "break" (= *la rupture*, from Althusser) in film?

Juliet wearing helmet and holding stick; her commune; Mao with a Vladimir tee-shirt — Juliet's political action and life-style have not been integrated; rock music is heard.

Shots of Kunstler intercut with the Sorbonne — Kunstler is idealistic and rich and "doesn't realize the travesty of the Bill of Rights."

Tennis game again; picture of children in China — Turn the trial into an act of resistance; it is not simple; we're trying to explain and define things, but our position at the trial may seem ridiculous.

Seale in jail; Yves and Ann reading *Vive la révolution*; judge; close-ups of jurors, eyes moving — Crimes against workers are listed. "All that's left them is management-organized leisure."

Judge keeps yelling, "Objection sustained." Gorin as judge and Godard as policeman enacting farcical stunts; black frames; film stock; Lenin and Brecht; Nagra tape recorder playing; postcard of Chinese peasants; light bulb; Lenin in tee-shirt; Seale's image intercut with all of the above — Black music is played. "Simply putting conclusions together does not give a true image of the facts on which they rest"; Lenin was against the idea of constructing world-images that were too complete"; racism and sexism are discussed.

Ann silkscreening women's liberation tee-shirts; Yves reading and not understanding a militant feminist speech; Ann sitting behind him and speaking each word of that speech separately while he mouths her words silently — Issues raised include sexual politics, the feminist's position in organizations, her personal stance, the male revolutionary's need to see things from her point of view.

Seale with gun at head and fist clenched; judge drawing over picture of naked woman; jurors' faces; gavel; Ann with raised clenched fist; cake brought in for Seale and snatched away; light bulb glowing and bursting; Dellinger wrestling with police on floor — The rupture means different things for blacks, as Seale demands strict adherence to bourgeois justice and wants to defend himself; the pacifist breaks with his own former ideology of nonviolence.

All defendents, except Seale, at a press conference chanting in unison; empty red chair for Seale; TV monitor; camera person and Godard and Gorin shown — While on bail, "we forced the enemy's TV and camera to film a political action politically."

Seale chained and struggling, gagged; judge and jurors in close-up — Blacks have the right to fight back if attacked.

Construction sites; Seale; Jackie in cars; apartment complexes; student strike; children playing; Chinese children — Analysis is given of the situation of youth and workers.

Courtroom — Black frames show the shots we did not know how to shoot; all that you see here is tainted by bourgeois ideology and imperialism, with color used as in any James Bond film.

Nagra; CBS tee-shirt; sentencing seen on TV monitor; characters in close-up; Seale in cell; Lenin; Berto behind bars; Chinese children — The press conference and media reception of the trial analyzed.

Vladimir and Rosa tee-shirts; red car with red sign in car engine (Communists = motor of the revolution) — Godard and Gorin summarize their concepts about political filmmaking, similar to the conclusions in PRAVDA.

38 TOUT VA BIEN

Producer:	Alain Coffier
Executive Producer:	Jean-Pierre Rassam
Production Companies:	Anouchka Films; Vicco Films, Empire Films (Rome)
Directors:	Jean-Luc Godard and Jean-Pierre Gorin
Screenplay:	Jean-Luc Godard and Jean-Pierre Gorin
Monologues based on:	Jean Saint-Geours' *Vive la société de consommation* (Manager's monologue); CGT Magazine, *La Vie ouvrière* (Union official's monologue); "Maoist" magazine, *La Cause du peuple* (Leftist worker's monologue)

Director of Photography:	Armand Marco
Process:	Eastmancolor
Screen Ratio:	1:66
Camera Operators:	Yves Agostini, Edouard Burgess
Sound:	Bernard Ortion, Gilles Ortion
Electricians:	Louis Parola, Robert Beulens, José Bois
Machinery:	Ferdinand Rocquet, André Saudemont, Eugéne Delsuc, Marcel Mercier
Special Effects:	Jean-Claude Dolbert, Paul Trielli, Roger Jumeau, Marcel Vantiegham
Script Continuity:	Marie-Noël Bon
Production Manager:	Alain Coffier
Production Assistants:	Armand Barbault, Volker Lemke, Jacques Perrier, Philippe Venault
Sets and Art Direction:	Jacques Dugied, Oliver Girard, Jean-Luc Dugied
Editing:	Kennout Peltier, Claudine Merlin
Sound Mix:	Antoine Bonfanti
Still Photography:	Alain Miéville, Anne-Marie Michel
Cast:	Yves Montand (Him), Jane Fonda (Suzanne), Yves Caprioi (Salumi boss), Elisabeth Chauvin (Geneviève), Castel Casti (Jacques), Eric Chartier (Lucien), Burgette (Georges), Yves Gabriel (Léon), Pierre Oudry (Fréderic), Jean Pignol (CGT steward), Anne Wiazemsky (Leftist woman), Marcel Gassouk (Second CGT steward), Didier Gaudron (Germain), Michel Marot (Communist Party representative), Hugette Miéville (Georgette), Luce Marnaux (Armande), Natalie Simon (Jeanne), Ibrahim Seck, Jean-René Defleurien (Leftist man), Louise Rioton (Lyse)
Filmed:	In studios and on location, Paris, December 1971–January 1972
English-Language Release Title:	*Tout va bien (Just Great)*
Running Time:	95 minutes
Released:	
Paris:	April 28, 1972
England:	London, December 1973
USA-New York:	Film Festival, October 10, 1972; general release, February 16, 1973
Distribution:	
England:	The Other Cinema
France:	Belstar, Pathé-Gaumont
USA:	New Yorker Films

Notes

The film had a budget of $1,200,000.

Synopsis

Red, white, and blue credits and titles, MAY 1968/MAY 1972/FRANCE

1972, open the film. Over close-up shots of a hand writing checks (sound of checks tearing), the voice off indicates what feature films materially need: stars (close-ups of Fonda and Montand); a story line, here about love (shots of a couple walking by a river, lines spoken from *Le Mépris*, couple fighting by a bathroom door); and the context of that story (shots of people in Metro, woman with a cow, worker at a lathe, student demonstrations, farmers burning potatoes, police dragging bloodied people out of a house). The voice off intermittently states, "Farmers farm. The bourgeoisie 'bourge'. Things move according to class."

Montand makes commercials. Fonda has a radio show with the American Broadcasting System, "Survey of France Today." The couple go to the Salumi meat packing plant, occupied by the workers, to interview the locked-in director. The entire two-story factory is seen in cross-section, with one wall cut off and the most influential offices on the left (boss upstairs, architects downstairs) and the butchers and meatpackers to the right. A large banner between the two floors reads: IT'S A GOOD IDEA TO LOCK UP THE BOSS — UNLIMITED STRIKE.

The couple make their way to the boss' office where they are locked in with him. He delivers a long, satirically filmed and acted monologue about worker-management relations today: The class struggle is passé. Marxism and collectivism do not protect workers against oppression. Collaboration between classes provides an improved standard of living and an evolutionary movement toward permanent material progress. We must seek a happy medium as we strive to rationalize life.

The CGT (= largest union in France) officials in the factory try to get to see the boss but are kept out. One CGT official reads a long statement defining workers' struggles primarily in terms of production figures, contracts, and the "complex problem of the food industry."

Various groups of workers, shown in close-up, explain their position: So-called bonuses are always taken out of the paycheck; the CGT denounces radicals as provocateurs and expects workers to let the union and party (French Communist Party; hereafter PCF) think for them; all the militancy the union provides is a May Day parade and occasional one-hour work stoppages. A woman on the phone tells her husband or lover that she is going to stay with the occupation and asks him to take care of her children, as she did when he was on strike.

The boss wants to urinate and the toilet is occupied. He can go to the dirty workers' toilet below but is given only three minutes to do so — the rule for workers. He runs desperately back and forth through the corridors till the time is up and he is forced back into his office. In desperation he throws a paperweight through his window to urinate outside (sound of stream of water). Workers at other windows look on.

Outside in the corridor, groups of women talk to Fonda. One has four children, problems with child care, another "shift" working at home every night, and a doctor who "scared her off the pill." Another woman sings a "left song," saying that workers want to fight back. Fonda wants to understand their working conditions. They say that she does not ask the right questions nor understand the complexity of their situation. In a long Brechtian sequence we see Fonda working on the line stuffing sausages. (Voice off: "The worst is the stink . . . Imagine performing the same motion all day.") Montand, shown pushing a meat cart, is described as being so bored that he is psychically paralyzed. Fonda is told that the bosses harass the workers and call this organization of a factory "natural." Reporters do not show struggle or how things change.

Luminously back-lit, Montand stands by his camera. In the background and also seen through the viewfinder, short-skirted women ceaselessly dance on the stage where he is filming a commercial. He delivers a long monologue about having been a New Wave screen writer, participating in the May 1968 events where he met Fonda, making commercials, planning a political film based on Brecht's "Notes to *Mahoganny*," and associating with and then drawing away from the PCF. At her studio, Fonda sits at the microphone and tries to read her story about the strike, but tears up her script. She gives a monologue telling how her reporting during the May events made her the station's "left specialist," but now they do not want stories on student politics or on workers. Furthermore, the network's style makes all the news sound the same. "I am an American correspondent in France, but I don't correspond to anything."

In their apartment, Montand and Fonda fight. He does not want her to bring her work problems, her writer's block, home. All they do, she says, is eat, go to the movies, fuck, and fight. She repeats that list and demands more than that in her image of the two of them. She says he can conceive of only one image of them (black and white photo of a woman's hand holding a penis), but she needs to be able to imagine that image along with a conception of him and her as they are while at work.

Intertitle: TODAY (1). Montand and another male photographer are filming on the top of a tall building. Montand thinks back to May 1968 and his desire to make political films in a new way. We see a series of tableaux-like, highly stylized sequences of the police confronting students with tear gas; students beating up an isolated policeman; youths standing around a pond near a drowned friend giving a eulogy for him (= Gilles Tautin, police victim of 1968); and the police rounding up lines of students with their hands over their heads. In this sequence, police cars burn in the background, and the voice off recites a litany of student and worker uprisings.

TODAY (2). Montand on the phone angrily says he feels like working and will not travel with her. Woman secretary asks him, "Is something wrong?"

Fonda visits a supermarket to write about what people buy and sell. Long lateral pans reveal cashiers checking out shopping carts. Many of the customers are black. Bells ring and the cash registers make a loud noise. A PCF salesman hawks a book on French history and democracy. A group of long-haired students enter and enact a guerrilla theater demonstration, getting the customers away from the checkouts, stacking carts full of merchandise, arguing with the PCF salesman, and throwing things on the floor. As the camera tracks to the right, we see police entering right. (At the far right, a policeman steals a skirt.) As the camera tracks left, a general fight with the police ensues.

TODAY (3). As Montand sits drinking coffee in a cafe, Fonda comes to the window; the roles are reversed and the shot repeated. The voice off declares that they "loved each other silently. They learned to think of themselves historically. Let each of us be our own historian. Me. You. France. 1972."

The camera tracks right and left over a barren strip of urban wasteland. A popular song praises the sun shining over France. Voice off: "You don't have to be a leftist to think this way." Final titles include FRANCE 1972/HISTORY/HIM HER/ME YOU.

39   LETTRE À JANE/LETTER TO JANE

Director:	Jean-Luc Godard
Screenplay:	Jean-Luc Godard
Cast:	Jean-Luc Godard and Jean-Pierre Gorin (Narrators). Still by Joseph Kraft from *L'Express*, 31 July-6 August, 1972, in an article about Fonda's tour to Hanoi.
Process:	16mm
Running Time:	60 minutes
Released:	
USA-New York:	Film Festival, October 10, 1972. New York general release (at Film Forum, with Oshima's *Diary of a Yunbogi Boy*), April 11, 1974
San Francisco:	San Francisco Film Festival, Autumn 1972
Distribution:	
England:	The Other Cinema
USA:	New Yorker Films
France:	Never shown (*See* 1976, Segal, "Godard et le groupe Dziga Vertov," Entry No. 1999)

Notes

The film seems to have been made specifically to accompany *Tout va bien* to international film festivals. Cost, $300.

Synopsis

Godard and Gorin deliver a commentary entirely in voice off, analyzing a photograph by Joseph Kraft which appeared in *L'Express* and showed Jane Fonda while on tour in North Vietnam. In fact, Fonda's tour was used by the North Vietnamese as a publicity vehicle to make known to the world the extent to which the United States had bombed their dikes. The photograph shows Fonda on the left looking with concern toward a helmeted Vietnamese soldier on the right, whose back is facing us. Another Vietnamese man is seen standing in the background, facing the camera. This figure is out of focus. The caption reads: "Jane Fonda questions the inhabitants of Hanoi about the American bombardments."

In the commentary, Godard and Gorin discuss journalism, the star system in film production, and the dependence of Third World countries such as North Vietnam on our press and our radical stars — in this case on Jane Fonda. Godard and Gorin talk about the rituals and codes of a certain kind of cinematic expression, that of helpless dismay in the face of immense social suffering. They discuss the political implications of photojournalistic form. They use the topic of Fonda's militant practice as a roundabout way of rephrasing the question, "What is the role of the intellectual in the revolution?" They examine the newsphoto of Fonda as a scientific experiment, first to see its form and then to see it as a kind of "social nerve cell." In this film, as in *Pravda*, the sound track cites the three kinds of social production that Mao said could generate correct ideas — the struggle for production, the class struggle, and scientific experimentation.

In discussing the photo as a "social nerve cell," Godard and Gorin note that the caption was written by *L'Express* writers untruthfully (Fonda was listening and not questioning) and without any contact with the North Vietnamese, who probably controlled the process of producing the photo but who did not control the distribution, and thus were limited in completing the act of communication they planned. Fonda was photographed by Joseph Kraft in her role as a star, as a certain kind of ideological merchandise, and Godard and Gorin said that if *L'Express* was able to lie in the caption, it was because the picture made that possible: "*L'Express* is able to avoid saying, "What peace?" — leaving this up to the picture alone."

The directors conclude that Fonda was being used in the photo solely as a star. She is in the foreground with a look on her face that conveys only a tragic sense of pity, and the Vietnamese are seen only out of focus or with backs turned. Such a photograph "imposes silence as it speaks . . . says nothing more than how much it knows . . . Film equals the editing of 'I see'. . . . [This expression that says] it knows a lot about things, that says no more and no less, is an expression that doesn't help one to see more clearly into one's personal problems; to see how Vietnam can shed some light on them, for example . . . " The voice off also asserts elliptically at this point that such an expression is a look that came into sound film with the New Deal, but the economic connections to film form are not here made explicit.

Godard and Gorin criticize Fonda because she does not evaluate or act out of the contradictions in her own situation and practice as an actress. They want her to question how she might become a militant actress, creating a new militant approach or style. Their political demand on her is primarily an aesthetic one.

In its visual aspect, the film often presents either a shot of the Kraft photograph or a close-up of a part of it. Also used are publicity stills from *Tout va bien*; pictures of Dziga Vertov, Bertolt Brecht, and Mao Tse-tung; a cigarette ad showing a cowboy; stills of Jane Fonda in *Klute* and Henry Fonda in *Grapes of Wrath* and *Young Mr. Lincoln*; atrocity photos from Vietnam; other silent and sound era film stars such as Lillian Gish and James Dean; the handwritten words "Lenin" and "Mao," plus Marx's picture, superimposed over a photo of student demonstrators with their hands over their heads, being rounded up by the police. In a montage sequence, we see Rodin's *The Thinker* juxtaposed over part of an image of massed corpses. Both this shot and the montage that follows symbolize the conflict between idealistic and dialectial materialism ways of thinking. After *The Thinker* comes images of Jane Fonda, Marlon Brando, Pompidou, Agnew, and Nixon, which are followed by shots of bookcovers of *Capital* and works by Engels, Lenin, and Mao; this montage concludes with the blurred image of the Vietnamese who was in Kraft's photograph, and then a black frame. Black frames are used throughout the film to indicate those structures, truths, and ways of thinking that the bourgeois media repress, not only in the content of what is being presented but in the visual form.

40 MOI, JE

Stills from this abandoned project, planned for production in video, are used to illustrate an interview with Godard. (1973, Durand, Entry No. 1777)

41 NUMÉRO DEUX

Producers:	Georges de Beauregard, Jean-Pierre Rassam
Production Companies:	Sonimage, Bella Productions, S.N.C., Gaumont
Director:	Jean-Luc Godard
Screenplay:	Jean-Luc Godard, Anne-Marie Miéville. Commentary over sequence of older women washing is a compilation of statements by Germain Greer; Miéville wrote woman's commentary; some of the little girl's words are the child's own.
Video Engineer:	Gérard Tiessedre
Director of Photography:	William Lubtchansky
Process:	Color, 35mm (16mm subtitled print in England)
Technical Collaborators:	Milka Assaf, Gérard Martin
Sound:	Jean-Pierre Ruh

Production Manager:	Marcel Mossoti
Song:	Léo Ferré
Cast:	Sandrine Battistella (Wife), Pierre Dudy (Husband), Alexandre Rignault (Grandfather), Rachel Stéfanopoli (Grandmother), (Vanessa, small girl), (Nicholas, boy)
Filmed:	Partly in Godard's studio, Sonimage, in Grenoble, 1975.
English-Language Release Title:	*Numéro Deux*
Running Time:	88 minutes
Released:	
Paris:	September 24, 1975 (France-Elyssés)
USA-Philadelphia:	November 4, 1976
Distribution:	
England:	The Other Cinema

Notes

Cost was about 600,000 F. (about $120,000), roughly the same cost as *A bout de souffle*. Godard said he was making a remake of *A bout de souffle*, thus the title, *Numéro deux*.

Synopsis

Among this film's many video techniques, computerized intertitles replace the titles letter by letter to create fleeting puns and word plays. Superimposed figures in silhouette reveal the listener, observer, or reverse shot of the incident portrayed, especially when the "listener" is a woman or child. The film depicts symbolic situations rather than dramatic ones. Three generations of a nuclear family (boy and girl, mother and father, grandmother and grandfather) enact scenes from family life and are shown in a small video image against a black field. Usually the dialogue is heard in voice off. The sequences in Godard's studio are the exception; the image takes up the full screen and we hear synch sound (in the first).

Some of the major situations presented in the film are indicated below (Image — Sound).

The sound track explicitly deals with the problems of fragmented family relations under capitalism, memory and isolation, age differences and communication between different age groups, the relation between sexuality and work, and the communications network that surrounds us. The film demonstrates the relation between structures of daily life and the social/economic/communications structure under which we live.

Image: Two children look off a balcony; a long shot shows an industrial city street — Sound track: "There was this landscape and a factory in it . . . There was this factory and around it they put a landscape." Unemployment facts and health hazards at work are discussed.

AT FIRST (intertitle). Godard, in shadow, speaks and is seen talking on the video monitor. Projectors run in the background, with a loud sound —

Godard says he is alone now with his machines and tells why he left Paris. In this library or print shop, he is both boss and worker. "In democracies," the body, the educational system, and the family are all like factories, and Godard is concerned with their "noise," short circuits, slips, and interferences, because these are the things that can teach us something. He talks about international film production, the news, and how this film was made.

Multiple TV monitors banked together alternate the following images: May Day union parade, with leader demanding better pay and better jobs and radical antiwar protestors breaking in to chant, "Ho Chi Minh"; Bruce Lee kung-fu movie; porn film, *Les Devoreuses de sexe*; Sautet's film, *Vincent, François, Paul . . . et les autres*; Bergman's *Scenes from a Marriage* — Woman's voice says, *"Numéro Deux* is not a film on the right or left, but the film before or after; before, are the kids; behind, the government, school teachers, and work."

SOON ON THIS SCREEN — "Is this film about sex *(cul)* or politics? Why always ask is it this or that? Perhaps it is both at the same time . . ."

NUMÉRO DEUX. Girl writes on board: "Avant d'etre née, j'etais néante." REPRODUCTION—"Did someone ever ask you if Papa is a factory or a landscape and Mamma a landscape or a factory? You put on some music. Why? To see the unbelievable. And what's the unbelievable? It's what you don't see."

Girl's view of sexuality: she sees her mother ironing, sees her parents having anal intercourse, and is washed in the bathtub by her mother — "Will I bleed when I'm older . . . Sometimes I think *that's* nice, sometimes stinky *(caca)* . . . Do all little girls have a hole?"

Boy, sitting at table, wants to be alone but mother wants him to join in with her and his sister, dancing around the living room — Anarchist folk song plays on record player; Godard's voice whispers, "Solitude."

The two children tell each other a murder story about a crime of passion.

Father talks to camera and later is seen in bathroom urinating in sink — He talks about his job and his relation to his wife, which depends on his job. The couple argue about who initiates lovemaking. Voice off asks where and how to change?

WORK. Girl's face is juxtaposed over shot of mother and father standing in bathroom and having anal intercourse — This "payment," which the man extracted from the woman because she slept with another man, was seen by the child, who heard her mother scream. "Family affairs, I guess," relates the man.

Woman and man by the washing machine — He tries to take over to carry out complicated instructions but cannot get the machine to run. She is angry at his presumption and gets machine to run.

He likes to look at her anus because she never sees it. She looks at his genitals in bed in the morning — He: "Your body is like a river. People talk of the violence the river does to the shore, but never of the violence the shore does as it contains the river." She: "Every morning when you leave, I see your ass going to work, a part of you you never see. I'd like to pay you or someone else to make love so that would be their real job, but we're not that rich."

Woman on the street asks the wife to come to a meeting for women prisoners in Chile — She reads the leaflet about torture. "There are other women. Me, too."

As woman listens to music, man tries to grab headphones off her so as to carry on an argument. She sits drinking coffee, constipated. She comes in from shopping, lies on bed exhausted, masturbates, and sends man away when he comes in and tries to join her — She: "If you don't get along with a man, you can always leave him, but what do you do when it's the state and the whole social system that's a rape?"

Shots of the grandmother peeling carrots, cleaning house, mopping floors, and washing herself (nude) at the sink are intercut with shots of the young wife sewing and doing housework — A feminist social analysis is given from Germaine Greer.

As he cooks, sits nude with family watching TV, or sits at a table facing us (genitals visible), the grandfather talks to camera in synch sound about his past life as a radical. HISTOIRE. CIMÉMA — One incident relates when he was in Dachau in a "red section, where the Communists were in control over a small sector of "a death camp where Hitler was the company boss and controlled the wages. I don't think the origins of the Party were there, but where?"

Grandfather argues with grandson about watching TV; grandfather shares phonograph headset with granddaughter and her mother — They listen to Ferré's song, "La Solitude," about mental and emotional escape; we hear the song in snatches.

Younger man talks to camera. He pauses in making love with his head between his wife's knees — "It's hard for me to do the housework, to see shit on her dirty underwear. For her, it's the factory; for me, it's home." She likes to make love that way, but he does not want to and says, "I feel smothered by all the 'I love you's' I say to you."

The younger man and woman wash dishes, her face in silhouette over the image. The grandmother washes the stairs. The younger woman performs oral intercourse — The younger woman tells her husband she couldn't stand the pace of an outside job and lists all her abilities used at home. "There's just too much and finally not enough . . . I thought I was producing, but the goods had already been sold in advance, at a loss. It's not him, it's someone behind him and between us: work."

Girl in bathtub — Father thinks about his role as householder and citizen. Girl asks, "When you're dead, will you still be my father?"

One TV monitor in Godard's studio shows one woman talking (not in synch); another monitor shows the girl, silent. Godard by his tape deck faces us. He manipulates the controls, and finally lays his head down in his arms on top of the deck. The woman protagonist's voice speaks in voice off — It is the woman who does the understanding but it is always the man who does the directing and explaining. "What's worse, I say it for him, and have him working in my place . . . To let other people speak for you is a crime, especially when you are unpaid." The woman's voice off reflects on the conjuncture of an individual's specific situation: "Still and already, already me. Today and tomorrow. Number 1, 2, and me, 3." Godard listens to the Ferré song about loneliness, music, and escape, and he ends in sleep or exhaustion as he assumes the pose of the total romantic artist struggling to "invent grammar" in his solitude.

42   ICI ET AILEURS

Producer:	Jean-Pierre Rassam, Anne-Marie Miéville, Jean-Luc Godard
Production Company:	Sonimage, Gaumont
Process:	16mm, Eastmancolor 7254
Filmed:	In Palestine, February 1970. Edited over 1970–1976. Some sections shot in Paris or Grenoble.
Running Time:	50 minutes
Released:	
Paris:	September 15, 1976
Distribution:	
France:	MK2-Diffusion
U.S.A.:	Showings in 1976 at Pacific Film Archives, Berkeley CA, and October, 1977, at Bleeker Street Cinema, N.Y., N.Y.

Notes

A bomb was discovered the first day in one of the two theaters where the film was playing, the Quintette, and the film was withdrawn immediately, leaving it to play only in the theater "14 Juillet."

The film cost about 120,000 francs, one-third being contributed by each of the producers. (1975, Roud, Entry No. 1922).

Synopsis

The film is made in three parts, and it's important to understand the movement which animates these three parts.

1. The film was begun in 1970. At the request of the PLO, Godard goes to the Middle East and films several hours of rushes. He returns to France. After the massacres in Amman (September 1970), he wants to edit the film, but he realizes he cannot do it.

The first part of the film is composed of these images which Godard went looking for in the Palestinian camps. In the end, he only retains five, which are like key images of the politics of the PLO. These images are the ones the PLO wants circulated in France. In this sense they are the images of any propaganda film. This is the *material* which the film must work with.

2. Between 1970 and 1975, Godard tries to find an order for editing his film, but he doesn't succeed. He is very marked by the fact that many of those whom he filmed have since died, and that as a filmmaker and a survivor he has their images at his disposal. Instead of giving up his film, then, he modifies it and adds to these images of Palestine other images of France, mainly an average French family (with the father unemployed) who are watching television. In France, this is a period of pulling back and taking stock for leftism (many dreams fell apart). It is also a period when one asks more questions than before about the media and their effect on people, about advertising, propaganda, etc.

The second part of the film, the longest and most complex, cannot be summarized here (see the accompanying text). It is an analysis of the "chains of images" in which we are all caught. One conclusion is that Godard denounces what he calls "making the sound too loud" (even the *Internationale*), which is to say, covering one sound with another and so becoming incapable of simply *seeing* what is in the images.

3. The third part of the film is a return to the images of the beginning. But with a dialectical change. There is no longer one, but two voices over, which allow themselves time to rerun the images (as on an editing table), to see both what the images really mean and what is wrong; to listen attentively to these images. What is involved, then, is the engagement of the filmmaker *as a filmmaker*. In effect, it is the very nature of cinema (the shift between here and elsewhere). What Godard says, very uncomfortably and very honestly, is that the real place of the filmmaker is in the AND. A "hyphen" has value only if it does not confuse what it unites.

Text and Images

(Soundtrack) "In 1970, this film was called *Victory*; in 1974 this film is called *Here and Elsewhere* . . . and elsewhere, and . . ." (Image track) *Et.*

(sound) "Five images and five sounds that have never been heard, or seen, on Arab land. The will of the people, plus . . . plus armed struggle, equals the people's war; plus, plus political work equals the education of the people; plus, plus the logic of the people equals popular war prolon . . . ged, prolon . . . ged, prolonged till the victory of the Palestinian people." (image) Five documentary images of the Palestinian camps.

(sound) "I returned to France . . . things weren't going well. Very soon, in France, you don't know what to do with the film; very quickly, as they say, contradictions explode, and you with them . . ." (image) Return to France, daily life.

(sound) "Probably by adding hope to dream, you must have made errors in addition." (image) Images of living Fedayeen/images of dead Fedayeen (Amman, 1970). Pocket calculator.

(sound) "Both . . . and, either . . . or." (image) Newspaper headlines, TV commercials.

(sound) "Too simple and too easy to simply divide the world in two. Yes, how does capital function? It adds, and what it adds are zeros. And since our dreams usually add up like a series of zeros, you have to say that the images of the total will have nothing to do with the totality of the images. Here as elsewhere. Poor idiot revolutionary! Millionaire in images! Millionaire in images of revolution! Today, we see that what finally happened in this film is what happens in any American or Soviet film." (image) Blackboard with zeros.

(sound) "Each time, one image comes to replace the other. Each time, the image after expels the image before and takes its place, while more or less keeping, of course, the memory." (image) The five images are run one after the other.

(sound) "O.K. now how to use one's time to occupy one's space? How to organize a schedule? How to organize a chain?" (image) Metaphor of the chain.

(sound) "How to manufacture one's own images, one's trademark *(image de marque)*, that is to say, an image which marks." (image) Camera ads.

(sound) "You have to abandon this system of questions and answers and find something else." (image) A scene of family life: the father returns home; he hasn't found work; his daughter asks him questions; he doesn't know how to answer.

(sound) "O.K., decompose one of these movements, and watch it slowly. Always a moment, a point in time, when one sound takes power over the others, a point in time when this sound seeks almost desperately to conserve its power . . . How did this sound take power? It took power because at a given moment, it had itself represented by an image . . ." (image) Argument about the sound on the TV, turned up *too-loud*. Examples of sounds that are too loud (the maid, the races, the TV, etc.). Nixon-Mafia/Dayan-strawboss.

(sound) "Any daily image would thus be part of a vague and complicated system where the whole world goes in and out at every instant." (image) A young worker reading a porn novel.

(sound) "It's thus that each of us becomes too numerous inside himself, and not outside, where we are replaced little by little . . ." (image) TV.

(sound) "One did like quite a few people, one took images, and one made the sound too loud . . . "It's the final struggle . . ." (image) The *Internationale*.

(sound) The five images from the beginning (and a few others) are rerun, but with a *new sound* given by Miéville's commentary, which simply describes what is to be seen. (image) The little girl reciting a poem in the ruins. The group of Fedayeen near the river. Learning to read, a woman repeats a union text. A pregnant woman is happy to give her son to the revolution. The burned bodies of Fedayeen. Munich. Crime against humanity.

"In 1970 this film was called *Victory*. In 1975, it's called *Here and Elsewhere*. Here, a French family that watches television; elsewhere, images of the Palestinian revolution. Here, today, noise and the image of this noise today. Elsewhere, yesterday first of all, abroad, then tomorrow. Here, very simple images, children watching television before doing their homework and after dinner. Elsewhere, very simple images: Fedayeen criticize the way they crossed the river under the Israeli machine guns. But why were we incapable of seeing and listening to these very simple images, and why did we, like everybody, say something else about them, something other than what they still said. No doubt, it's that we don't know how to see or hear, or else that the sound is too loud, and covers reality. Learning to see here, in order to hear elsewhere. Learning to hear oneself speak in order to see what the others are doing. The other, this elsewhere of our here."

(The above program notes from Bleecker Street Cinema, "La Semaine des *Cahiers*," Sunday, October 30, 1977, by William Kron (pseud. T.L. French) and Serge Daney, reprinted here in their entirety by permission of the authors, and the publisher, *The Thousand Eyes*, copyright 1977.)

The following is a further description of *Ici et ailleurs* by Richard Roud (1975, Entry No. 1922). (The order of Roud's statements has been altered to correspond to the film's chronological order as described by Kron.)

"The images shot back in 1970 are confronted, first of all, by Godard himself who on the sound track discusses the meaning or lack of meaning of those images. They are also confronted by images of 1975, a French family watching television. Last of all, they are confronted by Anne-Marie Miéville, who adds her own critique of Godard to his auto-critique.

"Most of the Palestinians in the shots from 1970 says Godard, are now dead — and death is represented in the film by a flux of images and sounds which hide the silence. But it's too easy, says Godard, to declare that Brezhnev and Nixon are wrong and that the poor are right, too simple to divide the world in two. We have to learn to *see*. To see that both the US and the USSR are capitalist systems. The world of today is too complex to be expressed in an image: we have replaced an image by a chain of images; each has its own place and so do we. But we've lost all control.

"The film is . . . about the eternal confrontation between sound and image (*son* et *image* = Sonimage), how sometimes the sound is so loud it drowns the voice one wants to come out of the image. These confrontations are not only theoretical or cinematic: there is also the confrontation between the Jews in Israel today and the Jews in the concentration camps during the war; somewhere Godard dug out the fact that the SS guards used to call the Jews who were at the end of their ropes 'Musulmans'.

"When he shows us intercut images of the German concentration camps and the Palestinian concentration camps, there is silence on the sound track. Silence is vital. For only when the sound is not too loud can we learn to see *here* in order to hear *elsewhere*. Six million Jews were killed in the last war, and 200,000 Palestinians have died in this one. Contradictions: we hear a tape of a speech by Hitler in which he refers in 1938 to Czechoslovakia as 'another Palestine'; we hear the Requiem for Auschwitz.

"Godard's is not a simplistic view of the problem. He is prepared to attack it with all its contradictions. The sound of Vietnam, the sound of Prague are [also] too loud — at which point the "Internationale" blares up on the sound track.

"The film runs about fifty minutes, but every minute is packed; on the other hand, watching it is more than an intellectual experience. Godard somehow manages to make this theorizing dramatically gripping, probably because of the many levels of internal drama. For example, he shows a pregnant Lebanese girl [sic] who tells us she is happy to be able to give her child to the revolution. But then Anne-Marie Miéville comes in on the sound track and says: 'That's not interesting. What's interesting is the *director*, not the person he is directing.'

"And then we hear Godard manipulating the girl, telling her to move left, then a little to the right, then to raise her head. Anne-Marie returns to chide him with the fact that the girl was not actually pregnant, that he chose purposely a young, beautiful intellectual to make his point more telling, and from this kind of distortion to facism the distance is not very far.

"In another scene we see a group of Fedayeen by the Jordan talking, Godard tells us, about the links with the land, the Palestinian earth. They weren't talking about that, interrupts Anne-Marie; they weren't talking about theory and practice; they were talking about love and death. But it isn't only Godard who comes in for criticism. In a scene where a Palestinian People's representative is talking to a group of people, Anne-Marie comments that he is too far from the people he is talking to; hence there is no dialogue, only *theater*."

(Reprinted by permission of Richard Roud, copyright 1975.)

43 COMMENT ÇA VA?

Producers:	Jean-Pierre Rassam, Jean-Luc Godard, Anne-Marie Miéville
Direction:	Jean-Luc Godard and Anne-Marie Miéville
Screenplay:	Jean-Luc Godard and Anne-Marie Miéville
Running Time:	78 minutes

Released: Showings in U.S. in 1976 at Pacific Film Archives and
                                   October 1977, at Bleeker Street Cinema, New York.

Notes

I have not been able to find further credits for the film, but since Écran 76,
No. 51 (October 15), p. 56, lists the same personnel working on Ici et ailleurs
and Six fois deux (Sur et sous la communication), presumably this is the Sonimage personnel that also produced Comment ça va?

Synopsis

Comment ça va? is a film about two workers in a newspaper plant who are
attempting to make a video-film about newspaper and its printing plant. But
it is also a film about the mass media, about the transmission of information
in the press, on the radio, on TV, in a film like this one. It is a film about
finding out who is really "looking," who is controlling the dissemination of
information, who is really making the film, this video-film.

The woman, a former union representative, is a typist; the man a journalist. They had the idea of making this film to show at cell meetings of the
Party in the Paris area so that their coworkers could begin to understand
how a newspaper functions. They thought it was important to make that
kind of information available to workers at a time when several major
newspapers were on strike and that it was necessary to counter the violent
attacks of the owners. They wanted to show how a newspaper run by
Communists would handle information.

In the process of making the film, the woman, Odette, convinces her
coworker that not only does he not understand what he is reporting, but also
that he does not see that he is being controlled by someone else's look in
the very way in which he presents the information. After an initial disagreement — he wanted to cut a section of the film where they had an
argument — she tries to show why he cannot really understand what he is
reporting, and that, in effect, his refusal to see how things really are is an
indication of his desire to keep his position. They go over the text, sentence
by sentence. Again, she tells him that there is something wrong in all that,
and that there is something which is controlling everything: the look.

He finally understands what she is trying to do and decides to back her up
in spite of the fact that he knows that the Political Bureau of the Party is dead
set against the project. This is what happens, and their coworkers who had
voted to give Odette support get cold feet when they hear of the bureau's
decision. The man then says that Odette left and that he never saw her again.

The film can be broken down into four major sections, parts of which are
repetitions; first Odette and the newspaperman watching the video-film,
arguing first about his decision to cut part of it because he did not want to
show the argument between them when she objected to his reading too fast

a text intended to illustrate a photograph of the Portuguese revolution; then various discussions about the photograph and another picture of a demonstration in France which she intended to contrast with the photograph from Portugal. In that segment, shots of Odette and the newspaperman watching the film on a TV monitor alternate with shots of the two of them in the film on the screen, and with the video images seen on the TV monitor: images of the activities in the office of the newspaper. In order to explain to the man what was wrong in the way he was dictating the text about Portugal, she asks him to reenact the scene, and she shows him how the movement of her hands differs from that of the eye because in effect the eyes are controlled by the structure of the sentence, prisoners of meaning. That's one thing which is wrong. She then objects to the text itself, pointing out that it does not indicate what his own position is about what he is writing, his point of view on the subject (the meaning of the photograph), and that by failing to let it show in his text, he is letting someone else's viewpoint control what he is saying.

The man then states that he is beginning to understand what Odette wanted to do: to start from an image, only one, in the same way as science starts from particles in order to find out how they fit together. Objecting at first that she should have asked other members of the committee to participate instead of asking outsiders (her neighbors), he finally agrees with her; workers in a printing plant are in no better position to judge the merit of what they are printing than workers in a munitions plant to judge the value of the armaments they are making. Their voices are heard commenting on the photograph, but they are never seen.

A second section begins with a long held shot of a couple seen periodically throughout the film: the very first shot of the film, the man is driving, then he is writing in a cafe; later he is working in a factory; the woman is seen talking to him on the phone, and later, at the beginning of the second part of the film, she is hanging clothes while he reads his paper; later on, there are shots of the two of them watching television, walking in the street, walking in the snow, and again in their apartment in front of the TV kissing, on the TV monitor, and at the end, he is writing (mostly repeat shots), and in the very last shot we see him listening to the newscast announcing Franco's death while a neighbor complains that the radio is too loud. "Non, ça va pas, non? Ça va pas?" ("Nothing is right.") This series of images functions as a counterpoint to the main part of the narrative — ironic in the way the relationship between the couple is totally oblivious to the struggle between the woman (Odette, whose face is never shown) and the newspaperman (the younger man's father).

After the shot of the young worker and the young woman at the breakfast table, Odette explains the photograph and relates it to a similar photograph taken in France four years earlier. This section, which includes one of the most elaborate montages in Godard's entire work, alternates, mixes, superimposes, and distorts video images of the two photographs and earlier shots of the newspaper office while different offscreen voices and Odette comment on the photographs. These short segments, which combine many special effects, most of which can only be produced with video equipment, are intercut with shots of the newspaperman and Odette listening to the sound track of the film.

This section is followed by another long alternation of shots of the newspaperman facing the camera with Odette's head in the foreground, listening to a discussion of their coworkers reacting to Odette's proposal. But soon, although he realizes that she has to make them see something in the picture, he understands that they still don't "see," still don't understand, and he begins to go through a pile of pictures, photographs, advertisements, war pictures, etc., which Odette had collected for her project. It is these pictures, shuffled in front of the camera which is absolutely still — a subtle variation of the postcard sequence in Les Carabiniers — which alternate with shots of him slowly stopping to listen to the discussion.

The last section includes the shots of Odette and the newspaperman waiting in a dimly lighted office for the decision of their coworkers in an adjacent office. But when the decision comes, she is not happy because she knows that the Political Bureau will overrule the workers' decision. And this is indeed what happens. Aside from the shots of the two of them waiting, and a few shots of the young couple, most of the images and sounds intercut with them are repeat shots from earlier scenes in the film or from the video-film (in the film). Explaining that he suddenly had decided to back up Odette, the man says:

> . . . In the final analysis, what was she saying, Odette, with this little video-film? She was saying that television and the press were corrupt, and since we were looking at them and reading them, our 'looking' was corrupt too, and our mouths, our hands too; in short, we had cancer, us especially, and we were not saying a thing about it.

Against the black screen:

A FILM BETWEEN THE ACTOR AND THE SPECTATOR/
changes to /
A FILM BETWEEN THE ACTIVE AND THE PASSIVE

(See 1977, Augst, Entry No. 2021. The above synopsis reprinted by permission of the author, Bertrand Augst, and Camera Obscura, copyright 1977.)

44   SUR ET SOUS LA COMMUNICATION

Six programs of two films each on Sundays on F.R. 3 (third channel on French TV) at 8:30 p.m. for 1 hour and 40 minutes

1. July 25, 1977:	*Y a personne* (60 min.)
	Louison (40 min.)
2. August 1, 1977:	*Leçons de choses* (50 min.)
	Jean-Luc (50 min.)
3. August 8, 1977:	*Photo et cie.* (85 min.)
	Marcel (20 min.)
4. August 15, 1977:	*Pas d'histoire*
	Nanas
5. August 22, 1977:	*Nous trois*
	René
6. August 29, 1977:	*Avant et après*
	Jacqueline et Ludovic
Producers:	Michel Raux, Jean-Luc Godard
Production Company:	Institut national de l'audio-visuel, Sonimage
Directors:	Anne-Marie Miéville, Jean-Luc Godard
Screenplay:	Jean-Luc Godard and Anne-Marie Miéville
Cost:	18 million old francs per program
Process:	Videotape, color
Video Engineer:	Gerard Teissedre
Camera Operator:	William Lubtchansky
Assistant Camera Operator:	Dominique Chapuis
Photography:	Anne-Marie Miéville
Technical Supervisor:	Henri False
Technical Advisor:	Joël Mellier
"Economic Manager":	Jean-Luc Godard
Assistant Director:	Philippe Rony
Production Manager:	Louisette Neil
Editing:	Jean-Luc Godard, Anne-Marie Miéville
Running Time:	1 hour and 40 minutes each show, unequally divided between two episodes

Synopsis

Y a personne: A still camera is fixed on job seekers coming for interviews into the "boss'" office at a private firm in Grenoble which produces television shows. Godard, speaking in voice off, proposes to them another form of work — to talk and to enact their gestures, occupations, and hobbies for TV spectators. The applicants include a woman who has never worked before, a welder, a woman "attachée de direction," a salesman who wants to go into administration, a female executive secretary, and a housewife. The wizened housewife starts out fumbling for words but becomes very lively and sings the "Internationale" at the boss' demand. The episode challenges the split between work and leisure, work and play.

Louison: In a field a tractor draws near, then stops. The driver gets down, plucks a piece of grass, tosses it away, moves off, and then comes back and gives a monologue. He talks about water, plants, and weather. He elaborates on his concerns, explains the production of one liter of milk, and compares blue collar work to farm work.

Leçons de choses: After leaving work, two workers argue in a cafe about their work. They communicate by using diverse kinds of documents. The first man has a system for explaining the world, which he demonstrates by images and sounds. The second, however, starts from images and sounds, and he assembles them to develop a certain idea about the world. Things shown on the screen are named another way. A young child becomes a "political prisoner" behind the iron grill surrounding a school courtyard. A river is a long "histoire" — a story or the course of history. The production line in a factory represents a "porn film," where people make gestures without love. "What they see is not the same as what people believe . . . The important things are in between. There. Here."

Jean-Luc: Godard is seen in a single static take as he is interviewed by a reporter from *Libération*, whose back is so intrusive in the foreground that it sometimes hides Godard's face. Godard, standing by a movie camera, tells his life story and comments on his role: "I'm the magpie, kids, and I'm at my wit's end. All year long, it's me who does the singing at dawn in my neighbor's garden: . . . You have to learn to resent this lack, this cynicism, this communication without love — so you will not be forced to work without love."

Photo et cie.: The tourist pays to photograph natives, but the professional reporter earns a commission and does not pay to photograph convicts and beggars. Through selected examples, Godard analyzes the process of taking photos of social events. He shows an examining magistrate's reconstruction of a crime, a group of doctors diagnosing a cancer in a medical consulting room, a political meeting with George Marchais. Documentary still photos can be read by their "mute clichés," and together photographs have "fixed in place forever" events of all kinds and from all areas of life. There is a long interview with a reporter who narrowly missed getting the Pulitzer Prize for having photographed prisoners being bayonetted in the stadium in Dacca. For 15 minutes he happily explains a reporter's techniques. When Godard, in voice off, asks what end this knowledge serves, the photographer says, "I'm not paid to ask what function I serve. When you get down to it, it's just my job." During his speech we see only the photo he took, the instant of execution. Similarly, he says that when photographing beggars, the "drama" is to decide whether to film them in black and white or in color.

Marcel: An amateur filmmaker tells of his desire to record nature, how he looks at and listens to a landscape, and how he works. He has a rugged sounding voice with a wonderful provincial accent. He says, since he has a "bad" voice, he would put a spoken commentary in his film only if he could find an "orator with a beautiful sounding voice."

Pas d'histoire: There is a large close-up of a woman's breast, at which a baby is nursing. Contrasting narratives — written, spoken, and drawn —

demonstrate the adult, patriarchical language imposed on children: e.g., "Don't pick your nose. Don't scrape your feet." Godard says that love demands a separation, a third term (image of Third World), which moves away from this voracious, misleading desire for fusion to a position which lets us understand and create. The third term can drive us crazy, yet is the source of communication. It is what is between, "that which separates me from the other. Because there's a separation, we can go from one to another. There is communication. There is distance. There is a river. There is a current."

Nanas: An old woman explains how since her electric bill has gone up while her income remains the same, she has no way to pay her bill.

Nous trois: A ten-minute shot sequence shows a letter being written from prison, telling how the letter writer survives by imagining his beloved. The film opens with the metaphor of prison bars over bars of lined school paper. Narrative tension is established as the viewer waits for the next word. The faces of the man, the wife, and another woman are shown in silent close-ups talking, laughing, thinking, or dreaming. In the editing, their faces merge and are blurred into the words. There is no sound.

René: A mathematician with the voice of a peasant talks to the camera.

Avant et après: In a 45-minute static take, a young man wearing headphones is seen sitting and speaking words Godard whispers to him. He finds it hard to pick up Godard's accent and intonation. It becomes clear that the young man symbolizes the communications apparatus, and his presence is intended to irritate the audience in a way which the TV industry does not. Godard speaks of the images of these very programs as being filmed in Grenoble but then having to be "decoded, recoded, and swallowed up" by Paris. To communicate with his next door garage mechanic in Grenoble, Godard finds he has to send that man's image to Paris. "The image needs a passport, a TV license." Godard wants to create an artisan, playful television; at times, he says, it should babble like a child. Yet this program had to be "loaned out" so as to reach us via Parisian channels, which are centralized, napoleonic, and imperialist.

Jacqueline et Ludovic: Long shot sequences of a man and woman talking present them in a three-quarter view standing by an empty etagere. The woman tells of her efforts to meet the Pope in a private audience, marry him, become Mrs. Montini, and never have sexual relations. She wants to be able to counterfeit money. "In the Vatican you ought to be able to do that. Everything is OK when it's a matter of helping out the poor." She hides. We see the man in long silences, which Godard tolerates without interrupting. These are insane people. Godard questions them in voice off but takes care not to say what we might say in his place. For example, when the man, Ludovic, says he turns the key in the lock three times before going to bed,

Godard says, "I do it twelve times and I never went to the hospital for that."

The descriptions of these programs were drawn from 1976, Collet, Entry No. 1967; 1977, Fox, Entry No. 2030; 1976, Forrester, Entry No. 1973; and 1976, Anon., *Téléjours*, Entry Nos. 1954, 1955, and 1956.

IV
Writings About Godard

1958

45 T.[ruffaut], F.[rançois]. *"Charlotte et Véronique." Cahiers du cinéma*, No. 83 (May), p. 41.
Truffaut admires Godard's ease, looseness, and grace in what would later be called *Tous les garçons s'appellent Patrick*.

1959

46 Douchet, Jean. "Un Cinéma des gens de lettres." *Arts*, No. 730.
Presumably a review of *A bout de souffle*. Cited 1974, Collet, Entry No. 1832.

47 Leblanc, Michel. Interview with Godard. *L'Etrave*, December.
Cited 1960, Moullet, Entry No. 81.

48 Manceaux, Michel. "Les Debuts de Jean-Luc Godard." *L'Express*, December 23.
Cited 1974, Collet, Entry No. 1832. Review of *Breathless*.

49 Truffaut, François. Review of *A bout de souffle*. *Radio-Cinéma-Télévision*, October 1.
Cited 1974, Collet, Entry No. 1832.

1960

50 Anon. "Censure: *Le Petit Soldat*." *Image et son*, No. 134, p. 19.
Cited 1963 *Index: 1946–1962, Image et son*, No. 158 (January), p. 64.

51 Anon. "Jean-Luc Godard: 'Je ne suis pas à bout de souffle.'" *Arts*, No. 767 (March 23), pp. 1–2.
Interview with Godard on *A bout de souffle*.

52 Anon. "Personality of the Month." *Films and Filming*, 7, No. 1 (October), 5.
Article on Belmondo and *Breathless*. Cited, 1976, Schuster, Mel, *Motion Picture Performers: Supplement No. 1*, p. 62.

53 Anon. "*Le Petit Soldat* de J.-L. Godard est interdit." *Le Monde*, September 14, p. 13.

Louis Terrenoire, Minister of Information, agreed with the majority of the Commission of Cinematographic Control and outlawed the film. His reasons are quoted in full.

54 Anon. "Two Actors: Interview." *Films and Filming*, 7, No. 1 (October), 13.
    Interview with Belmondo. Cited, 1976, Schuster, Mel, *Motion Picture Performers: Supplement No. 1*, p. 62.

55 Baby, Yvonne. "Un Entretien avec J.-L. Godard, le réalisateur du *Petit Soldat*." *Le Monde* (13 September), p. 13.
    In an interview, Godard discusses his portrayal of torture, Bruno's political stance, and the literary forebears—novelists of a philosophical-political bent —who influenced the film. Trans. 1967, Garnham, *Le Petit Soldat* script, Entry No. 2290.

56 Baby, Yvonne. "Mon Film est un documentaire sur Jean Seberg et J.-P. Belmondo." *Le Monde* (18 March), p. 12.
    Godard discusses his shooting method and planning, direction of actors, characterization of Patricia and Michel, and death as a theme.

57 Baroncelli, Jean de. "*A bout de souffle*." *Le Monde* (18 March), p. 12.
    Godard's filming by instinct fits the "romantic disorder" of his story. New Wave style and this film's place in it are discussed in detail.

58 Billard, Pierre, et al. "Petit lexique de la nouvelle vague." *Cinéma 60*, No. 45 (April), p. 98.
    Entry on Godard describes his early short films as "insignificant" and *A bout de souffle* as irritating, mean, feverish, and aggressive.

59 Borde, Raymond. "Cinéma français d'aujourd'hui." *Premier Plan*, Nouvelle Vague issue, No. 10, pp. 1–33.
    In this history of the *nouvelle vague* and analysis of its films, *A Bout de souffle* is characterized as an amateurish film full of gags and with unsympathetic characters, but also a film the public "fell for."

60 Carta, Jean. "Mort d'un enfant du siècle." *Témoignage chrétien* (8 April).
    Cited 1974, Collet, Entry No. 1832.

61 Charensol, Georges. "*A bout de souffle*: du côté de Hollywood." *Les Nouvelles littéraires*, March 24.
    Sartre, Sophia Loren, Cocteau, and Maurice Bessy liked the film. The *Cahiers* critics make U.S.-style films better than the American originals. *A Bout de souffle* has an infantile plot and characterization, but its constant wit, ellipses, and rapid, syncopated pace maintain interest.

62 Chauvet, Louis. Review of *A bout de souffle*. Le Figaro (18 March).
    Cited 1974, Collet, Entry No. 1832.

63 Chevallier, J. [acques]. "Films nouveaux: *A bout de souffle*." *Image et son: Revue du cinéma*, No. 130 (April), p. 18.

Discusses Godard's characterization, techniques, and use of a detective genre. Godard's genius in making 'low-budget' film lies in letting sound and image "just be." He is weakest when "stealing" shots from others' films. Godard's long takes, everyday dialogue, hand-held camera, outdoor shooting, and apparently incoherent pans catch every detail of the protagonists' comportment.

64   Choublier, Claude. Review of *A bout de souffle*. *France-Observateur* (24 March), p. 22.

Roger Vadim's ideals and Godard's notions about Vadim's *Sait-on jamais?* are, in fact, realized in *A bout de souffle*. This is an "extraordinary documentary about a boy and a girl today." The entire film technique and dialogue act to reinforce character, albeit not through verisimilitude.

65   Cortade, René. "*A bout de souffle:* naissance du cinéma vaudois." *Arts*, No. 767 (23 March), p. 7.

Everyone lauds "*A bout de souffle*, including Sartre, Sophia Loren, Kessel, Cocteau, and Henri Jeanson. New Wave plagiarism is now called citation. These directors project their own adolescent concerns on to themes about the sensitive soul vs. society. Godard's film relies on a "false audacity"; foolish, vulgar characterization and acting; sentimental music; low humor; and an irresponsible social and aesthetic rebellion.

66   Curtelin, Jean. "Mareé montant?" *Premier Plan*, No. 9.

Godard is compared to Rouch and Resnais in this early history of the New Wave from Melville through Godard. The anarchic *A bout de souffle* marks the beginning of new era in French cinema.

67   Ford, Charles. Review of *A bout de souffle*. *Le Bien public de Dijon* (4 June). Cited, 1968, Gauteur, Entry No. 1111.

68   Gruber, R. Review of *A Bout de souffle*. *Image et son*, No. 134, p. 2. Cited, 1963, *Index: 1946-61: Image et son,* No. 158 (January), p. 19

69   Guyonnet, René. "Les Rapports déchirés de deux personnages en exil." *France-Observateur* (17 March). Cited 1974, Collet, Entry No. 1832.

70   Lefèvre, Raymond, Review of *A bout de souffle*. *Image et son*, No. 130 (April), p. 4. Cited 1963, *Image et son index: 1946-63*, No. 158 (January), p. 19.

71   Lennon, Peter. "Three New French Films." *Films in Review*, 11, No. 6 (June-July), 367–68.

Belmondo plays a role similar to those of James Dean; "the American girl" is authentic; and Paris is well used as the background in *Breathless*.

72   Manceaux, Michel, Interview with Godard on *Le Petit Soldat*. *L'Express* (16 June), p. 38.

Godard describes his politics, the torture sequences from *Le Petit Soldat*, and the influence of Malraux and Bresson on that film. Trans. 1972, Brown, Entry No. 1658.

73 Marcabru, Pierre. "*A bout de souffle* de Jean-Luc Godard." *Combat* (19 March), p. 3.
This comedy of manners, morally, in its characterization, derives from Nietzsche. Phenomenologically, the discontinuous and elliptical narrative form and the unstable, lively camera technique echo Husserl.

74 Marcorelles, Louis. "Views of the New Wave." *Sight and Sound*, 29, No. 2 (Spring), 84–85.
The history of *Breathless* is given, plus an inaccurate plot summary. This "irresponsible" film depicts "a world of immorality, lived skin-deep."

75 Maresco, Serge. Review of *A bout de souffle. La Méthode*, No. 1.
Cited 1968, Gauteur, Entry No. 1111.

76 Martin, Marcel. "*A bout de souffle.*" *Cinéma 60*, No. 46 (May), pp. 117–119.
A bout de souffle is the most significant but not necessarily best New Wave film. It deliberately provokes a scandal by its content and characterization; it mocks us and all the rules of cinema. It establishes a whole new film style — totally original yet constantly referring to film history, especially U.S. cinema.

77 Martin, Marcel. "Nouvelle Vague: tentative de bilan." *Cinéma 60*, No. 44 (March), pp. 4–13.
A bout de souffle is discussed in passing.

78 Mauriac, Claude. "*A bout de souffle* de Jean-Luc Godard." *Le Figaro littéraire*, 15 (19 March), 16.
This is the revolutionary film we've been waiting for from the young filmmakers, as adventurous as Griffith. Godard's critical writings on *Hiroshima Mon Amour* and *Pickpocket* are cited and applied to this film. The acting, dialogue, rhythm, and original treatment of the criminal story make this a "rich, violent, and poetic" film.

79 Mosk[owitz, Gene]. "*A bout de souffle (Out of Breath)* (French)." *Variety* (27 January), p. 6.
Brief credits, Paris. The film is a "grabbag mixture of content, satire, drama and protest." Seberg's name, plus the action, make the film "even worth dubbing." Cutting style fits the quick and ruthless action.

80 Mosk[owitz, Gene]. "*A bout de souffle.*" *Variety* (4 February).
The film has little feeling and an unorthodox style. There's "too much palaver." Quoted at length in *Film Facts* (1961, Anon., Entry No. 92).

81 Moullet. Luc. "Jean-Luc Godard." *Cahiers du cinéma*, No. 106 (April), pp. 25–6.
An in-depth essay of Godard's artistic beginning, from his criticism through his short films and *A bout de souffle*, gives information about Godard's early career not available elsewhere and traces those aesthetic lines that would later characterize his whole work. Translated, 1967, Moulett, *Cahiers du Cinema in English*, Entry No. 938. That translation reprinted in 1968, Mussman, Entry No. 1168.

82   Nourissier, François. *"A Bout de souffle*: un cri de jeunesse." *Les Lettres françaises*, No. 817 (24–30 March), pp. 1 & 5.

The new generation of filmmakers, their background (WW II, criticism) and their relation to the *noveau roman* are described. Their films speak in the first person. Godard's characters define themselves by literary and cinematic reference, and Nourissier describes that literary and cinematic "mythology" which was in the New Wave filmmakers' milieu. He finds the comments in the press on Godard's characters' amorality foolish and says that Godard has presented a refreshingly ironic love story, making us laugh at his characters' posturing.

83   Nourissier, François. "Le Second Souffle." *La Nouvelle Revue française*, 16 (1), 321–27.

The "revolt" in *Cahiers du cinéma* against older filmmakers paralleled the revolt of the *noveau roman* in literature, and these film critics are now installed as the "new generation of French cineastes." Godard's references to literature in *A bout de souffle* are precise yet "inexplicable" either as coming from a young director whom "cinema has totally formed," or from his characters — a facile American woman or a tough guy hero. Also surprising is the sensuality and tenderness of the film's love story.

84   Pesce, Alberto. "A Berlino un occhio sul mondo." *Bianco e nero*, 21, No. 7 (July), 24–25.

Brief review of *A bout de souffle*, entitled *Fino all'ultimo respiro* in Italian, which won the prize for the best direction at Berlin.

85   Sadoul, Georges. "L'Important est de se poser des questions." *Lettres françaises*, No. 848 (3–9 November), p. 7.

Sadoul had seen *Le Petit Soldat* in a private showing along with others. Because the film is censored now, he describes the plot. Stylistically, the film does not match *A bout de souffle*. The dialogue is pretentious. The protagonist, like Hamlet, is not confused but uncertain. And like Gance's *J'accuse*, the film is nauseated at war. So far only Godard has filmed the most burning problem in France.

86   Sadoul, Georges. *"Quai des brumes, 1960."* Les Lettres françaises, No. 818 (31 March–6 April), p. 7.

Godard has burned up all the grammars of film. Sadoul describes the visual style of *A bout de souffle* and compares the plot and theme to *Quai des brumes*. Godard's protagonists are not likable nor admirable, not even motivated by Lafcadio's *acte gratuit*. But their relations and Godard's vision of Paris are fascinating.

87   Salachas, Gilbert. *"A bout de souffle."* Téléciné, No. 89 (May-June), pp. 3–12.

"Fiche No. 365." Credits, plot summary. The critic discusses the film's dramatic construction, discontinuity, marginality and psychology of the protagonists, and cinematic innovations — including composition of the image, framing, camera movements, editing, dialogue, background noise, and music. Is this a "little documentary about the times" or a personal reflection on inconsequential characters?

88   S.[eguin], L.[ouis]. "Quoi de neuf (suite): *A bout de souffle* — un plège à cons." *Positif*, No. 33, p. 49.

The New Wave, represented by Godard, did not deserve the Vigo Prize as much as did new U.S. films by Robert Wise and Lionel Rosogin. *A Bout de souffle's* protagonist has reprehensible politics. The film pretentiously tries to depict the "ambiguity and chaos" of life by wild camera movements and fabricated vivacity.

89   Tailleur, Roger. "C'est une oeuvre." *Positif*, No. 37, pp. 17–18.

In comparing *Le Trou* to *A bout de souffle*, Tailleur finds the former a masterpiece and the latter irritating, narcissistic, and empty.

90   Weightman, J.G. "The New Wave in French Culture." *Commentary: A Jewish Review*, 30, No. 3 (September), 230–33.

Sartre called *Breathless très beau*, yet the film is a "tribute to romantic nihilism." The critic faults Godard for creating such a shallow-minded, unimpressive, delinquent character as Michel Poiccard and for not taking "pyschological flimsiness itself" as the film's theme. The film partakes of a "long tradition of anarchic individualism running through French literature, a tradition which has re-emerged in various forms since commitment began to go out of fashion."

1961

91   Alpert, Hollis. "The Conscienceless Hero." *Saturday Review*, 44, No. 10 (11 March), 39.

Alpert attacks the critical praise *Breathless* has received. The characters are psychopathic and the film often lacks meaning. Is Godard parodying his characters as well as other films? Quoted at length in *Film Facts* (1961, Anon., Entry No. 92).

92   Anon. "Breathless." *Film Facts*, 4, No. 7 (17 March), 35–37.

Complete credits and synopsis of the film are given as well as citations from the reviews in the *New York Times*, the *Saturday Review, Time, Films in Review*, the New York Herald Tribune, and *Variety*.

93   Anon. "Cubist Crime." *Time*, 77, No. 18 (17 February), 62.

The filming and plot of *Breathless*, as well as the "existentialist" character of Michel Poiccard are briefly described. Godard "seems chiefly concerned with developing an abstract art of cinema, in which time and space are handled as elements in a four-dimensional collage."

94   Anon. "Movies Abroad: Larcenous Talent." *Time*, 77, No. 12 (17 March), 58–61.

Unusual biographical details are given about Godard's larcenous adolescence, the way he married Anna Karina, and his early filmmaking. Quoted at length in *Film Facts* (1961, Anon., Entry No. 92).

95   Anon. "Person of Promise." *Films and Filming*, 7, No. 12 (September), 23.

On Anna Karina and *Une Femme est une femme*. Cited, 1976, Schuster, Mel, *Motion Picture Performers: Supplement No. 1*, p. 395.

96 Anon. *Le Petit Soldat.*" *Cinéma 61*, No. 52 (January), pp. 12–20.
A synopsis of *Le Petit Soldat* written by Godard is given (scripts, No. 2286) followed by an interview with Godard at a seminar at the FFCC, when the censor's decision was not yet known.

97 Anon. Review of *A bout de souffle*. London *Times* (7 July), p. 15.
Cited 1961, *Times Index* (July-August), p. 50.

98 Anon. Review of *Breathless. Mademoiselle* (April), p. 52.
Cited Reader's Guide, 23, Part 2 (March 1961–February 1963), 1256.

99 Anon. Review of *Une Femme est une femme*. London *Times* (5 July), p. 17.
Cited 1961, *Times Index* (July-August), p. 50.

100 Anon. "What Is It? *Breathless.*" *Newsweek*, 57, No. 6 (6 February), 84.
A brief description of plot and characterization is given. The film is a "sometimes repellent but interesting what-is-it."

101 Archer, Eugene. "Nonconformist on the Crest of a New Wave." The *New York Times* (5 February), Sec. II, p. 7.
Archer defines what New Wave means and describes Godard's unorthodox filming style. Godard appeared in New York to accept the New York Critics award on behalf of Resnais for *Hiroshima mon amour*. Godard said of *Breathless* that Resnais, Rossellini, and Bresson were pointing the way to a new cinema and he wanted to end the old tradition in a spectacular way. *Une Femme est une femme*, dedicated to Lubitsch, was to be a comedy in close-up and a "film that could only be a film and could have no other meaning, no other description."

102 Aubriant, Michel. "Un Divertissement à trois personnages." *Paris-Presse-l'intransigeant* (8 September).
Cited 1974, Collet, Entry No. 1832.

103 Beckley, Paul V. "The New Movie: *Breathless.*" New York *Herald Tribune* (8 February).
The critic describes Godard's editing, the romance between the protagonists, and the crime story that Godard "does not come to grips with." Quoted at length in *Film Facts* (1961, Anon., Entry No. 92).

104 Bonnot, Gérard. "Un Naïf au cinéma: Jean-Luc Godard." *Les Temps modernes*, No. 186 (November), pp. 566–75.
Like a primitive, Godard has a freshness of vision, but he lacks an intelligent content. Bonnot discusses Godard's improvisation, camera work, direction, and projection of himself into his protagonists. Godard cannot "maintain discursive thought" in *Le Petit Soldat* and *Une Femme est une femme*, where he does not adequately deal with his themes — the Algerian situation and the paradoxes of female logic.

105 Bory, Jean-Louis. "Du cinéma pour la fine equipe." *Arts* (13 September).
Cited 1974, Collet, Entry No. 1832.

106 Cameron, Ian. Review of *A bout de souffle*. *Film* (British Federation of Film Societies), No. 29 (Summer), p. 10.
     Cited in Bowles, p. 60.

107 Capdenac, Michel. "Le Démon de la parodie." *Lettres françaises*, No. 892 (14–20 September), p. 7.
     Une Femme est une femme is pure cinema, although it never takes itself seriously. It's a "polychrome divertissement," full of parody and charming foolishness.

108 Collar, Georges. "Carta de Paris: *Le Petit Soldat*." *Arco* (Bogotá), 3, No. 12 (January-February), 38–40.
     The critic explains the censorship of *Le Petit Soldat* against the background of Francis Jeanson's support for the Algerian terrorists in France.

109 Collar, Georges. "Dos generaciones en el cine francés." *Arco* (Bogotá), 3, No. 12 (January-February), 34–41.
     Godard's work is just mentioned in this review of the films of the *nouvelle vague*. *A bout de souffle* is seen as morally limited but cinematically unique.

110 Collet, Jean. Review of *Une Femme est une femme*. *Signes du temps* (October).
     Cited 1974, Collet, Entry No. 1832.

111 Croce, Arlene. "Breathless." *Film Quarterly*, 14, No. 3 (Spring), 54–56.
     Discusses Godard's attitude toward the United States, seen both in his use of the B-film crime genre and in the characterization of Patricia ("the triumphant, actual artifact of a culture of which he [Michel], in his delusion is the copy, the dupe"). Faults critics for overemphasizing the film's "romantic nihilism." Rather Godard wanted to "produce slices of cinema — shots, fragments, iconography." Explains Godard's innovations and the cult of "Belmondoism."

112 Crowther, Bosley. "The Best Films of 1961." *New York Times* (31 December), Sec. II and X, p. 1.
     Lists *Breathless* in top ten; it's "a sordid, morbid," well-acted film in a "vivid, New-Wave style." Mostly foreign-language pictures are listed.

113 Crowther, Bosley. Review of *Breathless*. *New York Times* (8 February), p. 26.
     Brief credits. *Breathless* "is emphatically unrestrainedly vicious, completely devoid of moral tone, concerned mainly with eroticism and the restless drives of a cruel young punk to get along."

114 Crowther, Bosley. Review of *Breathless*. *New York Times* (12 February), Sec. II, p. 1.
     Cited in *New York Times Index*. I found an entry only for February 8.

115 D. [yer], P.[eter] J. [ohn]. "*A bout de souffle (Breathless)*, France, 1969." *Monthly Film Bulletin*, 28 (July), 90.
     Credits, film's origins, story line. Dreyer notes how this film fits in "the New Wave trend." He admires the "free, almost abstract technique of film narrative"

but finds the "expression of *Cahiers'* own American mystique" infantile and devoid of meaning or feeling.

116 Finetti, Ugo. "La donna è donna." *Cinema nuovo*, 10, No. 154 (November-December).
Cited 1967, Amengual and Estève, Entry No. 782.

117 Frizell, B. "On Screen," *Horizon*, 4 (November), 116.
On Belmondo, with reference to *Breathless.* Cited 1971, Schuster, Mel, *Motion Picture Performers*, p. 77.

118 Garrigou-Lagrange, Madeleine. *"Une Femme est une femme."* *Télécine*, No. 99.
Mixed review followed by comments by G.M. and M.R. (mixed) and G.S. (con). Quotations are included from reviews by Marcel Martin (1961, Entry No. 138) and Claude Mauriac, *Le Figaro littéraire* (16 September).

119 Gow, Gordon. *"Breathless."* *Films and Filming*, 7, No. 11 (August), 25.
Brief credits. Gow had assumed "the deliberate disjointedness expressed the central character's state of mind," but Godard told Gow in an interview that "he was out to destroy accepted conventions of filmmaking." Gow discusses the aptness of the jump cuts, acting, and dialogue (noting what is lost in the subtitling).

120 Hart, Henry. *"Breathless."* *Films in Review*, 12, No. 3 (March), 175–77.
"Godard's direction of *Breathless* is infantile, especially the dialogue." Cinematically, his "quick cuts" are interesting. However, the film "upholds and promotes the idea that theft, murder and amoral nihilism are legitimate reactions in contemporary society." Quoted at length in *Film Facts* (1961, Anon., Entry No. 92).

121 Hartung, Phillip T. "The Screen: Woe, Woe, Whoa." *Commonweal*, 73 (17 February), 553.
Breathless portrays two unlovable delinquents in a slight plot. It has a fresh quality.

122 Hatch, Robert. "Films." *The Nation*, 192, No. 10 (11 March), 223.
Breathless is a brilliant expression of what? That there's something wrong with French youth?

123 Haudiquet, Phillippe. "Critique: *Une Femme est une femme.*" *Image et son*, No. 145, p. 22.
Cited *Image et son: Index, 1946–1962* No. 158 (January 1963), p. 43.

124 Kael, Pauline. *"Breathless* and the Daisy Miller Doll." *The New Yorker*, 36 (11 February), 101 +.
Analyzes Godard's characterization of two "youthful representatives of mass society, . . . amusingly individualistic" but indifferent to human values. Patricia tries everything, but doesn't want to be bothered by anything. The music, the editing, the improvisation and the humor "convey the tempo and the quality of the [protagonists'] activities." Reprinted 1965, Kael, Entry No. 550.

125 Kauffmann, Stanley. "Adventures of an Anti-Hero." *The New Republic*, 144 (13 February), 20–21.

Godard asserts his own style and point of view with his first film, *Breathless*. The subject is the antihero, but it is the style that best shows us Michel's "playful violation of the bases of civilized behavior." Reprinted in 1966, Kauffmann, Entry No. 711.

126 Labarthe, André-S. "La Chance d'être femme." *Cahiers du cinéma*, No. 125 (November), pp. 53–56.

Labarthe reviews *Une Femme est une femme*, finding it a *nouveau roman*-style documentary in its use of Karina and its desultory dialogue and banal gags. Accidents and the purest form of cinema seize upon the smallest intonations and modulations in human interactions, thus capturing the "truth" of the characters. Brief credits. Excerpts in 1970, Collet, Entry No. 1425.

127 Lachize, Samuel. "*Une Femme est une femme*: le jeu de l'humor et du hasard." *L'Humanité* (9 September), p. 2.

In spite of all the in-jokes, this is an accessible, entertaining fantasy, albeit an ironic one, and is marked by brilliant cinematic improvisation, especially in the surprising use of color. It offers a tender homage to Karina.

128 Lebesque, Morvan. "*Une Femme est une femme*: un Godard audacieux prisonnier d'un Godard collégian." *L'Express* (14 September), p. 32.

In *Une Femme est une femme* we get many glimpses of this essentially lazy filmmaker's genius. He has invented a personal technique which could serve him better.

129 Lefèvre, Raymond. Review of *La Petit Soldat*. *Image et son*, No. 140–141, p. 19.

Cited 1963, *Image et son: Index: 1946–1962*, No. 158 (January), p. 64.

130 Macdonald, Dwight. "Films: The New Cinema, the Old Nonsense." *Esquire*, 56, No. 1 (July), 20–22.

Godard joins the other *Cahiers* critics as a filmmaker. *Breathless* has a banal plot (recounted ironically) which is "without either will or feeling." However, Macdonald finds the film exhilarating because of the way Godard handles the actors and because of his "stacatto" style. Godard's style is like that of the New Novelists: "It catches 'tropisms' on the wing; it doesn't describe, it states."

131 Manceaux, Michèle, "Entretien: un film est un film." *L'Express* (27 July), pp. 32–34.

Summarizes a discussion with Godard about *une femme est une femme*, the cinematic influences on him, his improvisation and use of actors. Coutard tells about working with Godard. Godard tells why he made *Le Petit Soldat*. He says his aesthetic goals are close to those of Jean Rouch. Trans. 1972, Brown, Entry No. 1658.

132 Manceaux, Michlèle. "Tournage: Michèle Manceaux vous raconte." *L'Express* (12 January), pp. 36–38.

See July 27 entry, Entry No. 131. Trans. in 1972, Brown, along with July 27 interview, Entry No. 1658.

133 Marcabru, Pierre. "De Jean-Luc Godard à Claude Autant-Lara: les paradoxes de la censure." *Combat* (21 October), p. 8.
Protests the censoring of both a "bad" film, Autant-Lara's about a conscientious objector, and Godard's *Le Petit Soldat*, a lucid and demystifying portrayal of the Algerian war where agitators from both sides "have almost the same face."

134 Marcabru, Pierre. "Jean-Luc Godard ou le cinéma des copains." *Combat* (9 September), p. 8
The *Cahiers* writers-turned-directors address only themselves. If *A bout de souffle* shows a certain disorderly invention, in *Une Femme est une femme*, Godard shows he just cannot master cinema. The film refers to U.S. musicals but lacks all their grace and spontaneity. The dialogue is infantile and vulgar.

135 Marcorelles, Louis. "Cinéma-spectacle ou cinéma-langage?" *France-Observateur* (19 October), pp. 26–27.
Interviews François Truffaut, who, in this discussion of the New Wave, notes Raymond Queneau's influence on the young filmmakers, especially on Godard's *Une Femme est une femme*. A photo of Godard is mislabeled "François Truffaut." The interview cogently summarizes New Wave aesthetics and cultural attitudes.

136 Marcorelles, Louis. Review of *Une Femme est une femme*. *France-Observateur* (14 October), p. 23.
The film explores a cartoon-strip aesthetic "without killing emotion." Marcorelles compares this to its cinematic antecedents, some of which are cited directly in the film. Everything exists only fugitively, in the instant, a sense which Godard maintains throughout the film by his imposition of a unique form of montage over the actors' improvisational acting style. It is a film that is both 100 percent abstract and "one of the most passionate documents about modern anxiety."

137 Martin, Marcel. "Entretien avec le petit soldat: Michel Subor." *Cinéma 61*, No. 52 (January), pp. 19–20.
Subor tells about his background and the censorship of this, his first leading role; he gives details about the production of *Le Petit Soldat*. It was shot in real interiors with extrasensitive, Afga-record film stock for 40 million F., using post-synchronized sound. Subor describes Godard's use of improvisation and the shooting of the assassination scene in busy Geneva streets.

138 Martin, Marcel. "*Une Femme est une femme*." *Cinéma 61*, No. 60 (October), pp. 100–102.
The New Wave has mastered film style and composition of the image, but their films, especially this one, often lack a subject, and are instead filled with gags for the initiate, i.e., readers of *Cahiers du cinéma*. This film lacks the choreographic and musical movement of American musical comedy. It uses color originally but is too heavily verbal.

139 [Martin, Marcel]. *"Le Soldat de Godard." Cinéma 61*, No. 52 (January), p. 12.

Introduction to special section on *Le Petit Soldat*.

140 [Martin, Marcel]. *"Le Soldat* de Godard: questions à l'auteur." *Cinéma 61*, No. 52 (January), pp. 16–18.

Interview with Jean-Luc Godard, who says that *Le Petit soldat* is not so much a political film as a psychological study of a man who refuses to be forced to do something. Subor himself shaped the role during the filming. Lack of experience with torture helped Godard, for he did not intend to evoke real torture but rather to reflect on the phenomenon of torture.

141 Mauriac, Claude. Review of *Une Femme est une femme. Le Figaro littéraire*, 16 (16 September).

Cited 1961, Garrigou-Lagrange, Entry No. 118, and 1974 Collet, Entry No. 1832.

142 Morgenstern, Joseph. "The Lively Arts." New York *Herald Tribune* (5 February).

Review of *Breathless*.

143 Murray, William. "New Outlook on the Contemporary Film World." *The New Leader*, 44, No. 13 (27 March), 20.

Breathless has a few rough spots, but Godard's style perfectly captures the nuances between the lovers and paints an exact portrait of their "detached, uncommitted, and self-centered" generation.

144 N.[ourisser] F.[rançois]. *"Le Petit Soldat*, de Jean-Luc Godard." *La Nouvelle Revue française*, 17, No. 1, 148.

It is a morally displeasing but technically exhilirating film. The censors just didn't want certain words said on the screen: *deserter, Algeria, F.L.N.* A Swiss like Godard has the right to describe the nefarious intrigues that go on in Geneva, but Parisians would reject the hero of that film, while still finding the character fascinating.

145 Pearson, Gabriel and Rhode, Eric. "Cinema of Appearance." *Sight and Sound*, 30, No. 4 (Autumn), 161–68.

Banal material in Godard's films is used not for its extrinsic merit but as a kind of vocabulary. The New Wave directors, especially Godard in *Breathless*, make us doubt our assumptions about plot development and make us pay attention to the director's "controlling mind." *See* 1961, Rhode, Entry No. 147.

146 Pesce, Alberto. "Berlino anno undici." *Bianco e nero*, 22, No. 7-8 (July-August), 110–11.

Brief review of *Une Femme est une femme*.

147 Rhode, Eric and Pearson, Gabriel. "Cinema of Appearance." *Sight and Sound*, 30, No. 4 (Autumn), 161–68.

See 1961, Pearson, No. 145.

148 Schneider, P.E. "Punk with Charm." *New York Times Magazine* (7 May), p. 81.
On Belmondo, with reference to *Breathless.*

149 Siclier, Jacques. *Nouvelle Vague?* Collection 7e Art. Paris: Editions Cerf. Pp. 70–71, 116–21.
Describes the genesis of the *nouvelle vague* and the economics of the film industry. *A bout de souffle* is "the manifesto of the *Cahiers* generation", but has an immoral, anarchistic protagonist. *Le Petit Soldat* is more accomplished stylistically but is "nauseatingly exhibitionist" in Godard's presentation of his personal obsessions and its lack of ideals or political stance. The *Cahiers* critics' films are "insidious in that they are organized not deliberately but instinctively around an ideology which readily feeds into fascism, that of the chosen being."

150 Siclier, Jacques. Review of *Le Petit Soldat. Sight and Sound*, 30, No. 3 (Summer), 120.
A bout de souffle was the *Cahiers* directors' "intellectual manifesto." *Le Petit Soldat* is its "ideological manifesto" in terms of attitudes toward politics, moral and social values, women, and the *acte gratuit.*

151 Siclier, Jacques. Review of *Une Femme est une femme. Télérama* (24 October).
Cited 1968, Gauteur, Entry No. 1111. Collet, 1974, Entry No. 1832, has an entry for an article by Sicilier entitled, "Le Film le plus ambitieux de J.-L. Godard," *Télérama*, No. 610, n.d. These are probably the same article.

152 Steen, T.M.F. "The Sound Track." *Films in Review* (August), p. 243.
Describes thematic use of Mozart's Clarinet Concerto in *Breathless.*

153 Steen, T.M.F. "The Sound Track." *Films in Review*, 12, No. 7 (August-September), 436–37.
"The music for *Breathless* was written by Martial Solal, an Algerian pianist, composer, and arranger of jazz music, who has also done a jazz score for the *L'Affair d'une nuit.*"

1962

154 Whitebait, William. "Night and Day." *The New Statesman*, N.S. 62 (14 July), 62.
Breathless is the most characteristic New Wave film. It breaks down narrative and cinematic continuity. The subject matter is jaded. The camera work and Belmondo's performance are fine.

155 Anon. "Biofilmographie: Jean-Luc Godard." *Vivre sa vie: L'Avant-Scène du cinéma*, No. 19 (October), p. 6.
Credits for *Les Carabiniers* and the proposed *Pour Lucrèce.*

156 Anon. "Biofilmographie: Pierre Braunberger." *Vivre sa vie:*

L'Avant-Scène du cinéma, No. 19 (October), p. 6.
   Biography of major Godard producer.

157   Anon. "Le Brave Petit Soldat." *Positif*, No. 46 (June), p. 77.
   Citations from *Les Lettres françaises* (29 September, 1960, p. 7, and 3 November,
   p. 7) about the censoring of *Le Petit Soldat* are given and responded to.

158   Anon. Interview with Godard. *Le Fait public* (2 January), pp. 9–11.
   Cited 1970, *Image et son*, No. 238 (April), p. 31.

159   Anon. Interview with Godard. *Film Ideal* (Madrid), No. 101.
   Cited 1970, Cameron, Entry No. 1399.

160   Anon. "La Prostituée" *L'Express* (28 August), p. 16.
   Announcement of *Vivre sa vie*, accompanied by publicity still.

161   Anon. Review of *Vivre sa vie*. London *Times* (15 September), p. 15.
   Cited 1962, *Times Index* (September-October), p. 51.

162   Anon. "*Vivre sa vie* et la press." *Vivre sa vie: L'Avant-Scène du cinéma*,
   No. 19 (October), pp. 31–32.
   Quotations from nineteen French reviews.

163   Aubriant, Michel. "Un Roman photo stendhalien fait triompher
   Jean-Luc Godard." *Paris-Presse-l'intransigeant* (30 August), p. 7 DP.
   Godard's problems at the Venice Film Festival are noted. Aubriant finds *Vivre
   sa vie* a poetic and cinematically innovative character study but totally deficient in
   presenting the social and moral context which its theme, prostitution, calls for.

164   Aubriant,   Michel.   "Le   Vrai   Sujet,   c'est   Anna   Karina."
   Paris-Presse-l'intransigeant (29 September), p. 12 DP.
   Vivra sa vie's topic of prostitution is only a pretext for improvising variations,
   some astounding, some tedious. Often Godard seems to mock his audience by his
   disconcerting negligence. This film is an homage to the vibrant Karina.

165   Baby , Yvonne. "Au festival de Venise: un portrait de femme dans le
   film de J. L. Godard, *Vivre sa vie*." *Le Monde* (30 August), p. 11.
   The press saw an uncensored version but the jurors did not. Godard can make
   something exceptional out of banality. The film is both Nana's diary and the
   interior history of her preserving her liberty in spite of humiliation; i.e., two ways
   of Godard's "interrogating life" itself.

166   Baroncelli, Jean de. "Un Palmarès sans surprise au festival de Venise."
   Le Monde (11 September), p. 11.
   Vivre sa vie wins Jury's Special Prize at Venice Festival.

167   Bellechase, André. Review of *Vivre sa vie*. *Carrefour* (12 September).
   Cited 1962, Anon., "*Vivre sa vie* et la presse," Entry No. 162.

168   B.[enayoun], R.[obert]. "Dictionnaire du cinéma français: Godard,
   Jean-Luc." *Positif*, No. 46 (June), p. 27.

Brief pejorative entry accusing Godard of logorrhea, misogyny, illiteracy, and bluff.

169 B.[enayoun], R.[obert]. *"Une Femme est une femme."* Positif, No. 43 (January), pp. 76–77.
There is a "Godard cult" among reviewers, who cannot see that this filmmaker is lazy, vulgar, and pretentious.

170 Benayoun, Robert. " 'Godard,' mon beau souci." *Positif*, No. 48 (October), pp. 37–38.
Brief pejorative review of *Vivre sa vie*, seen along with other Venice Festival films.

171 Benayoun, Robert. "Le Roi est nu." *Positif*, No. 46 (June), pp. 1–14.
The New Wave is the art form of Gaullism, that "ideal terrain for ultra-bourgeois" formalism. A debunking history of the New Wave from 1957–61 is given, discussing why the press lionizes these directors whose amateurism and incompetence are elevated to the level of style and whose films of citation have nothing to say. Godard is not even an anarchist because he "attributes no importance to what he says."

172 Billard, Pierre. Review of *Vivre sa vie*. *Candide* (12 September).
Cited 1962, *Vivre sa vie: L'Avant-Scène du cinéma*, Entry No. 162.

173 Bory, Jean-Louis. "Un Documentaire pensant mais lucide qui cache un film d'amour." *Arts*, No. 892 (19–25 September).
Bory discusses the following influences on and/or citations in *Vivre sa vie*: Montaigne, Sartre, Dreyer, Parain, and de Beauvoir. He analyzes Nana's character and her existentialism. The film is tightly constructed, but Nana's death provides a false ending. Prostitution probably leads to corpulent old age with a big car, but "Godard couldn't bear imagining that vision." Reprinted 1971, Bory, Entry No. 1553.

174 Brigante, Louis. "Venice 1962." *Film Culture*, No. 26 (Fall), p. 42.
Describes Godard's press conference in which he discusses *Vivre sa vie*. Three nude shots were removed from the film due to festival censorship.

175 Capdenac, Michel. "Jean-Luc Godard, *'Le Petit Soldat* ou la résistance à la tyrannie.' " *Les Lettres françaises*, No. 910 (18–24 January), p. 6.
Godard tells his intentions in the film and the influences on it. Like Rossellini, Godard wanted to make a realist film embedded in the concrete.

176 Carta, Jean. "Un Fascinant Portrait de femme." *Témoignage chrétien* (28 September).
Cited 1974, Collet, Entry No. 1832.

177 Cervoni, Albert. *"Vivre sa vie."* France-nouvelle, No. 884 (26 September–2 October), p. 31.
In a real auteur film the director also writes the script. Godard's sensibility in *Vivre sa vie* derives from love — for a woman, for human truths, and for life: Godyard's stylistic hallmark and goal are a controlled spontaneity. He combines a

subjective, personal camera style with a cinema verite kind of documentary which concentrates on social concerns.

178 Chapier, Henry. *"Vivre sa vie* ou les difficultes de rester soi-même." *Combat* (24 September).
Cited 1962, *Vivre sa vie: L'Avant-scène du cinéma*, Entry No. 162.

179 Chauvet, Louis. Review of *Vivre sa vie. Le Figaro* (29 August).
Cited 1974, Collet, Entry No. 1832.

180 Chauvet, Louis. Review of *Vivre sa vie. Le Figaro* (27 September).
Cited 1974, Collet, Entry No. 1832.

181 Chazal, Robert. Review of *Vivre sa vie. France Soir* (22 August).
Cited 1962, *Vivre sa vie: L'Avant-Scène du cinéma*, Entry No. 162.

182 Clay, Jean. Review of *Vivre sa vie. Réalités,* September.
Cited in 1962, *Vivre sa vie: L'Avant-Scène du cinéma,* Entry No. 162.

183 Cobast, C. "Critique: *Sept Péchés capitaux." Image et son*, No. 152, p. 37.
Cited 1963, *Image et son: Index: 1946–1962* No. 158 (January), p. 72.

184 Collet, Jean. "L'Acteur à son insu dans les films de la nouvelle vague." *Etudes cinématographiques: Théâtre et cinéma, 2: L'Acteur.* Ed. Claude Gautier. Nos. 14-15 N.S. (Spring), (Paris: Lettres Modernes-Minard), pp. 38–47.
Previously film acting had been subordinated to the requirements of the camera and the filming, and the directors sought either a stylized or a naturalized performance. Both of these extremes are now found in the New Wave films, where the actors are directed in "a dialectic of mannerism and improvisation." In this way *Une Femme est une femme,* like Rossellini's *Voyage to Italy,* is a document about its protagonist both as actress and as woman.

185 Collet, Jean. "La Bande sonore du film *Vivre sa vie." Revue du son*, No. 116 (December), p. 513.
Godard's direct-sound recording is described. Trans. 1972, Brown, Entry No. 1658.

186 Collet, Jean, et al. "Entretien avec Jean-Luc Godard." *Cahiers du cinéma*, "Spécial 'Nouvelle Vague," No. 138 (December), pp. 21–39.
In an interview with Jean Collet, Michel Delahaye, Jean-André Fieschi, André-S. Labarthe, and Bernard Tavernier, Godard discussed *Cahiers* critics' development into film directors, his use of improvisation and his direction of actors, his interest in theater and in certain other directors, and the techniques and goals of the *nouvelle vague* directors. (Mussman's version omits a long discussion of *Le Petit Soldat,* some of Godard's comments on his writing the scenario for and his current evaluation of *A bout de souffle,* his problems distributing *Une Femme est une femme,* some of his discussion about French television, and the international film industry. There are excisions of sentences and references throughout.) Reprinted 1968, Narboni, ed., No. 1170. A translation by Rose Kaplin in the *New York Film Bulletin*, was reprinted in *Cahiers du Cinema in English,* and also in 1968, Mussman,

Entry No. 1168. Trans. 1972, Milne, Entry No. 1713. Excerpts, 1970, Collet, trans. Vaughan, Entry No. 1425.

187 Collet, Jean. Interview with Godard on *Vivre sa vie*. *Télérama*, No. 663.
Cited 1974, Collet, Entry No. 1832.

188 Collet, Jean. "Le Portrait d'une ame." *Signes du temps*, n.d.
Review of *Vivre sa vie* cited 1975, Collet, Entry No. 1832.

189 Collet, Jean. Review of *Vivre sa vie*. *Télérama* (30 September).
Quoted 1962, *Vivre sa vie: L'Avant-Scène du cinéma*, Entry No. 162.

190 Corbin, Louise. "*Seven Capital Sins*." *Films in Review*, 13, No. 10 (December), 625–26.
In his sketch, *Sloth*, Godard "superficially kids about a profound psychological problem."

191 Cortard, Rene. Review of *Vivre sa vie*. *Candide* (26 September).
Cited 1962, *Vivre sa vie: L'Avant-Scène du cinéma*, Entry No. 162.

192 Delahaye, Michel. "Sérénade à trois." *Cahiers du cinéma*, No. 132, pp. 40–44.
Credits for *Les Sept Péchés capitaux*. The critic analyzes the genre of the omnibus film. In Godard's sketch, *La Paresse*, owning an automobile incarnates the sin of sloth. Godard's style is complex and entirely appropriate for the sketch's theme.

193 Doniol-Valcroze, Jacques. "Lettre à Jeander." *Libération* (6-7 October).
Cited 1974, Collet, Entry No. 1803.

194 Dort, Bernard. "Le Star et le comedien." *Etudés cinématographiques: Théâtre et cinema, 2: L'Acteur*. Ed. Claude Gautier. Nos. 14–15, N.S. (Spring), (Paris: Lettres Modernes-Minard), pp. 5–11.
In *A bout de souffle* Godard does not give the actors roles but rather "reduces" the environment to a reflection of character. He "surprises" the actors in their acting, filming the way they act, the way they invent a character. Today's cinema goes beyond using actors merely as visual elements in the scene and is open to letting them express both their knowledge of self and of society. However, the "epic style of the Brechtian actor seems as irreducible to film as the diction exercises of our classic stage actors."

195 Dort, Bernard. "Tours et detours de J. L. Godard." *France-Observateur* (27 September), pp. 22–23.
On the bad side, the theme of *Vivre sa vie* is banal; Godard ignores the reality of prostitution and tries to be an amateur philosopher; he lapses into the ritual of a Mass, following Rossellini's aesthetic and Dreyer's notions of sacrifice; his cinematic "innovations" often make the film "unreadable." On the good side, he romantically captures the grace and fragility of his beloved actress.

196 Douchet, Jean. "Venise 1962: *Vivre sa vie*." *Cahiers du cinéma*, No. 136 (October), pp. 44–46.

This praising review provides a plot summary, a discussion of the theme (interior vs. exterior aspects of Nana's life), and an indication of cinematic "distanciation" devices.

197 El Kaïm, Arlette. "Du cinéma consideré comme un assassinat." *Les Temps modernes*, 18, No. 199 (December), 145–47.
Godard, in *Vivre sa vie*, made a film to show off a woman, but nothing more. He throws titles around, multiplies images feverishly, and gives Nana dialogue consisting of his own vague and empty ideas "without ever making an effort to interiorize them" in the characterization.

198 Ferrero, Adelio. "Il destino di Nana." *Cinema nuovo*, 11, No. 159 (September-October).
Review of *Vivre sa vie*. Cited 1967, Amengual and Estève, Entry No. 782.

199 Fieschi, Jean-André. "La Difficulté d'être de Jean-Luc Godard." *Cahiers du cinéma*, No. 137 (November), pp. 14–25.
The title refers to Cocteau's book, *The Difficulty of Being*. Fieschi describes how Godard "finds himself" in cinema and art. The following themes in *Une Femme est une femme* and *Vivre sa vie* are traced: the crystallization of chaos; dream vs. reality; the difficulty of being; death's life; art's absorbing the artist; oppression and liberation or unhappiness and happiness as coincidental, equal, and even identical. Trans. 1967, *Cahiers du Cinema in English*, Entry No. 879. That trans. reprinted 1968, Mussman, Entry No. 1168.

200 G.[autier], G.[uy]. "Contre *Vivre sa vie*." *Image et son: Revue du cinéma*, No. 156 (November), pp. 42–43.
The film suffers from empty content, trite theme, vulgarized philosophy, pretentious division into tableaux, and tedious long takes of people's backs. Yet Godard does film with an ease, elegance of style, and seemingly personal vision.

201 Giroud, Françoise. "Un Message personnel." *L'Express* (20 September), pp. 23–24.
Vivre sa vie is analyzed in terms of its romanticism, cinematic originality, and personal tone.

202 Grousset, Jean-Paul. Review of *Vivre sa vie*. *Le Canard enchaîne* (26 September).
Cited 1962, *Vivre sa vie L'Avant-Scène du cinéma*, Entry No. 162.

203 Jeander. Review of *Vivre sa vie*. *Libération* (22 September).
Cited 1968, Gauteur, Entry No. 1111.

204 Kauffmann, Stanley. Review of *Seven Capital Sins*. *New Republic* (22 December).
Quoted 1963, Anon., *Film Facts*, Entry No. 245.

205 Koval, Francis. "Venice 1962." *Films in Review*, 13, No. 8 (October), 470–71.
Godard has flashes of brilliance in *Vivre sa vie*, but the plot is one of humdrum

"immorality." Godard seems obsessed to be original and to exhibit his wife's talents.

206 L.[efèvre], R.[aymond]. "Pour *Vivre sa vie.*" *Image et son: Revue du cinéma*, No. 156 (November), p. 42.
Godard has an aggressive, lucid style which gives each sequence in *Vivre sa vie* a new kind of richness and range of signification. The stylistic innovations are described.

207 Martin, Marcel. "*Vivre sa vie.*" *Cinéma 62*, No. 70 (November), pp. 105–106.
Brief credits. The film is a lovely hymn to Karina and to cinema itself. Yet it has irritating "tics." Rather than being a documentary about prostitution, it is a portrait of one individual's interior spiritual "adventure." Its structure is loose, haphazard, like a journal, with "insupportably boring" inserts of philosophy and a story by Poe.

208 Maurel, Christian. "Venise: chères idoles." *L'Express* (30 August), p. 17.
Brief review extolls *Vivre sa vie* as emotionally touching and stylistically brilliant.

209 Mauriac, Claude. "Un Peintre fait le portrait d'une femme." *Le Figaro littéraire*, 17 (22 September), 18.
In *Vivre sa vie* Godard creatively uses citations and an episodic structure. Each of the different segments is "meticulously composed" into the whole. The changes of tone permit us to approach this "portrait" as a series of sketches, from different angles and in different, contradictory styles.

210 Mesnil, Michel. "Du péché d'indifférence." *Esprit*, No. 12 (December), pp. 1018–23.
Vivra sa vie is full of philosophical pretentiousness. It fails as a character study. The distanciation is not Brechtian because it does not enrich or critique our reality and move us to action. Rather Godard "empties things of their truth, elicits our irony, our detachment." Other New Wave directors also misuse distanciation.

211 Miller, Claude. "*Vivre sa vie.*" *Télécine*, No. 108 (December-January), pp. 1–12.
"Fiche No. 413." Credits, plot summary. Miller analyzes the cinematic style, Nana's characterization, and cinematic influences on Godard. Godard's carefree style really hides a pessimistic attitude toward a woman who is shown seeking money, being degraded, and ending up lost. "Unnecessary" excesses include the following: the Poe story, the scene with Parain, the "logorrhea," and the intrusion of dry, abstract ideas. Godard cannot express ideas dramatically or cinematically in terms of action.

212 Milne, Tom. "How Art is True." *Sight and Sound*, 31, No. 4 (Autumn), 161–171.
Everyone is using improvisation in the film now to try to capture reality. Filmmakers want to grasp "the whole complexity of human nature . . . Gone are

the good old days of the great stars, when one knew exactly what one was going to get, and it was more than enough." In the use of improvisation, which has many pitfalls, Godard's *Une Femme est une femme* is superior to a film like Cassevetes' *Shadows*. In *Vivre sa vie*, the camera, not the actress, improvises. The virtue of Godard's and Truffaut's improvisation is that they constantly surprise us and show us new ways of seeing.

213 Milne, Tom. "Jean-Luc Godard and *Vivre sa vie*." *Sight and Sound*, 32, No. 1 (Winter), 9–12, 50.

In an interview taped when VIVRE SA VIE was shown at the London Film Festival, Godard talks about political commitment, the relation between fiction and documentary, being misunderstood by the public, Brecht, and his plans to film *Pour Lucrèce*. This interview is followed by Milne's review. Milne notes the Brechtian influence on *Vivre sa vie*, Godard's use of a static camera that "traps apparently unimportant details," and Godard's effort to "capture" Nana in a portrait by moving from her exterior to her soul. Interview reprinted 1968, Mussman, Entry No. 1168.

214 Mosk[owitz, Gene]. "*Seven Capital Sins*." *Variety* (11 April).

This satiric look at human foibles has "Rabelesian humor" and "tasteful nudity." Quoted 1963, Anon., *Film Facts*, Entry No. 245.

215 Mosk[owitz, Gene]. *Vivre sa vie (Live Her Life)* (French)." *Variety* (29 August).

Credits. Venice. The film treats the subject of prostitution in a serious, brisk, unsentimental, arty way.

216 Ollier, Claude. "*Les Sept péchés capitaux*." *La Nouvelle Revue française*, 19 (II), 922.

Godard's *La Paresse* is the only sketch in the film that is totally cinematic.

217 Pechter, William. "= Time^2." *Contact* (Sausalito, CA), No. 10 (June), pp. 74–81.

In-depth review of *Breathless* begins with a complete plot summary, which inclusively describes the visuals, the dialogue, the music, and the pacing. Analyzes Godard's mixture of humor and existential seriousness, the portrayal of a love relationship, Michel's characterization as a romantic hero, Patricia's evasiveness, the use of the Bogart myth, the jazz score, the jump cuts (a "spatial play on time"), and the episodic structure. It is a revolutionary film. Reprinted 1971, Pechter, Entry No. 1606.

218 Polac, Michel. Interview with Godard. *Arts*, No. 892 (19-25 September).

Cited 1974, Collet, Entry No. 1832. Brown (1972, Entry No. 1657), lists this entry: "*Arts*, No. 892, August 15 (?)." Question mark is Brown's.

219 Potenze, Jaime. "Cine: *Una mujer es una mujer (Une Femme est une femme*, Francia, 1961)." *Criterio* (Buenos Aires), 35, No. 1409 (9 August), 589.

New Wave films, of which this is an example, show talent but treat human relations, especially sexual ones, immorally, frivolously, and often boringly. The New Wave directors cannot "film a coherent drama or comedy," and their films are flawed by in-jokes, repetition, and vacuity.

220 Rabine, Henry. Review of *Vivre sa vie*. *La Croix* (29 September).
Cited 1974, Collet, Entry No. 1832.

221 Sadoul, Georges. "Je tremble pour *Vivre sa vie*, comme pour tous les films que j'aime." *Les Lettres françaises*, No. 941 (30 August-5 September), p. 7.
Reviews films shown at the Venice Film Festival. Sadoul fears *Vivre sa vie* might be dismissed, critically. It is neither a melodramatic nor a musical treatment of prostitution, but a denunciation of the condition of women under Western civilization done effectively in a restrained, Brechtian way.

222 Sadoul, Georges. "Ni 'melo' ni 'conventionnel.'" *Les Lettres françaises*, No. 945 (27 September–3 October), p. 8.
Discusses sources for *Vivre sa vie* (*Quai des brumes*, Brecht, Montaigne, *Lola Montès*, Poe, silent film). Some have found the ending "conventional," and the film "melodramatic." In fact, Godard uses the prostitution theme to critique the lumpenproletariat's role in the social organization, with an analysis similar to that found in *The Good Soldier Schweik* or *The Three Penny Opera* or in Engels' *The Origins of the Family, Private Property, and the State*.

223 Sadoul, Georges. "Venise 1962: festival decevant." *Les Lettres françaises*, No. 943 (13–19 September), p. 6.
Vivre sa vie won the Gold Lion and the Italian Critics Prize, although the festival officials censored and cut a number of shots.

224 LeSerpent. Review of *Vivre sa vie*. *Minute* (27 September).
Cited 1962, *Vivre sa vie: L'Avant-scène du cinéma*, Entry No. 162.

225 Shivas, Mark. Review of *Vivre sa vie*. *Movie*, No. 3 (October), p. 30.
Cited in Bowles, p. 552.

226 Steen, T.M.F., "The Sound Track." *Films in Review*, 13, No. 2 (February), 115–16.
Describes the innovations on the sound track of *La Femme mariée*—Legrand's score, Godard's use of ambient noise, and his editing the sound disconnectedly "every few seconds of screen time."

227 Truffaut, François. "Que chacun vive sa vie." *Vivre sa vie: L'Avant-Scène du cinéma*, No. 19 (15 October), p. 7.
Truffaut comments on the New Wave. *Vivre sa vie*'s emotional force comes from Godard's intuitively, rather than scientifically, pushing cinema to both its ultimate abstraction and ultimate concreteness.

228 Yvoire, Jean de. "*Vivre sa vie*." *Téléciné*, No. 107 (October-November), unnumbered.
Mixed review, with which H.A., G.S., and J.E.F. agree.

229   Zand, Nicole. "Entretien avec Jean-Luc Godard: 'Ce que je recherche, c'est exprimer des pensées plutôt que raconter des histoires.'" *Le Monde* (21 September), p. 13.
Finds Nana's death in *Vivre sa vie* melodramatic and theatrical, as were other situations in that film. In an interview Godard tells other endings he'd considered. The film is a "reconstituted documentary," "theater-verite." Godard says his goal is not to convey situations but an interior state.

1963

230   Alpert, Hollis. "Continental Comedy." *Saturday Review*, 46, No. 6 (9 February), 21.
Godard's skit "Laziness" in *Seven Capital Sins* is always amusing and "proves that Godard . . . is no flash in the pan." Quoted at length in *Film Facts* (1963, Anon., Entry No. 245).

231   Alpert, Hollis. "Irma and Nana." *Saturday Review*, 46, No. 25 (22 June), 31.
In *My Life to Live*, Karina's "artlessness" is affecting and beautiful. Godard's arbitrariness fails artistically although he clearly wished to use improvisation to infuse his tale of a prostitute with "life and meaning." Quoted at length in *Film Facts* (1963, Anon., Entry No. 239).

232   Anon. "A Beautiful Woman in Focus." *Christian Science Monitor* (16 December), p. 4.
Review of *My Life to Live*. Cited 1963, *Christian Science Monitor* annual index, 1963, p. 99.

233   Anon. "Breathlessly Lifeless." *Newsweek*, 62, No. 14 (30 September), 84.
The episodes in *My Life to Live* are "tiresome" and the dialogue "opaque"; the film as a whole "combines the flatness of documentary work with "theatrical banality."

234   Anon. Brief mention of the filming of *Les Carabiniers. L'Humanité* (1 January).

235   Anon. "Checklist 5—Jean-Luc Godard." *Monthly Film Bulletin*, 30 (August).
Filmography. It also lists the films Godard acted in from 1950–1963.

236   Anon. Interview with Godard. *Film ideal* (Madrid), (1 January).
Cited 1970, Cameron, Entry No. 1399.

237   Anon. "A Love Song: *My Life to Live.*" *Time*, 82, No. 13 (11 October), 113.
The film is an allegory about a woman who feels free and responsible for the first time in her life. The camera adores Karina, and Godard enlarges and liberates the language of film by many "new cinematic tricks." It is an accomplished, subtle, ironic, and emotional film.

238 Anon. "Movie Differences." *Movie*, No. 8, pp. 28–29.
Cited in Bowles, p. 552.

239 Anon. *"My Life to Live." Film Facts*, 6, No. 44 (5 December), 268–69.
Complete credits and one-paragraph synopsis of the film are given, as well as lengthy citations from the reviews in *Variety, Time*, the New York *Herald Tribune*, the *New York Times*, the *New Republic*, and the *Saturday Review*.

240 Anon. *"Le Petit Soldat* presente à Paris le 25 janvier." *Le Monde* (22 January), p. 15.
Announces opening of film after two years' censorship. January 24 premiere will be at Ciné-Club Universitaire with Godard talking afterward.

241 Anon. Review of *Les Carabiniers. Image et son: la saison cinématographique 1963*.
Cited 1973, Anon., *Image et son: Index: 1946–1972*, Entry No. 1746.

242 Anon. Review of *Le Petit Soldat.* London *Times* (27 June), p. 16.
Cited 1963, *Times Index*, May-June, p. 101.

243 Anon. Review of *Vivre sa vie. Film* (British Federation of Film Societies), No. 35 (Spring), pp. 30 and 32.
Cited in Bowles, p. 552.

244 Anon. "Les Robots sont là_____." *France-Observateur* (6 May).
Interview with Godard, cited 1975, *Les Temps modernes*, 20 No. 230, 187.

245 Anon. *"Seven Capital Sins." Film Facts*, 6, No. 7 (21 March), 31–32.
Complete credits. Reviews quoted from *Saturday Review*, the *New Republic*, the *New York Times, Variety*, and the New York *Herald Tribune*. A brief synopsis of each director's section of the film is given.

246 Aubriant, Michel. *"Les Carabiniers* de Jean-Luc Godard: un film à lire, les pieds dans des pantoufles." *Paris-Press-l'intransigeant* (6 June), p. 12E.
Godard fans call this film Brechtian or anticinema and a superior form of expression. In fact, *Les Carabiniers* is built on "banality, cliche, psychological incoherence, bad photography, . . . inaudible dialogue, disordered thinking, ugliness, . . . [and] actors transformed . . . into grimacing marionettes." Cited and refuted, 1963, Godard, Entry No. 2216.

247 Autera, Leonard. *"Les Sept Péchés capitaux." Bianco e nero*, 23, No. 5 (May), pp. 70–71.
Complete credits, review.

248 Baby, Yvonne. Interview with Godard on *Le Mépris. Le Monde* (20 December).
Godard talks about his relations with Carlo Ponti and Joseph E. Levine, and the latter's insistence on the addition of a nude scene. Godard had wanted Kim Novak and Frank Sinatra for the film, Levine wanted Mastroianni and Loren. *Le Mépris's* theme is misunderstanding; the cinematic technique is to "film a quick glance over a long space of time." Trans. 1972, Brown, Entry No. 1658.

249 Baker, Peter. "It's My Life." *Films and Filming*, 9, No. 4 (January), 44.
Brief credits. The theme of *Vivre sa vie* is that a prostitute doesn't necessarily have an ignoble soul. The film is dull and Godard's workmanship sloppy (e.g., filming the back of two conversing people's heads for several minutes in one take).

250 Baroncelli, Jean de. "*Les Carabiniers.*" *Le Monde* (4 June), p. 20.
The film flirts with Brecht but is closer to Jarry. Its satire falls flat, and it becomes a totally irritating, repetitious failure that nevertheless reveals its maker's talent.

251 Baroncelli, Jean de. "Critique: *Le Mépris.*" *Le Monde* (21 December).
Like a classical tragedy, the film has "acts" which respect the unity of time and place. The central section, a "vulgar scene of a couple. . .caught by surprise in their intimacy," is marked by "seriousness, sensibility, and profound emotion." Again Godard irritates us by his "usual extravagances" and "mania for citation."

252 Benayoun, Robert. "Godard ou le mythe de l'irresponsable." *France-Observateur* (31 January), p. 22.
Le Petit Soldat has a few eleventh-rate police scenes of action blemished by empty close-ups of the protagonist, many banal lectures and citations, and an irresponsible, apolitical, and studiously "innocent" directorial stance toward Algeria. Sources for Godard's citations are noted in passing. Godard's films are all facetious bluffs. Short excerpt trans. 1970, Collet, Entry No. 1425.

253 Benayoun, Robert. "Jusqu'à quand, Monsieur Godard?" *France-Observateur* (6 June), p. 21.
Godard's overwhelming ambition, disdain, laborious attempts at humor, lack of imagination, and empty thinking are evident in *Les Carabiniers.* This brute farce has nothing in common with Brechtian distanciation.

254 Benayoun, Robert. "Même Bardot n'a pas sauvé Godard." *France-Observateur* (24 December)., p. 18.
People criticize him for his prejudice against Godard, so he tried to like *Le Mépris.* After seeing the film, he had to buy Moravia's book because he couldn't believe the original novel could have been so pretentious and intellectually empty. There are a few beautiful cold photographs, but the tempo and the action around the theme of disdain are "distended."

255 Bertieri, Claudio. "Taccuino della XXIII Mostra." *Bianco e nero*, 23, No. 9-10 (September-October), ii.
Mention of *Vivre sa vie*.

256 Bory, Jean-Louis. "Bodart et Gardot." *Arts*, No. 942 (25–31 December).
Le Mépris is about the kind of woman who demands to be possessed or she'll disdain the man. Bardot has never been directed so well. The film is also a "meditation" on Homer, tragedy, and cinema. Reprinted 1971, Bory, Entry No. 1553.

257 Boys, Barry. "*Le Petit Soldat.*" *Movie*, No. 11 (August), pp. 18–20.
Bruno's ambiguities reflect the real perversities of the then intolerable political situation.

258 Bureau, Patrick. "Anna et les paradoxes." *Cinéma 63*, Special issue: "L'Acteur," No. 78 (July-August), pp. 56–65.
A discussion of Anna Karina's personality and career and an interview with her.

259 Capdenac, Michel. *"Le Petit Soldat*: irritante confusion." *Les Lettres françaises*, No. 963 (31 January–6 February), p. 7.
The film raises serious issues but does not treat them in depth. It is hard to take the protagonist's existential doubts and his refusal to murder on demand seriously, because his reflections are dominated by his monstrous, negative egotism.

260 Carroll, Walter J. "The Cinema: *My Life to Live.*" *The Villager* (Greenwich, Conn.), (10 October).
This is a sensitive, austere, well-acted portrait of a prostitute. Camera work is briefly noted.

261 Cervoni, Albert. "Godard et la torture." *France-nouvelle*, No. 903 (6–12 February), pp. 26–27.
Godard calls himself a sentimental leftist. Bruno's characterization in *Le Petit Soldat* is as insufficient as Sam Wood's "impartial" direction of *For Whom the Bell Tolls*. To portray France's political situation during the Algerian War, Godard uses psychological arguments and blames marginal organizations, but he never accuses or analyzes the roles of any of the governments.

262 Chapier, Henry. Review of *Les Carabiniers. Combat* (5 June).
Positive review. Quoted 1976, Anon., *"Les Carabiniers* et la presse," Entry No. 1931.

263 Chauvet, Louis. Review of *Les Carabiniers. Le Figaro* (5 June).
Negative review. Quoted in 1976, *"Les Carabiniers* et la presse," Entry No. 1931.

264 Clay, Jean. "Le Paradoxe de Jean-Luc Godard, nihiliste et créateur." *Réalités*, No. 212 (September), pp. 84–94.
Many biographical details about Godard's life, mannerisms, and personality are given and form the basis for analyzing Godard's cinematic direction and his work, which is "disguised autobiography." Godard has an "adolescent nostalgia for the absolute" and thus treats as major themes time and death. He "tries desperately to immobilize the movement of life." Godard is interviewed and describes his work as follows: *Le Mépris* is a tragedy in long shots; *Une Femme est une femme* is a comedy in close-ups. In *Le Mépris* he wanted "to put across the idea of a world, rather than a character," i.e., Homeric serenity vs. TV sets and flashing cars. People didn't like *Les Carabiniers* because they did not like to see "larvae" like themselves on the screen but rather wanted the catharsis of a "beautiful Zanuck-style war" Trans. 1964, Clay, Entry No. 380. Excerpts in 1968, Collet, Entry No. 1088; and these are trans. in 1970, Collet, Entry No. 1425.

265 Collet, Jean. *Jean-Luc Godard*. Series Cinéma d'aujourd'hui. No. 18. Paris: Editions Seghers.
For 1968 and 1974 revisions, see Entry Nos. 1088 and 1836. For 1970 trans. of

1968 French edition see Entry No. 1425. I have not been able to see this 1963 edition or the 1965 revision.

266 Collet, Jean. "Mourir sa mort." *Télérama*, No. 700 (16 June).
Review of *Les Carabiniers*. Quoted 1965, *Une Femme mariée: L'Avant-Scène du cinéma*, Entry No. 455.

267 Collet, Jean. "Où est la liberté?" *Signes du temps* (July), p. 33.
In *Les Carabiniers*, Godard puts war and bestiality on trial, and also the voracity of the eye for spectacle. He maintains a distance from his characters, uses a fable form, and rejects traditional pictorial cinematic style. Trans. 1972, Brown, Entry No. 1658.

268 Collet, Jean. "'La Question' de J.-L. Godard." *Signes du temps* (February).
Cited 1974, Collet, Entry No. 1832.

269 Comolli, Jean-Louis. "La Présence et l'absence." *Cahiers du cinéma*, No. 141 (March), pp. 54–58.
Provides an in-depth analysis of *Le Petit soldat* within the context of a romantic aesthetic. The mise en scene continually inverses all relationships, and Godard "ceaselessly mixes and explains one thing by its opposite, a presence by an absence."

270 Cournot, Michel. "En verité, Godard s'est devoué." *L'Express* (13 June), pp. 28–29.
Les Carabiniers is exasperating, ugly, badly written and acted, and poorly lit. Yet it is the first war film that shows war as ugly, ignoble, and petty, unlike all those other war films full of photogenic violence and emotion. Excerpt trans. 1970, Collet, Entry No. 1425.

271 Crist, Judith. "*My Life to Live*, with a Blank-Faced Heroine." New York *Herald Tribune* (24 September).
Paris theater. Brief credits. This is a tedious, pretentious effort, both in its artiness and in its treatment of prostitution.

272 Crist, Judith. Review of *Seven Capital Sins*. New York *Herald Tribune* (17 January).
Cited 1963, Anon., *Film Facts*, Entry No. 245.

273 Crowther, Bosley. "New Parisian Styles: Recent Movies from France Display More Artiness than Art." *New York Times* (29 September), Sec. II, p. 1.
In *Vivre sa vie*, Godard loses control, dissipates emotional development, and uses a banal theme.

274 Crowther, Bosley. Review of *Seven Capital Sins*. *New York Times* (17 January), p. 5.
Brief credits. Godard's skit, *Laziness*, in *Seven Capital Sins*, shows "in driest, drollest fashion" how sloth overcomes and cancels out lust. Quoted in *Film Facts* (1963, Anon., Entry No. 245).

275 Crowther, Bosley. Review of *Vivre sa vie*. *New York Times* (24 September), p. 43.
Brief credits. Godard's narrative innovations in *Vivre sa vie* are bold. Although he tries to convey an "external sense of the aloneness, inadequacy, and pathos" of the protagonist, Nana still "never emerges as more than an amiable, stupid, helpless thing preyed upon by a standard procurer . . ."

276 Durgnat, Raymond. Review of *Le Petit Soldat*. *Films and Filming*, 9, No. 11 (August), 23–24.
Cited in Bowles, p. 390.

277 Dyer, Peter John. *"Le Petit Soldat." Sight and Sound*, 32, No. 4 (Autumn), 195–96.
What Godard offers us in *Le Petit Soldat* "is not an apprehension of life, but of imminent death; not thought but a reflex of thought and, moreover, moviemania thought at that." The "discrepancy between subject and sensibility . . . makes *Le Petit Soldat . . .* a fantastic piece of sophistry."

278 Fieschi, Jean-André. "Godard: Cut-Sequence: *Vivre sa vie.*" Trans. Gary Broughton. *Movie*, No. 6 (January), pp. 21–25.
Includes script for sequences cut from English version. Cited in Bowles, p. 552.

279 Gill, Brendan. "No Surprises." *The New Yorker*, 39, No. 33 (5 October), 179.
My Life to Live is a dull, moralistic, inelegant story of prostitution, enlivened only by the shots of Karina's face.

280 Gilson, René. *"Les Carabiniers." Cinéma 63*, No. 78 (July-August), pp. 123–24.
This is a cinematic *Candide*, Godard's most inventive and intelligent film. Brief credits.

281 Giroud, Françoise. "Un Bon Jeune Homme." *L'Express* (31 January), pp. 15–16.
Le Petit Soldat is cold and detached because it looks at politics in an abstract, romantic way. The hero defines himself in citations. The style is inappropriately that of a U.S. gangster film or a comic strip, but the virtuoso long take of Bruno's photographing Veronica shows Godard's genius.

282 Graham, Peter. "The Face of 63—France." *Films and Filming*, 9, No. 8 (May), 13.
Article on Belmondo and Karina. Cited in Schuster, p. 165.

283 Hartung, Phillip T. "The Screen: What Makes Sammy Run?" *Commonweal*, 79 (18 October), p. 105.
Vivre sa vie is dull, its plot contrived, and is full of excessive close-ups and pretentious titles. The content is like a "documented case history" with "sordid undertones."

284 Houston, Penelope. *The Contemporary Cinema*. Baltimore: Penguin. Pp. 103–105.

A bout de souffle is discussed in terms of its amorality, shifts and jump cuts, and emphasis on the instant rather than on the story line. *Une Femme est une femme* is an "exhibitionist demonstration" of pure cinema; in *Vivre sa vie* this consciousness of watching a film and nothing else remains, but Godard's power is finely controlled.

285 Jeander. Review of *Les Carabiniers*. *Libération* (8 June).
Cited 1968, Gauteur, Entry No. 1111, and 1976, Anon., *"Les Carabiniers* et la presse," Entry No. 1931.

286 Jeander. Review of *Le Mépris*. *Libération* (27 December).
Cited 1968, Gauteur, Entry No. 1111.

287 [Jeanson, Henri]. "Godard (Jean-Luc), réalisateur, né à Paris le 30 décembre 1930" in "Petit dictionnaire de feu de la nouvelle vague." *Crapouillot*, No. 60 (April), pp. 66–67.
Jeanson gives an offhand, personal reaction to Godard's films and a witty commentary on Godard's sources and the criticism written about him.

288 Kauffmann, Stanley. "Wanton Women, Modest Men." The *New Republic*, 149 (12 October), 28–29.
My Life to Live is only a "collection of stylistic devices, without characterization, without credible motivation." The Brechtian devices do not help us understand anything. Reprinted in 1966, Kauffmann, Entry No. 711.

289 Lachize, Samuel. "Et tout ça pour quoi?: *Le Mépris* de Jean-Luc Godard." *L'Humanité* (26 December), p. 6
The characters in *Le Mépris* are terribly removed from everyday life. The couple's quarrel seems senseless, and generally the film's dialogue is either vulgar or esoteric. Godard had not wanted to use Bardot, but she is the only thing of interest in the film.

290 L.[efèvre], R.[aymond]. *"Le Petit Soldat." Image et son: Revue du cinéma*, No. 160 (March), pp. 53–54.
The film does not provoke audiences as it would have in 1960. The sound track varies between dialogue and reflection, fits the protagonist's multiple contradictions, and reflects Godard's own youth and political immaturity. Karina has a marvelous evanescence. The camera movement, angles and editing "evoke the aesthetic of the best comic strips."

291 Lennon, Peter. "One Man Unit." *Guardian* (12 January), p. 15.
Lennon describes Godard's filmmaking technique and "exasperating personality." In an interview on the site of filming *Les Carabiniers*, Godard discusses unions, the new film, his use of improvisation and private jokes, *Le Petit Soldat*, *Vivre sa vie*, and his reactions to U.S., French, and British directors.

292 Manceaux, Michèle. "Il était écrit qu'un jour Camille se mettrait à penser: *L'Odysée* de Godard." *L'Express* (26 December), pp. 20–21.
Le Mépris is seen as a masterly character study. The critic discusses the parallels to *The Odyssey*.

293 Marcabru, Pierre. *"Les Carabiniers:* un affreux Jojo à la guerre." *Arts,* No. 920 (12–18 June).

Like a 12-year-old who just got his first camera, Godard films mainly faces, especially that of the savage, porcine, naive Juross, "the son of Ubu." In this grim, Jarry-like farce about war, Godard fails because of a refusal to draw a lesson and lazy cinematic construction.

294 Marcabru, Pierre. "L'Univers des bandes dessineés." *Arts,* No. 901 (30 January–5 February).

Le Petit Soldat has a comic strip's fragmentary, naive, and schematic construction. Ironically that construction approaches the reality of the Algerian war in France, where "shifty, dangerous, and gullible characters play at cops and robbers." The ultrasensitive film stock allows Godard to film freely and loosely indoors, in a style that suits the disorder and precariousness of the characters' lives. The voice-over commentary is often boring and pretentious.

295 Marcorelles, Louis. "Review of *Les Carabiniers." Gazette de Lausanne* (29 January).

Cited 1965, *Une Femme mariée: L'Avant-Scène du cinéma,* Entry No. 455.

296 Mardore, Michel. "Jean-Luc Godard a repeint dans *Le Mépris* le sourire des statues grecques." *Lettres françaises,* No. 1,009 (26 December–1 January, 1964), pp. 1 and 7.

Asserts that Godard's modesty is combined artistically with provocative aggressiveness and vice versa. In an interview, Godard describes in detail the production problems with *Le Mépris* and discusses the major themes of the film and his borrowings from Moravia.

297 M.[artin], M.[arcel]. "La Censure et *Le Soldat." Cinéma 63,* No. 74 (March), pp. 22–23.

A number of cases of recent political film censorship are described. Godard's flip comments, cited here at length, irritated people after *Le Petit Soldat*'s premier at the Ciné-Club Universitaire. (e.g., "I'm for freedom, pure and simple, vs. any kind of socialism . . .") Martin faults Godard for accusing political activists of "opportunism," for preaching, and for a purely individualistic notion of freedom.

298 Martin, Marcel. "En écoutant Jean-Luc Godard." *Les Lettres françaises,* No. 936 (31 January–6 February), p. 7

Godard premiered *Le Petit Soldat* at the Ciné-Club Universitaire, and his flippant answers at a round table discussion afterward irritated many. Martin cites Godard at length.

299 Martin, Marcel. *"Le Petit Soldat." Cinéma 63,* No. 74 (March), pp. 129–31.

The film is irritating with its verbal deluge, pontificating tone, and political ambiguities. Martin describes the sections cut by the censors: details about Veronica's being tortured to death by the fascists and her words to Bruno, "You'll lose this war because you don't have an ideal."

300   Mauriac, Claude. *"Les Carabiniers* de Jean-Luc Godard." *Le Figaro littéraire* (15 June), p. 20.

At one point, Godard filmed 31 shots for this film in one day. The film shows the influence of Brecht and silent film directors. It has comic moments but deals with the subject of war in a derisory, irritating way. Godard should have been more demanding with himself.

301   Maurin, A. "La Projection du film *Vivre sa vie* de Jean-Luc Godard." *L'Humanité dimanche* (8 February), p. 2.

Includes interview with Godard and brief announcement.

302   Mekas, Jonas. "Movie Journal." *Village Voice* (26 September), p. 13.

My Life to Live is marred by excesses of formal control and Nana's philosophizing, her super-rational *cogito*. Drawing on Jung, Mekas faults Godard for not considering that "other mind," beyond logic and thinking, "the Dionysus mind." Happily, the film's beauty, especially in the shots of Karina's face, "overrides Godard's philosophy.

303   Melville, Jean-Pierre. "Le Cinémois de Jean-Pierre Melville." *Cinéma 63*, No. 75 (April), p. 4.

Melville doesn't like Godard's films and notes a conversation he had with Pierre Braunberger over Godard's forthcoming film on prostitution, *Vivre sa vie.*

304   Milne, Tom. "Indirections." *Sight and Sound*, 33, No. 1 (Winter), 12–13.

With *Les Carabiniers* Godard has been accused of insulting men who went to war, but underneath the coarse, mundane, and brutal portrayal of war lies a real concern.

305   M.[ilne], T.[om]. *"Petit Soldat, Le (The Little Soldier)*, France, 1960." *Monthly Film Bulletin*, (August), 111–112.

Credits, plot summary. In this "singularly honest film," we see everything through Bruno's mind, "with the slight dislocation that involves." Coutard's camera work gives a cool, precise, absorbed beauty similar to that of Bresson's films.

306   Monjo, Armand. "Une Pochade peu convaincante: *Les Carabiniers* de Jean-Luc Godard." *L'Humanité* (4 January), p. 2.

To mix fable and realism should be a good way to treat this subject, but Godard nihilistically mixes gags, satire, "easy scandal," and a general contempt for humanity. The best moments are those directly taken from the Joppolo play.

307   Monjo, Armand. Review of *Les Carabiniers*. *L'Humanité* (12 June).

Negative review. Cited 1968, Gauteur, Entry No. 1111. Monjo's review was quoted and refuted by Godard, 1963, *Cahiers du cinéma*, Entry No. 2216.

308   Monjo, Armand. Review of *Le Petit Soldat*. *L'Humanité* (30 January).

Negative review. Cited 1968, Gauteur, Entry No. 1111.

309   Mosk[owitz, Gene]. *"Les Carabiniers* (French-Italo)." *Variety (19 June).*

Brief credits. "Bee-stung lips on the women, the stolid one-dimensional characters of the men, the highly contrasted, dense lensing of Raoul Coutard all bring to life the early feel of silent films with their larger-than-life aspects and comments on humanity in its simplest aspects." Reprinted in part, April 24, 1968 (Entry No. 1163). Quoted at length in *Film Facts* (1968, Anon., Entry No. 1025).

310 Mosk[owitz, Gene]. *"Le Petit Soldat (The Little Soldier)* (French)." *Variety* (20 February).
Brief credits. Paris. The film is too full of jump cuts and shallow, impromptu performances, but it does have a strong visual effect. Quoted at length, 1967, Anon., *Film Facts*, Entry No. 804.

311 Ollier, Claude. Review of *Les Carabiniers. Mercure de France* (October).
Positive review. Quoted 1976, Anon., *"Les Carabiniers* et la presse," Entry No. 1931.

312 Phillipe, Jean-Claude. "Les Films de Fellini et Godard posent une question: qu'est-ce que le cinéma?" *Télérama*, No. 701 (23 June).
Cited 1967, Amangual and Estève, Entry No. 782.

313 Potenze, Jaime. "Cine: *Vivir su vida (Vivre sa vie*, Francia, 1962.)" *Criterio*, 36, No. 1423 (14 March), 193–94.
Vivre sa vie is a story of the solitude, sadness, and anxiety faced by those souls fallen into vice who have not found God. Notes Dreyer's influence and explains cinematic techniques that might give the viewer difficulty.

314 Risso, Elsa. "Cine: *Vivir su vida." Estudios* (Buenos Aires), No. 542 (March-April), pp. 143–44.
Vivra sa vie is compared to *A bout de souffle*, which had portrayed the search for love and the breakdown of communication and moral values characteristic of our times. Nana celebrates freedom and lucidity. It is essential that "her condition as prostitute was not brought about by social pressure or any kind of determination, rather a free act." She finds love but her body becomes an object of commerce, liberated finally by her death, like Joan of Arc. Karina's acting is superlative and we can see the influence of Dreyer and Brecht.

315 Rochereau, Jean. "Cinéma: *Les Carabiniers." La Croix* (14 June), p. 6.
It is incorrect to use an improvised, frivolous farce to treat such a grave subject, but sometimes, as in the postcard sequences, Godard finds the right "derisive symbols."

316 Sadoul, Georges. *"Les Carabiniers*: Un Croquis m'en dit plus qu'un long rapport." *Les Lettres françaises*, No. 981 (6–11 June), p. 8.
The war is obviously a 1960s reconstruction of WW II, with the "king" being Hitler. The postcard sequence and ending "dissipate the film's charm" and diminish its credibility. Still, it's a better film politically than *Le Petit Soldat.*

317 Sadoul, Georges. "Etrange mais vrai." *Les Lettres françaises*, No. 1,009 (26 December–1 January, 1964), p. 7
Le Mépris is reviewed, with particular attention paid to the character types played by Bardot, Lang, Piccolli, and Palance. Godard's fight over the nude scene

with producer Joe Levine is described in detail. The film is icy, distanced, and has a bitter wit. It stays with you a long time.

318 Sarris, Andrew. "Films." *Village Voice* (26 September), pp. 12–13.
In contrast to *Breathless*, *My Life to Live* "is more precise in its framing, more discreet in its camera movements, more conventional in its editing . . . more Bressonian." Nana's cinematic predecessors are Louise Brooks as Lulu, Falconetti as Jeanne d'Arc, and Olphus' Lola Montès. "Elsewhere, the peculiar mixture of fact and truth, Rossellini and Rouch, never quite jells for the audience" — especially with the abrupt, cold ending.

319 Le Serpent. Review of *Les Carabiniers*. *Minute*, n.d. (probably May 31 or early June).
Quoted and refuted by Godard, 1963, *Cahiers du cinéma*, Entry No. 2216.

320 Shivas, Mark. "Review of *Paris vu par —*." *Movie*, No. 14 (August), pp. 39–40.
Review of omnibus film in which Godard's *Montparnasse-Levallois* appeared. Cited in Bowles, p. 383.

321 Siclier, Jacques. Review of *Les Carabiniers*. *Télérama*, No. 700 (16 June).
Quoted in 1976, Anon., "*Les Carabiniers* et la presse," Entry No. 1931.

322 Simon, John. "31 Hath September." *The New Leader*, 46, No. 13 (30 September), 20.
Simon briefly dismisses *Rogopag*, where Godard, in *Le Noveau Monde*, showed the same "straining" effort at invention that had "made his *My Life to Live* insufferable."

323 Tallenay, Jean-Louis. "Le Vertige de la violence." *Télérama*, No. 682.
Cited 1974, Collet, Entry No. 1832.

324 T.[aylor], J.[ohn] R.[ussell]. "*Vivre sa vie (It's My Life)*, France, 1962." *Monthly Film Bulletin*, 30 (August), 19–20.
Credits, plot summary. The film reveals a "passionate romanticism embodied in the distancing framework." It's a portrait of Karina.

325 Vecchiali, Paul. "La Guerre tout court." *Cahiers du cinéma*, No. 145 (July), pp. 52–55.
Brief credits for *Les Carabiniers*. The public can't appreciate Godard's richness of content and purity of expression. *Les Carabiniers* refuses to reassure its audience. People are upset because Godard takes up the theme of war without "neutralizing" it, without proposing a solution, because he sees it as stupid and useless. It's an "atonal" cinema, an open modernist one. Behind all the bestiality, we understand the director's love for life.

326 Verdone, Mario. "Quattordici film meno due." *Bianco e nero*, 23, No. 9-10 (September-October), 11–12.
Brief review of *Vivre sa vie*.

327 Vianey, Michel. "En attendant Homère." *L'Express* (30 May), pp. 24–27.

This interview with Godard about *Le Mépris*, as well as with Palance, Lang, and Bardot, provides insights into Godard's working relations with actors. Palance dislikes Godard's disdain for actors; Lang admires Godard's work but finds the film's ending implausible (i.e., going on shooting with the producer dead); Bardot speaks of how fame has affected her life, often adversely, and of her leftist political concerns. Details are given about shooting several scenes at the Malaparte villa in Capri.

328 Wagner, Jean. "Jean-Paul Belmondo et son mythe." *Cinéma 63*, Special issue: "L'Acteur," No. 78 (July-August), pp. 36–55.

After *A bout de souffle*, Belmondo was very much in demand. Each of his roles is analyzed to disengage his "type" — a man who refuses myth, an amoral person who fears only being duped, a man who needs a woman's physical presence, an outsider, someone who flirts with death. His "perpetual derision hides a fragility, a fear of losing face." He first took on his role as Laslo Kovacs in Chabrol's *A double tour*.

329 Young, Colin. "Conventional-Unconventional." *Film Quarterly*, 17, No. 1 (Fall), 22–30.

Explicates *Vivre sa vie*'s narrative structure, with special attention to the interaction of the sound and visual tracks. Godard's visual style, type of dramatic development, and characterization are compared to those of Fellini and Antonioni. Godard's alienation tactics and his development of Nana are described. Regrettably, critics do not understand Godard's efforts to forge a new cinematic language. Interview with Godard cited.

330 Yvoire, Jean d'. "*Le Petit Soldat.*" *Téléciné*, No. 110 (April-May), unnumbered.

The film's style is supple and coherent; Bruno's characterization is basically apolitical; and woman is once again shown as betrayer and victim. Negative comments on the film are added by A.A., H.A., J.E.F., G.S., and H.L.

1964

331 No entry.

332 Allombert, Guy. Review of *La Femme mariée*. *Cinématographie française* (3 October).

Cited 1965, Anon., "Les Infortunes de la liberté," Entry No. 460.

333 Anon. "Belmondo, Jean-Paul." *Current Biography*, 26 (December), 3.

See annotation under 1965, Anon., "Belmondo, Jean-Paul," Entry No. 454.

334 Anon. "Breathless Man." *Time*, 84 (10 July), 76.

On Belmondo, with reference to his work with Godard.

335 Anon. "Encyclopédie permanente du cinématographe." *Positif*, No. 59 (March), pp. 59–60.

There are three entries devoted to Godard: "Godard (Ereintement)" cites an article Godard had recently written on Kubrick in *Cahiers du cinéma*; "Godard (Hagiographie)" discusses Collet's book, where politics is "transfigured by metaphysics"; and "Godard (Hérédité)" challenges Truffaut's statements praising *A Bout de souffle*.

336   Anon. "Une Escroquerie en trop." *Cinéma 64*, No. 83 (February), pp. 11 and 14.
  Sketch films abound. The best have sketches by Godard *(Le Grand Escroc, Anticipation)* but scandalously *"Le Grand Escroc"* was dropped from the rest of the film by the producers, who thought it "too philosophical."

337   Anon. "A Fad Is Not a Revolution: Gadget-Laden France Alters." *Variety* (29 April), pp. 61 and 80.
  The New Wave had brought fresh themes and techniques, but now looks to have been a passing fad. Why? Perhaps DeGaulle era prosperity has reduced "cerebral" interests in film, except now for Godard's *Contempt*.

338   Anon. "Free Love in Free Form" *Time*, 84, No. 19 (6 November), 105.
  A Woman Is a Woman is a "flashy little showpiece . . . full of daring artifice and visual horseplay." Examples of Godard's stylistic innovations are given.

339   Anon. "Glorious Nut." *Newsweek*, 64, No. 22 (30 November), 100.
  Godard has a lot of enthusiasm and nerve in the helter-skelter *A Woman Is a Woman*, but his adulation of Karina is tiresome and he uses all her worst takes. The critic provides some interesting background on the genesis of the film.

340   Anon. Interview with Godard. *Contre-champ*, No. 3.
  Cited 1967, Jacotey, Entry No. 898.

341   Anon. Interview with Godard. *Film ideal* (Madrid), (1 April).
  Cited 1970, Cameron, Entry No. 1399.

342   Anon. Interview with Godard. *Filmkritik*, No. 8
  Cited 1970, Cameron, Entry No. 1399.

343   Anon. Interview with Godard. *Filmstudio* (German), No. 44.
  Cited 1970, Cameron, Entry No. 1399.

344   Anon. Interview with Godard. *Script*, March.
  Cited, 1970, Cameron, Entry No. 1399.

345   Anon. Interview with Godard on *La Femme mariée*. *Le Monde* (26 November).
  Cited 1965, Anon., "Les Infortunes de la liberté," Entry No. 460.

346   Anon. Photo essay of *Le Mépris*. *Filmkritik*, 8 (August), 409–412.
  Cameron (1970, Entry No. 1399) says there is an interview with Godard in this issue.

347   Anon. Review of *Bande à part*. London *Times* (12 May), p. 15.
  Cited 1964, *Times Index*, May-June, p. 81.

348 Anon. "Screen Leadership for France: Native, 50%, U.S. 33%, Italy, 17%." *Variety* (29 April), p. 61.
Contempt, with 190,000 admissions, was a major box office grosser in France, and *Vivre sa vie* had 213,210 admissions.

349 Anon. "Three Year Check Shows Directors 'Lay Off' Plenty." *Variety* (29 April), p. 62.
Of the 154 French directors making films from 1961–63, only eight directed six films or more. Godard is among these.

350 Aprà, Adriano. "Jean-Luc Godard fra mundo classico e mundo moderno." *Filmcritica*, No. 151–52 (November-December), pp. 581–88.
Cited 1972, Brown, Entry No. 1657.

351 Aprà, Adriano. *"Le Mépris e Il disprezzo."* *Filmcritica*, No. 151–52, (November-December), pp. 611–13.
Analyzes differences between French and Italian versions of film. Cited 1972, Brown, Entry No. 1657.

352 Arbois, Janick. "Un Film-miroir." *Télérama*, No. 780.
Review of *La Femme mariée*. Cited 1974, Collet, Entry No. 1832.

353 Archer, Eugene. "France's Far-Out Filmmaker." The *New York Times* (27 September), Sec. II, p. 11.
Godard's personality, career, and relations with producers are briefly described on the occasion of his presenting *Band of Outsiders* and *A Woman Is a Woman* at the N.Y. Film Festival.

354 Archer, Eugene. "French New Wave." *New York Times* (4 November), p. 47.
Excerpts from Archer's September 19 review of *Une Femme est une femme* are given. It's provocative, avant-garde, very French, "and often thoroughly infuriating."

355 Archer, Eugene. Review of *Bande à part* and *Une Femme est une femme*. *New York Times* (19 September), p. 19.
Both *Bande à part* and *Une Femme est une femme* are "wildly original, stubbornly modern, characteristically French," often infuriating, and brilliant. Godard's films "offer rich rewards to a limited audience." Brief credits.

356 Arragon, Louis. "Der Film des Manets." *Film* (Hanover), (January), pp. 6–13.
Reviews *Pierrot le fou*.

357 Baby, Yvonne. "Entretien avec Jean-Luc Godard à propos d'*Une Femme mariée*: "L'Idée de la femme dans un société primitive de 1964." *Le Monde* (5 December), p. 16.
In an interview, Godard discusses his desire to make a classical or anthropological filmed-essay defining women. He explains his treatment of Charlotte's character. "It's a humanistic film about a world that isn't."

358 Baroncelli, Jean de. *"Une Femme mariée."* *Le Monde* (8 December), p. 16.

This is first-person filmmaking, a personal statement, but it lapses too often into the women's-magazine style and the consumer mentality that it seeks to criticize.

359 B.[ellour], R.[aymond]. "Godart or Not Godard." *Les Lettres françaises*, No. 1029 (14 May), p. 8.

Recognizing that what delights some people in Godard's films bores or infuriates others, Bellour describes the components of Godard's sensibility with reference to the thought of Merleau-Ponty. *Bande à part* "formulates extraordinary incidents in which we see how . . . living goes on and falls apart in that confusion conjured up and always renewed [by Godard] . . ."

360 Bellour, Raymond. "Jean-Luc Godard s'explique." *Les Lettres françaises*, No. 1029 (14 May), pp. 8–9.

In an interview, Godard discusses his love for literature and the literary influences on *Bande à part* (a U.S. detective novel and Queneau). He wanted to convey a lot of information constantly about many characters. And using literary and cinematic "citation" is not of a different order from, say, filming the Arc d'Triomphe — it's all part of the spectacle. *Le Petit Soldat* was an adventure film made by a student with no political sense, a little like Voltaire's Candide. Godard discusses his rapid filming, based on some concrete idea, sentiment, or bit of dialogue. "I film an instinctive world in a reflexive way."

361 Benayoun, Robert. "Godard jusqu'a plus soif." *France-Observateur* (13 August), p. 18.

Once again, says Benayoun, he finds all Godard's faults in a film, here *Bande à part*. He lists the "typical" ones. The characterization is like a "cemetery of empty clothes. Frey is reduced to a hat."

362 Billard, Pierre. *"Bande à parte."* *Cinéma 64*, No. 89 (September-October), pp. 105–108.

Brief credits. Godard was "king of the New Wave" until critics rejected this film because it did not have a "profound message" or "metaphysical ambitions." The elements of Godard's cinema, especially his "personal" camera style, are noted. It's not a coherent "vision" but he always has "his own universe and his own language" to offer us. Anarchically, he maintains the heterogenity of all the elements he works with and his own freedom as well.

363 Blasi, Ralph and Sarris, Andrew. "Jean-Luc Godard: Biofilmography." *New York Film Bulletin*, No. 46 (summer), pp. 20–24.

See 1964, Sarris, Entry No. 434.

364 Bontemps, Jacques. "L'Île au trésor." *Cahiers du cinéma*, No. 159 (October), pp. 55–56.

Bande à part is a banal and sad film, with certain moments of grace.

365 Borde, Raymond. "Knokke-le-zouette: le cinéma experiméntal in 1964." *Positif*, No. 60 (April-May), p. 58.

Brief mention of *Une Femme coquette*, shot in 16mm, on the streets of Geneva. De Maupassant's text is read in voice off on the soundtrack of that film. The film "does not have the exhibitionism Godard would reveal in Paris."

366 Bory, Jean-Louis. "Godard: le Maeterlinck des époux." *Arts*, No. 984 (9–15 December), p. 14.
The censors of *La Femme mariée* are really angry that Godard refused to dramatize and romanticize adultery. Like Molière, La Bruyère, and Maeterlinck, he accumulates details about *the* woman. The "insolent" montage and Méril's acting are fine. Reprinted 1971, Bory, Entry No. 1553.

367 Brightman, Carol. "Art vs. Sheer Artistry." *The New Leader*, 47, No. 18 (31 August), 32–33.
Le Mépris' fascination lies in its style. Godard, in a color cinemascope production, evinces all the intellectualisms and barbarisms and camera swipes and pans of a true auteur. *Le Mépris* opened the 5th Montreal Film Festival.

368 Brule, Claude. Review of *La Femme mariée*. *Candide* (December).
Cited 1965, *Une Femme mariée: L'Avant-Scène du cinéma*, Entry No. 458.

369 Bruno, E[duardo]. "*Une Femme mariée*." *Filmcritica*, No. 147–48 (August), pp. 360–62.
Reviews *La Femme mariée*.

370 Bruno, Eduardo. "Personaggi senza ombra ne *Il Disprezzo* di Jean-Luc Godard." *Filmcritica*, No. 141 (January), pp. 3–5.
Reviews *Le Mépris*.

371 Caen, Michael, et al. "Entretien avec Jean-Luc Godard." *Cinématographie française*, June-July, pp. 61–62.
In an interview with Michael Caen and Alain le Bris, Godard says he made *A bout de souffle* to demonstrate the futility of certain filmmaking taboos. He discusses the *nouvelle vague*; his films' relation to their audience; French cinema's modes of production and distribution, and its future.

372 Cervoni, Albert. "L'Age de Nylon." *France nouvelle*, No. 999 (9–15 December), pp. 22–23.
The French censors do not value the way *La Femme mariée* presents adultery in an analytical social context. The film's characters search for human contact, but advertising and consumerism have conditioned them to accept certain alienated rules of conduct and "prefabricated" emotions. Godard is both concrete and intellectual, personally sincere and socially concerned.

373 Cervoni, Albert. "Un Film dans le film." *France nouvelle*, No. 950 (2–8 January), pp. 19–20.
Discusses the filming of *Le Mépris* (nude scenes, filming in sequential order, etc.) and its aesthetics (Godard's use of Bardot, Lang, tragic conventions, quotidian visual details, and the flexible long take). The film makes us reflect on filmic conventions, the economic imperatives of the film industry, and the role of "performance" in an intellectual's public and private life.

374 Cervoni, Albert. "Godard à Annecy." *France nouvelle* (25 November), pp. 22–23.
Cited 1967, Amengual and Estève, Entry No. 782.

375 Chamberlin, Phillip. *My Life to Live.* Program Notes. Fall Film Series, University of California, Santa Barbara (4 October).
Credits. This film is not as much about prostitution as it is about a woman's quest for self-discovery. Godard demands "full attention of eye, ear, and mind." Extensive citation from Colin Young's article on the film from *Film Quarterly*, Fall 1963, Entry No. 329.

376 Chapier, Henry. Review of *La Femme mariée. Combat* (7 December).
Cited 1965, *Une Femme mariée: L'Avant-Scène du cinéma*, Entry No. 458.

377 Chauvet, Louis. Review of *La Femme mariée. Le Figaro* (5-6 December).
Quoted 1965, *Une Femme mariée: L'Avant-Scène du cinéma*, Entry No. 458.

378 Chazal, Robert. *"Une Femme mariée* (le mensonge tout nu.)" *France Soir* (5 December).
Brief credits. Macha Méril was aptly chosen for this film. It shows a lot of nudity and has a sound track filled with Godard's "inevitable literary and pseudophilosophic citations."

379 Chevallier, Jacques. *"Le Mépris." Image et son: Revue du cinéma*, No. 172 (April), pp. 100–101.
Godard has helped free cinema of its conventions but he is too mannered and in *Le Mépris* seems insincere. He seems to be a moralist but keeps us at arm's length by his distanciating wit. This article was excerpted from *Pourquoi*, the magazine of La Ligue de l'Enseignement.

380 Clay, Jean. "Jean-Luc Godard: The French Cinema's Most Negative Asset." *Réalités* (English), No. 158 (January), pp. 40–44.
Trans. from 1963, Clay, Entry No. 264. Excerpts of this trans., 1970, Collet, Entry No. 1425.

381 Coleman, John. "Borrowed Faces." *The New Statesman*, N.S. 68 (23 October), 626–27.
Les Carabiniers has a home-movie style and fails to provoke any serious thought on war by its so-called distanciation devices.

382 Coleman, John. "Venice 1964." *The New Statesman*, N.S. 68 (18 September), 414.
Coleman rejects *The Married Woman*, seen at Venice, for its distanciation techniques, but he likes Coutard's photography.

383 Collet, Jean. "Critique." *Télérama*, No. 729.
Review of *Le Mépris*. Cited 1974, Collet, Entry No. 1832.

384 Collet, Jean. Interview with Godard on *Bande à part. Télérama*, No. 761 (16 August), pp. 49–50.
Bande à part tries to capture the tone of certain novels, especially *Fool's Gold* and those of Raymond Queneau. Godard likes to impose restraints on himself, e.g., shooting rapidly and on a low budget, or, in *Le Mépris*, shooting in Italy with direct sound. Godard discusses the dialogue, acting, characterization, and themes in *Bande à part*. Trans. 1972, Brown, Entry No. 1658.

385 Cournot, Michel. "Après l'interdiction de *La Femme mariée:* Comment parler de l'adultère?" *France-Observateur* (8 October), pp. 15-16.

    The film is reviewed in the light of its recent censorship. Not sensual, it's like "Plato directly pictorialized." The dialogue consists of intellectual lectures delivered in cold tones — the antithesis of gross vulgarity and obscenity. The plot and theme are briefly summarized, especially the theme of "revealing those social factors which shape married women's awareness in 1964." The censors want the protagonists to be as abject as possible.

386 Crist, Judith. "Something for the Boys — A Bare Christmas." New York *Herald Tribune* (19 December).

    Brief credits. The critic discusses the nude sequence in *Contempt,* Godard's "childish" style, and the characterization in that film.

387 Crist, Judith. Review of *A Woman Is a Woman.* New York *Herald Tribune* (4 November).

    Cited 1970, Collet, Entry No. 1425.

388 [Crowther, Bosley]. "Paris to See Godard Film after Change in the Title." *New York Times* (4 December), p. 46.

    Notice about Godard's "lengthy" battle with censors over title of *La Femme mariée* and his decision to make certain changes.

389 Crowther, Bosley. Review of *Le Mépris. New York Times* (19 December), p. 25.

    Brief credits. Crowther discusses Camille's character and is puzzled why she leaves her husband. The other characters are described briefly.

390 Domarchi, Jean. *"Le Mépris."* Monde et la vie. No. 133 (June).

    Cited 1968, Gauteur, Entry No. 1111.

391 Eyles, Allen. Review of *Les Carabiniers. Films and Filming,* 11, No. 3 (December), 30.

    Cited in Bowles, p. 71.

392 Feinstein, Herbert. "An Interview with Jean-Luc Godard." *Film Quarterly,* 17, No. 3 (Spring), 8–10.

    Interview was originally given October 1963. Since then it is not clear if Godard will give his name to all three language versions of *Contempt.* Godard discusses *Breathless,* other directors who have had trouble with producers like Levine, and the story of *Contempt* and its political future in commercial distribution.

393 Fléouter, Claude. "Avec *La Femme mariée,* Jean-Luc Godard a volou faire un 'film de ethnologiste.' " *Le Monde* (25 August).

    In an interview, Godard defends his method of filming very rapidly. Godard feels this film is closest to *Le Petit soldat* in describing comportment without explaining it.

394 Fruchter, Norm. *"Bande à part." Film Quarterly,* 18, No. 2 (Winter), 54–55.

    Godard has returned to a conventional narrative form; he also "freezes and distances the action." He denies his trio of bumbling, gullible, and callous characters sympathy. The film is "compellingly dominated by Godard's sure narrative control and Coutard's barren, sombre, finally dominating, Paris suburbs."

395 Gauthier, Guy. *"Bande à part." Image et son: Revue du cinéma*, No. 178 (November), pp. 96–97.
The film is a "gratuitous accumulation of choice morsels, badly integrated into the whole." Although the image track is often banal, the sound track is rich, diverting, and full of gags. Godard has found new and moving ways to portray the incoherent relations between young people in an unstable world.

396 Gay, Pierre. "Revu et corrigé: *Le Mépris." Cinéma 64*, No. 86 (May), pp. 131–33.
Gay appreciates the disturbing incongruities in the film that keep it from being totally explicable. One of these is the disdain that Camille feels for Paul. Finally all that's left on the screen are Godard, Lang, and the cinema, "the privileged instrument for exploring human mystery."

397 Gilson, René. *"Le Mépris." Cinéma 64*, No. 83 (February), pp. 108–116.
This is the first time editors split to give a film four stars or a zero. A debate between editors Jean Collet, Pierre Billard, and Phillipe Esnault follows Gilson's review, which discusses the themes of misunderstanding and cinema in *Le Mépris*.

398 Giroud, Françoise. "Jean-Luc et Bérénice." *L'Express* (7–13 December), pp. 65–66.
As presented in art, adultery now has no cuckolded Othellos for husbands; women are beginning to discover their own physical autonomy and pleasure, and no one dies at the end of an affair. Rather the artist leaves things going on as before. All Godard's tics are here in *La Femme mariée*, integrated with humor and tenderness in a disquieting social statement.

399 Guégan, Gérard, et al. "Entretien avec J.-L. Godard." *Les Lettres françaises* (19 November), pp. 1, 8, 9.
In an interview with Gérard Guégan and Michel Petris, Godard says he abandoned plans to do a TV program in the United States, where he had visited recently. In France he'd like to do journalistic pieces or *Bérénice* or *Pour Lucrèce* on TV. He admires Renoir for creating both art and the theory that explains it. He discusses *Le Mépris, Bande à part*, realism, self-reflexivity, instinctive and open-ended filming (exemplified, Godard says, by *Vivre sa vie* and *Les Carabiniers*), and Rossellini's influence. He had wanted to make a film about France called *France la douce*, but it's changed to one about Communists and a provincial election and a student who's in the UEC in Paris (Communist Student Union). He discusses the critical reaction, especially on the left, to *Le Petit Soldat*. He admires Brecht for being an analyst and strategist at the same time, and finds Rossellini's historical films similar to Brecht's historical plays. Long interview.

400 Guégan, Gérard, et al. "Intrevista con Jean-Luc Godard." *Filmcritica*, No. 150 (October).
Interview by Guégan and Michel Petris with Godard. Possibly translated into Italian from 1974, Guégan, Entry No. 399. Cited 1974, Ferrero, Entry No. 1841.

401 Heifetz, Henry. *"Une Femme est une femme." Film Quarterly*, 18, No. 2 (Winter 1964/65), 56–57.

Brief plot summary is given. Comic use of color, pace, playful relation with audience give a "steady light touch." There is a "nostalgia for lost joy," and the "style distances and cornices the action." "In Godard, people always betray and vitality dies."

402 Jacob, Gilles. "Jean-Luc Godard." *Le Cinéma moderne.* Lyon: SERDOC. Pp. 127–134.

Cited BFI Bibliography.

403 Kauffmann, Stanley. "Spirits, High and Low." *The New Republic*, 151 (5 December), 23–24.

In *A Woman Is a Woman* Godard is supposed to be playing so well with film conventions that he has the right to ignore "literary" ones like a story. However, the film is "torpid and clumsy," and Godard distastefully displays his private life with Anna Karina. Reprinted 1966, Kauffmann, Entry No. 711.

404 Koval, Francis. "Venice 1964." *Films in Review*, 15, No. 8 (October), 464.

La Femme mariée and Godard's press conference are briefly described in negative terms.

405 Kustow, Michael. "Inside and Outside: *Bande à part.*" *Sight and Sound*, 34, No. 1 (Winter), 11–12.

In this highly theatrical film, unstable, mutable characters act out their dreams. "Godard makes us feel his awareness of the constant fragility of his fiction, the illusoriness of his medium."

406 Lachize, Samuel. "Choquer qui-peut! *Une Femme mariée* de Jean-Luc Godard." *L'Humanité* (12 December), p. 6.

Notes the kinds of criticism written about Godard. Godard still persists in a "disagreeable confusion" in his social analysis but he does depict many crucial social problems, here, consumerism and women's condition.

407 Lefèvre, Raymond. *"Le Mépris." Image et son: Revue du cinéma*, No. 172 (April), pp. 96–101.

"The New Wave has given us its masterpiece." Lefèvre relates the circumstances behind Godard's writing a script for *Le Mépris*. In the film, *contempt* influences relations between all the characters. Although many critics were shocked by it, the nude scene is dramatically necessary and as inoffensive as a Renaissance statue. Godard's use of tragedy, classical reference, Fritz Lang, and his cinematic self-reflexiveness are noted. Godard's statement made on the film's release is quoted at length. Followed by a negative comment by Jacques Chevallier (1964, Entry No. 379).

408 Lefèvre, Raymond and Warren, Jean-Paul. *"A bout de souffle." Image et son: Revue du cinéma*, No. 176-77 (September-October), pp. 3–8.

See 1964, Warren, No. 448.

409 Legrand, Gérard. "Sans attendre Godard." *Positif*, No. 59 (March), pp. 70–74.

Credits. Legrand reviews *Le Mépris* in terms of Moravia's story and the film's cinematography, characterization, parallels to *The Odyssey*, and critical reception. It is an inconclusive thesis film about cinema and contains all of Godard's boring anxieties.

410 Lovell, Alan. "Jean-Luc Godard: A Pessimist Who Has to Be Faced." *Peace News* (4 December), p. 5.

Godard is an irritating, often boring, but formidable filmmaker who has a good sense of the contemporary world but whose films are often marred by facile borrowings from the other arts and by "obtrusive cleverness." He strives to dramatize a philosophical position close to existentialism. Lovell analyzes the social themes and style of *Les Carabiniers* and *Bande à part*.

411 Marcorelles, Louis. "Godard's Half Truths." Trans. Ernest Callenbach. *Film Quarterly*, 17, No. 3 (Spring), 4–7.

Le Mépris is a triumph in France. Godard's concerns are style, cinema, the written word, travel, and social conscience. He is erratic, tormented, and uncertain. The critic examines Godard's use of language, especially in *Charlotte et son Jules*, his Brechtianism, and his use of cinema direct.

412 Mauriac, Claude. Review of *La Femme mariée*. *Le Figaro littéraire* (10 December).

Cited 1965, *Une Femme mariée: L'Avant-Scène du cinéma*, Entry No. 458.

413 M.[ilne], T.[om]. *"Bande à part (The Outsiders)*, France, 1964." *Monthly Film Bulletin*, 31 (December), 170–171.

Bande à part sets its characters in a dreamy fantasy into which reality and violent death intrude. Godard is a moralist and also an artist of the moment; he seizes intangible instants for our contemplation. Credits, plot summary.

414 Mosk[owitz, Gene]. *"Bande à part (Gang of Outsiders)* (French)." *Variety* (29 April), pp. 6 and 26.

This film avoids jump cuts and is more accessible than usual. Plot and characterization are described. The observation of adolescent yearning, good acting, "excellent lensing," and a low budget ($100,000) should make this film pay off. On page 76 is a customary "thank-you ad," here from Godard to Columbia. "All my thanks for helping me so nicely in the making of *Bande à part* . . . I was able because of your help to deliver a picture under budget and schedule."

415 Moskowitz, Gene. "Checklist of French Films." *Variety* (29 April), p. 60.

Georges de Beauregard "recently broke up partnership with Carlo Ponti in Rome-Paris Films." He sold his share of *Contempt* to Ponti and Joseph E. Levine's Embassy Films. Pierre Roustang specializes in sketch pictures and produced *Les Plus Belles Escroqueries du monde* this year with Vides Film (Rome) and Toho (Japan).

416 Mosk[owitz, Gene]. *"Le Femme mariée (The Married Woman)* (French)." *Variety* (16 September), p. 17.

Godard made two pictures in five months for Columbia, each at $100,000. He shot the first in three weeks, this in about four. At various times, it is comic, amoral, essay-like, or beautifully "crystal-like" in its lensing. However, the intertitles, ellipses and fragmentation make it at times lagging and repetitious, at times precocious. Macha Méril has a "zesty, offbeat" quality and spontaneity that makes us accept anything the protagonist does.

417 Mosk[owitz, Gene]. *"Le Mépris (Contempt)* (French-Italian) (Color)." *Variety* (1 January).
   The critic discusses Bardot's acting.

418 Moskowitz, Gene. "Sex Kitten Bardot Holding Her Own as Most Dependable French Export." *Variety* (29 April), p. 62.
   Bardot showed in *Contempt* that she is a good actress "when intelligently used." Anna Karina is well-esteemed in France aa a film actress, if not abroad.

419 Narboni, Jean. "Ouvert et fermé: *Le Mépris." Cahiers du cinéma*, No. 152 (February), pp. 66–69.
   Brief credits. Narboni discusses Godard's mastery over and acute sense of duration in the shots of the film.

420 Olivier, Anne. "Fritz Lang contre Prokosch." *France-Observateur* (5 March), pp. 13–14.
   Olivier, a collaborator of Lucien Goldmann, offers a structuralist analysis of *Le Mépris*. "Prokosch and Lang are the two main characters. It is by means of them that Camille discovers the only two realities of contemporary society: the old culture and the modern world, and between the two her husband's inconsistency and inanity as he participates in neither . . . Lang's humanist tradition nor Prokosch's dynamism and power." This seems to be the work of Annie Goldmann, reprinted in her book, 1971, Entry No. 1576.

421 Ollier, Claude. "Une Oeuvre et ses marges." *Cahiers du cinéma*, No. 153 (March), pp. 15–19.
   Le Mépris uses a technique of "discontinuity in the heart of continuity, absolute rigidity in the heart of discontinuity," both to affirm and simultaneously to negate that the world is livable.

422 People's Theater Arts Group. *Vivre sa vie (It's My Life).* Program Notes. Tyneside Film Society (Newcastle Upon Tyne), 365th Programme (27 September).
   Interview with Godard is cited extensively. The critic appreciates the effective Brechtian structure, Godard's mastery and economical use of a wide "range of cinema vocabulary," and Karina's moving and unsentimental portrait of a prostitute.

423 Pétris, Michel. "Il 'mito vissuto' di *Le Petit Soldat." Filmcritica*, No. 151–52 (November-December), pp. 589–90.
   Cited 1972, Brown, Entry No. 1657.

424 Pilard, Phillipe. *"La Femme mariée." Image et son: Revue du cinéma*, No. 179 (December), pp. 94–96.
   Brief credits and summary. Pilard discusses the censorship and the favorable

criticism written about the film. He compares it unfavorably to various other films and finds it interminable, pretentious, incoherent, and superficial.

425 Poitras, Robert. "De l'éxterieur à l'intérieur." *Objectif* (February-March), pp. 27–29.

Vivre sa vie is dominated by the character of Nana, whose loss and then recovery of her liberty is portrayed poetically through ellipses, which carry us directly to the heart of the matter.

426 Pons Maurice. "Monsieur Godard et la culture, ou l'*Odysée* selon Saint Jean-Luc." *Les Temps modernes*, No. 213 (February), pp. 1533–36.

Review of *Le Mépris*.

427 R.[abine], H.[enry]. *"Une Femme mariée."* *La Croix* (11 December), p. 7.

Godard irritates with his schoolboy mentality and his easy acceptance of adultery. He shows too much of that which he seems to condemn and films characters in an interview style only to have them express his own thoughts.

428 Roche. "Jean-Luc Godard divorce mais garde sa femme, Anna Karina, dans ses deux prochains films." *France-Soir* (5 December).

Godard tells his plans for *Alphaville* and *Pierrot le fou*.

429 Rochereau, Jean. Review of *La Femme mariée*. *La Croix* (11 December).

Cited 1968, Gauteur, Entry No. 1111.

430 R.[ochereau], J.[ean]. *"Du vent, du vent."* *La Croix* (10 September).

Cited 1968, Gauteur, Entry No. 1111.

431 Sadoul, Georges. "Le Doigt sur la plaie." *Les Lettres françaises* (10 December).

Critics who hated Godard now like *La Femme mariée*. In that film Godard examines all the different ways French is spoken. Citation is just part of the montage of the film. Méril incarnates a "tender and spiritual" soul in a world where publicity shapes desire and pleasure. Godard has both recreated *Madame Bovary* and made a work of pop art.

432 Sarris, Andrew, "A Movie Is a Movie Is a Movie Is a." *New York Film Bulletin*, No. 46 (Summer), pp. 17–19.

Discusses Godard's problems with the French censors. Describes Godard's modern, self-conscious filmmaking style, which combines personal, aesthetic, and formal concerns with social and psychological realism. Godard's cinema is an analytical, intellectualized, "European" reflection on U.S. cinema and can only comment on but never capture the directness of "American reflexes." Reprinted 1969, Sarris, Entry No. 1341. Reprinted 1967, Sarris, Entry No. 966 (paperback edition, 1969).

433 Sarris, Andrew. *"A Woman Is a Woman."* *The Village Voice* (12 November).

This very European film has an "analytically fragmented lyricism," which "comments on reality"; in this case, it documents "the sheer otherness of all women." Reprinted 1968, Mussman, Entry No. 1168; 1970, Sarris, Entry No. 1507.

434 Sarris, Andrew and Blasi, Ralph. "Jean-Luc Godard: Biofilmography." *New York Film Bulletin*, Godard issue, No. 46 (Summer), pp. 20–24.

Traces Godard's career from 1930–1964. Credits, some notes on Godard's career, brief descriptions of the films — noting both plot and film style. Comments and judgments on films written by Sarris, filmography by Blasi.

435 Sarris, Andrew, and Blasi, Andrew. "Waiting for Godard." *Film Culture*, No. 33 (Summer), pp. 2–8.

Godard's career is described for those who have only seen *Breathless*, comparing him to other New Wave directors and to the ideals postulated by their criticism. Godard's style is described in comparative terms, relative to that of numerous other directors. The critical response to his breaking all the "rules" is noted. A biofilmography by Blasi is given, with comments by Sarris. Five features have not yet appeared in the United States. Reprinted 1968, Mussman, Entry No. 1168.

436 Schlesinger, Arthur, Jr. "The Battle and Other Titillations." *Show*, 4, No. 10 (November), 86–87.

Briefly discusses *Contempt's* use of and departure from Moravia's novel *Ghost at Noon*, especially in the characterization. It is a dreary film.

437 Schneider, Edgar. Interview with Godard on *La Femme mariée*. *Paris-Presse-l'instransigeant* (2 December).

Cited 1965, Anon., "Les Infortunes de la liberté," Entry No. 460.

438 Shipman, D. "Belmondo." *Films and Filming*, 10–12 (September), 7.

On Belmondo, with reference to his work with Godard.

439 Simon, John. "Escapism into Art." *The New Leader*, 47 (23 November), 28–29.

Godard's camera "wallows" over Karina in *A Woman Is a Woman*. The characters and dialogue are "imbecilic" and Godard fills the film with "gimmicks" and "the usual New-Wave devices." Movies have become the great escape, and nonacting and distanciation are falsely hailed as virtues. Reprinted 1967, Simon, Entry No. 975.

440 Sonbert, Warren and Weinberg, Gretchen. Untitled, included in "Jean-Luc Godard: An Interview." *New York Film Bulletin*, No. 46, p. 13.

In an interview with Warren Sonbert, transcribed by Gretchen Weinberg, Godard discusses *Bande à part*, *Le Mépris*, *Une Femme est une femme*, and a future project [*Made in U.S.A.*], especially in terms of his cinematography. Reprinted 1967, Sarris, Entry No. 965.

441 Sontag, Susan. "On Godard's *Vivre sa vie*." *Moviegoer*, No. 2 (Summer/Autumn), pp. 2–10.

Godard's films are about ideas; they demonstrate or prove that something happened and do not analyze *why*. Sontag explains the function of Godard's distancing techniques in *Vivre sa vie*, which is a ("text") especially on the sound track, about lucidity and seriousness. She calls *The Oval Portrait* sequence and the conclusion the film's "one false step." Sontag includes as "appendix," a poem

Godard wrote for film's Paris advertisements. Reprinted 1968, Mussman, Entry No. 1168; 1966, Sontag, Entry No. 761.

442. S.[ussex]. A. *"Les Carabiniers (The Soldiers)*, France/Italy, 1963." *Monthly Film Bulletin*, 31 (December), 170–71.

Godard induces people to grasp the horror of war and see it with new eyes. He uses an "oblique approach," which consists of cool detachment and many cinematic devices, to achieve a Brechtian distanciation.

443 Taylor, John Russell. "The New Wave: Jean-Luc Godard." *Cinema Eye, Cinema Ear: Some Key Filmmakers of the Sixties.* New York: Hill and Wang. London: Metheun. Pp. 211–20.

Godard is not a great director but cinematically liberating. The fast and witty style in *A bout de souffle* keeps us at a distance from any amorality. *Une Femme est une femme* jokingly uses a big budget color film to make a home movie. *Vivre sa vie* is crisped, planned, and Brechtian, and draws our attention to Karina's small gestures. Critics found *Les Carabiniers* misanthropic because they did not understand its Brechtian "impulses" and arbitrary style.

444 Valdés, Hermán. "Crónica cinematográfica: Jean-Luc Godard." *Anales de la Universidad de Chile* (Santiago), 122, No. 132 (October-December), 176–80.

Analyzes the cinematic and narrative innovations in *A bout de souffle* and *Vivre sa vie*. The crime story in the former and the prostitution theme in the latter serve primarily as a formal pretext, a way of selecting and ordering in a given temporal succession certain details about the world that have moved Godard.

445 Vanier, Alan. "D'Une Improbable Vérité." *Les Lettres françaises* (20 August), p. 8.

Bande à part is so much an improvisation, it's hardly cinema. It lacks all coherence, and the characters do not come alive till late in the film.

446 Vasquez Rossi, Jorge. "Valoración del nuevo cine francés." *Universidad* (Sante Fe, Argentina), No. 59 (January-March), pp. 123–133.

Cited 1964, *Latin American Index*, 4, p. 93.

447 Verdone, Mario. "Da Bergman ad Antonioni." *Bianco e nero*, 25, No. 8–9 (August-September), 22–23.

Review of *La Femme mariée*.

448 Warren, Jean-Paul and Lefèvre, Raymond. *"A bout de souffle." Image et son: Revue du cinéma*, No. 176–177 (September-October), pp. 3–8.

Credits, Godard's biography, brief plot summary. François Truffaut is quoted from a Radio-Cinéma-Télévision broadcast, October 4, 1959, on his original treatment for the film and on the "new style" incarnated by Godard: original, spontaneous, rapidly filmed, elliptically edited. There is also a discussion of Godard's free and loose camera movements, shot sequences, and direction of actors. The characterizations of Michel and Patricia reflect "ambiguity, pluralism, and contradictions." A recurrent theme is death.

449 Weinberg, Gretchen and Sonbert, Warren. Interview with Godard. *New York Film Bulletin*, No. 46.
Reprinted 1967, Sarris, Entry No. 900. See 1964, Sonbert, Entry No. 440, for annotation.

450 Yvoire, Jean d', et al. *"Le Mépris." Télécité*, No. 115 (February-April), unpaged.
The content reflects Godard's own suffering and contemptuous attitude toward women and the public. The cinematic technique is subtle and brilliant. C.M. says it is not a psychological portrait but modern poetry. G.S. says it tries to pose as philosophy but is slickly commercial. J.P. says it is about cinema itself. J.E.F. praises the parts but dislikes the whole. H.A. agrees with Yvoire. A.A. says it is Godard's best so far. J.C. says the film has a puerile and a serious side. C.H. says the adolescent side is too irritating.

451 Zand, Nicole. "Godard: 'Je radiographie.'" *France-Observateur* (8 October), p. 16.
In an interview, Godard indicates the plot, the filming techniques, the theme, the few cuts made in *La Femme mariée*. He compares himself to other filmmakers, dramatists, and novelists who have dealt with infidelity. The film is like an IBM analysis of a consumer and woman.

1965

452 Ajame, Pierre. Review of *Pierrot le fou*. *Les Nouvelles littéraires* (15 November — in that week).
Rave review quoted in 1976, Anon., "Pour ou contre *Pierrot le fou*," Entry No. 1940.

453 Alpert, Hollis. Review of *The Married Woman*. *Saturday Review* (28 August), p. 28.
Cited *Reader's Guide*, 25 (March 1965–February 1966), 711.

454 Anon. "Belmondo, Jean-Paul." *Current Biography Yearbook 1965*, p. 25.
Biography of Belmondo, describing his films with Godard (*A bout de souffle, Pierrot le fou*). Reprinted from 1964, Anon., *Current Biography*, Entry No. 333.

455 Anon. *"Les Carabiniers." Une Femme mariée: L'Avant-Scène du cinéma*, No. 46 (March), pp. 42–43.
Credits. Synopsis. Brief history of the actors and the film's reception. Résumé of reviews.

456 Anon. "Encyclopédie permanent du cinématographie: contrechant (pour Godard)." *Positif*, No. 66 (January), pp. 108–109.
Criticizes Godard's statements to Gérard Guégan and Michel Pétris (1964, Guégan, Entry No. 400).

457 Anon. *"Une Femme mariée." Cinéma 65*, No. 92 (January), p. 106.
The film deserves two stars. The fragmented narrative is apt for portraying the

"multiple facets of an ungraspable truth," but Godard treats this trio in a derisory rather than objectively sociological way.

458 Anon. *"Une Femme mariée* et la presse." *Une Femme mariée: L'Avant-Scène du cinéma*, No. 46 (March), pp. 33–34.
Citations from thirteen French reviews. Brief credits for *Bande à part.*

459 Anon. "Godard on Pure Film." *Movie*, 2, No. 5 (March-April), 38.
Cited in Schuster, p. 165.

460 Anon. "Les Infortunes de la liberté: une femme et la censure." *Positif*, No. 67-68 (February-March), pp. 146–47.
The censorship of *La Femme mariée* is described in the context of too many such recent acts.

461 Anon. Interview with Godard. *Les Lettres françaises* (9 September).
In doing *Alphaville*, Godard had wanted to do Aldiss' *Crosière sans escale* or Van Vogt — plus Chandler. Finally he opted for a "western." The idea comes from Richard Matheson's *I Am a Legend.*

462 Anon. *"A Married Woman:* French Film." *Christian Science Monitor* (11 November), p. 6.
Christian Science Monitor 1965 Annual Index, p. 72.

463 Anon. "Off Course Odyssey: *Contempt." Time*, 85, No. 2 (8 January), 54.
"Godard muddles an already tricky narrative with personal mannerisms and outright irrelevancies."

464 Anon. "Passwords in Paris." *Newsweek*, 66 (30 August), 79–80.
The Married Woman teaches new ways of seeing and new insights into society, false consciousness, and personal relationships. Some problems are Godard's rambling, stream of consciousness whispers, and visual and verbal puns and inside jokes. Godard has made a "feast for today's audiences and tomorrow's directors" for under $100,000.

465 Anon. *"Pierrot le fou." Une Femme mariée: L'Avant-Scène du cinéma*, No. 46 (March), p. 60.
Complete credits. Brief synopsis. Résumé of reviews.

466 Anon. "Une Rencontre nommeé Godard." *Cinéma 65*, No. 92 (January), pp. 16–17.
"Journées Jean-Luc Godard" organized by the Ciné-Clubs of Annecy and the French Federation of Ciné-Clubs, were held November 6, 7, & 8 with a retrospective of Godard's work and a panel discussion, including Godard himself, after each film. A special program was televised, in a series run by Janine Bazin and André-S. Labarthe, of which a good part was filmed there.

467 Anon. Review of *Alphaville. Atlas*, 10 (September), 177–78.
Cited in *Humanities and Social Sciences Index*, 19 (April 1965-March 1966), 205.

468   Anon. Review of *The Married Woman.* London *Times* (8 April), p. 6.
Cited 1965, *Times Index* (March-April), p. 85.

469   Anon. Review of *Pierrot le fou. Paris-Match* (15 November — in that week).
Negative review quoted in 1976, Anon., "Pour ou contre *Pierrot le fou,*" Entry No. 1940.

470   Anon. Review of *Pierrot le fou.* London *Times* (3 September), p. 14.
Cited 1965, *Times Index* (September–October), p. 73.

471   Anon. "Slogans sur *Pierrot.*" Press dossier on *Pierrot le fou.* L'Agence FOG. 5 November. Written in Godard's style.
Reprinted 1976, Anon., *L'Avant-Scène du cinéma*, Entry No. 2333.

472   Anon. "That Old Feeling: *A Married Woman.*" *Time*, 86, No. 9 (27 August), 82.
Gives a description of the censors' changing *"The"* to *"A"*; a plot summary, with emphasis on the fragmented love-making sequences and the monologues; and a summary of Godard's weaknesses — redundancy, obtrusiveness, and self-indulgent attempts at visual and verbal humor.

473   Anon. *"Tous les garçons s'appellent Patrick."* Movie, No. 12 (Spring), p. 45.
Brief review, cited in Bowles, p. 525.

474   Anon. "Venice." *Sight and Sound*, 34, No. 4 (Autumn), 185.
Pierrot le fou implicitly contains Godard's examination of his own work to date. It also probes love and betrayal, "obviously based on personal experience."

475   Anon. *"A Woman Is a Woman:* French New Wave Film." *Christian Science Monitor* (4 March), p. 10.
Cited *Christian Science Monitor 1965 Annual Index*, p. 71.

476   Anon. "003 in 1984." *Newsweek*, 66, No. 19 (8 November), 109–113.
Is *Alphaville* an ill-contrived science fiction film, a melodramatic joke, or a romantic and lyrical consideration of feeling and "consciousness"? It's a cross between Orwell's *1984* and Oscar Wilde.

477   Aragon, Louis. "Collages dans le roman et dans le film." *Collages.* Series Miroirs de l'art. Paris: Hermann.
Union Catalogue 1963–67, Authors list #3, p. 188.

478   Aragon, Louis. "Qu'est-ce que l'art, Jean-Luc Godard?" *Les Lettres françaises*, No. 1096 (9–15 September), pp. 1 and 8.
Godard's work has been received like that of Delacroix, with jeers and personal attacks. The colors in *Pierrot le fou*, especially the obsessive reds, express horror, great beauty, and "the desperate order of passion." Citations serve the function of collages; not illustrations, "they are the film itself." Trans. 1972, Brown, Entry No. 1658.

479 Archer, Eugene. *"Cahiers* — An In Word that Means Far Out." *New York Times* (23 May), Sec. II, p. 9.
Describes the development of *Cahiers du cinéma* and the auteur theory.

480 Aubriant, Michel. Review of *Pierrot le fou*. *Paris-presse-l'intransigeant* (15 November — in that week).
Celebration of the film as a modernist masterpiece. Quoted in 1976, Anon., "Pour ou contre *Pierrot le fou*," Entry No. 1940.

481 Autera, Leonardo. "I debiti della 'nouvelle vague.'" *Bianco e nero*, 26, No. 1 (January), 1–9.
Godard's is the strongest artistic "voice" of the New Wave.

482 Baby, Yvonne. "Entretien avec Jean-Luc Godard: 'Dresser des embuscades dans la planification.'" *Le Monde* (6 May), p. 16.
In an interview on *Alphaville*, Godard discusses the theme of the film (borrowed from Lovecraft), the relation between present and future, his political conception in the film, the locations (a bank, La Défense, the Bull Machine Company), the characterization of Natacha.

483 Baby, Yvonne. Review of *Pierrot le fou*. *Le Monde* (31 August).
Positive review, cited in 1976, Anon., "Pour ou contre *Pierrot le fou*," Entry No. 1940.

484 Baroncelli, Jean de. *"Alphaville: une étrange aventure de Lemmy Caution."* *Le Monde* (7 May), p. 14.
Paris is made to seem like another world. Such a metamorphosis is due entirely to Godard's genius in mise en scene. His romanticism is ingenuous and his analysis lacks originality, but the film speaks with a fine personal voice.

485 Baroncelli, Jean de. Review of *Pierrot le fou*. *Le Monde* (9 November).
Quoted in 1976, Anon., *"Pierrot* et la presse," Entry No. 1940.

486 Bellour, Raymond. "Le Miroir critique." *La Nouvelle Revue française*, 26, No. 152 (August), 305–17.
Drawing on the example of Velasquez's *Las Meninas*, Bellour describes a kind of self-reflexive art which not only comments on its own processes of creation but also on the spectator's act of watching it — an art that offers up both itself and "its own mirror," *Le Mépris*, among other films, is analyzed in this context.

487 Benayoun, Robert. *"Alphaville:* la nébuleuse de l'épate-bourgeois." *Positif*, No. 71 (September), pp. 66–69.
Credits. Godard sells more of his tired cliches, reaching a new low in *Alphaville*, where, among other faults, the photography is overexposed.

488 Benismon, Jacques, et al. "Les Cravates rouges: convérsation avec Jean-Luc Godard." *Objectif*, No. 33 (August/September), pp. 3–16.
In an interview with Jacques Benismon, Christian Rasselet, and Pierre Théberge, Godard discusses *Le Mépris* and *Bande à part* in detail, noting the reasons for his cinematographic and narrative choices and comparing himself to other

filmmakers. He does not like to look at his old films because they often irritate him from a technical point of view and he sees things he'd like to do over. He identifies with the characters who are always in motion and he is proud of being an intellectual. He discusses his use of dance and music, his earlier films, and his love of digression.

489 Bérard, Jacques. *"Pierrot le fou." Téléciné*, No. 126 (December), pp. 23–34.
"Fiche No. 453." Complete credits. Two-page plot summary. Analyzes narrative construction, characterization, image track, use of color, sound track, and direction.

490 Billard, Pierre. "Lecture et réflexion faites." *Cinéma 65*, No. 94 (March), pp. 71–75.
Introduces a long taped statement by Godard but admits he is not a Godard admirer. He recognizes the way that cinema and life merge in Godard's personal and aesthetic stance, but he prefers a modernism like Brecht's or Resnais', in which the director uses amorality or fragmentation in art but works from a "non-chaotic vision of the universe" and creates art to help people recuperate sense from a fragmented world.

491 Bory, Jean-Louis. "Godard godardissime." *Arts*, No. 6, N.S. (3–9 November).
Pierrot le fou is, as Fuller defines cinema in the film, all color and movement. Belmondo's characterization sums up all Godard's thematic concerns. Like Virginia Woolf, Godard shows what is "between the acts." Reprinted 1971, Bory, Entry No. 1553.

492 Bory, Jean-Louis. "Terrible!" *Arts*, No. 1,005 (12–18 May), p. 10.
Enumerates the following sources for Lemmy Caution's characterization and *Alphaville*'s theme about love: Orwell, Huxley, Pascal, Céline, Eluard, comic strip, detectives Harry Dickson and Guy Léclair, Oedipus, Orpheus, and Theseus and the labyrinth. Too often Godard turns his work into caricature, with his puns, paradoxes, and gags. Reprinted, 1971, Bory, Entry No. 1553.

493 Capdenac, Michel. "Eddie Constantine de 1789 à 1989." *Les Lettres françaises*, No. 1080 (13 May), p. 7.
Godard uses cliches and stereotypes in *Alphaville* to destroy them. Like Eluard, whom he cites, Godard goes back to common speech to renew and transform it poetically.

494 Cervoni, Albert. "Le Printemps noir." *France nouvelle*, No. 1021 (12–18 May), pp. 26–27.
In *Le Mépris* Godard had succeeded in showing how capitalist structures of production corrupt intellectual integrity. In *Alphaville*, he uniquely captures the exterior signs of our social malaise, but he gives these a metaphysical dimension and ignores the real social forces at work.

495 Cervoni, Albert. "Jean-Luc le sage." *France nouvelle*, No. 1047 (10–16 November), pp. 23–24.

Pierrot was censored for youths because of vulgar language, and two out of three spectators walked out. Naive leftists had earlier rejected Godard as a fascist. Nevertheless, this not very salable film is a highly individual love story and also a moralist's evaluation of the real world, especially of Vietnam, advertising, and alienated daily life.

496 Chauvet, Louis. Review of *Pierrot le fou*. *Le Figaro* (15 November — in that week).

Negative review. Quoted in 1976, Anon., "Pour ou contre *Pierrot le fou*," Entry No. 1940.

497 Ciment, Michel. "Venise — 25e mostra: *La Femme mariée*." *Positif*, No. 66 (January), pp. 76–77.

Negative review.

498 Clark, Arthur B. *"Contempt." Films in Review*, 16, No. 1 (January), pp. 51–52.

The film is obscene, speciously anti-American, and degenerate, especially in its "truckling to Communists" and in the "debased" role played by Fritz Lang.

499 Clouzot, Claire. "Macha-la-chaste." *Cinéma 65*, No. 92 (January), pp. 108–109.

La Femme mariée is not the story of many women, just one. Macha Méril has a purity and unique grace. She's not very erotic but more like an androgenous mixture of adolescent and adult. She's chaste because there are no real men around her to seduce her. Why call Godard a misogynist when it's the men here who are so "gauche, banal, hypocritical, and sheepish"?

500 Coleman, John. "Good Godard." *The New Statesman*, N.S. 69, No. 1778 (9 April), 583.

What works in *La Femme mariée* is "the multi-layered surface of this skin-deep comedy." What doesn't are the painful "ethnographic interviews." Coleman notes which motifs in the opening sequence will recur: lovemaking, Charlotte's shallowness, classical theater, underwear, an advertising poster. All the visual details and most of the visual and verbal allusions and jokes "encrust the surface" of the film to portray a superficial life.

501 Collet, Jean. "Entretien avec Jean-Luc Godard." *Jean-Luc Godard*. Series Cinéma d'aujourd'hui, No. 18. Paris: Seghers.

Interview conducted September 12, 1963, after Godard had read opening essay for original 1963 edition of Collet's book. Godard describes how he became interested in film, his "instinct" to make films, and his aesthetic philosophy — similar to Rossellini's: "I think I am looking for something definitive, eternal, but under its least definitive, most fragile and living form." Godard has repeatedly used the theme of misunderstanding, culminating in *Contempt*, where he tried to "reduce the distance" between himself and his characters. He discusses his project for *Pour Lucrèce*. Reprinted 1968, Collet, Entry No. 1088, and 1974, Collet, Entry No. 1836. Trans. 1968, Mussman, Entry No. 1168. Trans. by Ciba Vaughan in 1970, Collet, Entry No. 1425. Vaughan and Mussman translations differ substantially.

502 Collet, Jean. Interview with Godard on *Alphaville. Télérama*, No. 801. Cited *Image et son*, No. 210, p. 22.

503 Collet, Jean. *Jean-Luc Godard.* Series Cinéma d'aujourd'hui, No. 18. Paris: Seghers.
I have not seen this edition. Revised from 1963 edition (Entry No. 265) and revised again in 1968 (Entry No. 1088) and 1974 (Entry No. 1836) in French; 1968 edition, trans. 1970 into English (Entry No. 1425).

504 Comolli, Jean-Louis. "A rebours?" *Cahiers du cinéma*, No. 168 (July), pp. 86–87.
Comolli analyzes the problems with any thematic criticism of *Alphaville*, for the film is a modernist puzzle. "The filmmaker's course is superimposed over that of the protagonist." Trans. 1966, Comolli, *Cahiers du Cinema in English*, No. 3 (March), Entry No. 670.

505 Comolli, Jean-Louis, et al. "Parlons de *Pierrot:* nouvel entretien avec Jean-Luc Godard," *Cahiers du cinéma*, No. 171 (October), pp. 18–35.
In this long interview with Jean-Louis Comolli, Michel Delahaye, Jean-André Fieschi, and Gérard Guégan, Godard discusses his first choices for actors for *Pierrot*; the "emergence" of a subject for his film while shooting; the characterization; the topic of adventure; convention and tradition vs. liberty in cinema; the references to Velasquez, Fuller, and Vietnam; politics and ideology in cinema; problems of aspiring directors in France; film criticism; the commentary on the image *within* Godard's films; going beyond mise en scene and auteur criticism; and film color and music. Reprinted in 1968, Narboni, ed., Entry No. 1170. Translated and commentary in 1970, Milne, Entry No. 1713. Extracts from Milne trans. in 1969, *Pierrot le fou* (script), Entry No. 2332.

506 Cournot, Michel. "Appelez le cinévidu." *Le Nouvel Observateur* (6 May), p. 28.
This witty science fiction satire is written in the "style" of *Alphaville* and tells about Paris being saved by Godard's films.

507 Cournot, Michel. Interview with Suzanne Schiffmann. *Le Nouvel Observateur* (6 May).
In an interview written in prose form without the questions, Schiffmann asserts that Godard's shooting style derives from his aesthetic stance. "He is obsessed by truth, reality. He wants to keep everything that has taken place during the shooting unless something comes from the equipment and not from "reality," either a camera noise or a noise made by the tracking dolly." Trans. 1972, Brown, Entry No. 1658.

508 Cournot, Michel. "*Pierrot le fou* de Jean-Luc Godard: pas du sang, du rouge!" *Le Nouvel Observateur* (3 November), pp. 36–37.
The critic appreciates the film for its lyrical beauty, its romanticism, and the character Marianne.

509 Cournot, Michel. "Victoire des maquis." *Le Nouvel Observateur* (20 October), pp. 39–40.

The weakest selection in *Paris vu par* is Godard's *Montparnasse-Levallois*, full of his "fascist misogyny."

510 Coutard, Raoul. "La Forme du jour." *Le Nouvel Observateur* (22 September).
Describes the demands Godard makes on cinematographers and labs. Trans. 1965, *Sight and Sound*, Entry No. 511. That trans. reprinted, 1968, Mussman, Entry No. 1168.

511 Coutard, Raoul. "Light of Day." *Sight and Sound*, 35, No. 1 (Winter), 9–11.
Trans. from 1965, *Le Nouvel Observateur* (22 September) (Entry No. 510). Reprinted 1968, Mussman, Entry No. 1168.

512 Crowther, Bosley. Review of *Alphaville*. *New York Times* (8 September), p. 51.
Godard "fails to follow through on a line of satiric development equal to his elaborate and colorful cinematic style" in *Alphaville*.

513 Crowther, Bosley. "Screen: *Alphaville*, Festival Picture, at the Paris." *New York Times* (26 October), p. 49.
Brief credits. *Alphaville* starts out well as Lemmy Caution moves into the mysterious city, but the film lapses into a hackneyed allegory about love and a robot society.

514 Crowther, Bosley. "Screen: Godard's *Married Woman*." *New York Times* (17 August), p. 39.
Brief credits. The structure of the film is fairly easy to understand. Godard takes an emotionally immature, shallow, pretty French woman and conveys her "subjective sensations" in unusual pictoral and verbal terms. It can be taken either solemnly or sardonically.

515 Crowther, Bosley. "What Is This Thing Called Love?" *New York Times* (22 August), Sec. II, p. 1.
The protagonist of *The Married Woman* is completely confused and maladjusted about emotions and sex. Her affairs and whole life are purely "tactile." The French censors thought it was a psychological and sociological treatise on how our civilization "baffles and overwhelms women." Crowther finds the film a "clever, sophisticated jibe" at a certain kind of superficial modern woman.

516 Curtis, Jean-Louis. "Adam, Ève, et Jean-Luc." *La Nouvelle Revue française*, 26, No. 146 (February), 319–22.
In *La Femme mariée*, "the trio that Godard presents to us is neither humorous nor pathetic, it's just mundane — that's Godard's view of the sexual revolution." *Le Mépris* had tried too hard to be self-reflexive. *La Femme mariée* does it with a more apt and lighter hand. Reprinted, 1967, Curtis, Entry No. 862.

517 Daix, Pierre. "L'Amérique à l'avant garde." *Les Lettres françaises*, No. 1063 (14 January), pp. 1 and 13.
Daix reports on the U.S. critical reception of *Le Mépris* (The *New York Times*

called it "doodling disguised as art.") Partly the cause may be the satiric portrayal of an American film producer, partly a disdain for Bardot and also for Fritz Lang's role in U.S. cinema. Pop art is elevated by the United States, and *Le Mépris* is vilified precisely because it criticizes such a tawdry buying and selling of intellectual and artistic capacity that pop art itself represents.

518 Delaney, M. "Jean-Luc Godard's Woman of Parts." *Saturday Night* (Toronto), 80 (November), 38–40, 45.
Cited 1964, *Canadian Periodicals Index*, 18, p. 208.

519 Delmas, Jean. "Godard et ses fans." *Jeune cinéma*, No. 7 (May), pp. 7–9.
Delmas is bored by the critical attention, mostly praise, given to Godard. He tries to ascertain why Godard has had popular success. For some, Godard is a witness to our confused times; for others, he attacks and opens up the narrow range of cinematic realism.

520 Denys, Richard. "Jean-Luc Godard." *Granta*, 71, No. 12457 (6 November), 8–11.
Cited in BFI bibliography.

521 Doniol-Valcroze, Jacques. "Jean-Luc Godard, cinéaste masqué." *Une Femme mariée: L'Avant-Scène du cinéma*, No. 46 (March), pp. 6 and 42.
This family friend tells about Godard's adolescence, cites Resnais on *A bout de souffle* as a "revolutionary" film, and cites Godard on his intent in *La Femme mariée*. Godard is the only one of his peers to continue in a low-budget mold. *La Femme mariée* is a carefully wrought melody and counterpoint — an analytical case history filled with tenderness.

522 Dorigo, Francesco. "Dal *nouveau roman* a *La Femme mariée*." *Cineforum*, 5, No. 46–47 (Spring), 461–484.
On Godard's modernism.

523 Dort, Bernard. "Godard ou le romantique abusif." *Les Temps modernes*, No. 235 (December), pp. 1118–28.
Analyzes *Le Mépris, La Femme mariée, Alphaville*, and *Pierrot le fou* and concludes that romanticism is a structural element of Godard's work. Godard tries to capture the surface of life but also maintains a myth of a lost ancient order whose people were fully themselves, an order now no longer accessible to us except via death and art. Excessive citations, love of U.S. cinema, characters "who play at cinema" all refer back to that once fuller reality grasped through art. Godard's work is a hall of mirrors with infinite exchanges between images of reality and characters who "play at truth" and never become autonomous figures.

524 Durand, Michel. Review of *Pierrot le fou*. *Le Canard enchâiné* (15 November — in that week).
Mixed, basically positive review. Quoted in 1976, Anon., "Pour ou contre *Pierrot le fou*," Entry No. 1940.

525 D.[yer], P.[eter] J.[ohn]. "*Femme mariée, Une (A Married Woman)*, France, 1964." *Monthly Film Bulletin*, 32 (May), 67–68.

Credits, plot summary. The film is often comic and is "not erotic but clinical." It extends the techniques developed in *Vivre sa vie* — "semi-improvised dissertations, restless wanderings, challenging confrontations." The performances are excellent in this portrayal of "mid-1960's labor-saving *angst*."

526   Egly, Max. "Jean-Luc Godard: *A bout de souffle*, 1969." *Regards neufs sur le cinéma*. Ed. Egly and Jacques Chevallier. Collection "Peuple et culture." Paris: Seuil. Pp. 216–23.
Brief credits and filmography. Plot summary. A character sketch of Michel and of Patricia is given. Godard takes up the "New Wave theme" of the relation between pleasure and love, once these are located outside morality, ethics, or social regulation. The film's cinematic innovations make it an important new work, even though it often may be disconcerting or irritating.

527   El Kaïm, Arlette. "*Alphaville* ou bêtafilm." *Les Temps modernes*, No. 229 (June), pp. 2292–93.
Alphaville is intellectually weak. This vacuous film does not merit its current critical acclaim.

528   Eyles, Allen. "*Bande à part*." *Films and Filming*, 11, No. 4 (January), 31.
Credits. This slight film, rejected by the Venice Film Festival, lags sometimes but is rewarding. Karina is "spineless" but Godard offers "incisive impressions of the central characters and the dreary or crispy cold settings."

529   Eyles, Allen. Review of *La Femme mariée*. *Films and Filming*, 11, No. 9 (June), 28–29.
Cited in Bowles, p. 155.

530   Failliot, Odile. "Analyse." *Télérama*, No. 791.
Review of *Bande à part*. Cited, 1974, Collet, Entry No. 1832.

531   Farin, Michel. "Des conteurs à *Alphaville*." *Etudes*, 323 (July-August), 84–95.
There is no outerworld in *Alphaville*. Constantine and Karina flee into pure imagination. Their love has no history; and it is the loss of history, not poetry, that the film really mourns.

532   Fieschi, Jean-André. "Après?" *Cahiers du cinéma*, No. 168 (July), p. 87.
Discusses *Alphaville* briefly as a legend for our times. Trans. 1966, Fieschi, *Cahiers du Cinema in English*, Entry No. 687.

533   Fieschi, Jean-André and Téchiné, André. "Fable sur *Pierrot*." *Cahiers du cinéma*, No. 171 (October), pp. 35–36.
Considers the film's formal innovations, its use of chance, and its themes. *Pierrot* seems an unexpected departure for Godard.

534   French, Phillipe. "*Une Femme mariée*." *Movie*, No. 13 (summer), pp. 2–5).
Brief plot summary. Godard neither holds Charlotte up to ridicule nor merely attacks mass society. Charlotte moves in a dream world and seems reduced to an

object. The lovemaking scenes are ritualized "immaculately told lies," and the interviews also elicit reflection on role playing. This intellectual, modernist work examines a number of philosophical issues, particularly how images and inventions in the twentieth century have become extensions of the self. Revised version, 1970, Cameron, Entry No. 1405.

535 Fuzellier, Etienne. *"Pierrot le fou." Education nationale*, No. 744, p. 30.
The critic tabulates the characteristic elements of Godard's style found in *Pierrot*. Ultimately *Pierrot* fails to satisfy us because it possesses neither rigor (like *Marienbad*) or human warmth (like *Juliet of the Spirits*). It has beauty and virtuosity, but the love story lacks interest.

536 Genêt. "Letter from Paris: June 2." *New Yorker*, 41, No. 17 (12 June), 116–118.
Summarizes the critical reaction to and the plot of *Alphaville*, "the most talked-of new French film." She tells the futuristic buildings it was filmed in.

537 Gill, Brendan. "Love and Marriage." *New Yorker*, 41, No. 27 (21 August), 99–100.
Being prolific allows an artist to take risks. Godard has made some very good and very bad films, mainly about the lack of communication in love and marriage. *The Married Woman* is an enjoyable, spare, beautifully photographed study of a troubled young woman who can't behave "for more than a few minutes at a time in a sensible fashion, much less in a conventionally honest one."

538 Giroud, Françoise. "Godard le fou." *L'Express* (8–14 November), pp. 56–57.
Through a cinematic language which integrates word, image, and color, *Pierrot* conveys the happiness and pain of loving. Godard films as spontaneously as he thinks. Unlike U.S. directors who tell stories, Godard is in the French tradition of poet-moralists.

539 Gozlan, Gérard and Liszek, Babette. "Jean-Luc Godard à la recherche de l'humain." *Miroir du cinéma*, No. 12–13.
Review of *Alphaville*. Cited, 1967, Amengual and Estève, Entry No. 782.

540 G.[uégan], G.[érard]. "Plein sud." *Cahiers du cinéma*, No. 169 (August), p. 7.
Guégan interviewed Godard, who was finishing *Pierrot le fou*, and who discusses his films, other filmmakers, and various authors.

541 Guégan, Gérard and Thevoz, Michel. *"Une Femme mariée." Cahiers du cinéma*, No. 163 (February), pp. 80–82.
See 1965, Thevoz, Entry No. 610. Trans. 1966, Guégan, Entry No. 697.

542 Haffner, Helmut. "Godard contra 'Goldfinger'." *Eckart-Jahrbuch* (Wittenberg), pp. 265–70.
Godard's "overinflated" critical reputation is discussed in this general article on the reception of films and filmgoing audiences in West Germany.

543 Hartung, Phillip T. "Dullsville: The Screen." *Commonweal*, 83 (12 November), 192–93.

Sees *Alphaville*, the opening film of the N.Y. Film Festival, as having a stimulating film technique but a self-indulgent content, filled with in-jokes, monotonous acting, preaching, and repeated situations.

544 Hartung, Phillip T. "*Les Girls:* The Screen." *Commonweal*, 81 (5 February), 611.

Contempt is panned as ridiculous and silly.

545 Hartung, Phillip T. "Summer Summary: The Screen." *Commonweal*, 82 (3 September), 637–38.

The Married Woman is photographically stunning but has a "confused" protagonist.

546 Hatch, Robert. "Films." *The Nation*, 201, No. 12 (18 October), 259.

The Married Woman is composed of "idiosyncratic montages of contemporary experience." Because the characterization is so weak, the film seems pornographic by concentrating on the sexuality of these people "in whom otherwise we take little interest."

547 Jacob, Gilles. "*Alphaville*." *Cinéma '65*, No. 97 (June), pp. 115–118.

Analyzes how the mise en scene expresses the film's humanistic concerns. It's the first French sci-fi film since *La Jeteé*, and perhaps Godard's best work to date.

548 Jacob, Gilles. "*Alphaville:* For or Against." *Sight and Sound*, 34, No. 4 (Autumn), 162.

Jacob summarizes the French press' conflicting reactions to *Alphaville*, which 160,000 people saw from May to August in first-run Paris cinemas. *La Femme mariée* ran for four weeks in first-run theaters to 70,000 spectators; *Bande à part*, five weeks, to 42,000.

549 Jacob, Gilles. "*Pierrot le fou:* selection du 'Godard's Digest.'" *Cinéma 65*, No. 101 (October), pp. 100–104.

Pierrot recapitulates gracefully Godard's major techniques and themes — including references to himself and his concerns, citations from literature and art, characters who search for liberty and betray each other, political statements about Vietnam, and problems of language, identity, and communication.

550 Kael, Pauline. "*Breathless* and the Daisy Miller Doll." *I Lost It at the Movies*. Boston: Little Brown. Pp. 127–32. Also, 1966, London: Jonathan Cape. Reissued 1969, New York: (Bantam) Grossett and Dunlap, Pp. 115–19.

Reprinted from 1961, Kael, Entry No. 124.

551 Kael, Pauline. "Godard Est Godard." *New Yorker*, 41, No. 34 (9 October), 43–46.

Kael writes a parody, in the form of a movie script, about Godard's appearance at the 3rd New York Film Festival.

552 Kauffmann, Stanley. "Conjugations of Love." *New Republic*, 152 (2 January), 21–22.

Contempt "seizes every chance to display Bardot." The argument sequence shows Godard's "egotism and bankrupt imagination." Palance acts badly, Lang well. Reprinted in 1966, Kauffmann, Entry No. 711.

553 Kauffmann, Stanley. "From France with Talent." *New Republic*, 153 (11 September), 25–27.

The photography of Macha Méril and Godard's "armory of experiment" are well used to develop the theme of modern love in *The Married Woman*. The film is a character study of a woman who is "secure because she is attractive but insecure because she does not understand the extent or meaning of her powers and appetites." Reprinted 1966, Kauffmann, Entry No. 711.

554 Kauffmann, Stanley. "The Future at Present." *New Republic*, 153 (20 November), 31–32.

Eddie Constantine, star of *Alphaville*, appeals to the French because he's made fifty detective movies in France about an FBI agent named Lemmy Caution. Part of the film is a "lively burlesque of tough private-eye nonsense." The rest is a boring thesis film. Sometimes Godard is "filmic"; sometimes he just gives us verbiage "accompanied by pictures, like a lecture with slides."

555 Klein, Gary. "In-quest of Jean-Luc Godard." *Isis*, No. 184 (2 June), pp. 16–19.

Cited 1972, Brown, Entry No. 1657.

556 Knight, Arthur. "Heating Up the Cold War." *Saturday Review* (13 November), p. 73.

In *Alphaville*, the action passages, conversations, "whisking" camera movements, elevator rides, and cars riding through the neon-lit city streets are all ultimately "wearying."

557 Lachize, Samuel. "Lemmy aux enfers: *Alphaville* de Jean-Luc Godard." *L'Humanité* (8 May), p. 8.

Godard's aesthetic and his use of citations, especially from poetry, serve his theme well—logic and machines vs. poetry and liberty.

558 Lachize, Samuel. "Ne rien raconter et tout dire: *Pierrot le fou* de Jean-Luc Godard." *L'Humanité* (6 November), p. 8.

This important film is a cinematically inventive poem about love and beauty in a world of violence and death. Regrettably the citations, hommages, and collages often lapse into buffoonery.

559 Lachize, Samuel. Review of *Pierrot le fou*. *L'Humanité* (11 November).

Cited in 1965, Anon., "*Une Femme mariée* et la presse," Entry No. 458. Also a similar review on November 3 is cited in 1976, Anon., "*Pierrot* et la presse, Entry No. 1939.

560 Lawson, J. Howard. Article on *A bout de souffle*. *Le Cinéma, art du XXe siecle*. Paris: Buchet-Chastel.

Cited 1967, Belmans, Entry No. 826.

561 L.[èfevre], R.[aymond]. *"Une Femme mariée" Image et son: la saison cinématographique 64*, special issue, No. 180-81 (January-February), p. 126.
Credits, brief plot summary. Godard aptly documents contemporary sensibility, especially in noting how it is shaped by advertising. However, his intellectual propositions are too insistent, and he has too many verbal digressions, especially one "indecent" monologue by the maid, Mme. Céline.

562 Lefèvre, Raymond. "L'Imaginaire politique." *Image et son: Revue du cinéma*, special issue "Cinéma et politique," No. 188 (November), pp. 81–89.
Le Petit Soldat and *Les Carabiniers* are discussed briefly in the context of how imaginative structures can aid the tasks of political films.

563 L.[èfevre], R.[aymond]. *"Les Plus Belles Escroqueries du monde."* *Images et son: la saison cinématographique 64*, No. 180–81 (January-February), p. 214.
Complains that Godard sketch was left out of French-release version.

564 Maillat, Phillipe. *"Une Femme mariée."* *Télécine*, No. 123 (June), pp. 15–28.
"Fiche No. 446." Credits, description of censorship, and plot summary are given. The critic describes the attacks on and praises for Godard, the film's genesis, the filming, each element of the cinematography, the characterization and themes, and Godard's role as ethnologist or first-person filmmaker. Godard juxtaposes elements in an intellectual construction that makes us see each element freshly, but his content is too often didactic, ambiguous, or even derisive.

565 Mardore, Michel. Review of *La Femme mariée.*" *Lui* (January).
Cited in 1965, *Une Femme mariée: L'Avant-Scène du cinéma*, Entry No. 458.

566 Martin, Marcel. "Femme entre eux." *Cinéma 65*, No. 92 (January) pp. 106–108.
There are too few feminist films and the subject of infidelity is posed here in dignified and everyday terms. But Godard bores us with his lectures, digressions, and citations. The fragmentation shows Godard's "lack of a fundamental theory, a vision of the world."

567 M.[artin], M.[arcel]. *"Pierrot le fou."* *Cinéma 65*, No. 99 (August), pp. 5–6.
Godard has great visual talent but fills his films with too much bric-a-brac and paperback and comic book culture. The key themes are the boredom of lovers, a violent world (Godard virulently attacks the U.S. presence in Vietnam), and the luxuriance of nature.

568 Matharan de Potenze, Sylvia. "Cine: *Pierrot le fou* (Francia, 1965)." *Criterio*, 91, No. 1548 (23 May), 536–37.
Godard has audaciously "expanded cinematographic language," but *Pierrot*, like Godard's other films, is flawed by an "incorrigible frivolity," and Godard's usual "obsessions and tics."

569 Mauriac, Claude. *"Pierrot le fou." Le Figaro litteraire* (11 November).
Cited 1967, Amengual and Estève, Entry No. 782.

570 Mazzocco, Robert. Review of *Alphaville, New York Review of Books*, 5,
No. 6 (28 October), 26–28.
Cited in Bowles, p. 11.

571 Méril, Macha and Godard, Jean-Luc. *Journal d' "Une Femme mariée."*
Paris: Denoël. 100 pages.
This is a photo journalistic presentation of stills from the film, emphasizing the
lovemaking sequences, Méril's face, and the underwear advertisements. The
monologues and various other lines from the film serve as the text, which is related
in the first person as the reflections of the character Charlotte. *See also* entry under
Godard Scripts, Entry No. 2323.

572 Milne, Tom. "Jean-Luc Godard, ou La Raison Ardente." *Sight and
Sound*, 34, No. 3 (Summer), 106–11.
Analyzes *La Femme mariée* in depth and takes up the following themes: the
shifting moral values, contradictions, inexplicable factors, fragmentation, and
dislocation of contemporary life; woman's condition in a consumer society where
she has no outlet for authentic expression; visual and verbal wit and the web of
meaning it forms; theatricality vs. sincerity; the transcience, tenderness, and
uncertainty of love. Reprinted 1972, Brown, Entry No. 1658.

573 Milne, Tom. *"Pierrot le fou." Sight and Sound*, 35, No. 1 (Winter), 6–7.
"After the carefully ordered disorder of *Le Femme mariée* and *Alphaville, Pierrot
le fou* looks like a return to the arbitrary insouciance of *Une Femme est une femme."*
The conception of the film is "purely romantic," the only unity coming from
Pierrot's attempt to understand and define his relation with Marianne.

574 Morandini, Morando. *"Les Plus Belles Escroqueries du monde (Le Più belle
truffe del mondo)." Bianco e Nero*, 26, No. 2 (February), 76–78.
Godard's sketch was not included in the Italian-release version.

575 Mortier, Michel. *"Une Femme mariée." Téléciné*, No. 120 (March), 33–39.
Godard treats his subject ambiguously and uses all his usual stylistic "man-
ias." Pro and con statements from HA., A.T., J.E.F., Ph.M., C.M., and G.S. as
well as extracts from reviews from nine French periodicals follow. (*Le Canard
enchaîné, Les Lettres françaises, La Croix, Signes du temps, Image et son, Le Figaro
littéraire, L'Humanité, Témoignage chrétien*).

576 Mosk[owitz, Gene]. *"Six in Paris." Variety*, date unknown.
Godard's sketch is "well-played and spouts clever dialogue in the midst of
much sound, movement, and work." Quoted at length, 1969, *Film Facts* (Anon.,
Entry No. 1255).

577 Mouillaud, Geneviève. "Les Essais de Jean-Luc Godard." *La Pensée*,
N.S., No. 122 (August), pp. 116–30.
The critic closely analyzes *Alphaville, Les Carabiniers, Le Mépris*, and *La Femme
mariée* in terms of the following aspects: collage technique, treatment of the human

body, use of Eddie Constantine, filmic citations, cinema verite techniques, use of real-life characters, love themes, treatment of women, vision of daily life, and Brechtianism.

578 Mouillaud, Geneviève. Review of *Pierrot le fou. La Pensée*, N.S., No. 122 (August).
Cited in 1965, Cervoni, Entry No. 494.

579 Natta, Enzo. "*Alphaville*: origini e sviluppi della fantasciensa." *Cineforum* (Venice), 5, No. 49 (November), 755–72.
Alphaville is analyzed from the following points of view: the development of cinematic and literary science fiction, Godard's career, an analysis of the film's plot (summary given), the theme of humans vs. robots—or human robots, cinematic language, and Godard's own comments on the film (interview cited, conducted by Natta).

580 Pilard, Phillippe. "Nouvelle vague et politique." *Image et son: Revue du cinéma*, special issue, "Cinéma et politique," No. 188 (November), pp. 90–101.
Godard falls victim to the dangers of "suspended meaning" just as others in the New Wave do.

581 Prédal, René. "*Alphaville*." *Jeune cinéma*, No. 8 (June-July), pp. 33–34.
Brief credits. This film is not as boring as Godard's two previous films, and the theme is both "solid" and well served by what are otherwise irritating Godard mannerisms (inserts, ads, intertitles). But the film is neither complete nor consistent.

582 Prédal, René. "Godard et la critique." *Jeune cinéma*, No. 8 (June-July), pp. 30–32.
Summarizes Godard's reception by both the film journals and the daily press. Godard's public is mostly film buffs, especially students and snobs who take Godard as their symbol. The critics seem to respect what they can't understand.

583 Price, James. "A Film Is a Film: Some Notes on Jean-Luc Godard." *Evergreen Review*, 9, No. 38 (November), 46–53.
Godard uses editing like Eisenstein, yet does not acknowledge him. Godard's films-within-films fit the characters' situations and comment on cinematic process. All the elements of Godard's self-conscious style, nonchalant tone, and "awareness of the camera . . . joined to awareness of location" are found in his early films. He makes the "spectator question the reality of a character or scene, answer, then reframe the question in another fashion." These films still convey surprisingly "strong feeling" and "traditional movie sentiment."

584 Ranieri, Tino. "Trieste: rassegna utile con qualche incertezza." *Bianco e nero*, 26, No. 10–11 (October-November), 90–91.
Review of *Alphaville*.

585 Rochereau, Jean. "*Alphaville*: ce monde où nous vivons." *L'Humanité* (15 May), p. 6.

The ambiance of contemporary Paris at night and the ultramodern interiors of a bank and a factory aptly contribute to this first good Kafkaesque film about France. It is marred by Godard's characteristic bad jokes and bad taste.

586 R.[opars]-W.[uilleumier], M.[arie]-C.[laire]. "De la mode." *Esprit*, 33, No. 2 (February), 368–70.

In *The Married Woman* Godard is searching for a new cinematic language to convey all the social aspects of the present moment, but he risks falling into the style of ads and TV images that he wants to comment on. Generally he is effective. Trans. in 1976, Ropars-Wuilleumier, Entry No. 1991.

587 [Ropars-] W.[uilleumier], M.[arie]-C.[laire]. "La Perte du langage." *Esprit*, 33, No. 9 (September), 315–17.

In *Alphaville*, "on the level of the image, because of the rhythmic union of night and light, when the world that is denounced acts as an explicit counterpoint to the political investigation, this vision of the world implicitly recreates poetry." But when the verbal discourse imposes meaning and not just a poetic rhythm, it contradicts the very theme of poetry. Then, because of the poverty of thought and the profusion of literary cliches, the film's subject—Alphaville—becomes satirized in a merely moralistic way. Trans. in 1976, Ropars-Wuilleumier, Entry No. 1991.

588 Roud, Richard. "Anguish: *Alphaville*." *Sight and Sound*, 34, No. 4 (Autumn), 164–66.

Contrasts Godard's use of the comic strip with his "great refinement and plastic beauty of style." The following contrasts are built into the film: light vs. dark, syrupy music vs. discordant noise, straight line vs. circle, romantic striving vs. classic formal perfection. The subtleties of the dialogue are lost in English titles, but Coutard brilliantly shows Paris as the Capital of Pain without trick shots or special effects. Reprinted 1966, Round, Entry No. 745.

589 Sadoul, Georges. *Dictionnaire des films*. Paris: Seuil.

See 1972, Sadoul, Entry No. 1726.

590 Sadoul, Georges. "Godard, Jean-Luc." *Dictionnaire des cinéastes*. Paris: Seuil.

See 1972, Sadoul, Entry No. 1727.

591 Sadoul, Georges. "A l'indicatif présent." *Les Lettres françaises*, No. 1080 (13 May), p. 7.

Alphaville's computer is compared to Dostoevsky's Grand Inquisitor. Plot summary given. Like *Les Carabiniers*, the film criticizes a war-like future. Godard has created an imaginary country, like Cocteau in *Orphée*, but here we recognize Paris. The philosophizing in this film is a little too elementary, and Eddie Constantino was not the appropriate hero for Karina to fall in love with.

592 Sadoul, Georges. "Pierrot mis à mort." *Les Lettres françaises* (11 November), p. 5.

Pierrot le fou is compared to three novels by Aragon—*Anicet*, *La Mise à mort*, and *Oedipe*.

593 Sainte-Marie, Gilles. "La Langage des signes." *Objectif*, No. 33 (August-September), pp. 36–38.

This is the text of a TV or radio program from CBF, April 2, 1965, on "Cinéma, miroir du monde." Godard uses apparently lax structures, e.g,, montage, to forge new instruments for investigating and appropriating reality and for shaping the means of communication. *La Femme mariée* has two themes—that of signs and of testimonials. Charlotte searches for her identity but only has the image of woman given to her by women's magazines and a consumer society. Brief credits.

594 Samson, Pierre. "A propos d'*Alphaville:* les méchanismes d'une imposture." *Les Temps modernes*, No. 230 (July), pp. 182–187.

Terrorist art thrives in bourgeois culture, especially under Gaulism. Godard designates diabolic attributes to technology, and his solutions are through individual adventure and a return to sentiment and love. He doesn't integrate his images of Paris in any coherent political way.

595 Sarris, Andrew. "*Alphaville.*"

Explanatory notes for 3rd New York Film Festival.

596 Sarris, Andrew. "Films." *Village Voice* (28 January).

Sarris discusses the production of *Contempt* and Godard's use of Moravia's novel.

597 Sarris, Andrew. "Films." *Village Voice* (30 September), p. 19.

In *The Married Woman*, Godard's coldly analytical, cubist, and collage style fits development of his characters, who are "completely consumed by impeccable images and imperfect ideas." However, the film lacks "order" even though it has wit and moments of brilliance (e.g., the nude sequences, the furtive assignation at the airport hotel).

598 Schlemmer, Isabelle. "*Alphaville.*" *Jeune cinéma*, No. 8 (June-July), p. 34.

The critic senses that Godard may have discarded the same poetry that Alpha 60 did. The sound track is harsh and frustrating, the film a "broken text of a dead civilization."

599 Schlesinger, Arthur, Jr. "Any Time for Comedy." *Show* (January), pp. 10–11.

The story of *A Woman Is a Woman* is hopeless; the tricks are impressive at first but finally "degenerate into an orgy of coyness, cuteness, and complacent exhibitionism." Richardson says he got his formal inspiration here for *Tom Jones*. Godard seeks the shock and discontinuity of "constant immediacy," but these discontinuities make the film lack power.

600 S.[eguin], L.[ouis]. "*Une Femme mariée.*" *Positif*, No. 67-68 (February-March), pp. 140–41.

Positif deliberately didn't review *Bande à part*. *Une Femme mariée* is just another example of Godard's misogyny, banality, and laziness.

601 S.[eguin], L.[ouis]. "Venise: *Pierrot le fou.*" *Positif*, No. 72 (December-January, 1966), pp. 21–23.
The film elicits no emotion, tells no story, and carries off no gag.

602 Le Serpent. Review of *Pierrot le fou*. *Minute* (18 November).
Negative review, quoted in 1976, Anon., "*Pierrot* et la presse," Entry No. 1939.

603 Shivas, Mark. "*Paris vu par.*" *Movie*, No. 14 (Fall), pp. 39–40.
Cited in Bowles, p. 583.

604 Simon, John. "Fake Death, Fake Love." *New Leader*, 48, No. 4 (15 February), 25.
In *Band of Outsiders*, sex is a "subhuman caprice," and the characters are "feelingless particles."

605 Simon, John. "Festival of Famine." *New Leader*, 48, No. 20 (11 October), 29.
Dismisses *The Little Soldier* for reducing politics to a game of cops and robbers and for "slobbering" over Anna Karina. Reprinted 1967, Simon, Entry No. 975.

606 Simon, John. "Gravity Defied." *New Leader*, 48, No. 18 (13 September), 31–32.
A Married Woman has much visual imaginativeness and beauty. Simon finds the protagonist "a cute little narcissist" and hates the sound track, the citations and puns. and the monologues. He likes the love scenes, the camera work, and the use of posters, headlines, and record jackets. Reprinted 1967, Simon, Entry No. 975.

607 Taylor, Stephen. "After the Nouvelle Vague." *Film Quarterly*, 18, No. 3 (Spring), 5–9.
All *Contempt* provides us is a number of situations, seemingly infinite options, "variously relevant details," and "unrelieved uncertainty." Social forces are portrayed but in an attenuated way—a tactic central to Godard's dramatic method. The confusion of languages in translation and the excessive use of quotations reinforce the film's theme: "the danger of forcing great works of the past—even the past itself—into conformity with your present circumstances."

608 Téchiné, André. "Blues du juke-box: *Montparnasse-Levallois.*" *Cahiers du cinéma*, No. 172 (November), pp. 52–53.
Credits. The film lacks Godard's typical, formal, imaginative innovations and control. He chose only to control decor, basic plot, and choice of actors. The same anecdote is used much more effectively in *Une Femme est une femme*.

609 Téchiné, André and Fieschi, Jean-André. "Fable sur *Pierrot.*" *Cahiers du cinéma*, No. 171 (October), pp. 35–36.
See 1965, Fieschi, Entry No. 533.

610 Thevoz, Michel and Guégan, Gérard. "*Une Femme mariée.*" *Cahiers du cinéma*, No. 163 (February), 80–82.

Brief credits. The critics examine Godard's internal references to and analysis of the function of the mass media. We always have a critical attitude toward all the characters. Godard's sense of an outsider derives from his being Swiss. As an ethnologist in this film, he looks at all the forms of communication in which our lifes are embedded. Translated in 1966, *Cahiers du Cinema in English*, Entry No. 762.

611 Th.[irard], P.[aul] L.[ouis]. *"Rogopag." Positif*, No. 72 (December-January 1966), pp. 108–109.

Brief credits. Godard's *Le Nouveau Monde* is a brief version of *Alphaville* and the worst film Godard ever made.

612 Thomas, John. Review of *A Woman Is a Woman. Film Society Review* (September), p. 12.

Cited in Bowles, p. 575.

613 Towne, R. "Bogart and Belmondo." *Cinema* (Beverly Hills), 3, No. 1 (December), 4.

Article on Belmondo. Cited 1976, Mel Schuster, *Motion Picture Performers: Supplement No. 1*, p. 62.

614 Tynan, Kenneth. Review of *The Married Woman. The Observer* (11 April).

The woman's moral concepts, or lack of them, are shaped by her job working for a fashion magazine, "a world of second-hand images." The film "always enlists the mind." Long excerpts reprinted in 1975, *Godard: Three Films*, Entry No. 2297.

615 Verdone, Mario. "Molti autori e 'mezzi' film." *Bianco e nero*, 26, No. 10-11 (October-November), 12–14.

Review of *Pierrot le fou*.

616 Walsh, Moria. *"Alphaville," America*, 113 (27 November), 694–95.

Finds Godard "preoccupied with camera pyrotechnics and silly 'inside' jokes" rather than evoking the "plight of rootless, alienated modern man."

617 Warren, P. "Le Cinéma de Godard." *Rélations* (Montreal), No. 299 (November), pp. 328–29.

Cited 1965, *Canadian Periodicals Index*, 18, p. 208.

618 Wellington, Frederick. "Three Films from Paris." *Film Comment*, 3, No. 3 (Summer), 30–33.

Brief credits for *La Femme mariée*. The film is full of "meat" and passionless characters. Godard uses advertisements to describe the characters' world and mentality, but it's all too boring. The directors of *La Peu douce, La Femme mariée*, and *Le Bohheur* all have a "hard and cruel" point of view.

619 Whitehead, Peter. Review of *Pierrot le fou. Films and Filming*, 12, No. 3 (December), 16 and 51–52.

Cited in Bowles, p. 392.

620 Zand, Nicole. "Interview with Godard." *Atlas*, 9, No. 1 (January), 56–57.
Cited in *Humanities & Social Sciences Index*, 19 (April 1965–March 1966), 205.

621 Zanelli, Dario. "Berlino: un passo avanti." *Bianco e nero*, 26, No. 10-11 (October-November), 78–79.
Review of *Alphaville*.

1966

622 Ajame, Pierre. Review of *Made in U.S.A. Les Nouvelles littéraires* (29 December).
Cited 1967, *L'Avant-Scène du cinéma*, Entry No. 801.

623 Alvarez, A. "The Delinquent Aesthetic." *Hudson Review* (Winter).
Cited 1967, Simon, Entry No. 910.

624 Anchis, Piero. Review of *Pierrot le fou. Cinema and Film*, 1, No. 1 (Winter), 33–38.
In Lincoln Center Library.

625 Anon. "Alphonse and Gaston: Le Clézio Talks to Godard." *Atlas*, 12, No. 3 (September), 54–56.
Interview between Godard and novelist Jean-Marie Le Clézio. Cited 1972, Green, Entry No. 1656.

626 Anon. *"Band of Outsiders." Film Facts*, 9, No. 5 (1 April), 44–46.
Complete credits and synopsis are given as well as quotations from reviews in the *New York Herald Tribune*, the *New York Times*, *Variety*, and *Time*.

627 Anon. "C Rating: National Catholic Office for Motion Pictures." *Catholic Film Newsletter*, 32, No. 2 (20 October).
Masculine-Feminine is condemned because "naturalism of style alone, without point of view or content, can neither support nor justify its vulgar and suggestive treatment." Reprinted 1969, Billard, Entry No. 1268.

628 Anon. "Encyclopédie permanent du cinématographe: Carre (dernier)." *Positif*, No. 74, pp. 87–88.
In this hostile look at Godard's career and the left critical reception of his work, Godard is criticized for his citations, his pretext of political engagement, and his pretentiousness. The article is followed by a photocopy of a newspaper clipping which tells of a 43-year-old Roger Godard being arrested for offering a young woman a "part in his next film."

629 Anon. "French Made 86 Features in 1965." *Variety* (4 May), p. 58.
Godard made three films this year: *Alphaville, Pierrot le fou*, and *Masculin-Féminin*.

630 Anon. Interview with Godard. *Amis du film et de la télévision*, No. 116.
Cited 1967, Belmans, Entry No. 826.

631 Anon. *"Masculine-Feminine* (The Children of Marx and Coca-Cola)." *Film Facts*, 9, No. 19 (1 November), 237.

Complete credits and one-paragraph summary of the film are given, as well as lengthy quotations from the reviews in the *New York World Journal Tribune*, the *New York Times, Time*, and *Variety*.

632 Anon. "Masters and Mavericks." *Newsweek*, 68, No. 14 (14 February), 94.

At the 4th New York Film Festival, people wore Godard buttons for their new culture hero. *Masculine-Feminine* is "an hilarious and moving film-poem" about a generation.

633 Anon. "People Are Talking About—." *Vogue*, 148 (1 October), 217.

Article on Belmondo. Cited in 1971, Schuster, Mel, *Motion Picture Performers*, p. 77.

634 Anon. "Pulp Fantasy." *Newsweek*, 67, No. 13 (28 March), 100.

Godard's flair for parody finally works. *Band of Outsiders* is "a well-integrated, quickly drawn and ironic study" of three "punk-heroes" acting out the fantasy of a grade-B gangster film.

635 Anon. Review of *Band of Outsiders. Time* (1 April).

Quoted 1966, Anon., *Film Facts*, Entry No. 626.

636 Anon. Review of *Made in U.S.A.* London *Times* (10 December), p. 13.

Cited 1966, *Times Index* (November-December), p. 75.

637 Anon. Review of *Masculine-Feminine.* London *Times* (10 May), p. 6.

Cited 1966, *Times Index* (May-June), p. 70.

638 Anon. Review of *Masculine-Feminine. Time* (7 October).

Quoted 1966, Anon., *Film Facts*, Entry No. 631.

639 Anon. Review of *Paris vu par.* London *Times* (17 February), p. 8.

Cited 1966, *Times Index* (January-February), p. 65.

640 Anon. Review of *Pierrot le fou.* London *Times* (7 March), p. 9.

Cited 1966, *Times Index* (March-April), p. 67

641 Anon. Review of *Pierrot le fou.* London *Times* (17 March).

Cited in 1967, Mainds, Entry No. 923.

642 Anon. Review of *Pierrot le fou.* London *Times* (14 April), p. 17.

Cited 1966, *Times Index* (March-April), p. 67.

643 Aprà, Adriano. "La semplicita della confusione." *Cinema and Film*, 1, No. 1 (Winter), 15–18.

In Lincoln Center Library.

644 Ardagh, John. "An Alpha for Godard?" *Guardian* (12 March), p. 7.

Interviews Godard and reports on the director's personality, living habits, and career. Godard sees *Pierrot* and *Alphaville* as very much about France today; he calls himself an old-fashioned romantic and a politically uncommitted leftist.

645 Argan, E.C. Article on Godard. *Filmcritica*, No. 165 (March).
Cited 1967, Baldelli, Entry No. 822.

646 Arnaud, André. "Copians flashes." *Salut les copians* (July).
Review of *Masculin-Féminin*. Trans. 1969, Billard, Entry No. 1268. Reprinted in *Cahiers du cinéma*, No. 195 (July 1966).

647 Baroncelli, Jean de. Review of *Masculin-Féminin*. *Le Monde* (23 April).
Trans. 1969, Billard, Entry No. 1268.

648 Benayoun, Robert. "*Pierrot le fou:* la machine à décerveler." *Positif*, No. 73 (February), pp. 93–96.
Credits. Benayoun is outraged at Godard's critical reception and his representing France at international festivals, for Godard's work is plagued by repetition, indifference to political nuances, and a puerile, Céline-like taste for blood and destruction. Neither Godard nor his supporter Aragon understand true collage.

649 Billard, Pierre. "Godard's valse triste." *L'Express* (18 April).
"There's something deliberately irritating, or naive, about this business of reproducing a certain reality exactly." Trans. 1969, Billard, Entry No. 1268.

650 Bond, Kirk. "3 from Godard." *Film Society Review* (March), pp. 11–17.
Cited in Bowles, p. 11.

651 Bory, Jean-Louis. "Ils tuent pour vous." *Le Nouvel Observateur* (14 December), pp. 50–51.
Analyzes the adverse reaction to *Made in U.S.A.* at its opening at an anniversary benefit for *Le Nouvel Observateur*. Situates the violence presented in the film within the context of the cultural and political history of France since WW II and relates cinematic violence to capitalist economic and state violence. Reprinted 1972, Bory, Entry No. 1653.

652 Bory, Jean-Louis. "Les Jeunes devant le jeune cinéma: face à l'amour un regard plus froid que celui de la caméra." *Arts*, No. 31 (27 April–3 May), pp. 60–61.
The Latin Quarter and Cinématèque provide a new serious-minded film public, to which the new French cinema offers disquieting, lyrical, fast-paced political and psychological studies. Godard, leader of this new cinema, portrays today's youth in *Masculin-Féminin* as banal, romantic, cynical, and ironically realistic. Godard and others of this movement have borrowed techniques from cinema-direct, but Godard's personality, especially his humor, emerges uniquely in his films. Excerpt trans. in 1969, Billard, Entry No. 1268.

653 Bragin, John. "*The Married Woman*." *Film Quarterly* 19, No. 4 (Summer), 42–48.
The film essentially transmutes the dramatic into the graphic. Bragin explicates the story line and its points of importance, especially the formal means by which Godard highlights his concerns. This film provides "an instantaneous

plunge into the fabric of the life of a character." Reprinted 1968, Mussman, Entry No. 1168.

654 Caen, Michael. "Eye of the Cyclone." Trans. Jane Pearce. *Cahiers du Cinema in English*, No. 2, pp. 274 +.
Trans. from 1966, Caen, Entry No. 655.

655 Caen, Michael. "*Pierrot le fou:* l'oeil du cyclone. *Cahiers du cinèma*, No. 174 (January). p. 74.
Brief credits. In *Pierrot le fou* Godard tries to say everything in each image. He questions his own, the characters', and the film's existence, and he uses a shooting method which is a phenomenolotigal exercise, somewhere between Céline and Husserl, to analyze the tangible proofs of existence. He ends up giving us pulsating episodes and still-lives, "which correspond to the calmer moments of a free fall." Trans. 1966, Caen, *Cahiers du Cinema in English*, Entry No. 654.

656 Capelle, Anne. "Des silences qui parlent trop." *Arts-loisirs*, No. 66 (28 December), pp. 48-49.
In this interview Godard is largely silent and tells Capelle to invent answers or to see his films, which will contain all the answers. "When I was a journalist I invented things . . . Now my films are like automatic writing."

657 Cervoni, Albert. "*Masculin-Féminin.*" *France nouvelle*, No. 1072 (4 May), pp. 24–25.
Godard's films (each listed and discussed) regularly comment on neocapitalism. In *Masculin-Féminin* Godard uses a television style, rather than an "artistic" one, to make us question what the truth is that the visual and verbal conventions of the media elicit. Godard admires youth's rejection of convention and false morality, their search for liberty, and their critical and demanding spirit. It is an important film.

658 Cervoni, Albert. "Un 'Truc politique.'" *France nouvelle*, No. 1105 (21 December), pp. 23–24.
Cervoni contrasts the more documentary-like Godard films with *Alphaville* and *Made in U.S.A.* These are more general philosophical reflections, using imaginary "societies transposed from the real world." *La Femme mariée* attacks surface manifestations of advertising and consumerism but does not give a more profound political analysis. *Made in U.S.A.* is limited by too improvised and rapid filming and by lack of an organizing principle.

659 Chapier, Henri. Review of *Masculin-Féminin*. *Combat* (24 April).
Trans. 1969, Billard, Entry No. 1268.

660 Chauvet, Louis. Review of *Masculin-Féminin*. *Le Figaro* (26 April).
Strongly negative review. Trans. 1969, Billard, Entry No. 1268.

661 Chelminski, R. "Power, Spell, and Free Spirit of Belmondo," *Life*, 61 (11 November), 111.
Article on Belmondo. Cited in 1971, Schuster, Mel, *Motion Picture Performers*, p. 77.

662 C.[hevassu], F.[rançois]. *"Pierrot le fou."* *Image et son: la saison cinématographique,* special issue, p. 150.

Credits, brief résumé. The film has been hailed as a French cinematic masterpiece, but it is only an innocent diversion which is an aesthetically pleasing but intellectually empty demonstration of collage technique, surrealist moments, and wit.

663 Cohn, Bernard. *"Paris vu par:* de tout pour faire un monde." *Positif,* No. 73 (February), pp. 102–105.

Review of *Montparnasse-Levallois,* credits. The dialogue is almost inaudible and the plot insulting to the female protagonist.

664 Coleman, John. "Alphaville and Alphieville." *The New Statesman,* 71, No. 1828 (25 March), 437.

Alphaville has almost no plot. It's hard even to give an account of the events. Godard only "toys with issues, ideas, images" in an evasive, amateurish, modish, pop art way. This film does an injustice to cinema, which is a basically realistic medium.

665 Collet, Jean. "Analyse: *Alphaville.*" *Télérama,* No. 851 (8 May), pp. 79–80.

Credits, setting described, plot summary. The themes are reduced language and the suppression of desire and love in a planned world. The film's poetry doesn't lie with that other-worldly kind depicted in the film but in the portrayal of the city, and in the film as a whole—with all its juxtapositions, tensions, and oppositions.

666 Collet, Jean. "Jean-Luc Godard, le cinéma, et la vie." *Etudes,* 324 (February), 196–202.

Godard's fame and the admiration/disgust he inspires among critics are described. People went to *Pierrot* for an adventure story and received a critique of cinema itself. Other films, especially *Alphaville, Le Mépris,* and *La Femme mariée,* are about language. Godard says we have to choose between the prefabricated "story," constantly being offered to us in different forms by a consumer society, and "the world of instantaneous, immediate living."

667 Collet, Jean. *"Masculin-Féminin* de Jean-Luc Godard." *Etudes,* 325 (July), 91–92.

The interest of the film is not in its subject matter (adolescence is often dealt with in film) but its technique. Godard is the first to understand the limits of certain narrative "methods" and to demonstrate and criticize these constantly. Both today's youth and the limits of language itself are treated seriously and "bitterly" in this film.

668 Collet, Jean. *"Masculin-Féminin."* *Télérama* [June], p. 72.

After the poetry of *Pierrot,* this is a new descent into hell, our own, where love is impossible and words have lost their meaning. These adolescents talk and talk — to live, to gain confidence, and to avoid facing silence, freedom, and love. Godard views another generation critically, lucidly, and tenderly. (There was no date on this clipping, which I received from Royal Brown.)

669 Collet, Jean. Review of *Masculin-Féminin*. *Signes du temps* (June).
Cited 1974, Collet, Entry No. 1832.

670 Comolli, Jean-Louis. "Contrariwise." Trans. Jane Pearce. *Cahiers du Cinema in English*, No. 3., pp. 57–58.
Review of *Alphaville*. Trans. from 1965, Comolli, Entry No. 504.

671 Cournot, Michel. "Les Orphelins de la parole." *Le Nouvel Observateur* (22 September).
Cited 1967, Amengual and Estève, Entry No. 782.

672 Crist, Judith. "Just Run-of-Godard-Mill." *World Journal Tribune* (19 September).
Reviews *Masculin-Feminine*. Brief credits. The acting excellently conveys the ambivalence and faults of late adolescence. Godard tries to shock us with explicit sexuality. Repetition and irrelevance water down the flashes of original wit.

673 Crist, Judith. Review of *Masculine-Feminine*. New York *Herald Tribune* (19 September).
Quoted 1966, Anon., "Masculine-Feminine." *Film Facts*, Entry No. 631. Reprinted 1969, Billard, Entry No. 1268.

674 Crist, Judith. Review of *Pierrot le fou*. *World Journal Tribune* (22 September).
Cited 1970, Collet, Entry No. 1425.

675 Crowther, Bosley. "Hollywood Woos Foreign Talent." *New York Times* (26 November).
Financing with Columbia for *The Married Woman* and *Band of Outsiders* is discussed. The films cost $100,000 and $120,000 respectively.

676 Crowther, Bosley. Review of *Masculine-Feminine*, *New York Times* (19 September), p. 57.
Masculine-Feminine is a "movie happening," in which Godard "seems to have little more concentration span than his saucy, good-looking youngsters, who evidently have none at all." Brief credits. Reprinted 1969, Billard, Entry No. 1268.

677 Crowther, Bosley. Review of *Pierrot le fou*. *New York Times* (22 September), p. 57.
Pierrot le fou offers some good color "sight-seeing" but is an overlong, rambling account of two indecisive lovers "bouncing around."

678 Curtis, Jean-Louis. "Le Fou d'Anna." *La Nouvelle Revue française*, 27, No. 160 (April), 689-94.
The crime story in *Pierrot* was just thrown in at parts like dabs of paint on a canvas. Similarly, just when the film seems to provoke emotion, it "freezes" it. Godard spoils the film's charm and romantic emotion with his tics, mannerisms, and childish games. Reprinted 1967, Curtis, Entry No. 862.

679 Dadoun, Roger. Review of *Pierrot le fou* and *Masculin-Féminin*. *Preuves*, No. 179 (January).
Cited 1968, Gauteur, Entry No. 1111.

680 Daix, Pierre. "Ce que Godard nous jette à la figure." *Les Lettres françaises*, No. 1162 (22–28 December), pp. 34–35.

Made in U.S.A. exposes both a political reality and the mechanisms of cinematic illusion. The film's theme "is not violence as such, but our complicity with it, our absence of reaction in the face . . . of the most massive crimes." The film is our *Guernica*.

681 Daix, Pierre. "Jean-Luc Godard: 'Ce que j'ai à dire.' " *Les Lettres françaises*, No. 1128 (21–27 April), pp. 16–17.

In an interview, Godard discusses *Masculin-Féminin* in terms of its use of the survey and public opinion poll. At this point, he feels like a prisoner in the French film industry, like a sniper shooting at it from inside. He explains his rejection of a cinema of "spectacle." Trans. in 1969, Billard, Entry No. 1268.

682 Delahaye, Michel. "Jean-Luc Godard et l'enfance de l'art." *Cahiers du cinéma*, No. 179 (June), pp. 65–70, 77.

Like Bernanos, Godard shows the relation between terror and banality, often using protagonists who are dead souls. Naiveté allows one to "dream, see, believe, do, and live." Godard looks at the generosity and sincerity of youth in *Masculin-Féminin* as well as their social conditioning, which has made the women characters successful "mutants," able to adapt, and the male protagonist weak and an outsider. Trans. 1967, Delahaye, *Cahiers du Cinema in English*, Entry No. 866.

683 Dupeyron, Georges. "Le Cinéma." *Europe*, 44, No. 449 (September), 243–44.

Discusses the interview technique in *Masculin-Féminin* and the romantic sentimentalism and spiritual purity of these adolescents. It's too vague and loose a film but does capture the externals of the neon world and life outside of the classroom, which is where 20-year-olds live.

684 Faccini, Luigi. Review of *Bande à part*. *Cinema and Film*, No. 1 (Winter), 27–32.

In Lincoln Center Library.

685 Faurecasten, Jean. "*Masculin-Féminin*." *Téléciné*, No. 129 (June-July), pp. 3–14.

"Fiche No. 459." Credits, resume, complete explication of film. Godard proceeds by juxtaposition, addition, and accumulation to present "the fluctuations of the personal, sentimental and lustful life" of Paul, who seems Godard's own self. The camera style and editing is austere, the sound track "expressionistic," the acting poor, the social view pessimistic, and the general tone one of romantic despair.

686 Ferrero, Adelio. "Jean-Luc Godard: monografía." *Cinestudio*, No. 17, unnumbered.

In British Film Institute Library.

687 Fieschi, Jean-André. "Afterwards." Trans. Jane Pearce. *Cahiers du Cinema in English*, No. 3, pp. 59–60.

Review of *Alphaville*. Trans from 1965, Fieschi, Entry No. 532.

688 Gambetti, Giacomo. "Rigore e coerenza di Jean-Luc Godard." *Bianco e nero*, 28, No. 7-8 (July-August), 37–43.

The "cultural session" of the 27th Venice Film Festival showed three Godard films — *Le Petit Soldat, Les Carabiners*, and *Bande à part* — and also Janine Bazin and André-S. Labarthe's TV documentary, *Jean-Luc Godard, ou le cinema de défi*, in the "Cinéastes de notre temps" series. This critical article reviews Godard's career to date.

689 Gauteur, Claude. "Jean-Luc Godard et *Le Mépris.*" In "Le Cinéma française: la nouvelle vague." *Image et son: Revue du cinéma*, No. 200 (December), pp. 67–89.

Discusses those New Wave films that incorporate other films, have their characters go to films, use filmmakers as protagonists, show film posters or cinemas. Godard's work is a veritable compendium of homages to other directors. New Wave directors, especially Godard, love private jokes and "citations" of other directors' shots, colors, and style. *Le Mépris is considered in detail.*

690 Goldman, Judith. "Godard — Cult or Culture?" *Films and Filming*, 12, No. 9 (June), 36–37.

Discusses audience reactions to Godard, the autobiographical elements in his films, and his antiwar scenes. Godard's citations are sometimes effective, sometimes elitist in-jokes. Fans enjoy recognizing an aesthetic continuity between Godard's films.

691 Goldmann, Annie. "Jean-Luc Godard: un nouveau réalisme." *Nouvelle Revue française*, 14, No. 165 (1 September), 558–65.

Goldmann analyzes the social themes and characterization (maladroit, romantic, male "outsiders" and rational and adoptive women) in each film through *Masculin-Féminin.* Godard denounces the ways in which our consumer society, dominated by advertising and technology, has damaged interpersonal relations, culture, and our relation to nature. Possibly reprinted in 1971, Goldmann, Entry No. 1576, as "Les Heros Godardien et le monde."

692 Goldmann, Lucien. *Le due avanguardia.* Rome(?): Argalia. P. 102.

Reference to argument about *Le Mépris* developed by Anne Olivier, 1964, Entry No. 420. Cited 1974, Ferrero, Entry No. 1841.

693 Gollub, Julia Podselver. "Nouveau roman et nouveau cinéma." Ph.D. dissertation, UCLA. *Dissertation Abstracts*, 26, 6712.

Does not deal extensively with Godard but notes that he regularly incorporates into his films the most superficial "tricks" of Brecht — subtitles, documentary sequences, actors addressing the camera, introduction of real personnages, private jokes, and characters that bear famous names. (p. 143).

694 Gow, Gordon, Review of *Alphaville*. *Films and Filming*, 12, No. 8 (May), 8 and 10.

Cited in Bowles, p. 11.

695 Grenier, R. "Son of Bogie," *Esquire*, 65 (January), 67.

On Belmondo and his films (*Breathless, Pierrot*). Cited 1971, Schuster, Mel, *Motion Picture Performers*, p. 77.

696 Guarino, Ann. Review of *Masculine-Feminine*. *Daily News* (20 September).
The film is too frank about sex and gets two stars. Excerpts reprinted in 1969, Billard, Entry No. 1268.

697 Guégan, Gérard. "Decollages." Trans. Jane Pearce. *Cahiers du Cinema in English*, No. 3, p. 56.
Review of *La Femme mariée*. Trans. from 1965, Guégan, Entry No. 541.

698 Guest, Harry. "Godard Quotation." Letters to Editors. *Sight and Sound*, 35, No. 4 (Autumn), 207.
Reader explains *Pierrot le fou*'s references to Rimbaud and to *Paul et Virginie*.

699 Harcourt, Peter. "Godard le fou (il s'appellée [sic] Pierrot)." *Views*, No. 11 (Summer), pp. 51–54.
Pierrot le fou "has an essentially imagistic style . . . based on the apparently haphazard." The "surrealistic association of violent death and tender love" reinforces Godard's theme that "life is the most beautiful when lived most freely as play in the face of the meaningless annihilation of death." Reprinted 1974, Harcourt, Entry No. 1843.

700 Hartung, Phillip T. "Lexicon of Youth: The Screen." *Commonweal*, 85 (7 October), 21–22.
Masculin-Féminin is well acted so that even the interminable conversations seem convincing. Excerpts reprinted in 1969, Billard, Entry No. 1268.

701 Hatch, Robert. "Films." *The Nation*, 202, No. 14 (4 April), 406.
Band of Outsiders deals with "dreamy heirs of Existentialism" who want to live inside a fantasy but can't. The film is "ingratiating . . . touching . . . and a little boring."

702 Hatch, Robert. "Films." *The Nation*, 203, No. 11 (10 October), 366.
Masculine-Feminine has an episodic structure and is full of change of pace and tone. The characters are ingratiating; Godard treats the young men better than the young women. No one has yet made a substantial work about "the alleged entropy of contemporary youth."

703 Haudiquet, Phillipe. *"Masculin-Féminin."* *Image et son: Revue du cinéma*, No. 195 (June), pp. 106–107.
It would have been a fine film if Godard had stuck to portraying his young hero and companions, but regretably Godard has tried to insert too many "notes" or "signs" that would depict a whole epoch. His cinema-direct, recognizable backgrounds and crowds on the street are just inserted, and do not capture or recreate any "atmosphere" at all. Trans. 1969, Billard, Entry No. 1268.

704 Hautecouverture, Michel. *"—Unissez-vous!"* *Positif*, No. 75 (May), p. 183.
In a letter to the editors, Godard is seen as the prime example of "cultural Gaullism," and the writer explains the political bases of certain critics' support.

705 H.[obson], H.[arold]. *"Alphaville*: New Godard Film." *Christian Science Monitor* (7 May).

Written from London. Film's interest resides in photography of contemporary Paris, subtle literary references, and Constantine's dour characterization of Lemmy Caution.

706 H.[ouston], P.[enelope]. "*Pierrot le fou*, France/Italy, 1965." *Monthly Film Bulletin*, 33 (June), 90–91.

Credits, plot summary. The film is built on contradictions and juxtapositions: long shots vs. sharp jabs of action; the romantic idyll of the sea vs. violence; "the shock of chance, coincidence, real death." Godard is a "modern romantic."

707 Jouffroy, Alain and Godard, Jean-Luc. "Miner le terrain." *L'Oeil*, No. 137 (May), pp. 34–42.

Cited *Arts Index* (November 1965–October 1967), p. 422.

708 Kael, Pauline. "Godard among the Gangsters." *New Republic*, 155 (10 September), 27–29.

"Godard's sense of the present is dominated by his movie past." Kael discusses in detail how *Band of Outsiders* is a nostalgic, poignant homage to the American gangster genre. The adolescent characters live within a gangster fantasy. Sadness pervades this lyrical portrayal of how their efforts to enact that fantasy failed. Reprinted 1968, Mussman, Entry No. 1168; 1968, Kael, Entry No. 1130.

709 Kael, Pauline. "Movie Brutalists." *New Republic*, 155 (24 September), 23–31.

Godard has strengths and weaknesses as a filmmaker, but too many young filmmakers try unsuccessfully to imitate this "hero," who appeals to them because of his young, "floating," artistically sensitive characters and his artistic independence. They are right to react against a Hollywood studio style, but to advocate rough messiness is "movie brutalism." Reprinted 1968, Kael, Entry No. 1138, and in 1969, Billard, Entry No. 1268.

710 Kael, Pauline. "Youth Is Beauty." *New Republic*, 155 (19 November), 24–30.

In *Masculine-Feminine*, the film structure and the cinematography aptly reinforce the romantic theme of young love and isolation "in a time of irreverance and hopelessness." Reprinted 1968, Kael, Entry No. 1131. *See* entry there. Also reprinted in 1970, Kael, Entry No. 1466.

711 Kauffmann, Stanley. *A World on Film: Criticism and Comment*. New York: Harper and Row.

"*Breathless*," pp. 238-241, reprinted from 1961, Kauffmann, Entry No. 125. "*My Life to Live*," pp. 241–42, reprinted from 1963, Entry No. 288. "*A Woman is a Woman*'" pp. 242–43, reprinted from 1964, Entry No. 403. "*Contempt*," pp. 243–44, reprinted from 1965, Entry No. 552. "*The Married Woman*," pp. 244–46, reprinted from 1965, Entry No. 553.

712 King, Adele. "Godard and Proust." Letters to Editor. *Sight and Sound*, 35, No. 2 (Spring), 102.

Two citations from Proust which appear in *Vivre sa vie* and *Bande à part* are noted.

713 Klein, Michael. *"Pierrot le fou."* *Film Quarterly*, 19, No. 3 (Spring), 46–48.
A "coolness" pervades the film — seen in the use of long shots, Karina's bored look, the failure of the love idyll, and the "strained intellectualization" of the Vietnam skit and the gun battles.

714 Kustow, Michael. *"Paris vu par."* *Sight and Sound*, 35, No. 2 (Spring), 91–92.
Brief review of omnibus film in which Godard's *Montparnasse-Levallois* appears.

715 Labro, Phillippe. ["One Evening, in a Small Cafe —"]. *Le Nouveau Candide* (17 January).
Interview with Godard on location while shooting *Masculin-Féminin*. Trans. in 1969, Billard, Entry No. 1268.

716 Labro, Phillipe. "Qui sont les enfants des années 60? Jean-Luc Godard repond à Phillipe Labro." *Elle*, No. 1051 (10 February), pp. 70–72.
Labro witnessed the filming of *Masculin-Féminin* and finds the film a powerful portrait of France, a study of the pains of love, and another indication of Jean-Pierre Léaud's importance to the New Wave. Léaud is like an anti-Belmondo. Godard has captured the exact tone of adolescent conversation, as destructive as it is tender. An excerpt from the dialogue is cited.

717 Lachize, Samuel. Review of *Masculin-Féminin*. *L'Humanité* (27 April).
Cited 1968, Gauteur, Entry No. 1111.

718 Laude, André. "Quand Macha s'en va-t-en guerre." *Les Lettres françaises*, No. 1162 (22-28 December), pp. 34–35.
In an interview Macha Méril says that Godard chose her only for her appearance but, in fact, they worked together well. She had scraps of paper for scripts, never knowing the situations in advance. Godard's films reflect only himself, not any star. Méril, now producing with Machafilms, seeks to make quality films "outside the system."

719 Lefèvre, Raymond. *"Pierrot le fou."* *Image et son: Revue du cinéma*, No. 192 (March), pp. 108–109.
Brief credits. It's a personal film about the desire to flee from an unlivable world into love, art, nature, and fantasy. The ending is one of despair.

720 Linder, Herbert. "Godard: Instinkt und Reflexion." *Filmkritik* (Munich), 10, No. 3 (March), 125–38.
Analyzes the relation between Godard's use of improvisation, mixture of fiction and documentary modes, and self-reflexivity about cinematic process.

721 Macciocchi, Maria A. *"Due o tre cose che so di li."* *L'Unita* (18 October).
Interview with Godard on *Deux ou trois choses*. Cited 1974, Ferrero, Entry No. 1841.

722 Macciocchi, Maria A. "Incontro con Jean-Luc Godard." *Filmcritica*, No. 172 (November), pp. 535–37.

Godard is interviewed on his sources for and ideological presuppositions in *Deux ou trois choses.*

723 Marcabru, Pierre. "Le Film le plus beau et le plus bête de l'année: *Made in U.S.A.*" *Arts et loisirs*, No. 66 (28 December–3 January, 1967).
     Cited 1967, Amengual and Estève, Entry No. 782.

724 Martell, Luigi. Review of *Masculin-Féminin, Cinema and Film*, 1, No. 1 (Winter), 39–42.
     In Lincoln Center Library.

725 Mauriac, Claude. "L'Écran miroir: *Masculin-Féminin.*" *Le Figaro littéraire* (28 April), p. 14.
     Godard has given the cinema and especially the camera their liberty and desanctified them because these are his tools. They allow him to see and hear. Godard's images capture the instant, here the warmth and despair and the fleeting quality of adolescence. His films move us because of their rapidity and incompleteness. In *Masculin-Féminin* he speaks from the depths of solitude. Trans. 1972, Brown, Entry No. 1658.

726 Metz, Christian. "Le Cinéma moderne et la narrativité." *Cahiers du cinéma*, No. 185 (December), pp. 43–68.
     Metz's long article is largely illustrated with full-page stills from Godard's films. In his discussion of cinema narratives and modernist innovations, Metz analyzes Godard's type of "realism," interest in Jean Rouch, self-reflexivity, concentration on the single shot, "abuses" of cinematic syntax, and also a successful challenging and reshaping of that syntax. In this article Metz refers to his own *"grande syntagmatique"* so that it is often an evaluation of how Godard transgresses that system.

727 Michaelson, Annette. "Film and the Radical Aspiration." *Film Culture*, No. 42 (Fall).
     Originally this was a lecture given at Lincoln Center, September 1976. The critic discusses the phenomenological effects of Godard's narrative pacing, manipulation, and dislocation in *Alphaville*. His work, like that of Resnais, "constitutes renderings of the agonistic dimension" of film. These renderings show in the most open and nonprescriptive way possible the possibility and dynamics of the medium. Reprinted 1970, Michaelson, Entry No. 1484, and 1967, Michaelson, Entry No. 933.

728 M.[ilne], T.[om]. "*Alphaville: une étrange aventure de Lemmy Caution (Alphaville)* France/Italy, 1965." *Monthly Film Bulletin*, 33 (May), 70–71.
     Credits, plot summary. Godard describes the destructive aspects of a technological society which is an extension of our own. He does this by using two legends — that of Lemmy Caution and that of Cocteau's Orpheus, who "recalls the existence of poetry."

729 Milne, Tom. "*Masculin-Féminin.*" *Sight and Sound*, 36, No. 1 (Winter), 44–45.
     Paul in *Masculin-Féminin* is an isolated, suffering romantic hero. Most of the sequences in the film are "shot with a fixed camera in a single take, the complexity

arising from the orchestration of references, visual and aural." Excerpts reprinted in 1969, Billard, Entry No. 1268.

730 Moravia. Review of *Pierrot*. *L'Espresso* (Rome), (22 May).
Cited 1967, Baldelli, Entry No. 822.

731 Mosk[owitz, Gene]. *"Masculin-Féminin* (French-Swedish)." *Variety* (4 May), p. 6.
In this "arty" picture, Godard "takes a look at local youth in his usual personal style," which includes "incidents, not story, inside jokes, despair, wit, and a sort of mixture of cinema truth interview and sociological methods." Leaud aptly plays a callow youth; the other actors and actresses are "photogenic and persuasive." Quoted 1966, Anon., *Film Facts*, Entry No. 631. Reprinted 1969, Billard, Entry No. 1268.

732 Otchakovsky-Laurens, Paul. "Et si vous voulez . . . *Masculin-Féminin." Jeune cinéma*, No. 15 (May), pp. 35–36.
Godard's films are still marked by both his irritating tics and his generous spirit. This sociological investigation presents characters and an environment that seem completely human, showing all the foolishness and contradictions around and within us.

733 Pacey, Ann. Review of *Pierrot le fou*. *The Sun* (England) (16 March).
Cited in 1967, Mainds, Entry No. 923.

734 Parinaud, André. "Spectacles: Jean-Luc Godard." *Arts-loisirs* (5 April).
In an interview, Godard discusses the influences on *Masculin-Féminin* (Marker, Rouch), his aesthetics, and the role that cinema plays in his own life and thought. "I'm an eye that looks and that stares at itself." Brief extract from dialogue of *Masculin-Féminin*.

735 Petrowski, Minou. Review of *Masculin-Féminin*. *Take One*, 1, No. 1 (September-October), 26–27.
Brief review. Cited in Bowles, p. 319.

736 P[hillipe], P[ierre]. *"Masculin-Féminin." Cinéma 66*, No. 107 (April), pp. 116–17.
In TV style, Godard offers a mannered, romanticized survey of adolescence. The film is generally "empty, graceless, . . . reactionary and puritanical."

737 Powell, Dilys. Review of *Pierrot le fou*. London *Sunday Times* (20 March).
Cited in 1967, Mainds, Entry No. 923.

738 Predal, René. *"Paris vu par . . ." Jeune cinéma*, No. 11 (January), p. 33.
In *Montparnasse-Levallois*, Godard allowed his actors the freedom of improvisation and his camera person complete liberty, just like a reporter at a news event.

739 Quigley, Isabel. Review of *Pierrot le fou*. *The Spectator* (25 March).
Cited in 1967, Mainds, Entry No. 923.

740 [Regard, Sylvain]. *"One or Two Things." Sight and Sound*, 36, No. 1 (Winter), 2–6.

Interview with Godard, trans. from 1966, Regard, *Le Nouvel Observateur*, Entry No. 741. This trans. reprinted 1968, Mussman, Entry No. 1168. Also 1967, Regard, trans. Jean Billard, *Take One*, Entry No. 955.

741 Regard, Sylvain. "La Vie moderne." *Le Nouvel Observateur* (12–18 October), pp. 53–56.

In an interview written as a prose text without questions, Godard discusses making two films at once (*Deux ou trois choses* and *Made in U.S.A.*), the Ben Barka affair, the relation between prostitution and urban development, newsreels, advertising, Vietnam and Cuba, actors, and the taboo on a "real" presentation of sexuality. Trans. 1966, Regard, *Sight and Sound*, Entry No. 740. Trans. reprinted, 1968, Mussman, Entry No. 1168. Trans. 1967, Regard, *Take One*, Entry No. 955.

742 Reichert, Helmut. "Film: Godards Effekte." *Civis: Zeitschrift für Christian-Democratische Politik* (Bonn), 12 (June), 28.

Cited 1967, IBZ, 3, Part 2 (G-K), p. 280.

743 Richetin, René. "Notes sur la coleur au cinema." *Cahiers du cinema*, No. 182 (September), pp. 60–67.

A filmmaker uses either natural, homologous colors or deliberately noninte-grated colors. In Godard's style, especially in *Pierrot* and *Le Mépris*, "the screen seems to be made larger, lit by its own luminescence."

744 [Ropars-] W.[uilleumier], M.[arie]-C.[laire]. *"Pierrot le fou." Esprit*, 34, No. 2 (February), 302–04.

Godard's cinematic poetry seeks to "arrest time" and capture the very "vibra-tions of space," the "structure rather than the effects of poetry." The poetic elements in the film — dance, word, music, painting — too often bear only their own meaning rather than become *cinematic* elements. Excerpt trans. 1970, Collet, Entry No. 1836.

745 Roud, Richard. "Introduction — Anguish: *Alphaville." Alphaville* [script]: *A Film by Jean-Luc Godard.* Ed. and trans. Peter Whitehead. New York: Simon & Schuster. Pp. 9–11.

Reprinted from 1965, Roud, *Sight and Sound*, Entry No. 588.

746 Roud, Richard. *"Masculin-Féminin:* Two (pre + re) views." *Sight and Sound*, 35, No. 3 (Summer), 113–116.

Roud wants to trace the relation of plot to theme and not try to evoke the visual style. Godard borrowed a de Maupassant story, *Paul's Girl*, for his main plot and included another, *The Signal*, as a Swedish film-within-a-film. Godard wanted to "do Paris in December" and had a number of young friends at the time. The theme is about "the children of Marx and Coca-Cola," and the story line is relatively unimportant. The mosaic technique brings in action which indirectly refracts on the characters' lives. Reprinted 1968, Mussman, Entry No. 1168; excerpts in 1969, Billard, Entry No. 1268.

747 Russell, Lee, pseud. *See* Wollen, Peter.

748 Sadoul, Georges. "Les Facettes d'un miroir brisé." *Les Lettres françaises*, No. 1163 (29 December–4 January), pp. 21 and 54.
Writing about *Made in U.S.A.* is like Sadoul's writing about *Guernica* in 1937, which the press either ignored or called a "propaganda poster." Sadoul discusses the film's plot, the evolution of Karina's roles, the comic book visual style, and the deliberately "fractured" political messages of the film.

749 Sadoul, Georges. "Godard ne passera pas." *Les Lettres françaises*, No. 1130 (5-11 May), p. 38.
Sadoul compares *Masculin-Féminin* to Diderot's *Rameau's Nephew*. He comments on two audience's — sociologists' and students' — reactions to the film, on Godard's depiction of the Parisian locale, and on the differences between the generations of the forties and sixties. By appearances the film may seem merely sociological, badly made, or just cinema verite, yet Godard reconstitutes reality for us in his own personal style.

750 Salachas, Gilbert. "*Masculin-Féminin*." *Télécine*, No. 128 (May-June), pp. 56–57.
Godard is inspired by the same two themes, romanticism and sociology. The film has an irritating style and reveals a bitter and mediocre mind. M.H., H.L., A.T., and J.E.F. all agree.

751 Salgues, Yves. ["Jean-Luc Godard as Seen Through the Eyes of Chantal Goya"]. *24 Heures* (29 December).
Goya describes her getting the role in *Masculin-Féminin*. Trans. 1969, Billard, Entry No. 1268.

752 Salmaggi, Robert. "*Band of Outsiders* at Beekman." New York *Herald Tribune* (16 March).
Brief credits. The film has familiar Godard trademarks, but the acting and characterization lag and get bogged down in a vapid plot.

753 Saltini, Vittorio. Review of *Pierrot le fou*. *Nuovi argomenti* (April-June).
Cited 1967, Baldelli, Entry No. 822.

754 Salvas, François. "*Pierrot le fou*: beau comme tout." *Objectif*, No. 37 (November-December), pp. 7–13.
Discusses the internal logic, lyricism, construction, symbolism, and characterization of the film. The Pierrot-Ferdinand duality represents the character's romantic stance, which pulls Ferdinand deeper into fantasy and writing and the search for eternity in love. Godard's editing style is discussed (he rarely cuts on a glance).

755 Sarris, Andrew. "Belmondo." *Gentleman's Quarterly* (Fall-Winter).
Sarris describes how Belmondo lives out the myth of virility seen in his films. Reprinted 1970, Sarris, Entry No. 1507.

756 Sarris, Andrew. "Berlin '66 ou Godard ist da." *Cahiers du cinéma*, No. 181 (August), p. 11.
Cited 1966, *Index analytique*, 1, p. A-0187.

757 Sarris, Andrew. "Films." *Village Voice* (24 March).
In *Band of Outsiders*, "Godard embroiders a conventional melodrama with unconventional freedom." He's sometimes excessively cerebral or his pranks go too far, but the characters are alive.

758 Sarris, Andrew. "Films." *Village Voice* (6 October).
Masculine-Feminine is filled with newspaper-like comments on every aspect of present life, but underneath there is a plot about the "wounded cry" of adolescents. Some of Godard's disconcerting habits are his constant mixing of tragedy and comedy, switching conventions, speaking through all his characters indiscriminantly, fragmentation, "improbably violent punctuation" to some of his scenes, and using "mock objectivity to mask irony if not outright indifference." However, he's really in touch with the world in these "dazzling exercises of style." Reprinted 1966, Sarris, *Film Culture*, Entry No. 759, and in 1969, Billard, Entry No. 1202.

759 Sarris, Andrew. Review of *Masculine-Feminine*. *Film Culture*, No. 42 (Fall), pp. 10–11.
Reprinted from 1966, Sarris, Entry No. 758.

760 Sharits, Paul J. "Red, Blue. Godard." *Film Quarterly*, 19, No. 4 (Summer), 24–29.
Offers a close textural analysis of the thematic use of color in *Une Femme est une femme* and *Le Mépris*. In the former film, color closely follows narrative and character development, while in the latter, the color is more deliberately symbolic. In *Le Mépris* "the leitmotif is . . . more complex, more visually apparent, and becomes, in itself, a formative theme."

761 Sontag, Susan. "Godard's *Vivre sa vie*." New York: Farrar, Straus, Giroux. Pp. 196–207; 1967. London. Eyre and Spottswoodie; Reissued 1969. Laurel Paperbacks. New York: Dell.
Reprinted from 1964, Sontag, Entry No. 441. Also reprinted in 1968, Mussman, Entry No. 1168.

762 Thevoz, Michel and Guégan, Gérard. "*A Married Woman*." Trans. Jane Pearce. *Cahiers du Cinema in English*, No. 3, pp. 54–59.
Trans. from 1965, Thevoz, Entry No. 610.

763 Thomas, John. "*Alphaville*." *Film Quarterly*, 20, No. 1 (Fall), 48–51.
Alphaville's content is not as important as the structure of its images. Light is the central visual theme, reinforced by a recurrent flashing light. Stairways, elevators, and corridors form a labyrinth. Godard uses a comic book, fairy story, parody form to eliminate psychological subtleties and the need to intellectualize. He offers us a "poetry of filmmaking that in itself is the answer to Alpha 60."

764 Thomas, John. "*The Married Woman*." *Film Society Review* (October), pp. 19–21.
Godard uses Beethoven's string quartets on the soundtrack as well as a sonata form to structure the film as a whole. The "thematic statements" are presented in a "cool, abstract close-up style" and the "variations" in a lighthearted, anything-for-a-jump-cut, throwaway approach."

765 Toti, Gianni. Review of *Les Carabiniers*. *Cinema and Film*, 1, No. 1 (Winter), 19-26.
In Lincoln Center Library.

766 Toti, Gianni. Review of *Pierrot le fou*. *Cinema 60*, No. 56 (February). Cited 1967, Baldelli, Entry No. 822.

767 Tynan, Kenneth. "Tomorrow Up to Date." *The Observer*, Weekend Review (20 March).
Plot summary of *Alphaville* given. Godard's moralizing and his erotic lyricism are "Tinkerbell stuff," but he is brilliant in his use of everyday Parisian locations to create an ominous technocratic world.

768 Vianey, Michel. *En attendant Godard*. Paris: Bernard Grasset. 224 pp. (1966 is edition date in front; January 7, 1967 is printing date in back of book.)
Vianey gives an impressionistic, overpersonalized account of the filming of *Masculin-Féminin*. Dialogue from the film and indications about the acting are included. Godard's own shooting notes are given. (*See* 1966, Godard, Entry No. 2248). Selections reprinted in 1969, Billard, Entry No. 1268.

769 Vlady, Marina. "Du *Nouvel Observateur* — à Godard." *Le Nouvel Observateur*, n.d., p. 46.
Godard had first wanted to film Balzac's *Le Lys dan la vallée*, then used the *Nouvel Observateur* articles on prostitution as a pretext to express himself on current society. His protagonist prostituted herself so as not to let mediocrity destroy her femininity, and Vlady says she'd do the same. Vlady received Godard's words, which she repeated, through a microphone in her ear. Reprinted 1967, *Deux ou trois choses que je sais d'elle: L'Avant-Scène du cinéma*, No. 70 (May), and 1971, *Deux ou trois choses* script, Entry No. 2343.

770 Weiler, A.H. "*Band of Outsiders*: Jean-Luc Godard's Film Shown at Beekman." *New York Times* (16 March).
Brief credits. This film is playing in New York two years after it was shown in the festival here. It is marred by personal and cinematic jokes and by directorial intrusion. The characters philosophize too much and are not credible. The acting is poor.

771 Whitehead, Peter. "*Paris vu par*." *Films and Filming*, 12, No. 8 (May), 53–54.
Review of *Montparnasse-Levallois*. Cited in Bowles, p. 383.

772 Whitehead, Peter. "*Pierrot le fou*." *Films and Filming*, 12, No. 9 (June), 16, 51–52.
Cited 1972, Green, Entry No. 1684.

773 Winsten, Archer. Review of *Masculin-Féminin*. *New York Post* (19 September).
The film is totally boring except for its "fine-looking, very young females." Reprinted in 1969, Billard, Entry No. 1268.

774 Wittig, Monique. "Lacunary Films." *New Statesman*, 72 (15 July), 102.
Wittig borrows her title from Straub and uses it to describe the discontinuity in Godard's films. This discontinuity works at the level of plot and character. The order is that of juxtaposition and not of some "inner logic." Wittig links this style to French literary figures from the Enlightenment and to Brecht.

775 [Wollen, Peter] Russell, Lee, pseud. "Lee Russell Writes." *New Left Review*, No. 39 (September-October), pp. 83–87.
Wollen finds that Wood (1966, Entry No. 776) raises the right issues but cannot deal with Godard adequately critically. Godard sees culture as threatened by vandalism and violence and offers romantic solutions of beauty and contemplation and/or action. The following themes are interrelated in the films: women, the present, crisscrossing of attributes and roles, freedom, cinema as instantaneity and permanence, culture vs. society, and the absence or defeat of politics.

776 Wood, Robin. "Society and Tradition: An Approach to Jean-Luc Godard." *The New Left Review*, No. 39 (September-October), pp. 77–83.
Godard's sense of tradition is seen in his cultural references and his characters, shown cut off from their past (e.g., the English lesson sequence in *Bande á part*). Like Eliot, Stravinsky, and Picasso, Godard builds up his own personal tradition, but with bitter self-doubt, even self-parody. *Alphaville*, *Pierrot le fou*, *Les Carabiniers*, *A bout de souffle* are discussed. Godard's creative energy makes his position positive rather than nihilistic. Followed by responses by Lee Russell [Peter Wollen]. *See* 1966, Wollen, Entry No. 775. Wood's article reprinted, 1968, Mussman, Entry No. 1168.

777 Young, Vernon. "The Verge and After: Film by 1966." *Hudson Review*, 19, No. 1 (Spring), 92–100.
Godard's ten films since *Breathless* lack a scale of values and use a negative and disdainful technique. Young catalogues the techniques that others find innovative, but he concludes that "Godard has no organizing power and has discovered no lucid category of image, largely because the butt of his bad jokes is film itself."

778 Zanelli, Dario. "I festival dell'estate: Berlino." *Bianco e nero*, 28, No. 9–10 (September-October), 81–82.
Review of *Masculin-Féminin*, shown at Berlin Festival.

1967

779 Akoun, André. "Les Films de Godard sont des retrouvaillés." *La Quinzaine littéraire*, No. 24 (15–31 March), pp. 43–45.
Like a hall of mirrors reflecting images of images, *Deux ou trois choses* has a structural rigor which does not derive from narrative. The collage technique aptly captures how messages circulate without "subjects" and "form the noise of our world." Godard's sensibility oscillates between revolutionary optimism and skeptical irony. Reprinted 1967, *Deux ou trois choses que je sais d'elle: L'Avant-Scène du cinéma*, No. 70 (May), and 1971, *Deux ou trois choses* script, Entry No. 2343.

780 Albèra, François. "*Masculin-Féminin.*" *Travelling J* (Laussane), No. 16 (April), pp. 51–58.

Credits. The film engages us on three entirely different levels: it interrogates language, looks critically at contemporary society, and shows the progress of Paul's infatuation. These three levels are "mixed because, in this film, the spectacle of life intermingles with its own analysis."

781 Amengual, Barthélemy. "Jean-Luc Godard et la remise en cause de notre civilisation de l'image." *Jean-Luc Godard — au delà du récit: Etudes cinématographiques*. No. 57–61. Ed. Michel Estève. Paris: Lettres Modernes-Minard. Pp. 113–77.
Godard has invented a new language apt for expressing and defining our epoch. An in-depth analysis is offered of *A Woman Is a Wonan, Les Carabiniers*, and *Pierrot le fou*. Amengual relates Godard's work to that of Brecht, Eisenstein, Méliès, Lumière, Sennett, comic strips, Bresson, Queneau, Flaubert *(Bouvard et Pécuchet)*, and Rossellini.

782 Amengual, Barthélemey and Estève, Michel. "Bibliographie selective." *Jean-Luc Godard — au delà du récit: Etudes cinématographiques*. No. 57–61. Ed Michel Estève. Paris: Lettres Modernes-Minard. Pp. 188–91.
Bibliography including books, interviews, scripts, and critical articles.

783 Anon. Article on *L'Amour en l 'an 2000*. London *Times* (12 July), p. 6.
Discusses audience receptivity to film, which contains Godard's sketch, *"Anticipation."* Cited 1967, *Times Index* (July-August), p. 72.

784 Anon. Article on *L'Amour en l 'an 2000*. London *Times* (4 August), p. 6.
Film receives Golden Thistle award. Cited 1967, *Times Index* (July-August), p. 72.

785 Anon. Article on *La Chinoise*. London *Times* (11 September), p. 6.
Cited 1967, *Times Index* (September-October), p. 73.

786 Anon. Article on *Loin du Viêtnam*. London *Times* (8 July), p. 11.
Film was disputed over and excluded from Venice Film Festival. Cited 1967, *Times Index* (July-August), p. 72.

787 Anon. "Biofilmographie de J.-L. Godard." *L'Avant-Scène du cinéma: Deux ou trois choses que je sais d'elle*, No. 70 (May).
Reprinted 1971, *Deux ou trois choses* script, Entry No. 2343.

788 Anon. "Box office de Jean-Luc Godard" and "Jean-Luc Godard et la Centrale Catholique du Cinéma." *Image et son: Revue du cinéma*, No. 211 (December), p. 74.
One table lists the attendance at first-run Paris theaters for Godard's features from *A bout de souffle* through *La Chinoise*. Another table lists the recommendations of the Catholic censors: most of Godard's films are "recommended for adults, with reservations," but the censors advise all adults to avoid *Le Mépris* and *La Femme mariée*.

789 Anon. "Brèves nouvelles du cinéma." *Cinéma international* (March-April), p. 620.
Brief mention of *La Chinoise* (being planned) and *Deux ou trois choses*.

790   Anon. "Dokumentation." *Cinema* (Union of Swiss Film Clubs), No. 49 (Spring), pp. 702–704.
Brief biography. Filmography through *Masculin-Féminin*, with a brief summary of each film.

791   Anon. Godard Filmography. *Image et son*, No. 211 (December).

792   Anon. "Godard, Jean-Luc, cinéaste." *Le Monde: Index analytique*, p. 536.
Lists articles on Godard. "Godard marries Wiazemsky, granddaughter of François Mauriac, article — July 25, p. 19."

793   Anon. "Gorin, Jean-Pierre." *Le Monde: Index analytique*, pp. 538–39.
Gorin's articles for 1967 while a journalist on *Le Monde* are listed, with these annotations: "*Cahiers marxistes-léninistes* publish Mao's 1942 text illuminating cultural revolution, Jan. 11, p. 2; books to read in '67, Jan. 13, p. 15; interview with A. Schwartz Bart about concentration camps, Feb. 1; interview with M. Robert about study of Freud, Feb. 8, pp. IV–V; biography of A. Carpentier, Feb. 22, p. IV; M.-T. Eyquem cited on electoral campaign in 17th arrondisment, Feb. 24, p. 5; interview with G. Dumezil on Roman religions, Mar. 15, p. VII; Who goes to the museum? Apr. 12, p. VI; magazine roundup — ethnology, sociology, psychoanalysis, linguistics, May 31, p. VI; article and interview with R. Kanters on science fiction, June 7, p. VII, and June 28, p. 11; International Pen Club Congress on Ivory Coast, August 3, p. 6; M. Tournier wins French Academy prize for best novel. Nov. 18, p. 10; review of P. Bordieu and A. Darbel's "L'Amour de l'art — les museés et leur public," April 12, p. VI; review of J.P. Faye's "Le Récit hunique," March 18, p. 111.

794   Anon. "Guerra et Godard à Sarcelles." *Cinéma 67*, No. 117 (June), pp. 108–109.
Announcement for a film festival, May 17–28, where Godard would show *Deux ou trois choses* and appear in person on May 25.

795   Anon. "International Movie Report." *Mademoiselle*, 64 (February), 116–19.
Cited *Reader's Guide*, 27 (March 1967–February 1968), 772.

796   Anon. Inverview with Godard. *El Moudjahid* (Algeria), (January).
Cited 1975, Hennebelle, Entry No. 1900.

797   Anon. Inverview with Godard on *La Chinoise*. *La Quinzaine littéraire* (15 March).
Cited 1968, Albèra, Entry No. 1013.

798   Anon. Interview with Godard on *Deux ou trois choses*. *Combat* (5 September).
Cited 1967, Chevassu, Entry No. 848.

799   Anon. Listing of articles on *La Chinoise*. *Le Monde: Index analytique*, pp. 252–53.
"Interview with Godard; *L'Humanité*'s review of film; film receives special

prize. Aug. 5, p. 8; Aug. 8, p. 9; Aug. 24, p. 10; Sept. 6, p. 16; Sept. 7, p. 11; Sept. 9, pp. 10–11; Sept. 11, p. 15."

800   Anon. Listing of interviews with Godard on *Deux ou trois choses. Le Monde: Index analytique*, p. 253.
Interviews: Jan. 21, p. 15; and Mar. 21, p. 16.

801   Anon. *"Made in U.S.A." Deux ou trois choses que je sais d'elle: L'Avant-Scène du cinéma*, No. 70 (May), pp. 47–50.
Credits. Synopsis of *Made in U.S.A.* by and interview with Godard. Résumé of reviews of *Made in U.S.A.*

802   Anon. "Des manifestations du mouvement Occident interrompent le projection du film *Loin de* [sic] *Viêtnam." Le Monde* (21 December), p. 12.
An extreme right-wing group, Occident, vandalized the cinema showing *Loin du Viêtnam.*

803   Anon. "New Film" London *Times* (23 January), p. 14.
Report on Godard's plans for *Deux ou trois choses.* Cited 1967, *Times Index* (January-February), p. 82.

804   Anon. *"Le Petit Soldat." Film Facts*, 10, No. 13, 164–65.
Brief credits, synopsis, and extensive quotations from reviews in the *New York Times*, New York *World Journal Tribune, Variety.*

805   Anon. *"Le Plus Vieux Métier du monde." Positif*, No. 87 (September), p. 57.
Review of *Anticipation*, cited in 1972, Anon., *Positif* cumulative index, Entry No. 1632.

806   Anon. Review of *L'Amour en l 'an 2000.* London *Times* (18 July), p. 6.
Review of *Anticipation.* Cited 1967, *Times Index* (July-August), p. 72.

807   Anon. Review of *Deux ou trois choses.* London *Times* (5 April), p. 10.
Cited 1967, *Times Index* (March-April), p. 66.

808   Anon. Review of *Deux ou trois choses* and *La Chinoise.* London *Times* (25 November), p. 19.
Cited 1967, *Times Index* (November-December), p. 69.

809   Anon. Review of *Loin du Viêtnam.* London *Times* (16 September), p. 7.
Cited 1967, *Times Index* (September-October), p. 73.

810   Anon. Review of *Masculin-Féminin.* London *Times* (22 June), p. 8.
Cited 1967, *Times Index* (May-June), p. 76.

811   Anon. Review of *A Woman Is a Woman.* London *Times* (23 March), p. 10.
Cited 1967, *Times Index* (March-April), p. 66.

812   Anon. "Synopsis of *Les Carabiniers."* Program Notes, 5th New York Film Festival (20–30 September).
In Museum of Modern Art clipping file.

813   Aprà, Adriano. "A proposito di un non riconciliato pero ausente." *Cinema and Film* (Rome), 1, No. 3, 323–24.
In Lincoln Center Library.

814   Ardagh, John. "An Alpha for Godard?" *Manchester Guardian* (12 March, p. 7.)
Godard's shy personality is described. Karina left him two years ago for actor Maurice Ronet, and now Godard lives by himself in a hotel near the Etoile and has an "office in the smart suburb of Neuilly." He says his documentary impulse enables him to stay close to his own times, and especially record the impact of modernity on French daily life. Godard is generous to friends, especially to rising talent. He likes cars and doesn't take holidays, but he keeps filming and going to films, about six or seven a week. He reads a lot and looks at paintings. He says he's on the left, but not really politically committed.

815   Aristarco, Guido. "Langage et idéologie dans quelques films de Godard." Trans. Barthélemy Amengual. *Jean-Luc Godard —au delà du récit: Etudes cinématographiques*, No. 57–61. Ed. Michel Estève. Paris: Lettres Modernes-Minard. Pp. 5–16.
Godard is brilliant at capturing the surface manifestations of contemporary society in all their complexity, but he is trapped in the confusion of what he conveys. His Brechtianism is only superficial, for he neither offers an analysis of what he shows nor provokes a coming to political awareness in the spectator. Examples are drawn primarily from *Le Petit Soldat*, *La Femme mariée*, and *Vivre sa vie*.

816   Armitage, Peter. "Honest to Godard." *Film* (British Federation of Film Societies), No. 50, pp. 13–14.
This review of Roud's and Cameron's books on Godard presents and criticizes the arguments put forth by Godard's admirers. "Multivalency" is not necessarily a "good thing." "Some richness may be merely confusion and it is easy to overwhelm the spectator by drowning him [sic] in 'noise'."

817   Autera, Leonardo. "I Film di pesaro." *Bianco e nero*, 28, No. 7–9 (July-September), 132.
Complete credits for *Made in U.S.A.*, which was shown in a cultural session outside the competition, at the Pesaro Film Festival.

818   Baby, Yvonne. "Dans ma journeé d'artiste." *Le Monde* (27 January), p. 25.
In an interview, Godard compares himself to a scientist. Except in China, artists can only "amuse." He discusses how to make political art. He cannot see why the left rejects "scientific" art and wants only sentimental films. Cinema, his kind, can prevent insanity by putting people in touch with reality. He discusses *Made in U.S.A.* and *Deux ou trois choses*.

819   Bachman, Gideon. "'Der Mensch ist Gott, weil Gott keine Ideale hat': Ein Gësprach mit Jean-Luc Godard über die Verantwortung des Künstlers in der Gesellschaftt." Trans. from English, Christa Maeker. *Film* (Hanover), (November), pp. 12–16.

Godard discusses art and science in abstract terms at some length, especially from the perspective of the sociology of knowledge.

820 Bagehot, Henry. "Who Kidnapped Ben Barka?" *Made in U.S.A.* London: Lorrimer. Pp. 9–13.
Known details about Barka's abduction are given as background to film script.

821 Baldelli, Pio. "Jean-Luc Godard." *Giovane critica*, No. 15 (Spring).
Cited 1967, Amengual and Estève, Entry No. 782.

822 Baldelli, Pio. "Des personnages au langage: originalité et limites d'une recherche esthétique." Trans. Jean Bastaire. *Jean-Luc Godard — au delà du récit: Etudes cinématographiques*. No 57–61. Ed. Michel Estève. Paris: Lettres Modernes-Minard. Pp. 35–47.
Belmondo represents a new kind of protagonist suited to express contemporary life (the loss of old values, living at a furious pace through a fragmented existence, etc.). The camera work and montage offer an "industrial still-life." They also "reveal" reality. Godard's ideas are second hand and are based in emotion — a melancholy, juvenile protest. The pros and cons in the Godard criticism, especially that based in a "linguistic" analysis of cinema, are evaluated.

823 Baroncelli, Jean de. *"Deux ou trois choses que je sais d'elle."* Le Monde (21 March), p. 16
This film is compared to *Made in U.S.A.* Both are poetic-sociological visions of our times. Godard's total break with traditional narrative cinema is explained.

824 Baroncelli, Jean de. "Godard et le analyse critique de notre société." *Le Monde* (27 January), p. 25.
Made in U.S.A. and *Deux ou trois choses* demand to be looked at in a new way. The former is a "filmed object" that directly bombards us with intellectual and sensory stimuli. Godard is trying to take film out of its "ghetto" and integrate it into the world.

825 Baroncelli, Jean de. *"Loin du Viêtnam."* Le Monde (19 December).
The importance of the film as a whole is discussed, and Godard's section briefly mentioned, negatively.

826 Belmans, Jacques. "L'Ethique et l'esthétique du chaos." *Jean-Luc Godard — au delà du récit: Etudes cinématographiques*. No. 57–61. Ed Michel Estève. Paris: Lettres Modernes-Minard. Pp. 83–99.
Belmans offers an analysis of the "negative" characters in Godard's films. Godard is unhappy rather than anarchistic, a moralist, an ethnologist of daily life. Death fascinates and repels him. Too often it's just his virtuosity that fascinates us and his work is empty.

827 Bertolucci, Bernardo. "Vérsus Godard." *Cahiers du cinéma*, No. 186 (January), 29–30.
Last summer Godard finished filming *Made in U.S.A.* on a Friday and started *Deux ou trois choses* the next Monday; he edited both simultaneously. *Made in U.S.A.* shows a plastic inventiveness but is paralyzed by ideological conformity.

Deux ou trois choses suffers from vulgarity and forcing the effect and being a bit too attentive to everything. Trans. 1967, Bertolucci, *Cahiers du Cinema in English*, Entry No. 828.

828 Bertolucci, Bernardo. "Versus Godard." Trans. Jane Pearce. *Cahiers du Cinema in English*, No. 10 (May), pp. 16–17.
Trans. from 1967, Bertolucci, Entry No. 827.

829 Billard, Ginette. "Interview with Georges de Beauregard." *Film Quarterly*, 20, No. 3 (Spring), 20–23.
Beauregard talks about how he came to produce *Breathless* and the difficulties he had with the censorship of *Le Petit Soldat*. He gives biographical data about Godard.

830 Billard, Pierre. "Le Bric-à-brac de Godard." *L'Express*, No. 815 (30 January—5 February), p. 46.
Made in U.S.A. has a painterly cohesiveness, but the colors "are there only to accompany a text." Godard's voice off commentary which is supposed to "reflect on politics" fails, throwing the film into "aesthetic chaos."

831 Billard, Pierre. "Cinéma: Pierre Billard a vu *Deux ou trois choses que je sais d'elle*." *L'Express*, No. 822 (20–26 March), p. 19.
Godard is concerned, anxious, and sad about the contemporary situation and gives us in *Deux ou trois choses* an inventory of social problems; but he does not understand society.

832 Blanquart, Paul. "Un Philosophe au cinématographe: *Made in U.S.A.*" *Signs du temps* (April), pp. 28–20.
The critic gives a close reading of the film's philosophical issues. Symbolically Paula kills off the poet, and no longer does a Belmondo-Pierrot-type protagonist echo Rimbaud. Godard is no longer celebrating an open Nature, full of marvels, but rather he is full of questions, looking forward to years of combat "with the fear perhaps of being already exhausted in advance."

833 Bontemps, Jacques. "Une Libre Variation imaginative de certains faits." *Cahiers du cinéma*, No. 194 (October), pp. 30–34.
The critic analyzes Godard's aesthetic presuppositions in *La Chinoise*, first with reference to Merleau-Ponty and then to Brecht. Trans. by Elisabeth Cameron, 1970, Cameron, Entry No. 1399.

834 Bontemps, Jacques, et al. "Lutter sur deux fronts." *Cahiers du cinéma*. No. 194 (October), pp. 13–26, 66–70.
In this key interview with Jacques Bontemps, Jean-Louis Comolli, Michel Delahaye, and Jean Narboni, Godard discusses the fictional nature of *La Chinoise*, his direction and editing, and the left's reactions to the film. He needs to discover "the scientific facts of film," which he sees as deriving not from a study of semiotics but of film technique and its dependence on the economic forces that shape modes of production, processing, and distribution, which forces he discusses in detail. He comments on Bunuel, Jerry Lewis, Bergman, Resnais, and Cassavetes, among others; proposes a film on *Pour Lucrèce* that would "teach what

theater is"; indicates a better ending for *La Chinoise*; and discusses what concepts underlie his future film, *Émile* [to be *Le Gai Savoir*]. Excerpts reprinted, 1968, Collet, Entry No. 1088. These in 1970, Collett, trans. Ciba Vaughan, Entry No. 1425. Entire article in 1968, Bontemps, *Film Quarterly*, trans. by D.C.D., Entry No. 1070.

835 Bory, Jean-Louis. "La Brûlure du présent." *Le Nouvel Observateur* (1 February), p. 44.

In *Made in U.S.A.*, Godard's puerile, comic strip satire analyzes in a Brechtian way, albeit obliquely, a political reality and also provides a critical perspective on how that reality is presented in day-to-day life and in film. Bory admires Godard's personal and political sincerity. Reprinted 1972, Bory, Entry No. 1653.

836 Bory, Jean-Louis. "A la hauteur de nos tourments." *Le Nouvel Observateur* (22 March), pp. 46–47.

Deux ou trois choses and *Made in U.S.A.* manipulate the written word, have a plastic beauty, and depict the Gaullist regime as a police state. In *Deux ou trois choses*, Godard the moralist depicts prostitution only to make us better understand the social and psychological oppression of advanced capitalism. Reprinted 1972, Bory, Entry No. 1653.

837 Bory, Jean-Louis. "Rapsodie pour un massacre." *Le Nouvel Observateur* (20 December).

Godard's sequence in *Loin du Viêtnam* is only a narcissistic "pirouette." The film as a whole has some use as a militant tool, but Godard's section seems to be almost purely about cinema. Reprinted 1972, Bory, *La Nuit complice*, Entry No. 1653.

838 Braucourt, Guy. "*Pierrot le fou* ou les héros de Jean-Luc Godard." *Jean-Luc Godard — au delà du récit: Etudes cinematographiques.* No. 57–61. Michel Estève. Paris: Lettres Modernes-Minard. pp. 101–112.

Analyzes the romantic aspects of the film: Ferdinand's character, death, the diary, the colors, nostalgia for a "lost time" vs. social reality, action vs. stasis, use of collage, and Godard's sense of nothingness.

839 Brochier, Jean-Jacques. "Godard, la critique et le public." *Images et son: Revue du cinéma*, No. 211 (December), pp. 71–73.

The accusations critics level against Godard are summarized.

840 Bruno, Eduardo. "Godard: Barthes come Berthomieu." *Filmcritica*, 18, No. 174 (January-February), 307.

In Lincoln Center Library.

841 C., L.. "Petit Journal du cinéma: l'evangile selon Jean-Luc." *Cahiers du cinéma*, No. 193 (September), p. 7.

Review of *L'Amour*, Godard's contribution to *Vangelo 70*. Plot and setting are briefly described.

842 Capdenac, Michel. "Beau et intelligent: *Made in U.S.A.* de Jean-Luc Godard." *Les Lettres françaises* (2 February), p. 19.

Godard's film has to be seen as making a totally modernist revolution in cinema, similar to that of Joyce, Picasso, and Schonberg. It's an intelligent and beautiful work that forces the viewer to participate. It leaves political echoes in the mind and heart.

843 Cardinal, Marie. *Cet eté-la: suivi en annexe du scénario de Jean-Luc Godard, "Deux ou trois choses que je sais d'elle."* Paris: Juillard. 185 pp.
Contains some material on the shooting of *Deux ou trois choses.*

844 Carreno, Richard D. *"Made in U.S.A." Cineáste*, 1, No. 3 (Winter), 3–4.
Cited in Bowles, p. 303.

845 Casty, Alan. *"Masculine-Feminine," Film Quarterly*, 20, No. 4 (Summer), 57–60.
In *Masculine-Feminine*, dislocated narrative structures, theatricality, and alienation devices join with "abrupt shifting and mixing of moods, tones, and emotions" to portray a living, incomplete love relationship. Casty analyzes the relationship between Paul and Madeleine in detail in the context of Godard's romantic aesthetic.

846 Caviglioli, François, et al. "Les 'Chinoise' de Paris désavouent Godard." *Le Nouvel Observateur* (20 September), pp. 22–24.
Michèle Dariá and François Caviglioli interview politically active students and faculty on *La Chinoise*. A "moderate" Maoist professor from the Ecole Normale Superieur comments on Godard's portrayal of "romantic" youth in *La Chinoise*. The professor does not denounce it as bourgeois and revisionist, but it does not touch him. Others, philosophy students at Nanterre, denounce Godard for portraying Maoists as irresponsible terrorists and people "playing at revolution." The critic also gathers responses from others as to the political intent and effect of the film.

847 Chatelet, François. "Godard, collectionneur de genie," in "Commentaires à propos de *2 ou 3 choses." Deux ou trois choses que je sais d'elle: L'Avant-scène du cinéma*, No. 70 (May), p. 43.
What's the film about? Vlady? Prostitution? It's about the city, here presented in tableaux that seem like harsh, gaudy posters. Reprinted 1971, *Deux ou trois choses* script, Entry No. 2343.

848 Chevassu, François. *"La Chinoise." Image et son: Revue du cinéma*, No. 210 (November), pp. 119–122.
Brief credits. Godard uses material from the other arts, but all elements in his films follow the rules of "pure" cinema. He is the only filmmaker committed to portraying the political aspects of our epoch. Regrettably in *La Chinoise* his political orientation is not clear; he shows us only characters who take up Marxism a la mode. All the political citations in the film make no cohesive sense other than to present the milieu in which the characters live.

849 Ciment, Michel. *"Loin du Viêtnam." Positif*, No. 89 (November), pp. 11–13.
The film was "finished a few days before it premiered in Montreal." Godard's short section is similar to *La Chinoise*, with a clear image but a confused ideology and artistic intent. The film as a whole is better than that.

850 Clouzot, Claire. "U.S. Festival Scene: New York." *Film Society Review*, 3, No. 3 (November), 12–18.
Cited 1972, Green, Entry No. 1684.

851 Cluny, Claude Michel. "Le Mort pris sur le vif." *Nouvelle Revue française*, No. 176 (August), pp. 312–16.
Deux ou trois choses preaches, but to whom? It offers a boring and incomprehensible "revolutionary aestheticism" and will not reach the public that needs it.

852 Coleman, John. "Nostra Mostra." *The New Statesman*, N.S., 74 (15 September), 330.
Coleman dismisses *La Chinoise*, shown at the 28th Venice Film Festival, as irresponsible, permissive nonsense.

853 Collet, Jean. *"Deux ou trois choses que je sais d'elle."* Etudes, 327 (July-August), 72–74.
Godard has found both a form to express urban chaos and a formal beauty to be set against chaos. "Prostitution replaces language and communication" in a consumer society, for the language of ads is a perpetual aggression waged against the human psyche. The woman and the city (*elle*) are shown by Godard struggling not to be "things."

854 Collet, Jean. "Les Films: *La Chinoise* de Jean-Luc Godard." *Etudes*, No. 327 (November), pp. 536–39.
La Chinoise is "violently polyphonic," with many kinds of signs offered as equivalents. Godard's version of cultural revolution is to provide a "semantic grid" to interpret these signs and "decode the familiar languages" of daily life. Godard's revolt is still that of a bourgeois.

855 Collet, Jean. "Jean-Luc Godard: *Made in U.S.A.*" *Etudes*, 326 (March), 374–77.
This is a first-person film with the "I" absent. *Po* = *poetic* and *political*, forbidden words, as in *Alphaville*. In the end, on a highway as in *Alphaville*, poetry is killed off, and the characters rediscover a moral sense as actors *in history* in the "year zero of the left."

856 Collet, Jean. "Le Jeune Cinéma français." *Travelling J* (Laussane), No. 16 (April), pp. 12–34.
Godard's work is mentioned in the context of an overview of the New Wave, with special reference to his low budgets, his sense of "discontinuity," his reflections on the nature of cinema, and his (all the New Wave's) romantic aesthetic sensibility.

857 Collet, Jean. "Qu'est-ce que le nouveau cinéma?" *Etudes*, 327 (September), 212–21.
Collet reports on the 3rd International Festival for a New Cinema, Pesaro, Italy, where Godard was the constant reference point. "*Made in U.S.A.* was projected the last night of the festival as the glorious prototype of the 'new cinema.'" Godard's films are appreciated both because they are revolutionary and a critique of that revolution.

858　Comolli, Jean-Louis. "A l'assaut de l'image." *Cahiers du cinéma*, No. 191 (June), pp. 67–68.

At the Festival of Hyères, Godard's *Anticipation* was finally shown in its true form, with whole sequences in blue, red, yellow, or red and certain images and scenes in negative, overexposed, dark, or distorted. This science fiction film on prostitution depends on the contrast between normal and abnormal, positive and negative, but all we had until now from the lab was a sepia print with one color shot at the end. Trans. 1972, Brown, Entry No. 1658.

859　Comolli, Jean-Louis. "Le Point sur l'image." *Cahiers du cinéma*, No. 194 (October), pp. 29–30.

At first it seems that *La Chinoise* has brilliantly clear images but confused ideas. However, instead, we see that the images were not intended to describe any political reality external to the film or even a political fiction; they *create* both the political concepts and the fiction. Trans. by Elisabeth Cameron in 1970, Cameron, Entry No. 1405.

860　Cournot, Michel. "Quelques evidentes incertitudes: entretien entre J.-L. Godard et M. Cournot." *Revue d'esthétique*, N.S., 20, No. 2–3, 115–22.

Godard discusses his growing difficulty with the film industry, his "war" films, French filmmaking, his early politics and his current "left anarchist" stance. This is a transcript of a talk given to University of Nanterre students in 1967 before the shooting of *La Chinoise*. Excerpts trans. 1970, Flash, Entry No. 1441.

861　Crowther, Bosley. Review of *Far from Vietnam*. *New York Times* (2 October), p. 58.

Brief credits. *Far from Vietnam* is unmitigated propaganda and brought the 5th New York Film Festival to a "noisy wind-up." "It indicates so clearly the total intemperance and blathering of radicals on both sides."

862　Curtis, Jean-Louis. *Cinéma*. Paris: Julliard.

"Contre le naturel et l'artifice," pp. 54–60, on *Le Mépris*, discussed *passim* (reprinted from *La Nouvelle Revue française*, 1963). "Le Fou d'Anna," pp. 173–82, on *Pierrot le fou* (reprinted from 1966, Curtis, Entry No. 678). Adam, Ève, and Jean-Luc," pp. 99–104, on *La Femme mariée* (reprinted from 1965, Curtis, Entry No. 516).

863　Dadoun, Roger. "Un Cinéma 'sauvage' et 'ingenu.'" *Image et son: Revue du cinéma*, No. 211 (December), pp. 3–12.

La Chinoise is a psychodrama or a journalistic cinema, one that has "banalized" the means of expression and not a serious intellectual or political one. "Social reality [is] seized in its masks or as mask . . . The photo plays a determinant role. It's the name-image, a magical nominalism captured in the image, in the icon." The citations function verbally as the photo does visually.

864　Daix, Pierre. "A propos de *La Chinoise*." *Les Lettres françaises* (6 September), pp. 18–19.

There are inconsistencies in the artistic structures of *La Chinoise* which result in the politics of the film seeming confused. Yet the film crucially raises the question of how to make the revolution in France in 1967.

865 Dariá, Michèle. "Une Provocation de type fasciste: le film, *La Chinoise*." *L'Humanité nouvelle*, 3, No. 66 (14 September), 14.
Analyzes *La Chinoise* from another Maoist or Marxist-Leninist perspective, criticizing bourgeois intellectuals who play at revolution. This film serves the bourgeoisie by "discrediting the real combatants in the working class and by paving the way for repression."

866 Delahaye, Michel. "Jean-Luc Godard and the Childhood of Art." Trans. Jane Pearce. *Cahiers du Cinema in English*, No. 10 (May), pp. 18–29.
Trans. from 1966, Delahaye, Entry No. 682.

867 Delahaye, Michel. "Jean-Luc Godard or the Urgency of Art." Trans. Jane Pearce. *Cahiers du Cinema in English*, No. 10 (May).
Trans. from 1967, Delahaye, Entry No. 868.

868 Delahaye, Michel. "Jean-Luc Godard, ou, l'urgence de l'art." *Cahiers du cinéma*, No. 187 (February), pp. 29–33.
Compares Godard to Sacha Guitry, another autobiographical, prolific artist with a prediliction for wordiness and provocation. Godard explores the role of sexuality in our culture and its relation to language and communication. He deconstructs reality into "signifying fragments . . . [which are] sufficiently connected so that each person can recognize her/his reality in them." Trans. 1967, Delahaye, *Cahiers du Cinema in English*, Entry No. 867.

869 Delmas, Jean. "Jean-Luc Godard, *Made in U.S.A.*: le cinéma politique traité par le mépris." *Jeune cinéma*, No. 21 (March), pp. 14–20.
Vehemently attacks those critics — Sadoul, Bory, Capdenac, and Jacob — who praised *Made in U.S.A.* as a political film. This film treats proletarian characters disdainfully, but more significantly it is incoherent and incomprehensible. Godard invokes Brecht falsely, for Brecht and Piscator advocated a collective spectacle aimed at leading spectators toward both political understanding and political action.

870 Delmas, Jean. Review of *La Chinoise*. *Jeune cinéma*, No. 25 (October).
Negative review. Cited 1968, Gauteur, Entry No. 1111.

871 Dorigo, Francesco. "Topografia dell'oggetto." *Bianco e nero*, 28, No. 2 (February), 30–61.
In a long article about the emphasis on "things" in modernist films, Godard's films are found similar to the *nouveau roman*.

872 Duboeuf, Pierre. "Le Jaune en péril." *Cahiers du cinéma*, No. 195 (November), pp. 69–70.
Reviews *La Chinoise*.

873 Duvigneau, Michel. "*La Chinoise*." *Télécine*, No. 135 (November), pp. 13–27.
"Fiche No. 475." Describes the apartment set and the characters in detail — including each one's motives, social background, and actions. Godard defines his aesthetics in extensive remarks quoted from a FLEC seminar at Pâques, 1967.

Discusses the following aspects of the film: its musical structure, similarity to and difference from the *Arabian Nights* and Apollinaire's *Calligrams*, borrowings from Lumière and Méliès, shock value, symbolism, and conflict between political and romantic aspects.

874 Ehrenstein, David. "Speak Out the Arts: Festival Feedback: Testament of Richard Po_____: Simple to Everyone Else." *Village Voice* (12 October).
   Made in U.S.A. is emotionless and seemingly shows Godard saying he cannot express complicated political issues but rather can only challenge meaning and language — so much so that nothing seems left. Yet here people too easily enjoy seeing easy answers and their own ideas dramatized — such as absorbing *The Battle of Algiers* after the war is over or Sidney Poitier as a social artifact. Thus *Made in U.S.A.* not only begins to deal with complex current political issues, it aptly discusses "the concept of dealing with issues."

875 Estève, Michel. "Le 'Cas' Godard." *Jean-Luc Godard: au-delà du récit: Etudes cinématographiques.* No. 57–61. Ed. Michel Estève. Paris: Lettres Modernes-Minard. P. 3.
   Editor's introduction to Godard issue.

876 Estève, Michel, ed. *Jean-Luc Godard: au-delà du récit: Etudes cinématographiques.* No. 57–61. Paris: Lettres Modernes-Minard. 191 pp.
   Godard issue, with bibliography. Each article annotated separately.

877 Estève, Michel. "Notes sur la festival de Venise." *Etudes*, No. 327 (November), pp. 528–31.
   The festival prizes went to modernist, intellectual, leftist *auteurs*. *La Chinoise* brings new aesthetic life to cinematic technique and narrative structure, but, like *Masculin-Féminin*, its political perspective is simplistic and it didactically presents a superficial message.

878 Faccini, Luigi. "L'infinito cinematografico: *La Chinoise.*" *Cinema and Film*, 1, No. 4 (August), 445–49.
   In Lincoln Center Library.

879 Fieschi, Jean-André. "The Difficulty of Being Jean-Luc Godard." Trans. Roberta Bernstein, *Cahiers du Cinema in English*, No. 12 (December), pp. 38–43.
   Reprinted 1968, Mussman, Entry No. 1168. Trans. from 1962, Fieschi, Entry No. 199.

880 French, Phillip. "On Being Young in Paris." *The Observer*, Review (25 June).
   Godard's documentary interests and his alienation devices serve his theme in *Masculine-Feminine*. His "attitude to the young [is] a mixture of admiration and horror, honest reporting and romanticising."

881 Ganne, Claude. "Filmographie de Jean-Luc Godard." *Image et son: Revue du cinéma*, No. 211 (December), pp. 87–92.
   Filmography with credits and Paris opening dates from *Opération béton* through *Weekend*.

882 Garnham, Nicholas. "Introduction." *Le Petit Soldat: A Film by Jean-Luc Godard*. English trans. and description of the action by Nicholas Garnham. Modern Film Scripts. New York: Simon and Schuster. Pp. 13–17.

Godard's films of action and instinct are usually followed by ones of personal meditation. Analyzes Godard's relentless camera style, the characterization of Bruno, and Godard's political and philosophical concerns. In Godard's films, love "is an escape from thought," a "terrifyingly flimsy" hope that usually lapses into despair.

883 Gauthier, Guy. "Godard par Godard." *Image et son: Revue du cinéma*, No. 211 (December), pp. 61–69.

Many short extracts from Godard interviews are cited to give a picture of Godard's aesthetic and political ideas. Source for each citation is given.

884 Giammanco, Roberto. "Importenza e estraniazione in Godard." *Giovane critica*, No. 14 (Winter).

Cited 1974, Collet, Entry No. 1832.

885 Giammanco, R.[oberto]. "Petit bourgeois d'Europe centrale." *Giovane critica*, No. 14 (Winter).

Cited 1967, Baldelli, Entry No. 822.

886 Giannoli, Paul. "Godard malgre Mauriac." *Candide* (7 August), pp. 27–31.

Cited in BFI Bibliography.

887 Gilliatt, Penelope. "Exponents of Modern Love." *The Observer*, Review (26 March).

Une Femme est une femme "is a film about the freedoms that are felt by people in love, which includes the sense of being able to behave without repercussions." It is shot in "child's poster-paint colors."

888 Godet, Sylvain. "Chemin principal et chemins lateraux." *Cahiers du cinéma*, No. 190 (May), pp. 63–64.

Brief credits. Godard uses montage, analogy, and juxtapositions of images and ideas to show workers and women, among others, the unity of their struggle. Unlike in *Pierrot*, the citations, lists, and fragmentation are integrated and elucidate reality in a modernist way. People in *Deux ou trois choses*, especially Vlady, are filmed as blank faces so that we have to see them as objects. There are no more "islands of solitude and tenderness" as in *Masculin-Féminin*.

889 Gough-Yates, K. Review of *Alphaville*. *Studio International* (January).

Cited 1970, Collet, Entry No. 1425.

890 Gregorio, Eduardo de. *"Made in U.S.A." Cinema and Film*, 1, No. 3, 325–26.

In Lincoln Center Library.

891 Hale, Wanda. "French Deserter's Exploits." New York *Daily News* (21 April).

Brief credits. The critic describes the background, plot, and themes of *Le Petit Soldat*.

892 Hartung, Phillip T. "The Screen." *Commonweal*, 87 (20 October), p. 88.
Far from Vietnam offers only ineffective anti-U.S. polemics. Godard noted, passim.

893 Hennebelle, Guy. "Interview de Jean-Luc Godard à Alger." *Cinéma international*, 16, No. 3 (September-October), 708–711.
The text, prepared by Guy Hennebelle, is of a conference Godard held at the Algerian Cinemathèque in connection with a retrospective of his films, January 1967. He discusses his political growth from *Le Petit Soldat* to the present, the psychological importance of making films for him, his use of frequently inaudible material on the sound track, and his imprssions of other filmmakers and of specific critics. He says that he uses a hand-held camera because he films without a script, and thus can qualify as an "amateur" and film without authorization from the French *Centre du cinéma*.

894 Hi.[lborne], B.[arbara]. "Godard, Jean-Luc." *Britannica Book of the Year: Biography Index, 1964–67.* Chicago: University of Chicago Press and Encyclopedia Britannica Co. P. 151.
At the 1967 Venice Film Festival, Godard personally introduced a film about his work entitled *The Cinema of Challenge*. Hilborne briefly describes Godard's career.

895 I.[bberson], J.[ack]. "*Masculin-Féminin*, France/Sweden, 1966." *Monthly Film Bulletin*, 34 (August), 122.
Credits, plot summary, and a critical listing of the social issues taken up by Godard in the film.

896 Jacob, Gilles. "Du cinéma atonal des marmottes." *Cinéma '67*, No. 113 (February), pp. 68–86.
Comparing himself to other critics, Jacob admires Godard's improvisation and "partial, biased, passionate, subjective vision." *Made in U.S.A.* shows the Americanization of the French mentality. Here Godard totally destroys narrative and characterization and uses abstraction, silhouettes, allegorical figures, still photos, and brute noise as well as a Schumann symphony to create a despairing vision of language, politics, sexuality, and creativity. Formally and thematically, this film is both continuous with and a new departure from Godard's previous work. Trans. 1972, Brown, Entry No. 1658.

897 Jacob, Gilles. "Hollywood sur Seine." *Sight and Sound*, 36, No. 4 (Autumn), 162–66.
Discusses funding and format of *Loin du Viêtnam*.

898 Jacotey, Christian. "Jean-Luc Godard ou l'aventure cinématographique." *Jean-Luc Godard — au delà du récit: Etudes cinématographiques.* No. 57-61. Ed. Michel Estève. Paris: Lettres Modernes-Minard. Pp. 71–81.
Godard both reproduces present day reality and contests it, along with the messages it conveys. His films are both documentaries and films of ideas, especially about cinema. Special attention is paid to *Le Mépris* and *Alphaville*.

899 Johnson, William and Kazloff, Max. "Shooting at War: Three Views." *Film Quarterly*, 21, No. 2 (Winter), 27–36.
See 1967, Kazloff, Entry No. 904.

900 Jouffroy, Alan. "Le Cahier de *La Chinoise.*" *Opus intèrnational*, No. 2, pp. 12–29.
See 1967, Godard, Entry No. 2346.

901 Juin, Pierre. Review of *La Chinoise. Télérama* (24 September).
Cited 1968, Gauteur, Entry No. 1111.

902 Juin, Pierre. "Sur le grand écran du palais des papes d'Avignon — *La Chinoise* de Jean-Luc Godard: des contours limités." *L'Humanité* (5 August), p. 7.
We see Maoist youth, possibly realistically, as dogmatic, lacking in social practice, and romanticizing the concept of cultural revolution. Godard's style is characteristically both irritating and creative, and we do not know which of the views here are his own. His treatment of politics is limited and schematic.

903 Karol, K.S. "The Ben Barka Fiasco." *Made in U.S.A.* London: Lorrimer. Pp. 13–14.
Brief discussion of political complexities of Barka affair. Background to film script.

904 Kazloff, Max and Johnson, William. "Shooting at Wars: Three Views." *Film Quarterly*, 21, No. 2 (Winter), 27–36.
Finds that *Les Carabiniers* has an overly abstract style "devoid of affect, causality, climax." Godard's section in *Far from Vietnam* comes across as a "genuine moment of conscience and self-examination." Johnson, however, finds *Far from Vietnam* generally extremely propagandistic, and Godard's section clumsy but credible.

905 Kustow, Michael. "Introduction." *Made in U.S.A.* London: Lorrimer. Pp. 15–19.
Introduces the film script by discussing the following topics: Godard's attitude toward the left, bright colors, the poets in the film, the protagonist's moving through a labyrinth, and her political development.

906 Kustow, Michael. "Without and Within: Thoughts on Politics, Society, and the Self in Recent Films." *Sight and Sound*, 36, No. 3 (Summer), 113–17.
Discusses the labyrinthine plot, the vivid colors, the death of the poets David Goodis and Richard P._____, the protagonist's coming to awareness, and the self-reflexive form in *Made in U.S.A.* Presents Godard's trailer for and synopsis of *Deux ou trois choses*, which Kustow calls "a comic strip in depth." Godard's commentary from that film is cited, and the critic concludes that Godard's cinematic poetry has advanced to be a unique combination of the personal and the public. Reprinted 1968, Mussman, Entry No. 1168.

907 Lachat, Pierre. "Versuch über Godard: Die Wirklichkeit in Ehren —

wir sind im Kino." *Cinema* (Union of Swiss Film Clubs), No. 49 (Spring), pp. 689–92.

Discusses the relation between reality and imagination in Godard's cinema and finds in Godard the "Romantic" artist.

908 Lachize, Samuel. "Dommage qu'elle soit une prostituée: *Deux ou trois choses que je sais d'elle* de Jean-Luc Godard." *L'Humanité* (22 March), p. 8.

Although unappealing to the average spectator, *Deux ou trois choses* artistically deals with major social issues. Godard does not pursue any solutions, but, in fact, people in the very districts he shows in the film are waging their own active political struggles.

909 Lachize, Samuel. "*Made in U.S.A.*: l'espoir dans la tormente et l'ambiguité." *L'Humanité* (28 January), p. 8.

Godard's pursuit of the truth has brought him further to the left, but this film is still marked by an irritating confusion which mixes everything up and explains nothing. For Godard, "cinema is not pleasure but a way of crying out" against a violent society, similar to Picasso in *Guernica*.

910 Lachize, Samuel. "Les Mauvaises Cibles: *La Chinoise* de Jean-Luc Godard." *L'Humanité* (6 September), p. 10.

The very talented Godard is the only filmmaker to investigate the principal social problems of our time, but he does so in a romantic, sentimental, and confused way. Maoist groups in France preach confusion and seek to weaken the Communist Party, which Godard ignores as being the first and principal supporter of Vietnamese independence.

911 Land[ry, Robert]. "*Far from Vietnam.*" *Variety* (4 October), p. 12.

Brief credits. The film is built on "the old 1915 atrocity film genre." The political points of this "tedious" film are traced out. It is "one-sided but often clever, demagogic while cerebral in its accents, preaching to the converted." It is sometimes "outrageously unfair."

912 Landry, Robert J. "Propaganda Boffs Buffs: A French Rap as N.Y. Fest Windup." *Variety* (4 October), p. 3 and 15.

The showing of *Far from Vietnam* elicited more explosive approval than boos. It has an unprecedented film style, here used for unabashed propaganda. The three Godard events (also *Les Carabiniers* and *Made in U.S.A.* were also shown) were sold out. Roud's "idolatry" of Godard and Godard's "fragmentation" are scored.

913 Latil-Le Dantec, Mireille. "Jean-Luc Godard ou l'innocence perdue." *Jean-Luc Godard – au delà du récit: Etudes cinématographiques.* No. 57–61. Ed. Michel Estéve. Paris: Lettres Modernes-Minard. Pp. 49–70.

Discusses idealism in Godard's works and the sense of a "paradise lost." This theme is related to that of a language which always lies or betrays us. Godard both attacks a world of "slogans" and uses slogans — like the surrealists — in an act of "dislocation" to allow us to understand and go beyond social, moral, and cultural structures. To this end, he also uses theatricality, poetry, and self-reflexive elements. Latil, Le Dantc compares Godard's work to that of Robbe-Grillet, and pays special attention to *Deux ou trois choses.*

914 Lazaro Romero, Ferdinand, "Tres actitudes morales del cine actual." *Arco*, 9, No. 75 (January), 45–56.
Three moral attitudes in film are analyzed: the defense of human nature (John Ford), the negation of a moral world (Jean-Luc Godard), and the search for a moral world (Igmar Bergman).

915 Lebesque, Morvan. "Les Buffons." *Le Canard enchaîné*, No. 2415 (1 February).
Makes an attack on Establishment culture in France in the form of a letter to Godard.

916 Leduc, François. "Deus ou trois choses — que j'aime de lui." *Jeune cinéma*, No. 23 (May), p. 39.
Everyone is always talking about Godard. The critic gives a brief history of his reactions to Godard's films.

917 Lefèvre, Raymond. *"Deux ou trois choses que je sais d'elle."* *Image et son: Revue du cinéma*, No. 207 (June), pp. 128–130.
Brief credits. Departing from one word, *ensemble*, Godard gives us fragments of traditional cinematic structure, of characters, and of Parisian life. At the same time that he discusses the new large apartment complexes *(grandes ensembles)*, he creates a new cinematic grammar and challenges us to integrate our aesthetic and social experience in a new way.

918 Lefèvre, Raymond. "Godard sans sous-titres." *Image et son: Revue de cinéma*, No. 211 (December), pp. 15–23.
Of the New Wave directors, only Godard and Renais still have reputations as "giants." Godard has created a new cinematic language as rich and supple as verbal language. Examines in detail all the various filmic ways that Godard fragments narrative continuity and what these techniques achieve. Has Godard created an aesthetic revolution or not?

919 Lennon, Peter. "La Vie *Weekend*: Peter Lennon Watches Godard at Work." *Manchester Guardian* (27 September), p.5.
Vivid reportage about the filming of the long traffic jam sequence.

920 Loubet, Christian. "Le Cinéma français entre l'esthétisme et la prétention politique." *Pedagogie*, 22, No. 2 (June), 538–44.
Cited 1967, *Index analytique*, 2, p. E.0112.

921 Loubière, Pierre. *"Made in U.S.A."* *Téléciné*, No. 133 (February-March), p. 61.
Brief credits. The film has all of Godard's stylistic devices and seems to take up a political theme, but it really neither deals with nor analyzes society. Furthermore, in his disdainful relation to the spectator, Godard implicity accepts as inevitable the separation between artist and public. Reviews are cited from *France nouvelle*, *Arts et loisirs*, *Le Canard enchaîné*, and *Les Lettres françaises*.

922 Macdonald, Michael C.D. "Being Hot." *Village Voice* (12 October), pp. 4 and 41.

A letter from a liberal protests the propagandistic distortions of *Far from Vietnam*. Macdonald tries to analyze the political status of the film's viewers.

923 Mainds, Roger. *"Alphaville: A Strange Adventure of Lemmy Caution."* *Screen Education Yearbook 1968*, Society for Education in Film and Television, pp. 128–136.

Credits, synopsis, biography, filmography, citations from Britsh press about *Alphaville*. The film is analyzed in terms of the following aspects: the context of Godard's career, parody of comics and film conventions, cinematic technique (emphasis on night scenes, sharp contrasts of black and white), themes (transitory values, mass media, surface aspects of our social milieu), emphasis on detail, and paucity of ideas in the film.

924 Manz. H.[ans] P.[eter]; Tecklenberg, W.[alter]; Lachat, P.[ierre]. "Ein Streitengespräch." Ed. S. Plattner. *Cinema* (Union of Swiss Film Clubs), No. 49 (Spring), pp. 700–702.

In a debate held in October 1, 1966, the issues raised dealt with Godard's disdain for people and for cinema, his amorality, his "existentialism," his formalism, his mis en scene, the autobiographical aspect of his films, his politics and social criticism, the examination of modes of communication, Godard's relation with Coutard, his use of Karina.

925 Marchi, Bruno de. "Godard, profezia e mistificazione." *Vita e pensiero*, 50, No. 12 (December), 1338–41.

Cited 1972, Brown, Entry No. 1657.

926 Marcorelles, Louis. *"Deux ou trois choses."* *Cinéma 67*, No. 116 (May), pp. 114–115.

This film is compared to works of Joyce, Brecht, Mozart, and McLaren. It is subjective and confusing but also sincere. Vlady totally embodies objectified woman in modern society.

927 Mascariello, Angelo. "Godard: la dissoluzionne del personaggio." *Filmcritica*, No. 181 (September), pp. 142–46.

Godard's formal innovations are discussed both in the context of contemporary literature and the perspectives established by his own films.

928 Matharan de Potenze, Sylvia. *"Masculino-Feminina (Masculin-Féminin, Francia-Suecia, 1966)."* *Criterio*, 90, No. 1525 (8 June).

Godard's cinematic innovations fit his theme — alienated youth in a "wintery, restless, exasperated, violent Paris." Although Godard coldly and precisely chooses what to show us about these adolescents, the film is "much less cynical than it seems on first viewing."

929 Mauriac, Claude. *"La Chinoise de Jean-Luc Godard." Le Figaro littéraire*, No. 1117 (11–17 September), p. 46.

Discusses the disconcerting mixture of adolescent nonchalance and deadly seriousness in the film. Godard is the post-Guttenberg poet of the new visual age.

930 Mauriac, Claude. *"Loin du Viêtnam." Le Figaro littéraire*, No. 1131 (18–24 December), pp. 38–39.

Tries to ascertain why the film as a whole has a derisory tone.

931 Mauriac, Claude. Review of *Made in U.S.A. Le Figaro littéraire* (2 February), p. 14.

Made in U.S.A. is confusing but exciting "pure" cinema which has great political significance for left culture. Vianey's account of filming *Le Mépris* and *Masculin-Féminin* is discussed. Godard's film editor and his secretary speak about him, noting that he visualizes a film exactly before he shoots.

932 Mayersberg, Paul. "Second Opinion: Jean-Luc Godard." London *Sunday Times*, Magazine section (9 April), p. 50.

Brief biography of Godard is given and his critical reputation described. Godard's traits come from his Swiss background, with his eclecticism, innocence, asceticism, and remoteness. Like the Geneva school of literary criticism, he is concerned with criticism as art and creates literature about literature.

933 Michaelson, Annette. "Film and Radical Aspiration." *The New American Cinema*. Ed. Gergory Battock. New York: E.P. Dutton. Pp. 83–102.

Reprinted from 1966, Michaelson, Entry No. 727. Also reprinted in 1970, Michaelson, Entry No. 1484.

934 M.[ilne], T.[om]. "*Une Femme est une femme (A Woman Is a Woman)*, France, 1961." *Monthly Film Bulletin*, 34 (May), 71.

This is uniquely lighthearted among Godard's films and weakest where it tries "to impose some sort of reality on what is basically fantasy material."

935 M.[ilner], M.[ax]. "Godard ambigu." *Esprit*, 35, No. 5 (May), 931–35.

Godard uses the titles from the "Ideés" series in *Deux ou trois choses* to comment on our "paperback civilization," in which people are the object of banal language which innundates them but in which they do not recognize themselves. Correlatives of this theme in the film are the banal conversations, Vlady's opacity, housing construction, state planning, and prostitution—"the degree zero of communication."

936 Mosk[owitz, Gene]. "*La Chinoise (The Chinese Girl)* (French-Color)." *Variety* (13 September).

Brief credits. Venice. Godard tries "to give a convoluted serio-comic look at all aspects of youthful leftist thinking." Zestful conversations and color animate the film.

937 Mosk[owitz, Gene]. "*Le Plus Vieux Métier du monde.*" *Variety* (24 May), p. 6.

Credits. Godard's *Anticipation* not evaluated. Cited 1969, Anon, "The Oldest Profession," *Film Facts*, Entry No. 1254.

938 Moullet, Luc. "Jean-Luc Godard." Trans. Roberta Bernstein. *Cahiers du Cinema in English*, No. 12 (December), pp. 22–23.

Trans. from 1960, Moullet, Entry No. 81. Reprinted in 1968, Mussman, Entry No. 1168.

939 Mussman, Toby. "Godard as Godard." *Medium*, 1, No. 2 (Winter), 20–32.

Godard requires that his audience fill in the gaps. This makes us engage the film intellectually and empathetically. We anticipate, evaluate, "second-guess," and question the characters. Godard places his own predilictions, cinematic techniques, metaphors, and methodological concerns directly before us—so that we experience all the filmed events in two ways, as an experience and as a discussion of experience, an "historical referencing" of events.

940 Mussman, Toby. "Jean-Luc Godard's Non-Endings." *Arts* (U.S.), 42, No. 2 (November), 20–22.

Godard's "technique of making patently arbitrary and artificial endings, or non-endings, is invoked in order to create a strong implication for analytic self-awareness as a necessary complement to both the telling of the story and the watching of it being told."

941 Narboni, Jean. "Notes on *Deux ou trois choses.*" Trans. Jane Pearce. *Cahiers du Cinema in English*, No. 10 (May), pp. 32–37.

Complete credits for *Made in U.S.A.*; partial credits for *Deux ou trois choses.* Trans. from 1967, Narboni, Entry No. 942.

942 Narboni, Jean. "Notes sur *Deux ou trois choses que je sais d'elle.*" *Cahiers du cinéma*, No. 186 (January), pp. 32–33.

Discusses Godard's "hesitant," parenthetical, improvised camera style which catches unexpected glimpses of our reality, and relates this cinema's past and future. Trans. 1967, Narboni, Entry No. 941.

943 Pennec, Claude. "L'Évangile selon Saint-Luc." *Arts-loisirs* (22 March), pp. 24–25.

Deux ou trois choses seemingly denounces prostitution and ads but depends on pretty women and ads for its visual style. How can a political film be effective with so Calvinist a sense of predestination and such tedium?

944 Perles, Yvette. "En marge d'Avignon." *Image et son: Revue du cinéma.* No. 211 (December).

These remarks were recorded by Yvette Perles during the press conference after *La Chinoise*'s premiere at Avignon, summer, 1967. No questions are noted, just Godard's comments. Godard says youth are not caricatured in *La Chinoise.* The actors were given great freedom, and Wiazemsky's conversation with Jeanson resembles real conflicts in South America between the Communist party and guerrilla insurgents. We do not need art for the masses, which would stupify the public, but rather an art to make people think. Godard defines himself as an anarchist.

945 Pilard, Phillipe. "Entretien avec Jean-Luc Godard." *Image et son: Revue du cinéma*, No. 211 (December), pp. 51–58.

Godard explains his political and personal alienation from the French film industry, which is dominated by U.S. economic and cultural control. His own independence has come from working within low budgets for small audiences. He discusses his critics and his dislike for Vianey's *En attendant Godard.* As a "journalist" he has always made films about youths. He defends himself against the charge of being politically confused.

946　Pilard, Phillippe. "Jean-Luc Godard: thèmes et variations." *Image et son: Revue du cinéma*, No. 211 (December), pp. 25–28.

The "star" Godard imposes his personality, concerns, and own voice on us. His films fit well into the New Wave. Pillard discusses Godard's themes — romantic quests, communication, social disorder, and contemporary mores — and his techniques — fable, documentary, reflections on film and art, and automatic writing. Godard's work is "more sociological than cinematographic."

947　Pinel, Vincent. "Filmographie de Jean-Luc Godard." *Jean-Luc Godard — au delà du récit: Etudes cinématographiques*. No. 57–61. Ed. Michel Estève. Paris: Lettres Modernes-Minard. Pp. 179–87.

This filmography runs from 1954 through *La Chinoise*, 1967.

948　Plattner, S. "Editorial." *Cinema* (Union of Swiss Film Clubs), No. 49 (Spring), p. 688.

The older critics had discussed but decided not to do a Godard issue. When younger writers joined the staff, they argued for Godard. The two opinions are represented in this issue.

949　Plattner, Samuel. "Sprache — Zitat — Warheit." *Cinema* (Union of Swiss Film Clubs), No. 49 (Spring), pp. 698–99.

Analyzes how Godard uses citation ("a dictionary of the consumer society") to create atmosphere, reflect on the relation between language and truth and modes of discourse, and provide a distanciation effect — either Brechtian or Absurdist.

950　Ponzi, Mauricio. "Un 'iposti: Godard nomatore." *Cinema and Film*, 1, No. 3 (1967), 353–55.

In Lincoln Center Library.

951　Pouillon, Jean. "Il faut bien que jeunesse se passe." *Les Temps modernes*, No. 256 (September), p. 575.

La Chinoise offers vague, reactionary sympathy for a stereotypical kind of rebellious youth. Looking at youth in this way, our society knows well how to "recuperate" them.

952　Pouillon, Jean. Review of *La Chinoise*. *Minute* (7 September).

Negative review. Cited 1968, Gauteur, Entry No. 1111.

953　R.[abine], H.[enry]. "*Made in U.S.A.*" *La Croix* (5 February), p. 5.

The brilliant colors do not reproduce reality; they signify — but what? Godard is compared to Ionesco and faulted with portraying a confused world in an unnecessarily confused way.

954　de Ravel d'Esclapon, Pierre-Felix. "La Logique interne de Godard." *Take One*, 1, No. 4 (April), 13–14.

Lists the aspects of Godard's work that evoke strong reactions: capturing things without judging them, gathering contradictions with a sort of positive cynicism, stripping down reality with a certain asceticism, using Brechtian tactics not to evaluate life but to evaluate Godard's own theatricality, and filming people who do or say anything with an intent similar to Surrealist automatic writing.

955 Regard, Sylvain. "Modern Life." Trans. Jean Billard. *Take One*, 1, No. 3 (February), 7–10.

Author is listed as Godard in *Take One*. Trans. from 1966, Regard, *Le Nouvel Observatuer*, Entry No. 741. Also trans. 1967, Regard, *Sight and Sound*, Entry No. 740. That trans. reprinted, 1968, Mussman, Entry No. 1168.

956 Revel, Jean-François. "Le Cinéma et ses prophetes." *L'Express*, No. 822 (20–26 March), p. 93.

Negative review of Michel Vianey's *En attendant Godard*.

957 Ropars-Wuilleumier, Marie-Claire. *"La Chinoise."* Esprit, 35, No. 11 (November), 783–86.

The visual track in *La Chinoise* illustrates the characters' political discourse, but all references to social reality as well as the impossibility of the fiction satirize the characters, their bourgeois comfort, and finally their discourse itself — that is, Marxism-Leninism. Reality and fiction annul each other. It is a didactic film without a lesson. Reprinted 1970, Ropars-Wuilleumier, Entry No. 1502.

958 [Ropars-] W.[uilleumier], M.[arie]-C.[laire]. "La Forme et le fond." *Esprit*, 35, No. 4 (April), 670–72.

The contradictions, both formal and thematic, that permeate *Made in U.S.A.* make it a miccrocosm reflecting the totality of the "democratic" world, with its complicity in violence, its politics in debris, and its incapacity to express itself in words and discursive thought.

959 Ropars-Wuilleumier, Marie-Claire. "La Forme et le fond ou les avatars du récit." *Jean-Luc Godard — au delà du récit: Etudes cinématographiques*. No. 57–61. Ed. Michel Estève. Paris: Lettres Modernes-Minard. Pp. 17–34.

Godard uses cinema as a creative form of thought. That form is obtrusive and self-reflexive, used methodically to investigate the means of communication. "While his works take their fullest form through a profound attention to the ephemeral, unformulated instant, his personal needs lead him to transform this instant into a formulated absolute . . .; it is in the success of the search for this absolute that the significant power of his language disappears." Reprinted 1970, Ropars-Wuilleumier, Entry No. 1502. Trans. 1972, Brown, Entry No. 1658.

960 Roud, Richard. "Godard." *Making Films*, 1, No. 4 (October), 17.

People still dislike plotless films. Godard's genius is to exploit simultaneously all the contradictions inherent in the art: "visual vs. narrative, fiction vs. documentary, reality vs. abstraction."

961 Roud, Richard. *Jean-Luc Godard*. Collection Cinema World. New York: Doubleday.

Second edition updated, 1970, Roud, Entry No. 1505. See that entry for annotation.

962 Sadoul, Georges. "Deux ou trois choses d'un grand ensemble." *Les Lettres françaises*, No. 1175 (23–29 March), pp. 20 and 22.

Deux ou trois choses is described in terms of art and film history, its themes, and its fragmentation. It is "a series of rapid visions mingled with soliloquies and reflections about two or three things." Trans. 1972, Brown, Entry No. 1658.

963 Salmaggi, Bob. "Exasperating Godard Opus." *World Journal Tribune* (27 April).
Brief credits. *Le Petit Soldat* tires us with its nervous photography, tedious dialogue, and ludicrous situations. Quoted at length in 1967, Anon., *Film Facts*, Entry No. 804.

964 Sarris, Andrew. "Films." *Village Voice* (9 November), p. 33.
Les Carabiniers is compared to Richard Lester's *How I Won the War*; Godard's film "shows considerably more beauty and feeling." *Les Carabiniers* sees war "entirely from the point of view of the poor slobs who fight."

965 Sarris, Andrew, ed. *Interviews with Film Directors.* Indianapolis: Bobbs-Merrill. Reissued 1969. Discus Edition. New York: Avon. Pp. 208–227.
Reprints two interviews with Godard that appeared in the *New York Film Bulletin*, No. 46, 1964. One was from *Cahiers du cinéma*, No. 138, trans. Rose Kaplin (1962, Collet, Entry No. 186); the other by Warren Sonbert and Gretchen Weinberg (1964, Sonbert, Entry No. 440).

966 Sarris, Andrew. "Jean-Luc Godard." *Interviews with Film Directors.* Indianapolis: Bobbs-Merrill. Reissued 1969, New York: Avon. Pp. 202–208.
Reprinted from 1964, Sarris, Entry No. 432. Also appears in 1969, Sarris, Entry No. 1341.

967 Sarris, Andrew. "The New York Film Festival." *Village Voice* (12 October), p. 31.
"The individual artists in *Far from Vietnam* obviously surrendered their individual consciences for the sake of a collective statement." The film wasn't worth it. Reprinted 1967, Starr, *Film Culture*, Entry No. 977; 1970, Sarris, Entry No. 1507.

968 Schlappner, Martin. "Spiel, Abenteur, Schicksal: Jean-Luc Godard." *Filme und ihre Regisseure.* Bern and Stuttgart: Huber. Pp. 119–151.
Overview of Godard's work, with special attention paid to his use of improvisation.

969 Segal, A.[braham]. "Biofilmographie de Jean-Luc Godard." *Deux ou trois choses que je sais d'elle: L'Avant-Scène du cinéma*, No. 70 (May).
Complete biography of Godard through 1966. Reprinted 1971, *Deux ou trois choses* script, Entry No. 2343, where it is updated to 1970.

970 Segal, Abraham. "Godard: essai collage." *Image et son: Revue du cinéma.* No. 211 (December), pp. 31–37.
Citing Mao and comparing Godard to Lumière, Segal examines in depth how Godard uses a modernist form to create a radical political art. Discusses in detail Godard's cinematographic distanciation techniques. Fiction and documentary merge in films that give a cinematic existence to names, words, books, sounds, cars, and ideas.

971 S.[eguin], L.[ouis]. *"Deux ou trois choses que je sais d'elle."* *Positif*, No. 85 (June), pp. 62–63.

Brief hostile review. The first sentence contains nineteen pejorative adjectives.

972 Shepard, Richard D. *"Made in U.S.A.*: Full of Imagery and Message." *New York Times* (28 September).

Brief credits. *Made in U.S.A.* seen at New York Film Festival. It's a crime story that deals with "life's meaningless incidents" and also the inadequacy of the right's and the left's emotional and aesthetic stances.

973 Simon, John. "The Festival Concluded." *The New Leader*, 50, No. 22 (6 November), 32–33.

Simon saw *Made in U.S.A.* and *Les Carabiniers*, but his contempt for Godard is so great he cannot say it all here. He cites John Coleman of the *New Statesman*, with whom he agrees, and refers readers to his own essay, "Godard and the Godardians" in *Private Screenings* (Entry No. 974).

974 Simon, John. "Godard and the Godardians: A Study in the New Sensibility." *Private Screenings*. New York: Macmillan. Pp. 272–296. Reissued 1971, Berkley Medallion Books. New York: Berkley Publishing Co. Pp. 306–332.

Rejects a "new sensibility" that accounts for a revolution in contemporary arts. Godard's "shock effects" do not broaden our perceptions or understanding, do not clothe old things in new forms. Lists Godard's cinematic and narrative devices, behind which Godard has "nothing." Godard eschews psychology and celebrates cruelty and amorality. Godard's philosophical utterances are banal and hollow. Gratuitousness can be neither poetic nor suspenseful. Godard's presentation of social problems is either oversimplified or obfuscating. Improvisation and chance mean Godard neglects to "shape or reshape reality." Simon refutes Susan Sontag, Pauline Kael, Andrew Sarris, John Tomas, Richard Roud, John Russell Taylor, and A.A. Alvarez on Godard.

975 Simon, John. *Private Screenings*. New York: Macmillan. Reissued 1971. Berkley Medallion Book. New York: Berkley Publishing Co. [Page numbers here refer to Berkley edition.]

"Escapism into Art," pp. 151–56, reprinted from 1964, Simon, Entry No. 439. "Festival of Famine," pp. 208–209, reprinted from 1965, Entry No. 605. "See Naples and Live," pp. 166–67. "Godard and the Godardians: A Study in the New Sensibility." pp. 306–332, reprinted from a lecture at Williams College, Williamstown, Mass. *See* Entry No. 974. "Gravity Defied," pp. 205–208, reprinted from 1965, Entry No. 606.

976 Sontag, Susan. "Godard" (broadside). Program notes for New Yorker Theater Godard retrospective (1 November).

One side of broadside consists of statements by Godard selected from Roud's *Godard*, plus a brief filmography. Sontag, on the other side, describes Godard as the greatest director working in cinema today. She discusses his output, her preferences among his films, and "Godard's insouciant mixture of tonalities, themes, and narrative techniques." Godard changes "the familiar boundaries between moral passion and aestheticism." Godard directly inserts ideas into cinema, explores all aspects of language, and uses the image to stand as exactly equivalent to a word or text.

977 Starr, Francis; Sarris, Andrew; and Mekas, Jonas. *"Far from Vietnam."* *Film Culture*, No. 46 (Fall), pp. 32–34.

Describes the film in detail and provides heavily ironic comments in a "Dick-and-Jane" style on the film's politics. Sarris' review from *The Village Voice* (October 12) is reprinted, followed by a cartoon by Mekas attacking Sarris' review. Sarris' article reprinted from 1967, Sarris, *Village Voice*, Entry No. 967, and reprinted in 1970, Sarris, *Confessions of a Cultist*, Entry No. 1507.

978 Téchiné, André. "De trois films et d'une certaine parole." *Cahiers du cinéma*, No. 189 (April), pp. 50–51.

Cited 1968, Gauteur, Entry No. 1111.

979 Téchiné, André. "L'Unique et le pluriel." *Cahiers du cinéma*, No. 190 (May), p. 64.

People are overwhelmed by miltiple significations in an urban environment. If cinema is to recoup reality, how should we remake film for that task? The form of *Deux ou trois choses* reflects the theme of being trapped within a profusion of images, yet it also reenacts it. Godard tries to seize everything and has been seduced by "abundance, profusion, (and) original confusion."

980 Tecklenburg, Walter. "Godard und die Tradition." *Cinema* (Union of Swiss Film Clubs), No. 49 (Spring), pp. 693–95.

Discusses Godard's incorporation of film history into his films.

981 Thévoz, Michel. "Collage de la mujer casada." *Revista de belles artes* (Mexico), No. 14 (March-April), pp. 46–50.

La Femme mariée aptly directs the spectator not only to look at his/her own "reflection" but also to consider spectacle itself (this film, the ads around us, TV, other films — both documentary and fiction), challenging how we "direct ourselves toward it and how we live in it." The self-reflexive aspect of Godard's art, with reference to *La Femme mariée* and *Le Mépris*, is analyzed in detail.

982 Th.[irard]. P.[aul]-L.[ouis]. "De A à Z: *La Chinoise*." *Positif*, No. 89 (November), p. 62.

This is the first Godard film for a long time that hasn't been boring and irritating, but it still rests too heavily on mythology. Jeanson should have asked "la Chinoise" if she'd seen *Le Petit Soldat*.

983 Thirard, P.[aul]-L.[ouis]). "L'Opposant dans le vent." *Positif*, No. 83 (April), pp. 40–42.

Credits. Leftist critics mistakenly praise *Made in U.S.A.*, for it only presents more Godard and no thesis. The form of the film has little value, and the content mocks politics because it refuses to present a political judgment.

984 T[ompson], H.[oward]. Review of *Les Carabiniers*. *New York Times* (28 September), p. 58.

Brief credits. The critic could see "no discernible" reason why this bad Godard film, made in 1962, was shown at the New York Film Festival.

985 Thompson, Howard. Review of *Le Petit Soldat*. *New York Times* (21 April), p. 48.
Brief credits. *Le Petit Soldat* has a "steely glitter," a fine sense of flying in cars around Geneva, "sickenly horrendous torture session," and inhuman characters we cannot care about. Quoted at length 1976, Anon., *Film Facts*, Entry No. 804.

986 Thompson, Richard. "Jean-Luc *Cinema* Godard." *December*, 9, No. 2–3 (Western Springs, Ill.), unpaged.
In this lengthy (18-page) article, Thompson analyzes Godard's work primarily in terms of cinematography and characterization. He provides an in-depth analysis of the following films: *Breathless, A Woman Is a Woman, My Life to Live, Le Petit Soldat, Contempt, Band of Outsiders, The Married Woman,* and *Alphaville*. The essay describes each film and assesses Godard's cinematic achievements within the context of film history.

987 Thomson, David. *Movie Man*. New York: Stein and Day; London: Secker & Warburg. Pp. 178–185, 206–207.
Godard "synthesizes the two categories of cinema: the film director and the scientist." Thus he is both the "last great artistic director" and the "first great new filmmaker." Thematically Godard shows "the complete dissolution of the humanistic tradition," and visually all his shots make us as aware of cinematic convention as of the story. In film such as *Pierrot le fou*, Godard is the ultimate "democratic" director, with every connotation bearing equal weight.

988 Tournès, Andrée. "Les Fioretti de Saint Jean-Luc." *Jeune cinéma*, No. 21 (March), pp. 20–21.
En attendant Godard by Michel Vianey is supposed to be about the filming of *Masculin-Féminin* but is overly filled with trivial accounts of personalities and interviews with cast and crew. It answers no essential questions.

989 Truffaut, François. "La Savate et le finance ou deux ou trois choses que je sais de lui." *Deux ou trois choses que je sais d'elle: L'Avant-Scène du cinéma*, No. 70 (May), p. 45.
Coproducer of Godard's thirteenth film, Truffaut compares Godard to other filmmakers and discusses his revolutionary effect on audience expectations about films. Reprinted from 1967, Truffaut, *Les Lettres Françaises*, Entry No. 990. Reprinted 1971, *Deux ou trois choses*, Entry No. 2343.

990 Truffaut, François. "La Savate et le finance ou deux ou trois choses que je sais de lui." *Les Lettres Françaises*, No. 1174 (16 March), p. 21.
Reprinted 1967, Truffaut, *L'Avant-Scène*, Entry No. 989. See annotation there. Also reprinted in 1971, *Deux ou trois choses* script, Entry No. 2343.

991 Vialle, Gabriel. "Deux ou trois choses que nous savons de d'*elles, elles*, les femmes, depuis qu'*il*, Jean-Luc Godard nous en a parle—." *Image et son: Revue du cinéma*, No. 211 (December), pp. 39–49.
Godard often treats the theme of "love" or "the couple" with a moralistic temperament. His scenes of lovemaking, undress, and even nudity are exceptionally modest — against which modesty he challenges bourgeois hypocrisy about sexuality. The prostitution motif becomes an "anguished warning" about the

course of society. Godard's female protagonists reflect an "epoch in total trans-formation, with the woman herself completely changing her own concept of her role."

992 Vianey, Michel. *"Waiting for Godard." Harper's Bazaar* (June). pp. 58–62.
In excerpts from his book, Vianey describes Godard and the making of *Masculin-Féminin* by aphoristic descriptions of things seen or heard, quotations, etc. A rebus by Godard that was the preface to the book is included. Trans. by Sandy Petrey. *See* 1966, Vianey, Entry No. 768.

993 Weinberg, Jean. "A la memoire de *Pierrot le fou." Jeune cinéma*, No. 21 (March), pp. 21–22.
We cannot learn much from *Pierrot*. It is more about violence and irresponsibil-ity than it is beautiful, lyrical, or sentimental — which are the qualities for which most critics have praised it.

994 Whitehead, Peter. Review of *A Woman Is a Woman. Films and Filming*, 13, No. 8 (May), 30.
Brief review. Cited in Bowles, p. 575.

995 Winsten, Archer. *"Le Petit Soldat* at the New Yorker." *New York Post* (21 April).
The film is plagued by too much talking.

996 Zimmer, Christian. "Totalisation du vrac." *Les Temps modernes*, No. 252 (May), pp. 2101–2106.
Discusses the relation between documentary and modernist impulses. *Made in U.S.A.* and *Deux ou trois choses* are "realistic" in the form of a catalogue, each image standing for itself, giving its message in a stripped-down way in separate shots. In *Made in U.S.A.* the op art colors don't support the confused political message. *Deux ou trois choses* is "decentered," and each spectator is supposed to complete the work, with Godard giving indications about the social and artistic production of meaning in contemporary life.

1968

997 Adler, Renata. "Adler Loves Godard — Sort Of." *New York Times* (27 October), Sec. II, pp. 1 and 20.
The reasons for Godard's violently mixed and contradictory reputation are described in the context of both popular and avant garde cinema. What should we do with *Weekend*, which is grand in its conception and power in certain moments and intellectually insulting in others? Reprinted 1971, Alder, Entry No. 1535.

998 Adler, Renata. "Debate Rages over Centre du Cinéma." *New York Times* (25 May), p. 27.
Describes the debates in the Etats-Généraux in Paris in detail. Godard and Truffaut have not been seen there since May 20.

999 Adler, Renata. "Film Festival: *Weekend*: Godard Film Captures Despair and Violence." *New York Times* (28 September), p. 36.

The plot fragments in *Weekend* lead nowhere. It is a despairing work, like Beckett's, but also "rich, overloaded, really epic, . . . an appalling comedy." Reprinted 1971, Adler, Entry No. 1535.

1000   Adler, Renata. "Fracas at Festival." *New York Times* (26 May), Sec. II, pp. 1 and 22.
   Background of and details about Cannes strike are given. Godard wanted continuous free projection of films in the city. Adler feels "art does not function well in the service of politics, it does not work by majority rule". Reprinted 1971, Adler, Entry No. 1535.

1001   Adler, Renata. "Godard Stalking Reality through the Movies." *New York Times* (6 December), Section 1, p. 50.
   The filming of several sequences of *One A.M.* is described — a girl carrying a phonograph and playing soul music through the streets of Harlem, the Jefferson Airplane performing on a hotel roof; Tom Hayden going up and down in an elevator marked "no passengers." Adler notes the future structure of the film and the aesthetic intent of each of these sequences. The police interrrupted the rock performance, ordering the amplifiers to be shut off. Reprinted 1971, Adler, Entry No. 1535.

1002   Adler, Renata. "How Movies Speak to Young Rebels." *New York Times* (19 May), Sec. II, pp. 1 and 14.
   Criticizes bourgeois adolescents for advocating a "style" or "aesthetic" revolution; they "simply bring the system down upon their heads." In *La Chinoise* there is a tremendous casualness on the part of the radicals as to where all this will lead. Reprinted 1971, Adler, Entry No. 1535.

1003   Adler, Renata. "How Their World Might Ideally Be." *New York Times* (2 June), Sec. II, pp. 1 and 26.
   The mood and issues debated by the Etats-Généraux are described and participants named. Reprinted 1971, Adler, No. 1535.

1004   Adler, Renata. "*One American Movie.*" *New York Times* (20 November), p. 42.
   Describes Godard shooting this film in the United States for Public Broadcasting Laboratories.

1005   Adler, Renata. "Renata Adler and Godard." *New York Times* (5 May).
   Les Carabiniers is an understated, great movie that aptly uses the banal to express what Borges calls "worn metaphors." "War really looks diffuse, meaningless, with great pockets of peace in it." Reprinted 1971, Adler, Entry No. 1535.

1006   Adler, Renata. Review of *Les Carabiniers*. *New York Times* (26 April), p. 31.
   Brief credits. *Les Carabiniers* is a "comment that works both at the allegorical level and at the real — on war, symbols, the quality of modern life, and the meaning of photography." Reprinted 1971, Adler, Entry No. 1535.

1007   A[dler], R.[enata]. Review of *La Chinoise*. *New York Times* (4 April), p. 58.

In *La Chinoise* Godard has caught in beautiful, flat photography the hurt, intelligent, and gentle look of the young who have joined a political struggle outside their own class; their talk is almost entirely of ideas, often violent ones. Brief credits. Reprinted 1971, Adler, Entry No. 1535.

1008 Adler, Renata. Review of *Deux ou trois choses. New York Times* (26 September), p. 60.

Deux ou trois choses offers beautiful, precise visual details to depict the most mundane aspects of urban life, but Godard's voice off commentary is affected and tedious. Brief credits. Reprinted 1971, Adler, Entry No. 1535.

1009 Adler, Renata. Review of *Far from Vietnam. New York Times* (7 June), p. 32

The narration of *Far from Vietnam* is banal and ugly. The content consists of "political stereotypes in a rage." Exceptions are interviews with Ho Chi Minh, Fidel Castro, and Mrs. Norman Morrison. Brief credits. Reprinted 1971, Adler, Entry No. 1535.

1010 Adler, Renata. "The Ten Best Films of '68." *New York Times* (22 December), Sec. II, p. 3.

There were more serious, fewer entertainment films this year. *Les Carabiniers* is among Adler's top ten, *La Chinoise* in the second ten.

1011 Adrian, Alan Aaron. *"Pierrot le fou." Cinema*, 4, No. 4 (December), 37.

Cited in Bowles, p. 392.

1012 Agel, Henri. "Les Monographies cinématographiques de 1950-1968." *Information littéraire*, 20, No. 5 (November-December), 209–224.

Cited 1969–70, *Index analytique*, 4, p. F-161.

1013 Albèra, François. "Godardorama." *Travelling J* (Lausanne), No. 21 (May-July), pp. 16–24.

Credits for *La Chinoise* and *Weekend*. Discusses the following aspects of Godard's aesthetic development: debt to U.S. cinema, fragmentation of the narrative, *La Chinoise*'s use of an adventure film's dramatic structure, the combination of Méliès and Brecht, a "musical" composition of images, "starting again at zero," and *Weekend* as a war film. A note is given on recent critical writings published on Godard, with an attack on Jacques Pollack-Lederer (*see* 1968, Pollack-Lederer, Entry No. 1173).

1014 Alpert, Hollis. "Film Ferment: *La Chinoise* and *Far from Vietnam*." *Saturday Review* (30 March), p. 39.

Brief review of *Far from Vietnam*: "Conscience is fine, but at the moment it is not enough—nor are arrogance and pretentiousness." *La Chinoise* is feelingless, its characters sophomoric, and its politics merely a fantasy. Quoted at length, 1968, Anon., *Far from Vietnam*, *Film Facts*, Entry No. 1032.

1015 Améry, Jean. "Jean-Luc Godard oder das Misverstandnis der kunstlerschen Freiheit." *Merkur* (Stuttgart), 22, No. 239 (March), 234–43.

First with the *Cahiers* critics and now in Germany, film studies have just wanted to analyze the autonomous art work. With the decline of popular front films, the "dream of resistance and revolution was played out." The New Wave, like the fields of marketing and public relations in the fifties, packaged a commercially successful product with sex and violence. In his pursuit of aesthetic advances and artistic liberty, Godard uses so many distancing effects that he "neutralizes the theme, *any* theme."

1016 Anon. "Additif à la biofilmographie de J.L. Godard." *A bout de souffle: L'Avant-Scène du cinéma*, No. 78 (March).
Brief credits for *Anticipation, La Chinoise, Weekend*. A record was made by Columbia in 45 rpm of the music from *A bout de souffle*.

1017 Anon. Article on Godard's failing to arrive in Britain for a lecture. London *Times* (21 October), p. 3.
Cited 1968, *Times Index* (September-October), p. 92.

1018 Anon. Article on *One Plus One*. London *Times* (27 November), p. 1.
Film banned in Edinburgh. Follow-up articles on November 28, p. 2; November 29, p. 10; and November 30, p. 10. Cited 1968, *Times Index* (November-December), p. 86.

1019 Anon. Article on *One Plus One*. London *Times* (29 November), p. 10.
Film to be shown at London Festival. Cited 1968, *Times Index* (November-December), p. 71.

1020 Anon. "*A bout de souffle* et la presse." *A bout de souffle: L'Avant-Scène du cinéma*, No. 79 (March), pp. 45–46.
Citations from reviews.

1021 Anon. "*The Beautiful Swindlers.*" *Film Facts*, 11, No. 24 (January), 530.
Credits. Godard's segment "was deleted for the picture's Paris premiere in August 1964 [and] . . . was later released in France as a short titled *Le Grand Escroc (The Great Swindle)*. Initially set for US release by Continental, the film was held in limbo until Jack Ellis took over distribution."

1022 Anon. Brief review of Roud's *Godard*. *Film Quarterly*, 21, No. 4 (Summer), 55.
Cited in Bowles, p. 629.

1023 Anon. "Cannes Officials Close Festival." *New York Times* (19 May), p. 26.
Godard, Léaud, and Truffaut fought physically with local residents in the main auditorium of the Cannes festival to keep Renais' film from being projected. Léaud held the curtain shut. Previously Malle, Godard, Truffaut, and Polanski had declared solidarity with students and strikers.

1024 Anon. "*Les Carabiniers.*" *Cue* (27 April).
This original antiwar film mixes comedy and brutality, surrealism and realism. The postcard sequence is excessive and wearing.

1025 Anon. *"Les Carabiniers." Film Facts*, 11, No. 11 (July), 183–84.
Credits, synopsis, Godard's view of the film, festivals it was shown at, lengthy citations from reviews in the *New York Times, Time*, and *Variety*.

1026 Anon. *"La Chinoise." Cue* (6 April).
This well-acted, original film lacks depth.

1027 Anon. *"La Chinoise." Time*, 91, No. 17 (26 April), E10 and 108.
La Chinoise visually is a successful cinematic demonstration of "minimal art." The characters are so much "a satire on themselves" that the film has little depth.

1028 Anon. *"La Chinoise (The Chinese Girl)." Film Facts*, 11, No. 10 (June), 146–48.
Credits, synopsis, extensive quotations from reviews in the *New York Times, Saturday Review, Time, Variety*, and briefly from *New York Magazine*.

1029 Anon. "Diary Note" on *One Plus One*. London *Times* (30 November), p. 10.
Cited 1968, *Times Index* (November-December), p. 71.

1030 Anon. "Directors: Infuriating Magician." *Time*, 91 (16 February), 90–91.
The Museum of Modern Art's retrospective of Godard's fifteen features reveals Godard's cinematic inventiveness and daring, as well as his "preening and perversities" and bookishness. Godard's technical innovations are described, as well as his youth (he is characterized as a rebellious young freeloader, even a thief). His latest films—*Two or Three Things, La Chinoise*, and *Weekend*—are "not bad at all" but often "incoherent."

1031 Anon. "Encyclopédie permanente du cinématographe: Godard (distribution)." *Positif*, No. 94 (April), pp. 50–51.
Godard protested the imperialism of French film distributors, especially COMACICO, that inhibit the growth of national film industries in Africa. Yet *Weekend* was produced by Copernic, a subsidiary of COMACICO.

1032 Anon. *"Far from Vietnam." Film Facts*, 11, No. 14 (15 August), 262–64.
Credits, synopsis, lengthy citations from reviews in *Variety, Saturday Review, the New York Times*, and *Time*.

1033 Anon. *"Far from Vietnam* and *Green Berets." Time*, 91, No. 25 (21 June), 84.
Both films "preach to the converted" and lack a scenario and also common sense. In *Far from Vietnam*, Godard is fascinated with only himself and his own ideas.

1034 Anon. "Four New Movies Rated Condemned by Catholic Office." *New York Times* (4 October), p. 34.
Weekend was condemned by the Legion of Decency. The film, they said, had artistic force and a certain truth in its criticism but it was "a coldly intellectual exercise," "often adolescent," and "dangerously simplistic in its attack on traditional morality and existing social values."

1035 Anon. "Godard Campus Tour Canceled." *Film Society Review* (March), p. 11.

Godard's tour of 18 campuses with *La Chinoise*, "at top lecture fees," was canceled without explanation after only five campuses were visited.

1036 Anon. "Godard in Gotham." *Variety* (4 October), p. 15.

Godard's films shown in the New York Film Festival from 1963 to 1967 are listed: 1963, *Rogopag*; 1964, *A Woman Is a Woman, Band of Outsiders*; 1965, *Alphaville, Le Petit Soldat, Montparnasse-Levallois*; 1966, *Masculin-Féminin, Pierrot le fou*; 1967, *Les Carabiniers, Made in U.S.A., Loin du Vietnam*.

1037 Anon. "Godard Is Missed at Festival Here." *New York Times* (28 September).

The article comments on the actors' and spectators' uneasy and varying reaction to the "ideological pressure" resulting from the earlier closing of Cannes Film Festival.

1038 Anon. "Godard, Jean-Luc." *International Who's Who 1968–69*, 32. London: Europe Publications. P. 486.

Brief entry, mainly listing films.

1039 Anon. "Godard visita Cuba: breve reseña gráfica." *Cine Cubano*, No. 48., pp. 34–40.

Godard had wanted to come to Cuba for the Cultural Congress in Havana in January but was filming then. He came with Anne Wiazemsky, Feb. 3–11, and said he had decided to film a few scenes in Cuba to use in his next picture. The article is primarily a photo series illustrating Wiazemsky's and Godard's visit.

1040 Anon. "Half-Done Godard Film Fails to Irk Its Brit. Producer." *Variety* (10 July).

London. Michael Pearson of Cupid Productions affirms that Godard, now "indisposed" in Paris, will return to complete *One Plus One*. Difficulties have plagued the film.

1041 Anon. Interview with Godard. Lausanne: Centre de Initiation au Cinéma de Lausanne.

Interview conducted September 1968, in Locarno. Cited 1969, Collet, Entry No. 1282.

1042 Anon. "Jean-Luc Godard Biography." New York Film Festival Program.

This mentions Godard's participation in the New York Film Festivals and his influence on "almost all the films seen at the National Student Film Festivals, sponsored by Lincoln Center."

1043 Anon. "New Movies: *Les Carabiniers*." *Time*, 91, No. 20 (17 May), 101.

Within the timeless context of a folk tale, Godard develops the worn metaphor that "in a war, winner takes nothing." "Lean, clean, performances" are played out against Coutard's "haunted landscapes."

1044 Anon. "New Movies: Society as a Slaughterhouse." *Time*, 92 (November), 100–101.
Review of *Weekend*. Godard "makes his movies like a kid with his first camera," incorporating digressions, sight gags, and nose-thumbing at the audience. Examples from a plot summary demonstrate "Godardian overkill."

1045 Anon. "*The Oldest Profession*." *Film Facts*, 11, No. 14 (15 January), 483–84.
Credits, synopsis—including that of Godard's sketch *Anticipation*. Criticism cited from the *New York Times* and *Variety*.

1046 Anon. "Paris Filmmakers Protest a Dismissal." *New York Times* (14 February), p. 55.
François Truffaut leads French filmmakers to protest Langlois' firing.

1047 Anon. "Primo film inglese di Godard: parallelo fra creazione e distruzione." *Bianco e nero*, 29, No. 5–6 (May-June), X.
One Plus One was announced as a film that would be about a young French woman (Anne Wiazemsky), a right-wing Texan, and a leftist black man.

1048 Anon. *Program Notes to Accompany Two Godard Premiers ("A Movie Like Any Other" by Godard, and "Two American Audiences" by Mark Woodcock)*, *Philharmonic Hall, Lincoln Center, December 29, 1968.* New York: Leacock and Pennebaker. 22 pp.
The notes consist of an interview with Godard, who talks about the relation of film to social change, Hollywood film, distribution, film form, his cinematographic technique, the political aspects of *La Chinoise*, his chance to direct *Bonnie and Clyde*. Interview possibly was conducted by Leacock and Pennebaker.

1049 Anon. "Quotesmanship: What's Being Said About Directing." *Action*, 3, No. 3 (July-August), 20.
Brief Godard statement quoted from Roud's book, *Godard*. Entry No. 961.

1050 Anon. Review of *One Plus One*. London *Times* (26 November), p. 6.
Cited 1968, *Times Index* (November-December), p. 71.

1051 Anon. Review of *One Plus One*. London *Times* (2 December), p. 62.
Godard punches producer Ian Quarrier on stage of NFT, saying final song ruined the film and asking audience to leave.

1052 Anon. Review of *One Plus One* Premier. *International Herald Tribune* (2 December).
Report of Godard's hitting Quarrier in the jaw. Cited 1968, *Esquire*, 72, No. 1, 72.

1053 Anon. Review of Roud's *Godard*. *Cinema*, 4, No. 3 (Fall), 47.
Cited 1968, *Guide to P.A.*, p. 144.

1054 Anon. Review of Roud's *Godard*. *Film Quarterly*, 21, No. 4 (Summer).
Brief review. Cited Bowles, p. 629.

1055 Anon. Review of Roud's *Godard. International Film Guide*, 5, p. 263.
Cited in Bowles, p. 629.

1056 Anon. Review of Roud's *Godard. Take One*, 2, No. 1 (September-October), 27.
Cited in Bowles, p. 144.

1057 Anon. Review of *Seven Capital Sins. Cinema*, 4, No. 1 (Spring), 46.
Brief review cited in Bowles, p. 450.

1058 Anon. "*Weekend.*" *Film Facts*, 11, No. 17 (October), 255–57.
Credits, synopsis, lengthy citation of reviews from *Time*, the *New York Times*, *Variety* and *New York Magazine*.

1059 Anon. "*Weekend.*" London Times (4 July), Sec. C, p. 13.
Cited 1968, *Times Index* (July-August), p. 81.

1060 Archer, Eugene. "What Makes Us Hate, or Love, Godard?" *New York Times* (28 January), Sec. II, p. 17.
This article reviews Godard's whole career. Godard is influential, "alas." Godard hates his audiences but loves movies. *Breathless* worked but *A Woman Is a Woman* was an expensive failure. When *My Life to Live*, $40,000, succeeded, Godard found his metier in low budget films and the sheer bulk of his production helped him rise to fame. Godard's other films and his relations with producers are noted. His cinema is personal, confused, and irritating.

1061 Aumont, Jacques. "L'Etang moderne." *Cahiers du cinéma*, No. 199 (March), pp. 59–60.
Brief credits for *Weekend*. The camera and use of color makes us aware of the film's artifice and our role as spectators. Two formal categories clash to provide the dynamics of the film—nostalgic romanticism vs. the representation of a mechanized, inhuman society.

1062 Aumont, Jacques and Collet, Jean. "Le Dur Silence des galaxies — *Weekend.*" *Cahiers du cinéma*, No. 199 (March), pp. 60–61.
The critics discuss the relation between decomposition and imagination in Godard's work. *Weekend* carefully transgresses most taboos but still leaves us inside "the cinematic taboo of see-but-don't touch, dream-but-don't-live."

1063 Beaulieu, Janick. *Alphaville: le phénomène Jean-Luc Godard.* Limbourg (Québec): Editions Janickvonocinéma. 65 pp.
Cited 1971, Allard, Entry No. 1537.

1064 Benedikt, Michael. "*Alphaville* and Its Subtext." *Jean-Luc Godard: A Critical Anthology.* Ed. Toby Mussman. New York: E.P. Dutton. Pp. 312–20.
In the mise en scene, the use of Eluard, and the treatments of love and poetry, Godard deliberately engages the surrealist tradition, both formally and thematically, in *Alphaville*.

1065 Billard, Pierre, et al. *"L'Express* va plus loin avec Alain Robbé-Grillet." No. 876 (1–7 April), pp. 38–46.

In an interview conducted by Pierre Billard, Jean-Louis Ferrier, Christiane Collange, and Madeleine Chapsal, Robbe-Grillet compares Godard to the U.S. sculptor, Lichtenstein, and finds Godard a great modernist and humanist. Robbe-Grillet discusses modernism in literature and film. He finds the sequence of Mireille Darc in her underwear talking to an "analyst" in *Weekend* extremely lovely and erotic.

1066 Bochner, Mel. *"Alphaville*: Godard's Apocalypse." *Arts*, 42 (May), 14–17.

Cited *Art Index* (November 1967–October 1968), p. 232.

1067 Bochner, Mel. *"Alphaville* or the Death of Dick Tracy." *Jean-Luc Godard: A Critical Anthology*. Ed. Toby Mussman. New York: E.P. Dutton. Pp. 206–212.

Presents a montage of citations, descriptions, impressions of the mise en scene, characterization, and themes in *Alphaville*.

1068 Bochner, Mel. Review of *Breathless*. *Arts* (U.S.), 42 (May).

Cited 1970, Collet, Entry No. 1425.

1069 de Bonis, Jacques. *"Weekend* au mois de mai." *La Nouvelle Critique*, No. 18 (October), pp. 59–62.

The critic cites a number of reviews to indicate there are two major misunderstandings about Godard, that he is too much of a modernist or too much of a naturalist. A rather lyrical appreciation of *La Chinoise* and *Weekend* is offered.

1070 Bontemps, Jacques, et al. "Struggle on Two Fronts: A Conversation with Jean-Luc Godard." Trans. D.C.D. *Film Quarterly*, 22, No. 2 (Winter), 20-35.

Translated from 1967, Bontemps et al. Entry No. 834.

1071 Bory, Jean-Louis. "Un Poete en colère." *Le Novel Observateur*, date unknown.

Review of *Weekend*. Reprinted 1972, Bory, Entry No. 1653.

1072 Bragin, John. *"La Chinoise* and *La Cine e vicina." Film Society Review*, 4, No. 1 (September), 26–36.

The two films are analyzed in the context of the leftist political situation in France and Italy. "In *La Chinoise* the formal fabric of the film is set in continuous tension with Ideas."

1073 Burton, Scott. "The Film We Secretly Wanted to Live: A Study of *Masculin-Féminin." Jean-Luc Godard: A Critical Anthology*. Ed. Toby Mussman. New York: E.P. Dutton. Pp. 261–73.

Masculin-Féminin offers a "natural history of adolescence." Formally, it depends on monologues, interrogations, disruptions of causality, omnipresent crowds and city noises, performance and exhibition, elusive details at the very edge of the screen and/or on it only momentarily, intermittant violence and death which exist only peripherally for us and at the edge of our awareness. We have a "growing distaste" for the selfish Madeleine and see Paul "caught in a sexual web of his own spinning."

1074 Cadeau, Charles. "Lettres de lecteurs." *Positif*, No. 93 (March), pp. 69–70.

A reader's vehement political attack on *La Chinoise* is answered by Michel Ciment and Paul-Louis Thirard, who found it a "tolerable" film.

1075 Canby, Vincent, "Screen: A Bit of Godard." *New York Times* (8 November), p. 42.

Godard's 15-minute sketch *Anticipation* is the "only decently funny episode" in *The Oldest Profession*. Plot summary of *Anticipation* is given and brief credits for the whole film. Quoted 1969, Anon., *Film Facts*, Entry No. 1254.

1076 Capdenac, Michel. "Jean-Luc Godard et Alain Resnais au trebuchet." *Les Lettres françaises*, No. 1241 (17–23 July), p. 18.

Reviews *Jean-Luc Godard par Jean-Luc Godard* and Godard issue of *Etudes cinématographiques*, No. 57–61. Examines the similarity between Godard's writing style and the concerns in his early criticism, and his filmmaking style and the themes in his films: e.g., delight in classification and formulae; mixing of humor and seriousness; rejection of closed or constraining systems; critical apprehension of style, which is also a critical apprehension of reality.

1077 Capdenac, Michel. "Petit lexique pour *Weekend.*" *Les Lettres françaises*, No. 1215 (3–9 January), p. 15.

Discusses the elements of Godard's apocalyptic, virulent satire in *Weekend* and deals with Godard's literary and artistic citations, sources, and parallels.

1078 Carson, L.M. Kit. "The American Journey of Jean-Luc Godard." *Eye*, 1, No. 7 (September), 58–61.

Godard's tour at the following places is described: Berkeley-Oakland (March 7), New York (February 21), Austin (March 8), and Kansas City (March 11). Carson reevaluates *Breathless*, describes details about Godard's behavior and reception on the tour, and quotes Godard's statements.

1079 Cervoni, Albert. "*Loin du Viêtnam*: une reflexion politique." *Cinéma 68*, No. 122 (January), pp. 97–99.

Analyzes cinematic styles and political perspectives in the film.

1080 Champlin, Charles. "Godard's *Pierrot le fou* Due at Los Feliz Theater." *Los Angeles Times* (17 November), p. 22.

Brief credits. The events are often parodies, yet there is always a sure sense of cinema, and Godard conveys much "that is in the deepest sense terrifying" about our civilization. Cited at length in 1969, Anon., *Film Facts*, Entry No. 1256.

1081 Cheminée, Philippe. "De *La Chinoise* de Jean-Luc Godard . . . à la Chine de Mao Tse Tung." *Parole et société* (formerly *Christianisme social*), Nos. 1–2, pp. 78–82.

A critical look at Godard's politics.

1082 Christagau, Robert. "Godard: Master of the Clean Home Movie." *Ramparts*, 6, No. 11 (15 June), 59–60.

The critic reviews Godard's impact on the public (the *Breathless* cult), noting that Maoists won't like *La Chinoise*. "The fragility of what moves and heartens Godard about his young cadre" is expressed in his throwaway style (he's rumored to be completing a feature in Super-8, home-movie style). He shows certain contradictions as a given in his bourgeois Maoist youths and examines how each character embodies those contradictions.

1083 Clouzot, Claire. "Godard and the U.S." *Sight and Sound*, 37, No. 3 (Summer), 111–114.

As seen from his films, Godard first admired U.S. culture and films and then rejected Hollywood psychological drama and the "Americanization" of the world. Leacock-Pennebaker, distributors of *La Chinoise*, set up a tour of 20 universities with Godard and the film. He visited only six. Clouzot was his interpreter in Berkeley and reports on the political discussion there. Godard was "non-heroic" and the students, "literal minded."

1084 Cluny, Claude Michel. "Les Megots de Godard." *Nouvelle Revue française* No. 191 (16 August), pp. 668–72.

Neither *Weekend* nor *La Chinoise* scandalized the public. Revolution is a product to be consumed. In Godard's work, citations "contaminate" the dialogue. Other recent films are compared to Godard's.

1085 Cluny, Claude Michel. "Un Week-end loin du Viêtnam." *La Nouvelle Revue française*, 16, No. 183 (18 March), 499–503.

Loin du Viêtnam, the first consciously collective film for its makers, testifies how far intellectuals are from understanding the war; consequently its form is fragmentary, metaphoric, and incomplete. We cannot admit the reality of massacre and Godard refuses the role of voyeur. *Weekend*, however, shows he does not know what to film or even to caricature. Hanoi was right not to let him come.

1086 Cobast, Claude. "Entretien avec Antoine Duhamel." *Image et son: Revue du cinéma*, No. 215 (March), pp. 105–107.

Duhamel contrasts the way he wrote music for *Pierrot le fou* and *Weekend*.

1087 Collet, Jean. "Cache-cache terrible." *A bout de souffle: L'Avant-Scène du cinéma*, No. 79 (March), p. 6.

A bout de souffle "unmasks" its characters, glances, fleeting moments, and the beautiful route toward death during which all the pirouettes of characters and cinematic technique are shown to be possible.

1088 Collet, Jean. *Jean-Luc Godard*. Revised edition. Series Cinema d'aujourd'hui, No. 18. Paris: Editions Seghers. 191 pp.

Trans. 1970, Ciba Vaughan, New York: Crown. See Entry No. 1425. For previous editions, see 1963, Collet, Entry No. 265; 1965, Collet, Entry No. 503; later edition, 1974, Collet, Entry No. 1836. Since I have not been able to have constant access to the 1968 French version, references are annotated under the 1970 English translation.

1089 Collet, Jean. "Weekend." *Etudes*, 328 (April), 555–63.

Godard didn't want to prove anything but wanted to present a nightmare. To multiply the adventures promised by bourgeois advertising, the first "couple" has to disappear; others always take their place—thus the hippie orgie is the realization of the original couple's fantasy. Collet gives a close analysis of each of the major sequences.

1090 Collet, Jean and Aumont, Jacques. "Le Dur Silence des galaxies — *Weekend.*" *Cahiers du cinéma*, No. 199 (March), pp. 60–61.
See 1968, Aumont, Entry No. 1062.

1091 C.[omolli], J.[ean]-L.[ouis]. "Première semaine: l'affair Langlois." *Cahiers du cinéma*, No. 199 (March), p. 33.
A day-by-day account is given of Langlois' dismissal, starting Friday, February 9, and the filmmakers' protest. Police wounded Godard as he led a protest of 3,000 on February 14 in the Trocadero.

1092 Corliss, Richard. "Film Chronicle." *National Review*, 20, No. 26 (2 July), 664–65.
Review of *La Chinoise*. Cited 1972, Green Entry No. 1684.

1093 Cd.[Cornand] A.[ndré]. "*Loin du Viêtnam.*" *Image et son: la saison cinématographique*, No. 219 (September-October), pp. 122–23.
Credits, résumé. Film tries to unite too many diverse elements, but it is politically important.

1094 Crist, Judith. Review of *La Chinoise. New York Magazine* (29 April).
Cited 1968, Anon., *La Chinoise, Film Facts*, Entry No. 1028.

1095 Crist, Judith. Review of *Weekend. New York Magazine* (21 October).
Cited 1968, Anon., *Weekend, Film Facts*, Entry No. 1058.

1096 Davis, R[onald] G. "Movies: *Far from Vietnam.*" *Ramparts*, 6, No. 8 (March), 64–65.
Godard's statement is the most important in the film, indicating how we can "understand the world through Vietnam." "The most important and successful sections are those which are contrived," but the film as a whole is not well crafted to make a political point.

1097 Dawson, Jan. "*One Plus One.*" *Sight and Sound*, 38, No. 1 (Winter), 32–33.
Summarizes the major moments in this film, which she says defines a political-aesthetic line only in terms of rejection. There is no narrative line or even dialectical relation between sound and image. It is an intellectual's "fantasy" denouncing culture and things intellectual. The film and its ideas "demand to be edited and organized," unless it is intended as "a metaphor for England, with extremists of every persuasion coexisting lifelessly side by side."

1098 Dawson, Jan. "*Weekend.*" *Sight and Sound*, 37, No. 3 (Summer), 151–152.
Individual sequences are analyzed to discuss Godard's technique and intent.

The film is poetic, intellectual, and Brechtian. "Nothing in it exists when it's not being looked at," and the "form, or formlessness [is] perfectly fitted to its subject."

1099   Delahaye, Michel. "Fin d'un festival: Cannes." *Cahiers du cinéma*, No. 203 (August), p. 26.
Details Godard's role in the closing of the 1968 Cannes Festival.

1100   Delmas, Jean. "Cette nostalgie révolutionnaire qui s'appelle: chine." *Jeune Cinéma*, No. 32 (September), pp. 10–15.
Criticizes the political confusion in *La Chinoise*, the concentration on personalities, and the weakness and paucity of Godard's ideas.

1101   Dufour, Ferdinand. *"Le Weekend*: un utile exercise de liberté." *Cinéma 68*, No. 126 (May), pp. 94–97.
Weekend is built on drastic switches in rhythm and tone, a mixture of horror and fantasy; but the denunciatory content and the plastic expression always match. Selects key moments in the film and analyzes them in depth.

1102   Durgnat, Raymond. Review of *Far from Vietnam*. *Films and Filming*, 14, No. 5 (February), 20–21.
Cited in Bowles, p. 152.

1103   Ehrenstein, David. "Other Inquisitions: Jean-Luc Godard's *Pierrot le fou." Jean-Luc Godard: A Critical Anthology*. Ed. Toby Mussman. New York: E.P. Dutton. Pp. 221–231.
The film takes up and finds cinematic ways to express a number of romantic themes: the outsider, the last and ultimate couple, the death of love, the diary, the doppelgänger, despair, and the sea.

1104   Ehrenstein, David and Blum, Peter. "Two or Three Things We Know About Godard." *December*, 10, No. 1, 164–73.
Provides a close reading of *Pierrot le fou* and *Masculine-Feminine*, primarily in terms of their romantic themes. "The easy point-making effects of montage are bypassed [in *Masculine-Feminine*], just as those of narrative have been." Analyzes the relation between cinematography and narrative dislocation, on the one hand, and Godard's political concerns, on the other, in *Made in U.S.A.* and *Two or Three Things I Know about Her*. His conclusions are that Paula is maintained by a sense of morality in the former film and that Godard finally retreats into silence. "a state of aesthetic bliss," at the end of the latter.

1105   Eliscu, Lita. "Vietnam Déjà Vu: A Review of Godard's *La Chinoise*." *Evergreen Review*, 12, No. 56 (July), 66–68.
Godard uses a brilliant, Cubist technique but is totally cool and intellectual about his subject. "Technique is all" in *La Chinoise*.

1106   Ellison, Harlan. Review of *Les Carabiniers*. *Cinema*, 4, No. 3 (Fall), 45.
Cited in Bowles, p. 71.

1107   Farber, Manny. *"La Chinoise." Artforum*, 7 (Summer).
La Chinoise irritates with its puerile acting, "pettily pendantic debates," and

out of date "modern painting devices." *Les Carabiniers* is a primeval, pastoral comedy, with throwbacks to Sennett and many other directors. It has "beautiful, bleak photography" and is "likeable and terrestrial." Reprinted 1971 as *"La Chinoise* and *Belle de jour,"* *Negative Space,* Entry No. 1569.

1108 Farber, Manny. "The Films of Jean-Luc Godard." *Artforum,* 7, No. 2 (October), 58–61.

Godard starts his films with the "basic intellectual puzzle pretty well set in his mind," but "the form and manner of execution changes totally with each film. The unique style of each film is described. Godard's films have the following constants: talkiness, boredom, ping-pong motion, a Holden Caufield hero, mockery, moralizing, and dissociation. The critic discusses Godard's formal patterning, his use of factors, and his contribution to film history. Reprinted 1971, Farber, Entry No. 1569.

1109 Federman, Raymond. "Jean-Luc Godard and Americanism." *Film Heritage,* 3, No. 3 (Spring), 1–10, 48.

Analyzes how Godard challenges these aspects of U.S. cultural imperialism: our exportation of U.S. goods and mores; the U.S. cinema's *mythos* and spectacle; love of bigness; "sub-urbanization"; personal shallowness, alienation, and prostitution resulting from the pressure to imitate U.S. ways; and international political violence and manipulation.

1110 Finler, Joel. "L'Affaire Godard." *International Times* (13–31 December), p. 24.

Discusses Godard's appearance at the National Film Theater, London. The producers had added a new ending, so Godard was having his version simultaneously screened at the more radical Open Festival. He asked the NFT audience not to see the film and to donate their money to Eldridge Cleaver. He infuriated them and ended up punching producer Ian Quarrier. Finler weighs the complications on all sides in this scandal over *One Plus One.*

1111 Gauteur, Claude. "Godard et ses critiques." *Image et son: Revue du cinéma,* No. 213 (February), pp. 88–94.

The critic provides an extensive bibliography of the reviews of Godard films from French periodicals. Each is identified as pro or con or mixed.

1112 G.[authier], G.[uy]. *"La Chinoise."* *Image et son: La Saison cinématographique,* No. 219 (September-October), pp. 37–38.

Brief credits. Godard's political immaturity keeps us from totally accepting this otherwise artistically accomplished and prophetic film. The critic contrasts reactions on first viewing the film and on seeing it after May '68. First it just seemed a portrait of adolescent rebellion; later, a portrayal of a "radically new attitude toward the old world."

1113 Genêt. "Letter from Paris: January 24." *New Yorker,* 43, No. 50 (3 February), pp. 80–81.

Benjamin has beauty, sensuality, and perfect taste; the opposite is true of *Weekend.* Criticizes the "fetishization" of Godard by his admirers. A brief plot summary of *Weekend* is given. Godard totally avoids offering any "sane, constructive solutions in this his maddest film."

1114 Gilliatt Penelope. "The Folly of Soldiers." *New Yorker*, 44 (11 May), 157–60.
> War needs stupid men to "do the top brass' dirty work" and make a profit for the capitalists." *Les Carabiniers* is a Brechtian film about false consciousness and Godard here is a "great intellectual cartoonist . . . who goad[s] by deforming the familiar and by pretending callousness." Godard implicitly comments on language, newspaper photography, and cinema. Reprinted 1969 Gilliatt, Entry No. 1269. Excerpts reprinted and analyzed in 1969, Bobker, Entry No. 1270.

1115 Goldwasser, N. "*Made in U.S.A.:* The Paper Tiger in Your Tank." *Cineaste*, 1, No. 4 (Spring), 16–18.
> Cited in Bowles, p. 303.

1116 Greenspun, Roger. "*Les Carabiniers.*" *New York Free Press* (16 May), pp. 9–10.
> Brief credits. Discusses Godard's reputation at the New York Film Festival and his scanty showings in New York. Also discusses Renata Adler as a critic and notes how favorable *Times* reviews helped *Les Carabiniers*, a film with much to say both about the class struggle and about how movies work.

1117 Greenspun, Roger. "*La Chinoise.*" *New York Free Press*, No. 17 (18 May), pp. 8 and 10.
> "Godard supresses character in favor of ideas" in a misanthropic way. All the "political talk, capsule histories of art and literature, and graphic-arts demonstrations" give *La Chinoise* "a kind of defensive busyness." This film is "a calculated and sentimental manipulation of youth."

1118 Greenspun, Roger. "Movies: *Weekend.*" *New York Free Press*, 1, No. 41 (17 October), 8.
> Brief credits. The interruptions, which other critics found most intrusive in the latter half of *Weekend*, are significant dislocations in the film's movement from "bourgeois to antibourgeois." They are bold dramatic lies, especially the monologues, which break the fiction to wonderfully redirect it. Reprinted 1972, Brown, Entry No. 1658.

1119 Guerlain, Quentin. "*La Chinoise*: A New Film by Jean-Luc Godard." *Cinema*, 4, No. 1 (Spring), 34–35.
> Cited 1972, Green, Entry No. 1684.

1120 Guerlain, Quentin. "*Made in U.S.A.*" *Cinema*, 4, No. 1 (Spring), 50.
> Cited 1972, Green, Entry No. 1684.

1121 Haskell, Molly. "Film Notes." *Cahiers du Cinema in English*, No. 9 (March), pp. 62–64.
> Describes *Les Carabiniers*, where Godard's portrayal of war is a "masterpiece of ugliness and irony."

1122 Haskell, Molly. "Omegaville." *Film Heritage*, 3, No. 3 (Spring), 23–26, 30.
> Godard is like a New Novelist. "*Two or Three Things* is as disinfected of cruelty

as it is devoid of pleasure. As an essay it lacks persuasiveness, as an exercise, surprise. As a personal statement, it is deviously impersonal . . ."

1123 Hatch, Robert. "Films." *The Nation*, 206, No. 16 (15 April), 517–18.
The reviewer admires the aesthetics of *La Chinoise* and rejects the politics. It is "an ideology-induced 'trip' experienced by a group of students." The characters are "extraordinarily real—vulnerable, honorable, and frightening."

1124 Hatch, Robert. "Films." *The Nation*, 206, No. 20 (13 May), 645–46.
Les Carabiniers is like an amateur movie made about characters living at the city dump. The film lacks zest, and the distanciation is not Brechtian because the viewers are not made to understand themselves or modern war "through the fractures of the illusion."

1125 Henahan, Donald. "Boos Great Film by Godard Here." *New York Times* (30 December), p. 26.
Audience booed and hissed *A Film like Any Other*. The house manager of Philharmonic Hall, against the will of Leacock-Pennebaker's distribution manager, offered the audience their $2.50 ticket price back. Only 100 of the 1,000 there stayed to see the second reel.

1126 Hobson, Harold. "Putting Out Its Tongue." *Christian Science Monitor* (29 July).
In London, the new quarters of the Institute of Contemporary Arts opened up with *Weekend*. "This, says Godard, is bourgeois society; and the ICA smiles approvingly."

1127 Houston, Penelope. "The Muddle Is the Message." *Spectator*, 220 No. 7280 (5 January), 17.
Review of *Far from Vietnam*. "One's left wondering about the film's collective voice, . . . and whether it's design or accident that allows this eccentric devaluation of the currency of dissent."

1128 Houston, Penelope. "The Show Must Come Off." *Spectator*, 220, No. 7300 (24 May), 713.
The Cannes Festival closing indicates the politicization of French directors and their dissatisfaction with French bureaucratic cultural structures, yet they get no more than emotional support from international directors and producers who need the festival as a marketplace. Gives a detailed, unsympathetic, eyewitness account of the closing.

1129 Jussawalla, Adil. "Kindly Leave the Stage." *The Listener* (12 December).
Godard's appearance at the NFT is reported on.

1130 Kael, Pauline. *"Band of Outsiders." Kiss, Kiss, Bang, Bang.* Boston: Little, Brown. Pp. 112–15. Reissued 1969. Bantam Books. New York: Grossett and Dunlap. Pp. 137–41.
Reprinted from 1966, Kael, Entry No. 708.

1131 Kael, Pauline. *"Masculine-Feminine." Kiss Kiss Bang Bang.* Boston:

Little, Brown. Pp. 127–30. Reissued 1969. Bantam Books. Grossett & Dunlap. Pp. 155–59.

Discusses the modern rituals of courtship and the nuances of the personal relations in *Masculine-Feminine*. "The theme is the fresh beauty of youth amidst the flimsiness of pop culture and pop politics." Notes the "Americanization," the seemingly extraneous episodes, easy sex vs. feminine mystery, and "talk as a form of preliminary sex play." Reprinted from 1966, Kael, Entry No. 708. Also in 1970, Kael, Entry No. 1466.

1132 Kael, Pauline. "A Minority Movie." *New Yorker*, 44 (6 April) 156–66.

Godard intuitively seizes and dramatizes new social elements, projecting his feelings on them. He often irritates by using a "shorthand" style and by assuming the audience's intellectual involvement, e.g., in his use of verbal humor, Brechtian distanciation devices, the *acte gratuit*, and digressions about literature, politics and film. In *La Chinoise*, Godard satirizes his characters' politics and relationships. An important filmmaker today, Godard makes his pop art graphic style serve his social themes. Reprinted 1969, Kael, Entry No. 1309; 1970, Kael, Entry No. 1464.

1133 Kael, Pauline. "Movie Brutalists." *Kiss Kiss Bang Bang*. Boston: Little, Brown, Pp. 14–17. Re-issued 1969. Bantam Books: Grossett & Dunlap. Pp. 15–24.

Reprinted from 1966, Kael, Entry No. 709.

1134 Kael, Pauline. "Weekend in Hell." *New Yorker*, 44 (5 October), 141–45.

Godard goes beyond didacticism in *Weekend* to reach a "truly apocalyptic" fervor and rage. Many of the "big scenes" are brilliant; others are flops — including the Mozart musicale, the garbage men's speeches, the killing of a real pig, and the "prattling of figures from literature." Godard is to film as Joyce is to literature. When others try to follow him they can't. "It's the strength of his own sensibility that gives his techniques excitement." Reprinted 1969, Kael, Entry No. 1310; 1970, Kael, Entry No. 1465.

1135 Kauffmann, Stanley. "Stanley Kauffmann on Films: Activism Can Be Fun." *New Republic*, 158 (27 April), 22 and 39.

Godard plays with ideas, literature, cinematic devices, art, suicide, murder, and politics in *La Chinoise*. The critic discusses the film's characterization and acting, as well as its cinematography, in terms of Godard's usual style. The content is either an irresponsible treatment of or an "inconsequential divertissement on a serious theme." Reprinted 1971, Kauffmann, Entry No. 1588.

1136 Kauffmann, Stanley. "Stanley Kauffmann on Films: The Long Weekend." *New Republic*, 159 (19 October), 28 and 40.

Weekend is reviewed as part of 6th New York Film Festival. Kauffmann praises Sontag's essay in *Partisan Review* but finds Godard "irresponsible in his use of explosive political ideas and callow in his literary display." Sontag tries to give order to Godard's method, which is "essentially impulsive and whimsical." The improvisation in *Weekend* grows tired about halfway through the film. Reprinted 1971, Kauffmann, Entry No. 1588.

1137 Kauffmann, Stanley. "Stanley Kauffmann on Films: Tell the Real Lies." *New Republic*, 158 (2 March), 26 and 37.

Far from Vietnam, shown at the last New York Film Festival, was "blithe about hard political issues," for it "assumed that the problem of communism only bothers squares."

1138 Kauffmann, Stanley. "Stanley Kauffmann on Films: War—Fact and Fancy." *New Republic*, 158 (1 June), 26 and 41.
Godard made *Les Carabiniers* "in a childlike way, with few actors, minimum verisimilitude, fabulist simplicity, and home-movie techniques." He uses many Brechtian devices, but simplistically, for he tells us nothing we don't know about war. Reprinted 1971, Kauffmann, Entry No. 1588.

1139 Kernan, Margot. "*Made in U.S.A.*: Jean-Luc Godard's Walt Disney Movie." *Film Heritage*, 3, No. 3 (Spring), 31–34.
Discusses the following aspects of the film: fascinating "pop surfaces," irritating literary affectations, "bits of amusing dialogue," billboards and Disney — "the familiar landscape of fantasy," "splendid camerawork," shallow and self-conscious Brechtianism, and flimsy philosophy and politics.

1140 Knight, Arthur. "Jean-Luc Godard." *Saturday Review* (30 November). Godard has the rare ability to get through to today's youth.
Pierrot le fou is uneven, elusive, contemporary, poetic, and sensual.

1141 Kotlowitz, Robert. "Films: Short Takes." *Harpers*, 237, No. 1418 (July), 108–109.
Favorably describes the relations among the characters of *La Chinoise* and Godard's cinematic technique. The characters' "sharp exchanges . . . suggest a whole state of mind, of living. . . . They mean what they say, they make things happen."

1142 Lambert, Gavin. "*La Chinoise*." *Cinema*, 4, No. 2 (Summer), 67.
Cited 1972, Green, No. 1684.

1143 Lefèvre, Raymond. "*La Chinoise*: l'anti *Weekend*." *Cinéma 68*. No. 126 (May), pp. 92–93.
Brief credits. Left-wing "verbal diarrhea," visual austerity, and extreme Brechtian distanciation characterize this film. In content and style, it is the dialectical opposite of *Weekend*.

1144 Lefèvre, Raymond. "*Week-End*." *Image et son: Revue du cinéma*, No. 213 (February), pp. 117–121.
Weekend is the most beautiful horrible film, poetic crazy film, comic tragic film. It is "inventive, lucid, cynical, insolent." Godard shows the class basis of eroticism, weekend exoduses, and his protagonists' psychology. In the provinces the world is totally crazy, inhabited by symbolic or allegorical characters.

1145 Lerman, L. "International Movie Report." *Mademoiselle*, 66 (January), 62–65.
Cited *Reader's Guide*, 27 (March 1967–February 1968), 772.

1146   Lottman, Herbert R. "Cinema Verite: Jean-Luc Godard." *Columbia University Forum*, 11, No. 1 (Spring), 23–29.
   Cited 1972, Green, Entry No. 1684.

1147   MacBean, James Roy. "Godard's *Week-End*, or the Self-Critical Cinema of Cruelty." *Film Quarterly*, 22, No. 2 (Winter), 35–43.
   The film pushes spectacle to its limit and uses it for ritual (Godard is compared to Artaud) and for revolutionizing the way we look at art and at the relation between art and life (Godard is compared to Brecht). Cannibalism, consumerism, alienation, self-destructiveness, and empty sexual contact—Godard depicts all as real or symbolic traits of the bourgeoisie. This film is similar to *Les Carabiniers* in that the passage from civilization to barbarism is seen as linked to our human concern with images of things. Reprinted 1975, MacBean, Entry No. 1907.

1148   MacBean, James Roy. "Politics and Poetry in Two Recent Films by Godard." *Film Quarterly*, 21, No. 4 (Summer), 14–20.
   In *Two or Three Things* the modern city is seen as flooding us with visual and verbal signs that threaten to "drown what is real." The film taxes the audience's aural endurance. In the film Godard examines the cinematic means needed to transpose a social analysis into art. Compares *La Chinoise* to *Hamlet* and provides a close analysis of key sequences. There Godard depicts the infantile excesses of characters who are committed to a political stand, one with which both he and the audience sympathize. Reprinted 1975, MacBean, Entry No. 1907.

1149   Manchel, Frank. Review of Roud's *Godard*. *Film Society Review*, May, p. 39.
   Brief mention of the book.

1150   Marchi, Bruno de. "Appunti su Godard." *Vita e pensiero*, 51, No. 1 (January), 45–51.
   Cited 1972, Brown, Entry No. 1657.

1151   Matharan de Potenze, Sylvia. "*Los Carabineros (Les Carabiniers*, Francia, 1963)." *Criterio*, 91, No. 1550 (27 June), p. 439.
   This year we can see all the previously unseen Godard films. *Les Carabiniers* reveals war to be as stupid, violent, and passionless as the two protagonists.

1152   Mauriac, Claude. "Le Film que je n'ai pas tourné." *Le Figaro littéraire*, No. 1154 (14–23 June), p. 39.
   Every filmmaker was out filming during the May events (photo of Godard, May 7, Blvd. St. Germain). Mauriac tells of his experiences on the streets.

1153   Mauriac, Claude. "*Week-End*." *Le Figaro littéraire*, No. 1135 (15–21 January), pp. 34–35.
   A conversation about the film, overheard in a restaurant, is cited at length. No one was watching TV there till an interview with *Weekend*'s actors came on; then everyone was silent. Godard is the only filmmaker in France that gets that much attention—either admiration or disapproval.

1154 Mayersberg, Paul. "Godard's Last Weekend." *New Society*, No. 301 (4 July), p. 23.

Offers an aesthetic and thematic explication of the film. "Godard's anti-romance of the road is, like most films with a journey structure, preoccupied with landscape."

1155 McFadden, Patrick. *"Le Petit Soldat & Les Carabiniers."* Film Society *Review* (March), pp. 19–22.

Credits. Godard is a political agnostic and these two films, "little messages of desperation," comment on the "intellectual agonies that shook Europe after the collapse of France in the 1940's. . . . Godard does not feel an *a priori* responsibility for all men; they are *not* his brothers."

1156 Medjuck, Joe. *"Weekend." Take One*, 1, No. 11.

This is the most violent film yet made. It is intellectual, sparse in its editing, masterful in its long takes.

1157 M.[illar], G.[avin] O. *"Week-End*, France/Italy, 1967." *Monthly Film Bulletin*, 35 (August), 116–117.

Credits, plot summary. Godard's social pessimism sees death as "the logical end of animal competition."

1158 Millar, Gavin and Reisz, Karel. "Personal Cinema in the Sixties: Jean-Luc Godard." *The Technique of Film Editing.* 2nd Ed. London: Focal Press. New York: Hastings House. Pp. 345–58.

See 1968, Reisz, Entry No. 1179.

1159 Milne, Tom. "Godard's Barbarians." *The Observer*, Review (7 July).

The couple's actions in *Weekend* are described, as are the switches in tone. Godard's rage and satire is as sharp and savage as Swift's.

1160 Monréal, Guy. "Qui n'a pas son petit Godard?" *L'Express* (15–21 July), pp. 51–52.

Summarizes Godard's activist roles, tells the difficulties in filming *One Plus One*, and describes the production, cost and content of the *cinétracts*, shot in July. Describes an omitted "drama" that was to be part of *One Plus One*.

1161 Morgenstern, Joseph. "The Frowzy War." *Newsweek*, 71 (13 May), 98.

Antiwar films have "no value as a cautionary tale." *Les Carabiniers* wisely deflates itself as it deflates war, making its points with clarity but in an "uncompromisingly comic" way. It combines hyperbole with "tawdry little episodes."

1162 M[orgenstern], J[oseph]. "The Godard Generation." *Newsweek*, 71, No. 16 (15 April), 100 and 103.

Like *The Graduate*, *La Chinoise* is a "painfully funny" picture of today's youth who are yearning for "simplicity, purity, and a sense of purpose." Godard uses "logorrhea as a comic device," and his vignettes "provide us with unexpected new insights into reality."

1163 Mosk[owitz, Gene]. *"Les Carabiniers* (French-Italo)." *Variety* (24 April).

Reprinted in part from June 19, 1963 (Entry No. 309), when reviewed by Mosk in Paris. The film is good for Godard buffs, shows visual know-how, and offers a biting look at humanity.

1164 Mosk[owitz, Gene]. *"Le Weekend* (French-Color)." *Variety* (10 January), pp. 6 and 20.
Brief credits. This technically brilliant picture has just too much poured into it. After a promising first part, it turns into a series of adventures. It needs more coherence and less verbiage.

1165 Mussman, Toby. "Chronology and Filmography of Jean-Luc Godard." *Jean-Luc Godard: A Critical Anthology.* Ed. Toby Mussman. New York: E.P. Dutton, Pp. 310–317.
Brief statements about Godard's life and a complete filmography are given by year from 1930 through 1967 (*Weekend*).

1166 Mussman, Toby. "Duality, Repetition, Chance, the Unknown, Infinity." *Jean-Luc Godard: A Critical Anthology,* Ed. Toby Mussman. New York: E.P. Dutton. Pp. 300–308.
Analyzes Godard as a modernist artist and finds Godard's technique appropriate for "mirroring" psychic conditions in the modern world.

1167 Mussman, Toby. "Introductory Notes." *Jean-Luc Godard: A Critical Anthology.* Ed. Mussman. New York: E.P. Dutton. Pp. 11–23.
Cited as "excerpts from a longer essay," but no source given. Elements of analysis, reflection, and action are always found in Godard's aesthetic. He is a "classicist" of the cinema, balanced between seriousness and humor, personal and historical statement. His films demand re-viewing and challenge the distinctions many critics draw between art, intellectuality, and entertainment.

1168 Mussman, Toby, ed. *Jean-Luc Godard, A Critical Anthology.* New York: E.P. Dutton. 319 pp.
This important early anthology brings together critical articles from *Cahiers du cinéma* in English, interviews with Godard, and analyses of individual films. Each article is annotated here under the date of its original appearance.

1169 Mussman, Toby. "Notes on *Contempt." Jean-Luc Godard; A Critical Anthology.* Ed. Mussman. New York: E.P. Dutton. Pp. 152–69.
This in-depth analysis of the film deals primarily with Paul's and Camille's characterization and the "lifelike" treatment of the theme: mistrust destroying an ideal love.

1170 Narboni, Jean, ed. *Jean-Luc Godard par Jean-Luc Godard: articles, essais, entretiens.* By Jean-Luc Godard. Collection *Cahiers du cinéma.* Paris: Pierre Belfond. 414 pp.
Introduction and notes by Narboni. Filmography. See also 1968, Godard, Entry No. 2263; 1972, Milne, Entry No. 1713.

1171 Nusser, Richard. *"Weekend." After Dark* (December), p. 60.
Godard has turned cinema into an effective vehicle for social criticism both by

his imaginative use of the medium and by his devastating portrait of contemporary bourgeois society.

1172 Pierre, Michel, et al. "Godard vu par des enfants de Marx (sans Coca-Cola)." *Jeune cinéma*, No. 31 (May), pp. 16–21.

Michel Pierre, Pierre Saint-Germain, and Patricia Vermeren, university students at Reims, revaluate Godard and discuss most of the political issues raised by his films (through *Weekend*) in the light of their own recent politicization. Godard's use of Brechtian techniques comes under fire because his political cinema "is not under the command of a clearly defined ideology."

1173 Pollack-Lederer, Jacques. "Jean-Luc Godard dans la modernité." *Les Temps modernes*, 23, No. 262 (March), 1558–89.

Godard's modernism is attacked at length from a left perspective. Modernism merely appropriates everything superficially on the level of the present and does not show reality as the intersection of real conflicts and contradictions, especially class conflicts. Modern artists can only portray capitalism in terms of the transformations successively unfolding across its surface. Society's real processes, and history itself, thus remain invisible.

1174 Polt, Harriet R. *"Masculine-Feminine." Film Society Review*, February, pp. 15–17.

Godard has taken a close look at the sixties, but his weaknesses are shallowness and not going beyond a "masterly revelation of egoistic alienation." *Masculine-Feminine* has a weak theme but is "fun."

1175 Powell, Dilys. "The Manic Side of Godard." *Sunday Times* (7 July).

Weekend is a fantasy of violence which goes too far, especially in the killing of the goose and pig. "Horror at violence can be aroused without resort to actual violence."

1176 Prédal, René. "A Cannes, samedi 18 Mai." *Jeune cinéma*, No. 32 (September), pp. 17–18.

Godard's role in halting the Cannes Festival is noted briefly.

1177 Price, James. "Mod Apocalypse." *Spectator*, 221, No. 7307 (12 July), 62.

Summarizes *Weekend's* plot. Godard attacks Western materialism but treats key figures — the black, the Algerian, and the hippies — ambiguously. He aims to shock and repel as he "insists on our either rejecting Western civilization or rejecting this film."

1178 R., A. "The Godard Revolution: La Révolution de Godard." Program Notes, Canadian National Film Theater, Ottawa (November-December), 15 pp.

A film series was planned to show Godard's films paired with films that influenced him. The program notes briefly cite interviews with Godard and articles about the films.

1179 Reisz, Karel, and Millar, Gavin. "Personal Cinema in the Sixties:

Jean-Luc Godard." *The Technique of Film Editing*. 2nd ed. London: Focal Press. New York: Hastings House. Pp. 345–358.

In-depth examination of Godard's editing technique in the context of New Wave film style.

1180 Rondolino, Gianni. "I festival dell'autunno-Bergamo: si al film di ricera." *Bianco e nero*, 29, No. 1-2 (January-February), 91–93.

Praising review of *Deux ou trois choses*, shown at Bergamo Film Festival.

1181 [Ropars-] W.[uilleumier], M.[arie]-C.[laire]. "Le Cru et le cuit." *Esprit*, 33, No. 3 (March), 524–26.

This close formal reading of *Weekend* analyzes its determinant structures and its mythic dimension, seen in Lévi-Strauss' terms. "It is less a matter of denouncing, in a purely intellectual operation, the myths of occidental civilization than of plunging into that civilization via a purely aesthetic operation, into a mythic world that reveals that civilization to itself."

1182 [Ropars-] W.[uilleumier], M.[arie]-C.[laire]. *"Loin du Viêtnam."* *Esprit*, 33, No. 4, 700–703.

Each of the sections is described and the author identified. The film shows us our distance from the war and how hard it is to talk about the real situation there; it asks us to measure our involvement with Vietnam. Reprinted 1970, Ropars-Wuilleumier, Entry No. 1532.

1183 Rosenbaum, Jon. "Cities and Carwrecks: Godard." *Film Society Review*, 4, No. 2 (October), 38–44.

Brief credits for *Deux ou trois choses* and *Weekend*. *Deux ou trois choses* is a "mosaic," an antifilm, an investigation, and a statement of the gap between what Godard would like to film — his cosmic vision — and what he can do. *Weekend* is a "shocking" fable (plot summary given), shows life as a "prison," and creatively evaluates and revitalizes film history.

1184 Rosenbaum, Jon. *"Jean-Luc Godard: A Critical Anthology*, Edited by Toby Mussman." *Film Society Review*, 4, No. 4 (December), 42–43.

Mussman's book is better than Roud's or Cameron's but suffers from mistranslations, mislabeling of stills, use of original rather than updated pieces (e.g., Sontag on *Vivre sa vie)*, and generally restricted sources. The material by and interviews with Godard are valuable, as are some of the individual reviews. Yet the reviewers oversimplify issues rather than understand Godard's unique and original sense of film history.

1185 Rossell, Deac. "Flashing Back in Godard Duo about Soldiering." *Boston After Dark* (1 January), p. 12.

Review of *Le Petit Soldat* and *Les Carabiniers* finds Godard to be a Calvinist, an exponent of despair.

1186 Roud, Richard. "Cannes '68." *Sight and Sound*, 37, No. 3 (Summer), 115–117.

Important details are given about the mood of the festival and why it was shut down by Truffaut, Godard, Lelouch, and Berri.

1187 Roud, Richard. "The Films of Jean-Luc Godard: A Lecture." Museum of Modern Art, N.Y. (31 January).

Godard has redefined the medium of cinema. Roud discusses documentary and fiction and Lumière and Méliès. He relates the fate of deMaupassant's *La Femme coquette* in Godard's early short and its sequel (and conclusion) as the film-within-the-film in *Masculin-Féminin*. Godard's interest in and unique editing of movement can be seen in clips of Karina dancing. Godard always uses professional actors. Roud analyzes the interaction between realism and formal innovation and pays close attention to *Deux ou trois choses*, finding it Godard's best film — saying "a lot" and having a satisfying pattern which does not so much express the content as structure it.

In a question and answer period, Roud discusses Godard's problems with censors, his lawsuit with a U.S. novelist over *Made in U.S.A.*, his increasing politicization, his use of color and sound and cinemascope, and his "banality."

The transcript of the interview, available from the Museum of Modern Art, is uncorrected and full of misspellings, often hard to read.

1188 Roud, Richard. "Godard on Film" Museum of Modern Art announcement for film series running from 15 February to 18 February.

The series showed Godard's films alongside those of directors who influenced him or those which provide a contrasting treatment of a similar theme.

1189 Roud, Richard. *"One Plus One." Sight and Sound*, 37, No. 4 (Autumn).

A brief report is given on the financing and shooting of the film. Godard shot the Rolling Stones sequence in June, seemingly abandoned the film, but returned in the third week of July to film the sequences in Battersea.

1190 Sachs, C. "Days in May: A Chronicle of the Events at This year's Cannes Festival." *Cinema*, 4, No. 3 (Fall), 6–12.

Cited 1968, *Guide to Performing Arts*, p. 144.

1191 Salachas, Gilbert. *"Loin du Viêtnam." Téléciné*, No. 139 (February), pp. 32–33.

Brief credits. A brief, favorable review of this "polyphonic" film is followed by citations of reviews in *Combat, France nouvelle, Témoignage chrétien*, and *L'Humanité*.

1192 Salachas, Gilbert. "Week-End." *Téléciné*, No. 139 (February), p. 33.

Brief credits. Godard vomits up a whole epoch in this excessive, often nauseating, and sometimes enigmatic film. Reviews are cited from *Télérama* and *Témoignage chrétien*.

1193 Salmaggi, Robert. *"The Married Woman."* New York *Herald Tribune* (17 August).

Brief credits and review.

1194 Sarris, Andrew. "Film: The Illusion of Naturalism." *Drama Review/TDR*, 13, No. 2 (Winter), 108–12.

Sarris begins his essay with a discussion of the conversation about Lumière and Méliès from *La Chinoise* and concludes that "the fundamental motivation of Naturalism in the cinema is to escape the influence of theater; yet, ironically, there is a growing nostalgia among knowledgeable film aestheticians for direct sound and all it implies of the essential theatricality of the cinema." Reprinted 1973, Sarris, Entry No. 1813.

1195 Sarris, Andrew. "Films." *Village Voice* (4 April).
La Chinoise has charm and shows what Godard feels, unlike his other recent films. Godard reveals the chasm between thought and action and uses Anne Wiazemsky for her facility in expressing "the inexorable intolerance of youth." Reprinted 1969, Sarris and Alpert, Entry No. 1338. Reprinted 1970, Sarris, Entry No. 1507.

1196 Sarris, Andrew. "Films." *Village Voice* (23 May).
Sarris describes the origins of the phrase, "Waiting for Godard," the fame of Godard at the Montreal Film Festival in 1963, where *Les Carabiniers* was screened along with *Le Petit Soldat*, and the reluctance of the New York critical establishment to back Godard. *Les Carabiniers* uses antiquarianism to cover Godard's doubts about "the continuing originality of his style." It also reveals Godard's basically anal, infantile personality.

1197 Sarris, Andrew. "Films." *Village Voice* (21 November), pp. 51–52.
Weekend has many "admirable set pieces," but the characters are treated with contempt and the ending is weak. Thematically the film suffers from "witless bourgeois baiting and coy Pirandellianism." Godard's melancholy reveals that his romantic sensibility is located somewhere before the revolution. Reprinted 1969, Sarris, Entry No. 1339. Reprinted 1970, Sarris, Entry No. 1507.

1198 Sarris, Andrew. "Jean-Luc vs. Saint Jean." *Film Heritage*, 3, No. 3 (Spring), 27–30.
Notes regretfully the following changes of emphases in Godard's work — from love of cinema to rejection of Hollywood, emotion to passivity, and joyful experimentation to boring "exercises in self-flagellation."

1199 Schickel, Richard. "The Trying Genius of M. Godard." *Life*, 64, No. 15 (12 April), 12.
Godard's reputation and his recurrent theme of the True Believers is noted. The teens in *La Chinoise* are absurd creatures portrayed in a realistic, comic, and chilling way. Godard's style is unseductive and he tries to keep you constantly "off balance." Reprinted 1972, Schickel, Entry No. 1728, with an afterthought.

1200 Schlesinger, Arthur, Jr. "*Weekend.*" *Vogue*, 152 (15 September), 74.
Cited *Reader's Guide*, 28 (March 1968-February 1969), 783.

1201 Segal, Abraham. "Jean-Luc Godard: montage à partir d'un entretien avec Jean-Luc Godard." *Image et son: Revue du cinéma*, No. 215 (March), pp. 72–82.
An interview with Godard, conducted January 24, 1968, is printed in bold type, without the questions. Segal intersperses it with quotations from various authors and from Godard's films. In the interview Godard discusses how he manipulates sound and how he writes dialogue and directs the actors' lines. He would like to read a novel on film and to film all the ideas about and forms of theater in a project on *Pour Lucrèce*. He discusses his interests in language, in

separating sound from image, and translation. He describes his use of music, the technical devices he favors, and his plans for a forthcoming film based mainly on sound, *Le Gai Savoir.*

1202 Sequin, Louis, "L'Art du scruple: *Loin du Viêtnam.*" *Positif,* No. 93 (March, pp. 10–15.
Complete credits for film. Long review of the film finds Godard's section the poorest.

1203 S.[eguin], L.[ouis]. "Trouvé, certes, mais où?" *Positif,* No. 93 (March), pp. 39–42.
Credits for *Weekend.* Godard's films are like a Mass, a ritual that is always the same and demands belief in the cult. Always "immediately readible," Godard gives us the same banal obsessions from Céline to Mao, from prostitution to married life. Analyzes *Weekend* and scathingly dismisses all its elements, referring to other better films.

1204 Sémeniako, Michel. "Tourner avec Godard." *Travelling J* (Lausanne), No. 21 (May-July), pp. 13–16.
The actor who played Henri in *La Chinoise* writes on Godard. Godard's only way of communicating with the world is through film, and he uses whatever's around in his films. Gives a detailed description of Godard's direction, shooting method (he rarely looked through the viewfinder, having complete confidence in Coutard), and editing (to remove anything "explanatory"). Much gossipy information about Godard's habits is given. (The author of article is listed as Sémeniako, but it seems to be the text of an interview, written in prose form by François Albèra.)

1205 Sheed, Wilfred. "Films." *Esquire,* 69, No. 1 (January), 24.
Les Carabiniers, which appeared at the New York Film Festival, is a weary, banal war movie.

1206 Sheed, Wilfred. "Films." *Esquire,* 69, No. 6 (June), 56–58.
Godard appeared among a group of critics discussing his work at a round table discussion in New York, where he mainly attacked the imperialism of "American-type movies." Sheed liked the idea behind *La Chinoise* but felt Godard treated his characters so facetiously that they were as grotesque as any villains.

1207 Siegel, Joel E. "Between Art and Life: The Films of Jean-Luc Godard." *Film Heritage,* 3, No. 3 (Spring), 11–22, 47, 48.
Discusses the following aspects of Godard's work: critical reception; the films' modernism, poetry, emotion, and honesty; abstraction and ideas; pretentious cultural illusions; failures (e.g., *The Married Woman* and *Alphaville* are "too tidy"); and the best, most elusive films — two of which, *Band of Outsiders* and *Contempt,* are analyzed in detail.

1208 Simon, John. "Bull in the China Shop." *Film Heritage,* 3, No. 3 (Spring), pp. 35–47.
A briefer version of this appeared as "Sugar , Spice and Speciousness." *The New Leader,* May 6, 1968 (Entry No. 1211). Reprinted with postscript added after "student unrest in France," 1971, Simon, Entry No. 1618.

La Chinoise suffers from visual and verbal "logorrhea" and false and unbelievable characters, dialogue, and situations. Godard is not an essayist because he lacks a point of view — we do not know whether to take the characters and their politics seriously or find them in consequential. Simon dislikes the film's pace and non sequiturs, the interviews, the collegiate humor, the lack of a story, the reference to yet no real understanding of cultural figures, the abuse of the French language, and the bad acting.

1209 Simon, John. "The Question of Violence." *New York Times* (17 March), Sec. II, p. 17.
Pierrot le fou is plotless, its characters mindless and feelingless, and its ending ridiculous. Because he doesn't know "where he's going with his scene, his film, his oeuvre," Godard pretentiously and vacuously goes off in all directions at once. Reprinted 1970, Collet, Entry No. 1425.

1210 Simon, John. Review of Roud's *Godard. Book World* (26 May), p. 7.
Roud's *Godard* is "frilly, pretentious, ill-written, and foolish" and gives "an idea of what, nowadays, passes for film criticism."

1211 Simon, John. "Sugar, Spice, and Speciousness." *New Leader*, 51, No. 10 (6 May), 24–26.
Finds *La Chinoise* formless. (He describes three main types of scenes.) Godard simultaneously writes and shouts contradictory political messages at the audience. Briefer version of 1968, Simon, *Film Heritage*, Entry No. 1208. Reprinted in expanded form, 1971, Simon, Entry No. 1618.

1212 Solokov, Raymond A. "'The Truth 24 Times a Second.'" *Newsweek*, 71 (12 February), 90–91.
It is difficult to know anything about Godard's life, even though his impact on film is immense. Solokov describes Godard's early career and the making of *Breathless*. Godard's recurring themes and motifs include stark apartments, violence, intertitles, characters addressing the camera, the "outsider," and politics. Reactions to his films by both critics and ordinary viewers are noted.

1213 Sontag, Susan. "Godard." Program Notes. The Films of Jean-Luc Godard: A Retrospective Tribute, University Art Museum, University of California, Berkeley, CA. (March-April-May).
One side of broadside is reprint of Sontag's article. Other side is the film program plus an announcement that Godard and his wife, Anne Wiazemsky, would be on campus March 4–7 to present *La Chinoise* and that Godard would deliver a lecture on March 4. He would also hold informal office hours and participate in daytime seminars.

1214 Sontag, Susan. "Going to the Movies: Godard." *Partisan Review* (Spring), pp. 290–313.
In an important in-depth study, Sontag analyzes Godard's career and films in terms of the following aspects: modernism, Godard's sensibility, his literariness, his critique of and break with the formal structures of narrative cinema, his use of theatrical structures — often for a political end, his similarity to and differences from Brecht, his use of the first person, absorption of chance, recording temporality and the present, and a "cool" staying outside the characters and

the action. In particular Godard explores language — its ideology, duplicity, banality, deformation, prostitution, visual quality, and coerciveness. Reprinted 1969, Sontag, Entry No. 1347.

1215 Souchon, Michel. "Vers un noveau statut de l'O.R.T.F.?" *Etudes*, 329 (August-September), 179–192.
Useful facts are given about the ORTF precisely at the time when it forbid *Le Gai Savoir* and when the Etats Généraux was trying to reorganize it.

1216 Stackhouse, J. Foster. *"La Chinoise." Take One*, 1, No. 9, 22.
A brief poem reviewing the film calls it Godard's most Brechtian film — thought-provoking yet "easy to take."

1217 Sternberg, Jacques. "Révolution culturelle au Festival de Cannes." *Le Figaro littéraire*, No. 1154 (14–23 June), pp. 40–41.
Complete diary, with hour-by-hour countdown, is given for the disruptions of the Cannes Festival.

1218 Stuttner, Wolfgang. "Techniche epicizzanti nel cinema di Godard." *Cinema and Film*, 11, No. 5–6 (Summer), 124–46.
In Lincoln Center Library.

1219 Svendson, Juris, et al. "Talking Politics with Godard." *San Francisco Express Times* (14 March), pp. 8–9.
In an interview with Juris Svendson, Tom Luddy, and David Mairowitz, Godard discusses his discovery of "aesthetic imperialism" or "the gestapo of film structures." He wants art that will work in the same direction as left political action, not against it. In this context, he specifically discusses *Far from Vietnam, Salt of the Earth,* and Chinese movies ("rather bad"). Reprinted 1970, Flash, *Kinopraxis*, Entry No. 1441.

1220 Swados, Harvey. "How the Revolution Came to Cannes." Magazine Section. *New York Times* (9 June), pp. 128–32.
Radical writer Swados describes the ambiance at Cannes, the social and political climate in France, the Langlois affair, the directors' strike at the festival, the reaction to the militants' announcement at the closing (Godard was denounced by cries of "Millionaire! Millionaire!"), and the last event, a speech by Henri Langlois in homage to Georges Sadoul.

1221 Taddei, Nazareno. *"Week-end*: una donna e un uomo dal sabato alla domenica." *Bianco e nero*, 29, No. 5-6 (May-June), 122–27.
Credits. In-depth review of *Weekend*.

1222 Thomas, Kevin. Review of *Six in Paris. Los Angeles Times* (9 October).
Six in Paris is a cut above the usual anthology film, but Godard's sketch is the most conventional thing he's done. Cited at length in 1969, Anon., *Film Facts*, Entry No. 1255.

1223 Truffaut, François. "Le Scenario d'origine de François Truffaut (texte

intégral inédit)." *A bout de souffle: L'Avante-Scène du cinéma*, No. 78 (March), pp. 47–49.
    Truffaut's original scenario, partially used by Godard for *A bout de souffle*.

1224   Tynan, Kenneth. "Shouts and Murmers." *The Observer*, Review (27 October).
    Godard insulted the British by sending a telegram minutes before he was to speak at the National Film Theater, saying to give his fee to the poorest man the organizers could find on the streets.

1225   Whitley, John. "Interview: John Whitley Watches Godard, at Work on His First British Film, Put Some Revolutionary Theories into Practice." London *Sunday Times* (23 June).
    Godard is interviewed at a recording session for *One Plus One*. He discusses his use of long takes, U.S. cultural imperialism in England, his improvisational method, and his ideas about political filmmaking and film viewing.

1226   Winkler, Richard. *"Far from Vietnam." Movie*, No. 15 (Spring), pp. 34–36.
    Cited in Bowles, p. 152.

1227   Winsten, Archer. *"La Chinoise* at Kips Bay Theater." *New York Post* (4 April), p. 66.
    La Chinoise is a film in beautiful color that gets bogged down in theoretical conversations and leaves the audience "hoping something interesting will happen."

1228   Winsten, Archer. "Reviewing Stand: *Weekend* at 72nd Playhouse." *New York Post* (1 October), p. 28.
    Godard takes off in all directions, "kicking normal audiences in the teeth." There's good color photography and a certain intelligence, action, and force.

1229   Wood, Robin. "Godard and *Weekend." Movie*, No. 16 (Winter), pp. 29–33.
    Brief plot summary. Wood is suspicious of the audience's accepting with "only half-shocked amusement" Godard's repudiation of everything Wood has "always believed in, worked for, and found worth living for." Godard doggedly shows what is real about our age, but with habitual distanciation. Thus, his humor both functions as a healthy way to seek clarity in an age of despair and also expresses a "holding back from commitment." Abridged slightly and reprinted, 1970, Cameron, Entry No. 1405. Reprinted 1972, *Weekend* and *Wind from the East* script, Entry No. 2353.

1230   Woodside, Harold G. *"One Plus One." Take One*, 2, No. 1 (September-October), 24–25.
    Conducts an internal dialogue trying to discover what Godard means to him. Improvisations make Godard's films "awareness in pure form." Either you relate to them or you don't.

1231 Wright, Ian. "A Warning from Battersea." *Manchester Guardian Weekly* (1 August), p. 14.

Financing of *One Plus One* is described as are facts about its production. It was stopped for one month after Godard had shot 2-½ hours of rushes with the Stones. Wright is on location at Battersea for the shooting of the Black Power sequences.

1232 [Youngblood, Gene]. "Godard in Hollywood." *Take One*, 1, No. 10 (June), pp. 13–17.

Symposium with Vidor, Fuller, Bogdanovich, Corman, and Godard (Kevin Thomas, moderator), reprinted from *Los Angeles Free Press*. See 1968, Youngblood, Entry No. 1233. There is also a comment by D.A. Pennebaker, dated April 1968, on Godard's being wooed by producers while in Hollywood.

1233 Youngblood, Gene. "Godard: 'We Are All Outside of Hollywood.' " *Los Angeles Free Press* (22 March), pp. 10–11.

Third of four-part series. A panel, "Godard in Hollywood," at USC, February 28, included Godard, King Vidor, Peter Bogdanovich, Sam Fuller, Roger Corman, and Moderator Kevin Thomas, critic. The directors discuss Hollywood's "deterioration," Godard's use of Hollywood conventions and incorporation of aspects of the filming process into his films. He discusses low budget filmmaking, problems with state-controlled filmmaking in Eastern Europe, his social commentary, and his use of actors and of chance. Reprinted 1968, Youngblood, Entry No. 1232.

1234 Youngblood, Gene. Interview with Godard. *Los Angeles Free Press* (8 March).

Cited 1970, Collet, Entry No. 1425. First of four parts.

1235 Youngblood, Gene. "Jean-Luc Godard: 'A Film Is Not a Work of Art.' " *Los Angeles Free Press* (29 March), pp. 24–25.

Fourth of four parts. Godard appeared at a USC panel discussion on February 29 with four student filmmakers — Armand Ballester and Eli Hollander of UCLA and Caleb Deschanel and Steve Mannes of USC — and Lewis Teague and Moderator Gene Youngblood. Godard discusses *Les Carabiniers*, the use of sound, the motives of the early *auteur* critics, his direction of actors in *La Chinoise,* and his films as reflecting his "life of ideas." He denies that the *Red Desert* influenced *Contempt* and defends his treatment of the "love story" in *La Chinoise*. He's trying to change the world by changing the way people come to see his movies.

1236 Youngblood, Gene. "Jean-Luc Godard: 'Hollywood Should Shoot in 8mm.' " *Los Angeles Free Press* (15 March), pp. 2 and 25.

Second of four-part series. Godard appeared at a press conference at USC, Tuesday, February 27, with Agnes Varda, translator Mark Woodcock, and USC filmmaker and instructor Charles Lippencott. Topics covered include financing films, reception and distribution, censorship, and specific films — both Godard's and those of others. Godard's future projects include a film on education, which "started out as Rousseau's *Emile,"* a film on the death of Trotsky, and an adaptation of Kierkegaard's *Diary of a Seducer*.

1237 Zimmer, Christian, "Cent-mille rizières." *Les Temps modernes,* No. 261 (February).

Cited 1972, Brown, Entry No. 1657. Review of *Loin du Viêtnam.*

1238 Zimmer, Christian. "Les Livres de cinéma: Jean-Luc Godard: 'Poésie et vérité.' " *Le Monde* (14 September), Supplement, p. 6.

Review of *Jean-Luc Godard — au delà du récit: Etudes cinématographiques,* No. 57–61. Only Bresson has equally stubbornly pursued a private vision in film. Godard is a moralist who lives in cinema as the Ideal. His interviews are of a piece with the films; both are monologues. Zimmer feels Amengual and Bladelli unjustly accuse Godard of not surmounting the problems of adolescence. Godard's moralism lies in his forcing spectators to evaluate film language. Brief mention of *Godard par Godard.*

1969

1239 A., H. *"One Plus One (Sympathy for the Devil)." Image et Son: la saison cinématographique,* No. 230-21 (September-October), p. 211.

Brief credits and résumé of the film. Godard is criticized for his superficiality and terrorism.

1240 Alder, Renata. "A Gentle and Humble Godard: Belmondo Plays Pierrot to Anna Karina." *New York Times* (9 January), p. 21.

Brief credits. *Pierrot* is a whimsical, poetic, slightly erratic film, a personal love story with oddly no sex scenes.

1241 Amette, Jacques-Pierre. "Du parti pris des choses dans le cinéma contemporain." *La Nouvelle Revue française,* 34, No. 199 (July), 154–55.

Describes the "devotion to objects," including filming women as an object, in *La Femme mariée, La Chinoise,* and *Les Carabiniers.*

1242 Amette, Jacques-Pierre. "Les Spectacles: *One Plus One." La Nouvelle Revue française,* No. 200 (August), pp. 308–309.

Amette hates all the stale current cinema. Although Straub, Godard, and Malle also do not know what kind of films to make for our time, these are the only directors who give a few indications of what that cinema might be.

1243 Amiel, Mireille. *"One Plus One*: egale combien?" *Cinéma 69,* No. 138 (July/August), pp. 120–22.

One Plus One is full of "laborious repetitions" and "few ideas." A little, but not enough, of Godard's humor, talent, and visual sense shows through. Credits.

1244 Anon. Article on Godard's filming at Essex University. London *Times* (13 February), p. 3.

About filming student section of *One Plus One.* Cited 1969, *Times Index* (January-February), p. 87.

1245 Anon. "Five Directors — Five Films." *Popular Photo* (October), p. 116.

Cited *Reader's Guide,* 29 (March 1969-February 1970), 794.

1246   Anon. "Godard Buffs Riot at Philharmonic Re Garbled 2-Language Soundtrack." *Variety* (January [first week]), p. 23.

Last Sunday, December 29, an audience of 1,000 enjoyed Mark Woodcock's 30-minute documentary that contained an interview with Godard about *La Chinoise*. No one, however, could understand the mixed English and French soundtrack of *A Film like Any Other*. Leacock and Pennebaker's manager, David McMullin, was booed at the end of the first reel. The Philharmonic officials promised refunds and only 100 people stayed for the second half of the film. Source: Lincoln Center Library of the Performing Arts clipping file.

1247   Anon. "Godard, Danny the Red, Barcelloni Plot Chinese-Proverbial 'Western'." *Variety* (26 March), pp. 2 and 95.

Rome. Tells about the production and casting of *Wind from the East*.

1248   Anon. "Godard, Jean-Luc." *Current Biography*, 30 (May), 12.

See 1970, Anon., "Godard, Jean-Luc," Entry No. 1367.

1249   Anon. "Godard por Solanas, Solanas por Godard." *Cine del tercer mundo*, No. 1 (October).

Fernando Solanas and Godard discuss each other's work. Cited 1974, Ferrero, Entry No. 1841.

1250   Anon. "Godard's *Devil* Has No Distrib. as Yet." *Variety* (16 July).

London. *One Plus One* has been entered in its fourth film festival, including London, Rio, Berlin, and Edinburgh.

1251   Anon. "Grove Press into Pics More; 4 Deal with J-L Godard." *Variety* (2 July), pp. 3 and 15.

Grove will pay Godard after the films are delivered, but they will accept whatever he makes — tentatively four features and a documentary. Two are in script-outline form.

1252   Anon. "Die Kunst ist eine Idée der Kapitalisten." *Film* (Hanover), No. 4 (April), 22–26.

In an interview dated August 1968, Godard discusses the Etats Généraux of filmmakers, the cinétracts, the efforts to show films to workers in May '68, and later developments in political filmmaking. He discusses Chinese film, agitational film, alternate forms (video, TV, 8mm), *La Chinoise*, the film he's going to make in September. Excerpts trans. 1970, Flash, Entry No. 1441.

1253   Anon. "No Word on Godard's Pro-Arab Feature." *Variety* (31 December), p. 1.

Paris. Brief report on proposed *Their Just Fight* [*Till Victory*].

1254   Anon. "The Oldest Profession." *Film Facts*, 11, No. 24 (15 January), 483–84.

Complete credits, synopsis, and quotations from the *New York Times* and *Variety* reviews of the omnibus film containing Godard's *Anticipation*.

1255   Anon. "*Paris vu par. Six in Paris*." *Film Facts*, 12, No. 5, 119–20.

Credits. Plot summaries. Reviews quoted from the *Los Angeles Times, Chicago Tribune, Variety*, and the *New York Times*.

1256 Anon. *"Pierrot le fou." Film Facts*, 12, No. 1, 1–4.
Credits, synopsis, film's history in USA and brief summaries of the criticism written on the film (six favorable reviews, three mixed, six negative), extensive quotations from reviews in the *Village Voice*, the *New Republic*, the *Los Angeles Times*, and *Time*.

1257 Anon. *"Pierrot le fou*: Godard on Screen." *Christian Science Monitor* (19 February), p. 6.
Christian Science Monitor 1969 Annual Index, p. 63.

1258 Anon. Review of *Two or Three Things*. *Newsweek* (18 May), p. 107A+.
Cited *Reader's Guide*, 30 (March 1970-February 1971), 797.

1259 Anon. "7 Days and 7 Nights Making 12 Days and 12 Nights in all." *Good Times*, 2, No. 42 (30 October).
Cited API, 1, No. 1–2, 27.

1260 Anon. "Wanton Flow. *Time*, 93, No. 3 (17 January), 67–68.
"Wanton flow is the film's [*Pierrot le fou*] main source of entertainment." The film's major asset is Karina's and Belmondo's performances. Weakest are the "melodramatic slice-of-life interludes." pretentious monologues, and shrill anti-Americanism. Quoted at length, 1969, Anon., *Film Facts*, Entry No. 1256.

1261 Autera, Leonardo. "L'Equilibrio difficile del festival di Berlino." *Bianco e nero*, 30, No. 9–10 (September-October), 29, 32 and 36.
Credits. *Le Gai Savoir*, shown at Berlin Festival, is praised as a modernist work. *Amore e Rabbia* was also shown there.

1262 Ayala Blanco, Jorge. *"Jean-Luc Godard y Los Carabinieros." Revista de belles artes* (Mexico), No. 26 (March-April), pp. 65–70.
That the New Wave directors only live and think film is both their strength and limitation. Godard's beginnings as a cinephile and critic are described as well as the postwar environment which gave rise to his political skepticism and anti-heroism. Godard's weapon of attack is verbal and film language. From *A Bout de souffle* on, his films are a series of questions, of negations, "an anguished response to that which he cannot do." His achievement is to rephrase completely the problems of cinematic language and, in a film like *Les Carabiniers*, to confront us with that kind of mental emptiness which is a prime source of violence.

1263 Baconnier, Fernand. "Bilan: les films de, sur, autour de, dans l'esprit de Mai." *Télécine*, No. 151-52 (March-April), pp. 26–34.
Description and analysis of *Une Film comme les autres*. Godard refuses to present the images of May with direct sound, but rather uses a student-worker political discussion to reinterpret those sounds and images and thus to create a new dialogue and the idiom which will "prolong that of May."

1264 Bensky, L. "A Tale of 2 Festivals." *Dock of the Bay*, 1, No. 15 (11 November).
Cited API, 1, No. 1, 28.

1265 Berardini, Aldo. Review of *Deux ou trois choses*. *Cineforum*, 9, No. 82, 85–96.
Review of film discussing its politics and modernism.

1266 Berg, Gretchen. "Fritz Lang on Godard and *Contempt*." *Take One*, 2, No. 2 (22 June), 12–13.
In an interview originally conducted in 1967, Lang compares his filmmaking style with that of Godard, especially in terms of Godard's preference for natural locations over sets, his improvisation, and his low shooting ratio.

1267 Berry, Leonard J. "Politics at the Festival: The Screen." *Commonweal* (24 October), p. 103.
The New York Film Festival concentrates on political film. *Le Gai Savior* is briefly described, and Godard's attack on language noted.

1268 Billard, Pierre. "About *Masculine-Feminine*." *Masculine-Feminine: A Film by Jean-Luc Godard*. New York: Grove Press. Pp. 187–288.
Billard gives the following critical documents to provide a background for the published screenplay: the De Maupassant stories and the disclaimer legally allowing De Maupassant's heir, Robert Esmenard, to sell those rights again because the film hardly followed the stories: 1966, Godard, Entry No. 2248; selections from 1966, Vianey, Entry No. 768; 1966, Labro, Entry No. 715; 1965, Salgues, Entry No. 751; 1966, Daix, Entry No. 681; 1966, Sadoul, Entry No. 749; 1968, Billard, Entry No. 649; 1966, Baroncelli, Entry No. 647; 1966, Chapier, Entry No. 659; 1966, Chauvet, Entry No. 660; 1966, Bory, Entry No. 652; 1966, Haudiquet, Entry No. 703; 1966, Arnaud, Entry No. 646; 1966, Roud, Entry No. 746; 1966, Milne, Entry No. 729; 1966, Moskowitz, Entry No. 731; 1966, Crowther, Entry No. 676; 1966, Winsten, Entry No. 773; 1966, Crist, Entry No. 673; 1966, Guarino, Entry No. 696; 1966, Sarris, Entry No. 758; 1966, Hartung, Entry No. 700; 1966, Anon., *Catholic Film Newsletter*, Entry No. 627; 1966, Kael, Entry No. 709.

1269 Billard, Perre. "Jean-Luc Godard choisit le néant." *L'Express*, No. 932 (19–25 May), pp. 67–68.
One Plus One is "derisively symbolic," aimed to force spectators out of passive complicity with a cinema of consumption. It's a "huge cry of powerless anger, which sees the revolution slip away from it."

1270 Bobker, Lee R. *Elements of Film*. New York: Harcourt Brace & World. Pp. 129–31, 213–15, 249–52.
Contains the following: (1) Godard, "Montage mon beau souci, "trans. reprinted from *Film Culture*, No. 22–23 (Summer 1961), Entry No. 2206. (2) Bobker, "Jean-Luc Godard," lists five key elements in Godard's films related to camera technique, social commentary, unconventional narrative, and cinematic inventiveness. (3) "Penelope Gilliatt." Bobker reprints and analyzes excerpts from "The Folly of Soldiers," 1968, Gilliatt, Entry No. 1114.

1271 Bonneville, Leo. "Connaissez-vous les cinéastes." *Sequences*, No. 56 (February), pp. 62–66.
Cited 1969–70, *Index analytique*, 4, p. F. 303.

1272 Bory, Jean-Louis. "L'Anglais tel qu'on le filme?" *Le Nouvel Observateur* (12 May).
See 1973, Bory, Entry No. 1761.

1273 Burch, Noel. *Praxis du cinéma.* Paris: Editions Gallimard.
See entry under English translation, 1973, Burch, Entry No. 1765.

1274 Cameron, Ian, Ed. *The Films of Jean-Luc Godard. Movie* Paperbacks Series. London: Studio Vista. 192 pp. U.S. edition. New York: Praeger, 1970.
I have listed all the entries for this book under 1970 because that was the only edition I was able to consult.

1275 Canby, Vincent. "Film Festival: *Le Gai Savior*, A Godard Abstract: Movie Suggests That Language Be Remade." *New York Times* (29 September), p. 54.
Brief credits. Canby discusses Godard's theme of "de-education particularly in relation to language and the meaning of words," describes Godard's visual technique, and finds *Le Gai Savior* one of Godard's "most beautiful, most visually lucid movies."

1276 Canby, Vincent. "Godard Treatise." *New York Times* (28 September).
Brief credits. *Le Gai Savior* is a "beautiful and visually lucid," abstract discourse about the "need for de-education." Godard simply extends "ideas he has been playing with," includes lots of puns in "typically Godardian whimsy," and cuts to visual inserts that here "make complete sense." Reprinted 1970, Canby, Entry No. 1407.

1277 Cassagnac, J.-P. "Comme les autres comme avant ———." *Cinéthique*, No. 1 (January), pp. 30–31.
Une Film comme les autres is rare as a film that makes us "continue" its discourse completely in our own present political reality. It respects a "whole practice of clandestine struggle" as well as respects "images, sound, voices and words."

1278 Chevassu, François. "Digression en forme d'ajout: cinéma et télévision ou le malentendu Godard." *Image et son: Revue du cinéma*, No. 224 (January), p. 8.
A long footnote to the editorial praises Godard for his as yet inadequately understood visual essay style and television aesthetics.

1279 C.[ohn], B.[ernard]. "*Amore e rabbia: L'Amore.*" *Positif*, No. 110 (November), p. 50.
Godard's easily forgettable sketch in *Vangelo 70* has a young man and woman discussing the usual death, philosophy, war, and politics.

1280 C.[ohn], B.[ernard]. *"Le Gai Savoir." Positif,* No. 110 (November), p. 52.

The origins of the title in Nietzsche are discussed. "Godard accumulates obscenities, paradoxes, and astute insights." Cohn values the effort to make the soundtrack free of and equal to the visual track.

1281 Collet, Jean. "Le Cinéma et le crise de mai." *Etudes,* 330 (February), 239–251.

Complete information is given on the revolt in French filmmaking in 1968 — discussing the Cinémathèque and Malraux's role in firing Langlois, the repressive aspects of the ORTF and the CNC (Centre National de la Cinématographie), the Etats Généraux, and "Godard's consecrating the month of June to make small films in 8mm and 16mm to prove the possibility of collective creation.

1282 Collet, Jean. Review of *One Plus One. Télérama,* No. 1009.
Cited 1974, Collet, Entry No. 1832.

1283 Cott, Jonathan. "Inverview with Godard." *Rolling Stone,* No. 35 (14 June), pp. 21–23.

"Love, consciousness, tenderness, and art . . . formed the silent horizon" of Godard's films through *Pierrot.* Now Godard's films question the relation between art and politics. Godard discusses his political development, his rejection of spectacle, his current political concepts of filmmaking. He explains his killing of the pig and use of Yippie guerrillas in *Weekend.* The Stones' practicing in *One Plus One* and the entire form of that film were like a "scientific experiment" for correct political art. He discusses working outside the system and his reaction to an older kind of filmmaking, including his own past films. Reprinted 1970, Flash, Entry No. 1441.

1284 Cowie, Peter. *"Breathless." Seventy Years of Cinema.* New York: A.S. Barnes. Pp. 228–29.

Brief credits. Plot and stylistic characteristics are described. "Godard's cinema is governed by the *episode.*" Godard records the "garish and pretentious and expendable."

1285 Crofts, S. "The Films of Jean-Luc Godard." *Cinema* (England), 3 (June), 27–32.
Cited in Schuster, p. 167.

1286 D., R. "Godard's *Weekend." Helix,* 10, No. 7 (20 October), 18.
This is a brilliant film even if Godard is too aloof to be a committed Marxist.

1287 Darling, Brian. "Jean-Luc Godard: Politics and Humanism." Mimeographed paper. British Film Institute Education Department Seminar (17 April). 4 pp.

The major themes in Godard's films are identity, the constraints and lies of language, violence, and the domination of the media by capitalism and U.S. imperialism. "Language, society, betrayal and prostitution, are all forms of violence, of domination of one by another."

1288 Dawson, Jan. *"Le Gai Savoir."* *Monthly Film Bulletin*, 36 (August), 162–63.
Credits, brief description of film. Godard's "sought-after degree zero of sounds plus images is in fact zero plus Mao Tse Tung." Finds the film repetitious, inaccessible, and often aesthetically and emotionally ineffective.

1289 Deehan, B. " — If You Can Absorb It!" *Distant Drummer*, No. 54 (11–18 October), pp. 1 and 8.
Godard puts viewers through a series of violent incidents, including animals' being killed while filmed, and makes us complicit in the violence. There is a political message to the film, but it is also Godard's finale within the arena of lush, bourgeois filmmaking before going on to pure "filmed doctrine," as in *Le Gai Savoir*.

1290 Ebert, Roger. Review of *Six in Paris*. *Chicago Sun-Times* (29 October).
Godard shows his preoccupation with automobiles in an amusing sketch.

1291 Elleson, N. "4 Vietnam Films." *Old Mole*, 1, No. 27 (December).
Possibly contains a review of *Far from Vietnam*. Cited in API, 1, No. 1–2, 27.

1292 Fargier, Jean-Paul, et al. "Deux heures avec Jean-Luc Godard." *Tribune socialiste*, No. 396 (23 January), pp. 18–19.
In an interview with Fargier and Bernard Sizaire, written without questions as a prose statement, Godard discusses the role of filmmaking during May '68 and what it means to see these films now. He presents a political analysis of filmmaking and film form, and of culture as a whole in France. There's never been a revolutionary film made inside the system. He comments on the cinétracts, *Le Gai Savior, La Chinoise*, and *Un Film comme les autres*.

1293 Fargier, Jean-Paul. "Une Double Catharsis." *Cinéthique*, No. 1 (January), pp. 30–31.
Other citations on the sound track of *Un Film comme les autres* include words of Michèle Firk and personal reflections of Godard. The film integrates discussion and commentary as simple elements of a composition, which is intended to wash over the spectator as a "therapeutic experience." It isn't trying to inculcate an idea, as the cinétracts did. The silent documentary sections seem like "phantom events, irrevocably past." The only locus of struggle can be the present, which we construct for ourselves during those silences.

1294 Fieschi, Jean-André. "Un Film en trois." *La Quinzaine littéraire* No. 65 (January 15), pp. 28–29.
Le Gai Savoir, One Plus One, and *Un Film comme les autres* are seen as a "tryptich" which reflects the political uncertainty, questioning of cinema itself, and provisional resolutions which characterize these times. Gives a close formal analysis of the three films, with particular attention to *Un Film comme les autres*.

1295 Fox, J. "Godard and Truffaut Ten Years Later." *Commentator* (Canada), 13 (July-August), 21–22.
Cited in 1969 *Canadian Periodicals Index*, 22, p. 217.

1296 Gilliatt, Penelope. *"Les Carabiniers." Film 68/69.* Ed. Hollis Alpert and Andrew Sarris. New York: Simon and Schuster. Pp. 94–98.
Reprinted from 1968, Gilliatt, "The Folly of Soldiers," Entry No. 1114.

1297 Goldmann, Annie. "Les Déserts de la foi." *Revue de l'Institut de sociologie* (Brussels) No. 3, pp. 463–73.
Cited 1969–70, IBZ, 7, Part B - Subjects "A-Franchreich," p. 707.

1298 Goldman, Lucien. "Note sur quatre films de Godard, Buñuel, et Pasolini." *Revue de l'Institut de sociologie* (Brussels), No. 3, pp. 475–77.
Cited 1972, IBZ, 7, Part B - Subjects "G-K," p. 1352.

1299 Gow, Gordon. *"Le Gai Savior." Films and Filming,* 15, No. 12 (September), 56–57.
Cited in BFI Bibliography.

1300 Gow, Gordon. Review of *Le Gai Savoir. Films and Filming,* 15, No. 2 (September), 56–57.
Credits given. Cited in Bowles, p. 177.

1301 Green, Calvin. "L'Homme Politique: Man and Revolution at the New York Film Festival." *Cineáste,* 3, No. 2 (Fall), 2–5, 36.
Brief review of *Le Gai Savoir.*

1302 Greenspun, Roger. "Movies: *Pierrot le fou.*" *New York Free Press* (23 January), pp. 9 and 12.
Brief credits. Greenspun discusses *Pierrot's* romanticism in its plot about escape, themes of time and eternity, and terms of formal use of chance. The film "disappoints as a whole" because it lacks cohesiveness.

1303 G.[uarner], J.[osé]-L.[uis]. "Godard, Jean-Luc." *Enciclopedia ilustrada del cine,* II. Eds. Salvador Clotas, José-Luis Guarner, Joaquin Jorda. Barcelona: Editorial Labor. Pp. 50–51.
A brief biography is given. Describes Godard's romanticism, his penchant for making "filmed essays," the dialectic between distanciation and emotion in the films, self-reflexivity, the juxtaposition of disparate elements, and the autobiographical aspect of the films.

1304 Gubern, Roman. *Godard polémico.* Series Cinématografica, No. 3. Barcelona: Tusquets Editorial. 116 pp.
Analyzes in depth the relation between Godard's modernist innovations and his social and political insights. Godard's biography and films are discussed in terms of the filmmaker's "ethics and aesthetics" (e.g., the tension between individualism and major social problems is resolved in favor of the latter after *Masculin-Féminin*). Discusses each aspect of Godard's style and what is achieved by it and then analyzes chronologically Godard's "filmic itinerary." Filmography through *One Plus One* is given, plus a list of the films in which Godard acted.

1305 Hans. "Le Gai Savoir (The Gay Knowledge) (French-Color)." *Variety* (9 July).

This intellectual nonsense and totally unfilmic film raised much talk at the Berlin Film Festival.

1306 Hatch, Robert. "Films." *The Nation,* 208, No. 4 (27 January), 126.
Reviews *Pierrot le fou.*

1307 Houston, Penelope. "70." *Sight and Sound,* 39, No. 1 (Winter), 3–5.
Le Gai Savoir is mentioned.

1308 Jouffroy, Alain. "Le Guérillero et le savant." *Le Fait public,* No. 2 (January).
In an interview, Godard discusses information systems, especially TV and cinema, at length. To make films is always a theoretical act. Even those who don't think so have a theory: they're "making films for the public." TV and news production has been left in the hands of engineers and bureaucrats. Godard says that things which seem regressive from a certain perspective (certain kinds of political films, auteurism) may have a positive aspect (mobilizing people, freeing cineastes from serfdom to producers). Reprinted 1974, Collet, Entry No. 1836.

1309 Kael, Pauline. "A Minority Movie (*La Chinoise*)." *Films 68/69: An Anthology of the National Society of Film Critics.* Ed. Hollis Alpert and Andrew Sarris. New York: Simon and Schuster. Pp. 65–72.
Reprinted from 1968, Kael, Entry No. 1132.

1310 Kael, Pauline. "Weekend in Hell (*Weekend*). *Film 68/69: An Anthology of the National Society of Film Critics.* Ed. Hollis Alpert and Andrew Sarris. New York: Simon and Schuster. Pp. 32–39.
Reprinted from 1968, Kael, Entry No. 1134. Also reprinted in 1970, Kael, Entry No. 1464.

1311 Kauffmann, Stanley. "Stanley Kauffmann on Films." *New Republic,* 160 (22 February), 22 and 34.
Pierrot le fou's trite narrative is only "a scaffolding for acrobatics, cinematic and metaphysical." It has all Godard's standard devices but is boring because Godard can't seem to develop any one theme profoundly. Reprinted 1971, Kauffmann, Entry No. 1588. Quoted at length in *Film Facts* (1969, Anon., Entry No. 1256).

1312 Kezich, Tullio. "*Amore e rabbia.*" *Bianco e nero,* 30, No. 7–8 (July-August), 130–32.
Credits. Title of Godard's sketch is here given as *L'Amore/L'Aller et retour/andata e ritorno/des enfants prodigues/dei figli prodighi.*

1313 Knight, Arthur. Review of *Two or Three Things. Saturday Review* (22 November), p. 68
Cited 1971, MMRI, p. 173.

1314 Leblanc, Gérard, et al. "Un Cinéaste comme les autres." *Cinéthique,* No. 1 (January), pp. 8–12.
In an interview with Gérard Leblanc and J.-P. C., Godard discourages

starting a new journal, emphasizes inexpensive communication, a news leaflet, perhaps. He talks about collectivity, *Un Film comme les autres*, Jean-David Pollet as a bourgeois filmmaker, his sympathy with the situationists. He feels that filmmakers and film workers should keep more in touch, form an underground network. He calls himself an "anarchist" in the sense of supporting workers councils, land redistribution, sharing the work, etc. Trans. 1970, Jack Flash, *Kinopraxis*, Entry No. 1441.

1315 L.[efèvre], R.[aymond]. *"One Plus One." Image et son: Revue du cinéma*, No. 229 (June/July), pp. 149–50.
Why does Godard bore spectators so? He may be reflecting an incoherent world or saying that cinema is dead.

1316 Lerman, L. "International Movie Report." *Mademoiselle* (January), p. 74.
Cited *Reader's Guide*, 28 (March 1968-February 1969) 783.

1317 MacBean, James Roy. "Politics, Poetry, and the Language of Signs in Godard's *Made in U.S.A." Film Quarterly*, 22, No. 3 (Spring), 18–25.
Made in U.S.A. is compared to Antonioni's *Red Desert*. MacBean discusses Godard's use of Karina, the lack of depth in her role and in the visuals, the comic-strip style, and sign-conflict in the films. Words are undercut by noise or by other words spoken simultaneously; they conflict with visual signs (the long conversation in the bar). The mise en scene is Brechtian. The relation between the emotional tone of the film and its political dimension is explored. Reprinted 1975, MacBean, Entry No. 1907.

1318 Macdonald, Dwight. *"Breathless." Dwight Macdonald on Movies.* Englewood Cliffs, N.J.: Prentice-Hall. Pp. 372–75.
Godard's jerky staccato style perfectly renders "the convulsive style of this kind of life." Like the New Novelists, Godard catches "tropisms." The New Wave subordinates plot to character, suggests mood rather than tell a story, and restores the preeminence of camera and montage. (July 1961).

1319 Malmfelt, A.D. *"Pierrot le fou." Film Society Review*, 4, No. 6 (February), 34–40.
Traces Godard's reputation in the United States from 1966, when *Pierrot* was shown at the New York Film Festival, to 1969, when it opened commercially. In *Pierrot*, Godard's "arbitrariness works." This kind of destructiveness — in both content and cinematic technique — culminates in *Weekend*.

1320 Mancini, Michele. "Conversazione 1, 2, 3, 4." *Godard*. Series Paperbacks/Cinema. Rome: Trevi. Pp. 53–101.
A series of four interviews in which Godard talks about what he'd like to do, other filmmakers and the influences on him, realism, the reception of his films, his politics, Brecht, the Italian version of *Le Mépris*, Italian cinema, and ideology.

1321 Mancini, Michele. "Filmografia." *Godard*. Series Paperbacks/Cinema. Rome: Trevi. Pp. 126–137.
Filmography from *Operation béton* (1954) through *Weekend* (1967).

1322 Mancini, Michele. *Godard.* Series Paperbacks/Cinema. Rome: Trevi. 137 pp.
  Contains interviews, critical articles, translations into Italian from sound-tracks and filmography.

1323 Mancini, Michele. "Il paradosso." *Godard.* Series Paperbacks/Cinema. Rome: Trevi. Pp. 7–52.
  Critical article analyzing Godard's politics and style.

1324 Martin, Marcel. "L'Enfant terrible: *One Plus One* de Jean-Luc Godard." *Les Lettres françaises.* No. 1329 (14 May), p. 16.
  Martin discusses *Une Film comme les autres, Le Gai Savoir,* and *One Plus One.* He respects Godard's political commitment and desire to provoke, but finds that the structure of *One Plus One* does not achieve what seem to be Godard's political aims.

1325 Mauriac, Claude. "Cette homme est dangereux." *Le Figaro littéraire* (28 July).
  Cited 1974, Collet, Entry No. 1832.

1326 McKegney, Michael. "Film: *Le Gai Savoir & Pigpen.*" *Village Voice* (6 November).
  Godard's notion that "we must return to pristine simplicities in order to progress artistically and politically" is really "sentimental and reactionary nonsense."

1327 Meccoli, Domenico. "Il XVIII festival di Berlino, più per registri che per studenti." *Bianco e nero,* 29, No. 9–10 (September-October), 52.
  Notoriety made *Weekend* the "star" of the Berlin Festival and sparked a pro- and anti-Godard battle among critics.

1328 Micciché, L. "Solanas: un cineasta militante." *Cinema 60* (Italian), No. 73–74 (December 1969-February 1970).
  In an interview, Solanas discusses Godard. Cited 1974, Ferrero, Entry No. 1841.

1329 Morgenstern, Joseph. "Fugue for Sweethearts." *Newsweek,* 73, No. 4 (27 January), 86.
  Pierrot le fou has some brilliant moments such as the cocktail party, Karina's "music hall" numbers, and Belmondo's talking about the book he wants to write which could capture the essence of life (= Godard's aesthetic). Unfortunately Godard clutters the film with a murder plot, weak slapstick, torture scenes, and a "desperate comic protest against the U.S. role in Vietnam." Reprinted 1970, Morgenstern, Entry No. 1488.

1330 Moskowitz, Gene. "Godard the Wrecker Is at It Again; This Time It's Rio; But Parisians Ignore His Advice, Send Party." *Variety* (26 March).
  Paris. Godard and *Etats généraux* unsuccessfully asked that films not be sent to Rio Film Festival since Brazilian filmmakers were boycotting it and revolutionary films had been ruled out of the festival.

1331 Oudart, Jean-Pierre. "Dans le texte." *Cahiers du cinéma*, No. 213. (June), pp. 59–60.

Godard gives each of the elements in *One Plus One* — music, gesture, verbal text, and camera movement — an "absurd autonomy" and gives them both an aggressive, "sexualized" connotation and a political one. The interweaving of these connotative elements makes up the fragile structure of this "deconstructed" work. Credits.

1332 Pechter, W.S. "For and Against Godard." *Commentary: A Jewish Review*, 47, No. 4 (April), 59–63.

Discusses the pro- and anti-Godard positions. Too often Godard's "Brechtian" devices are mannerist paradoxes and conceits, or else they increase, not decrease, pathos. In his best films Godard calls on the silent film tradition of expressionism and montage and maintains a unity of thematically interwoven ideas and an abstract rigor, but his imaginative energy often fails. Images of death pervade his films, and in *Weekend* he, like Eisenstein, sacrifices art to didacticism. Reprinted 1971, Pechter, Entry No. 1606.

1333 Reed, Rex. "Rex Reed at the Movies: And Now Some Sacred Cows to Kill." *Holiday*, 45, No. 5 (May), 22.

Pierrot le fou is fun, especially because Godard allows Belmondo a whole range of technicolor antics and directs Karina with such irony and affection. Reed disliked *Weekend* but finds *Pierrot* "a New Wave picnic."

1334 Rispoli, Paola. "Cinema provocazione." *Filmcritica*, No. 194 (January), pp. 8–12.

Young people are making political movies that are revisionist or even "American." Godard says he has been concentrating on scientific experimentation, in Mao's sense, in the arts, and this information should be offered to all people who want to use film and video in the class struggle. There is a possibility for worker resistance within the film industry. We should do without directors and have three or four people making movies together equally. Godard discusses the possibilities for and the attempts at making films with workers. Trans. 1970, Flash, Entry No. 1441.

1335 Rocha, Glauber. "Brazil's Cinema Novo: An Interview with Glauber Rocha," by Michel Delahaye, Pierre Kast, and Jan Narboni. *Evergreen Review*, 13, No. 73 (December), 28–32, 67–71.

Cited 1972, Green, Entry No. 1684.

1336 Ross, Walter S. "Splicing Together Jean-Luc Godard." *Esquire*, 72, No. 1 (July), 42–46, 72–75.

Ross interviewed Godard as he was going back to London to exhibit *One Plus One*. The title of the film *(Un et un)* was scribbled on the walls in May '68. Ross tells about Godard's production of cinetracts. Godard discusses his politics and his films' effect (or lack of it) on audiences. Ross combines citations from articles and reviews, observations made by those who know Godard, and his own research to present a detailed biography of Godard's early career through *Breathless.* Through such an impressionistic collage, Ross also presents a picture of the filmmaker's personality, work habits, filmmaking technique, and political concepts, especially those in *La Chinoise*. Godard's film editor, Agnès Guillemot, is quoted at length, especially for her first-hand observations about Godard.

1337   Roud, Richard. *"Le Gai Savior." Sight and Sound*, 38, No. 4 (Fall), 210–11.
At first one would reject *Le Gai Savior* and feel "cheated." Yet one can also find similarities to earlier Godard films. The film tires to explore the ideological assumptions behind language. Roud compares its method and intent to Walter Benjamin's criticism, Bach's "The Art of the Fugue," and Noam Chomsky's structural analysis of language. The film provoked "disasterous reactions at Berlin." Reprinted 1972, Brown, Entry No. 1658.

1338   Sarris, Andrew. "Andrew Sarris *(La Chinoise)." Film 68/69: An Anthology by the National Society of Film Critics*. Ed. Hollis Alpert and Andrew Sarris. New York: Simon and Schuster. Pp. 65–72.
Reprinted from 1968, Sarris, *Village Voice*, Entry No. 1195.

1339   Sarris, Andrew. "Andrew Sarris *(Weekend)." Film 68/69: An Anthology by the National Society of Film Critics*. Ed. Hollis Alpert and Andrew Sarris. New York: Simon and Schuster. Pp. 39–42.
Reprinted from 1968, Sarris, Entry No. 1197. Also reprinted in 1970, Sarris, Entry No. 1507.

1340   Sarris, Andrew. "Films: How Good Is Godard?" *Village Voice* (23 January).
Sarris discusses Godard's reputation and his drive to make one film each yearly for the Venice and Berlin Festivals. *Pierrot* is the "metaphorical expression of passion being cooled by existence." Love is sublimated into art, art translated into love. "Belmondo and Karina and Coutard and Antoine Duhamel (music) translate Godard's most tentative ideas into sensuous spectacle." Reprinted 1970, Sarris, Entry No. 1507. Quoted at length in 1969, Anon., *Film Facts*, Entry No. 1256.

1341   Sarris, Andrew. "A Movie Is a Movie Is a." *The Emergence of Film Art*. Ed. Lewis Jacobs. New York: Hopkinson and Blake. Pp. 313–18.
Reprinted from 1964, Sarris, Entry No. 432; Also in 1967, Sarris, Entry No. 966.

1342   Schechter, D. "2 × 1 Equals Go Home." *Old Mole*, 1, No. 24 (23 October).
Probably a review of *One Plus One*. Cited API, 1, No. 1-2, 27.

1343   Segal, Abraham. *"Alphaville." Image et son: Revue du cinéma*, No. 233, pp. 1–5.
Credits, plot summary. *Alphaville* mixes conventional genres. Analyzes Alpha 60's words, Godard's theme of language, and his use of sharp contrasts in the lighting. Now that Godard is making cinetracts, the cine clubs that enthusiastically projected those early films of social critique are challenged to follow him in his "resistance and struggle."

1344 Sheed, Wilfred. "Films." *Esquire*, 71, No. 1 (January), 36–40.
Traffic is the right metaphor to satirize the contemporary political-social situation. *Weekend*, however, declines at its conclusion when it situates itself in prehistory, fetish, and taboo. (The National Catholic Film Office denounced the film as "antihuman.")

1345 Simon, John. "Unmagnificent Seven." *The New Leader*, 52, No. 19 (13 October), 23.
Le Gai Savior shows "two blank faces surrounded by blackness pretentiously jabbering away about the evils of language."

1346 Sontag, Susan. "El cine de Godard." *Sur* (Buenos Aires), No. 316–17 (January-April), pp. 124–41.
Trans. of 1968, Sontag, Entry No. 1347, by Edgardo Cozarinsky.

1347 Sontag, Susan. "Godard." *Styles of Radical Will*. New York: Farrar, Straus & Giroux. Reissued 1970. Delta Books. New York: Dell.
Reprinted from 1968, Sontag, Entry No. 1214. Also reprinted in Spanish trans. 1969, Sontag, Entry No. 1346.

1348 Teague, Lewis. "New York Film Festival." *Los Angeles Free Press*, 6, No. 77 (7 November), 44–46.
Positive, brief description of *Le Gai Savior* is given.

1349 Th.[irard], P.[aul]-L.[ouis]. *"One Plus One." Positif*, No. 108 (September), p. 72.
The film is so "babbling" that it may cost Godard any chance for future production monies. That in itself inspires a certain "paradoxical respect."

1350 Turroni, Giuseppi. "Michele Mancini: *Godard." Bianco e nero*, 30, No. 7–8 (July-August), 144–145.
Reviewer of Mancini's book discusses the usefulness of her interviews with Godard as a way of coming to grips with and better understanding Godard's "modernity."

1351 Turroni, Giuseppe. "La rivola degli studenti." *Bianco e nero*, 30, No. 3–4 (March-April), 9–16.
Godard's Brechtian cinema and Pasolini's theory of a "cinema of poetry" are analyzed in the light of New Left militancy, especially among university students.

1352 Verdone, Mario. "Cinema di idee." *Bianco e nero*, 29, No. 1-2 (January-February), 15–16.
Along with other films shown at the 28th Venice Film Festival, the critic reviews *La Chinoise* briefly in terms of its formally experimental aspect.

1353 Volpi, Gianni. "Cinema as a Gun: An Interview with Fernando Solanas." *Cinéaste*, 3, No. 2 (Fall), 18–26, 33.
Solanas tells his areas of disagreement with Godard, as well as mutual concerns.

1354 Weightman, John. "Whatever Happened to Godard?" *Encounter*, 33, No. 3 (September), 56–59.

Reviews Godard's work through *Le Gai Savior*, in which film Godard's "vapid verbalization [is] . . . a form of cinematographic suicide." *Le Petit Soldat, The Married Woman, A Woman Is a Woman*, and *Masculine-Feminine* are fragmentary films that seem to fumble for a theme. In *La Chinoise, Weekend, One Plus One*, and *Le Gai Savior*, Godard "has exchanged his romantic admiration of the outlaw for a muddled and uninteresting obsession with the concept of revolution, which he is handling about as badly as possible."

1355 Weiler, A.H. "Godard to Direct *Little Murderers* Film." *New York Times* (29 May), p. 50.

Godard signed to direct Feiffer's *Little Murderers* as his first American-made, English-language feature, with script written by writers of *Bonnie and Clyde*, Robert Benton and David Newman.

1356 Weiler, A.H. Review of *Six in Paris*." *New York Times* (3 March), p. 26.

Godard's sketch for *Six in Paris*, "Montparnasse et [sic] Levallois," is brief and comic, although poorly subtitled. Plot is described. Brief credits. Quoted at length in 1969, Anon., *Film Facts*, Entry No. 1255.

1357 Whitehead, Peter. "*Week-End*." *Films and Filming*, 15, No. 5 (February), 34.

Cited in Bowles, p. 561.

1358 Winsten, Archer. "*Pierrot* at 72nd Street." *New York Post* (9 January).

The joys of *Pierrot* lie in its celebration of "color, form, and pure emotion."

1359 Wolf, William. "*Pierrot le fou*." *Cue* (10 January).

"Godard dissipates the original strengths" of the film with in-jokes and literary and cinematic imitation.

1360 Wollen, Peter. *Signs and Meaning in the Cinema*. Bloomington: Indiana University Press. Revised edition, 1972.

In 1972, Wollen looks at his evaluation of Godard in 1969 (as the apex of cinematic communication and expression) and explains the historical necessity for and possibility of "a recasting of the semiological foundations of art." Godard's importance lies in his "systematic challenging of the assumptions underlying the adoption of a style or point of view."

1970

1361 Alexandre, Jean-Louis. "Cinéma et citation." *Cinéma* 9 (OctoberNovember), pp. 20–26.

Describes Godard's in-group jokes, cinematic citations, use of the word as a visual image, "avalanche" of quotations in *Pierrot le fou*, use of real cineastes and philosophers, and lengthy monologues. Because he often suppresses the "quotation marks" and does not let us know when he uses cinematic and literary citation, Godard disquiets us and causes us to question the whole nature of citation.

1362 Anon. Article on Godard. *Triumfo* (Spain), (26 September).
Cited 1972, de Gregorio, Entry No. 1687.

1363 Anon. Brief review and credits of *Vent d'est*. *Bianco e nero*, 31, No. 5-6 (May-June).
This film strives to politicize film form by becoming a nonfilm.

1364 Anon. "*British Sounds* Banned from TV." London *Times* (28 April), p. 9.
Cited 1970, *Times Index* (March-April), p. 89.

1365 Anon. "Collision of Ideas." *Time* (18 May).
The various sections of *Sympathy for the Devil* are described, and the film is placed in the context of Godard's work since *Le Gai savior*. The film's symbolism and political statements are too simple, but the photography and images are "crazily beautiful," the work of cinema's "foremost pop essayist." Reprinted 1971. Denby, David, ed. *Film 70/71*. New York: Simon and Schuster.

1366 Anon. "Godard chez les Feddayin." *L'Express* (26 June-2 August), pp. 44–45.
Godard responds to an interview in Amman, where he is making a film at the request of "the Central Committee of the Palestine Revolution." The film will be entitled, "The Methods of Thinking and Working of the Palestine Revolution." The film must be made as a result of political discussion, not just sympathy.

1367 Anon. "Godard, Jean-Luc." *Current Biography Yearbook, 1969*, p. 167.
Godard's address is listed as c/o *Cahiers du cinéma*. Biographical details, descriptions of the films, and critical opinions are given, with sources for data noted at the end.

1368 Anon. Godard: *See You at Mao/Pravda — 2 Films by Jean-Luc Godard and Comrades of the Dziga-Vertov Group*. Grove Press/Evergreen Films press releases.
Graphics, descriptions of films, recent filmography (from *Made in U.S.A.* through 1970).

1369 Anon. "Godard/Weekend." *Times Now*, 1, No. 7 (18 June), 21.
Cited API, 2, No. 4, 39.

1370 Anon. "Godard's *Weekend*." *Helix*, 10, No. 7 (20 October).
Cited in API, 1, No. 1–2, 27.

1371 Anon. "The New Movie: Godard Film at New Yorker." *New York Post* (1 May), p. 40.
Review of *Two or Three Things*.

1372 Anon. "Pasticciacco '70 a Bergamo." *Bianco e nero*, 31, No. 9-10 (September-October), 71.
Godard's *Lotte in Italia* is mentioned as entered in the Bergamo Film Festival (2–10 September) competition.

1373 Anon. Review of *La Chinoise*. London *Times* (14 April), p. 10.
Cited 1970, *Times Index* (July-August), p. 97.

1374 Anon. Review of *Contempt*. London *Sunday Times* (26 April).
Contempt's themes are the complexities of marriage and work, which are set
off against the personage of Fritz Lang, who has faith in the "ancient Greek
unquestioning acceptance of nature and reality." Godard's characteristic cinematic touches are tedious and distracting but the film is fresh and brilliant.

1375 Anon. Review of *Lotte in Italia*. London *Times* (15 September), p. 13.
Cited 1970, *Times Index* (September-October), p. 99.

1376 Anon. Review of *Le Mépris*. London *Times* (1 May), p. 8.
Cited 1970, *Times Index* (May-June), p. 90.

1377 Anon. Review of *Two or Three Things*. *Commonweal*, 93, No. 20 (February), p. 496.
Positive review. Cited MMRI, 1971, p. 173.

1378 Anon. Review of *Two or Three Things*. *Sightlines*, 5, No. 2
(November-December), p. 29.
Cited 1971, MMRI, p. 173.

1379 Anon. Review of *Vent d'est*. London *Times* (12 May), p. 11.
Cited 1970, *Times Index* (May-June), p. 90.

1380 Anon. "*Sympathy for the Devil*." *RAT*, 19 June, p. 20.
Cited API, 2, No. 2, 30.

1381 Anon. "*Sympathy for the Devil (One Plus One)*." *Fifth Estate*, 4, No. 3 (19
March), 7.
The reviewer discusses the steps by which the song is built during the Stones'
rehearsal, and finds the film "an impressive visual and aural orchestration of
incredibly diverse parts."

1382 Anon. "*Vent de l'est* [sic] — Italy/France/West Germany 1969." Program Notes. 8th New York Film Festival.
Credits. Brief synopsis. Godard biography. Recent quotes from Godard.

1383 Anon. "*Weekend*." *Nola Express*, 1, No. 56 (29 May), 24.
Cited API, 2, No. 2, 30.

1384 Anon. "What Directors Are Saying!" *Action*, 5, No. 4 (July-August),
31.
Brief Godard quotation from Collet's *Jean-Luc Godard*.

1385 Armes, Roy. "Jean-Luc Godard." *French Cinema since 1946. Vol 2: The
Personal Style*. Rev. ed. London: A. Zwemmer; New Jersey: A.S. Barnes.
Pp. 69–93.
Provides an explication of each of Godard's films in chronological order.

Armes discusses genre, acting, citation, political themes, visual aspect, and mood and tone. He evaluates the "success" or partial success of the films. He then describes Godard's work as a whole — personal note, flaunting of cinematic convention, immediacy, opposition to French "quality" filmmaking, subject matter (gestures, hackneyed plots, women), distancing strategies, use of film itself as a theme, love of everything about cinema, and presentation of "undigested elements."

1386 Barr, Charles. *"A bout de souffle."* *The Films of Jean-Luc Godard.* Ed. Ian Cameron, New York: Praeger. Pp. 11–16.
   Brief plot summary. In the sequence where Godard acts as informer, Barr sees Godard's "indifference to surface naturalism," the director's intervening and reminding us of the film as film, the characters' self-consciousness about their roles, and something like Hamlet's ghost in Godard's relation to Michael. This is the only Godard film where the social environment that is the background to the protagonist's seeking freedom or love is not sketched in sharp political or analytic terms.

1387 Beauregard, Georges de, Raoul Coutard, Agnès Guillemot, François Truffaut, and Jean Clay. "Witnesses: Notes on Godard." *Jean-Luc Godard.* Ed. Jean Collet. Trans. Ciba Vaughan. New York: Crown. Pp. 163–78.
   Friends and coworkers of Godard separately provide biographical insights. Truffaut's reminiscences were taped in 1963 and reviewed and "completed" by him for the 1968 edition. Trans. from 1968, Collet, Entry No. 1088.

1388 Benhari. /GRMI. "Breaking Wind." *Good Times*, 3, No. 41 (16 October), p. 15.
   The critic imagines a porn scene which censors might have cut from *Breathless* as well as a subsequent possible interview in *Réalités*, where Godard explains "the function of the deleted pissoir sequence." There was a strongly negative response in the audience to *Wind from the East* in Berkeley, but "the herb" and the critic's own political reflections let him glimpse Godard's intent.

1389 Bernardini, Aldo. "Testi di film." *Bianco e nero*, 31, No. 7-8 (July-August), 153.
   The Grove Press edition of the *Masculine-Feminine* script, edited by Pierre Billard, is reviewed.

1390 Biggin, B. "No Sympathy for Jean-Luc Godard." *Philadelphia Freepress*, 3, No. 6 (16 February), 15.
   Cited API, 2, No. 1, 19.

1391 Billard, Pierre. "Le Cinéma perpendiculaire." *L'Express.* Special issue. No. 965 (May), pp. 92 and 94.
   Godard's militant filmmaking is described in terms of "rupture," "research," "reportage," "refusal" (of traditional forms of production and expression), and "retreat." Alternative cinema in France since 1968 is described.

1392 Björkman, Stig. *"Deux ou trois choses que je sais d'elle."* Trans. Kersti French. *The Films of Jean-Luc Godard.* Ed. Ian Cameron. New York: Praeger. Pp. 140–46.

Brief plot summary. Godard's collage technique allows him to treat interconnected political and social themes with a new realism and also personal hesitation. Reprinted 1975, *Godard: Three Films* (scripts), Entry No. 2297.

1393 Björkman, Stig. *"Masculin-Féminin."* Trans. Kersti French. *The Films of Jean-Luc Godard.* Ed. Ian Cameron. New York: Praeger. Pp. 119–22.
Brief plot summary. Done "completely in long shot," the film invites us to look "outside the picture." Godard harshly treats the themes of objectivity, freedom, feelings, and deceit. He shows "teenagers . . . trying to assume adult attitudes while retaining the irresponsibility which is their adolescent privilege."

1394 Blinder, Henry. "Directing the Director." *Montage*, 1, No. 4 (30 April), 15.
Cited in BFI Bibliography.

1395 Bory, Jean-Louis. "L'Écran d'Arlequin." *Le Nouvel Observateur* (22 June)..
Review of *La Contestation (Vangelo 70).* See 1974, Bory, Entry No. 1830.

1396 Boston, J. *"See You at Mao." People's World*, 33, No. 19 (9 June), 11.
Cited API, 2, No. 2, 30.

1397 Bradford, C. *"Sympathy for the Devil." Harry*, 1, No. 14 (14 May), 14.
Cited API, 2, No. 2, 30.

1398 Burg, V. "Jean-Luc Godard: Revolutions in Celluloid." *Phoenix*, 2, No. 36 (3 November), 10.
Ralph Thanhauzer made a short film of Godard and Gorin in the United States last spring. Burg describes Godard's interview with Sarris at Grove Press, encounters with audiences in Cambridge and Berkeley, and story board for *Palestine Will Win* [*Till Victory*]. Godard is cited at length. Thanhauzer's film, not mentioned by name here, is *Godard in America*.

1399 Cameron, Elisabeth. "Filmography and Bibliography." *The Films of Jean-Luc Godard.* Ed. Ian Cameron. New York: Praeger. Pp. 184–92.
Bibliography provides data not available elsewhere.

1400 Cameron, Ian. *"Les Carabiniers." The Films of Jean-Luc Godard.* Ed. Ian Cameron. New York: Praeger. Pp. 40–53.
Brief plot summary. Cameron describes in detail how Godard's cinematic technique, characterization, tone, and "what he has chosen to omit" in his portrayal of war work together to "rob war of any emotional value." Cameron relates that to the critique of "cinema as voyeurism" within the film itself.

1401 Cameron, Ian. *"Le Gai Savior." The Films of Jean-Luc Godard.* Ed. Cameron. New York: Praeger. Pp. 172–77.
Brief plot summary. *Le Gai Savior* deals with governmental control and abuse of education, mass communication, culture; the search for a new cinematic language adequate to Godard's political-aesthetic concerns; and language itself. "The film is a notebook for Godard and not something made for an audience. The sheer polyphonic verbiage defeats . . . the will to concentrate."

1402 Cameron, Ian. "Introduction." *The Films of Jean-Luc Godard.* Ed. Ian Cameron. New York: Praeger. Pp. 6–10.

Discusses the following aspects of Godard's work: violent critical reaction to it, relation between low budget and style, assemblage method, fragmentation, emotion, incorporation of Godard's own uncertainties, use of direct statement, and political and moral stance.

1403 Cameron, Ian. *"Made in U.S.A.".* *The Films of Jean-Luc Godard.* Ed. Ian Cameron, New York: Praeger. Pp. 131–39.

Brief plot summary. The critic lists fifteen political themes found in the film. The film is "centerless," yet the illogical and meaningless series of events which make up the plot seem very well defined. The passing allusions and references at the film's periphery, which seem more important, are made very difficult to grasp (e.g., the tape recordings of Richard Po).

1404 Cameron, Ian. Review of *Wind from the East. Movie,* No. 18 (Winter), p. 40.

Cited in Bowles, p. 572.

1405 Cameron, Ian, ed. *The Films of Jean-Luc Godard.* Movie Paperbacks Series. New York: Praeger. 192 pp.

U.S. edition of 1969, London: Studio Vista edition. Each article annotated separately.

1406 Canby, Vincent. "Godard Film in Festival: *Wind from the East* at Alice Tully Hall." *New York Times* (12 September), p. 31.

Wind from the East reviewed, brief credits. "The form is often fascinating. The content, however, is almost pure junk."

1407 Canby, Vincent. "Godard Treatise." *New York Times* (5 June), p. 22.

Reprinted from 1969 (September 28), Canby, Entry No. 1276.

1408 Canby, Vincent. "Movies? They Are No Joke, Mes Amis." *New York Times* (31 May), Sec. II, p. 1.

Gives an update on the financially troubled, "revolutionary" *Cahiers du cinéma* and mentions Godard's three "Maoist" films made outside France — *See You at Mao, Wind from the East,* and *Pravda.*

1409 Canby, Vincent. "The Screen: Two or Three Things at the New Yorker." *New York Times* (1 May), p. 47.

In 1966, Godard was filming one film in the morning, the other in the afternoon. *Two or Three Things* marks Godard's start as a "formal movie essayist." Canby briefly describes the structure and content of the film, which he finds intellectually lucid, humorous, beautiful, and Brechtian.

1410 Canby, Vincent. "What Godard Hath Wrought." *New York Times* (29 March), Sec. II, p. 1.

The ten sequences of *Sympathy for the Devil* are described. Canby admires the beautifully and carefully composed Rolling Stones sequences, which he finds more constructive in effect than the rest of the film is negative.

1411 Carroll, Kathleen. *"Sympathy for the Devil:* A Rolling Stone Tale of Our Times." *Daily News* (NY?), (27 April).

The content of the film is described and the story behind its two endings is related. It is an "impersonal personal statement about our confusing world." Museum of Modern Art clipping file.

1412 Carroll, Kent E. "Film and Revolution: An Interview with Jean-Luc Godard." *Evergreen Review*, 14, No. 83 (October), 47–51, 66–68.

Carroll interviews Godard and Gorin, who tell the ideology behind the Dziga Vertov group. This is one of the most complete statements of their political principles. Reprinted with material added from original manuscript, 1972, Brown, Entry No. 1658.

1413 Chapier, Henri. "Le Collectif Godard s'amuse à Prague." *Combat* (5 February).

Cited 1972, de Gregorio, Entry No. 1687.

1414 Chase, Tony. "Starting Again from Zero." *Montage*, 1, No. 4 (30 April), 4–6.

Cited in BFI Bibliography.

1415 Christie, Ian. "Current Non-Fiction and Short Films: *British Sounds."* *Monthly Film Bulletin*, 37 (October), 208–209.

Credits, description of the film's six sections, brief history of its being made for London Weekend Television and then shelved. The film "assumes a Marxist orientation in the audience." Godard successfully structures the very elements of the film didactically.

1416 Ciment, Michel, et al. "Entretien avec Emile de Antonio." *Positif*, No. 113 (February), p. 37.

De Antonio found the traveling shots around the Stones and the crane shot at the end of *One Plus One* brilliant, but thought otherwise it was an uninteresting, antipolitical film.

1417 C.[iment], M.[ichel]. *"Vento dell'est."* *Positif*, No. 119 (September), p. 33.

Brief review. Ciment understands the aesthetic intent of *Vent d'est*, but he thinks the film offers no real communication with its spectators.

1418 Cohen, Richard. *"Le Gai Savoir."* *Women's Wear Daily* (5 June).

This is a barren film about the reeducation of an intellectual.

1419 Coleman, John. "Sing Revolution." *The New Statesman*, N.S. 79 (24 April), 593.

Le Mépris has a silly plot, cultural pretentiousness, and ravishing photography. Is it an homage or a joke?

1420 Collet, Jean. "Bibliography." *Jean-Luc Godard*. Ed. Jean Collet. Trans. Ciba Vaughan. New York: Crown. Pp. 204–15.

This is primarily an English-language bibliography and lists works under the following categories: books, screenplays, interviews, articles by Godard in English, general articles, articles film-by-film, peripheral but relevant articles.

1421 Collet, Jean. "Bio-Filmography." *Jean-Luc Godard.* Ed. Jean Collet. Trans. Ciba Vaughan. New York: Crown. Pp. 179–204.

Gives biographical information, complete film credits, and one-paragraph summaries of the films chronologically from 1930 to 1969–70, with Godard's proposed version of *Little Murderers.*

1422 Collet, Jean. "Interview with Jean-Luc Godard." *Jean-Luc Godard.* Trans. Ciba Vaughan. Series Cinéma d'ajourd'hui in English, No. 18. New York: Crown. Pp. 83–94.

Trans. from 1968, Collet, Entry No. 1088. It probably appeared in the 1965 edition as well. Also trans. by Toby Mussman, 1968, Entry No. 1103. There is a big variation between the Mussman and Vaughan translations. The interview was conducted September 12, 1963, after Godard had read the opening essay for Collet's book, and is "somewhat edited" for the English version. In the interview, Godard describes how he became interested in film, his "instinct" for making films, his philosophy, similar to Rossellini's: "I think I am looking for something definitive, eternal, but under its least definitive, most fragile and living form." He says he repeatedly uses the theme of misunderstanding, culminating in *Contempt*, where he "tries to reduce the distance" between himself and his characters. He discusses his project for *Pour Lucrèce.* Reprinted 1974 (complete French text), Collet, Entry No. 1836.

1423 Collet, Jean. "Jean-Luc Godard: An Essay by Jean Collet." *Jean-Luc Godard.* Series Cinéma d'aujourd'hui in English, No. 18. Trans. Ciba Vaughan. New York: Crown. Pp. 1–79.

First analyzes Godard's way of thinking. Godard has "consented to look at things with a fresh and personal eye." His "beautiful vision of things is above all a just vision." The following aspects of Godard's style are considered: improvisation, direction of actors, shot-sequences, tableaux, theatricality, "clash" of shots, citations, wit, authorial intrusion, Brechtianism, filmed glances, mixtures of modes of discourse, polyphonic construction, cinema's "assassinating" life, and Godard's attack on cinema itself. Godard is a politically revolutionary filmmaker because he puts the means of communication on trial. Trans. from 1968, Collet, Entry No. 1088.

1424 Collet, Jean. "Second Interview with Godard." *Jean-Luc Godard: An Investigation into His Films and Philosophy.* Ed. Collet. Trans. Ciba Vaughan. Series Cinéma d'ajourd'hui in English, No. 18. New York: Crown. Pp. 97–103.

In an interview conducted in the studio during the filming of *La Chinoise*, May 12, 1967, Godard discusses the politics of international film production and distribution, the need to "educate" film audiences, the taboos and missing subjects in French cinema ("films about manual labor and intellectual labor"), and the problems with the French government's cultural policies. Trans. from 1968, Collet, Entry No. 1088. French version reprinted, 1974, Collet, Entry No. 1836.

1425 Collet, Jean,. ed. *Jean-Luc Godard: An Investigation into His Films and*

Philosophy. Trans. Ciba Vaughan. Series Cinéma d'ajourd'hui in English, No. 18. New York: Crown. 218 pp.

Trans. from 1968, Collet, Entry No. 1088. Bibliography in U.S. edition is mainly of English language articles. Earlier French editions 1963, 1965 (Paris: Seghers), Entry Nos. 265 and 503. Later French edition, 1974, Collet, Entry No. 1836.

1426   Comuzio, Ermanno. "Visti a Bergamo." *Bianco e nero,* 31, No. 9–10. (September-October), 119.

Credits for *Lotte in Italia* and brief negative review. The film is too "academic."

1427   Cournot, Michel. "Jean-Luc ex-Godard." *Le Nouvel Observateur,* No. 292 (15 June), pp. 42–44.

No one would discuss Godard as a filmmaker after *La Chinoise,* yet he made eight films from 1968–70. Describes what Godard's political and aesthetic assumptions were in each film of that period and evaluates the films and Godard's political practice. Trans. into Spanish, *Triumfo* (26 September), 1970.

1428   Cozarinsky, Edgardo. "*Une Femme est une femme.*" *The Films of Jean-Luc Godard.* Ed. Ian Cameron. New York: Praeger. Pp. 26–31.

Brief plot summary. "Meaning [is] not imprisoned in the work, but alluded to, pointed at, juggled with, even contradicted." The characters have no roots or solidity. Godard "incorporates into the film all the dead matter, the opaque, meaningless surfaces of experiences." The film has a reserved romanticism, especially in the presentation of Karina with her bad French and her portrayal of "frail emotions and stubborn will."

1429   Crist, J.[udith]. Review of *Sympathy for the Devil. New York Magazine* (18 May).

In *Sympathy for the Devil,* Godard's political thinking and humor are heavy handed, and "his redundancies and studied ironies are more tedious than artistic in their ultimate effect."

1430   Davidson, Lee. "No Sympathy for Godard." *Berkeley Tribe,* 2, No. 5 (6–13 February), 18.

Cites all the positive examples of a political and countercultural movement in the United States and Cuba and Vietnam. Rejects Godard's films not for what they contain but for what they lack — a positive, loving look at revolution.

1431   Dawson, Jan. "*Deux ou trois choses que je sais d'elle (Two or Three Things I Know about Her).*" *Monthly Film Bulletin,* 37 (December), 244–45.

Credits, plot summary. Different levels of film are described — Paris, industrial society, prostitution, consumer culture, misuse and limitation of language. Godard emphasizes that objects both define and obstruct human relationships.

1432   Dawson, Jan. "Raising the Red Flag." *Sight and Sound,* 39, No. 2 (Spring), 90–91.

Provides an in-depth analysis of *British Sounds* as militant cinema. She describes the film's fate at the hands of London Weekend Television. This film is not an object of consumption but a stimulus to analysis, discussion, and action.

1433 Durgnat, Raymond. "Asides on Godard." *The Films of Jean-Luc Godard.* Ed. Ian Cameron. New York: Praeger. Pp. 147–53.
 Repudiates Godard's Calvinism, his withdrawal from reality and "confused indifference," his visual and verbal "philosophical" gags, and his flipness, nastiness, and con games.

1434 Durgnat, Raymond. *"One Plus One."* *The Films of Jean-Luc Godard.* Ed. Ian Cameron. New York: Praeger. Pp. 178–83.
 Brief plot summary. *"One Plus One* is an audio-visual meditation on the remoteness of radical action. . . . Because inertia is its topic, it's no accident that the stylistic conception . . . recalls Warhol."

1435 Eckstein, G. " 'Cinemarxism': The Jokes Fall Flat." *Dissent: A Quarterly of Socialist Opinion*, 17, No. 6 (November), 574–75 and 590.
 One Plus One dispenses with action, depends on a collage of images and words, and makes the actors into "auxiliaries" of the filmic medium. "Godard is clearly a contemporary of McLuhan in his emphasis on the Medium . . . Like the actors, the message is largely drained of meaning."

1436 Editors. "Le Cinéma dans la politique: debat." *Positif*, No. 113 (February), pp. 22–23.
 The editors discuss Godard's efforts to forge a new political film language, with particular reference to *One Plus One*.

1437 Ehrenstein, David. "Anna Karina." *Film Culture*, No. 48–49 (Winter-Spring), pp. 52–53.
 "Anna Karina in her clumsy, inept attempts to portray characters gives totally of herself, fills the screen with beauty, makes it come alive."

1438 Ehrenstein, David. "Film: *Sympathy for the Devil (One Plus One)."* *Village Voice* (9 April).
 The characters and their fragmented roles are described. The critic appreciates this as an "open" art work that is more like a modern painting than a traditional film. It's a "series of raw materials" and should not be judged according to "structure" or "intention."

1439 Elsaesser, Thomas. *"One Plus One."* *Brighton Film Review*, No. 21 (June).
 Cited 1971, *Screen*, 12, No. 4 (Winter), 23.

1440 Erlich, R. "Cine Marxism." *Los Angeles Free Press*, 7, No. 28 (10 July), 36.
 Cited in API, 2, No. 3, 30.

1441 Flash, Jack [pseudo. for Augst, Bertrand and Degener, David], trans. and ed. *Kinopraxis*, No. 0, unpaged broadside. (2533 Telegraph Ave., Berkeley, CA.).
 Reprinted English-language interviews with Godard and those translated by Flash from French. See 1969, Cott, Entry No. 1283; 1969, Godard, "Premiers *Sons Anglais*," Entry No. 2267; 1967, Cournot, Entry No. 860; 1969, Leblanc, Entry No.

1314; 1968, Svendson, Entry No. 1219; 1969, Rispoli, Entry No. 1334; 1969, Anon., "Die Kunst ist eine Idee der Kapitalisten," Entry No. 1252; 1968, Godard, "Un Prisonnier qu'on laisser taper sur sa casserole," Entry No. 2264; 1970, Martin, Entry No. 1479. Also included is the text of an unedited videotaped interview that Godard made March 19, 1969, for French television "Cinéma Six," never shown (1970, Godard, Entry No. 2270).

1442 Flatley, Guy. "Godard Says Bye-Bye to Bardot and All That." *New York Times* (17 May), p. D-11.
Interviews Godard and Gorin and covers their appearance at Yale. He decries the passing of the "old" Godard of *Breathless*, discusses Gorin's influence on Godard, the two filmmakers' desire to film ongoing political struggles, their negative opinions of Belmondo, Z, *Battle of Algiers*, Coutard, Bunuel, other New Wave directors, and Godard and Gorin's positive opinions of Chinese films and Jerry Lewis.

1443 Gallagher, T.A. "Film: *2 or 3 Things I Know about Her.*" The *Village Voice* (7 May), pp. 59 and 63.
Provides a romantic appreciation of the film. It is a documentary which is also a meditation on art and an "ecstatic experience" for the viewer.

1444 Gambetti, Giacomo. "Il XXIII prevedibile festival de Cannes." *Bianco e nero*, 31, No. 5-6 (May-June), 74, 76 and 105.
Controversy over *Vent d'est* at Cannes Festival is described. Credits more complete than French ones.

1445 Gauthier, Guy, "Une Reapparition de Jean-Luc Godard." *Image et son: Revue du cinéma*, No. 245 (December), pp. 136–37.
A brief transcription is given of a radio program where Godard proposed a scenario for a film about the death of an immigrant laborer in a factory whose death was hushed up afterward.

1446 Gilliatt, Penelope. "Godard." *New Yorker*, 46 (2 May), 102–109.
In *Two or Three Things*, Godard is "a poet with a temperament of range and urgency held in check." Analyzes Vlady's Brechtian role and the "split between the subjective and the objective." *Sympathy for the Devil* has humorous, puerile, accurate parodies, depicts a "dispensible" world, and mantains a tension between "crass images" and "finely calibrated" thought. Reprinted 1971, Gilliatt, Entry No. 1574.

1447 Gilliatt, Penelope. "*See You at Mao* and *Pravda*." *New Yorker*, 46 (30 May), 81–85.
"The fight he sets up between words and images is a concrete metaphor for political struggle and our own sense of concrete reality . . . You are not a unity, say these films. You are trying to be a unity, but the fact is you are not." Reprinted 1972, Brown, Entry No. 1658.

1448 Goldcrab, M. "*One Plus One*: Godard." *Good Times*, 3, No. 10 (5 March), 17.
The film will be shown for a benefit for the Cinema Workshop for Bay Area filmmakers.

1449 Goodwin, Michael, et al. "inter/VIEW with Godard." inter/VIEW 1, No. 11, p. 6.

Selection from an April 7 interview with Godard and Gorin conducted by Goodwin, Tom Luddy, and Naomi Wise. They discuss political filmmaking and Godard's films, some made with Gorin, from *La Chinoise* through *Wind from the East*.

1450 Green, Calvin. Review of Roud's, Cameron's, and Collet's books on Godard. *Cinéaste*, 4, No. 1 (Summer), 29–30.

Cited in Bowles, pp. 623, 629, and 643.

1451 Greenspun, Roger. "Godard's *Mao* and *Pravda* Begin Run." *New York Times* (22 May), p. 36.

Briefly explains the themes and the "self-abnegation" of these films, noting the change in Godard's use of symbols and camera movement.

1452 Greenspun, Roger. "Screen: *Sympathy for the Devil* (1 + 1)." *New York Times* (27 April), p. 42.

Brief credits. Significance of change in ending is explained. "The film seems to be determined to be the prospective text of some ultimate, infinitely complex collectivism." Reprinted 1972, Brown, Entry No. 1658.

1453 Griselda. "*One Plus One*." *inter/VIEW*, 1, No. 8, 12.

Cited in Bowles, p. 372.

1454 Guarner, José Luis. "*Le Mépris*." Trans. Nicholas Houghton. *The Films of Jean-Luc Godard.* Ed. Ian Cameron. New York: Praeger. Pp. 54–60.

Brief plot summary. Analyzes in depth the tightly interwoven themes: voyeurism, misunderstanding, Prokosch's grossness vs. Lang's nobility (a direct comment on film production), watching vs. participating in the world, and harmony vs. destruction. Contrasts Godard's technique in developing Paul and Camille.

1455 Guarner, José Luis. "*Pierrot le fou*." Trans. Nicholas Houghton. *The Films of Jean-Luc Godard.* Ed. Ian Cameron. New York: Praeger. Pp. 94–103.

Brief plot summary. The film's action is always shown subjectively and in a fragmented way, and meaning is only implicit, never explicit, in the film. Godard's distancing is different from Brecht's and is used for romantic ends. Godard uses a double monologue structure and doubles each character as well. The characters "try to behave like characters in fiction" so as to avoid a mediocre existence, and Godard opposes a chaotic, violent world to that of contemplation, nature, and self-reflection.

1456 Guitar, J. "*Sympathy for the Devil*." *Saint Louis Outlaw*, 1, No. 9 (27 November), 6.

Cited API, 2, No. 4, 40.

1457 Hamalian, Leo. Review of *One Plus One*. *Journal of Popular Culture*, 4, No. 1 (Summer), 308–13.

Cited in Bowles, p. 372.

1458 Haycock, John W. *"See You at Mao." Boston After Dark* (29 April), pp. 1 and 6.
Review.

1459 Henderson, Brian. "Toward a Non-Bourgeois Camera Style." *Film Quarterly*, 24, No. 2 (Winter), 2–14.
The critic provides an in-depth analysis of the cinematographic innovations of Godard's later period — lateral tracking shots, planimetric compositions, collage and montage as organizing principles, the separation of and struggle between sound and image, and kinds of sequence structures and their overall effect. Henderson discusses the political efficacy of the visual "flatness" in *Weekend*. Reprinted 1976, Nichols, ed., Entry No. 1989.

1460 Herridge, Frances. "Godard in English at Muray [sic] Hill." *New York Post* (27 April).
Brief credits. *Sympathy for the Devil*, performed in alternate versions on alternate nights, is like an impressionist painting rich in provocative imagery. Many "isolated scraps of the today-scene" show a revolution in process.

1461 Hillier, Jim. *"Masculin-Féminin." The Films of Jean-Luc Godard*. Ed. Ian Cameron. New York: Praeger. Pp. 123–30.
Godard discards plot and character in *Masculin-Féminin* because they "deform the truth by presupposing attitudes, behavior, reactions to events." He uses flashes of insight, accidents, improvisation, collage, reminiscences, and cultural references which bring into the film the aesthetic and moral issues raised by mass culture, personal freedom, and Godard's own life. In all of Godard's films, escape, living vicariously, and the separateness of human beings are treated in a stylized way. Here and in *Pierrot* and *La Chinoise*, violence and politics are present but unintegrated factors in the characters' lives, representing the gulf between idea and action.

1462 Isaac, Dan. "The Social Gospel of Jean-Luc Godard." *Film Culture*, No. 48–49 (Winter-Spring), pp. 49–52.
La Chinoise presents its author as "the aestheticized man trying to come to terms with political reality through the artistic medium of film (the medium is the means)." *La Chinoise*'s virtue and fault is that it presents so much conceptual material from so many different angles.

1463 Jacobson, D. *"Weekend." Williamette Bridge*, 3, No. 18 (1 May), 21.
Cited API, 2, No. 2, 30.

1464 Kael, Pauline. "A Minority Movie: *La Chinoise.*" *Going Steady*. Boston: Little, Brown. Pp. 76–84.
Reissued 1971. New York: (Bantam) Grossett & Dunlap. Pp. 91–102. Reprinted from 1968, Kael, Entry No. 1132.

1465 Kael, Pauline. "Weekend in Hell: *Weekend.*" *Going Steady*. Boston: Little, Brown. Pp. 138–44.
Reissued 1971. New York: (Bantam) Grossett & Dunlap. Reprinted from 1968, Kael, Entry No. 1134. Also in 1969, Kael, Entry No. 1309.

1466 Kael, Pauline. "Youth Is Beauty." *Renaissance of the Film*. Ed. Julius Bellone. New York: Collier-Macmillan. Pp. 166–72.

Article on *Masculine-Feminine* reprinted from 1966, Kael, Entry No. 710. Also in 1968, Kael, Entry No. 1131.

1467 Kauffmann, Stanley. "Stanley Kauffmann on Films." *The New Republic*, 162 (9 May), 24.

Reviews *Two or Three Things I Know about Her*. Reprinted 1971, Kauffmann, Entry No. 1588.

1468 Kauffmann, Stanley. "Stanley Kauffmann on Films." *The New Republic*, 162 (6 June), 19 and 30.

Sympathy for the Devil is how a puritan portrays the role of sex in revolution. Both this film and *See You at Mao* are made of "blocks of material, juxtaposed but not joined." This collage method suits both Godard's artistic temperament and his political intent; it's a "propaganda form . . . of the rock-television-cinema age." Reprinted 1971, Kauffmann, Entry No. 1588.

1469 Kent, Leticia. "What Makes Susan Sontag Make Movies?" *New York Times* (11 October), p. 13D.

Sontag says "Godard's conversion should be respected," but she's "one of the fans he's left behind."

1470 Larcher, Diana. "Arts/Entertainment." *Christian Science Monitor* (4 May).

Reviews *See You at Mao*.

1471 Leblanc, Gérard. "Quelle avant-garde? (note sur une practique actuelle du cinéma militante)." *Cinéthique*, No. 7–8, pp. 72–92.

Vent d'est is more for the petit bourgeois intellectual than for the working class, who have other fights to fight beyond that of ideology in film. The intellectual, however, is in danger of substituting fantasy for a real knowledge about a class-structured society. *Vent d'est* has as its starting point not the people but the concrete situation of a cineaste analyzing bourgeois ideological hegemony in terms of cinema.

1472 Linden, George W. *Reflections on the Screen*. Belmont, California: Wadsworth.

Godard's anachronisms are "borrowings from the stage that often fit ill with film form." (p. 12) *Breathless* is based on "newspaper form." (p. 37). Godard makes amateur, boring films, like *Band of Outsiders*, when he narcissistically "confuses expression with self-expression." (pp. 15 and 222–23, 230–31).

1473 MacBean, James Roy. "*See You at Mao*: Godard's Revolutionary *British Sounds*." *Film Quarterly*, 24, No. 2 (Winter), 15–23.

Uses Louis Althusser as a reference point to explicate how *British Sounds* exposes and attacks bourgeois ideology. Embedded in the class struggle, the film does not attempt to be realistic but rather strives to bring us to grips with reality by presenting a concrete analysis of a concrete situation. Reprinted 1975, MacBean, Entry No. 1907.

1474   Maggi, Gilbert. "Cinéma et anarchie." *Sequences*, No. 60 (February), pp. 15–23.
Cited 1969–70, *Index analytique*, p. F. 303.

1475   Manceaux, Michèle. "Godard ne plaisante plus." *Le Nouvel Observateur* (16 February), p. 35.
Godard is leaving to film in Palestine. He's reputed to be masochistic and self-destructive, and he has cut himself off from all but a few militants. His films from 1968 have not been seen by anyone, except on the editing table. Last week he showed *Pravda* in a little theater in the Musée d'Art Moderne. The film is confused but still poetic. Godard's new aesthetic is described.

1476   Marcorelles, Louis. "Protest in Differing Accents." *Le Monde Weekly* (24 June), p. 7.
Brief history and description of *Vangelo 70*, with Godard's episode *L'Amour*. The editing and the photography of the woman resemble *La Femme mariée*. Godard seems to be seeking after the absolute in this beautiful little film about the impossibility of love.

1477   Marias, Julian. "Los cauces." *Visto y no visto: Cronicas de cine, II, 1965–67*. Madrid: Ediciones Guadarrama. Pp. 307–311.
A bout de souffle was recently seen for the first time and is superior to *Alphaville*. Michel and Patricia are "vaguely" or "weakly" motivated characters, a recurring feature of modern fiction, the history of which Marias briefly traces.

1478   Marias, Julian. *"Pierrot el loco."* *Visto y no visto: Cronicas de cine, II, 1965-67*. Madrid: Ediciones Guadarrama. Pp. 398–402.
Pierrot le fou owes little to the Lionel White thriller it supposedly was based on (*Obsession* in English; *Le Démon d'onze heures*). It's a beautiful, deliberately capricious film. Although full of cultural references, it portrays an adolescent world. The actors just don't have either the freshness of innocence or the "destiny" of maturity. Dated January 15, 1967.

1479   Martin, Marcel. "Le Groupe 'Dziga Vertov': Jean-Luc Godard parle au nom de ses camarades du groupe: Jean-Pierre Gorin, Gérard Martin, Nathalie Billard et Armand Marco." *Cinéma 70*, No. 151 (December), pp. 82–88.
In an interview Godard criticizes notions of parallel distribution and advocates giving cameras to workers. He discusses film as a blackboard and calls for new relations between film and viewers, especially in terms of film form. Reprinted 1970, Flash, Entry No. 1441.

1480   Mayersberg, Paul. *"Pierrot le fou."* *The Films of Jean-Luc Godard*. Ed. Ian Cameron. New York: Praeger. Pp. 104–105.
The film "is brilliant but wrong. . . . We don't want poetry on the screen; we want stories, action and characters."

1481   McBride, Joseph. *"See You at Mao."* *Sight and Sound*, 39, No. 3 (Summer), 136–37.

Describes Godard's radical career since 1968, the film *See You at Mao*, and Godard's and Gorin's appearance at the University of Wisconsin.

1482 Mekas, Jonas. "Movie Journal." *Village Voice* (30 April), p. 55.
Two or Three Things and *Far from Vietnam* (here called *Out of Vietnam*) are mentioned favorably in passing. "Godard has found his own polemical film language, a language understandable to a certain semi-intellectual audience."

1483 Mekas, Jonas. "Movie Journal." *Village Voice* (4 June), pp. 54 and 58.
"With *Pravda*, Godard abandons commercial cinema and joins the underground," where there are "much higher and stricter standards." It is a film of romantic "nostalgia for Revolution, for truth," which doesn't give the truth but rather "creates a pattern of sounds and images and voices which sets you in the mood" to search for revolution and truth.

1484 Michaelson, Annette. "Film and the Radical Aspiration." *Film Culture Reader*. Ed. P. Adams Sitney. Praeger Film Books. New York: Praeger. Pp. 404–22.
Originally, 1966, Michaelson, Entry No. 727. Also reprinted 1967, Michaelson, Entry No. 983.

1485 Milne, Tom. "Godard in Sunlight." *The Observer*, Review (26 April).
The plot of *Contempt*, just then showing in England, is given and the sensuous color photography praised. *Contempt* is much better than the later films of "cultural terrorism."

1486 Milne, Tom. "*Le Mépris*." *Sight and Sound*, 39, No. 3 (Summer), 163–64.
In *Le Mépris*, "for the first time in his work, Godard proceeds beyond the image of the actuality of death . . . to contemplate [the] eternity of peace and oblivion. . . . But, then, to him, God is a camera." The relation of all the characters to *The Odyssey* is discussed.

1487 Morgenstern, Joseph. "Coming Together." *Newsweek* (30 March), p. 88.
Godard describes a political revolution in *Sympathy with the Devil* and performs an aesthetic one. The critic discusses the film as antiart and sees the Stones as a metaphor for our "spiritual apartness and technological togetherness."

1488 Morgenstern, Joseph. "Fugue for Sweethearts." *Film 69/70: An Anthology by the National Society of Film Critics*. Ed. Joseph Morgenstern and Stefan Kaufer. New York: Simon and Schuster. Pp. 140–42.
Reprinted from 1969, Morgenstern, Entry No. 1329.

1489 Morgenstern, Joseph. "Paris When She Sizzles." *Newsweek*, 75, No. 20 (18 May), 104 and 107A.
Two or Three Things shows people trapped in the capitalist city, where they "are encouraged to be good consumers and to want goods, but are themselves unwanted goods." Godard uses the prostitution motif to observe how "human

appetites, sexual and otherwise, . . . are not being fulfilled in urban life." "Godard explores the intense life in objects, the near-death in people." Vlady plays with "Brechtian cool."

1490 Morley, Sheridan. Review of Jean Collet's *Jean-Luc Godard*. *Films and Filming*, 17, No. 1 (October), 72.
Cited in Bowles, p. 629.

1491 Morley, Sheridan. Review of Richard Roud's *Godard*. *Films and Filming*, 16, No. 12 (September).
Brief review. Cited in Bowles, p. 629.

1492 Moscariello, A. *Il cinema di Godard*. Rome(?): Partisan.
Book on Godard. Cited 1974, Ferrero, No. 1841.

1493 Mosk[owitz, Gene]. *"Le Vent de l'est (Wind from the East)* (Italo-French-Color)." *Variety* (20 May), pp. 28 and 30.
Brief credits. Cannes. "It is a rather tedious essay that carries many of his methods to an anarchic end . . . Mainly for film festivals, schools, or cinematheques."

1494 Moyer, R. *"Sympathy for the Devil."* *Nola Express*, 1, No. 55 (15 May), 3.
Cited API, 2, No. 2, 30.

1495 Perkins, V.[ictor] F. *"Vivre sa vie."* *The Films of Jean-Luc Godard*. Ed. Ian Cameron. New York: Praeger. Pp. 32–39.
Brief plot summary. The distanciation tactics and cinematic and narrative technique are described in detail. Nana seems a sleepwalker, unable to cope with complexity. "While the film's greatest strength lies in its examination of a temperament, Godard's devices continually destroy context so that Nana's oscillations of mood and attitude fail to cohere into a portrait."

1496 Plasticman. "Godard: Art and Politics." *Good Times*, 3, No. 18 (1 May), 8–9.
Godard's press conference "last Thursday" after showing of *See You at Mao* in Berkeley is discussed. Two people threw tomatoes at Godard. The only people trying to do independent filmmaking, Godard said, are those at Newsreel, but they wrongly emphasize distributing political films before knowing how to produce a politically just film. Grove is paying Godard and Gorin $8,000 for the tour.

1497 Potenze, Jaime. "Cine: *Week-End* (Francia, 1968)." *Criterio*, 93, No. 1606 (October 22), 769–70.
Weekend is a masterful, anarchic critique of bourgeois life and an apocalyptic, pessimistic projection of where real factors subtly destroying modern society will lead. A rational metaphor is followed by pure Absurdism. The critic explicates the social themes behind selected sequences.

1498 Rasch, B. *"Sympathy for the Devil."* *Daily Planet*, 1, No. 16 (22 June), 17.
Cited in API, 2, No. 2, 30.

1499 Rocha, Glauber. "Cinema Novo vs. Cultural Colonialism: An Interview with Glauber Rocha." *Cinéaste*, 4, No. 1 (Summer), 2–9.
Cited 1972, Green, Entry No. 1684.

1500 Rocha, Glauber. Untitled. *Manchete* (Brazil), No. 938 (31 January).
Cited in 1974, Fargier, Entry No. 1840.

1501 Ropars-Wuilleumier, Marie-Claire. *De la littérature au cinéma: genèse d'une écriture*. Paris: Armand Colin.
Godard, along with Resnais, is held as an exemplar of a kind of filmmaking which has at least reached the complexity of great literary fiction. The entire book is an in-depth structural analysis of modes of literary communication from the nineteenth century novel to the *nouveau roman* and cinematic communication from the silent film through the inception of the sound era to today's *cinéma d'écriture* (Godard and Resnais). With Godard, cinema achieves the liberty of "Joycean associations."

1502 Ropars-Wuilleumier, Marie-Claire. *L'Écran de la memoire: essais de lecture cinématographique*. Collection Esprit "La Condition humaine." Paris: Seuil.
"La Forme et le fond ou les avatars du récit," pp. 91–11, reprinted from 1967, Entry No. 959. "*La Chinoise*," pp. 148–51, reprinted from 1967, Entry No. 957. "*Loin du Vietnam*," pp. 217–20, reprinted from 1968, Entry No. 1182. "Le Cru et le cuit," pp. 152–55, reprinted from 1968, *Esprit*, 36 (March), reviews *Weekend* by discussing Godard's use of myth.

1503 Ross, M. "*Sympathy for the Devil*." *Los Angeles Free Press*, 7, No. 16 (17 April), 34.
Cited API, 2, No. 2, 30.

1504 Roud, Richard. "Cannes '70." *Sight and Sound*, 39, No. 3 (Summer).
Wind from the East is the most remarkable and self-assured film of the many politically oriented films that were shown in the Directors' Fortnight.

1505 Roud, Richard. *Jean-Luc Godard*. Second Edition. Collection Cinema One. London: Secker and Warburg. Bloomington: Indiana University Press.
Revised version of 1967, Roud, Entry No. 961. Looks at Godard's work in terms of dialectics and polarities, urban themes, and the nomadic characters who are "outsiders." Looking at each feature film in detail, Roud analyzes their moral and political preoccupations, and particularly the use of the prostitution metaphor to discuss society as a whole. The tension in Godard's work between documentary impulses and abstraction is analyzed, as is fragmentation in *Deux ou trois choses* and *Made in U.S.A*. *La Chinoise*, *Le Gai Savoir*, and *One Plus One* are considered Godard's political films and analyzed in detail. There is a description and analysis of Godard's short films and sketches, a feature not found in the other Godard monographs and anthologies. A complete filmography is given.

1506 S.[ainsbury], P.[eter]. "Jean-Luc Godard." *Afterimage*, No. 1 (April).

Godard is compared to Vertov. Godard's bourgeois detractors attack his formlessness, and his bourgeois supporters have extrapolated from his content but now leave him behind. His films have always rejected the notion of the complete, encapsulated work of art expressing or reflecting life from a distance. Now his films are "fragments, experiments, provisional solutions to problems, . . . aids to discussion," relating to life but not reflecting it, and part of a larger, definable political and philosophical strategy.

1507 Sarris, Andrew. *Confessions of a Film Cultist: On the Cinema, 1955–1969.* New York: Simon and Schuster.
   "*A Woman Is a Woman,*" pp. 167–70, reprinted from 1964, Sarris, Entry No. 433. "Belmondo," pp. 262–68, reprinted from 1966, Entry No. 755. "The New York Film Festival" (discusses *Far from Vietnam*), pp. 317–18, reprinted from 1967, Entry No. 967. "*La Chinoise; Madigan,*" pp. 349–52, reprinted from 1968, Entry No. 1195. "*Weekend,*" pp. 400–406, reprinted from 1968, Entry No. 1197, also reprinted in 1969, *Film 68/69*, Entry No. 1339. "*Pierrot,*" pp. 423-27, reprinted from 1969, Entry No. 1340.

1508 Sarris, Andrew. "Films in Focus: Godard and the Revolution." *Village Voice* (30 April), pp. 53, 61, 63–64.
   Sarris quotes the entire Grove Press press releases on Godard's forthcoming tour, starting April 15, to U.S. universities with Jean-Pierre Gorin, the film *See You at Mao*, and Kent E. Carroll of Grove; and also on the forthcoming (April 26) release of *Sympathy for the Devil* and *One Plus One* on alternate nights. Sarris then comments on Godard's current reputation in the United States and on the "showbiz gossip" about Godard the man. Godard and Gorin see themselves as the only truly revolutionary filmmakers (Cuba has "barred Godard from its shores"). In *See You at Mao*, Sarris finds that Godard has a passion for primary colors more than for political activity, especially in the assembly line sequence and at the end. Godard discussed *Pravda*, his uncompleted *One A.M.*, and the Weathermen. Sarris comments on the left's anti-Zionism. Quoted in *Vent d'est* Program Notes, 8th New York Film Festival, 1970.

1509 Schaefer, Jim. "Godard Should Stay Home." *Liberated Guardian*, 1, No. 8 (11 August), 17.
   The Stones' sequences in *One Plus One* is brilliant but other sequences reveal that "Godard has very little feeling for black culture, especially American black culture." *Le Gai Savoir* extends his modernist overthrow of traditional modes of cinema and "brings his notion of revolution as process to fruition." *See You at Mao* and *Pravda* prove he should make films "within the confines of French culture."

1510 Schechter, Joel. "Brecht and Godard in Ten Scenes from *The Decline and Fall of Aristotle.*" *Yale/Theater*, 3, No. 1 (Fall), 25–30.
   Review of *Weekend*. Godard's film is intransigently anti-Aristotelian. Godard's Brechtianism is clear in his project for *Pour Lucrèce* and in ideas about political theater in *La Chinoise*.

1511 Silber, Irwin. "Godard: Pretentious Polemics." *Guardian*, 22, No. 35 (13 June), 17.
   Cited API, 2, No. 2, 29.

1512 Silber, Irwin. *"Pravda* and *See You at Mao." Guardian*, 22, No. 35 (13 June), 17.
Cited API, 2, No. 2, 30.

1513 Silverstein, Norman. "Godard and Revolution." *Films and Filming*, 16, No. 9 (June), 97–98, 100, 102–105.
Cited in BFI Bibliography.

1514 Simon, John. "Jean-Luc Raves Again." *The New Leader*, 53, No. 10 (11 May), 32–33.
Compares *Sympathy for the Devil* to *Woodstock*. Godard gives us a "tenth rate piece of pop-music, . . . bits of appalling political-philosophic comic strips, . . . and his homely and untalented wife." Reprinted and condensed, with no reference to *Woodstock*, 1971, Simon, Entry No. 1618.

1515 Simon, John. "Propaganda and Pretension." *The New Leader*, 53, No. 19 (5 October), 23.
The 8th New York Film Festival consisted of either leftist or homosexual propaganda. Its "obligatory Godard film" was *Wind from the East*, sloppily made, hollow and inflammatory — and also poorly dubbed.

1516 Simsolo, Noël. *"Les Carabiniers." Image et son: Revue du cinéma*, No. 244, pp. 17–20.
Credits, plot summary. Made at the same time that Godard was planning to film *Pour Lucrèce* as a reflection on theater and life, *Les Carabiniers* has many theatrical elements — which Simsolo analyzes. In *Les Carabiniers* Godard finds ways to deprive the spectator of an illicit pleasure in the portrayal of war. This film indicates Godard's future militancy.

1517 Simsolo, Noël. *"Le Petit Soldat." Image et son: Revue du cinéma*, No. 244, pp. 101–106.
Tells the history of the film, noting the actors' relation to Godard and his trouble with censors then and throughout his career. Bruno is a person searching for his identity. Three sequences are analyzed to show the multiple meanings Godard gets from photographing faces, and these meanings are contrasted with what the characters say and what Bruno's voice-off commentary tells.

1518 Simsolo, Noël. *"Pierrot le fou." Image et son: Revue du cinéma*, No. 244, pp. 107–115.
Credits, complete plot summary. A description is given of the following persons' careers: Jean-Paul Belmondo, Antoine Duhamel, Lionel White, Georges de Beauregard, and Raymond Devos. The film was censored for under 18 year olds because of "intellectual anarchism." This work of pure cinema attacks narrative and moves by forms, colors, and composition to present a "savagely" emotional account of love, the sun, and death. Simsolo asks questions aimed to provoke a debate on the film.

1519 Spiers, David. "Review of Cameron's book, *The Films of Jean-Luc Godard. Screen*, 11, No. 2 (March-April), 86–88.
Cited in Bowles, p. 623.

1520   Steel, Ronald. "Where's the Relevance?" *Film Society Review*, 6, No. 2 (October), 33–39.
   Cited in 1972, Green, Entry No. 1684.

1521   Steele, L. "2 or 3 Things I Know about Godard." *Los Angeles Free Press*, 7, No. 30 (24 July), 19.
   Cited API, 2, No. 3, 30.

1522   Strick, Phillip. *"Le Mépris (Contempt) (Il disprezzo)."* *Monthly Film Bulletin*, 37 (July), 141–42.
   Credits, plot summary. Discussion of how Godard develops the theme of anguished lost love. The critic prefers that strain in Godard which treats "love, life and tragedy on a grand *Hollywoodisé* scale — references to Hitchcock, Hawks, Garbo and all."

1523   Tanner, Alain. "Alain Tanner dietro il muro." *Bianco e nero*, 31, No. 1-4 (January-April), 115–16.
   Tanner says he owes most to Godard, who has revolutionized cinema.

1524   Thirard, Paul-Louis. "Deux films 'maoistes': *Le Peuple et ses fusils* & *Pravda.*" *Positif*, No. 114 (March), pp. 1–7.
   With militant films, the critic should analyze the form, the politics presented, the adequacy of the independent mode of production and distribution — and should give this cinema militant support. In *Pravda* Godard admirably explores how to create a new cinematic language for political reportage, but his formal propositions are tentative and hesitant. His analysis of Czech revisionism is inadequate and dogmatic. Where did that revisionism begin? Prague Summer itself was a move toward liberal capitalism, not communism.

1525   Vaughan, Ciba, trans. *Jean-Luc Godard: An Investigation into His Films and Philosophy*. Ed. Collet, Jean. Series Cinéma d'aujourd'hui in English. New York: Crown. 218 pp.
   Trans. from 1968, Collet, Entry No. 1088; *see also*, 1970, Collet, Entry No. 1425.

1526   Walker, John. Review of *Contempt*. *Films and Filming*, 16, No. 10 (July), 40–41.
   Brief review. Cited in Bowles, p. 95.

1527   Walker, Michael. "Pierrot le fou." *The Films of Jean-Luc Godard*. Ed. Ian Cameron. New York: Praeger. Pp. 106–118.
   Analyzes in depth how *Pierrot le fou*'s cinematic techniques develop the fantasy of escaping a dehumanized urban society. He also analyzes the ambiguity of the heroine's feelings and the difficulty the hero has in understanding her, the film's celebration of freedom and search for a lost happiness, the sense of dislocation and despair, the portrait of self-destructive humanity, and the overtones of war.

1528   Wallington, Mike. *"La Chinoise, ou plutôt à la Chinoise."* *Monthly Film Bulletin*, 37 (November), 216–17.

Credits, plot summary. "Violent" formal aspects express new concepts — ideological ones — in a new way.

1529 Westerbeck, Colin J., Jr. "Movies: Sympathy for Godard." *Manhattan Tribune* (16 May), p. 10.
Reviews *One Plus One* and *Le Gai Savoir*.

1530 Winkler, Richard. *"Le Petit Soldat." The Films of Jean-Luc Godard*. Ed. Ian Cameron. New York: Praeger. Pp. 17–20.
Brief plot summary. Considers the theme of illusion and of reality as developed through the character of Bruno Forestier. Reprinted 1975, *Godard: Three Films*, Entry No. 2297.

1531 Wood, Robin. *"Alphaville." The Films of Jean-Luc Godard*. Ed. Ian Cameron. New York: Praeger. Pp. 83–93.
Brief plot summary. Godard tries to fuse the vitality of Lemmy Caution and pop culture with "the sense of tradition embodied in the arts." The film's structure is based on two oppositions — light vs. darkness, straight line vs. circle — "around which group themselves pairs of opposed ideas: isolation/togetherness, technology/art, emotional death/love." Wood dislikes Godard's treating violence and brutality humorously and associating all positive values with violence.

1532 Wood, Robin. *"Bande à part." The Films of Jean-Luc Godard*. Ed. Ian Cameron. New York: Praeger. Pp. 61–70.
Brief plot summary. Why are Godard's films so obscure and uneven? It is partly because of his method of working, partly because of his Brechtian bent, and partly due to his search for cinematographic "freedom." Cameron examines the film's characterization, cinematography, switches of tone, and theme (i.e., becoming lost in daydreams and pursuing melodramatic solutions).

1533 Zettler, Mike. *"Sympathy* Due." *Kaleidoscope-Milwaukee*, 3, No. 4 (1-14 May), 12.
Cites reviews of *Sympathy for the Devil* to describe it in advance of its showing.

1534 Zimmerman, Paul D. "Shooting from the Hip." *Newsweek*, 77, No. 19 (10 May), 116.
Godard artistically delivers his Maoist manifesto in *Vladimir and Rosa* with humor, pop culture politics, and an explicit interrogation of the very concept of political filmmaking. The film suffers from its simplistic message and its doctrinnaire, academic, and often boring tone.

1971

1535 Adler, Renata. *A Year in the Dark: A Year in the Life of a Film Critic, 1968–69*. Berkley Medallion Books. New York: Berkley Publishers.
"Jean-Luc Godard's *La Chinoise*," pp. 127–28, reprinted from 1968, Adler, Entry No. 1007; "War, Foreign Languages, and War Again on Sundays," pp. 159–61, about *Les Carabiniers*, Entry No. 1005; "Godard's *Les Carabiniers*," pp. 148–49, Entry No. 1006; "Style Politic II: *La Chinoise* on Sunday," pp. 170–71, Entry No. 1002; "Faces at the Cannes Festival," pp. 174–77, Entry No. 1000; "How Their

World Might Ideally Be," pp. 177–81, Entry No. 1003; "Very *Far from Vietnam*," pp. 186–87, Entry No. 1009; "Intense Whisper: *Two or Three Things I Know about Her*," pp. 270–72, Entry No. 1008; "A Terminal Smashup: *Weekend*," pp. 273–74, Entry No. 999; "*Weekend*, and Antagonizing Audiences," pp. 299–302, Entry No. 997; "Godard Stalks the Real through Movies: Report," pp. 319–22, about the filming of *One A.M.*, Entry No. 1001.

1536 Alessandrino, Paulo. "Godard." *Actuel*, 13 (October), 52–55.
Dziga Vertov had a unique approach to using montage for "newsreels." Godard's group explores the aesthetic problems of political cinema rather than make films for workers. *Le Gai Savior, British Sounds, Pravda, Luttes en Italie, Vent d'est* and *Vladimir and Rosa* are discussed in these terms. An original chart made by Godard, with his characteristic intellectual wit, is included. It delineates "the current situation of French cinema (situation of class struggle)."

1537 Allard, Pierre. "Godard: A Select Bibliography." *Take One*, 2, No. 11 (May-June), 11.
Lists books devoted to Godard, selected magazine interviews, and scenarios in English and French.

1538 Altman, Robert (photographer). "Dziga Vertov Notebook." *Take One*, 2, No. 11 (June), 7–9.
Photo essay of Godard and Gorin's notebooks for *Till Victory*, the Palestine film.

1539 Anon. Article on Godard's accident. London *Times* (10 June), p. 1.
Cited 1971, *Times Index* (May-June), p. 92.

1540 Anon. Article on Godard's condition after accident. London *Times* (11 June).
Cited 1971, *Times Index* (May-June), p. 92.

1541 Anon. Article on Godard's progress after his motorcycle accident. London *Times* (30 June).
Cited 1971, *Times Index* (May-June), p. 92.

1542 Anon. "*La Chinoise* et la critique." *La Chinoise: L'Avant-Scène du cinéma*, No. 114 (May), pp. 39–40.
Lengthy quotations from eight reviews.

1543 Anon. "*La Chinoise*/Godard." *Saint Louis Outlaw*, 1, No. 11 (22 January), 9.
Cited API, 3, No. 1, 50.

1544 Anon. "Godard Recuperating after Cycle Accident." *Variety* (14 July).
Paris. Godard reportedly has a budget of $1.2 million for *Tout va bien*, which will be made in both French and English in France.

1545 Anon. Interview with Godard. *Liberated Guardian*, 1, No. 19 (1 March), 17.
Cited API, 3, No. 1, 58.

1546   Anon. "Marketing the Revolution." *Liberated Guardian*, 2, No. 1 (1 June), 14.
Cited in API, 3, No. 2, 58.

1547   Anon. Recent Filmography. *Take One*, 2, No. 10 (March-April), p. 27.
Brief listing of films and partial credits from 1966–1970.

1548   Anon. "Revolutionary Cinema." *Liberated Guardian*, L, No. 21 (15 April), 56.
Cited in API, 3, No. 2, 60.

1549   Anon. *"Vladimir and Rosa."* *Film Facts*, 14, No. 23, 632–34.
Synopsis and quotations from reviews (*Newsday,,Village Voice, New York Times*).

1550   Aprà, Adriano, ed. and trans. *Il cinema è il cinema*. Rome(?): Garantzi.
This book of articles by and interviews with Godard is introduced by Pier Paolo Pasolini and contains both original material, translations from the French, notes, and an extensive bibliography. Cited 1974, Ferrero, No. 1841.

1551   Aristarco, Guido. *"Vento de l'est*, pensare e non essere pensati." *Cinema nuovo* (Florence), 20, No. 210 (March-April), 95–96.
Reviews *Vent d'est*.

1552   A.[rmes], R.[oy]. "Jean-Luc Godard." *A Concise History of the Cinema. Volume 2: Since 1940*. Peter Cowie, ed. London: A.S. Zwemmer. New York: A.S. Barnes. Pp. 114–16.
Godard is the most audacious, prolific, and influential of the New Wave filmmakers. He's come to a dead end but has still "made audiences and film directors reexamine the basic qualities of the medium."

1553   Bory, Jean-Louis. *Des yeux pour voir*. Paris: L'Union Générale des Editions.
This collection contains reviews primarily from *Arts*. "Pour et contre Godard," pp. 90–117, see 1971, Bory, Entry No. 1555; *"Vivre sa vie,"* pp. 90+, 1962, Entry No. 173; *"Le Mépris,"* pp. 96+, 1963, Entry No. 256; *"Bande à part,"* pp. 101+; *"Une Femme mariée,"* pp. 101+, 1964, Entry No. 366; *"Alphaville,"* pp. 107+, 1965, Entry No. 491; *"Pierrot le fou,"* pp. 112+, 1965, Entry No. 492.

1554   Bory, Jean-Louis. "Jean-Luc Godard selon deux points de vue." *Dossier du cinéma, cinéastes, I*. Ed. Jean-Louis Bory and Claude Michel Cluny. Paris: Editions Casterman. Pp. 97–99.
Godard relies on shocking audiences emotionally and visually and forces them to think about cinema by denying them illusion, identification, anecdote, and logic. Living inside a world of cinema, Godard uses it to explore and reveal his own thought, books and historical events as experienced by him, and cinematic process itself. Juxtaposition, collage, and rapid filming allow Godard to "gallop after time, after events," but such a style also precludes mature reflection and a truly polished artistic work.

1555 Bory, Jean-Louis. "Pour et contre Godard." *Des yeux pour voir*. Paris: L'Union Générale d'Éditions. Pp. 90–117.

Analyzes the following films: *Vivre sa vie* (it is philosophical and respectful of its protagonist); *Le Mépris* (it is about Woman, as Bardot incarnates her, and about Cinema); *Bande à part* (briefly commented on); *La Femme mariée* (it was censored for treating marriage, not adultery, as the problem); *Alphaville* (it was a pamphlet that had to transform itself into a mythological adventure tale to convey its message); and *Pierrot le fou* (color and movement provide the visual description of emotion).

1556 Buckley, Peter. "*Two or Three Things I Know about Her*." *Films and Filming*, 17, No. 4 (January), 51–52.

Brief credits. Godard sticks objects and people together as equals, finds all symbols empty and manipulable at will, attacks society cynically and in a cliched way, and never offers a solution.

1557 Byron, Stuart. "Agitprop Gratuit: Who Cares?" *Village Voice* (29 April).

Vladimir and Rosa has a diverting, pseudo-Brechtian format and expressionless, macho heroes. The film is too private. Quoted at length in *Film Facts* (1971, Anon., Entry No. 1549).

1558 Canby, V.[incent], "From Roz to Bela Lugosi." *New York Times* (16 May), Sec. II, p. 1.

Godard's *Vladimir and Rosa* has some comic moments but his "ruminations" about revolutionary filmmaking are "very, very bland."

1559 Canby, Vincent. "Godard's Social Mix, *Vladimir and Rosa*." *New York Times* (30 April), p. 45.

Brief credits. *Vladimir and Rosa* is played energetically and with childlike exuberance — a burlesque political cartoon. It often tires with its stern didacticism, and technically it is poor, often, literally, pale and fuzzy. Quoted at length in *Film Facts* (1971, Anon., Entry No. 1549).

1560 Cast, David. "Godard's Truths." *Film Heritage*, 6, No. 4 (Summer), 19–22.

Analyzes *Pravda* and *See You at Mao* by comparing them to the theories and work of the early Russian filmmakers. Now an "aesthetic moralist," Godard searches to find images' true meanings; we need "true texts over true images," Godard says. Yet the vivid and clear images contrast with Godard's poorly articulated politics.

1561 Casty, Alan. *The Dramatic Art of the Film*. New York: Harper & Row.

Discusses the following aspects of Godard's work: his symbolic use of color (p. 118), unusual methods of character development (p. 131), and Brechtianism (pp. 172–77).

1562 Ciment, Michel. "Bergame (reprise)." *Positif*, No. 123 (January), p. 68.

Brief mention of the showing of *Lotte in Italia* at the Festival of Bergamo.

1563 Cocks, Jan. *"One Plus One." Film 70/71.* Ed. David Denby. New York: Simon and Schuster. Pp. 208–209.
Review.

1564 Dawson, Jan. Review of the Pennebaker Completion. *Monthly Film Bulletin*, No. 451 (August).
Cited 1974, Collet, Entry No. 1832.

1565 Diamant, Ralph. *One P.M." Take One*, 2, No. 10 (March-April), 25.
Detailed explication of the film praises the Leacock-Pennebaker sections over Godard's: "the 'lesser lights' rebelled against what they saw as a rip-off."

1566 Diamant, Ralph. "One P.M. Movie Review: Godard, Leacock Pennebaker." *Berkeley Tribe.* No. 79 (22 January), 17.
In the part of *One P.M.* which is Godard's own footage we see that Godard distorted ideas, showed his politics were "nothing but rhetoric, and robbed the people he filmed of their dignity." But in the part filmed *about* Godard, we see a "struggle, as Godard's crew resists his direction." Review is written by member of American Documentary Films.

1567 Duflot, Jean. Article on Godard. *Politique-Hebdo*, No. 17 (28 January).
Cited 1972, de Gregorio, Entry No. 1687.

1568 Elsaesser, Thomas. "Godard's Sounds." *Monogram*, 2 (Summer), 7.
Cited in Schuster, p. 168.

1569 Farber, Manny. *Negative Space.* London: Studio Vista. New York: Praeger. Reissued 1975, as *Movies.* New York: Stonehill Publishing Co.
"Jean-Luc Godard," pp. 259–68, reprinted from 1968, Farber, No. 1108. *"La Chinoise* and *Belle de jour,"* pp. 269–74, reprinted from 1968, Farber, Entry No. 1107.

1570 Felheim, Marvin. *"Masculine-Feminine* as Genre" in "Critical Approaches to *Masculine-Feminine."* Paper presented at Midwest Modern Language Convention, November.
Masculine-Feminine can be analyzed for its newsreel approach, Godard's philosophical position, or its propagandistic aspects. Also Godard uses a typical screen-romance-with-an-unhappy-ending plot, upon which the other episodes obliquely reflect. Satirizing romance implicitly satirizes many films that have conditioned us.

1571 Gégauff, Paul. "Salut les coquins." *Lui*, January, pp. 25–26, 29, 38, 89, 96, 98, 106, 108.
In British Film Institute Library.

1572 Gelmis, Joseph. Review of *Vladimir and Rosa. Newsday* (30 April).
Godard has long been arrogant, fanatically didactic, and against entertainment. This film is dull and "shoddily put together." Cited at length in 1971, Anon., *"Vladimir and Rosa," Film Facts*, Entry No. 1549.

1573 Gilliatt, Penelope. "Godard Proceeding." *New Yorker*, 47 (8 May), 116–19.

Vladimir and Rosa is a Brechtian didactic film with humor, hesitancy, and grace. "Godard shows the inside of things by remaining outside, and he remains light." Reprinted 1972, Gilliatt, Entry No. 1680.

1574 Gilliatt, Penelope. *"Two or Three Things I Know about Her." Film 70/71.* Ed. David Denby. New York: Simon and Schuster. Pp. 205–208.
Reprinted from 1970, Gilliatt, Entry No. 1446.

1575 Glaessner, Verina. *"Vent d'est." Time Out* (London), No. 94 (3–12 December), p. 49.
Cited in BFI Bibliography.

1576 Goldmann, Annie. *Cinéma et société moderne: le cinéma de 1968 à 1968: Godard, Antonioni, Resnais, Robbe-Grillet.* Paris: Editions Anthropos.
"Problèmes méthodologiques," pp. 35–55, discusses the ways that modern art presents indices of culture — as "homologues that are not conceptual and do not refer to a totalizing concept" but rather gain sense only from the structure of the work as a whole, or, less successfully, as "classifying concepts," e.g., the bourgeoisie or Gaullist France in *Weekend.* "Le Héros godardien et le monde," pp. 79–85, looks at Godard's rejection of contemporary civilization. *"A bout de souffle,"* pp. 86–92, sees Michel as a forerunner of "youth in revolt." *"Le Petit Soldat,"* pp. 93–98, discusses the theme of people's blindness and indifference to a barbarous society. *"Vivre sa vie,"* pp. 99–103, describes Nana as an object of consumption who believes a vague, sentimental "mythology" of individual liberty, which only serves to make her interiorize and thus accept the course of her life. *"Les Carabiniers,"* pp. 104–111, discusses Godard's use of abstraction, description of the mechanisms and effects of authoritarianism, and characters who have false consciousness. In the future he would set these types in the setting of the consumer society. *"Le Mépris,"* pp. 112–31, reprinted from 1964, Olivier, Entry No. 420. *"Bande à part,"* pp. 132–37, sees the film as a nostalgic, tender, chaste film where purity wins out over evil. The camera work and imagery predominate. Godard is ironic, at a distance from his characters, and easy going. *"Une Femme mariée,"* pp. 138–45, looks at Godard's portrait of a consumer society and his protagonist's adapting to it. *"Alphaville,"* pp. 146–50, states that Godard should have placed more emphasis on Natasha's coming to awareness than on her falling in love. *"Masculin-Féminin,"* pp. 150–55, sees the film not as a real narrative or series of portraits but as an effort to describe social types. *"Pierre le fou,"* pp. 156–62, relates Ferdinand's character to that of Michel Poiccard, both romantic rebels. *"Deux ou trois choses que je sais d'elle,"* pp. 163–68, finds that Godard destroyed the Brechtian aspect of the film by inserting his own monologue, which brought in a pathetic, subjective element and made the film end on a "veritable profession of faith." *"Made in U.S.A.,"* pp. 169–72, discusses why both the theme and the structure of the film are based on incoherence. *"La Chinoise,"* pp. 173–78, discusses the film as prophetic and takes its protagonists seriously as "real revolutionaries," albeit treated critically and skeptically by Godard. *"Week-End,"* pp. 179–83, finds the film a cinematic *pièce-a-thèse,* using caricature and a description of a "global structure."

1577 Goodwin, Michael and Tom Luddy. "The Dziga Vertov Group in America." *Georgia Straight* (Vancouver), 5, No. 67 (18 May), 20–21.
Excerpts reprinted from 1971, Goodwin, et al., Entry No. 1578. Cited API, 3, No. 2, 66.

1578 Goodwin, Michael, et al. "The Dziga Vertov Film Group in America." *Take One*, 2, No. 10 (March-April), 8–27.

Tom Luddy, Naomi Wise, Michael Goodwin interview Godard and Groin on political filmmaking. For longer version and entry, see 1972, Goodwin, Entry No. 1681.

1579 Goodwin, Michael, et al. "Dziga Vertov Group Interview." *Gold Coast Free Press*, 1, No. 11 (1 July), 17.

Michael Goodwin and Tom Luddy interview Godard. Cited in API, 3, No. 3, 39.

1580 Gould, Haywood. "Jean-Luc Godard and the Sensibility of the Sixties." *The Image Maker*. Ed. Ron Henderson. Richmond, Va.: John Knox Press. Pp. 66–74.

Analyzes Godard's work in terms of modern alienation and dissatisfaction with social conditions, the mass media, and advertising.

1581 Green, Ron. "*Pravda*." *Take One*, 2, No. 11, (May-June), 13.

Green explains the relation between Godard's visual symbolism and his critique of revisionism in Czechoslovakia. This symbolism depends on the use of red and the right-left axis of the frame.

1582 Greenspun, Roger, "Film: Portraits of Two Artists." *New York Times* (27 November), p. 23.

Brief credits. In *Two American Audiences*, Godard tells what he thought he was doing in *La Chinoise*, but neither his words nor the chopped up inserts of that film "explain" that film.

1583 Haycock, Joel. "Notes on Solanas and Godard" (1st of 2 parts). *Film Society Review*, 7, No. 3 (November), 30–31.

Describes critically the development of Marxist aesthetics in French film journals, especially in the newly founded *Cinéthique*, which will not review capitalist movies but considers mostly the work of Godard.

1584 Haycock, Joel. "Notes on Solanas and Godard" (2nd of 2 parts). *Film Society Review*, 7, No. 4 (December), 31–36.

Godard's collective works autonomously politically. Discusses the political importance of Godard's later films, which "attempt to present modes of analysis for social material." *Un Film comme les autres, See You at Mao*, and *Pravda* are reviewed and compared to Solanas' *La hora de los hornos*, which uses documentary images without reflection. Reprinted from *Camera People*, n.d.

1585 Henderson, Brian. Godard's Paradigm." Mimeographed paper, Student Conference on Film Study, sponsored by Oberlin College in April.

Analyzes the radio messages at the end of *Weekend* and the relation of the four films mentioned to the history and "expressive possibilities of narrative cinema and of the realization of those possibilities over four decades." The films are *Potemkin, The Searchers* (called *Prisoners of the Desert* in French), *Johnny Guitar*, and *The Legend of Gosta Berling*.

1586 Jahiel, E.[dwin]. *"Masculine-Feminine* by Jean-Luc Godard," in "Approaches to *Masculine-Feminine."* Paper presented at Midwest Modern Lanugage Association Convention, November.
Discusses Godard's borrowings from de Maupassant and Brecht, use of "interrogation," and antifeminism. Each episode combines "theatricality, violence, and sex".

1587 Jouffroy, Alain. "Un Affaire à régler avec le monde entier." Press Book presented by Parc-Films and Athos Films for *La Chinoise* (May 1967), published in *La Chinoise: L'Avant-Scène du cinéma*, No. 114 (May), pp. 8–11.
Godard's political development (as a "Robinson Crusoe of Marxism-Leninism") is described and the political efficacy of *La Chinoise* evaluated. *See* 1967, Jouffroy, Entry No. 937. Also excerpts in 1970, Collet, Entry No. 1425.

1588 Kauffmann, Stanley. *Figures of Light: Film Criticism and Comment.* Harper Colophon Books. New York: Harper & Row.
"La Chinoise (April 27, 1968)," pp. 66–70, reprinted from 1968, Kauffmann, Entry No. 1135. *"Les Carabiniers* (June 1, 1968)," pp. 81–82, reprinted from 1968, Entry No. 1138. *"Weekend* (October 19, 1968)," pp. 109–112, reprinted from 1968, Entry No. 1136. *"Pierrot le fou* (February 22, 1969)," pp. 138–40, reprinted from 1969, Entry No. 1311. *"Two or Three Things I Know about Her* (May 9, 1970), pp. 258–60, reprinted from 1970, Entry No. 1467. *"Sympathy for the Devil, See You at Mao* (June 6, 1970)," pp. 264–66, reprinted from 1970, Entry No. 1468.

1589 Kauffmann, Stanley. "Stanley Kauffmann on Films." *New Republic,* 164 (1 May), 24 and 34.
Vladimir and Rosa is the "most effective agitprop of Godard's political films." It's based on caricature, street theater, and "cinematic hijinks." Cartooning suits Godard. However, the critic regrets that Godard "has foresaken ambiguity for certainty."

1590 Kavanagh, Thomas M. *"Le Gai Savoir." Film Quarterly*, 25, No. 1 (Fall), 51–53.
"The word is unmasked as the far from innocent — and far from simple — unit of ideological discourse"

1591 Koch, Christian. "Cinema in Context" in "Approaches to *Masculine-Feminine."* Paper presented at Midwest Modern Language Convention, November.
Offers a description of the film as part of a whole communication system, noting the changes we must strive for in that system so that viewers have full feedback. He proposes certain guidelines for teaching the film.

1592 Krebs, Albin. "Notes on People." *New York Times* (10 June), p. 37.
A brief report of Godard's motorcycle accident and his suffering hip fractures is given. The unidentified woman driving the cycle was run over by a bus after they'd been hit by a van.

1593 Laiman, Leah. *"Vladimir and Rosa." Show*, 2, No. 5 (July), 55.
Godard demands the spectator be interested in revolution — both political and cinematic.

1594   Lebel, Jean-Patrick. "A propos de Godard." *Cinéma et idélolgie.* Paris: Editions Sociales. Pp. 44–49.
Cited BFI Bibliography.

1595   Lokin, Jules. *"Wind from the East." Take One*, 2, No. 10 (March-April).
Brief review. The film is a powerful allegory, "an impressive collage of visual and aural dialectics, synthesizing the spirit of the revolution."

1596   Luddy, Tom. *"British Sounds." Take One*, 2, No. 11 (June), 12.
Detailed description of the film, interpreted from a left perspective.

1597   Luddy, Tom. *"A Film like Any Other." Take One*, 2, No. 10 (March-April), 14.
Explication of the film and the political context in which it was made. Its fate at its New York screening pleased Godard.

1598   MacBean, James Roy. *"One Plus One*, or the Praxis of History." The *Parisan Review*, July.
Close analysis of the film explains the political intent of the film in Marcusian terms. MacBean praises this film for tendencies he will denounce later in his book, which nevertheless contains this same essay. Reprinted 1975, MacBean, Entry No. 1907.

1599   MacBean, James Roy. *"Vent d'est*, or Godard and Rocha at the Crossroads." *Sight and Sound*, 40, No. 3 (Summer), 144–50.
Godard's attack on the "bourgeois concept of representation" is analyzed in depth. MacBean discusses the following concepts which *Vent d'est* raises to a conscious level and provides a political analysis of: acting style, depth of field, traditional relations between image and sound, film as vicarious experience and as fantasy, passive reception of film vs. using it as a tool of political analysis, and the "cult of spontaneity" in political action. Reprinted, slightly abridged, 1972, Godard, *Weekend* and *Wind from the East* script, Entry No. 2353. Also reprinted 1975, MacBean, Entry No. 1907; reprinted in 1976, Nichols, ed., Entry No. 1989.

1600   Mansfield, Joseph. "Open vs. Programmatic Cinema in *Masculine-Feminine*" in "Approaches to *Masculine-Feminine*." Paper presented at Midwest Modern Language Convention, November.
Godard seemingly identifies with Paul, rejecting interviews and finally cinema verite. Godard uses drama to comment on the relation between theater and reality, and he refers in other ways to "both honest and deceptive art." Godard escapes "dogmatism and deception" as his artistic vision extends beyond that of this characters.

1601   Martin, Marcel. "200. Godard, Jean-Luc (1930–)." France. Screen Series. London: A.S. Zwemmer. New York: A.S. Barnes. Pp. 66–67.
Brief filmography. Martin says that Jean-Henri Roger codirected *British Sounds.*

1602   Mellen, Joan. *"Vladimir and Rosa." Cinéaste*, 4, No. 2 (Winter), 39.
Negative review. "Godard reveals a singular contempt for his audience" in this film in which "image increasingly militates against idea."

1603 Mellen, Joan. *"Wind from the East." Film Comment*, 7, No. 3 (Fall), 65–67.

Wind from the East does not have a formal organizing principle that adequately expresses notions of causality. It also needs a myth, a controlling metaphor, or a situation about lived experience to bring this Maoist ideology to life. An authoritarian tone rather than persuasiveness, and the advocating of terrorism, damage the revolutionary cause. Credits.

1604 Moore, Judity. "Godard Burns Italian Art Film Org., Deserts Its Program at Mid-Point." *Variety* (31 March).

Godard was to participate in a conference for greater appreciation and wider distribution of art films. He showed up for the opening press conference in Rome, but failed to go to Turin for the showing of *Le Gai Savoir*.

1605 Nichols, Bill. *"Struggles in Italy." Film Quarterly*, 25, No. 1 (Fall), 56–57.

The political progress of the young bourgeoise in the film is described, as is Godard and Gorin's use of black leader (Gorin not credited here). Does the protagonist's solitariness represent the political limitations of the intellectual who "thinks" his/her way to political correctness? Godard would be well off now to face the problems of the working class directly.

1606 Pechter, William S. *Twenty-Four Times a Second*. New York: Harper & Row.

"=Time²," pp. 17–36, reprinted from 1962, Pechter, Entry No. 217. "For and Against Godard," pp. 242–253, reprinted from 1969, Pechter, Entry No. 1332. Godard is also mentioned passim, pp. 311–12, 314–15, and provides the conclusion for the book — in which Pechter tries to define both film greatness and great criticism.

1607 Pontaut, A. *"Godard, la lutte des classes et le vent qui rend fou." Le Magazine Maclean* (Montreal), 11 (December), 56.

Review of *Vent d'est* and discussion of Godard's politics. Cited 1972, *Canadian Periodicals Index*, 25 (publ. in 1974), p. 185.

1608 Rambaud, Patrick. "Deux ou trois choses que je pense de lui_____." *Actuel*, 13 (October), 55 and 57.

Godard's political filmmaking career is traced. His films are an aesthetic and political failure for they are overly verbal and made only for militants.

1609 Reed, Rex. *Big Screen, Little Screen*. New York: Macmillan.

Pierrot le fou owes everything to Belmondo, who romps in a "sun-ripened technicolor, New Wave sandbox." (pp. 219–20). Reed saw *Wind from the East* and hated it, crowded into an off-Broadway cinema after the New York Film Festival Committee had "violently rejected [the film] as trash." (p. 403).

1610 Rice, Susan. *"Le Gai Savoir." Take One*, 2, No. 10 (March-April), 11.

This interesting film demands a knowledge of French and of many contemporary intellectual and political figures. Godard seems to be giving up on creating a significant popular art. This is the last of his films that is illuminating and even whimsical rather than bitter and preachy.

1611 Robe. *"Vladimir and Rosa* (French-Color)." *Variety* (28 April).
This is a "totally confused film by Jean-Luc Godard about his usual paranoic anti-Americanism."

1612 Rondolino, Gianni. *Cinema e pubblicita nell'opera di Jean-Luc Godard.* Torino: Accademia delle scienze. 44 pp.
The critic discusses Godard's critical articles and traces the theme of advertising in Godard's films from *A bout de souffle* through *One Plus One.* Godard is similar to a pop artist who sees mass advertising as a unique element of modern life, which his art both reflects and criticizes. Reprinted 1972, Rondolino, Entry No. 1720.

1613 Roud, Richard. *"Sympathy for the Devil."* Monthly Film Bulletin, 38 (April), 83.
Credits, brief description. This series of fragments has no "meaning" but is Godard's attempt to go back to an aesthetic zero in the cause of developing a political art.

1614 Salem, James M. *"Breathless (1961)."* A Guide to Critical Reviews: Part IV: The Screenplay from "The Jazz Singer" to "Dr. Strangelove." Metuchen, N.J.: Scarecrow Press. P. 152.
In a bibliography listing reviews in the U.S. press of U.S. and foreign feature films, Salem curiously cites reviews for *Breathless* but for none of Godard's other films.

1615 Seguin, Louis. "Les Rencontres de Hyères en 1971: *Vladimir et Rosa."* *Positif,* No. 129 (July-August), pp. 62–63.
Balanced evaluation of the film, which is finally negative. "Godard's revolutionary fantasies are turned once again to amuse the class in power."

1616 [Sery, Patrick]. "Les Films du groupe 'Dziga-Vertov.'" *Le Monde* (8 April), p. 21.
Godard asked Sery to rectify the error of the previous week when Sery called the films presented at Brussells Godard's and not the Dziga Vertov Group's films.

1617 Sery, Patrick. "Jean-Luc Godard: 'Le Cinéma est un moment de la révolution." *Le Monde* (1 April), p. 17.
Godard visits European capitals and provincial French film societies to show and discuss his political films, which have no distributors. His interaction with one audience is cited at length.

1618 Simon, John. *Movies into Film: Film Criticism 1967–70.* New York: Dial Press.
"La Chinoise," pp. 249–60, originally 1968, Simon, Entry No. 1208; briefer version 1968, Entry No. 1211; here a postscript added after "student unrest" in France. *"Sympathy for the Devil,"* pp. 272–74, reprinted from 1970, Entry No. 1592.

1619 S.[imsolo], N.[oël]. *"Vent d'est."* Image et son: la saison cinématographique, No. 252–53 (September-October), pp. 287–88.
Credits, brief résumé. Discusses Godard's relation to the original Dziga Vertov's work. Cinematically the film is "magnificent, modern, effective." Politically Godard is still searching.

1620 Tuten, Frederic. "Conversation with Chairman Mao." *The Adventures of Mao on the Long March.* New York: Citadel Press. Pp. 103–21.

In this fictional interview, Mao speaks as an authority on contemporary U.S. and European culture and makes aesthetic and political pronouncements on *Breathless* and *La Chinoise.*

1621 Villelaur, Anne. "Jean-Luc Godard." *Dossiers du cinéma: cinéastes 1.* Ed. Jean-Louis Bory and Claude Michel Cluny. Paris: Casterman. unpated.

Discusses and refutes critics who have praised Godard. *Weekend* is certainly not an image of civilization in chaos. Like the rest of Godard's work, it is just "a bric-a-brac, a melange of petty snobisms and petty, confused ideas."

1622 Weiler, A.H. "Jane Fonda Signs for French Film." *New York Times* (16 April), p. 27.

Yves Montand and Jane Fonda have signed to do *Tout va bien.* Production information and plot of that film are given.

1623 Westerbeck, Colin Jr. "A Terrible Duty Is Born." *Sight and Sound*, 40, No. 2 (Summer), 81–83.

The critic analyzes Godard's films in terms of their self-conscious reference to cinematic tradition. Particularly in *Two or Three Things* and *Wind from the East* this reference and constant awareness about cinema itself function politically.

1624 Williams, Christopher. "Politics and Production: Some Pointers through the Work of Jean-Luc Godard." *Screen*, 12, No. 4 (Winter), 6–24.

This in-depth study of Godard's aesthetics and political intent sees Godard's cinema as providing "a multiplicity, a meeting place of a whole number of differing kinds and degrees of consciousness." The various elements in *Vivre sa vie* are listed and that film discussed in detail. Godard's post-1968 aesthetic-political development is closely followed. Bibliography.

1625 Williamson, Bruce. "*Le Gai Savoir.*" *Film 70/71.* Ed. David Denby. New York: Simon and Schuster. Pp. 209–210.

Godard's film is tedious and meaningless.

1626 Winsten, Archer. "The New Movie: *Vladimir and Rosa* in Town." *New York Post* (30 April), p. 28.

Godard drones on through another whole film about revolution and the evils of capitalism, etc.

1627 W.[olf], W.[illiam]. "*Vladimir and Rosa.*" *Cue* (1 May).

There are clever moments and a strong idea, but the film is boring and plodding.

1972

1628 Anon. "Entretien avec Godard-Gorin." *Politique-Hebdo*, No. 26 (27 April).

Montand and Fonda were chosen as stars (Mao himself also acts self-consciously as a star); they could see the complete story board of the film each day.

Godard and Gorin compare and contrast *Tout va bien* with traditional filmmaking and also with Godard's old films, especially in terms of the film's relation to the spectator. Long extracts reprinted 1974, Collet, Entry No. 1836.

1629 Anon. "Godard Back to Commercial Pix with *All Is Well*." *Variety* (26 April), pp. 1 and 69.
Production information is given about *Tout va bien*.

1630 Anon. "Godard-Gorin: Production of Distribution." *The Animator*, 1, No. 1 (December), 1–2.
In a press conference with questioners not identifed, Godard and Gorin discuss working collectively, *Tout va bien*, *Letter to Jane*, Deleuze and Guattari's theories, and the place of cinema within capitalism.

1631 Anon. Godard issue, *Filmmuseet*, magazine of the Danish Film museum (March-April-May).
In Museum of Modern Art clipping file.

1632 Anon. "Godard (Jean-Luc)." *Positif (Index du Numéro1 au Numéro134)*, No. 141 (August), p. 18.
Lists all articles printed on Godard in *Positif* from *A bout de souffle* to *Vladimir and Rosa*.

1633 Anon. "*One P.M.* at the Whitney Museum." *New York Post* (11 February).
Reviewer finds film "slanted and inconclusive" and even museum curator finds it "very difficult."

1634 Anon. Review of *La Chinoise, Two or Three Things, Weekend. Cinéaste*, 5, No. 3 (Summer), pp. 42, 47, 34.
MMRI, 1972, p. 39, 256, 276.

1635 Anon. Review of Collet's *Jean-Luc Godard*. *International Film Guide*, 9, p. 473.
Brief mention; cited in Bowles, p. 629.

1636 Anon. Review of *Tout va bien*. New York *Daily News* (2 May).
Tout va bien is reviewed from France. It is just another Godard film, this one with poor, one-dimensional acting. (Museum of Modern Art clipping file.)

1637 Anon. Review of *Tout va bien*. *Politique Hebdo* (11 and 25 May).
Cited 1972, de Gregorio, Entry No. 1687.

1638 Anon. Review of *Tout va bien*. *Témoignage chrétien* (4 May).
Cited 1972, de Gregorio, Entry No. 1687.

1639 Anon. Review of *Vent d'est*. *Monthly Film Bulletin*, 39, No. 456 (January), p. 18.
MMRI, 1972, p. 262.

1640   Anon. Review of *Weekend*. *The Listener*, 88, No. 2271 (5 October), p. 453.
   Mixed review of *Weekend*. Cited MMRI, 1972, p. 268.

1641   Anon. Review of *Wind from the East*. *Catholic Film Newsletter*, 37, No. 4 (February), p. 23.
   Negative review. Cited MMRI, 1972, p. 276.

1642   Anon. "Revolt in the Fishbowl." *Newsweek* (6 November).
   Review of *Tout va bien*.

1643   Anon. *"Tout va bien."* *Christian Science Monitor* (13 October), p. 4.
   In *Tout va bien*, a fine cinematic sense is brought into play on basically "oppressive material." *Letter to Jane* is "interminable."

1644   Anon. "13. *Tout va bien: Just Great*." Program Notes. Los Angeles International Film Exposition, Sunday, November 12.
   Brief credits, plus Godard and Gorin's aphoristic comments on the film.

1645   Aristarco, Guido. "Kje je Godard?" *Ekran*, 10, No. 96–97, 269–70.
   Godard's recent development is discussed. IIFP, 1974, p. 280.

1646   Aristarco, Guido. "Marx, le cinéma, et la critique de film." Trans. Barthélemy Amengual." *Etudes cinématographiques*, No. 88-92. Paris: Lettres Modernes-Minard. Pp. 56–58, 170–71, 181, 184–85, 215.
   Discusses Godard's Brechtianism and Godard's having "one eye cast on Pirandello," especially in *Weekend* and *La Chinoise*. Godard's later films have a firmer ideological foundation. They investigate entire historical perspectives and use Brechtian techniques more profoundly.

1647   Baby, Yvonne. "Jean-Luc Godard: 'Pour mieux écouter les autres.'" *Le Monde* (27 April), p. 17.
   In an interview on *Tout va bien*, Godard discusses his post-1968 filmmaking, his working with Gorin, and the audience response expected from *Tout va bien*. Long extract reprinted 1974, Collet, Entry No. 1836.

1648   Baroncelli, Jean de. *"Tout va bien* de Jean-Luc Godard et Jean-Pierre Gorin." *Le Monde* (3 May), p. 26.
   The "love story" and the political episodes are not quite convincing, but the manner of telling is brilliant, and, as the filmmakers desired, "political" in that it contributes to the renovation of cinematographic language.

1649   Baudry, Pierre. "La critique et *Tout va bien*." *Cahiers du cinéma*, No. 240 (July-August), pp. 10–18.
   An in-depth Marxist analysis is offered of the ideological presuppositions of the articles written on *Tout va bien* in an essay similar in its organization to Brecht's "Dreigroschenprozess" (trans. in French as "Sur le cinéma").

1650   Beh, Sieh Hwa. *"Vivre sa vie."* *Women and Film*, No. 1, pp. 70–73.

Examines Godard's style, his view of prostitution, and his extension of the prostitution metaphor to cover women's situation in general. Reprinted in 1976, Nichols, ed., Entry No. 1989.

1651 Belilos, Marlène, et al. Press conference on *Tout va bien.* Trans. Tony Rayns. *Cinema Rising*, No. 2 (May), p. 15.

Extracts are given of Godard and Gorin's press conference, where they were questioned by Marlène Belilos, Michel Bojut, Jean-Claude Deschamps, and Pierre-Henri Zoller. Godard and Gorin elaborate on what they mean by the "political production" of films. German version of this, 1973, Belilos, Entry No. 1759, in a longer version.

1652 Bory, Jean-Louis.. "L'Évangile selon Jean-Luc." *Le Nouvel Observateur* (8 May), p. 77.

With *Tout va bien*, Godard has decided to speak again to a broader audience. *Coup pour coup* better portrayed the experience of a strike, but the subject of *Tout va bien* is really the worn-out intellectual, i.e., Godard. The final moral, a call to civic duty, is one of those old platitudes that bears repeating. Yet to label Godard Brechtian does not mean this film portrays the situation in France as well as his films in 1966–67 did. Reprinted 1975, Bory, Entry No. 1880.

1653 Bory, Jean-Louis. *La Nuit complice: 1966–1968.* Paris: 10/18, L'Union Générale d'Editions.

This collection primarily contains reviews from *Le Nouvel Observateur*, including "A l'hauteur de nos tourments" (1967, Entry No. 836), pp. 103–106; "Ils tuent pour vous: *Made in U.S.A.*" (1966, Entry No. 651), pp. 47–56; "La Brûlure du présent: *Made in U.S.A.*" (1967, Entry No. 835), pp. 77–79; and "Un Poète en colère: *Weekend*" (1968, Entry No. 1071), pp. 146–70. "Rhapsodie pour un massacre: *Loin du Viêtnam* (1967, Entry No. 837), pp. 134–38.

1654 Breton, Émile. "Sur le Programme politique." *La Nouvelle Critique*, No. 56 (September), pp. 64–70.

Because *Tout va bien* does not refer back to and even represses a preexisting concrete Marxist analysis which can and does explain the class situation in France, the film "reinserts petit bourgeois humanism all too naturally into the deep structure of the film's discourse."

1655 Brown, Royal. "*La Chinoise*: Child's Play." *Focus on Godard.* Ed. Royal Brown. Film Focus Series. Englewood Cliffs, N.J.: Prentice-Hall. Pp. 168–73.

La Chinoise has a political content but is ambiguous in its political orientation. "Godard very clearly delineates between the calm, adult, and rather natural world of the liberals . . . and the frenetic, active, theatrical, and rather childlike world of the radicals." Brown closely analyzes the sequence between Anne Wiazemsky and her real-life teacher Francis Jeanson.

1656 Brown, Royal. "Chronology." *Focus on Godard.* Ed. Royal Brown. Film Focus Series. Englewood Cliffs, N.J.: Prentice-Hall. Pp. 10–24.

Provides an extensive chronology of Godard's life and career from 1930–72.

1657 Brown, Royal S. "Filmography" and "Bibliography." *Focus on Godard.* Ed. Royal S. Brown. Film Focus Series. Englewood Cliffs, N.J.: Prentice-Hall. Pp. 174–88.
 Gives a filmography from 1954–1972, a brief indication of Godard's unfinished films, and entries in the following bibliographic categories: film scripts, selected stills, works by Godard (including interviews), books on Godard, general articles, reviews of specific films. Multilanguage entries are given.

1658 Brown, Royal S., ed. *Focus on Godard.* Film Focus Series. Englewood Cliffs, N.J.: Prentice-Hall. 188 pp.
 All articles in this book are annotated separately here.

1659 Brown, Royal S. "Introduction: One Plus One Equals." *Focus on Godard.* Ed. Royal S. Brown. Film Focus Series. Englewood Cliffs, N.J.: Prentice-Hall. Pp. 5–19.
 Godard works within French modernism or the "debourgeoisification" of the narrative arts. His films eschew narrative and remain "anchored in the instant." Against a background of chaos and banality . . . Godard juxtaposes a varied layer of idealism that runs the gamut . . . from poetic involvement and even romanticism to radical political action."

1660 Brown, Royal S. "Jean-Luc Godard: Nihilism versus Aesthetic Distanciation." *Focus on Godard.* Ed., Royal Brown. Film Focus Series. Englewood Cliffs, N.J.: Prentice-Hall. Pp. 109–22.
 Godard's art contains paradoxes: nihilism vs. moral radicalism, distanciation vs. autobiography. Godard's cinematic allusions maintain their "external, objective identity." His films have an abstract beauty and a cinematic virtuosity, and he revolutionarily uses music as "more or less another pure aesthetic element." Until the Dziga Vertov Group films he created both a new cinematic language and a superior artistic reality to replace the negative one he observed.

1661 Bruno, Eduardo. "G. comme Godard: *Tout va bien*: Cinema/practica militante." *Filmcritica*, 23, No. 227 (September), 268–71.
 Gives a political analysis of the film, and discusses its use of Brechtian techniques.

1662 Buffa, M. "Crepa padrone, tutto va bene." *Filmcritica*, 24, No. 231 (January-February), 43–45.
 Reviews *Tout va bien.* Cited IIFP, 1973, p. 254.

1663 Byron, Stuart. "**Tout va bien** (at the Harvard Square)." *The Real Paper*, n.d.
 The dramatic struggle of the characters is not convincing, but the cinematography is fascinating. (Museum of Modern Art clipping file).

1664 Capdenac, Michel. "Deux histoires d'amour." *Les Lettres françaises* (10 March), pp. 14–15.
 Tout va bien's exaggeration does not help create an effective satire or a dynamic social criticism. The situation of the couple has great potential but is diluted into nothing.

1665 Carlini, F. "Politica/cinema/actilop." *Bianco e nero*, 33, No. 7–8 (July-August), 45–54.
> About political filmmaking in France since May '68. Cited, IIFP, 1973, p. 108.

1666 Carroll, Kathleen. "Latest Godard Film Is 45-Min. Atrocity." *(Daily) Sunday News* (29 October), Leisure Sec., p. 12.
> Fonda and Montand in *Tout va bien* "look like two characters in search of a film that's not worth finding." Shown with *Letter to Jane* where Godard "drowns in his own rhetoric." Clipping from Lincoln Center Library Godard file.

1667 Casetti, F. "Oltre l'inscrizione, la scrittura." *Bianco e nero*, 33, No. 7-8 (July-August), pp. 81–92.
> Semiological analysis of Straub and Godard. Cited, IIFP, 1973, p. 311.

1668 Chevalier, M. "Auto-distruzione della rappresentazione. *Film critica*, 23, No. 227 (September), 271–74.
> "Suggests that representation defeats its own purpose in *Tout va bien*." IIFP, 1973, p. 254.

1669 Clouzot, Claire. *Le Cinéma français depuis la nouvelle vague*. Paris: L'Alliance française/Ferdinand Nathan. Passim.
> Deals with Godard's career and films under the following categories: (1) the genesis of the New Wave, especially the *"Cahiers* group," the themes of their films (romantic, personal, love), and the stylistic characteristics of their films (mise en scène, photography, camera movement, editing, choice of actors, direction); (2) fictional French political filmmaking — its themes, sources, characters, decors, and visual styles; (3) the Dziga Vertov Group's collective work and *Cinéthique*'s interest in it; and (4) *Tout va bien*.

1670 Collet, Jean. *"Tout va bien." Etudes*, 336 (June) 902–905.
> The formal strategies of the film effectively create a structure to convey its political concepts. A close reading of the film is offered.

1671 Conway, James. "Jean-Luc Godard Wants to Live for the Revolution, Not Die for It." *New York Times* (24 December), Magazine sec., pp. 20–24.
> The author accompanied Godard and Gorin for several days from a Lincoln Center appearance to one at Rutgers University. Anecdotes of Godard's past outrageous behavior are related, as well as extensive, provocative quotations from Godard's and Gorin's conversations. *Tout va bien* and *Letter to Jane* are briefly described.

1672 Curtis, Thomas Quinn. "Godard's Absorbing *Tout va bien*." *International Herald Tribune* (28 April), p. 17.
> This brilliantly photographed, obliquely autobiographical film is a provocative and absorbing portrayal of "what threatens to be another lost generation." Curtis also discusses the unedited Palestine footage.

1673 Daniel, Joseph. *Guerre et cinéma: grandes illusions et petits soldats, 1895–1971*. Cahiers de la fondation nationale des sciences politiques, No. 180. Paris: Armand Colin. Pp. 350–61, 388–95.

Examines in detail the censorship of *Le Petit Soldat* in the context of other films about the Algerian war. Describes the plot of and critical reactions to *Les Carabiniers*. In discussing films about the Vietnam war, Daniel mentions *Masculin-Féminin, Pierrot, Made in U.S.A., La Chinoise*, and *Loin du Viêtnam*, with a detailed analysis of the last two.

1674 Degand, Claude. *Le Cinéma — cette industrie.* Paris: Editions Techniques et Economiques. 272 pp.
This is a useful study for understanding the New Wave's "fate" in the 1960s, the French CNC's relation to the film industry, film costs, distribution, and the dependence of European film industries on U.S. investment.

1675 Delain, Michel and de Vericourt, Guillemette. "La Censure clandestine." *L'Express* (14–20 February), pp. 58–59.
No film about May 1968 has been commercially released due to censorship; to insure its release, *Tout va bien* will use stars. Godard's ten films since 1968 were seen at the Festival of Hyères in 1971, but have probably been seen by only 25,000 people in total. The head of the Board of Censors, Pierre Soudet, claims that French films have not effectively criticized French society because filmmakers lack the talent to do so.

1676 Delmas, Jean. *"Tout va bien." Jeune cinéma*, No. 64 (July-August), pp. 42–44.
There is no reason to "pit" this film against *Coup pour coup*. Godard and Gorin effectively use middle class characters as protagonists so as to introduce into the film an honest "dimension of reflection" on the class position of who is speaking. This class position can be defined, come to terms with, and altered as the protagonists enter into the workers' struggle.

1677 Eisenschitz, Bernard. *"Tout va bien*: un film plein de talent." *La Nouvelle Critique*, No. 56 (September), pp. 64–70.
Evaluates the pros and cons of the film from a leftist perspective — looking at its content, its formal challenge to bourgeois cinema, its dividing audiences both along class lines and along the lines of those who will or will not accept its formal concerns. The conditions of and struggle against class exploitation are finally "mystified" in the film, which ends up being more about the couple's "love story."

1678 Evan, Martin. "Gorin, Jean-Pierre: des travailleurs artistiques de l'information." *Le Monde* (27 April), p. 17.
Gorin is interviewed on *Tout va bien*, released April 28. He discusses Brecht's influence, working with Godard, and Godard's past work.

1679 Gallagher, T.A. "What Lies between the Objects?" *Village Voice* (24 August), p. 51.
Reviews *Godard on Godard*; Milne's notes, photos, and index enhance the book's critical value. For the *Cahiers* critics, according to Gallagher, cinema was an "imprint of a mythology," the tracing of a path toward existential salvation." Gallagher discusses Godard's attitudes toward gesture, Rossellini, others' films, relation between theme and expression, and — by implication — Bazin.

1680   Gilliatt, Penelope. *"Vladimir and Rosa*: Godard Proceeding." *Film 71/72: An Anthology by the National Society of Film Critics.* Ed. David Denby. New York: Simon and Schuster. Pp. 159–62.
Reprinted from 1971, Gilliatt, Entry No. 1573.

1681   Goodwin, Michael and Marcus, Greil. *Double Feature: Movies and Politics.* New York: Outerbridge and Lazard. Pp. 9–68.
This is a much longer version of a series of interviews, some of which were published in *Take One.* A biographical commentary is inserted at various points. April 1970, interview: Godard and Gorin discuss the failure of *One A.M.*; group filmmaking; the achievements and limitations of *La Chinoise,* Brecht, and *One Plus One.* Second interview at Leacock-Pennebaker studios: Godard and Gorin contrast *One A.M.* to *Struggles in Italy;* they also discuss super-8 and magnetic sound. April 23, interview in Berkeley: Godard and Gorin express disdain for the ecology issue, discuss Godard's political evolution and what he has learned, and explain the financing and distribution of their militant films (especially *Vent d'est* and the Palestine film). At a press conference in Berkeley, Godard and Gorin encounter hostile students, discuss their politics and the political failure of *La Chinoise* and *One Plus One,* Godard's career, underground and political filmmaking, and ruling class artistic form (e.g., *Z*). April 24, interview with NET and Tom Hayden: Godard and Gorin do a political critique of their having involved U.S. radicals in *One A.M.* Originally published in an abridged version in 1971, Goodwin et al., *Take One,* Entry No. 1578.

1682   de Graff, T. "Nana of de realiteit in een klein frans tehuis." *Skrien,* No. 29-30 (Spring), pp. 28–31.
Analysis of *Vivre sa vie.* Cited in 1972, IIFP, p. 244.

1683   Grande, Maurizio. *"Lotte in Italia*: Practica-teoria-practica transformata." *Filmcritica,* 23, No. 227 (September), 275–77.
A political analysis of the film. Godard's reflection on film language is seen as his specific contribution to political theory.

1684   Green, James Ronald. "Political Evolution in Five Films of Jean-Luc Godard." Ph.D. dissertation, SUNY at Buffalo. *Dissertation Abstracts,* 33, 3584A.
Takes the following films and applies a different critical methodology to each. He considers *Pierrot le fou*'s relation to the Romantic tradition, *Masculin-Féminin* as an ethnographic film, *La Chinoise* as concrete poetry, *Made in U.S.A.* as a political statement, and *Deux ou trois choses* as a comment on everyday life similar to Henri Lefevre's *Everyday Life in the Modern World.*

1685   Greenspun Roger. "Film Fete: Miss Fonda, Montand in *Tout va bien.*" *New York Times* (11 October), p. 51.
Brief credits. Discusses the thematic use of the tracking shot and Godard and Gorin's political concerns. Godard's old camera techniques are here, but too simplified and too much in the service of a linear argument. Excerpts reprinted 1973 (17 February), Greenspun, Entry No. 1783.

1686   Greenspun, Roger. Review of *One P.M. New York Times* (11 February), p. 27.

Brief credits. Greenspun describes the film and finds it lacking both in content and cinematography, with an especially irritating use of the zoom lens.

1687 Gregorio, Eduardo de. "Sur le diapositif du film." *La Nouvelle Critique*, No. 56 (September), pp. 64–70.

Godard's critics violently disagreed about what *Tout va bien* did or did not accomplish, but all used the term "political analysis" in their arguments. Gregorio discusses the techniques of cinematic distanciation which manages the way various modes of political discourse are presented to us in the film. The camera work, the juxtaposition of stereotypes, the discussion of certain political issues are presented in the film within a structure that invites the spectator to make her/his own analysis by using that very structure.

1688 Harcourt, Peter. "The Loss of Community: Six European Directors." *Cinema Journal*, 12, No. 1 (Fall), pp. 2–10.

"A comparison of the respective world-views of six directors." IIFP, 1973, p. 311.

1689 Henderson, Brian. "*Weekend* and History." *Socialist Revolution*, 12 (November-December), 57–92.

Provides an in-depth study of class-typing in *Weekend* and evaluates the political efficacy of such a narrative tactic. He sets his argument in the context of concepts developed by Brecht, Lukács, Engels, and Benjamin.

1690 Hennebelle, Guy. "*Vive le cinéma.*" *Écran*, 9 (November), p. 14.

"Apropos the TV program *Vive le cinéma*, first banned but later broadcast by ORTF, Hennebelle expresses his disagreement with the concepts of *Cahiers du cinéma* and Jean-Luc Godard." IIFP, 1974, p. 280.

1691 K., H.W. "*Tout va bien.*" *Women's Wear Daily* (11 October).

Tout va bien and *Letter to Jane* are patronizing and doctrinaire.

1692 Kinder, Marsha, and Beverle Houston. "*La Chinoise*" (1967). *Close-Up*. New York: Harcourt, Brace, Jovanovich, Pp. 217–21.

La Chinoise has qualities of "humor, complexity, and inventiveness," which the later Dziga Vertov Group films lack. In *La Chinoise* we are very clearly asked to criticize the limitations of the characters, yet seriously to consider the questions of aesthetics and politics which they and the film as a whole raise.

1693 Kinder, Marsha and Beverle Houston. "*Contempt* (1963)." *Close-Up*. New York: Harcourt, Brace, Jovanovich. Pp. 262–67.

The following aspects of the film are analyzed: the connection between art and human relations, aesthetic issues in adaptation, Godard's autobiographical statements about his marriage, his relations with producer Joseph E. Levine and director Fritz Lang, the three-act structure, the symbolic use of color, and the melodramatic or parodic use of music.

1694 Kinder, Marsha and Beverle Houston. "Jean-Luc Godard: *Breathless* (1959)." *Close-Up*. New York: Harcourt, Brace, Jovanovich. Pp. 208–212.

The emphasis on the present in *Breathless* fits Michel's character, the gangster myth, the use of newspapers, the documentary function of the film, and the sense of spontaneity, mobility, and speed.

1695 Kinder, Marsha and Beverle Houston. *"A Married Woman: Fragments of a Film Made in 1964." Close-Up.* New York: Harcourt, Brace, Jovanovich. Pp. 212–17.

"The film simultaneously mocks conventions of film and of bourgeois culture." A shallow woman's fragmented life is presented in a film form which examines and comments on language, the documentary convention of the interview, and the convention of the lovemaking sequence. "The focus on the body stresses people's separateness."

1696 Knudson, M. *"Tout va bien* — eller Alt går som smurt." *Kosmorama*, 18, No. 110 (September), 263–64.

"An analysis of *Tout va bien* as compared with Marin Karmitz' *Coup pour coup*." IIFP, 1973, p. 235.

1697 Kovacs, Steven. *"Tout va Bien." Take One*, 3, No. 4 (June), 34–36.

Godard's political subject matter is as impressive as his cinematic technique, a fact played down by bourgeois reviewers. However, the reunion of the couple at the end is so mechanical it reveals Godard's inability to develop the theme of the couple's relationship adequately. We get no real sense of how their activities at the factory affected them.

1698 Leblanc, Gérard. "Lutte idéologique en *Luttes en Italie." VH 101*, No. 9 (Autumn), pp. 73–79.

This in-depth evaluation of Godard and Gorin's use of visual style to present a political analysis in *Luttes en Italie* critiques their political analysis from a Marxist-Leninist point of view.

1699 Leblanc, Gérard. "Sur trois films du Groupe Dziga Vertov." *VH 101*, No. 6, pp. 19–36.

The films of the Dziga Vertov group demand to be studied in terms of the historical and material context in which they were made. *Vent d'est* reflects both real contradictions in cinematic practice and of contradictions within the general assembly that had gathered to make the film. Leblanc describes that "assembly" in terms of the student left and Maoist lines that had developed in France since May 1968. The assembly's political conflicts are not resolved, merely represented in the film. This indicates the filmmakers' subjective incapacity to produce the analyses for which they see the necessity. Leblanc examines in detail the image codes in the film and their relation to social structure.

1700 Lefèvre, Raymond. *"Tout va bien." Image et son: Revue du cinéma*, No. 262 (June-July), pp. 101–102.

The film uses the Montand character to reflect on Godard's experiences as a filmmaker. It will certainly not please the Communists or the labor unions. Godard and Gorin have mastered the adaptation of Brechtian distanciation to cinematic form. The film also admirably explores the reality of a couple's relation to economic infrastructures.

1701 Lesage, Julia. *"Tout va bien* and *Coup pour coup*: Radical French Film in Context." *Cinéaste*, 5, No. 3 (Summer), 47–50.

A critique of the French Communist party and a presentation of working women's demands, usually ignored by trade unions, are two political themes developed in both films.

1702   Locke, Richard, "Books of the Times: A Filmmaker's First Career." *New York Times* (21 June).
This review of *Godard on Godard* begins with a brief review of Godard's career. Godard is a ferocious, epigrammatic, captious, intellectual artist obsessed with words. The book disappoints because it has none of the qualities of Godard's films, where he incorporated criticism into "intensely provocative, funny, intelligent, heartfelt, glacial collages." The critical writings are inaccessible.

1703   Lou Sin Groupe d'intervention idéologique. "Le Groupe Dziga Vertov (1)."*Cahiers du cinéma*, No. 238–239 (May-June), pp. 34–38. (First of two articles.)
A Marxist-Leninist political analysis is offered of Godard's post-1968 work, with special attention paid to *Pravda, Vent d'est,* and *Luttes en Italie* (the text of which film follows).

1704   [Lou Sin Groupe]. "Le Groupe Dziga Vertov (2)." *Cahiers du cinéma*, No. 240 (July-August), pp. 4–9.
An aesthetic analysis of the achievements and limitations of the 1969 Dziga Vertov Group films is given from a Marxist-Leninist perspective. Screenplays of *Pravda* and *Vent d'est* follow.

1705   Lou Sin Group. "Luttes de classes sur le front cinématographique en France: *Coup pour coup* et *Tout va bien.*" *Cahiers du cinéma*, No. 238-39 (May-June), pp. 5–32.
This in-depth Marxist-Leninist analysis of *Tout va bien* and *Coup pour coup* considers both films by raising the following political and aesthetic issues as problems: empiricism and cinematic realism; and revisionism, including *Coup pour coup*'s anarcho-syndicalist politics and "ultra-democratic" form of filming. *Tout va bien* is an example of a Brechtian kind of critical realism, and it also offers within it a critique of cinematic realism; yet Godard's work is still limited to the topic of subjective ideological transformation. Two appendices to the article are an essay on Mao's philosophy of knowledge by Tcheou Hsiué-li (1971) and Brecht's "Notes to the Opera *Mahagonny*."

1706   MacBean, James Roy. "Godard and the Dziga Vertov Group: Film and Dialectic." *Film Quarterly*, 26, No. 1 (Fall), 30–44.
Discusses *Till Victory*, Godard's decision to work collectively, the people whom art does and does not serve in a society, filmmaking *for* militants, and the role of editing in the Dziga Vertov Group films. In-depth analyses are provided for *Pravda, Struggle* [sic] *in Italy,* and *Vladimir and Rosa.* Reprinted in 1975, MacBean, Entry No. 1907.

1707   Marcus, Greil and Michael Goodwin. *Double Feature: Movies and Politics.* New York: Outerbridge and Lazard. Pp. 9–68.
See 1972, Goodwin, Entry No. 1681.

1708   Marie, Michel. "Qu'est-ce qui ne va donc pas?" *La Nouvelle Critique*, No. 56 (September), pp. 71–72.

Gorin and Godard refuse to "illustrate" a political situation or line in *Tout va bien*. They are trying to work out a new theory of cinematic/ideological codification and a new form of political expression. Their content rests on an "anarchist ideology, very slightly tinted with Maoism."

1709 Martin, Marcel. "Tout va bien — pour la capital!" *Écran*, 7 (July-August), 44–45.
Review of *Tout va bien*. Cited, IIFP, 1972, p. 236.

1710 Mauriac, Claude. "Retour sur Jean-Luc Godard." *Le Figaro* (27 May).
Cited 1974, Collet, Entry No. 1832.

1711 Merrill, Martha. "Black Panthers in the New Wave." *Film Culture*, Nos. 53-54-55 (Spring), pp. 134–45.
At the London Film Festival, Godard gives a political speech, asking the audience to demand their 10 shillings back and send it to Eldridge Cleaver's defense fund. Ian Quarrier is interviewed, as are "Jenny" and "Jane" of Open Films (to whom Godard lent his own copy of *One Plus One* to be shown free outside the National Film Theater). Merrill also interviews Richard Roud and Godard himself about the film and that event. (Article written Winter 1968.)

1712 Miccichè, L. *Il nuovo cinema degli anni '60.* Rome(?): ERI.
Book on new films of the sixties with reference to Godard. Cited 1974, Ferrero, Entry No. 1841.

1713 Milne, Tom, ed. and trans. *Godard on Godard.* London: Secker and Warburg. New York: Viking. 292 pp.
Trans. of 1968, Godard, Entry No. 2263. In this edition, Milne provides commentary and notes for each of Godard's articles. He has paired stills from Godard's films with those from films Godard has written about, so that we see past cinematic moments that might have influenced Godard's own work.

1714 Morandini, Mordando. "Francia/cinema." *Bianco e nero*, 33, No. 7–8 (July-August), 15–16.
In an in-depth article on French militant cinema and debates in France between *Cahiers du cinéma* and *Cinéthique*, the critic analyzes *Vent d'est* as a film based on "analogues."

1715 Mosk[owitz, Gene]. "*Tout va bien (All is Well)* (French-Color)." *Variety* (17 May), p. 28.
Brief credits. Discusses Brechtian distanciation and agit-prop themes in film. Comments on the film's treatment of the couple and of history.

1716 Nourissier, François. "Godard-Gorin: le souffle court." *L'Express* (2–7 May), pp. 88–89.
Godard and Gorin opened *Tout va bien* in Paris while everyone else was at Cannes, and the press was insulted by the invitations sent out for the press screening. The narration is "anti-aesthetic," the ideological monologues babbling or grotesque, and the strike sequences less effective than those in *Coup pour coup*. *Tout va bien* is just a "social cocktail" based on provocation.

1717 Quinnell, Ken. "Learning the Lingua Franca." *Nation* (Sydney, Australia), No. 335 (4 March), p. 19.
Weekend shows Godard's political transition. The film critiques bourgeois sexuality and a social system which engenders violence. Godard dominates contemporary cinema. His newest work has moved toward stasis and semiotic rigor.

1718 Renaud, Tristan. "La Nouvelle Vague à bout de souffle: une rupture dans la continuité." *Cinéma 72*, No. 163 (February), pp. 66–74.
A brief history of the New Wave is given. Cinematically these directors used fast stock, shot on location, and rejected traditional lighting. *A bout de souffle*, though it looks ordinary today, was an important breakthrough and the group's "manifesto." In the end, the New Wave's realism was superficial and its social engagement also superficial.

1719 Rice, Susan. "*Vladimir and Rosa.*" *Take One*, 2, No. 11 (June), 14.
"Godard still likes a pretty face and is willing to exploit it." It is less frenetic, complex, and colorful than the other political movies by Godard. It is earnest and often humorous, but too laborious.

1720 Rondolino, Gianni. "Cinema publicita nell'opera di Jean-Luc Godard." *Atti dela accedemia delle scienze di Torino*: Classe di scienze morale, storiche, e filogogiche, 106, pp. 55–98.
Reprinted from 1971, Rondolino, Entry No. 1612.

1721 [Ropars-] W.[uilleumier], M.[arie]-C.[laire]. "Une Fiction materialiste." *Esprit*, 40 (June), 1059–62.
The dialectical construction of *Tout va bien* is examined and found lacking in several crucial areas. Godard has always been concerned with the problem of "how to say it," but his characters, and ultimately the film, cannot find a language for the left, which would express what "left" means.

1722 Rosenbaum, Jonathan. "Paris Journal." *Film Comment*, 8, No. 3 (September-October), 2 and 76–77.
Godard and Gorin's irreverant invitation to the press for *Tout va bien* is reprinted. The film's compositions are "neutral." All is planned. The Montand character seems Godard's self-portrait; and the film has a sense of calm and assurance as it challenges and rebukes but offers no guide for the future.

1723 Rosenbaum, Jonathan. "Theory and Practice: The Criticism of Jean-Luc Godard." *Sight and Sound*, 41, No. 3 (Summer), 124–26.
In analyzing *Godard on Godard*, Rosembaum considers "the dense network to be found between Godard's reviews, other films Godard saw, and the ones he would eventually make. Considering several films in detail, Resembaum demonstrates how Godard's films criticize, imitate, and respond to genre conventions.

1724 Roud, Richard. "Godard is Dead, Long Live Godard-Gorin —*Tout va bien!*" *Sight and Sound*, 41, No. 3 (Summer), 122–24.
Discusses what the directors mean when they say they are making a materialist film. Montand and Fonda and a story of the "private lives" of a

bourgeois couple are used to draw audiences into the film. Godard's unique sense of camera movement, sound, and editing have reemerged.

1725 Roud, Richard. "Introduction." *Godard on Godard*. Trans and ed. Tom Milne. New York: Viking. Pp. 7–10.

Considers Godard's reputation as a critic, his polemics, the continuity of his writing with his early filmmaking, the auteur critics' role in introducing us to film history and "bring[ing] some order to the enormous corpus of films," and Godard's criticism as a cinematic "diary" or portrait of himself.

1726 Sadoul, Georges. *Dictionary of Films*. Trans., ed., and updated by Peter Morris. Berkeley: University of California Press.

Morris' critical additions are bracketed in the text. Brief credits, plot summary, and critical summary are given for each entry. *"A bout de souffle,"* p. 1: Sadoul discusses the protagonists' roles, the unconventional editing style, and "the vision of Paris." Morris notes the breakthrough in film form. Brief credits. *"Pierrot le fou,"* p. 284: "Godard's style attempts to evoke this absence of precision in the struggles of love and life." (Sadoul) *"Vivre sa vie,"* pp. 406–407: Morris finds this a touching and complex mixture of "social document, theatricality, and interior drama in the Bresson manner." *"Les Carabiniers,"* p. 52: Michel Cournot is quoted. *"Le Mépris,"* p. 216: Sadoul calls this a "taut, vibrant and sensitive [film], whose tragedy unfolds relentlessly." *"Bande à part,"* p. 23: Morris quotes Pauline Kael. *"Alphaville, une étrange aventure de Lammy Caution,"* p. 8: Richard Roud is cited. *"Masculin-Féminin,"* p. 212: Scott Burton is cited, calling the film a social document which ambivalently shifts back and forth from improvisation to "considered, articulated design." Revised from 1965, Sadoul, Entry No. 589.

1727 Sadoul, Georges. "Godard, Jean-Luc." *Dictionary of Film Makers*. Trans., ed., and updated by Peter Morris. Berkeley: University of California Press. Pp. 100–101.

Sadoul and Morris describe Godard's political movement from an early anarchism "to revolutionary political commitment pervaded by a deep sense of nihilism." The critics explain how Godard's innovations in and questioning of cinematic form are related to his political stand. Brief filmography through 1970. Revised from 1965, Sadoul, Entry No. 590.

1728 Schickel, Richard. *"La Chinoise." Second Sight: Notes on Some Movies, 1965–70*. New York: Simon and Schuster. Pp. 171–74.

Schickel's 1968 *Life* article (Entry No. 1199) is reprinted here with an afterthought that as Godard "became more and more a committed revolutionary . . . [Schickel] lost his taste for him entirely."

1729 Schneider, Pierre. "Paris: On the Frontiers of Francophilia." *New York Times* (10 July), p. 36.

Describes *Tout va bien.*

1730 Sery, Patrick. *"Tout va bien!* Rien ne va plus." *Cinéma 72*, No. 167 (June), pp. 148–50.

Brief credits. Godard's move to political filmmaking and association with Gorin are described and criticized. *Tout va bien* is beautiful to look at but is the work of intellectuals who are flirting with the left. We see "Godard's subconscious facism" in his *grande guignol* treatment of the workers and his "disdain for their realities."

1731 Silverstein, Norman. "Godard's Maoism." *Salmagundi*, No. 18 (Winter), pp. 15–30.

Using a close analysis of *See You at Mao*, Silverstein equates Godard's Maoism with Structuralism.

1732 Solomon, Stanley J. *The Film Idea.* New York: Harcourt, Brace, Jovanovich. Pp. 238–40, 357.

Breathless is described in terms of its "impulsive and destructive" characters and its "clinical" documentary approach (pp. 238–40). Godard has some success portraying character by limiting the background, depicting it abstractly, or using just a "few vivid allusions." (p. 357).

1733 Sorlin, Pierre. "Cinema et société." *Etudes*, 336 (January), 121–29.

Review of Annie Goldmann's *Cinéma et société moderne*, with a brief discussion of why she chose to analyze modernist films, especially Godard's. See 1971, Goldmann, Entry No. 1576.

1734 Stone, Oliver. "Film: Riding the Crest of Chaos." *Village Voice* (11 May), pp. 85 and 87.

Seen nine years later, the once-beloved *Breathless* now irritates the reviewer because of its easy and soft portrayal of characters who are basically a "flaunting young hoodlum" and a "tenuous, uncommitted" young woman who lives a "walking daydream." Godard's imaginative use of inconsequential moments in the bedroom sequences still establishes his style as both realistic and "curiously erotic."

1735 Sweeny, Louise. "Marxist Filmmaker with a Capitalist Accent." *Christian Science Monitor* (12 December), Sec. II, p. 7.

In an interview, Godard tells about on his working with Gorin and his problems with Paramount's reneging on the distribution of *Tout va bien*.

1736 Thirard, Paul-Louis. *"Tout va bien,* a vignt ans, dans les Aurès?" *Positif*, No. 140 (July-August), pp. 73–75.

Complete credits. Negative review.

1737 Thomsen, C. Braad. "Den röda duken." *Chaplin*, 14, No. 4 (No. 115), 146–151.

"Godard's development since May 1968 up to his latest film, *Tout va bien.*" IIFP, 1974, p. 28.

1738 Tinazzi, G. "La critica della gaia scienza." *Il Ponte*, No. 6 (June).

Article on Godard. Cited 1974, Ferrero, Entry No. 1841.

1739 de Vericourt, Guillemette and Delain, Michel. "La Censure clandestine." *L'Express* (14–20 February), pp. 58–59.

See 1972, Delain, Entry No. 1675.

1740   Vianey, Michel. "Deux petits soldats: entretien avec Godard-Gorin." *Le Nouvel Observateur* (17 April), pp. 49–52.
    Godard and Gorin discuss political filmmaking, their films since 1968, the ORTF, *Tout va bien* and its reflection of French film acting styles. Excerpts from *Tout va bien* dialogue given.

1741   Wollen, Peter. "Counter-Cinema: *Vent d'est.*" *Afterimage*, No. 4 (Autumn), pp. 6–16.
    Analyzes *Vent d'est* using Brecht's famous table contrasting Epic and Aristotelian drama. Wollen faults the film for totally rejecting emotion. Political art must also appeal to its viewer's *desire* for change. Trans. 1974, Wollen, *Skrien*, Entry No. 1862.

1742   Young, Vernon. *On Film: Unpopular Essays on a Popular Art.* Chicago: Quadrangle Books.
    In "I've Been Reading These Critics," pp. 324–27, Young attacks Annette Michaelson's defense of *Alphaville*, Roud's book on Godard, and Godard's breaking up the Cannes Festival. Young puts into the same category Godard, Robbe-Grillet, and the New American Cinema. In "The Verge and After," pp. 280–81, Godard is scored for lacking workmanship, moral values, lucidity, organizing power, "the gauche redundancy of his humor and his antagonism toward form and the reality principle alike."

1743   Zimmer, Christian. "Affaires mal reglées." *Les Temps modernes*, 29, No. 312-13 (July-August), 324–28.
    Zimmer analyzes narrative deconstruction and the rejection of spectacle in *Tout va bien* and their relation to the film's self-reflexivity and political intent.

1973

1744   Amengual, Barthélmey. "Ciméma et language." *Cinéma 73*, No. 173 (February), pp. 59–64.
    Mentions *Deux ou trois choses* in passing.

1745   Andrews, Nigel. "*Tout va bien.*" *Financial Times* (9 November).
    Describes how Godard and Gorin tried to make a commercially appealing film but have not had luck getting British distribution.

1746   Anon. "Godard, Jean-Luc." *Image et son: Revue du cinéma*: (Index 1946–1972), issue outside of series, ADV 13, pp. 49 and 129.
    Index lists articles in *Image et son* on Godard and reviews of his films through *Tout va bien*. Incomplete and frequently incorrect.

1747   Anon. "Note, Filmography." *Film Dope*, 3 (August), 109.
    On Belmondo. Cited 1976, Schuster, Mel, *Motion Picture Performers: Supplement No. 1*, p. 62.

1748   Anon. Review of Brown's *Focus on Godard. Velvet Light Trap*, No. 9 (Summer), pp. 53–54.
    Cited 1973, FLI, 1, No. 3, p. 14.

1749 Anon. Review of *Sympathy for the Devil. Cue*, 43, No. 1 (7 January), 42.
Negative review. Cited *Media Review Digest, 1974–75*, p. 250.

1750 Anon. Review of *Tout va bien. Crawdaddy*, No. 24 (May), pp. 89+.
Cited 1973, *Popular Periodical Index*, No. 1 (January-June), p. 74.

1751 Anon. Review of *Tout va bien. Cue*, 33, No. 37 (30 September), 37.
Cited *Media Review Digest, 1974–75*, p. 265.

1752 Anon. Review of *Tout va bien. New York Magazine*, 6 (19 February), 81.
Cited 1973, *Popular Periodal Index*, No. 1 (January-June), p. 74.

1753 Anon. Review of *Tout va bien. The Observer* (4 November).
Tout va bien is "both too loaded and too jokey."

1754 Anon. Review of *Tout va bien.* London *Times* (2 November), p. 13.
Cited 1973, *Times Index* (October-December), p. 146.

1755 Anon. Review of *Tout va bien.* New York *World*, 2 (10 April), 51.
Cited 1973, *Popular Periodicals Index*, No. 1 (January-June), p. 74.

1756 Anon. Review of *Two or Three Things. Cue*, 43, No. 37 (30 September), 37.
Mixed review. Cited *Media Review Digest, 1974–75*, p. 263.

1757 Anon. *"Tout va bien." Catholic Film Newsletter* (28 February).
Godard's return with this film will hardly appeal to even the most politically committed.

1758 Apon, A. "Methoden & Technieken van Brechts epies theater."
Skrien, No. 38–39 (November-December), pp. 3–9.
"Brecht's theories in regard to epic theatre, and examples of practice of his theories and methods in recent films, particularly *Il conformista* and *Tout va bien.*" IIFP, 1973, p. 254.

1759 Belilos, Marlène, et al. *"Tout va bien."* Trans. Gabriele Voss and Hübner, Christophe. *Filmkritik* (Munich), 17, No. 7 (July), 316–29.
In an interview with journalists and directors from Swiss TV (Marlène Belilos, Michel Boujut, Jean-Claude Deschamps, and Pierre-Henri Zoller), Godard and Gorin discuss the political aspects of their filmmaking practice, how they came to work together, and how they worked with Montand and Fonda on *Tout va bien.* They note the influences of Brecht and Vertov. Godard asked Sartre why the latter couldn't personally make a connection between political activity and literary research. Briefer version of this in English, 1972, Belilos, Entry No. 1651.

1760 Blonsky, Marshall and Browne, Nick. "The Rhetoric of the Specular Text." Mimeographed paper presented at the Student Conference on Film Study, American Film Institute, Kennedy Center, Washington, D.C., April. The conference was organized by Christian Koch, Communications Department, Oberlin College, Oberlin, Ohio.

Deux ou trois choses is seen as challenging bourgeois ideology (what is given as natural) and the codes of cinematic realism. It is contrasted to *Young Mr. Lincoln.*

1761 Bory, Jean-Louis. "L'Anglais tel qu'on le filme." *Ombre vive.* Series Cinéma, No. 3. Paris: 10/18, L'Union Générale d'Editions. Pp. 66–69.
Review of *One Plus One* (reprinted from 1969, Bory, Entry No. 1272), relates the aesthetics of "decomposing" the elements of the film to Godard's political intent, especially vis-à-vis Black Power. It's not new for Godard, but some of the sketches are admirable.

1762 Boujut, M. "Godard's Molotov Cocktail." *Lumière*, 23 (May), pp. 14–18.
Godard and Gorin discuss *Tout va bien.* Cited IIFP, 1973, p. 254.

1763 Browne, Nick and Blonsky, Marshall. "The Rhetoric of the Specular Text." Mimeographed paper. Student Conference on Film Study, Washington, D.C., April.
See 1973, Blonsky, Entry No. 1760.

1764 Broz, J. "Nonkonformismus Jane Fondové." *Film & Doba*, 19, No. 10 (October), 525–27.
The acting and opinions of Jane Fonda are described and background given to *Tout va bien* and *Letter to Jane.* Cited 1973, IIFP, p. 308.

1765 Burch, Nöel. *Theory of Film Practice.* Trans. Helen R. Lane. New York: Praeger.
Godard's disjunctive techniques, use of chance, and "dialectical" incorporation of different types of material are mentioned in passing. Closer attention is paid to the following: Godard's mixing styles and materials — "an essential structural element in his films" (pp. 60-61), André-S. Labathe's copying this technique in his TV documentary on Godard (pp. 59–60), the shifting relation between camera and actor in Godard's films (p. 119–20), Godard's "moving beyond the subject" of the film — especially in *Pierrot le fou* (pp. 148–50), and Godard's "cinema of ideas" (p. 162). Trans. from 1969, Burch, Entry No. 1273.

1766 Burk, Debbie. "*Breathless* (1959) *(A bout de souffle.) Cinema Texas Program Notes*, 4, No. 34 (15 March).
Reprinted 1975, Burk, Entry No. 1884. See annotation there.

1767 Calendo, J. "*Tout va bien.*" *inter/VIEW*, No. 31 (April), p. 39.
Cited IIFP, 1973, p. 254.

1768 Canby, Vincent. "He and She and Godard." *New York Times* (25 February), Sec. II, p. 4.
Feature article on *Tout va bien.* Even though the political message will turn off most viewers, there are some moving, witty moments in the scenes between Fonda and Montand. Godard's poetry is still there, and he is "closer to a new kind of film that makes most other politically and socially concerned movies seem like sentimental garbage," e.g., films such as *Save the Tiger.* Reprinted 1974, Canby, Entry No. 1831.

1769   C.[argin], P. "Workers' Cinema: *Carry on Girls* and *Tout va bien.*" *Film* (British Federation of Film Societies), Series 2, No. 9 (December), p. 18.

Tout va bien is compared and contrasted to a commercial entertainment film, also intended for the working class.

1770   Casty, Alan. "Godard." *Development of the Film: An Interpretive History.* New York: Harcourt, Brace, Jovanovich. Pp. 328–34.

Godard is described as an innovator who has revealed new ways to see and use film. As a result of improvisation and "shaping his films to reveal the consciousness of the director," Godard's films are shifting and erratic, sometimes brilliant and intelligent, sometimes lax and repetitious. Godard's Brechtianism, exaggerations, themes, social commentary, shifting of tone, comic-strip parodies, and "radical simplfications" are explained, as Casty discusses briefly most of the feature-length films through *Wind from the East.* Elsewhere Godard's influence on Makavejev is mentioned in passing (p. 402).

1771   Charest, G., et al. "Elle est atrice, elle est femme, et pourtant . . . elle tourne; elle s'appelle Anna Karina." *Cinéma Québec*, 3, No. 3 (November), 30–32.

In an interview with G. Charest and A. Leroux on *Vivre ensemble*, Karina says Godard only used improvisation from "a solid base," that is, professional actors.

1772   Coleman, John. "Stars and Strikes." *New Statesman*, 86 (9 November), 709.

Gorin seems to have had a major role in making *Tout va bien* because of Godard's accident. Godard was overrated before, then went naively political. Gorin tried to make *Tout va bien* popular but couldn't. Yet Montand comes off well, and the film is funny.

1773   Comsa, D. "Cei trei oameni furioşi: Fonda-tatal, Fonda-fiica, Fonda-fiul." *Cinema* (Bucharest), 11, No. 5 (May), 32.

Militant activities of Fonda family. Background to *Letter to Jane.* Cited 1973, IIFP, p. 308.

1774   Crist, Judith. "Tiger in a Cage." *New York Magazine*, 6 (19 February), 81.

Tout va bien is a naive and heavy-handed propaganda film.

1775   Currie, R.H. "Circles, Straight Lines, and Godard." *Journal of Modern Literature*, 3, No. 2 (April), 229–40.

A poem written about Godard's aesthetic is printed along with stills from his films.

1776   Dayan, Daniel and Alcira Kreimer. "The Geography of Film." Mimeographed paper presented at the Student Conference on Film, Washington, D.C. Kennedy Center, April. Conference organized by Christian Koch, Communications Department, Oberlin College, Oberlin, Ohio.

The paper discusses the ideological consequence of a "naturalized" or taken-for-granted urban background. Godard turns all the elements of our milieu into objects for intellectual and political consideration. Nothing is "natural" to him.

1777   Durand, Philippe. "Juin 1973: Jean-Luc Godard fait le point." *Cinéma pratique*, No. 124–60 (July-August), 156–60.
In an interview, Godard discusses the relation between the uses and filmic codes of home-moviemaking, commerical filmmaking, sports newscasting, and the film he'd like to make (about his family). He discusses financial independence, the variation in sound quality among different film or TV formats, and ways to break out of ideological formations (Ask, "En vue de quoi?" instead of "Quel vue?" — "For what purpose?" instead of "Which shot?"). Story board from *Moi-je* is shown in photos. Reprinted, 1974, Collet, Entry No. 1836.

1778   Escobar, R., "Crepa padrone, tutto va bene." *Cineforum*, 13, No. 122 (April-May), 343–57.
Review of *Tout va bien*. Cited IIFP, 1974, p. 334.

1779   Fonda, Jane. "Vietnam-Tagebuch." *Films und Fernsehen*, 2, No. 11, 11–16 and 43.
Fonda describes her stay in Vietnam. IIFP, 1974, p. 400.

1780   Friedrich, Jörg. "A bout de souffle du mai 68: Godard's *Tout va bien*." *Filmkritik*, 17, No. 12 (December), 578–82.
Tout va bien's class stand is analyzed from a Marxist viewpoint. Cited in IIFP, 1973, p. 254.

1781   Gledhill, Christine. "Notes for a Summer School: Godard, Criticism, and Education." *Screen*, 14, No. 3 (Autumn), 67–74.
Cited IIFP, 1973, p. 311.

1782   Goldstein, Laurence. "Familiarity and Contempt: An Essay on the Star Presence in Film." *Centennial Review*, 17, No. 3 (Summer), 256–74.
Analyzes in detail the aesthetics of film acting and of audience response to stars. Traces modernist attacks on identification and the struggle to "make contact with genuinely new modes of experience" by using new, impersonal art forms. Concludes with a discussion of Montand's and Fonda's function in *Tout va bien*.

1783   Greenspun, Roger. "Godard's *Tout va bien* Opens at Two Theaters." *New York Times* (17 February), p. 39.
Brief credits. Plot summary given. The film is full of ideological demonstrations and proceeds via linear argument. It lacks excitement and vision. Excerpted from 1972 (11 October), Greenspun, Entry No. 1685.

1784   Guback, Thomas. Review of Claude Degand's *Le Cinéma — cette industrie. Cinéaste*, 4, No. 4, 57–58.
See 1972, Degand, Entry No. 1674.

1785   Hennebelle, Guy. "Books to Change the French Cinema?" Trans. Rénee Delforge. *Cinéaste*, 6, No. 1, 40–45.
Translated from 1973, Hennebelle, Entry No. 1787.

1786 Hennebelle, Guy. "Un Cinéma pour attiser le feu." *Écran*, 19 (November), pp. 40–41.
"On the need to revive French political cinema." IIFP, 1973, p. 103.

1787 Hennebelle, Guy. "Situation de la critique en France: des livres pour changer le cinema français." *Cinéma Québec*, 3, No. 2 (October), 37–43.
Reviews a series of new books on cinema to give an overview of French political filmmaking since WW II. Both the Communist Party and those intellectuals seeking a deconstructed political art (i.e., Godard's Dzega Vertov Group) are scored, the former as revisionist, the latter as ultraleftist. Trans. 1973, Hennebelle, Entry No. 1785.

1788 Hennebelle, Guy. "Vers un renouveau du cinema français entre le ultragauchisme délirant et le révisionisme masqué." *Cinéma Québec*, Nos. 6-7 (March-April), 20–29.
Discusses French political films, both militant and commercial and looks at *Coup pour coup, Tout va bien*, and *Beau masque* in terms of the contemporary political climate in France. In *Tout va bien*, no real relation is established between the estranged couple and the strike.

1789 Hudson, Christopher. "Poor Pamela." *Spectator*, 231, No. 7585 (10 November), 616.
Tout va bien gives us only the "scraps" of a love story. Young children should see it as "a prime example of the turgidity of intellectualized revolutionary politics."

1790 Illuminati, A. "Jean-Luc Godard o l'impegno impossibile." *M-L*, No. 15 (December).
Article on Godard, Cited 1974, Ferrero, Entry No. 1841.

1791 Ioskevich, I. "Za sotsiologiiata na kinozhanrovete." *Kinoizkustvo*, 28 (December), 49–57.
Cited 1973, FLI, 1, No. 4, 163.

1792 James, S. "*Tout va baien.*" *Films and Filming*, 20, No. 3 (December), 47–48.
Cited IIFP, 1973, p. 254.

1793 Kahniutin, I. "Kosmaït na bdesheto." *Kinoizkustvo*, 28 (September), 50–63.
Review of *Alphaville*. Cited in 1973, FLI, 1, No. 4, p. 163.

1794 Karina, Anna. "I Didn't Always Understand Him (Jean-Luc Godard)." *Film*, 2, No. 2 (May), 16.
Cited 1976, Schuster, Mel, *Motion Picture Performers: Supplement No. 1*, p. 395.

1795 Kauffmann, Stanley. "Films." *New Republic* (10 March), p. 28.
Summarizes the couple's story from *Tout va bien* and finds the film merely repeats Godard's other work "in technique, anti-technique, and idea."

1796   Klein, Gillian. *"Tout va bien."* *Film Quarterly*, 26, No. 4 (Summer), 35–41.
Godard's development in political filmmaking is described, as is *Tout va bien*'s Brechtianism. "The structure and not merely the content of the film is ideological."

1797   Klein, Michael. *"Letter to Jane."* *Film Quarterly*, 26, No. 4 (Summer) 62–64.
Letter to Jane is analyzed both in terms of its visual style and the specific political criticism raised on the sound track.

1798   Kleinhans, Charles. *"Two or Three Things I Know about Her."* *Women and Film*, 1, No. 3-4, 66–71.
The film is discussed in terms of the way its form and characterization convey a sociopolitical analysis of contemporary life. Godard's political stance is evaluated.

1799   Kolkein, R.P. "Angle and Reality: Godard and Gorin in America." *Sight and Sound*, 42, No. 3 (Summer), 129–33.
During a two-day visit at the University of Maryland, Godard and Gorin discuss the relation between fiction and didacticism in *Tout va bien*, Brechtianism, cinematic technique, Jane Fonda in *Letter to Jane*, use of videotape, editing, and camera angle.

1800   Kreimer, Alcira and Daniel Dayan. "The Geography of Film." Mimeographed paper, Student Conference on Film Study.
See 1973, Dayan, Entry No. 1776.

1801   Lehman, Peter. "An Analysis of Jean-Luc Godard's *Pierrot le fou*." *Velvet Light Trap*, No. 9 (Summer), pp. 23–29.
Godard is the most sophisticated filmmaker to treat the subject of the interrelation between people and environment. In *Pierrot le fou* Godard raises environmental "cliches" to our conscious awareness, to an archetypal level. A close reading of the film is given by Lehman.

1802   Lesage, Julia. *"Tout va bien, Coup pour coup*: fransk film i kontekst." *Fant*, 7, No. 1 (No. 24), 16–26.
Cited in IIFP, 1973, p. 108. See 1972, Lesage, Entry No. 1701.

1803   Mate, Ken, et al. "Let's See Where We Are." *Velvet Light Trap*, No. 9 (Summer), pp. 30–36.
In an interview with Ken Mate, Russell Campbell, Louis Alvarez, and Maureen Turim, and also at an open question and answer session at the University of Michigan (November 1972), Godard and Gorin discuss their post-1967 film career, *Tout va bien* as a commercial film, their use of Fonda, their working collectively, workers' responses to *Tout va bien*, the flow of desire in the film, their image construction, and their reactions to other films, to the Black Panthers, and to *Cahiers du cinéma*.

1804   Mellen, Joan. *"Double Feature: Movies and Politics."* *Cinéaste*, 5, No. 4, 56–57.

Strongly negative review of Goodwin and Marcus book. See 1972, Goodwin, Entry No. 1681.

1805 Mellen, Joan. "Film and Style: The Fictional Documentary." *Antioch Review*, 32, No. 3, 403–25.

Discusses *Tout va bien, Letter to Jane, Deux ou trois choses*, and *Vladimir and Rosa*. Acknowledges Godard's cinematic talent but faults him for not portraying concrete and complex experiences in a dramatic way, for not engaging the audience's feelings, and for haranguing them with either self-evident or private political maxims. Reprinted 1975, Mellen, Entry No. 1911.

1806 Milne, Tom. "Jean-Luc Godard." *International Film Guide 1974*. Ed. Peter Cowie. London: The Tantivy Press. New York: A.S. Barnes. Pp. 27–36.

Finds parallels between Godard's pre-*Weekend* and post-*Weekend* films. He indicates the intellectual concerns in *A bout de souffle*, the perplexity in *Le Petit soldat*, the attempts to grasp "the reality and fantasy of life" in *Une Femme est une femme*, the more sophisticated cinematic language deriving from Brecht in *Vivre sa vie*, the "note of personal distress" in the films of 1964–1966, and Godard's starting from scratch in the films from 1967 on. The political films are judgmental, visually unwatchable, and one-dimensional. Complete filmography through 1973, in which proposed projects are not distinguished from completed films.

1807 Ongare, A. "Jane Fondová o sobé." *Film & Doba*, 19 No. 10 (October), 528–29.

In an interview translated from *Ciné-revue*, Fonda discusses politics and film production. Background to *Letter to Jane*. Cited 1973, IIFP, p. 308.

1808 Pearce, R. "Seeing as a Political Act: Godard's Pre-Revolutionist Films from *Breathless* to *Weekend*." *Performance*, 1 (May-June), 7–12.
Cited 1973, FLI, 1, No. 4, 63.

1809 Phinny, R.M. "*Charlotte et son Jules*." *Film/AV News*, 30 (April), 14.
Cited 1973, FLI, 1, No. 2, p. 21.

1810 Poel, P.H. van de. "Godard: wij moeten politieke films maken, wij moeten films politiek maken: *Voices/Vent d'est/Tout va bien/Letter to Jane*." *Skoop*, 9, No. 5 (October), 18–19.
Cited in IIFP, 1973, p. 311.

1811 Roger, R. "*Tout va bien*." *Jugend, Film, Fernsehen*, 17, No. 3, 157–58.
Cited in FLI, 1973 annual, p. 393.

1812 Sarris, Andrew. "Films in Focus." *Village Voice*, 18 (22 February), 61.
As with Bergman, Sarris admired Godard's earlier films but not these obfuscating and pessimistic later ones. In *Tout va bien*, Godard and Gorin sabotage Fonda's and Montand's "sympathetically charismatic icons . . . under the guise of working class egalitarianism."

1813 Sarris, Andrew. *The Primal Screen*. New York: Simon and Schuster. Pp. 51, 99–100.

Reprint of 1968, Sarris, "Film: The Illusion of Naturalism," Entry No. 1194. Godard mentioned elsewhere, passim.

1814 Schmid, Georg G. "French Avant-garde Film, 1968–1968: A Contribution to French Cultural History." *Zeitgeschichte* (Salzburg), 1, No. 1, 51–63.
Cited in Dietrich's 1975, IBZ, 2, Part 2, p. 188.

1815 Silber, Irwin. "Anarchist Outlook Mars Film on Workers." New York *Guardian* (7 March), p. 18.
The factory sequences in *Tout va bien* indicate what Godard learned from May '68: the class struggle is increasing, and the European Communist parties will only act as trade union bureaucracies well within the parameters of the bourgeois state. However, the supermarket sequence posits ultraleftist solutions and implies that the masses are like sheep. Godard refuses to see the necessity of a vanguard party.

1816 Snyder-Scumpy, Patrick. "Godard: Easy on the Mao." New York *Crawdaddy*, No. 24 (May), pp. 89–90.
"The politics of *Tout va bien* are the condiment that gives life to an emotionally human dish." The political themes and the techniques used to convey them are described.

1817 T.[ermine], L. "Crepa padrone, tutto va bene." *Cinema nuovo*, 22, No. 222 (March-April), 126–29.
Review of *Tout va bien*. Cited in IIFP, 1973, p. 255.

1818 Termine, L. "Inventati dal libero docenti itre evi della storia del cinema." *Cinema nuovo*, 22 (November-December), 414–18.
Cited, 1973, FLI, 1, No. 4, 163.

1819 Thomas, Tony. *"Tout va bien." The Militant* (9 September).
Generally a plot summary.

1820 Thomsen, Christian–Braad. "Christian–Braad Thomsen samtalar med Jean-Pierre Gorin." *Filmrutan*, 16, No. 2, 79–86.
Gorin describes his association with Godard in detail. He tells of a long film, *Communication*, which they planned together but never made. Cited in IIFP, 1973, p. 311. Reprinted, 1974, Thomsen, *Jump Cut*, Entry No. 1857.

1821 Thomsen, C[hristian]–B[raad]. "Godards filmkritik." Trans. A. Munkesjoe. *Chaplin*, 15, No. 1 (No. 120), pp. 15–16.
"A view of Godard's film criticism, provoked by the publication of the book *Godard on Godard*." IIFP. 1973, p. 311.

1822 Thomsen, Christian–Braad. "En milstolpe i den politiska filmkonsten." Trans. P. Budtz. *Filmrutan*, 17, No. 2, 73–79.
"An extensive study of the political film *Tout va bien*." IIFP, 1974, p. 334.

1823 Thon, K. "Jane Fonda i Oslo." *Fant*, 7, No. 1 (24), 11–14.
Report on Jane Fonda's press conference in Oslo about the Vietnam war; background to *Letter to Jane*. Cited 1973, IIFP, p. 308.

1824 Toiviainen, S. "Aina vain Godard." *Filmihullu* (Helsinki), No. 5, p. 26.
Cited in FLI, 1973 annual, p. 163.

1825 Westerbeck, Colin, Jr. "Tout ne va pas bien." *Commonweal*, 97 (5 January), 300–302.
The critic compares Godard and Warhol since both intend to outrage audiences. Godard has been more original in using montage, creating cinematic essays, and advancing cinematic art. Westerback evaluates and praises the post-1968 films, noting that while Godard's influence is great, his films can rarely be seen.

1826 White, Michael A. "*Bien*: Godard Comes Full Circle." *Columbia Daily Spectator* (20 February).
The tracking shots in *Tout va bien* are excellent cinematic equivalents of Brechtian distancing devices. The film is both a "partisan critique of apparatus" and an examination of "the contradictions involved in political filmmaking."

1827 W.[olf]. W.[william]. "*Tout va bien*." *Cue* (24 February).
This is "agitprop with style."

1974

1828 Anon. Review of *Godard on Godard. Monogram*, No. 5, pp. 34–36.
Cited 1974, FLI, 2, No. 2, p. 16.

1829 Anon. "*Tout va bien*." *Skrien*, No. 40–41 (January-February), pp. 4–12.
Sequence-by-sequence analysis of *Tout va bien*. Cited 1974, IIFP, p. 334.

1830 Bory, Jean-Louis. *L'Écran fertile: janvier 1970–juin 1971*. Series Cinéma, No. 4. Paris: 10/18, L'Union Générale d'Editions. Pp. 111–15.
"L'Écran d'Arlequin" (reprinted from 1970, Bory, Entry No. 1395) briefly mentions the themes of Godard's sketch, *L'Amour* for *Vangelo 70*, called *La Contestation* in French.

1831 Canby, Vincent. "*Tout va bien*: He, She, and Godard." *Film 73/74: An Anthology by the National Society of Film Critics*. Ed. Jay Cocks and David Denby. New York: Simon and Schuster. Pp. 161–64.
Reprinted from 1973, Canby, Entry No. 1768.

1832 Collet, Jean. "Bibliographie." *Jean-Luc Godard*. Ed. Jean Collet. Series Cinéma d'aujourd'hui, No. 18. Paris: Seghers. Pp. 193–204.
This bibliography of primarily French-language works is organized under the following categories: articles by Godard, interviews, texts of films, general articles on Godard, critiques of films (by film through *Tout va bien*), books on Godard.

1833 Collet, Jean. "Bio-filmographie." *Jean-Luc Godard*. Ed. Jean Collet. Series Cinéma d'aujourd'hui, No. 18. Paris: Editions Seghers. Pp. 177–191.
Writing in chronological order, Collet notes important events in Godard's life

and the credits and a brief plot summary for each film through *Tout va bien* and Godard's separation from Gorin.

1834 Collet, Jean. "Lexique." *Jean-Luc Godard*. Series Cinema d'aurourd'hui, No. 18. Paris: Editions Seghers. Pp. 68–79.
Collet is "playing with signs to facilitate access to Godard's use of the imaginary [in a Lacanian sense]," and he lists and discusses the following words in terms of Godard's themes and styles: air, love, money, arms, blue, countryside, castration, cinema, water, family, woman, fire, newspaper, struggle, darkness, workers, poetry, red, knowledge, sex, aging, cars.

1835 Collet, Jean. "Présentation: Jean-Luc Godard par Jean Collet." *Jean-Luc Godard*. Series Cinéma d'aujourd'hui, No. 18. Paris: Editions Seghers. Pp. 1–67.
Collet's essay, dated July 1972, is divided into the following sections, listed here with a brief indication of the content of each: "Godard aujourd'hui?" — Collet's view of Godard's political filmmaking; "Petit detour par la chambre noire" — Godard's theory of cinema as seen in *Le Mépris*; "Quelques images d'*A bout de souffle*"; "Du côté de *Pierrot le fou*" — the negation of time; "Les Armes du *Petit Soldat*" — history as nightmare, as a succession of visions; "*Une Femme est une femme, Le Gai Savior*, et le cinema decomposée" — self-reflexive, deconstructed cinema; "Le Miroir brisé" — Lacanian approach to describing the achievement of Godard's deconstruction; "Prendre la parole" — the power of the word or *logos* in Godard's films; "Les Citadelles de la parole" — the relations between city, country (the city's "double") theater and cinema; "La Decouverte de la télévision" — greater emphasis in TV on the sound track and on the present, the decline of cinema in the 60s, TV looked at from a McLuhanesque and Lacanian perspective; "Un Cinéma qui dit *nous*" — *Tout va bien*.

1836 Collet, Jean, ed. *Jean-Luc Godard*. Series Cinéma d'aujourd'hui. Paris: Editions Seghers. 204 pp.
Includes a long essay by Collet, one by Jean-Paul Fargier, Godard filmography, bibliography, and biography.

1837 Degand, Claude. "Bilan economique du cinéma française depuis la guerre." *Écran*, No. 21 (January), pp. 26–33.
Economic background of French film production. Cited 1974, FLI, p. 126.

1838 Degand, Claude. "O.R.T.F.: l'agonie du monopole." *Écran*, No. 26 (June), pp. 8–9.
Background of French governmental control of the media. Cited 1974, FLI, p. 126.

1839 Farassino, Alberto. *Jean-Luc Godard*. Series Il castoro cinema. Florence: La Nuova Italia. 151 pp.
Critical monograph that includes bibliography and filmography.

1840 Fargier, Jean-Paul. "Godard *avec* Vertov." *Jean-Luc Godard*. Ed. Jean Collet. Series Cinéma d'aujourd'jui, No. 18. Paris: Editions Seghers. Pp. 80–122.

The original books of the Cinema d'aujourd'hui Series fell under the ideology of the auteur, which type of criticism — its genesis and presuppositions — Fargier analyzes. Collective production of films challenges the bourgeois concept of "creation." Different types of political filmmaking are analyzed. Fargier answers the charge from the left of Godard's formalism and elitism and discusses sections of Dziga Vertov Group films to show their work in revealing, analyzing, and creating codes and "revolutionary" relations between sound and image. In *Tout va bien*, Godard and Gorin show that struggle goes on, but they cannot conceive of a revolutionary role for artists and intellectuals beyond one's acting as a subject conscious of one's place in history, contemplating others' struggles, and occasionally acting in a "spontaneously" revolutionary way. Written April-May 1972.

1841 Ferrero, Adelio. *Godard: tra "avanguardia" e "rivoluzione."* Series Problemi-libri, No. 16. Palermo: Palumbo Editore. 149 pp.
    This book examines and evaluates the critical polemic over Godard, Godard's view of women, his themes of solitude and introspection, his Brechtianism, his politicization in May '68, the Dziga Vertov Group's search for a new politicized cinematic language, and Godard's return to a more authentic Brechtianism in *Tout va bien*. Selected bibliography and complete filmography are given.

1842 Green, R.[on]. "Programming Works by a Single Filmmaker: Jean-Luc Godard." *Film Library Quarterly*, 7, No. 3–4, 17–27.
    Gives a general background about Godard and describes useful themes to program films around (escape, left politics, youth v. age, everyday life, advertising, leisure and labor, prostitution, use of color, cinema and print, communications media, sound variations, and cinematic truth). Gives a sample program based on "the changing role of women in Godard's films."

1843 Harcourt, Peter. "Godard le Fou: A Glimpse of the Struggle between Love and Politics in the Films of Jean-Luc Godard." *Six European Directors: Essays on the Meaning of Film Style.* Baltimore: Penguin. Pp. 212–54.
    Reprinted from 1966, Harcourt, Entry No. 699.

1844 Henderson, Brian. "*Godard on Godard*: Notes for a Reading." *Film Quarterly*, 27, No. 4 (Summer), 34–36.
    In his early criticism, Godard especially referred to the eighteenth century as a way to defend cinema as structured discourse, used to create heightened emotion. In "Bergmanorama" Godard began to prize chance and spontaneity more, dealing with these both as the capturing of a fleeting reality and as rhetorical devices used by a skillful director to naturalize film discourse. Godard sets up and explores the paradoxical equations — fiction-reality and fiction-documentary.

1845 Jørgensen, U. "Soldaterne." *Kosmorama*, 20, No. 120 (April), 218–19.
    Reviews *Les Carabiniers*. Cited in IIFP, 1974, p. 165.

1846 Kleinhans, Charles, "*Tout va bien (Everything's OK or Just Great)* — Jean-Luc Godard and Jean-Pierre Gorin." Program Notes. Film Center, School of the Art Institute, Chicago, May 8, 4 pp.
    The basic lesson of the film is that people and society are historical in nature. The critic describes the political positions found in the film and also the way

Godard and Gorin present the "cracks" in French life such as wildcat strikes, student rebellion, and middle class dissatisfaction with the quality of life.

1847 Korte, W. "Godard's Adaption of Moravia's *Contempt*." *Literature-Film Quarterly*, 2, No. 3 (Summer), 284–89.
    "Godard's transformation of Moravia's psychological novel into a highly formalized film challenges conventional ideas of the cinema." IIFP, 1974, p. 261.

1848 Lesage, Julia. "Godard and Gorin's *Wind from the East*: Looking at a Film Politically." *Jump Cut*, No. 4 (November-December), pp. 18–21.
    Wind from the East forces a political response both in terms of its formal construction and the content it deals with. Aspects of the contemporary French political situation that relate to the film are discussed, and a number of sequences are analyzed in detail.

1849 McCabe, Colin. "Realism and the Cinema: Notes on Some Brechtian Theses." *Screen*, 15 (Summer), 7–27.
    Compares the function and mechanisms of Brecht's own film, *Kuhle Wampe*, and Godard and Gorin's *Tout va bien*, which McCabe considers the more "Brechtian" of the two films. In both films, "the discourses are caught up in certain modes of life which are linked to the place of the agent in the productive processes . . ."

1850 Peary, Gerry. "Jane Fonda on Tour: Answering *Letter to Jane*." *Take One*, 4, No. 4 (July), 24–26.
    Describes a slide show on women in Vietnam presented by Jane Fonda as part of her tour through the United States on behalf of the Indo-China Peace Campaign. The various photos in that slide show are analyzed in the light of Godard and Gorin's critique in *Letter to Jane*.

1851 Petersen, L. "Her går det godt." *Kosmorama*, 20, No. 122 (September), 320.
    Reviews *Tout va bien*. Cited in IIFP, 1974, p. 334.

1852 Petrie, Graham. "Dickens, Godard, and the Film Today." *Yale Review*, 54, No. 2, 185–201.
    Godard is briefly compared to Dickens: "Only one film . . . comes close to paralleling the multidimensional effects of *Bleak House* or *Little Dorrit*, and this is Godard's *Weekend*."

1853 Rayns, T.[ony]. "The Godard Film Forum." *Film* (British Federation of Film Societies), Series 2, No. 10 (January), pp. 18–19.
    Discusses a large retrospective of Godard's work since *Loin du Viêtnam*, shown along with contrasting, related works. The organizers had hoped to use the festival as a "catalyst to larger concerns," but the floor discussions centered primarily on Godard's aesthetics.

1854 Sail, Nourdine. Interview with Godard. *Maghreb-Information* (27–28 April).
    Cited, 1975, Hennebelle, Entry No. 1900.

1855 Sail, Nourdine. Interview with Godard. *Maghreb-Information* (11–12 May).
Cited, 1975, Hennebelle, Entry No. 1900.

1856 Simons, Steven. *"Tout va bien." Film Comment*, 10, No. 3 (May-June), 54–59.
Analyzes the film as Brechtian — not only in its techniques and self-reflexive aspects, but also in moral and political intent. (Stanley Cavell's notions on Godard's Brechtianism and on cinema in general are refuted.) *Tout va bien* is a visual and aural masterpiece and is a landmark in the search for an adequate political film form.

1857 Thomsen, Christian–Braad. "Filmmaking and History." *Jump Cut*, No. 3 (September-October), pp. 17–19.
Interview with Jean-Pierre Gorin. Trans. from 1973, Thomsen, Entry No. 1822.

1858 Uhde, Jan. "The Influence of Bertolt Brecht's Theory of Distanciation on the Contemporary Cinema, Particularly on Jean-Luc Godard." *Journal of the University Film Association*, 26, No. 3, 28–30 and 44.
Defines the mechanisms of cinematic illusion and identification and points out a few early attempts by the avant garde to break these down. Godard was the first film director of international fame to use distancing techniques, which he specifically adopted from Brecht, and he has greatly influenced other directors in this. Brecht and Godard share political concerns. Uhde traces the cinematic ways that Godard destroys identification and achieves a distancing effect.

1859 Van Gelder, Lawrence. "Comment on Stills." *New York Times* (12 April), p. 18.
Godard and Gorin's *Letter to Jane* is sometimes foolish, sometimes illuminating, but it is far superior to the other study of still photography it was shown with, Nagisa Oshima's *Diary of a Yunbogi Boy.*

1860 Warhol, Andy. "Anna Karina." *Interview* (March), p. 6.
Cited 1976, Schuster, Mel, *Motion Picture Performers: Supplement No. 1*, p. 395.

1861 Wise, Naomi, et al. "Raymond Chandler, Mao Tse Tung, and *Tout va bien." Take One* (8 May), pp. 22–24.
In an interview with Michael Goodman and Naomi Wise in Berkeley, June 1972, Gorin discusses Jerry Lewis, *Tout va bien* as a big-scale production and a comic film, working with Godard and photographer Armand Marco and their future plans.

1862 Wollen, Peter. "Contra-cinema: *Vent d'est.*" Trans. E. Burcksen. *Skrien*, No. 40–41 (January-February), pp. 13–18.
Trans. from 1972, Wollen, Entry No. 1741.

1863 Wood, Robin. "Chabrol's New Beginning." *Times Educational Supplement*, No. 3076 (10 May), p. 78.
Cited 1974, FLI, 2, No. 2, p. 53, under "Godard, Jean-Luc."

1975

1864 Almendarez, Valentin. *"Alphaville." Cinema Texas Program Notes,* 9, No. 4 (18 November), 22–24.
Describes the stance of Godard lovers and Godard detractors. Godard's method is to make each cinematic and thematic element of equal significance. Black and white in *Alphaville* indicates that Lemmy, agent of emotion and imagination, lays siege to the city of light and reason, but the film reaffirms that each action contains its opposite. Bibliography on *Alphaville* is given.

1865 Amiel, M.[ireille]. *"Numéro deux*: One Plus One." *Cinéma 75*, No. 203 (November), 60–63.
In *Numéro deux*, by a technique of "analytical realism," Godard dissects the anxieties we feel on the daily level, which are "simple" to identify but impossible to escape as long as "it's the whole social state" that tears us apart. Godard is not an original theoretician but has the intuition and sensibility to express most sharply moments we all experience.

1866 Anon. Compliation of interviews about *Numéro deux. Écran 75*, No. 11 (November), pp. 52+.
Godard tells about building the Sonimage studios, his setting up a news information service, his turning to video, and his ongoing interest in visual education. Trans. into German, 26th Berlin Festival Program Notes.

1867 Anon. "Conversazione: J.-L. Godard." Trans. J. Grapow. *Film critica,* 26 (October-December), 368–73.
Review of *Numéro deux* and probably a translation of interview with Godard. Cited 1975, FLI, p. 400.

1868 Anon. "Due esempi (conclusione)." *Filmcritica,* 26 (Ocbober-December), 357–59.
Review of *Numéro deux*. Cited in 1975, FLI, p. 400.

1869 Anon. Interview with Godard. *Télécine,* No. 202 (September-October).
Long interview with Godard about establishing Sonimage Studios. Trans. into Italian, 1976, Tassone, Entry No. 2006.

1870 Anon. Interview with Godard on *Numéro deux. Pariscope*, No. 383.
Cited 1975, Collet, Entry No. 1887.

1871 Anon. Interview with Godard on *Numéro deux. Télérama* (27 September-3 October), p. 66.
Cited 1975, Garsault, Entry No. 1896.

1872 Anon. "Jean-Luc Godard: Paroles —." *Télécine* (September-October).
Cited 1975, Breton, Entry No. 1883.

1873 Anon. *"Numéro deux —* Jean-Luc Godard." *Unifrance Film News* (October).

Quotations translated into English from reviews of *Numéro deux* in *Télérama, Le Monde,* and *Figaro.*

1874 Anon. Review of Collet and Fargier's 1974 edition of *Jean-Luc Godard. Cinéma Québec,* 4, No. 5, 31.
  Cited 1975, FLI, p. 62.

1875 Baby, Yvonne. "Un Entretien avec Jean-Luc Godard: faire les films possibles là où on est." *Le Monde* (25 September), p. 15.
  This interview deals with the politics of Godard's filmmaking, the kinds of messages that one is able to send and receive, and the theme of sexuality in *Numéro deux.* Our environment consists of "images, sounds, and a salary." *Numéro deux* portrays "movements, relations, comings and goings," and a couple who "live in a symbiotic relationship to other equally fundamental couples: parents/children . . . factory/home." Trans. Oct. 1975, Charles Cameron Ball, in Museum of Modern Art Library file. Parts of Ball trans. in MOMA program notes for *Numéro deux,* "Perspectives on French Cinema," March 4–27, 1976.

1876 Baroncelli, Jean de. "La Sortie de *Numéro deux*: la galaxie Godard." *Le Monde* (25 September), p. 1.
  We've missed Godard's angry, irritating, generous films since *Weekend,* but *Numéro deux* brings us back to his old concerns and style. Words and language dominate the film, which deals in a profoundly political way with that area of life where politics is excluded. Trans. into German, 1976, 26th Berlin Film Festival Program Notes.

1877 Bechtold, C.[harles]. *"A bout de souffle." Cinématographe,* No. 13 (May-June), pp. 40–42.
  Cited 1975, FLI, p. 1.

1878 Bechtold, Charles. *"Numéro deux." Cinématographe* (month unknown), p. 30.
  Credits. Examines the distance Godard has come in his career in terms of the way he treats the human body, the culpable woman, children, and cinematic time. "Godard never tells stories but always The Story (or History)."

1879 Bohn, Thomas W. and Stromgren, Richard. "Jean-Luc Godard." *Light and Shadows: A History of Motion Pictures.* Port Washington, N.Y.: Alfred Publishers. Pp. 350–352.
  Brief description of Godard's career. He is seen to "challenge accepted precepts of film form and function," but, "like Truffaut, he usually manages to mask his own political position in ambiguity."

1880 Bory, Jean-Louis. "L'Évangile selon Jean-Luc." *La Lumière écrit: mai 1971–décembre 1972.* Series Cinéma, No. 5. Paris: 10/18, L'Union Générale d'Editions. Pp. 256–62.
  Reprinted from 1972, Bory, Entry No. 1652.

1881 Bory, Jean-Louis. "Les Nouvelles Billes de Godard." *Le Nouvel Observateur* (25 Sept), p. 93.

Numéro deux utilizes the rage, brutality, and grossness of *Weekend* to here make an apt comment on sexuality. Godard has elaborated a new form which brings to film the simultaneity of novels like those by Dos Passos and Woolf and also captures the multiple ways in which the media "confound" our daily life.

1882 Braucourt, Guy. "*Numéro deux:* propos de Jean-Luc Godard." *Écran 75*, No. 41 (15 November), pp. 51–52.

Review. Credits. Compilation of statements by Godard from interviews in *Pariscop, Le Monde, Libération, Politique–Hebdo, Télérama, Le Film français, Téléciné.* Braucourt says the film marks "the return of the greatest of the ethnologists examining French reality." Godard says of the film that the text was assembled and politically evaluated by others, not him; the working conditions on the film were gentler than before, less aggressive, more collective and creative for everyone; and it was like a family film, an amateur film where everyone was a *bricoleur.*

1883 B.[reton], É[mile]. "Jean-Luc Godard: *Numéro deux.*" *La Nouvelle Critique*, No. 89, N.S. (November), pp. 91–92.

The film is very sad in many ways, but it is exciting to see Godard open up all these possibilities for videotape to "speak."

1884 Burk, Debbie. "*Breathless* (1959) *(A bout de souffle).*" *Cinema Texas Program Notes*, 8, No. 49 (15 April), 1–5.

Reprinted from *Cinema Texas Program Notes*, 4, No. 34 (15 March 1973). Complete credits. The origins of the New Wave and Godard's life before making *Breathless* are described. The shooting of the film, the cinematic technique, and his use of "private" allusions are analyzed.

1885 Chauvet, Louis. "A travers Aphorismes et symbols." *Le Figaro* (29 September).

Reviews *Numéro deux* by having someone ask him questions about it. Generally Chauvet says he does not understand what Godard is trying to do.

1886 Christensen, J.P. "Godard genfoedt." *Kosmorama*, 21, No. 128, 264–65.

oreview of *Numéro deux.* Cited 1975, FLI, p. 400.

1887 Collet, Jean. "*Numéro deux.*" *Etudes*, 346 (November), 596–98.

A desperate, isolated, lost, and powerless artist "responds to capitalism's perversions with a perverse film," the "motor" of which is "an aggressive sadism vis-à-vis the spectator."

1888 Delameter, J.H. "Jean-Luc Godard's *Pierrot le fou.*" *Film Heritage*, 10, No. 3, 5–12.

Cited 1975, FLI, p. 422.

1889 Delilia, Hervé, et al. Interview with Godard. *Politique–Hebdo* (18 September).

This interview with Hervé Delilia and Roger Dosse is cited at length in 1976, Berlin Film Festival Program Notes, Entry No. 1942, and is entitled, "The Adventurer with Kodak and Polaroid." Godard tells how he became familiar with the political songs of Leó Ferré, composer of "La Solitude" in *Numéro deux*, while Godard was working with the left papers *La Cause du peuple* and *J'accuse*. Gorin, he said, came from an old Trotskyist family and was still tied to them, whereas Godard, the bourgeois, had early become independent of his parents. Anne-Marie Miéville provided the woman's perspective in *Numéro deux*. ("I always made the films of others; now, thanks to another, I can begin to make my own.")

1890 Delmas, Jean. *"Numéro 2." Jeune cinéma*, No. 89 (September-October), pp. 28–30.
The film fits in the trajectory of Godard's examination of cinema, but Godard's consideration of the relation between sexuality and politics is superficial.

1891 Dias, A. "Cuspir na comida." *Celuloide*, 18 (February), 17–18.
Credits. *Weekend* is reviewed. Cited 1975, FLI, p. 584.

1892 Evan, Martin. "Breathless Again." *Manchester Guardian Weekly* (9 June), p. 10.
Godard talks about what it's like to return to Switzerland to live and about his efforts to get back his own identity. He discusses the political aspects of his and Anne-Marie Miéville's current video set-up and of his economic dealings. Gaumont, their producers, won't open up its distribution network to them.

1893 Evan, Martin. "Le Remake de *A bout de souffle*: rencontre avec Godard sur un îlot de socialisme." *Le Monde* (8 May), p. 13.
Martin visited Godard at the Sonimage Studios in Grenoble. Godard talked about leaving Paris, his past relation with Gorin, film finance and production (Gaumont was financing him and he'd wanted to do a monthly TV news show for them, but they refused), and *Numéro deux*. Trans. into Italian, 1976, Tassone, *La Biennale*, Entry No. 2006.

1894 Fell, John L. *Film: An Introduction.* New York: Praeger.
Godard is mentioned in passing throughout the book, with particular attention paid to his theatricality and Brechtianism (pp. 80–81 and 104) and the moral implications of his camera style and reference to other images and names. (pp. 206–209).

1895 Filpo, E. *"Numéro deux." Amis du film et de la télévision*, No. 234 (November), p. 33.
Cited 1975, FLI, p. 400.

1896 Garsault, Alain. "Une Rentrée ratée: la nouvelle vague — *Numéro deux*." *Positif*, No. 176 (December), p. 52.
The film is wordy and misanthropic, and it defines humanity at the level of the toilet.

1897 Gearing, N. *"Vladimir and Rosa." Monthly Film Bulletin*, 42, No. 499 (August), p. 185.
Credits, review. Cited IIFP, 1975, p. 361.

1898 Gilliatt, Penelope. "Humanism Breaks Camp." *New Yorker* (14 August), pp. 93–95.

Twenty five of Godard's films are being shown in retrospective at Carnegie Hall Cinema. *Pierrot* is reviewed, the love story summarized. Godard is a late romantic agnostic, and this film teaches "something new about didactics, about play, about thinking and recall."

1899 Greene, Naomi. "Brecht, Godard, and Epic Cinema." *Praxis: A Journal of Radical Perspectives on the Arts*, 1, No. 1 (Spring), 19–24.

Godard's "work is marked by . . . a conflict between his bent, . . . that is primarily intellectual, toward Brechtian anti-realism and his unconquerable ability to make the reality he films around him live with great intensity."

1900 Hennebelle, Guy. "La Révolution aesthetique du 'god-art'." *Quinze ans de cinéma mondiale: 1960–1975.* Paris: Cerf. Pp. 385–407.

Godard's merit is in attacking Hollywood cinema and U.S. cultural imperialsm. In many of his films he has tried to bring French social problems to the screen when others did not, but he has no real historical perspective and merely "contemplates the chaos of the world from the point of view of his own chaos." His themes of love and death and his marginal characters reveal his basic romanticism. He moved from a fascist anarchism in *Le Petit Soldat* to a humanist anarchism in films such as *Le Mépris* and *Une Femme mariée* to a left-wing anarchism, especially in the films of 1966–67. With the Dziga Vertov Group, he lapsed into a terrorist, ultraleftist aesthetic position. There is not necessarily a conjunction between his modernist formal achievements, which we can admire, and the ideological content of his films.

1901 Humphries, Reynold. "*Numéro deux*: Godard's Synthesis — Politics and the Personal." *Jump Cut*, No. 9 (October-December), pp. 12–13.

In a review of *Numéro deux*, Humphries describes how Godard provides an analysis of sexual politics and its relation to structures of mass communication, the family, production relations, and the state.

1902 J., G. "Numéro 2." *L'Express* (6–12 October).

This brief notice calls *Numéro deux* a sad, empty, lazy film.

1903 Kauffmann, Stanley. "*Tout va bien* (March 10, 1973)." *Living Images: Film Comment and Criticism.* New York: Harper & Row. Pp. 179–81.

Reprinted from 1973, Kauffmann, Entry No. 1795.

1904 Lefèvre, Raymond. "Numéro deux." *Image et son: Revue du cinéma*, No. 300 (November), pp. 98–99.

Credits. Godard has chosen isolation and a salaried position in Grenoble to be able to express his liberty as a filmmaker. The various kinds of shots that are in the film are described: those of the kind to be seen in the commercial cinema — violence and pornography — and those depicting three generations. Godard discusses his own solitude, but also by the film he calls us to a new, more real kind of communication. Cited at length in 1976, 26th Berlin Film Festival Program Notes, Entry No. 1942.

1905 Lellis, George. *"Alphaville* (1965)." *Cinema Texas Program Notes*, 9, No. 4 (18 November), 17–21.
Complete credits. *Alphaville* "deals with the conversion of the energy of human movement to the matter of film." The critic discusses the contradictions and conversions within the film: Godard loves the technology he decries. He uses but cannot construct a detective film narrative. Constantine, the tender savior, is robot-like throughout. The music is both sentimental and Pavlovian. There is a tension between the mechanical side of the film medium and the humanistic message.

1906 Levitin, Jacqueline Doreen. "Jean-Luc Godard: Aesthetics as Revolution." Ph.D. dissertation, State University of New York at Buffalo. *Dissertation Abstracts*, 36, 1976, 6344A.
Explores the relation between film aesthetics and social revolution ("revolutionary" defined as "challenging the established relations of power and established codes"). *Deux ou trois choses* analyzes alienation under capitalism primarily as a problem of communication rather than of class. This leads Godard to idealize the role of the filmmaker in social change. *Le Gai Savior* declares Godard's political intent and shows the direction he will take in manipulating the aesthetics of cinema as his form of political struggle. However, the film stumbles in finding images to illustrate "the revolutionary energy of the unconscious." Nevertheless, in contrast to *Deux ou trois choses*, it shows the need for the filmmaker constantly to criticize the ideological voice within any presentation of information. Jean-Pierre Gorin and Godard use Brecht in *Tout va bien* to explore the ideological implications of the Hollywood love story. "By presenting their story as a model of the contradictions in industry and in media, the film draws parallels between the codes of behavior for the worker, the codes of representation in the media, and the codes governing love relationships." (Citations here from dissertation abstract, dissertation not consulted.)

1907 MacBean, James Roy. *Film and Revolution*. Bloomington: Indiana University Press.
"Politics and Poetry in *Two or Three Things I Know about Her* and *La Chinoise*," pp. 13–27 (from Entry 1148). "Politics, Poetry, and the Language of Signs in *Made in U.S.A.*," pp. 28–44 (from Entry No. 1317). *"Weekend*, or the Self-Critical Cinema of Cruelty," pp. 45–60, (from Entry No. 1147). *"One Plus One*, or the Praxis of History," pp. 79–98 (from Entry No. 1598). "*See You at Mao*: Godard's Revolutionary British Sounds, pp. 99–115 (from Entry No. 1473). "Godard and Rocha at the Crossroads of *Wind from the East*," pp. 116–138 from Entry No. 1599. "Godard/Gorin/The Dziga Vertov Group: Film and Dialectics in *Pravda, Struggle* (sic) *in Italy*, and *Vladimir and Rosa*," pp. 139–165 (from Entry No. 1706). *"Le Gai savior*: Critique Plus Auto-Critique du Critique," pp. 61–78: "In criticizing *Le Gai savior* for failing to be effective as art, I . . . perhaps was simply not ready to accept the degree to which Godard had moved beyond mere *subversion of the narrative* . . ., and that he now sought to lay the foundations of a truly revolutionary art which would no longer conveniently neglect the much-needed task of making the revolution *chez soi* . . ." "*Tout va bien* and *Letter to Jane*: The Role of the Intellectual in the Revolution," pp. 166–180: Godard and Gorin are faulted for becoming isolated from concrete struggles. *Letter to Jane* has a "more-radical-than-thou"

tone and is disturbing in its sexual politics. The filmmakers seem afraid to put themselves in a situation they cannot control, although in *Tout va bien* they do seem to indicate that "the revolution has to be rooted in strong feelings" rather than just in arguments and words.

1908 Magny, J. *"Numéro deux." Télécine*, No. 202 (September-October), pp. 7–10.

Credits. Article analyzes the film, discusses its production, and relates it to Godard's previous work.

1909 Mayne, Judith S. "The Ideologies of Metacinema." Ph.D. dissertation, State University of New York at Buffalo. *Dissertation Abstracts*, 1975, 1134A.

Metacinema is a cinema whose object is to analyze the ways in which cinematic forms function. Mayne analyzes three films which explore the nature of film language within a specific ideological context, namely, Vertov's *Man with a Movie Camera*, Godard's *Deux ou trois choses*, and Godard and Gorin's *Tout va bien*. The films are analyzed both semiotically and ideologically, with particular attention given to the codes of montage, sound/image, off-screen space, and matching shots. Discusses the ways that film reproduces and is a vehicle for various ideologies and how it also produces an ideology, the impression of realism.

1910 McCabe, Colin. "The Politics of Separation." *Screen*, 16, No. 4, 46–61.

On *Tout va bien* and *Deux ou trois choses*. Cited 1976, FLI, 4, No. 2, p. 40.

1911 Mellen, Joan. "Film and Style: The Fictional Documentary." in *Latin America Cinema: Film and History*. E. Bradford Burns, ed. Los Angeles: UCLA Latin American Center. Pp. 67–92.

Reprinted from 1973, Mellen, Entry No. 1805.

1912 Mercier, Marie-Claude. *"Vivre sa vie." Image et son: Revue du cinéma*, No. 297 (out of series), pp. 161–65.

A summary of film is given, along with complete credits, a brief biography of Godard, and an examination of the film in the context of Godard's later work. This film exemplifies Godard's working on a small budget, his experimentation, his social concerns, and his forcing us to reflect on cinematic process and processes of communication in general. Suggestions are given by the critic on how to teach the film.

1913 Mesnil, Michel. *"Numéro deux*? la plaine." *Esprit*, 43 (November), 701–704.

The film has a contemporary leftist "taste for bitterness," yet still despair is not fashionable for the bourgeoisie, who want entertainment — which this film denies them totally. Godard's style has much in common with the *nouveau roman*, and he is one of the few French filmmakers to be innovative in form. His concepts are still both exciting and confused.

1914 Minish, Geoffrey. "Jean-Luc Godard's *Numéro deux*." *Take One*, 4, No. 12 (December), 36.

The film cost $120,000, about the same as *Breathless*. The reviewer is not sympathetic to Godard's investigation of family life, nor to the format of the film, except when a televised May Day parade is equated with extracts from a film by Claude Sautet. Workers know they are exploited and don't need this film. Quoted in Museum of Modern Art Program Notes.

1915 Monaco, James. *"Le Gai Savior:* Picture and Act — Godard's Plexus." *Jump Cut,* No. 7 (May-July), pp. 15–17.
In this close analysis of the film, Monaco finds that Godard's principal aims are to fuse "method" and "sentiment," analyze film form, build politically correct images ("starting from zero"), and "reconstruct the expression of self."

1916 Mosk[owitz, Gene]. *"Numéro deux (Number Two)."* Variety (8 October), p. 20.
Brief credits. Paris. Describes the fragments about a family — man, wife, two children, two grandparents — whose roles Godard questions in the film.

1917 Pearson, L. "Waiting for Godard at the Front: The Palestinian Cinema Institution." *Canyon Cinemanews,* No. 3 (May-June), pp. 5–7.
Cited 1975, FLI, p. 228.

1918 Pearson, L. "Waiting for Godard at the Front: The Palestinian Cinema Institution." *Canyon Cinemanews,* No. 6 (November-December), p. 13.
Cited 1975, FLI, p. 228.

1919 Perlemutter, Ruth. *"Le Gai Savior:* Godard and Eisenstein — Notions of Intellectual Cinema." *Jump Cut,* No. 7 (May-July), pp. 17–19.
Godard's and Eisenstein's notions of disjunction, juxtaposition, and montage to create an intellectual effect are compared and contrasted. "The problem to solve [in *Le Gai Savior*] — the one that has been called into question throughout by a series of formal involvements with genre distortions, movements in and out of contexts and systems of thoughts, satirizations of discourses, and different levels of reflecting consciousnesses — is the pushing of film as tool into political action and the pulling of it back into the realm of art."

1920 Petrat, J. "Bertolt Brecht et le cinéma: des rapports difficiles et inaboutis." *Cinéma 75,* No. 203 (November), pp. 66–71.
Filmography. Brecht's "Geschichtsunterricht" and *Numéro deux* are compared to indicate both Brecht's concern with film and his influence on films today. *Numéro deux* is hailed as the first "non-Euclidean" film.

1921 Rosenbaum, Jonathan. *"Letter to Jane."* Monthly Film Bulletin, 42, No. 498 (July), 157.
Credits. Review of *Letter to Jane.* Cited IIFP, 1975, p. 262.

1922 Roud, Richard. "Godard Image." *Manchester Guardian Weekly,* 16 August, p. 19.
Roud visited Godard in Grenoble at the Sonimage lab on Rue de Belgrade, financed for £120,000 by Godard and Anne-Marie Miéville, Gaumont films, and producer Jean-Pierre Rassam. Roud also saw *Ici et ailleurs,* which Godard plans to

distribute on videotape cassettes. In structure, the film takes images of the Palestinians shot in 1970 and discusses them in terms of how we receive television images, the director's manipulation of the original actors and images, the relation of leaders to people, our relation to history — both to the concentration camps and to Vietnam, and our place in the "chain" of the world's images.

1923 Tallenay, J.-L. Interview with Godard on *Numéro deux*. *Télérama*, No. 1341.
Cited 1975, Collet, Entry No. 1887.

1924 Theuring, G. "Legende zu einer alten Postkarte: *Pierrot le fou.*" *Filmkritik*, 19 (September), 430–31.
Cited 1975, FLI, p. 422.

1925 Van Wert, William. "Theory and Practice of the Ciné-Roman in France." Ph.D. dissertation, Indiana University. 1976 *Dissertation Abstracts*, 36 (February 1976), 4816A.
In differentiating and concentrating critical attention on the "literary" New Wave, Van Wert discusses Brecht's influence, economic and cultural background, and increasing political commitment of the New Wave. Godard's work is mentioned frequently in passing; although he is not of this group, the general tendencies described apply to him.

1926 Whyte, Alistair. "Interview with Anna Karina (1973)." *Jean-Luc Godard: Three Films — A Woman is a Woman, A Married Woman, Two or Three Things I Know about Her.* Icon Editions, New York: Harper & Row. Pp. 191–92.
Karina denies that the character Julie in *Vivre ensemble* bears any relation to her parts for Godard, which were "very different everytime." Living with Godard, she said, was like being in "a very good school."

1927 Whyte, Alistair. "Introduction." *Jean-Luc Godard: Three Films — A Woman is a Woman, A Married Woman, Two or Three Things I Know about Her* (scripts). Icon Editions. New York: Harper & Row. Pp. 7–15.
Godard's detractors attack his rejection of cinematic conventions and his developing social and political awareness. These three films "clearly illustrate" both aspects of Godard's work. Whyte explains the following aspects of the three films: parody of and illusions to the cinema, literary quotations, humor, lyricism, use of Karina, abstraction, consumerism and false values, documentary style and intent, chronological dislocation, objects, prostitution, and social and philosophical reflection.

1928 Wollen, Peter. "Two Avant-Gardes." *Studio International*, 190, No. 978 (November-December), 171–75.
See 1976, Wollen, Entry No. 2012, for entry.

1929 Zimmer, Christian. "Lecture au laser pour system clos." *Les Temps modernes*, 31, No. 353 (November), 958–67.
Numéro deux can be analyzed in the way that personal "histories" repeat structures gained from society's history and from fictions (both = *l'historie*) and

vise versa. *Numéro deux* unmasks bourgeois "idealisations" about infancy, love and the elderly. The second discourse in the film, which stresses the notion of second-order experience and repetition, is a discourse about the media and technology — a discourse in which Godard implicates himself — often negatively, as a hidden manipulator, as a machine, as someone who attacks but is also trapped within that language secreted by bourgeois ideology. The film is compared to Fassbinder's work and André Téchiné's, *Souveiners d'en France*.

1976

1930 Anon. "Affiche: *Les Carabiniers.*" *L'Avant-Scène du cinéma*, Special Godard issue, No. 171-72 (July-September), p. 2.
Original poster to advertise film.

1931 Anon. "*Les Carabiniers* et la presse." *L'Avant-Scène du cinema*, No. 171-72 (July-September), pp. 41–42.
Quotations from French reviews.

1932 Anon. Article on *Sur et sous la communications. Le Monde* (14 August).
"The Association of Journalists and Reporters responded with an extreme violence to the episode, 'Photo and Cie.'" (1976, Collet, Entry No. 1967).

1933 Anon. "Godard, Jean-Luc: *Numéro deux.*" *Christian Science Monitor* (12 March), p. 26.
Christian Science Monitor 1976 Annual Index, p. 231.

1934 Anon. "Godard Newest to Suffer Censoring by Bomb; Closed." *Variety*, 284 (29 September), 44.
On showing of *Comment ça va?*. Cited 1976, FLI, 4, No. 3, p. 46.

1935 Anon. Interview with Godard. *Filmkritik*, 20 (June), 245.
Cited 1976, FLI, 4, No. 2, p. 63.

1936 Anon. "Mexico and Godard in Joint Film Vidtape for Theatrical Transfer." *Variety*, 282 (17 March), 30.
Cited 1976, FLI, 4, No. 2, p. 63.

1937 Anon. "*Numéro deux.*" *1000 Eyes* (April).
Brief announcement relates the theme and style of the film, at which showing Godard was to appear in person on Sunday, April 11.

1938 Anon. "Perspectives on French Cinema (4–27 March): *Numéro deux.*" Program Notes, Museum of Modern Art.
Introduction was given by Jacques Doniol-Valcroze, Association of French Film Directors, who selected new films for this program, presented with the cooperation of the French Film Office in New York. "The *cinema d'auteur* remains lively . . . and is always progressing" in France. Credits.

1939 Anon. "*Pierrot* et la presse." *L'Avant-Scène du cinéma*, Godard special issue, No. 171-72 (July-September), p. 110.

Reviews are quoted from *Le Monde* (1965, Baroncelli, Entry No. 485); *Minute* (1965, Le Serpent, Entry No. 602); *L'Humanité* (1965, Lachize, Entry No. 559); *France-Soir*; and *Arts* (1965, Bory, Entry No. 491).

1940   Anon. "Pour ou contre *Pierrot le fou*." *L'Avant-Scène du cinéma*, special Godard issue, No. 171-72 (July-September), p. 109.

Following reviews are cited: *Le Monde* (1965, Baby, Entry No. 483); *Paris Match* (1965, Anon, Entry No. 469); *Le Figaro littéraire* (1965, Mauriac, Entry No. 569); *Le Figaro*, 1965, Chauvet, Entry No. 496); *La Canard enchaîné* (1965, Durand, Entry No. 524); *Les Nouvelles littéraires* (1965, Ajame, Entry No. 452); and *Paris-Presse-l'intransigeant* (1965, Aubriant, Entry No. 480.)

1941   Anon. Program Notes for *Numéro Deux*. Philadelphia premiere, April 11, at which showing Godard was to appear in person.

Available in Museum of Modern Art clipping file.

1942   Anon. Program Notes No. 17: *Numéro deux*. 6th Internationales Forum des Jungen Films, 26th Internationale Filmfestspiele, Berlin, 27 June–4 July.

Credits. Brief description of film is given, as well as extensive citations and translations of interviews and articles from the French. Filmography.

1943   Anon. Review of MacBean's *Film and Revolution*. *Audience*, 8 (March), 14–15.

Cited 1976, FLI, 4, No. 1, p. 14.

1944   Anon. Review of MacBean's *Film and Revolution*. *Quarterly Review of Film Studies*, 1, No. 2, 155–62.

Cited 1976, FLI, 4, No. 3, p. 26.

1945   Anon. Review of Monaco's *The New Wave*. *American Film*, 1 (September), 74–75.

Cited 1976, FLI, 4, No. 3, p. 26.

1946   Anon. Review of Monaco's *The New Wave*. *Audience*, 9 (September), 8.

Cited 1976, FLI, 4, No. 3, p. 26.

1947   Anon. Review of Monaco's *The New Wave*. *Film and Literature Quarterly*, 9, No. 3, 60–62.

Cited 1976, FLI, 4, No. 3, p. 26.

1948   Anon. Review of Monaco's *The New Wave*. *Millimeter*, 4 (July-August), 73–74.

Cited 1976, FLI, 4, No. 3, p. 26.

1949   Anon. Review of Monaco's *The New Wave*. *New York Times* (29 August), Sec. 7, p. 8.

Cited 1976, FLI, 4, No. 3, p. 26.

1950 Anon. Review of Monaco's *The New Wave*. *Rolling Stone*, No. 218, (29 July), 55.
Cited 1976, FLI, 4, No. 3, p. 26.

1951 Anon. Review of Monaco's *The New Wave*. *Take One*, 5, No. 3, 41-42.
Cited 1976, FLI, 4, No. 3, p. 26.

1952 Anon. Review of Monaco's *The New Wave*. *Variety*, 283 (23 June), 35.
Cited 1976, FLI, 4, No. 2, p. 19.

1953 Anon. "Slogans sur *Pierrot*." *L'Avant-Scène du cinéma*, Godard special issue, No. 171-72 (July-September), p. 111.
From 1965, Anon., "Slogans sur *Pierrot*," Entry No. 471.

1954 Anon. "*Sur et sous la communication*." *Télé 7 Jours* (25 July), p. 20.
The TV guide describes the first and second episodes — *Ya personne* and *Louison*. This is the first program of the series, with two tapes each Sunday night starting at 8:30 and lasting in total 1 hour 40 minutes.

1955 Anon. "*Sur et sous la communication*." *Télé 7 Jours* (1 August), p. 34.
The second program in the series, shown at 8:30 on Sunday nights, presents tapes 3 and 4. *Leçons de choses*, and *Jean-Luc*.

1956 Anon. "*Sur et sous la communication*." *Télé 7 Jours* (8 August), p. 35.
This is the third program in the series, showing the fifth and sixth tape made by Godard and Anne-Marie Miéville: *Photo and Cie* and *Marcel*.

1957 Beal, Greg. "*A Woman Is a Woman (Une Femme est une femme)* (1961)." *Cinema Texas Program Notes*, 10, No. 4 (19 April), 18–25.
An in-depth essay examines the film in terms of Godard's playing with cinematic language. The following aspects are discussed: jump cuts, Karina as Godard's wife, references to other films, documentary aspects, long-winded jokes, direct sound and off-screen sound, use of cinemascope and Eastmancolor, interference with the narrative. Summary filmography through 1975 and brief reading list are given.

1958 Bonitzer, Pascal. "J-M. S. et J.-L. G.." *Cahiers du cinéma*, No. 264 (February), pp. 5–10.
Straub and Huillet's work and Godard's *Numéro deux* and *Ici et alleurs* are analyzed in Lacanian terms of *jouissance* (pleasure), the lack (the dark spaces in the montage and on the screen, the woman's voice) and chains of signifiers which Godard traces back in terms of the social apparatus of seduction (i.e., TV, films, ads). These directors attack "the old phallic complicity of the glance."

1959 Branigan, Edward. "The Articulation of Color in a Filmic System: *Two or Three Things I Know about Her*." *Wide Angle*, 1, No. 3, 20–31.
Godard uses highly saturated primary colors in a formalized, discontinuous way that does not reinforce any theme, mood, psychological state of the characters, or dramatic development. The color is nonreferential, and "the excessive

repetition of color tends to sever it from its object." It is also associated with repetition and regularity of shape.

1960 Braucourt, Guy. *"Ici et ailleurs* et *Six fois deux." Écran 76,* No. 51 (15 October), 56–57.
Credits. The films are briefly described, favorably, and the extremely hostile reactions from the press are noted.

1961 Britton, Andrew. "Godard and Politics — Living Historically: Two Films by Jean-Luc Godard." *Framework,* No. 3 (Spring), pp. 4–15.
In-depth political and aesthetic analysis of *Tout va bien* and *Vent d'est.*

1962 Campbell, Marilyn. "Life Itself: *Vivre sa vie* and the Language of Film." *Wide Angle,* 1, No. 3, 32–37.
To render the exterior aspects of Nana's soul, Godard concentrates on and makes noticeable his means of expression. In particular, he draws attention to the following aspects of filmic discourse: the face as abstraction and locus of fleeting individual gestures, methods of story telling, visual sense of depth, and tension between documentary and fiction.

1963 Casebier, Allan. "Exploiting Expectation: Audience Capacities." *Film Appreciation.* New York: Harcourt, Brace, Jovanovich. Pp. 62–73.
"The Godard equivalent of Brechtian alienation is *dislocation."* Dislocating techniques here include unusual use of color, space, editing, camera style, and genre conventions. Dramatically, the characters behave or react with unexpected casualness. The shots from an opening sequence of *Breathless* are analyzed in detail.

1964 Ch.[evallier] J.[acques]. *"Numéro deux." Image et son: la saison cinématographique,* No. 309–319 (October), p. 263.
Credits and brief résumé are given, followed by analysis of the film as a reflection on forms of communication.

1965 Clément, Catherine B. "Devoirs de vacances pour l'examen de communication." *Le Monde* (20 or 29 August).
Review of *Sur et sous la communication.* "Godard ruminates, and teaches, on the screen about me/you/the other/others." Cited 1976, Collet, Entry No. 1966.

1966 Collet, Jean. "Le Crime dans l'information." *L'Avant-Scène du cinéma,* Godard special issue, No. 171-72 (July-September), pp. 3–4.
Introduction to screenplays of *Les Carabiniers* and *Pierrot le fou* in terms of the multiple ways Godard chooses to present information and shape/comment on meaning.

1967 Collet, Jean. "Godard, au jourd'hui: du bon usage de la télévision." *Etudes,* 345 (November), 507–518.
Collet gives a close, praising explication and description of each program of *Sur et sous la communication,* telling how Godard combines a Lacanian perspective with an analysis of the media. Godard is not just content with changing the contents of television — having the insane, the peasantry, children, prostitutes,

old women speak — but what he's changing is our relation to these people, and giving us a code to communicate with them.

1968 Cd.[Cornand], A.[ndré]. *"Comment ça va." Image et son: Revue du cinéma*, No. 308 (September), p. 118.
Godard is an isolated, ideologically confused, bitter leftover from May '68 who has refused to join in the major political struggles of today. Brief comments also on first two programs of *Sur et sous la communication*.

1969 Daney, Serge. "Le Thérrorisé (pédagogie godardienne)." *Cahiers du cinéma*, Nos. 262-63 (January), pp. 32–40.
Since '68, Godard's (and Gorin's) films have been those of a school teacher. Now the milieu presented in *Numéro deux* is the family. Godard never ignores the discourse of others but takes it at its word, literally, and examines it. He seeks out another image, sound, and discourse to counterbalance and struggle against the "already-said." Yet there is still a tyranny of the teacher over the student. Daney finds Godard's feminism strange in that Godard places in women's mouths, from 1968 on, the words of the law (here, Marxist or feminist) in a mere role reversal of patriarchy. Trans. into Italian, 1976, *La Biennale*, B76, pp. 26–31. Trans. 1977, Daney, Entry No. 2029.

1970 Daniel, Jean-Louis and Van de Putte, Christine. *"Numéro deux." La Biennale: un laboratorio internazionale*, B76 (Venice), pp. 32–35.
Godard's treatment of family politics considers both sexuality and our ties to and similarity with machines.

1971 Deleuze, Gilles. "A propos de *Sur et sous la communication*: trois questions sur *Six fois deux*." *Cahiers du cinéma*, No. 271 (November), pp. 5–12.
In an interview, Deleuze comments on the creative richness of Godard's solitude. Godard's current concerns are to expand upon/attack older notions of labor power and information. He particularly makes us attend to and listen to those who cry out, stutter, or are silent — whose voice is lost. Among the many images around us, we usually only attend to a few — because verbal information directs us to just a few. Godard's dominant syntactic word is not *is*, as in Western thought, but *and* — not a dialectical *and* but one indicating an irreducible multiplicity and the frontier of possibilities for revolution.

1972 Foery, Raymond. "Everything's OK with Godard." *1000 Eyes*, No. 7 (February), p. 15.
Godard's career is briefly described in this review of *Tout va bien*, Godard's "first film of recent years to be somewhat less than totally propagandistic." The reviewer enjoys Godard's renewed "cinematic imagination and visual irony." Credits.

1973 Forrester, Viviane. "Les Cent Jours de Godard." *Le Nouvel Observateur* (9 August), p. 49.
Credits for *Sur et sous la communication*. Godard and Anne-Marie Miéville's twelve TV programs are described in terms of production and the first episode, which shows in a stylized way the relation of employee to employer and the effect

of unemployment and of alienated labor on one's sense of self. A brief comment by Godard is cited; he calls the programs "the ingredients for salad, not the salad."

1974 Giannetti, Louis D. *Understanding Movies*. 2nd Edition. Englewood Cliffs, N.J.: Prentice-Hall.

Discusses in passing the following aspects of Godard's films: lighting (p. 23), color (p. 28), use of film stock (pp. 39, 41), formal composition (pp. 51, 59, 81), tracking shots (pp. 116, 118), New Wave innovations in editing (pp. 178–80), sound track (pp. 197–98), "literary" language (p. 214), documentary interest (pp. 226, 305), self-reflexivity and relation to Vertov and Brecht (pp. 247–48, 421–22), lack of script (p. 313), avant garde aspects (p. 411), relation to Marxist art (p. 425), and auteur theory (p. 437).

1975 Gilliatt, Penelope. "Profiles: The Urgent Whisper." *New Yorker*, 52, No. 36 (25 October), 47–58.

Godard's quarters in Grenoble, his demeanor, and his past films are described by Gilliatt, who compares his personal stance to that of Brecht. Godard discusses the political reasons why a filmmaker must be original.

1976 Giraud, Thérèse. "Retour du même." *Cahiers du cinéma*, Nos. 262-63 (January), pp. 20–26.

Godard explores political commitment in terms of sexuality in *Numéro deux*, not "alongside" sexuality, as in *Tout va bien*. What does everyone in a family experience of sexuality? In *Numéro deux*, the images are encircled by black, a metaphor for ideology. Giraud analyzes the content of the film from a feminist psychoanalytic perspective. Trans. into Italian, 1976, *La Biennale*, B76, pp. 36–39.

1977 Goldwasser, Noë. "Godard Is Still at It." *Village Voice* (23 February).

Georges de Beauregard, producer of *Breathless*, financed *Numéro deux*. Godard says that the film was shot in video for a "television that doesn't yet exist" and could be titled, "The Sexual Economy of the Inhabitants of Lower Grenoble."

1978 Gross, L. "Film après noir." *Film Comment*, 12 (July-August), 44–49.
Review of *Alphaville*. Cited 1976, FLI, 4, No. 3, p. 6.

1979 Hennebelle, Guy. "Un Charabia indigeste." *Écran 76*, No. 51 (15 October), pp. 57–58.

Strongly negative review of *Ici et ailleurs* attacks Godard followers, especially those on the left.

1980 Lefèvre, R.[aymond]. "*Weekend*." *Image et son: Revue du cinéma*, No. 308, 134–39.
In-depth analysis. Cited 1976, FLI, 4, No. 3, p. 226.

1981 Le Peron, Serge. "*Numéro deux*: entre le zéro et l'infini." *Cahiers du cinéma*, Nos. 262-63 (January), pp. 11–14.

Numéro deux examines the way images are formed, what they contain, and the sociopolitical-familial conjuncture in which we receive them — that is, television. Within the images is inscribed the impossibility of certain rapports in our society — between men/women, young/old, there/here, etc. Le Peron describes the visual/audio impact and mechanisms of the film. Trans. into Italian, 1976, *La Biennale*, B76, pp. 40–42. Trans. into German, 1976, 26th Berlin Film Festival Program Notes, Entry No. 1942.

1982 Lesage, Julia. "The Films of Jean-Luc Godard and Their Use of Brechtian Dramatic Theory." Ph.D. Dissertation, Indiana University. *Dissertation Abstracts*, 37A Part 4 (October), 1845A.
   The dissertation examines Godard's leftist modernist aesthetic, his translation of (invention of equivalents for) Brechtian distanciation tactics, the social and political concerns which are part of a Brechtian work, and Godard's relation to other modernist tendencies besides Brechtianism. Topics considered at length include an aesthetic overview of Godard's films, influences on Godard, Godard's political evolution, Maoism in France, Brecht's theories and reception in France, Godard's awareness of Brecht, general aesthetic problems in comparing film and theater, and a close analysis of the Brechtian elements in four pre-1968 films (*Les Carabiniers*, *La Femme mariée*, *Vivre sa vie*, and *Deux ou trois choses*) and three post-1968 ones (*Le Gai Savoir*, *Vent d'est*, and *Pravda*).

1983 Lesage, Julia. "Visual Distancing in Godard." *Wide Angle*, 1, No. 3, 4–13.
   The following aspects of Godard's visual style are discussed: dislocating shots, framing and composition, documentary reflections, symbols and emblems, the written word, cinematic citation, the long take, color control, and modernist and Brechtian distanciation. There are serious printing errors and omissions that render some sentences inaccurate or unintelligible in the article.

1984 Lesage, Julia. "*Vladimir and Rosa*." *Revolutionary Films, Chicago '76*. Chicago Film Center, School of the Art Institute. Pp. 36–37.
   Godard and Gorin invented a range of visual tactics for a "Brechtian" cinema. A long women's liberation sequence raises sexual-political concerns in a "visually symbolic and verbally explicit way."

1985 Magny, Joel. "*Numéro deux*." *La Biennale: un laboratorio internazionale*, B76 (Venice), pp. 1–10.
   Credits. Analyzes Godard's political and aesthetic "itinerary" and his method of reeducating people about both the political content of his films and cinema as a whole.

1986 Manns, T. "Paris brev." *Chaplin*, 18, No. 1 (142), 27–28.
   Review of *Numéro deux*. Cited 1976, FLI, 4, No. 2, p. 114.

1987 Martini, E. "L'immagine della citta nel cinema." *Cineforum*, No. 151 (January-February), pp. 19–33.
   Cited 1976, FLI, 4, No. 2, p. 63.

1988 Mast, Gerald. *A Short History of the Movies*. 2nd Edition. Indianapolis: Bobbs-Merrill. Pp. 379–84.
   Godard both likes to capture irrational, inexplicable, fleeting moments and to "flirt with Brechtian devices and politics." His unconventional narrative techniques, unusual ways of developing character, capriciousness, arid debates and

discussions, formalist concerns, and attack on film conventions for radical ideological reasons are described through brief analyses of *Les Carabiniers, Weekend*, and *La Chinoise*.

1989 Nichols, Bill, ed. *Movies and Methods: An Anthology*. Berkeley: University of California Press.

James Roy MacBean, *"Vent d'est* or Glauber and Rocha at the Crossroads," pp. 91–106, reprinted from 1971, MacBean, Entry No. 1599; Sieh Hwa Beh, *"Vivre sa vie,"* pp. 180–85, reprinted from 1972, Beh, Entry No. 1650; Brian Henderson, "Toward a Non-Bourgeois Camera Style," pp. 422–38, reprinted from 1970, Henderson, Entry No. 1459.

1990 Rohdie, Sam. "Notes from a Pedant." *Quarterly Review of Film Studies*, 1, No. 2, 155–62.

Cited 1976, FLI, 4, No. 3, p. 87.

1991 Ropars-Wuilleumier, Marie-Claire. "On Fashion" and "Loss of Language." Trans. Dorothy Hoekzema. *Wide Angle*, 1, No. 3, 14–19.

Trans. from 1965, Ropars-Wuilleumier, Entry No. 586 and Entry No. 587.

1992 Rosenbaum, Jonathan. "Journals: Jonathan Rosenbaum from London." *Film Comment*, 12, No. 1 (January-February), 2, 4, and 63.

Discusses *Numéro deux* along with *Winstanley*, Fassbinder's films, and Nabokov's version of a film script for *Lolita*.

1993 Rosenbaum, Jonathan. *"Numéro deux." Sight and Sound*, 45, No. 2 (Spring), 124–25.

Cited 1976, IIFP, 4, No. 2, p. 63.

1994 Schwartz, Stan. *"Numéro deux." Film Quarterly*, 30, No. 2 (Winter), 61–63.

Explains Godard's aesthetic-political intent, offers a close analysis of the title sequence and discussion of what the title means, finds the film a Brechtian analysis of contradictions and "dualisms," makes comparisons to Bergman, and analyzes the opening and closing sequences in Godard's studio.

1995 [Segal, Abraham]. *"British Sounds." L'Avant-Scène du cinéma*, No. 171-72 (July-September), p. 60.

Credits, stills accompanied by explanations, extensive description of film, brief remarks by Godard. Godard discusses extent to which the film is or is not "political."

1996 [Segal, Abraham]. *"Cinétracts." L'Avant-Scène du cinéma*, No. 171-72 (July-September), pp. 54–58.

Segal describes how these short films were fabricated and reproduced and he explicates several of the ones made by Godard.

1997 [Segal, Abraham]. *"Un Film comme les autres." L'Avant-Scène du cinéma*, No. 171-72 (July-September), p. 59.

Brief résumé. Long citation from 1969, Fargier, Entry No. 1293.

1998 [Segal, Abraham]. *"Le Gai Savoir,"* *L'Avant-Scène du cinéma*, No. 171-72 (July-September), pp. 52–53.

Provides credits, a brief history, and a plot summary of the film, which Segal briefly compares to *Comment ça va?*.

1999 [Segal, Abraham]. "Godard et le groupe Dziga Vertov." *L'Avant-Scène du cinéma*, No. 171-72 (July-September), pp. 47–52.

A complete history is given of Godard's political filmmaking career from 1967 on. Sources are often from English-language publications.

2000 [Segal, Abraham]. *"Luttes en Italie."* *L'Avant-Scène du cinéma*, No. 171-72 (July-September), pp. 66–68.

Credits. Plot summary, quoted from 1971, Goodwin et al. Entry No. 1578. Stills accompanied by lines from the film. Segal comments on the concepts the images are supposed to symbolize and notes a progression in what the black frames represent. He compares *Luttes en Italie* to *Les Carabiniers* and to other Dziga Vertov Group films.

2001 [Segal, Abraham]. *"Pravda."* *L'Avant-Scène du cinéma*, No. 171-72 (July-September), pp. 64–65.

Credits. Stills accompanied by explanations. Plot summary quoted from a text signed by Godard and distributed as program notes at a showing at l'A.R.C., Musée d'Art Moderne, February 1970. Godard concluded that the film was filmed in an opportunistic way, and the montage still was too individualistic; but he had here learned to simplify images and find some specific ones to use in future films.

2002 [Segal, Abraham]. *"Vent d'est."* *L'Avant-Scène du cinéma*, No. 171-72 (July-September), pp. 61–63.

Credits. Stills accompanied by explanations and lines from the film. The political symbolism of the visual track is explained. Cohn-Bendit and Godard describe the film's history.

2003 [Segal, Abraham]. *"Vladimir and Rosa."* *L'Avant-Scène du cinéma*, Special Godard issue, No. 171-72 (July-September), pp. 69–70.

Credits, plot summary, and commentary. In real life, the Chicago 7 trial had transformed the judicial process into a circus or boxing ring, in a Brechtian way. Godard and Gorin utilize a commedia dell'arte style, comment on the mode of political action characteristic of each defendant, and examine their own goals and aesthetics. The film's derisive tone reflects the Dziga Vertov Group's removal from organized political struggles.

2004 Skorecki, Louis. "Questions/Réponses." *Cahiers du cinéma*, No. 262-263 (January), pp. 27–31.

Numéro deux forces the spectator into a new relation with the images and the sounds beyond merely "reading" them. Trans. into Italian, 1976, *La Biennale*, B76, pp. 22–25.

2005 Sotiaux, D. *"Numéro deux."* *APEC: Revue belge du cinéma*, 13, No. 6, 75–76.

Cited 1976, FLI, 4, No. 3, p. 153.

2006 Tassone, Aldo. "Due o tre cose che Godard ha detto di se." *La Biennale: un laboratorio internazionale*, B76, pp. 18–22.
Extensive citations from interviews with Godard (questions not included) about *Numéro deux* are translated into the Italian from *Le Monde, Télérama*, and *Télécine*.

2007 Teegarden, J. Review of *Numéro deux*. *Audience*, 8, No. 11 (May), p. 4.
Negative review. Cited *Media Review Digest, 1977*, p. 149.

2008 Thompson, Kirsten. "Sawing through the Bough: *Tout va bien* Seen as a Brechtian Film." *Wide Angle*, 1, No. 3, 38–51.
Initially criticizes Colin McCabe's application of Brecht's idea of "separation of the elements" to *Tout va bien* and concludes with her own concept of what it means to call a film Brechtian. *Tout va bien*'s "separation of the elements on the local level of stylistic devices" includes narrative "interruptions"; contradictions — which are the content of the film and which also arise from "the juxtaposition of technical devices which defy Hollywoodian norms"; and "refractions" — the film's way of emphasizing the way an action is shown. On the global level of the "story," *Tout va bien* breaks up traditional coded patterns of narrative conventions and interferes with narrative causality.

2009 Toubiana, Serge. "Le Hasard arbitraire." *Cahiers du cinéma*, Nos. 262-63 (January), pp. 15–19.
Film criticism, which needs to believe that the cinematic art *progresses*, cannot deal with Godard's always returning to zero, always asking, "What is cinema?" Compares *Numéro deux* to *The Guttenberg Galaxy*. Rather than being plunged into an imaginary world we are faced with images that don't seem to come from anywhere or go anywhere. Analyzes the political function of such a film and questions the role of a "minority" public reception of Godard's (and Straub's) work. Trans. into German, 1976, 26th Berlin Film Festival Program Notes (Entry No. 1942), into Italian, 1976, *La Biennale*, B76, pp. 1–5.

2010 Walsh, Martin. "Godard and Me." *Take One*, 5, No. 1 (February), 14–17.
In an interview with Jean-Pierre Gorin, November 1974, in London, Ontario, Martin Walsh and Gorin discuss Gorin's post-Maoist and post-Godard plans, especially in terms of Gorin's possibly making a comedy in Hollywood.

2011 Wolfe, Charles. Program Notes for *Breathless*. "Films from the Archive." Showing, Museum of Modern Art Department of Film, October 8-9.
Credits. The critic discusses the way Godard uses and transforms genre, conventions. We feel that beneath the characters' mannerisms "there is nothing more to reveal."

2012 Wollen. Peter. "The Two Avant-Gardes." *Edinburgh '76 Magazine: Psycho-Analysis/Cinema/Avant-Garde*, No. 1, pp. 77–85.
Godard and Gorin's work is described in terms of the history of two often hostile tendencies in experimental film, one coming from the visual arts (the Coop movement) and one coming from Eisenstein — that is, one seeking new forms to

express a new, politically revolutionary content. Reprinted from 1975, Wollen, Entry No. 1928.

1977

2013 Anon. *"Les Cahiers du cinéma*, 1968–1977: Interview with Serge Daney," *The Thousand Eyes* (October), pp. 19–31.
Daney gives key background information of the politicization of cultural circles in France after 1968, militant filmmaking, and the impact of the women's movement on political films there.

2014 Anon. "Godard Dug Up." *CTVD: Cinema-TV-Digest*, No. 38 (Summer), pp. 11–12.
Ici et ailleurs opened in two Paris theaters on September 15, 1976, but was withdrawn from one when a bomb was found in the theater on opening day.

2015 Anon. "Godard, Jean-Luc." *Who's Who in France 1977–78*, 13. Paris: Editions Jacques Lafitte. P. 782.
Gives information not available elsewhere: Godard's father's name (Paul); the fact that *Vivre sa vie* won both the Japanese and the German critics prizes as the best foreign film; dates of Godard's marriage to Karina (March 2, 1961) and to Wiazemsky (July 21, 1967), and his current address (13 Rue Henri-Duhamel, 3800 Grenoble, Switzerland).

2016 Anon. *Numéro deux*. Sixth International Forum of Young Films, 26th Berlin Film Festival, Program Notes, No. 17 (27 June–4 July).
Trans. from 1975, Delilia, et al. Entry No. 1889, and 1975, Anon., compilations of interviews about *Numéro deux*, Entry No. 1866.

2017 Anon. Review of *Numéro deux*. London *Sunday Times* (28 January), pp. 9, 30, 38.
Cited 1977, *Times Index* (January), p. 57.

2018 Appelbaum, Sam and Gerry Mead. *"Band of Outsiders, Le Gai Savoir."* Program Notes, Film Center, School of the Art Institute, Chicago, June 9. Pp. 1–7.
Godard uses "the cliches of a gangster film as its [*Band of Outsiders'*] skeleton," but his real subject, treated with spontaneity and seeming casualness, is "the poetry of human relationships." *Le Gai Savior* shows two youths who take up "an intensive dialectical analysis of bourgeois language-assumptions and reactionary definitions of truth, art, time, and love." Brief credits.

2019 Appelbaum, Sam and Gerry Mead. *"Une Femme est une femme, Camera-Oeil* from *Loin du Viêtnam, Weekend."* Program Notes, Film Center School of the Art Institute, Chicago, June 1. 8 pp.
Discusses the relation of *Une Femme est une femme* to the musical genre, its vitality and Godard's treatment of women. *Loin du Viêtnam* is described and the relation between Godard's political stance and aesthetic project is noted. *Weekend* reveals Godard's fascination with the New Left. Although he attacks narrative and

cinematic illusion, "the story, and cinema, survive." A close explication of *Weekend* is given.

2020 Appelbaum, Sam and Gerry Mead. *"Vladimir and Rosa."* Program Notes, Film Center School of the Art Institute, Chicago, June 22. Pp. 3–6.

This film pretends to be "distanced," but Godard and Gorin really "enforce" their line through games, repetitions, and caricatures — which are then related to the meaning of the Chicago 7 trial as Godard and Gorin see it. They have adopted the self-images of New Leftists, but the film "is simply a game, a recirculation of phrases and images whose impact has already been spent."

2021 [Augst, Bertrand]. *"Comment ça va? (How Is It Going?)*, 1976, Jean-Luc Godard." Pacific Film Archives program notes.

Summary and description of the film.

2022 Barath, Esther. *"Numéro deux."* Workprint: *Filmwomen Newsletter* (Boston), 4, No. 6 (November), 1.

Little coverage was given to New England premier of this powerful and accessible "questioning of incest taboos, male/female stereotypes of sexual behavior, and the demands of time and a consumer-oriented society upon communication."

2023 Bourget, Jean-Loup. *"Numéro deux."* Program Notes, Film Center, School of the Art Institute, Chicago, June 30 and July 1, pp. 1–4.

Brief credits. The unresolved contradiction in the film between Godard's love expressed for the characters, acting themselves, and his mechanical, boring presentation of sexual activity is echoed by other "binary oppositions" throughout the film: (1) organic v. mechanical, (2) factory v. landscape, (3) words v. images, (4) images v. their frame, (5) the "framing" of the film v. its central part, (6) Godard v. the machines, (7) *Numéro deux* v. the audience.

2024 Bourget, Jean-Loup. *"Pierre le fou."* Program Notes, Film Center, School of the Art Institute, Chicago, June 22. Pp. 1–3.

The following literary and cinematic influences on or citations in the film are noted: Ferdinand Céline, Samuel Fuller, Rimbaud, Faulkner, Jack London, Raymond Chandler, Fritz Lang, Gene Kelly, and Godard's own films.

2025 Butler, Jeremy. *"All the Boys Are Called Patrick, Une Historie d'eau, Montparnasse-Levallois* from *Six in Paris, Anticipation* from *The Oldest Profession, La Chinoise."* Program Notes, Film Center, School of the Art Institute, Chicago, May 26. 8 pp.

The following aspects of Godard's work are described: early film career, shorts, prostitution metaphor, and political development.

2026 Butler, Jeremy. *"Tout va bien, Letter to Jane."* Program Notes, Film Center, School of the Art Institute, Chicago, June 23. Pp. 4–7.

Critiques Kristin Thompson's (1976, Entry No. 2008) evaluation of *Tout va bien* as Brechtian. Instead, *Letter to Jane* is more genuinely political in a Brechtian way and "exists largely as the medicine that the sugar-coating of *Tout va bien* momentarily conceals."

2027 Butler, Jeremy. *"Vivre sa vie."* Program Notes, Film Center, School of the Art Institute, Chicago, June 2. Pp. 1–3.

Godard wanted to unite documentary and fiction in a *theatre verite*, partly following the traditions of Flaherty and Eisenstein, partly following Brecht's ideas of epic theater. The prostitution motif is discussed.

2028 Carlin, Warren. *"Two or Three Things I Know about Her."* Program Notes, Godard Retrospective, Film Center, School of the Art Institute, Chicago, May 25, pp. 4–5.

Describes the social protest contained in the film; Godard's charges are "overdone, [but] still timely."

2029 Daney, Serge. "The T(h)errorized." Trans. T.L. French and Charles Cameron Ball. *The Thousand Eyes* (October), pp. 33–43.

Trans. from 1976, Daney, Entry No. 1969.

2030 Fox, Terry Curtis. "Looking for Mr. Godard: Grenoble Savage — How It Goes with Godard." *Village Voice* (31 October), pp. 1 and 41.

Godard's reception in the United States is described from 1966, when *Bande à part* played four days in New York, to 1968, when he was a "surefire hit," to now, when his uncritical "feeling for Palestinians" will irritate New Yorkers. *Numéro deux* and *Comment ça va* are more discourse than story, but they do try to present both analysis and emotion.

2031 French, T.L. "The Tinkerers." *The Thousand Eyes*, Special *Cahiers du cinéma* issue to accompany "La Semaine de *Cahiers*" film showings at the Bleecker St. Cinema, October 30–November 3.

In the introduction to the series, French describes the significance of the word *bricoleur* as applied to Godard and the *Cahiers* critics, especially in their later development. By using a Lacanian approach to language, Serge Daney (see 1976, Daney, Entry No. 1969) can effectively criticize Godard's current form of isolation and turning words into things, talking to whomever will listen and not having a sense of audience in *Numéro deux*.

2032 Heller, Lucy. *"Alphaville."* Program Notes, Film Center, School of the Art Institute, Chicago, June 16. Pp. 1–3.

"Alphaville is composed of endless circles that seem to be straight lines until one is caught in them. . . . Perhaps in the last scene as Lemmy and Natasha drive down a gently curving nighttime highway as she learns to say 'I love you,' they are not driving away from Alphaville but back into it, back into the circle of the present."

2033 Lesage, Julia. *"Cinétracts/A Film Like Any Other."* Program Notes, Film Center, School of the Art Institute, Chicago, June 29, pp. 5–8.

The historical background, political-aesthetic intent, and content of the 1968 films are described. Brief credits.

2034 Lesage, Julia. *"The Married Woman, British Sounds, Pravda."* Program Notes, Godard Retrospective, Film Center, School of The Art Institute, Chicago, June 15. 4 pp.

"In contrast to *Vivre sa vie*, there is a certain nonchalance to the tone of *The Married Woman*, a kind of antiseptic Mr. Clean-quality to the bourgeois life style we see and a great deal of wit in the way that Godard comments on that life style and the false consciousness it engenders." *British Sounds* and *Pravda* are described in terms of the following: emblematic images, critique of revisionism, distrust of traditional cinematic expression, audience response, the sound track, and the relation between "scientific experimentation and the class struggle" in political film.

2035 Lesage, Julia. *"Le Nouveau Monde* from *Rogopag, Les Carabiniers."* Program Notes, Film Center, School of the Art Institute, Chicago, May 8. Pp. 1–5.

Rossellini's influence on *Le Nouveau Monde* and *Les Carabiniers* is described, as are "the major visual structural elements" of both films. "The truth about war (or any other external phenomena), says the Brechtian Godard in *Les Carabiniers*, lies under the surface in the social and economic relations which engender war and which it, in turn, engenders."

2036 Lesage, Julia. *"Wind from the East."* Program Notes, Film Center, School of the Art Institute, Chicago, June 17. Pp. 3–6.

The political symbolism in the film is explicated by a list of representative images, followed by a summary of the concepts they represent, usually ones that were presented in voice off on the film's sound track.

2037 Lev, Peter. Review of Monaco's *The New Wave. Quarterly Review of Film Studies*, 2, No. 2 (May), 227+.

Cited 1977, "Index (Vol. 2)," *Quarterly Review of Film Studies*, 2, No. 4 (November).

2038 Leyda, Jay, ed. *Voices of Film Experience: 1894 to the Present.* Research by Doug Tomlinson and John Hagan. New York: Macmillan. Pp. 170–72.

Excerpts are printed from the following interviews with Godard: (1) 1962, *Cahiers du cinéma* (December), Entry No. 186; trans. 1972, Milne, Entry No. 1713. (2) 1966, Regard, Entry No. 741; trans. 1966, *Take One*, Entry No. 740. (3) 1962, Milne, *Sight and Sound* (Winter), Entry No. 213. (4) 1965, Godard *Cinéma 65* (March), Entry No. 2230. (5) 1965, *The Observer* (5 September).

2039 McFarland, John. *"Contempt."* Program Notes, Film Center, School of the Art Institute, Chicago, June 29. Pp. 1–5.

The film portrays a conflict between an "artistic and a conqueror mentality"; it pays tribute to the classical idea of beauty but shows the passing of older conventions, especially in film. Each of the characters and what they represent is described. Brief credits.

2040 McFarland, John. *"Masculine-Feminine."* Program Notes, Film Center, School of the Art Institute, Chicago, June 23. Pp. 1–4.

The critic analyzes Godard's literary sources, Godard's response to Paris in 1965, Paul as Godard's alter ego, and the innovative aspects of the interview sequences.

2041 Mead, Gerry and Sam Appelbaum. *"Band of Outsiders, Le Gai Savior."*

Program Notes, Film Center, School of the Art Institute, Chicago, June 9. Pp. 1–7.
See 1977, Appelbaum, Entry No. 2018.

2042 Mead, Gerry and Sam Appelbaum. *"Une Femme est une femme, Caméra-Oeil* from *Far from Vietnam, Weekend."* Program Notes, Film Center, School of the Art Institute, Chicago, June 1. 8 pp.
See 1977, Appelbaum, Entry No. 2019.

2043 Mead, Gerry and Sam Appelbaum. *"Vladimir and Rosa."* Program Notes, Film Center, School of the Art Institute, Chicago, June 22. Pp. 3–6.
See 1977, Appelbaum, Entry No. 2020.

Undated

2044 Anon. *"British Sounds, Pravda, Six Cinetracts."* No title, pp. 41–42.
Brief credits and description of each film. Reviews cited, some at length. For *British Sounds*: Ian Christie, *Monthly Film Bulletin*; Chris Williams, *Screen*; Michael Goodwin, *Rolling Stone*. For *Pravda*: Peter Sainsbury and Godard, *Afterimage*, No. 1; *Take One*. For *Six Cinetracts*, Simon Hartog and Peter Sainsbury, *Afterimage*, No. 1. Godard's statement on the making of *Pravda* is cited at length. (Museum of Modern Art clipping file.)

2045 Anon. Commentary on *Les Carabiniers*. London, National Film Theater.
Cited BFI Bibliography.

2046 Anon. Commentary on *Charlotte et son Jules*. London, National Film Theater.
Cited BFI Bibliography.

2047 Anon. Commentary on *Deux ou trois choses que je sais d'elle*. London, National Film Theater.
Cited BFI Bibliography.

2048 Anon. Commentary on *Une Femme coquette*. London, National Film Theater.
Cited BFI Bibliography.

2049 Anon. Commentary on *Une Femme est une femme*. London, National Film Theater.
Cited BFI Bibliography.

2050 Anon. Commentary on *Les Fils prodigues* in *Vangelo '70*. London, National Film Theater.
Cited BFI Bibliography.

2051 Anon. Commentary on *Le Grand Escroc* in *Les Plus Belles Escroqueries du monde*. London, National Film Theater.
Cited BFI Bibliography.

2052 Anon. Commentary on *Made in U.S.A.* London, National Film Theater.
Cited BFI Bibliography.

2053 Anon. Commentary on *Montparnasse-Levallois* in *Paris vu par.* London, National Film Theater.
Cited BFI Bibliography.

2054 Anon. Commenatry on *Le Nouveau Monde* in *Rogopag.* London, National Film Theater.
Cited BFI Bibliography.

2055 Anon. Commentary on *La Paresse* in *Sept Péchés capitaux.* London, National Film Theater.
Cited BFI Bibliography.

2056 Anon. Commentary on *Pierrot le fou.* London, National Film Theater.
Cited BFI Bibliography.

2057 Anon. Fifth New York Film Festival (program notes). Lincoln Center for the Performing Arts, September 20–30.
Synopsis of *Made in U.S.A.* Although the plot is confusing, this is a realistic portrayal of what we know of contemporary political assassinations carried out by private police. The Hegelian discussion of language in a bar indicates that all is inextricably linked; all things are manifestations of a general situation. Even the heroine may be just a killer.

2058 Anon. "Jean-Luc Godard's *Vladimir and Rosa.*" Publicity brochure for Grove Press Distributors.
These reviews are quoted: Stuart Byron, *Village Voice;* Stanley Kauffmann, *New Republic;* Vincent Canby, *New York Times;* Michael Goodwin, *Rolling Stone;* Tom Luddy, *San Francisco Chronicle;* Paul D. Zimmerman, *Newsweek.*

2059 Anon. "I situazionisti dicono 'no' a Godard." *Cinema 60* (Italian), No. 64.
Cited 1974, Ferrero, Entry No. 1841.

2060 Aubervilles, B.P. Review of *Alphaville. Miroir du cinéma,* No. 12-13, p. 95.
Cited in 1967, Delmas, review of *Made in U.S.A.* Entry No. 869.

2061 Blue, James. Excerpts from future book on directing nonprofessional actors in film. Mimeographed. Museum of Modern Art clipping file.
Interviews Godard on directing actors. Godard compares his directing to that of Bresson and Renoir. He discusses his use of Eddie Constantine, Brigitte Bardot, Jack Palance, and the maid who recited Céline in *La Femme mariée* (directed via a microphone in her ear). "I want them to find what they have to do . . . They like themselves on the screen when they see the film, but they don't like to work with me very much, mainly because I never say much to them." Also interviews Richard Grenier, who had a bit part in *Pierrot.* Reprinted 1968, Mussman, Entry No. 1168.

2062 Brown, Royal. *The European New Wave and Music*. New York: Alfred A. Knopf. Forthcoming.

Godard satirizes film music and musicals in *A Woman is a Woman*. Godard's method is to have composers write whole scores to be "edited" with the film, rather than separate musical snippets for specific sequences. Apparently Paul Misraki did not see *Alphaville* before he wrote the score.

2063 Carreno, Jose Maria. "Semana de cine frances con Godard y Rohmer." *Film ideal* (Madrid), No. 222-23, 31–36.

Cited 1970, Cameron, Entry No. 1399.

2064 Carrol, Kathleen. Review of *Pierrot le fou*. New York *Daily News*.

Cited in *Film Facts*, 12, No. 1, p. 2.

2065 Chicheportiche, Roland. *"Weekend."* Paris: Institut des Hautes Etudes Cinématographiques. 8 pp.

Analysis of film.

2066 Collet, Jean. Interview with Godard on *Le Petit Soldat*. *Radio-Cinéma-Télévision*, No. 549.

Cited 1974, Collet, Entry No. 1832.

2067 Comolli, Jean-Louis. Review of *Alphaville*. *Cahiers du Cinema in English*, No. 3, pp. 57–59.

Cited Bowles, p. 11. Trans. from 1965, Comolli, Entry No. 504.

2068 Desclercs, Joannick. *"Masculin-Féminin."* Paris: Institut des Hautes Etudes Cinématographiques. 9 pp.

Analysis of film.

2069 Font, Ramon. "Jean-Luc Godard y la problematica de la imagen." *Film Ideal*, No. 222-23, pp. 126–44.

Cited 1970, Cameron, Entry No. 1399.

2070 Gelmis, Joseph. Review of *Pierrot le fou*. *Newsday*.

Cited in *Film Facts*, 12, No. 1, p. 2.

2071 Goodwin, Michael. Review of *British Sounds*. *Rolling Stone*.

Cited in Grove Press publicity brochure. (1970?)

2072 Kernan, Margot. *A Film Course Study Guide: The Politics of Revolution*. New York: Grove Press Film Division. Pp. 3–10.

A publicity and information booklet for the films distributed by Grove: *See You at Mao, Wind from the East, Pravda*, and *Vladimir and Rosa*. (probably 1972 or 1973)

2073 Kernan, Margot. *A Film Course Study Guide: Radical Voices*. New York: Grove Press Film Division. Pp. 3–4, 19–20.

Review of *Weekend* for Grove Press publicity pamphlet. (probably 1971 or 1972)

2074 *The Movies*, 1, No. 3.
Godard issue; cited 1968, Collet, Entry No. 1088.

2075 Neyrinck, Jean-Marie. Thesis on Godard in Nancy, France.
Mentioned in correspondence with Royal Brown. Neyrinck's address in 1972 was 19, Rue F. Mirguet, 57 Serémange, France.

2076 Patterson, G.G. *My Life to Live. Current Film Notes.*
The film, now showing at the New Yorker, is interesting mainly as a camera study of Karina and a rebellion against filmmaking "rules." It's a "fascinating oddity." (Lincoln Center Library clipping file.)

2077 Piton Geneviève. *"Le Mépris."* Paris: Institut des Hautes Etudes Cinématographiques. 9 pp.
Analysis of film.

2078 Potenze, Jaime. *Alphaville* (Id., Francia, 1964). *Criterio*, 38, No. 1494, 149.
Potenze attacks critics who think Godard can do no wrong and who find *Alphaville*, which is in fact a failure, the work of a poet.

2079 Prokosch, Mike. "Two or Three Films of Jean-Luc Godard." *On Film*, 1, No. 0 (sic), 91–94.
In *Weekend*, the protagonists' deneration and the decay of culture in general is indicated by the increasing aimlessness and depersonalization of the film. It is the "end of cinema" and of "the story," especially that kind of American cinema Godard had loved, with its development of a character's social situation psychologically. *Two or Three Things* still uses one character as an "entree to the analysis of social reality." *Le Gai Savior* has only a "nominal narrative with nominal identification figures," and it deals instead with images and words and "second-hand events," dialectically presented but not integrated into a general truth for us. It's even less cohesive than Eisenstein's work. Credits given.

2080 Shivas, Mark. Review of *A Woman Is a Woman. Movie*, No. 7, p. 26.
Cited in Bowles, p. 575, and BFI Bibliography.

2081 Simsolo, Noël. "La Révolution par le film selon J.-L. Godard., ou comment contester le cinéma de consommation." *Cinéma pratique*, No. 97.
Cited 1974, Collet, Entry No. 1832.

V
Writings by Godard

1950

2082 "Chronique du 16 mm." *La Gazette du cinéma*, No. 5 (November).
Signed J.-L.G. Cited 1974, Collet, Entry No. 1832.

2083 *"Ditte Menneskebarn." La Gazette du cinéma*, No. 5 (November).
Signed J.-L.G. Cited 1974, Collet, Entry No. 1832.

2084 *"La Femme à écharpe pailletee." La Gazette du cinéma*, No. 5 (November).
Signed H. Lucas. Cited 1974, Collet, Entry No. 1832.

2085 *"Gaslight." La Gazette du cinéma*, No. 5 (November).
Cited 1974, Collet, Entry No. 1832.

2086 *"The Great McGinty." La Gazette du cinéma*, No. 5 (November).
Signed Hans Lucas. Cited 1974, Collet, Entry No. 1832.

2087 "Joseph Mankiewicz." *La Gazette du cinéma*, No. 2 (June).
Godard discusses Mankiewicz's stories about marriage, narrative devices, direction of actors, and similarity to and differences from Moravia. Reprinted 1969, Narboni, ed., Entry No. 1170. Trans. and commentary 1972, Milne, Entry No. 1713.

2088 *"Panique dans les rues." La Gazette du cinéma*, No. 4 (October).
Kazin is tied to theater; for him the screen equals the stage rectangle and his direction merely "accentuates the phenomenon of the proscenium." His impersonality and absence of style reveal his "affectionate contempt for art." Signed J.-L.G. Reprinted 1968, Narboni, ed., Entry No. 1170. Trans. and commentary 1972, Milne, Entry No. 1713.

2089 "Pour un cinéma politique."*La Gazette du cinéma*, No. 3 (September).
Godard discusses the look and physical gestures of youth in political films, especially Soviet films, which move between the poles of exhortation and revolutionary action. Reprinted 1968, Narboni, ed., Entry No. 1170. Trans. and commentary 1972, Milne, Entry No. 1713.

2090 *"Que viva Mexico!" La Gazette du cinéma*, No. 4 (October).
Kenneth Anger's editing is a "contemptible . . . deed. Signed Hans Lucas. Reprinted 1968, Narboni, ed., Entry No. 1170. Trans. and commentary 1972, Milne, Entry No. 1713.

2091 *"La Ronde." La Gazette du cinéma*, No. 4 (October).
"This fragile mosaic of emotions is reserved for rose-colored spectators."
Signed Hans Lucas. Reprinted 1968, Narboni, ed., Entry No. 1170. Trans. and
commentary 1972, Milne, Entry No. 1713.

2092 *"Le Trésor, Vendemiaire, Le Manteau, The Land, Vinti anni d'arte muto."*
La Gazette du cinéma, No. 5 (November).
Signed H. Lucas. Cited 1974, Collet, Entry No. 1832.

2093 *"Works of Calder* et *L'Histoire d'Agnès." La Gazette du cinéma*, No. 4
(October).
" . . . the cinema . . . consists simply of putting things in front of the camera.
. . . *Works of Calder* is a propaganda film on behalf of objects." Signed Hans Lucas.
Reprinted 1968, Narboni, ed., Entry No. 1170. Trans. and commentary 1972,
Milne, Entry No. 1713.

1952

2094 "Les Bizarreries de la pudeur: *La Flamme qui s'éteint* (Rudolph Mate)."
Cahiers du cinéma, No. 10 (March).
"The classically constructed script . . . enables one to remain very close to the
actress and to share her inner emotions. . . . Thus cinema plays with itself. An art
of representation, all it knows of the interior life are the precise and natural
movements of well-trained actors." Signed Hans Lucas. Reprinted 1968, Narboni,
ed., Entry No. 1170. Trans. and commentary 1972, Milne, Entry No. 1713.

2095 "Défense et illustration du découpage classique." *Cahiers du cinéma*,
No. 15 (September).
Godard discusses the moral element in art, the relation of the artist to nature
and the moment, swiftness of action in U.S. comedy, filming faces and glances
(the "nuances of the soul"), and sticking close to "psychological reality." Classical
American cinema also has "contempt . . . for photographing a world seized by
accident" and uses language only as "a reflection of passions." Signed Hans
Lucas. Reprinted 1968, Narboni, ed., Entry No. 1170. Trans. and commentary
1972, Milne, Entry No. 1713.

2096 *"Les Petites Filles modèles." Les Amis du cinéma*, No. 1 (October).
Rohmer discusses his film, adapted from a story by the Countess de Ségur,
with Godard. Signed N.B. Reprinted 1968, Narboni, ed., Entry No. 1170. Trans.
and commentary 1972, Milne, Entry No. 1713.

2097 "Que'est-ce que le cinéma?" *Les Amis du cinéma*, No. 1 (October).
"Artistic creation does not mean painting one's soul in things, but painting
the soul of things." Signed Hans Lucas. Reprinted 1968, Narboni, ed., Entry No.
1170. Trans. and commentary 1972, Milne, Entry No. 1713.

2098 "Suprématie du sujet: *L'Inconnu du nord-express* (Alfred Hitchcock)."
Cahiers du cinéma, No. 10 (March).
Hitchcock's achievements are discussed against the background of classics of
literature and film and against Godard's own definitions of good cinema. "Cer-

tainly the camera defies reality, but does not evade it; if it enters the present, it is to give it the style it lacks." U.S. films effectively "make the subject the motive for the mise en scene." Signed Hans Lucas. Reprinted 1968, Narboni, ed., Entry No. 1170. Trans. and commentary, Milne, Entry No. 1713.

1956

2099   "Le Chemin des écoliers: *The Man Who Knew Too Much (L'Homme qui en savait trop)* (Alfred Hitchcock)." *Cahiers du cinéma*, No. 64 (November).
Hitchcock knows that suspense means waiting, and he fills it with asides. "The extraordinary serves as a foil for the ordinary, which, left to its own devices, would engender nothing but dullness." Reprinted 1968, Narboni, ed., Entry No. 1170. Trans. and commentary 1972, Milne, Entry No. 1713.

2100   "Mirliflores et bécassines: *The Lieutenant Wore Skirts (Chéri ne fais pas le zouave), Artists and Models (Artistes et modèles)* (Frank Tashlin)." *Cahiers du cinéma*, No. 62 (August-September).
Godard discusses the difficulty of manipulating "the grotesque" in a comic film, forcing uneasy spectators to laugh at vapid situations embellished by rich, bitter, and devastating invention. Reprinted 1968, Narboni, ed., Entry No. 1170. Trans. and commentary 1972, Milne, Entry No. 1713.

2101   "Montage, mon beau souci." *Cahiers du cinéma*, No. 65 (December).
"To splice on a look — this is practically the definition of editing . . ." Reprinted 1968, Narboni, ed., Entry No. 1170. Trans. Nell Cox, *Film Culture*, 1971. Cox trans. reprinted in 1968, Mussman, Entry No. 1168. Trans. and commentary 1972, Milne, Entry No. 1713. Trans. 1966, *Cahiers du Cinema in English*, Entry No. 2245.

2102   "Le Retour de Frank James de Fritz Lang, 1956." *A l'Ufoleis*.
Cited 1974, Collet, Entry No. 1832.

1957

2103   "Les Acteurs françaises: de bons produits sans mode d'emploi." *Arts*, No. 619.
Cited 1974, Collet, Entry No. 1832.

2104   "Biofilmographie de Jean Renoir: *La Nuit de carrefour, Swamp Water, Elena et les hommes.*" *Cahiers du cinéma*, Renoir issue, No. 78 (December).
"If *Elena et les hommes* is 'the' French film *par excellence*, it is because it is the most intelligent of films. Art and theory of art at one and the same time; beauty and the secret of beauty; cinema and apologia for cinema." It is a "Mozartian" film. Reprinted 1968, Narboni, ed., Entry No. 1170. Trans. and commentary 1972, Milne, Entry No. 1713.

2105   "Le Cinéaste bien-aimé: *The True Story of Jesse James (Le Brigand bien-aimé)* (Nicholas Ray)." *Cahiers du cinéma*, No. 74 (August-September).
Ray composes shots to enclose actors but not stifle them. He edits to insert suddenly "in a scene with several characters, a shot of one of them who is only

participating indirectly in the conversation he is witnessing." His sensitivity to decore equals Griffith's. Reprinted 1968, Narboni, ed., Entry No. 1170. Trans. and commentary 1972, Milne, Entry No. 1713.

2106 "Le Cinéma et son double: *The Wrong Man (Le Faux Coupable)* (Alfred Hitchcock)." *Cahiers du cinéma,* No. 72 (June).

This film is analyzed in depth, discussing how the mise en scene proceeds from and develops "inevitability." "The beauty of [the] . . closeups, with their searching attention to the passage of time, comes from the sense that necessity is intruding on triviality. . . . In [the] transitions Hitchcock analyzes feelings and subjective impressions too insignificant to find their way into an important scene. . . . A film comprising only such notations would be nothing; but one in which they are thrown into the bargain — that film is everything." Reprinted 1968, Narboni, ed., Entry No. 1170. Trans. and commentary 1972, Milne, Entry No. 1713.

2107 "Des preuves suffisantes: *Sait-on jamais* (Roger Vadim)." *Cahiers du cinéma,* No. 73 (July).

The stereotypical plot is summarized. Vadim's strength was to make the characters alive by presenting "only things he knows well" and to "describe himself with all his qualities and defects through these characters." Reprinted 1968, Narboni, ed., Entry No. 1170. Trans. and commentary 1972, Milne, Entry No. 1713.

2108 'Les Dix Meilleurs Films de 1956." *Cahiers du cinéma,* No. 67 (January).

Reprinted 1968, Narboni, ed., Entry No. 1170. Trans. and commentary 1972, Milne, Entry No. 1713.

2109 "Futur, présent, passé: Magirama (Abel Gance, Nelly Kaplan)." *Cahiers du cinéma,* No. 67 (February).

Godard dismisses Abel Gance and Nelly Kaplan's "polyvision." "The triple screen . . . may in certain scenes provoke supplementary effects in the sphere of pure sensation, but no more." Reprinted 1968, Narboni, ed., Entry No. 1170. Trans. and commentary 1972, Milne, Entry No. 1713.

2110 "*Hollywood ou mourir: Hollywood or Bust:* un vrai cinglé de cinéma (Frank Tashlin)." *Cahiers du cinéma,* No. 73 (July).

Frank Tashlin gets his freshness and invention from having drawn comic-strips. Reprinted 1968, Narboni, ed., Entry No. 1170. Trans. and commentary 1972, Milne, Entry No. 1713.

2111 "Au petit Trot: *Courte-tête* (Norbert Carbonnaux)." *Cahiers du cinéma,* No. 70 (April).

The "crazy-operetta genre" is hard unless one is Tati. Carbonneaux's only success comes here from pitting the actors against their own roles, resulting in a "monologue" tone. Reprinted 1968, Narboni, ed., Entry No. 1170. Trans. and commentary 1972, Milne, Entry No. 1713.

2112 "La Photo du mois: *Logare.*" *Cahiers du cinéma,* No. 76 (November).

Cited 1974, Collet, Entry No. 1832.

2113 "Rien que le cinéma: *L'Ardente Gitane* (Nicholas Ray)." *Cahiers du cinéma*, No. 68 (February).

The film is "semi-successful" because Ray did not take it seriously. Even if a director is amusing himself by taking it easy, that's still got to be serious work. Reprinted 1968, Narboni, ed., Entry No. 1170. Trans. and commentary 1972, Milne, Entry No. 1713.

2114 "Signal. *Forty Guns (Quarante tueurs)* (Samuel Fuller)." *Cahiers du cinéma*, No. 76 (November).

The film won't be released in France. It has an incomprehensible plot, but each scene, in black and white Cinemascope, is "Bursting with daring conventions," reminding Godard of Gance, Stroheim, and Murnau. Reprinted 1968, Narboni, ed., Entry No. 1170. Trans. and commentary 1972, Milne, Entry No. 1713.

2115 "60 Metteurs en scéne francais." *Cahiers du cinéma*, No. 71 (May).

Bresson is cited: "There is a sublime awkwardness, which remains indifferent to virtuosity — it is from this that emotion is born in the spectator . . ." Carbonneaux has a "slack but personal . . . mercurial style." Leenhardt "doesn't like good films, but makes them." With Jacques Tati, "French neo-realism was born. . . . He sees problems where there are none, finds them." Reprinted 1968, Narboni, ed., Entry No. 1170. Trans. and commentary 1972, Milne, Entry No. 1713.

2116 "Tournage: *Will Success Spoil Rock Hunter (Le Diable dans sa poche)* (Frank Tashlin)." *Cahiers du cinéma*, No. 74 (August-September).

Letter Tashlin wrote to Godard about Tashlin's next film. Reprinted 1968, Narboni, ed., Entry No. 1170. Trans. and commentary 1972, Milne, Entry No. 1713.

1958

2117 "Ailleurs: *Une Vie* (Alexandre Astruc)." *Cashiers du cinéma*, No. 89 (November).

Godard admires the film's rushed pace, the novelistic conception of character, a mise en scene that always lets us know what the off-screen space is as well, the emphasis on strong horizontal and vertical movements, and effects of "premeditated violence." Reprinted 1968, Narboni, ed., Entry No. 1170. Trans. and commentary 1972, Milne, Entry No. 1713.

2118 "Un Athlète complet: *Un Américain bien tranquille* (J.L. Mankiewicz)." *Arts*, No. 679 (22 July).

The Quiet American is a writer's film, with little added in the shooting. Its main quality is a constant Giraudoux-like play on words and on the difference between languages. Reprinted 1968, Narboni, ed., Entry No. 1170. Trans. and commentary 1972, Milne, Entry No. 1713.

2119 "Au-delà des étoiles: *Bitter Victory (Amère victoire)* (Nicholas Ray)." *Cahiers du cinéma*, No. 79 (January).

"One is no longer interested in objects, but in what lies between the objects and which becomes an object in its turn. Nicholas Ray forces us to consider as real something one did not even consider as unreal, something one did not consider at all." Reprinted 1968, Narboni, ed. Entry No. 1170. Trans. and commentary 1972, Milne, Entry No. 1713.

2120 "B.B. Rhénane: *Liane, l'esclave blanche.*" *Arts,* No. 700 (10 December).
Review of *Liane – White Slave,* contrasted to Jean Rouch's *Treichville.* Reprinted 1968, Narboni, ed., Entry No. 1170. Trans and commentary 1972, Milne, Entry No. 1713.

2121 "Bergmanorama." *Cahiers du cinéma,* No. 85 (July).
A Bergman film is "one twenty-fourth of a second metamorphosed and expanded over an hour and a half." *Summer Interlude* and *Summer with Monika* are discussed at length and the latter contrasted to Visconti's *Senso.* Some filmmakers see a wide range of things (Bergman, Rossellini, Welles); others "fix their attention on the precise point that interests them" (Visconti, Lang, Hitchcock). Reprinted 1968, Narboni, ed., Entry No. 1170. Trans. and commentary 1972, Milne, Entry No. 1713. Trans. 1966, *Cahiers du Cinema in English,* Entry No. 2237.

2122 "Un Bon Devoir: *The Killing (L'Ultime Razzia) (Stanley Kubrick).*" *Cahiers du cinéma,* No. 80 (February).
The film interests us only for its systematic dislocation of the chronology of events and its newsreel-style camera work. Reprinted 1968, Narboni, ed., Entry No. 1170. Trans. and commentary 1972, Milne, Entry No. 1713.

2123 "Une Bonne Copie: *The Wayward Bus (Les Naufragés de l'autocar)* (Victor Vicas)." *Cahiers du cinéma,* No. 81 (March).
The minor film has "the look of hurriedly prepared homework, which is far from displeasing." Reprinted 1968, Narboni, ed., Entry No. 1170. Trans. and commentary 1972, Milne, Entry No. 1735.

2124 "*La Chatte.*" *Arts,* No. 668.
Cited 1974, Collet, Entry No. 1832.

2125 "Désespérant: *La Femme en robe de chambre* (J.L. Thompson)." *Arts,* No. 680 (30 July).
Since Hitchcock, British cinema has been pretentious and insipid. Reprinted 1968, Narboni, ed., Entry No. 1170. Trans. and commentary 1972, Milne, Entry No. 1713.

2126 "Les Dix Meilleurs Films de 1957." *Cahiers du cinéma,* No. 79 (January).
Reprinted 1968, Narboni, ed., Entry No. 1170. Trans. and commentary 1972, Milne, Entry No. 1713.

2127 "17 jeune metteurs en scène donnent leur mot de passe." *Arts,* No. 724 (27 May).
Cited 1974, Collet, Entry No. 1832.

2128 "*Un Drôle de dimanche* (Marc Allegret)." *Arts,* No. 698 (26 November).

This "terribly bungled" film might have been saved by a better script or by Jean-Paul Belmondo. Reprinted 1968, Narboni, ed., Entry No. 1170. Trans. and commentary 1972, Milne, Entry No. 1713.

2129 "Ésotérisme farfelu: *Les Temps des oeufs durs* (Norbert Carbonnaux)." *Cahiers du cinéma*, No. 82 (April).
  The director is lazy with the script and gags, wakes up during shooting, and is fine at editing. This film has some dazzling, poetic bits every fifteen minutes or so. Reprinted 1968, Narboni, ed., Entry No. 1170. Trans. and commentary 1972, Milne, Entry No. 1713.

2130 "Une Fille nommeé Durance: *L'Eau vive* (François Villiers)." *Cahiers du cinéma*, No. 85 (July).
  Villiers' "textbook approach and tentative direction of the actors . . . at least do nothing to spoil the flavor of what they set out to achieve" in the commercially sponsored "Provençal saga" about a shepherdess and a hydroelectric dam. Reprinted 1968, Narboni, ed., Entry No. 1170. Trans. and commentary 1972, Milne, Entry No. 1713.

2131 "'Georges Franju." *Cahiers du cinéma*, No. 90 (December).
  Le Tête contre le mur is filmed by a dionysian director who shows the reality behind madness. Reprinted 1968, Narboni, ed., Entry No. 1170. Trans. and commentary 1972, Milne, Entry No. 1713.

2132 "Ignorés du jury: Demy, Resnais, Rozier et Varda dominent le festival de Tours 1958." *Arts*, No. 700 (10 December).
  Four films not awarded prizes were the best: Jacques Demy's *Le Bel indifférent* ("the beauty of inevitability"); Alain Resnais' *Le Chant du styréne* ("a brilliantly mounted film . . . a piece of jewelry"); Agnès Varda's *Ô saisons, ô châteaux* ("good . . . in the genre of fashionable splendor, or vice versa"); and Jacques Rozier's *Blue Jeans*. Reprinted 1968, Narboni, ed., Entry No. 1170. Trans. and commentary 1972, Milne, Entry No. 1713.

2133 "Jean-Luc Godard fait parler Astruc: *Une Vie*, c'est la folie derrière le réalisme." *Arts*, No. 684 (20 August).
  Astruc discusses adaptation of literary works, use of color and widescreen, and his plans. Reprinted 1968, Narboni, ed., Entry No. 1170. Trans. and commentary 1972, Milne, Entry No. 1713.

2134 "Jean-Luc Godard fait parler François Reichenbach." *Arts*, No. 685 (27 August).
  Reichenbach discusses his plans to make a feature-length documentary in the United States. Reprinted 1968, Narboni, ed., Entry No. 1170. Trans. and commentary 1972, Milne, Entry No. 1713.

2135 "Jean Rouch remporte le prix Delluc." *Arts*, No. 701 (17 December).
  Moi, un noir is vital in opening up "the possibilities for a new cinema" in France. Reprinted 1968, Narboni, ed., Entry No. 1170. Trans. and commentary 1972, Milne, Entry No. 1713.

2136 "Malraux mauvais français?" *Cahiers du cinéma*, No. 83 (May).

Léonide Keigel's documentary about Malraux will regretfully not represent France at Cannes. Reprinted 1968, Narboni, ed., Entry No. 1170. Trans. and commentary 1972, Milne, Entry No. 1713.

2137 "Mizoguchi fut le plus grand cinéaste japonais: la Cinémathèque lui rend hommage après sa mort." *Arts*, No. 656 (5 February).
Special attention is paid to *Ugetsu Monogatari*. Reprinted 1968, Narboni, ed., Entry No. 1170. Trans. and commentary 1972, Milne, Entry No. 1713.

2138 "*Monika* (Ingmar Bergman)." *Arts*, No. 680 (30 July).
"[Bergman's] camera seeks only one thing: to seize the present moment at its most fugitive . . ." His camera movements are integrated into the psychology of his characters, precisely able to evoke a specific feeling. *Monika* "already is *Et Dieu – créa la femme*." Reprinted 1968, Narboni, ed., Entry No. 1170. Trans. and commentary 1972, Milne, Entry No. 1713.

2139 "Petit journal du cinéma." *Cahiers du cinéma*, No. 83 (May).
Cited 1974, Collet, Entry No. 1832.

2140 "La Photo du mois: *Les Cousins*." *Cahiers du cinéma*, No. 89 (November).
Brief announcement of a forthcoming "deeply hollow and therefore profound film" by Claude Chabrol: *Les Cousins*. Reprinted 1968, Narboni, ed., Entry No. 1170. Trans. and commentary 1972, Milne, Entry No. 1713.

2141 "Retrospective Ophuls." *Cahiers du cinéma*, No. 81 (March).
The story of Ophuls' *Caught* is "cruel and delicate," "the technique already *Le Plaisir*." Reprinted 1968, Narboni, ed., Entry No. 1170. Trans. and commentary 1972, Milne, Entry No. 1713.

2142 "La Ronde de l'aube." *Arts*, No. 682.
Cited 1974, Collet, Entry No. 1832.

2143 "Saut dans le vide: *Montparnasse 19* (Jacques Becker)." *Cahiers du cinéma*, No. 83 (May).
This "negative" film makes us demand, "What is cinema?" It investigates Modigliani's unbalanced mind in a clumsy but moving way to penetrate the secret of artistic creation. Reprinted 1968, Narboni, ed., Entry No. 1170. Trans. and commentary 1972, Milne, Entry No. 1713.

2144 "Les Seigneurs de la forêt." *Arts*, No. 702 (24 December).
Cited 1974, Collet, Entry No. 1832.

2145 "Si le roi savait ça." *Arts*, No. 680.
Cited 1974, Collet, Entry No. 1832.

2146 "Sympathique: *Raffles sur la ville* (Pierre Chenal)." *Cahiers du cinéma*, No. 82 (April).
This thriller has good dialogue and an accuracy of tone as French policemen are shown as ordinary people. Reprinted 1968, Narboni, ed., Entry No. 1170. Trans. and commentary 1972, Milne, Entry No. 1713.

2147 "Télégramme de Berlin." *Cahiers du cinéma*, No. 86 (August).
Stream of conscious impressions sent by Godard from the 1958 Berlin Film Festival. Signed Hans Lucas. Reprinted 1968, Narboni, ed., Entry No. 1170. Trans. and commentary 1972, Milne, Entry No. 1713.

2148 "Travail à la chaîne: *The Long Hot Summer (Les Feux de l'été)* (Martin Ritt)." *Cahiers du cinéma*, No. 85 (July).
Ritt cannot make use of excellent actors. Reprinted 1968, Narboni, ed., Entry No. 1170. Trans. and commentary 1972, Milne, Entry No. 1713.

2149 "Voyez comme on danse: *The Pajama Game (Picnic en pyjama)* (Stanley Donen)." *Cahiers du cinéma*, No. 85 (July).
The dance sequences seem to have the "grace of actuality" rather than purely mathematical precision. When the actors dance here they are not then purely dancers doing their act, nor dancers playing a role (e.g., Gene Kelly), but actors who remain in character and suddenly feel the need to dance. Reprinted 1968, Narboni, ed., Entry No. 1170. Trans. and commentary 1972, Milne, Entry No. 1713.

1959

2150 "L'Afrique vous parle de la fin et des moyens: *Moi, un noir.*" *Cahiers du cinéma*, No. 94 (April).
Plot briefly described. The Nigerians in *Moi, un noir* refer to themselves by movie star names, including Dorothy Lamour, Eddie Constantine, Edward G. Robinson, and Tarzan. Rouch's art is consonant with chance; he makes characters out of his actors, after having organized the action "logically in the manner of Rossellini." Reprinted 1968, Narboni, ed., Entry No. 1170. Trans. and commentary 1972, Milne, Entry No. 1713.

2151 "*Auberge du sixième bonheur.*" *Arts*, No. 712 (4 March).
Signed Hans Lucas. Cited 1974, Collet, Entry No. 1832.

2152 "Une Bête humaine: *Un Simple Histoire* (Marcel Hanoun)." *Arts*, No. 717 (8 April).
This 16mm (and therefore "amateur") film interestingly utilizes a "morbid," clinically presented mise en scene to produce suspense and to develop a true story about a poor woman. Reprinted 1968, Narboni, ed., Entry No. 1170. Trans. and commentary 1972, Milne, Entry No. 1713.

2153 "*Bobosse.*" *Arts*, No. 716 (1 April).
Cited 1974, Collet, Entry No. 1832.

2154 "*Boris Barnett.*" *Cahiers du cinéma*, No. 94 (April).
This agreeable "Sovcolor" comic opera has methodically planned long shots, a few precise, graceful camera movements, and a lot of style. Reprinted 1968, Narboni, ed., Entry No. 1170. Trans. and commentary 1972, Milne, Entry No. 1713.

2155 "Le Brésil vu de Billancourt: *Orfeu negro* (Marcel Camus)." *Cahiers du cinéma*, No. 97 (July).

The film contains no poetry, no adventure, no close look at Rio, no authentic dialogue. It is amiable and sincere and artificially photographed, neglecting the soft, grey light to give the decor instead a "hard, repellent look" by means of filters. Reprinted 1968, Narboni, ed., Entry No. 1170. Trans. and commentary 1972, Milne, Entry No. 1713.

2156   "Cigarettes, whiskey, et p'tites pépées." *Arts*, No. 712 (4 March).
Signed Hans Lucaso Cited 1974, Collet, Entry No. 1832.

2157   "Cannes 1969." *Cahiers du cinéma*, No. 96 (June).
Rossellini's *India* is a "technician's film," logical, beautiful, and true. Reprinted 1968, Narboni, ed., Entry No. 1170. Trans. and commentary 1972, Milne, Entry No. 1713.

2158   "Chacun son Tours." *Cahiers du cinéma*, No. 92 (February).
Godard discusses the need to take short films seriously, sets out the short film's aesthetic principles, and reviews the best short films seen at Tours in 1968. These were Varda's *Du côte de la côte*, Demy's *Le Bel indifférent*, Rozier's *Blue Jeans*, and Resnais' *Le Chant du styrène*. Reprinted 1968, Narboni, ed., Entry No. 1170. Trans. and commentary 1972, Milne, Entry No. 1713.

2159   "Un Cinéaste, c'est aussi un missionnaire: Jean-Luc Godard fait parler Roberto Rossellini." *Arts*, No. 716 (1 April).
Godard interviews Rossellini, who states, "In the final analysis, intelligence, too, is a convention; and behind the intelligence I seek to show not only how it works but why it works that way. I would like to show the animal side of intelligence, just as in *India 58*, I showed the intelligence in animal behavior. I never calculate. I know what I want to say, and I look for the most direct way of saying it." Reprinted 1968, Narboni, ed., Entry No. 1170, who says Godard made up this interview. Trans. and commentary 1972, Milne, Entry No. 1713.

2160   "Le Conquérant solitaire: *Les Rendez-vous du diable* (Haroun Tazieff)." *Cahiers du cinéma*, No. 93 (March).
This feature-length documentary on volcanos pleases Godard for its "naive and barbaric charm" and "childlike technique," the photographer's need to authenticate by means of film, the reality of his having risked death, and the incredible colors in the mise en scene. Reprinted 1968, Narboni, ed., Entry No. 1170. Trans. and commentary 1972, Milne, Entry No. 1713.

2161   "Dépassé: *Asphalte* (Hervé Bromberger)." *Arts*, No. 711 (25 February).
This film about returning to the old home town lacks a good script and "a good eye." Reprinted 1968, Narboni, ed., Entry No. 1170. Trans. and commentary 1972, Milne, Entry No. 1713.

2162   "Des larmes et de la vitesse: *Le Temps d'aimer et le temps de mourir (A Time to Love and a Time to Die)* (Douglas Sirk)." *Cahiers du cinéma*, No. 94 (April).
Goddard loves Sirk's "delirium" — the "mixture of medieval and modern, sentimentality and subtlety, tame compositions and frenzied cinemascope." This

film is one of the greatest in film history. Reprinted 1968, Narboni, ed., Entry No. 1170. Trans. and reprinted 1972, Milne, Entry No. 1713.

2163 "Les Dix Meilleurs Films de 1958." *Cahiers du cinéma*, No. 92 (February).
Reprinted 1968, Narboni, ed., Entry No. 1170. Trans. and commentary 1972, Milne, Entry No. 1713.

2164 *"Les Dragueurs." Arts*, No. 722 (13 May).
Cited 1974, Collet, Entry No. 1832.

2165 "Dura Lex: *La Loi* (Jules Dassein)." *Cahiers du cinéma*, No. 93 (March).
"If Billy Graham were a filmmaker, he would doubtless be called Jules Dassein." Reprinted 1968, Narboni, ed., Entry No. 1170. Trans. and commentary 1972, Milne, Entry No. 1713.

2166 "Ennuyeux: *Le Grand Chef* (Henri Verneuil)." *Arts*, No. 715 (25 March).
Howard Hawks filmed a brilliant sketch on the same story (O'Henry's "The Capture of Red Chief"), but that wasn't seen in France. This version is terrible. Reprinted 1968, Narboni, ed., Entry No. 1170. Trans. and commentary 1972, Milne, Entry No. 1713.

2167 "Entretien avec J.-P. Mocky." *Arts*, No. 709.
Cited 1974, Collet, Entry No. 1832.

2168 "Entretein avec René Clément." *Arts*, No. 713 (11 March).
Cited 1974, Collet, Entry No. 1832.

2169 *"Esclave de son désir." Arts*, No. 712 (4 March).
Signed Hans Lucas. Cited 1974, Collet, Entry No. 1832.

2170 "Etonnant: *Moi, un noir* (Jean Rouch)." *Arts*, No. 713 (11 March).
Rouch "does not track down truth because it is scandalous but because it is amusing, tragic, graceful, eccentric, what you will. . . . He now sees that reportage derives its nobility from being a sort of quest for a Holy Grail called mise en scene." Reprinted 1968, Narboni, ed., Entry No. 1170. Trans. and commentary 1972, Milne Entry No. 1713.

2171 "Exclu l'an dernier du Festival, Truffaut réprésentera la France à Cannes avec *Les 400 Coups*." *Arts*, No. 719 (22 April).
This manifesto of the *Cahiers* critics-turned-directors, written in first person plural, speaks of "our" victory in Truffaut's film being the only French entry at Cannes. Godard describes the kind of cinema he and his peers have attacked, that previously recognized as "quality" by the Establishment. Reprinted 1968, Narboni, ed., Entry No. 1170. Trans. and commentary 1972, Milne, Entry No. 1713.

2172 "Fade et grotesque: *Le Vent se lève* (Yves Ciampi)." *Arts*, No. 708 (4 February).
This "insipid and grotesque" film is badly acted and badly directed. Re-

printed 1968, Narboni, ed., Entry No. 1170. Trans. and commentary 1972, Milne, Entry No. 1713.

2173 "Faiblard: *Faibles femmes* (Michel Boisrond)." *Arts,* No. 710 (18 February).
   Monotonous film with four "zombies for actors" and boring direction fails as a comedy. Reprinted 1968, Narboni, ed., Entry No. 1170. Trans. and commentary 1972, Milne, Entry No. 1713.

2174 *"Le Fauve est lâche." Arts,* No. 707.
   Cited 1974, Collet, Entry No. 1832.

2175 "Franc-tireur: *Tarawa Beachhead (Tarawa, tête de point)* (Paul Wendkos)." *Cahiers du cinéma,* No. 96 (June).
   This adaptation of a David Goodis novel has a hackneyed script but sharply handled action sequences. Reprinted 1968, Narboni, ed., Entry No. 1170. Trans. and commentary 1972, Milne, Entry No. 1713.

2176 "Gentillet: *Vacances à Paris* (Black Edwards)." *Arts,* No. 719 (22 April).
   Edwards should have written the script but "still manages an idea per shot." Reprinted 1968, Narboni, ed., Entry No. 1170. Trans. and commentary 1972, Milne, Entry No. 1713.

2177 "Hiroshima, notre amour." *Cahiers du cinéma,* No. 97 (July).
   Cited 1974, Collet, Entry No. 1832.

2178 *"Houla-Houla." Arts,* No. 706.
   Cited 1974, Collet, Entry No. 1832.

2179 "Jean Renoir: 'La Télévision m'a révélé un nouveau cinéma.' " *Arts,* No. 718 (15 April).
   Godard interviews Renoir, who discusses his production of *Le Testament du Docteur Cordelier,* filmed live for French television. Godard calls Renoir the "groundswell behind the New Wave" and says "he [Renoir] still leads the world in sincerity and audacity." Reprinted 1968, Narboni, ed., Entry No. 1170. Narboni says Godard made up the whole interview. Trans. and commentary 1972, Milne, Entry No. 1713.

2180 "Le Jeune Cinéma à gagné." *Arts,* No. 719 (22 April).
   Cited 1974, Collet, Entry No. 1832.

2181 *"Les Jeux dangereux." Arts,* No. 706.
   Cited 1974, Collet, Entry No. 1832.

2182 "Un Loi obscure: *La Tête contre les murs." Cahiers du cinéma,* No. 95 (May).
   Like Lang and the German Expressionists, Franju uses the long shot logically and precisely. He turns the camera on faces and objects "long enough to brand them deeply, as the sinner was once branded by the executioner . . ." Reprinted 1968, Narboni, ed., Entry No. 1170. Trans. and commentary 1972, Milne, Entry No. 1713.

2183 "Magnifique: *Les Cousins* (Claude Chabrol)." *Arts*, No. 713 (11 March).

From a theoretically beautiful script by Paul Gégauff, Chabrol created the "practical beauty" of a mise en scene where the characters were put through a series of exploits which "reveal[ed] them at each instant under a new light." Reprinted 1968, Narboni, ed., Entry No. 1170. Trans. and commentary 1972, Milne, Entry No. 1713.

2184 "Pas désagréable: *Les Motards* (Roger Pierre, Jean-Marc Thibault)." *Arts*, No. 715 (25 March).

This comic film needs better direction to develop its gags fully. Reprinted 1968, Narboni, ed., Entry No. 1170. Trans. and commentary 1972, Milne, Entry

2185 "Le Passe-temps retrouvé: *The Perfect Furlough (Vacances à Paris)* (Blake Edwards)." *Cahiers du cinéma*, No. 95 (May).

It's an amiable, banal film with one idea per shot. Reprinted 1968, Narboni, ed., Entry No. 1170. Trans. and commentary 1972, Milne, Entry No. 1713.

2186 "Petit journal du cinéma." *Cahiers du cinéma*, No. 94 (April).
Cited 1974, Collet, Entry No. 1832.

2187 *"Le Petit Prof'* . . . ne rime à rien (Carlo Rim)." *Arts*, No. 711 (25 February).

This overambitious history of twentieth century France has cramped shots, wooden dialogue, and almost no direction of actors. Reprinted 1968, Narboni, ed., Entry No. 1170. Trans. and commentary 1972, Milne, Entry No. 1713.

2188 "La Photo du mois: *Les 400 Coups.*" *Cahiers du cinéma*, No. 92 (February).

Announcement for forthcoming film, with a list of attributes applied to it. Reprinted 1968, Narboni, ed., Entry No. 1170. Trans. and commentary 1972, Milne, Entry No. 1713.

2189 "La Photo du mois: *La Ligne de mire* (Jean-Daniel Pollet). *Cahiers du cinéma*, No. 93 (March).

Looking for poetry, Pollet breaks convention and allows his actors complete freedom to improvise their scenes. Reprinted 1968, Narboni, ed., Entry No. 1170. Trans. and commentary 1972, Milne, Entry No. 1713.

2190 "Portrait de Rossellini." *Arts*, No. 716 (1 April).
Cited 1974, Collet, Entry No. 1832.

2191 *"Les 4 du Moana."* *Arts*, No. 716 (1 April).
Cited 1974, Collet, Entry No. 1832.

2192 *"Ramuntcho."* *Arts*, No. 711 (25 February).
Cited 1974, Collet, Entry No. 1832.

2193 "Remarquable: *La Tête contre les murs* (Georges Franju)." *Arts*, No. 715 (25 March).

Franju seeks out the bizzare, seeing in it a convention behind which one discovers a basic truth, "the true face of reality." Reprinted 1968, Narboni, ed., Entry No. 1170. Trans. and commentary 1972, Milne, Entry No. 1713.

2194 "Sainte simplicité: *Goha* (Jacques Baratier)." *Arts*, No. 723 (20 May).
The film has no profound subject but an engaging clumsiness and lack of technical virtuosity. "Its blunders are beautiful." Reprinted 1968, Narboni, ed., Entry No. 1170. Trans. and commentary 1972, Milne, Entry No. 1713.

2195 "Super Mann: *Man of the West (L'Homme de l'ouest)* (Anthony Mann)." *Cahiers du cinéma*, No. 92 (February).
There are three kinds of westerns: of images *(The Searchers)*, of ideas *(Rancho Notorious)*, of images and ideas *(Man of the West)*. Mann's mise en scene and camera work seem simultaneously to "discover and define" ideas and emotions. Reprinted 1968, Narboni, ed., Entry No. 1170. Trans. and commentary 1972, Milne, Entry No. 1713.

2196 "Tourné avec ses seuls amis en marge de la production courante, *Le Bel Age* de Pierre Kast sera un film pirandellian." *Arts*, No. 711 (25 February).
Kast's career, especially the influence of Raymond Queneau, is described. He tells how he plans to make a film about a real-life group of friends, financed outside the industry, and costing only as much as three shorts. Reprinted 1968, Narboni, ed., Entry No. 1170. Trans. and commentary 1972, Milne, Entry No. 1713.

2197 "Les Tripes au soleil." *Arts*, No. 722 (13 May).
Cited 1974, Collet, Entry No. 1832.

2198 "Les Vignes du seigneur: *Pourvu ou'on ait l'ivresse* (J.-D. Pollet)." *Arts*, No. 706 (21 January).
Review of a short film about boredom in suburban dance halls. Reprinted 1968, Narboni, ed., Entry No. 1170. Trans. and commentary 1972, Milne, Entry No. 1713.

1960

2199 Article or interview on *Le Petit Soldat*. *Libé*ration, April,
Cited in *Image et son*, No. 211, p. 65.

2200 "Les Dix Meilleurs Films de 1969." *Cahiers du cinéma*, No. 104 (February).
Reprinted 1968, Narboni, ed., Entry No. 1170. Trans. and commentary 1972, Milne, Entry No. 1713.

2201 "Entretien avec Robert Bresson." *Cahiers du cinéma*, No. 104 (February).
Cited 1974, Collet, Entry No. 1832.

2202 "Frère Jacques." *Cahiers du cinéma*, No. 106 (April).

Eulogy for Jacques Becker. Reprinted 1968, Narboni, ed., Entry No. 1170. Trans. and commentary 1972, Milne, Entry No. 1713.

2203 "Tournage: *Le Petit Soldat*." *Cahiers du cinéma*, No. 109 (July).

Announcement for film with a brief character description of Bruno. Reprinted 1968, Narboni, ed., Entry No. 1170. Trans. and commentary 1972, Milne, Entry No. 1713.

1961

2204 "But 'Wave' Adds Brightness." *Films and Filming*, 7, No. 12 (September), 7 and 36.

In a "recorded interview," written in essay form without questions, Godard discusses his role as a *Cahiers* critic, his entry into filmmaking, the production of *A bout de souffle*, and his reaction to the censorship of *Le Petit Soldat*. He compares studio and location shooting, shooting from a script vs. improvisation, working with established vs. unknown actors. He dislikes using actors who cannot speak the language, and he would like to do, but cannot get a producer for, a historical film in which all the actors speak Latin.

2205 "Les Dix Meilleurs Films de 1960." *Cahiers du cinéma*, No. 116 (February).

Reprinted 1968, Narboni, ed., Entry No. 1170. Trans. and commentary 1972, Milne, Entry No. 1713.

2206 "Montage, mon beau souci." Trans. in *Film Culture*, No. 22-23 (Summer).

Reprinted 1969, Bobker, Entry No. 1204.

2207 "*Le Petit Soldat*." *Cinéma 61*, No. 52 (January), pp. 12-14.

A synopsis of the film, written by Godard. *See* 1961, *Le Petit Soldat*, Entry No. 2256.

1962

2208 "Les Dix Meilleurs Films de 1961." *Cahiers du cinéma*, No. 128 (February).

Reprinted 1968, Narboni, ed., Entry No. 1170. Trans. and commentary 1972, Milne, Entry No. 1713.

2209 "Du stylo à la caméra." *Etudes cinématographiques: Théâtre et cinéma (2) — l'acteur*, No. 14-15. Paris: Lettres Modernes, Minard. P. 49.

In response to a questionnaire, Godard said that good direction of actors was a crucial element in film, a "sculptural investigation of human form, and a moral or political investigation of human liberty." The greatest directors of actors were Welles, Cukor, Bergman, and Renoir; Cocteau influenced his directing of actors the most. He discusses his use of little-known actors and his directing techniques.

2210 "Questions and Answers on Peace and War." *Film: Book 2: Films of Peace and War.* Ed. Robert Hughes. New York: Grove Press. P. 168.
Godard briefly answers questions about "the most effective" films dealing with peace and war, and those films that need to be made and by whom.

2211 "*Vivre sa vie.*" *Vivre sa vie: L'Avant-scène du cinéma,*" No. 19 (October), p. 1.
Advertisement for *Vivre sa vie* written in two verticle columns, one word per line. Column one: "A film about prostitution which tells how a young and beautiful Parisian shopgirl yields her body but keeps her soul while she glides like an apparition through"/Column two: "a series of adventures which introduce her to all profound human emotions possible and which were filmed by Jean-Luc Godard and played by Anna Karina Vivre Sa Vie." Reprinted 1970, Collet, Entry No. 1361.

1963

2212 "Un Conte de faits." *Cinéma '63*, No. 74 (March), pp. 26-28.
Godard describes *Les Carabiniers* and tells how the film is Brechtian. Reprinted 1968, Collet, Entry No. 1023. Trans. 1970, Collet, Entry No. 1361.

2213 "Dictionnaire des cinéastes américaines." *Cahiers du cinéma,* special issue on U.S. cinema, No. 150-51 (December 1963-January 1964).
Godard wrote entries on Richard Brooks, Charlie Chaplin, Stanley Kubrick, Richard Leacock, Jonas Mekas, Orson Welles, Billy Wilder. Reprinted 1968, Narboni, ed., Entry No. 1170. Trans. and commentary 1972, Milne, Entry No. 1713.

2214 "Les Dix Meilleurs Films américains du parlant." *Cahiers du cinéma,* special issue on U.S. cinema, No. 150-51 (December 1963–January 1964).
Scarface, The Great Dictator, and *Vertigo* occupy top rank. Reprinted 1968, Narboni, ed., Entry No. 1170. Trans. and commentary 1972, Milne, Entry No. 1713.

2215 "Les Dix Meilleurs Films de 1962." *Cahiers du cinéma,* No. 140 (February).
Reprinted 1968, Narboni, ed., Entry No. 1170. Trans. and commentary 1972, Milne, Entry No. 1713.

2216 "Feu sur *Les Carabiniers.*" *Cahiers du cinéma,* No. 146 (August), pp. 2–4.
Godard cites and answers the critics one by one for their total misunderstanding of *Les Carabiniers.* Trans. 1964, Alan Ulrich, *New York Film Bulletin,* No. 46; that trans. reprinted in 1968, Mussman, Entry No. 1103. Reprinted in French 1968, Narboni, ed., Entry No. 1170. Trans. 1972, Milne, Entry No. 1713. Reprinted 1976, *L'Avant-Scène du cinéma,* No. 171-72 (July-September), pp. 39–41.

2217 "Godard on Pure Film." *Cinema* (Beverly Hills), No. 2-5 (March-April), pp. 38.
Cited in Schuster, p. 165.

2218 *"Le Mépris."* *Cahiers du cinéma,* No. 146 (August), p. 31.
Godard discusses the multiple literary influences on his forthcoming film. Reprinted 1968, Narboni, ed., Entry No. 1170. Trans. and commentary 1972, Milne, Entry No. 1713.

2219 "Note per *Il disprezzo."* Trans. A.A. *Filmcritica,* No. 138 (October), pp. 579–87.
Godard presents a character analysis of Camille, Paul, Prokosh, Lang, Francesca (the translator). He describes the sets, the photography, the kind of direction needed, and the difference between *Le Mépris* and Moravia's novel.

2220 "L'Odyssée selon Jean-Luc." *Cinéma 63,* No. 77 (June).
Godard gives his proposed scenario for *Le Mépris,* noting especially the characterization of Camille and the use of red, yellow, and blue.

2221 "Sept hommes à debattre." *Cahiers du cinéma,* No. 150-151 (December 1963-January 1964), pp. 12–23.
Godard, Luc Moullet, Jacques Rivette, Claude Chabrol, François Truffaut, Pierre Kast, and Jacques Doniol-Valcroze discuss American film, especially westerns, *films noir,* and musicals. Godard defines himself as an *auteur* because he makes his films "alone," and he notes that at the beginning of his career he thought of himself positively in relation to U.S. cinema but now realizes how hard it is to be "free" inside the world of cinema.

1964

2222 "Les Dix Meilleurs Films de 1963." *Cahiers du cinéma,* No. 152 (February).
Reprinted 1968, Narboni, ed., Entry No. 1170. Trans. and commentary 1972, Milne, Entry No. 1713.

2223 "Entretien avec Antonioni." *Cahiers du cinéma,* No. 160 (December).
Cited 1974, Collet, Entry No. 1832. Trans. 1966, *Cahiers du Cinema in English* Entry No. 2242.

2224 *"La Femme mariée."* *Cahiers du cinéma,* No. 159 (October), pp. 13–14.
Godard briefly lists what "cinema has meant to different filmmakers. People demand filmmakers make novels, music, paintings, philosophy and yet also feel one kind of film should exclude certain aspects developed under another genre. Godard plays with those "rules" in *La Femme mariée.* He has made this film to show subjects as objects, to make life's spectacle finally be confronted with its own analysis. Reprinted 1968, Narboni, ed., Entry No. 1170. Trans. and commentary 1972, Milne, Entry No. 1713.

2225 *"Orphée"* in "Le Chiffre sept: homage à Jean Cocteau." *Cahiers du cinéma,* No. 152 (February).
Godard admires Cocteau for discovering himself in film, rediscovering Méliès as the only way to create cinema, and not distinguishing between "cinema-verite and cinema-lie." Reprinted 1968, Narboni, ed., Entry No. 1170. Trans. and commentary 1972, Milne, Entry No. 1713.

1965

2226 "Apprenez le François." *L'Avant-Scène du cinéma*, No. 48 (May).
Godard presents stream of consciousness impressions of Truffaut and Truffaut's films. Reprinted 1968, Narboni, ed., Entry No. 1170. Trans. and commentary 1972, Milne, Entry No. 1713.

2227 "Chacun ses dix." *Cahiers du cinéma*, special issue: "Crise du cinéma français," No. 161-162 (January), p. 126.
Ophuls, Rouch, and Cocteau are in first place as Godard lists the ten best French films since the Liberation. Reprinted 1968, Narboni, ed., Entry No. 1170. Trans. 1972, Milne, Entry No. 1713.

2228 "Conversazione con Antonioni." *Centrofilm*, No. 36-37, pp. 56–65.
In Lincoln Center Library. Probably trans. from 1964, Entry No. 2223.

2229 "Les Dix Meilleurs Films de 1964." *Cahiers du cinéma*, No. 165 (February).
Reprinted 1968, Narboni, ed., Entry No. 1170. Trans. 1972, Milne, Entry No. 1713.

2230 "Le Dossier du mois." *Cinéma 65*, No. 94 (March), pp. 48–70.
In this long article, which is the compilation of Godard's remarks over a series of several days at the *Journées Jean-Luc Godard* at Annecy, Godard provides a complete account of his aesthetic and filmmaking principles and tactics. Some of the topics covered are American cinema; the autobiographical element in his films, his efforts to make a gangster film (especially *A bout de souffle)*, his theme of the difficulty of communication and his questioning the nature of cinema; cinema verite (e.g., the scene where Subor interviews Karina in *Le Petit Soldat*); Brecht's influence on *Vivre sa vie*, cinematic citation, direction of actors; and the political aspects of his films. Godard comments on each of his films through *Le Mépris* and *Bande à part*.

2231 "Jean-Luc Godard Interviews Michelangelo Antonioni." *Movie*, No. 12 (Spring), pp. 31+.
Trans. from 1964, No. 2223. Cited in Schuster, p. 165.

2232 "Jean-Luc Godard: Lemmy Caution erre dans le futur comme dans le *Labyrinthe* de Borges." *Les Lettres françaises*, No. 1077 (22–28 April), pp. 1 and 7.
Science fiction is a genre generally rejected in France. "Reality is often too complex to be transmitted in a direct manner." *Alphaville* is a study in light and shadow, a kind of a "western." Godard had always wanted to use Eddie Constantine and that actor needed a secret agent role. As in the title of a novel by Richard Matheson, Constantine becomes his own legend. We have to find the factors for resisting the mechanization of thought, factors which already exist.

2233 "Mon film, un apologue." *Une Femme mariée: L'Avant-Scène du cinéma*, No. 46 (March), pp. 42–43.
In an important early definition of his aesthetic stance, Godard defines his

intent in *Les Carabiniers* and his debt to Lumière and Brecht, i.e., using realism to reinforce a mental or imaginary construct.

2234 *"Montparnasse-Levallois." Cahiers du cinéma,* No. 171 (October).
This story is similar to the side of life seen in *Bande à part* and in the novels of Raymond Queneau. It demands a fluid sense of feeling existence physically, letting the actors play characters who "live off the cuff." What's important is the atmosphere between characters. Reprinted 1968, Narboni, ed., Entry No. 1170. Trans. and commentary 1972, Milne, Entry No. 1713.

2235 *"Pierrot mon ami." Cahiers du cinéma,* No. 171 (October), pp. 17–18.
In a lyrical, stream of consciousness fashion, Godard lays out some aesthetic notions, especially the romantic one of trying to express or capture life. He expresses concern that his act of filming life means that the vital and sincere aspects have eluded him. Reprinted 1968, Narboni, ed., Entry No. 1170. Trans. 1965, Joachim Neugroschel, *Cahiers du Cinema in English* (October). Neugroschel trans. reprinted 1968, Mussman, No. 1168. Other trans. and commentary 1972, Milne, Entry No. 1713.

2236 [Response to] "Qui? Pourquoi? Comment?: questionnaire," *Cahiers du cinéma,* special issue: "Crise du cinéma français," No. 161-62 (January), pp. 14, 36.
Godard talks about finance, production, unions and French government "advances on the box office receipts." Reprinted 1968, Narboni, ed., Entry No. 1170. Trans. and commentary 1972, Milne, Entry No. 1713.

1966

2237 *"Bergmanorama." Cahiers du Cinema in English,* No. 1 (January), pp. 56+.
Cited in Schuster, p. 165. Trans. from 1958, Entry No. 2121.

2238 "Chronique d'un hiver." Press pamphlet advertising *Masculin-Féminin.*
Godard discusses other filmmakers — especially documentarists, Giraudoux, and his young friends. Trans. in 1969, Billard, No. 1268.

2239 "Deux arts en un: René Allio et Antoine Bourseiller repondent à Jean-Luc Godard et Michel Delahaye." *Cahiers du cinéma,* No. 177 (April), pp. 51–57, 76–78.
Godard and Delahaye interview Allio and Bourseiller. Godard asks questions about the relation of theater, music, and painting to film. He talks about literature and film, the Left Bank and the Right Bank tendencies in the New Wave, dubbing the dialogue vs. filming with synch sound, his own concept of developing a character and the relation of that to his direction of actors. Much of this interview echoes Godard's own plans to film the rehearsal of *Pour Lucrèce*. Godard also discusses film syntax and cinematography and raises a critique of the bourgeois culture industry. Trans. 1966, *Cahiers du Cinema in English*, Entry No. 2251.

2240 "Les Dix Meilleurs Films de 1965." *Cahiers du cinéma*, No. 174 (January).

Reprinted 1968, Narboni, ed., Entry No. 1170. Trans. 1972, Milne, Entry No. 1713.

2241 "Grace à Henri Langlois." *Le Nouvel Observateur*, No. 61 (12 January).

Godard discusses cinema in terms of spectators, access to films, finance, and documentary and fiction. Only Langlois has brought all of film history to France and he is treated "wretchedly." Godard aims his words at the Ministers of Culture and Finance. Reprinted 1968, Narboni, ed., Entry No. 1170. Trans. and commentary 1972, Milne, Entry No. 1713.

2242 "An Interview with Antonioni," *Cahiers du Cinema in English*, No. 1 (January), pp. 19+.

Cited in Schuster, p. 165. Trans. from 1964, No. 2223.

2243 "Lettre au ministre de la 'Kultur.' " *Le Nouvel Observateur* (6 April).

Godard protests to Malraux the banning of Rivette's *La Religieuse*, and he accuses Malraux of cowardice and fear. Reprinted 1966, *Cahiers du cinéma*, No. 177 (April) and 1968, Narboni, ed., Entry No. 1170. Trans. and commentary 1972, Milne, Entry No. 1713.

2244 "Miner le terrain." *L'Oeil*, No. 137 (May), pp. 34–42.

Cited *Art Index* (November 1965–October 1967), p. 422. With Alain Jouffroy. See 1966, Jouffroy, Entry No. 707.

2245 "Montage, Mon Beau Souci." *Cahiers du Cinema in English*, No. 3, pp. 45+.

Cited in Schuster, p. 166. Trans. from 1956, Entry No. 2101.

2246 "My Anger Has to Strike." *Atlas*, 11, No. 6 (June), 375.

Cited 1972, Green, Entry No. 1684.

2247 "La Question: entretien avec Robert Bresson." *Cahiers du cinéma*, No. 178 (May), pp. 26–35.

Godard and Michel Delahaye speak with Bresson about *Au hazard Balthazar* (in which Anne Wiazemsky appeared). Godard expresses interest in Bresson's improvisation and his exploring "several veins at once." Formally innovative are Bresson's use of ellipsis, inversion of image and sound, decisions as to where to edit, use of filmmaking to find new ideas about film, use of professional vs. nonprofessional actors, and use of foreign accents. This "moralistic" cinematography develops the theme of humanism vs. inquisition. The two directors interact as practicing filmmakers, particularly in discussing direction of actors. Trans. Jane Pease, 1967, *Cahiers du Cinema in English*, No. 8 (February), pp. 5–27.

2248 Shooting notes for *Masculin-Féminin*. Reprinted in 1966.

Vianey, Entry No. 768; excerpts trans. in 1969, Billard, Entry No. 1268.

2249 "Le Testament de Balthazar." *Cahiers du cinéma*, No. 178 (May), pp. 58–59.

Godard and M. Merleau-Ponty compiled a statement of Bresson's philosophy from his own words.

2250 "Trois milles heures de cinéma." *Cahiers du cinéma*, No. 184 (November), pp. 46–48.
Godard's diary contains descriptions of conversations, impressions of many films seen, his sound engineer's evaluations for *Deux ou trois choses* and *Made in U.S.A.*, and fleeting insights into his aesthetics. The article includes photos from films to illustrate his opinions on various films and directors; there are different stills in the U.S. *Cahiers du Cinema in English*. Trans. 1967, Jane Pease, *Cahiers du Cinema in English*, No. 10 (May), pp. 10–15. That trans. reprinted 1968, Mussman, Entry No. 1168.

2251 "Two Arts in One: A Conversation." *Cahiers du Cinema in English*, No. 6 (December), pp. 25+.
Cited in Schuster, p. 166. Trans. from 1966, Entry No. 2239.

1967

2252 "Godard: *La Chinoise.*" *Jeune cinéma*, No. 25 (October), pp. 16–19.
Text of a press conference given after the showing of *La Chinoise* at the Venice Film Festival, 1967, with the questions and the names of those who asked them also given. Godard agrees with a critic who applauds his having learned from Brecht and who says Godard is the only one to be creating cinema. Going back to zero with every film, Godard says, forcibly leads one to confront political issues. *La Chinoise* is no more about French youth than *Scarface* is about Chicago. Godard discusses the relation of the film to his own political stance, the characters he identifies with, the influence of Brecht in France, the Chinese cultural revolution, and his contact with actual Communist and Maoist groups before the film and their reaction after the film.

2253 "Impressions anciennes." *Cahiers du cinéma*, No. 187 (February).
Article was written in 1964 and printed when *Mediterranée* was released commercially. "Here are smooth, round shots abandoned on the screen like pebbles on the beach." Reprinted 1968, Narboni, ed., Entry No. 1170. Trans. and commentary 1972, Milne, Entry No. 1713.

2254 "Jean-Luc Godard commente *Deux ou trois choses que je sais d'elle.*" *Les Lettres françaises*, No. 1174 (16 March), pp. 20–21.
Includes "Lettre à mes amis pour apprendre à faire du cinéma ensemble." See Entry No. 2256 for complete listing of reprinting and translations.

2255 "Jean-Luc Godard über seinen Film, *Deux ou trois choses que je sais d'elle.*" *Film Club* (Städisches Kulturamt und Volkschule Kaiserlauten), 15, No. 10 (October), 1–3.
No name for interviewer given, written in essay form. Godard finished shooting *Made in U.S.A.* on August 11 and began shooting *Deux ou trois choses* August 8. He discusses the prostitution theme and Vlady as an actress (he planned the film with her in mind).

2256 "Lettre à mes amis pour apprendre à faire du cinéma ensemble." *Deux ou trois choses que je sais d'elle: L'Avant-Scène du cinéma*, No. 70 (May).

Graphically written as a poem. Life and filmmaking are a child's game reserved for big people to play. Reprinted from 1967, *Les Lettres françaises*, No. 1174 (16 March), Entry No. 2254. Reprinted 1968, Narboni, ed., Entry No. 1170. Reprinted 1971, in *Deux ou trois choses* script, Entry No. 2343. Trans. and commentary 1972, Milne, Entry No. 1713.

2257 "Ma démarche en quatre mouvements." *Deux ou trois choses que je sais d'elle: L'Avant-Scène du cinéma*, No. 70 (May).

Godard wants to describe the various "complexes" and their parts (including Juliette) in *Deux ou trois choses* as both objects and subjects, from the outside and then the inside, so as to arrive at certain structures and thus "bring us closer to life than at the outset." Poet Francis Ponge and philosopher Maurice Merleau-Ponty are cited. Reprinted 1968, Narboni, ed., Entry No. 1170. Reprinted 1971, *Deux ou trois choses* script, No. 2343. Trans. and commentary 1972, Milne, Entry No. 1713.

2258 "Manifeste." Press-book de *La Chinoise* (August).

We should modestly provoke, economically and aesthetically, "two or three Vietnams in the . . . Hollywood-Cinecittà-Mosfilm-Pinewood-etc. empire." Reprinted 1968, Narboni, ed., Entry No. 1170. Trans. and commentary 1972, Milne, Entry No. 1713.

2259 "On doit tout mettre dans un film." *Deux ou trois choses que je sais d'elle: L'Avant-Scène du cinéma*, No. 70 (May).

Godard describes his political concerns and theories about prostitution as seen in *Deux ou trois choses*; the relation between improvisation, documentary, and self-reflexivity; and his secret ambition — to be in charge of the French newsreel services. Reprinted 1968, Narboni, ed., Entry No. 1170. Reprinted 1971, *Deux ou trois choses* script, No. 2343. Trans. and commentary 1972, Milne, Entry No. 1713.

2260 "Three Thousand Hours of Cinema." Trans. Jane Pease. *Cahiers du Cinema in English*, No. 10 (May), pp. 10–15.

Trans. from 1966, Entry No. 2217. Reprinted in 1968, Mussman, Entry No. 1168.

2261 With Michel Delahaye. "Interview with Robert Bresson." *Cahiers du Cinema in English*, No. 8 (February), pp. 67+.

Cited in Schuster, p. 166. Trans. from 1960, No. 2201.

1968

2262 "Conférénce de presse: l'affaire Langlois." *Cahiers du cinéma*, No. 199 (March), pp. 34–41.

At a press conference protesting Langlois' dismissal, Godard discusses the continuity between Vichy and German film censorship and current French laws for financing and censoring films. Also present are Alexandre Astruc, Claude Chabrol, Jean Renoir, Jacques Rivette, Pierre Kast, Jacques Doniol-Valcroze, and a Mr. Kiejman. Date: February 17, 1968.

2263 *Jean-Luc Godard par Jean-Luc Godard: articles, essais, entretiens.* Introduction and notes by ed., Jean Narboni. Collections des *Cahiers du cinéma.*

> Also listed under 1968, Narboni, ed., Entry No. 1170. Book-length collection of Godard's essays and interviews. Trans. and commentary 1972, Milne, Entry No. 1713.

2264 "Un Prisonnier qu'on laisse taper sur sa casserole." *La Nouvelle Critique*, No. 18 (October), pp. 62–63.

> In December 1967, at the Besançon Week of Marxist Thought, Godard describes his early development, his lionization as a filmmaker, and his beginning to feel trapped inside the system. Film is the most "economically and culturally enslaved" art. Both film and TV are defined by image and sound. Trans. 1970, Flash, Entry No. 1441.

1969

2265 "Cinema-provcazione." *Filmcritica*, 20, No. 194 (January), 8–12.

> "A conversation taped at Paris by Paola Rispoli" is printed as a prose statement by Godard without the interviewer's questions. See 1969, Rispoli, Entry No. 1334. Trans. 1970, Flash, Entry No. 1441.

2266 "Lettera ai miei amici." *Cineforum*, 9, No. 82 (February), 82–84.

> In Lincoln Center Library.

2267 "Premiers 'Sons Anglais.' " *Cinéthique*, No. 5 (September-October), p. 14.

> Signed "on behalf of the Dziga-Vertov Group, Jean-Luc Godard," this manifesto defines the purposes of *British Sounds*: "The bourgeoisie creates a world to match its image, but it also creates an image to match its world . . . that it calls a reflection of reality. . . . A political film is obliged to discover what it has invented." Trans. 1970, Flash, Entry No. 1441.

1970

2268 "Godard on Godard." *Montage*, 1, No. 3 (16 April), 7, 10–11.

> Cited in BFI Bibliography.

2269 "Notes on *Pravda*." *Afterimage*, No. 1 (April).

> "Political tourism means filming images and sounds and at random. In editing we raised ideas on a politically more correct use of political cinema. It was wrong to film in an opportunistic, wasteful way, yet it was positive not to have abandoned the film. We [Godard and Gorin] learned in the editing to pick out simple images that are not 'too complete,' and to create images and sounds that are of and in the struggle and open to criticism and transformation."

2270 Soundtrack of videotaped Cinema Six show, dated March 19, 1969, signed on reel by I.P.N., never shown on French TV. Trans. Jack Flash. *Kinopraxis*, No. 0, broadside.

Godard provides a political analysis of the director as a "cultural product willed by the state, tolerated by imperialism"; of the image, which is made by people who accept it "piously"; of commercial cinema, a "drug"; of the failure to make Communist films in France. Everyone should make films but they don't know how to. The solution is to stop making movies for imperialism, sabotage the work one is hired to do for O.R.T.F.

2271 "What Is to Be Done?" Trans. Mo Tietelbaum. *Afterimage*, No. 1 (April).
Thirty-nine sentences on how to make a materialist film, with references to Lenin, Brecht, Dziga Vertov. Photos from Palestine film footage. Comments on *British Sounds*. Dated January 1970.

1971

2272 "Dziga Vertov Notebook." *Take One*, No. 11 (June), 7–9.
Photoessay by Robert Altman of the notebooks for *Till Victory*.

2273 "Godard Interviews Solanas." *Liberated Guardian*, 1, No. 19 (11 March), 17.
Cited API, 3, No. 1, 58.

1972

2274 "Che faire?" *Bianco e nero*, 33, No. 7-8 (July-August), 143–44.
List of points on how to make a Marxist film in a political way. Signed Godard and Gorin.

2275 Press release on *Tout va bien*. Coauthored with Jean-Pierre Gorin. Trans. Steve Hardy. *Cinema Rising*, No. 2 (May), p. 14.
The press release irreverently states the political intent of this "realistic love story," a "historical film" for the progressive bourgeoisie.

1974

2276 "L'Adolescent et l'homme." *L'Avant-Scène du cinéma*, No. 145 (March), p. 48.
Review praising Nicholas Ray. Reprinted from 1956, *Image et son* (July).

1975

2277 "Jean-Luc Godard paroles —." *Téléciné*, 202 (September-October), 11–13.
Godard describes his experiences working with video.

2278 "Warum ich hier spreche —." *Filmkritik* (Munich), 19, No. 9 (September), 420–29.
At Cannes in May 1975, Jean-Luc Godard talked about *Numero Deux*, then

being shot. He said that *Tout va bien* was 95 percent Gorin's, that *A Bout de souffle* came out of fascism and a fascistic part in himself. He discusses production at length and especially the history of the Palestine film, now released as *Ici et ailleurs*.

1976

2279 *"Pravda."* Program Notes from showing at l'A.R.C., Musée d'Art Moderne, Paris, February 1970.

Plot summary and evaluation are quoted in their entirety in 1976, Segal, Entry No. 2001.

VI
Screenplays, Descriptions, Scenarios, and Photo-Essays of Godard's Films

(Unless noted otherwise, the title of the film is also the title of the published text.)

CHARLOTTE ET SON JULES

2280 1961. *L'Avant-Scène du cinéma*, No. 5 (June), pp. 52–54.
Screenplay.

UNE HISTOIRE D'EAU

2281 1961. *L'Avant-Scène du cinéma*, No. 7 (September), pp. 60–62.
Screenplay. Complete filmography through 1960. Two films in preparation include *Eva* and *France la douce*.

A BOUT DE SOUFFLE

2282 1960. Francolin, C. *A Bout de souffle*. Paris: Seghers.
Novel based on film.

2283 1968. *L'Avant-Scène du cinéma*, No. 79 (March), pp. 1–49.
Screenplay, plus Truffaut's original scenario and quotations from reviews.

2284 1972. Translated into Italian *(Fino all'ultimo respiro)* in *Cinque film*. Ed. Gianni Rondolino. Rome: Einaudi.

2285 1974. Paris: Ballard.
Screenplay.

LE PETIT SOLDAT

2286 1961. *"Le Soldat* de Godard: le film." *Cinéma 61*, No. 52 (January), pp. 13–16.
This prose scenario of the film in ten sequences is presumably a version written by Godard *("etabli"* by Godard); its goal is to inform readers about the content of a censored film.

2287 1961. *Cahiers du cinéma*, No. 119 (May), pp. 23–37, and No. 120 (June), pp. 5–30.
Dialogue of film in two parts.

2288 1961. Translated into Italian. *Cinéma 60*, No. 8–9 (February-March).

2289 1967. "Extraits de dialogues." *Image et son*, No. 211 (December), pp. 76, 77, 81.
Extracts.

2290 1967. Intro. Nicholas Garnham. Modern Film Scripts. London: Lorrimer. New York: Simon and Schuster. 95 pp.
Complete credits. Filmography. Dialogue. Description of the action, mise en scene, camera movement, and size of figure in image.

2291 n. d. French dialogue script in British Film Institute Library.
Cited BFI Bibliography.

2292 n. d. Saint Benoit, Claude. Paris: Julliard.
Novel made from film. Cited 1972, Brown, Entry No. 1657

UNE FEMME EST UNE FEMME

2293 1959. "Commentaire de Jean-Luc Godard au disque du film," in 1968, Narboni, Entry No. 1170, pp. 275–84.
A ten-inch record was made but never released commercially. "It consists mainly of snatches of dialogue, interspersed with music from the film and Godard's observations on it." (1972, Milne, Entry No. 1713, where translation of record appears, pp. 165–71).

2294 1959. "Scenario." *Cahiers du cinéma*, No. 98 (August), pp. 46–51.
The original treatment for the film, based on an idea by Geneviève Cluny, is given and varies only slightly from the final film version. Trans. 1967, Michael Benedict, *Cahiers du Cinema in English*, No. 12 (December), pp. 35–37. That translation reprinted 1968, Mussman, Entry No. 1168, pp. 50–59. Reprinted 1968, Narboni, Entry No. 1170, pp. 260–68. Trans. 1972, Milne, Entry No. 1713, pp. 155–60.

2295 1964. *Filmcritica*, No. 150 (October).
Script.

2296 1968. Collet, Entry No. 1088, pp. 120–30.
The scenario and dialogue for two sections of the film are given. First is the quarrel between Émile and Angéla in the apartment, from the point where he rides his bike around her to the point after the exiting of the two plainclothes policemen who had been looking for terrorists.
The other section is the sequence with Alfred and Angéla in the bar from the point where they order drinks to where they are interrupted by two blind beggars. Trans. 1970, Collet, Entry No. 1425, pp. 114–26.

2297 1975. *Jean-Luc Godard: Three Films — A Woman Is a Woman, A Married Woman, Two or Three Things I Know about Her*. Intro. Alistair Whyte. Trans. Jan Dawson, Susan Bennett, and Marianne Alexander, respectively. Icon Editions. New York: Harper & Row. 192 pp.
Complete credits. Dialogue. Description of action, mise en scene, camera movement, and size of figure in image. (The latter two aspects are not described as fully for *A Woman is a woman.*)

2298 n.d. French dialogue script. British Film Institute Library.
Cited BFI Bibliography.

LA PARESSE

2299 n.d. French dialogue script in British Film Institute Library.
Cited BFI Bibliography.

VIVRE SA VIE

2300 1962. *L'Avant-Scène du cinéma*, No. 19 (October), pp. 5–30.
Screenplay.

2301 1962. "Nana et le philosophe." *L'Express* (20 September), p. 24.
The dialogue between Nana and Brice Parain in *Vivre sa vie* is reprinted.

2302 1962. "Scenario." Trans. Louis Brigante. *Film Culture*, No. 26
(Winter), p. 52.
Godard's ideas before filming *Vivre sa vie* changed somewhat before the final
version. Godard: "I want to prove that existence presupposes essence, and vice
versa . . ." Brigante translation reprinted 1968, Mussman, Entry No. 1168, pp.
77–80.

2303 1963. *Filmcritica*, No. 130 (February).
Script.

2304 1964. *Vivre sa vie: Die Geschichte der Nana S.* Drehbuch. Series
Cinemathek, 9. Hamburg: Marion von Schroeder.
Screenplay.

2305 1972. Translated into Italian *(Questa è la mia vita)* in *Cinque film*.
Ed. Gianni Rondolino. Rome (?): Einaudi.

LE NOUVEAU MONDE

2306 n.d. Italian dialogue script available in British Film Institute Library.
Cited BFI Bibliography.

LES CARABINIERS

2307 1963. "Un Conte de faits." *Cinéma 63*, No. 74 (March), pp. 26–28.
In an introduction to the scenario of the film, Godard discusses the fable form
and the savagery of the characters. Everything filmed represented *ideas*. The film
was influenced by both Lumière (camera reduced to its elemental function) and
Brecht (not showing real things but showing how things really are). Reprinted
1968, Collet, Entry No. 1088, pp. 78–79; trans. 1970, Collet, Entry No. 1425, pp.
128–29.

2308 1964. *Filmcritica*, No. 150 (October)
Dialogue. Critical annotations are given which describe the mise en scene

and the characterization. In Italian. Reprinted 1969, Mancini, Entry No. 1321, pp. 103–23.

2309   1965. *L'Avant-Scène du cinéma,* No. 46 (March).
Synopsis and photos.

2310   1970. Collet, Entry No. 1425. "Scenario: Act I: Nature (The Peasants' Cabin)," pp. 130–32. Translated from 1968, Collet, Entry No. 1088, pp. 133–34.
Collet contrasts in two parallel columns the original scenario by Godard and the final dialogue in the sequences where the carabiniers show the king's letter and explain what "mobilization" means.

2311   1976. *L'Avant-Scène du cinéma,* Godard special issue, No. 171-72 (July-September), pp. 5–38.
Complete credits. Complete text of a 15-page typed notebook containing the Rossellini and Grualt scripts (typed), which were pasted in sections and followed by Godard's handwritten comments (some of the characters' names vary from the film version). Complete screenplay and description of visual track of the film version of *Les Carabiniers.*

2312   n.d. *Film ideal* (Madrid), No. 222-23, pp. 47–168.
Scenario and introduction. Cited 1970, Cameron, Entry No. 1399.

2313   n.d. French dialogue script in British Film Institute Library.
Cited BFI Bibliography.

2314   n.d. "Protokoll." Series Cinemathek, Ausgewählte Filmtexte. Frankfurt-am-Main: Verlag Filmkritik. 100 pp.
Complete credits, scenario, and dialogue in German. Camera movements and length of scenes are noted, as are settings.

LE GRAND ESCROC

2315   1965. *L'Avant-Scène du cinéma,* No. 46 (March), pp. 37–41.
Screenplay.

LE MÉPRIS

2316   1963. *Filmcritica,* No. 139-40 (November-December), pp. 719–40.
French text in an Italian magazine. The visuals are described and the characters' lines are sometimes summarized. The action or the cinematography is often interpreted from the spectator's point of view: e.g., "We understand that . . ." or, "This sequence lasts 25 or 30 minutes. It's difficult for me to tell exactly and in chronological order what happened."

2317   1963. "L'Odysée selon Jean-Luc." *Cinéma 63,* No. 77 (June).
Godard's proposed scenario. See 1963, Godard, Entry No. 2220.

BANDE À PART

2318 1964. *Filmcritica*, No. 150 (October).
Script.

2319 1965. *Film*, 2, No. 2 (February).
Script in German.

LA FEMME MARIÉE

2320 1964. *Filmcritica*, No. 151-152 (November-December).
Script.

2321 1965. *L'Avant-Scène du cinéma*, No. 46 (March), pp. 5–32.
Screenplay.

2322 1965. *The Married Woman: A Jean-Luc Godard Film.*
Text based on English subtitles by Ursule Molinario. Berkley Medallion Books. New York: Berkley Publishing Co. Unpaged.

2323 1965. Méril, Macha and Godard, Jean-Luc. *Journal d' "Une Femme mariée."* Paris: Denoël. 100 pp.
Photo essay from stills and lines from film.

2324 1966. *Eine verheirate Frau.* Cinemathek, 15. Hamburg: Marion von Schroeder.

2325 1972. Translated into Italian *(Un donna sposata)* in *Cinque film*, ed. Gianni Rondolino. Rome (?): Einaudi.

2326 1975. *Godard: Three Films.* Entry No. 2268.
Complete credits.

ALPHAVILLE

2327 1965. "Une Nouvelle Adventure de Lemmy Caution." Trans. Peter Whitehead. Entry No. 2238. Pp. 77–97.
In this rather lengthy scenario, Godard describes the action as he would finally shoot it, with only a few variations. He describes the intent of certain kinds of shots and compositions; e.g., "true documentary images from everyday life . . . [are given] a novel, rather strange, mysterious quality." This treatment is also translated into Italian, 1965, *Filmcritica*, No. 159-60 (August-September).

2328 1966. English trans. and screenplay by Peter Whitehead. Intro. by Richard Roud. London: Lorrimer. New York: Simon and Schuster. 102 pp.
Complete credits. Dialogue. Description of the action and mise en scene. Partial description of camera movement, angle, and size of figure in image.

2329 1968. Collet, Entry No. 1088, pp. 134–36.
Alpha 60's slide-lecture in the Institute of General Semantics and the interrogation of Ivan Johnson by Alpha 60 are given from Godard's working documents. Trans. 1970, Collet, Entry No. 1425.

PIERROT LE FOU

2330 1966. Translated into Italian as *Il bandito delle 11*. *Filmcritica*, No. 165 (March).
Film script.

2331 1967. "Extraits de dialogues." *Image et son*, No. 211 (December), pp. 75–85.
Extracts from dialogue.

2332 1969. English translation and description of action by Peter Whitehead. London: Lorrimer. New York: Simon and Schuster. 104 pp.
Complete credits. Dialogue. Partial description of mise en scene. Camera movement and size of figure in image minimally noted. Action described at length.

2333 1976. *L'Avant-scène du cinéma*, special Godard issue, No. 171-72 (July-September), pp. 71–109.
Complete credits, screenplay, many stills.

2334 n.d. French dialogue script in British Film Institute Library.
Cited BFI Bibliography.

MASCULIN-FÉMININ

2335 1968. *Filmcritica*, No. 187 (March), pp. 173–85.
Part one of two parts. French dialogue script printed in an Italian magazine. Part two in 1968, *Filmcritica*, No. 189 (May-June), pp. 306–14.

2336 1969. Edited Pierre Billard and Robert Hughes. New York: Grove Press. 288 pp.
English trans. of script, plus other documentation, including the de Maupassant story on which film was based.

2337 n.d. French dialogue script in British Film Institute Library.
Cited BFI Bibliography.

MADE IN U.S.A.

2338 1967. "Extraits de dialogues." *Image et son*, No. 211 (December), pp. 75–85.

2339 1967. Screenplay. Introduction by Michael Kustow. London: Lorrimer. 87 pp.
English trans. gives dialogue but not cinematography. Out of print.

2340 1968. Collet, No. 1088, pp. 137–39. "Scène final."
From Godard's working documents, dialogue is given from the point after Paula Nelson has killed David Goodis and listens to her own voice on the tape recorder to the point where Philippe Labro says, "Right and left are a completely outdated equation; the questions shouldn't be posed in those terms anymore." Trans. 1970, Collet, No. 1425, pp. 135–38.

DEUX OU TROIS CHOSES QUE JE SAIS D'ELLE

2341 1967. *L'Avant-Scène du cinéma*, No. 70 (May), pp. 9–36.
Screenplay. Complete description of the mise en scene and camera movement; noise track and size of figure in frame also noted.

2342 1967. Cardinal, Marie and Jean-Luc Godard. *Cet été là: Deux ou trois choses que je sais d'elle.* Paris: Julliard.
Scenario and notes about shooting of film.

2343 1971. Collection Point-Films. Paris: Editions du Seuil, Avant-Scène.
Reprint of Entry No. 2341, with additional critical material.

2344 1972. Trans. into Italian (*Due o tre cose che so di lei*) in *Cinque film*, ed. Gianni Rondolino. Rome (?): Einaudi.

2345 1975. *Godard: Three Films.* Entry No. 2268.

LA CHINOISE

2346 1967. "Le Cahier de *La Chinoise*." Presented by Alain Jouffroy. *Opus international*, No. 2, pp. 12–29.
These are Godard's shooting notes from the film and consist of key words and bits of dialogue that indicate Godard's major political intent. Stills from film included.

2347 1967. *Filmcritica*, No. 182 (October), pp. 471–96.
French dialogue in Italian magazine.

2348 1968. Collet, Entry No. 1088, pp. 104–107. "Présentation."
Godard's prose description indicates plot and characterization. Trans. 1970, Collet, Entry No. 1425, pp. 138–40.

2349 1968. Collet, Entry No. 1088, pp. 139–46. "Scenario."
Godard's working dialogue is given for the following sequences: the naming of the Aden-Arabi cell and Henri's having been beaten up; Guillaume's explanation of the proper role of a militant actor; Véronique's monologue on being a radical student; Véronique and Guillaume's words of love; Guillaume's discussion of Méliès and Lumière; and the group's definition of a Brechtian, theoretically correct art. Trans. 1970, Collet, Entry No. 1425, pp. 140–48.

2350 1971. *L'Avant-Scène du cinéma*, No. 114 (May), pp. 7–40.
Screenplay.

2351 1972. Translated into Italian (*La cinese*) in *Cinque film*, ed. Gianni Rondolino. Rome (?): Einaudi.

WEEKEND

2352 1968. Collet, Entry No. 1088, pp. 115–19. "Présentation."
In a working summary of the film, Godard notes themes and intent, details of characterization, some of the events, and an ending different from the final version of the film. Trans. 1970, Collet, Entry No. 1425, pp. 148–54.

2353 1972. (with *Wind from the East*) Ed. Nicholas Fry. Trans. Marianne Sinclair and Danielle Adkinson. New York: Simon and Schuster. 188 pp.
Complete credits. Dialogue. Description of camera movement, mise en scene, and action.

CAMERA-OEIL

2354 1967. *Filmcritica*, 18, No. 183-84 (November-December), 560–61.
Script (*Lontano dal Vietnam*).

2355 1968. *Peace News* (5 January), p. 7.
Text of Godard's monologue.

LE GAI SAVOIR

2356 1968. "Extraits de la piste sonore." *Cahiers du cinéma*, No. 200-201 (April-May), pp. 53–55.
Extracts from the Union des Ecrivains dialogue script, plus stills from the film.

2357 1969. *Le Gai savoir: mot à mot d'un film encore trop réviso.* No. 2. Paris: Union des Ecrivains. Unpaged.
Dialogue and stills, especially of the photos with grafitti written over them.

CINÉTRACTS

2358 1968. "The kings of imperialism have transformed technological progress and sexuality into instruments of repression." *Art and Confrontation: The Arts in an Age of Change.* Trans. Nigel Foxell. Greenwich, Conn.: New York Graphic Society, Ltd. Pp. 190–97.
A series of photos show eight shots from a cinétract, with writing on an image — often over a woman's body or cartoon — similar to that in *Le Gai savoir*. The book attributes the film to Chris Marker, but it is clearly Godard's.

2359 1976. Photos and descriptions of several *cinétracts* by Abraham Segal. *L'Avant-Scène du cinéma*, No. 171-72, special Godard issue (July-September), pp. 54–58.

SYMPATHY FOR THE DEVIL/ONE PLUS ONE

2360 1970. "*Eins und Eins.*" *Film*, January, pp. 13–24.
Dialogue or screenplay in German. Cited BFI Bibliography.

PRAVDA

2361 1971. Translated into Italian. *Ubu*, No. 8 (January).

2362 1972. *Cahiers du cinéma*, No. 240 (July-August), pp. 19–30.
Text of voice over commentary, with accompanying photos keyed to lines in text.

VENT D'EST

2363 1970. *"Ostwind." Film*, December, pp. 21–28.
Dialogue or screenplay in German. Cited BFI Bibliography.

2364 1970. Translated into Italian *(Vento dell'est)*. *Marcatre*, No. 2 (July).
Complete translation.

2365 1972. *Cahiers du cinéma*, No. 240 (July-August), pp. 31–50.
Text of voice over commentary and dialogue, keyed to many photos from film.

2366 1972. (with *Weekend*). New York: Simon and Schuster. *See* Entry No. 2323.

LOTTE IN ITALIA/LUTTES EN ITALIE

2367 1970. *Cineforum*. No. 97-98 (November-December), pp. 475–89.
Script of Italian version.

2368 1972. *Bianco e Nero*, 33, No. 7-8 (July-August), 107–37.
Complete script of Italian-language version of film, with dialogue, credits, and indications about the visual track.

2369 1972. *Cahiers du cinéma*, No. 238-39 (May-June).
Voice over dialogue and commentary keyed to photos.

TOUT VA BIEN

2370 1972. Brief excerpts. *Cinema Rising*, No. 2 (May). In English.

2371 1972. Brief excerpts. *"Deux Petits Soldats." Le Nouvel Observateur* (17 April).

LETTER TO JANE

2372 1972. [Godard] Jean-Luc and Jean-Pierre [Gorin]. "Enquête sur une image." *Tel Quel*, No. 52 (Winter), pp. 74–90.
Complete text is given of *Letter to Jane*, including reproduction of Kraft photo, and an additional conclusion not presented in the film. Speakers not indicated and only a few of the visuals are noted.

2373 1973. *Women and Film*, 1, No. 3-4, 45–51.
Almost complete translation into English, although entitled, "Excerpts."

2374 1974. "Befragung eines Bildes." *Filmkritik,* 18, No. 7 (July), 290–307.
German translation.

2375 1974. "Onderzoek naar een beeld." *Skrien,* No. 40-41 (January-February), pp. 20–29.
Trans. of 1972, *Tel Quel* script, Entry No. 2242, into Swedish.

NUMÉRO DEUX

2376 1975. "Propos d'auteur: extraits de la bande sonore du film de Jean-Luc Godard, *Numéro Deux.*" *Cinéma 75,* No. 203 (November), pp. 4–5.
Extracts from sound track of film.

VII
Godard's Film Performances and Other Film-related Activities

Film Performances

1950

2377 *Quadrille*; d: Jacques Rivette

1951

2378 *Présentation (Ou Charlotte et son steack)*; d: Eric Rohmer

1954

2379 *Operation béton* — narration; d: Godard

1955

2380 *La Femme coquette* — prostitute's client; d: Godard

1956

2381 *Kreutzer Sonata*; d: Eric Rohmer

2382 *Coup du berger*; d: Jacques Rivette

2383 *Charlotte et son Jules* — Jules' voice; d: Godard

2384 *Une Histoire d'eau* — man's voice; d: Godard

1958

2385 *Paris nous appartient* — Godard's silhouette; d: Jacques Rivette

1959

2386 *Le Signe du lion*; d: Eric Rohmer

2387 *A Bout de souffle* — informer; d: Godard

1961

2388 *Cléo de 5 à 7* — with Anna Karina in comic sequence; d: Agnès Varda

1962

2389 *Vivre sa vie* — voice-off narration about prostitution; "Oval Portrait" narration; d: Godard

2390 *Le Nouveau Monde* — pill taker; narration; d: Godard

1963

2391 *Schérézade*; d: Pierre Gaspard-Huit

2392 *Le Grand escroc* — himself; d: Godard

2393 *Le Mépris* — Fritz Lang's assistant director; d: Godard

1964

2394 *Bande à part* — narration; d: Godard

2395 *Jean-Luc Godard, ou le cinéma de défi* — television program about Godard filmed largely at Journeés Jean-Luc Godard, Annecy, November 6–8; d: Janine Bazin, André-S. Labarthe, and Hubert Knapp.

1965

2396 *Pour le plaisir* — television program, using many clips from Godard's films and describing his work; d: Jacques Doniol-Valcroze

1966

2397 *L'Espion*; d: Raoul Levy

2398 *Deux ou trois choses que je sais d'elle* — narration; d: Godard

2399 *Made in U.S.A.* — narration, voice of Richard Politizer; d: Godard

1967

2400 *Caméra-Oeil* — himself; d: Godard

1967-68

2401 *Le Gai Savior* — narration; d: Godard

1968-70

2402 *One P.M.* — himself, director of *One A.M.*; d: Richard Leacock and David Pennebaker

1968

2403 *Two American Audiences: Godard on Godard* — himself, at N.Y.U.; d: Mark Woodcock

1969

2404 *Pravda* — narration; d: Dziga Vertov Group

2405 *Vent d'est* — narration; d: Dziga Vertov Group

2406 *Luttes en Italie* — narration; d: Dziga Vertov Group (Jean-Pierre Gorin)

1970

2407 *Godard in America* — himself, with Gorin, on tour in U.S., seen in encounters with audiences in Cambridge and Berkeley. He explicates the notebooks and story board of *Till Victory* in a manner similar to the explication of a photograph in *Letter to Jane*; d: Ralph Thanhauser.

2408 *Vladimir and Rosa* — himself; U.S. policeman; narration; d: Dziga Vertov Group

1972

2409 *Letter to Jane* — narration; d: Godard and Gorin

1975

2410 *Numéro deux* — himself; narration; d: Anne-Marie Miéville and Godard

1976

2411 *Ici et ailleurs* — himself; narration; d: Miéville and Godard

2412 *Sur et sous la communication* — himself; narration; off-screen questioner; d: Miéville and Godard

VIII
Archival Resources

Listed below are established film archives, with an indication of relevant holdings. Many university film departments in the United States have prints of selected Godard films and tapes of his appearances here or of private interviews with him and/or Gorin. I have several such tapes, but do not know the locations of the other material, except by vague word of mouth. Much of the interest in Godard in the late sixties and early seventies in the United States was generated by radicalized film buffs in the university counterculture, and recorded interviews on cassettes are regrettably ephemera that probably disappeared with the dismantling of alternative newspaper offices.

BERLIN

2413 Deutsche Film- und Fernsehakademie Berlin, Bibliothek.
1000 Berlin 19, Pommernallee 1, Germany.
Contains German newspaper and tradespaper clipping files.

2414 Deutsche Kinemathek Stiftung.
1000 Berlin 19, Pommernallee 1, Germany. Phone: 3036-233 and 234.
Contains dubbed German versions of a few Godard films, stills, German press books, and program leaflets.

BEVERLY HILLS

2415 The Charles K. Feldman Library.
American Film Institute Center for Advanced Film Studies, 501 Doheny Road, Beverly Hills, CA 90210. Phone: 213-278-8777.
Contains biography clipping file on Godard and files on individual film festivals.

2416 Margaret Herrick Library.
Academy of Motion Picture Arts and Sciences and Academy Foundation, 8949 Wilshire Blvd., Beverly Hills, CA 90211. Phone: 213-278-4313.
Contains biography and clipping files on director and individual films, 160 indexed periodicals, general subject files (e.g., French motion picture industry), and clipping files and programs for individual film festivals.

COPENHAGEN

2417 Danish Film Museum.
St. Søndervoldstroede, 1419 Copenhagen K, Denmark. Phone: ASTA-6500.
Contains stills, scripts, clipping files on films and director, 250 periodicals indexed since 1960, and a fairly representative collection of Godard's films.

GRENOBLE

2418 Jean-Luc Godard and Anne-Marie Miéville, Sonimage Studios.
2 Rue de Belgrade, Grenoble, Switzerland. Also 72 Rue de Rochechouart, 75009 Paris, France.

LONDON

2419 British Film Institute, National Film Archive and Library,
81 Dean Street, London W1 V 6AA, England. Phone: 01-437-4355.
Library contains clipping files of reviews from British and some foreign papers, an extensive bibliography of Godard (See Preface) available on request, English dialogue scripts of Godard films shown at the National Film Theater, and 250 film periodicals indexed since 1950. The archive has a few Godard films which are available for viewing to bona fide researchers for a small fee.

NEW YORK

2420 Lincoln Center Library for the Performing Arts, New York Public Library.
111 Amsterdam Avenue/Lincoln Center, New York, NY. Phone: 212-799-2000.
Contains extensive clipping files on director and films, and extensive collection of film periodicals. Photocopying is expensive.

2421 Department of Film, Museum of Modern Art, 11 West 53 Street, New York, N.Y. 10019. Phone: 212-956-6100.
Contains several Godard films, a clipping file on the director and one on each film. Fee for screenings. To use the facilities in this small space, appointments must be made with the Film Study Center (956-4212) or with the Stills Archivist (956-4209) in advance.

OTTAWA

2422 Canadian National Film Archive.
395 Wellington, Ottawa K1A-ON3, Canada. Phone: 613-995-1311.
Contains books, press clippings, references to periodical articles (60 periodicals indexed), stills, and a few scripts.

PARIS

2423   Centre National de la Cinématographie, Service des Archives du Film.
78390 Bois d'Arcy, Paris, France. Phone: 460-20-50.
   Contains prints of several Godard films, extensive stills, scripts (including that of the uncompleted *Moi, je*). Requests for use of this material should be made in writing in advance.

2423b   Institut des Hautes Études Cinématographiques.
92 Champs Elysées, Paris VIII, France. Phone: 539-22-86.
   Library contains complete documentation about French film production.

PHILADELPHIA

2424   Free Library of Philadelphia, Theater Collection.
Logan Circle, Philadelphia, PA 19103.
   Contains clipping files from local and New York papers on director and individual films, periodical collection.

POONA, INDIA

2425   National Film Archives of India.
Law College Road, Poona 411004, India. Phone: 58516.
   Contains a few Godard films with English subtitles.

WASHINGTON, D.C.

2426   The Library of Congress, Motion Picture Section.
Washington, D.C. 20540. Phone: 202-246-5840.
   Contains viewing prints (35mm), pressbooks, synopses, and stills.

WIESBADEN

2427   Deutsches Institut für Filmkünde.
602 Wiesbaden-Biebrich, Schloss, Germany. Phone: 69074-75.
   Contains international periodical collection, files of newspaper clippings on director and individual films, stills from films, and portrait stills.

IX
Distributors of Godard's Films

The films are listed here according to the title under which they are distributed, English or French. They are then indexed under French-language title, to which the English-language title in the index will also refer.

2428   Contemporary/McGraw-Hill Films, 1211 Avenue of the Americas, New York, NY 10021
Alphaville, Breathless, Pierrot le fou, Vivre sa vie, A Woman Is a Woman

2429   Corinth Films, 410 East 62nd Street, New York, NY 10021 Phone: 212-421-4470
Alphaville, Breathless, Les Carabiniers, My Life to Live, Le Petit Soldat, Pierrot le fou, A Woman is a Woman

2430   EYR Program, 45 West 45th Street, New York, NY 10036
Le Gai Savoir

2431   FACSEA, 972 5th Avenue, New York, NY 10021
Les Carabiniers, Histoire d'eau

2432   Grove Press Films, 196 W. Houston Street, New York, NY 10014
British Sounds (See You at Mao), Pravda, Vladimir and Rosa, Weekend, Godard in America (d: Ralph Thanhauser)

2433   Leacock-Pennebaker, 56 W. 45th Street, New York, NY 10036
La Chinoise, A Film like Any Other, One P.M., Two American Audiences (d: Mark Woodcock)

2434   Macmillan Audio-Brandon Films, 34 MacQuesten Parkway South, Mount Vernon, NY 10550
Contempt, The Oldest Profession, Rogopag

2435   New-Line Cinema, 121 University Place, New York, NY 10003
Sympathy for the Devil, Wind from the East

2436   New Yorker Films, 43 W. 61st Street, New York, NY 10023
Les Carabiniers, La Chinoise, Far from Vietnam, Letter to Jane, One P.M., Six in Paris, Tout va bien, Two or Three Things I Know about Her

2437   The Other Cinema Ltd., 12-13 Little Newport Street, London WC 2H
British Sounds, Cinetracts, Le Gai Savior, Letter to Jane, Numéro deux, Pravda, Tout va bien, Vladimir and Rosa, Vent d'est

2438   Pyramid Films, PO Box 1048, Santa Monica, CA 90406
All the Boys Are Called Patrick

2439   Swank Motion Pictures, 201 S. Jefferson Avenue, Saint Louis, MO 63166
Band of Outsiders, The Married Woman, Masculine-Feminine

2440   Tywman Films, 329 Salem Avenue, Dayton, OH 45401
Le Gai Savoir

X
Film Title Index

XI
Author Index